Praise for 'The Complete Walt Disney

"Seriously thorough." —*Family Circle*

"Highly recommended." —*New York Daily News*

"Should leave fans of Mickey

"A thorough overview, with in nice souvenir." —*Boston Globe*

"Far and away the best guide t —*St. Louis Post-Dispatch*

"A fantastic planning tool... A depth of information... Unusua vacationers will want to save it

"Our favorite Disney guidebod

"Endless tips and trivia." —*Knoxville News-Sentinel*

"Very detailed descriptions of each attraction. Among the gems are fun facts and little things to look for." —*Florida Times Union (Jacksonville)*

"Stunning photos... Looking through this book is simply fun. It will make you more knowledgeable, while immersing you in the magic of Disney World." —*Kirkus Reviews*

"In-depth insider knowledge... The magic of Disney radiates from the pages... All the information needed to ensure your vacation is the experience of a lifetime... Definitely the book to purchase to help plan out your trip." —*Midwest Book Review*

"The ultimate Walt Disney World guidebook... Everything you could possibly need to know to plan and pull off the best Disney trip ever... Colorful, easy-to-navigate... Leaves no stone unturned." —*Writer's Digest*

"Visually engaging... What sets apart the Neals' book are the color photographs of rides, rooms and characters." —*Library Journal*

"In this case, 'complete' is not hyperbole, it is a fact... Makes a trip to Disney seem more like an adventure full of surprises, instead of a whine-filled money drain." —*MomMostTraveled.com*

"The best reference available for planning a Disney vacation." —*Orlando Vacation Rentals*

"Well-written and illustrated, with sumptuous colour photographs." —*Florida Review and Travel Guide (United Kingdom)*

Awards and honors

Outstanding Family Product. Disney's iParenting Media Awards.*

Travel Guide of the Year. 2012 ForeWord Reviews Awards; 2012 Next Generation Indie Book Awards; 2012, 2011, 2010 International Book Awards; 2011, 2010, 2009, 2008 National Independent Excellence Awards; 2012, 2010 Benjamin Franklin Awards (silver medalist); 2009 ForeWord Reviews Awards (silver medalist); 2009 Living Now Book Awards (silver medalist); 2008 National Best Book Awards (finalist)

Travel/Family Activity Book of the Year. 2010 Living Now Book Awards; 2009 Living Now Book Awards (silver medalist)

Nonfiction Book of the Year. 2009 National Independent Excellence Book Awards; 2008 Writer's Digest International Book Awards

Book of the Year. 2012 Eric Hoffer Book Awards (finalist)

Best Interior Design. 2010 International Book Awards (finalist)

Reference Book of the Year. 2009 Writer's Digest Int'l Book Awards (silver medalist)

Best Southeast Nonfiction. 2008 Independent Publisher Book Awards (silver medalist)

* *The Complete Walt Disney World is the only guidebook ever honored by the Walt Disney Co.*

The Complete Walt Disney World 2015

ISBN 978-0-9903716-0-1

Writing and research: Julie Neal
Photography: Mike Neal
Additional photography and research: Micaela Neal

Produced by Coconut Press Media Inc.
Published by Keen Communications, LLC
Manufactured in the United States of America
Distributed by Publishers Group West

Acknowledgments

Our thanks to Jason Lasecki, Jonathan Frontado, Juliana Cadiz, Bebee Frost, Darrell Fry, Matt Gottfried, David Hillstrom, Laura Spencer, Charles Stovall and Benjamin Thompson for a variety of assistance, as well as: Ngonba Anadou, Mandee Andrichyn, Odalys Aponte, Kevin Baker, Richard Bogart, David Brady, Vince Burkhead, Mike Colangelo, Michael Colavolpe, Brian Cotten, Amy and Mitch Crews, Jason Dobbins, Todd Ferrante, Andrea Finger, John Frost, Jay and Kisha Garcia, Phran Gauci, Lorraine Gorham, Matt Hathaway, Jamie-Lyn Hawkins, Holland Hayes, David Hobart, Walter Iooss, Rob Iske, Eric Jacobson, Kristie A. Jones, Kristine Jones, Chris Kraftchick, Kathy Mangum, Roberto Martinez, Bob Miller, Tony Morreale, Doobie and Rebekah Moseley, Nenette Mputu, Charles Ridgway, Kathy Rogers, Joe Rohde, Debbie Sacleux, Susan Schofield, Steve Schussler, Theron Skees, Jason Surrell, Rheo Tan, Paul Tomayko, Alicia Vaughn, Terry Ward, Chris Weaver, John Wetzel, Herb and Debbie Wright, Kevin Yee and all the Disney resort managers and park duty managers.

To Jodi Chase, Melissa Personette, Jeff and Dawn Riordan, Mike Pollard, Jenn Wakelin and everyone else who helped us get through a difficult time. Also, belatedly, to Dave Herbst. May your "Rat on the Mouse" please the heavens. Just keep those facts straight.

The Complete
Walt Disney
World® 2015

Julie and Mike Neal

Foreword

Let's face it. A trip to Walt Disney World is a big investment. You're spending your hard-earned money so you can grow closer as a family or group, and reap the benefits of shared magical moments for years to come. That's why planning your trip is so crucial.

If you've looked around the Internet you've no doubt discovered there are many planning resources available to you. So in this day of ubiquitous smart phones and tablets, why rely on an actual printed-on-paper guidebook?

There is something to be said about holding a guidebook in your hands, about spreading it out on your dining room table and devouring its many details together as a family. A printed guide is easy to bookmark, tab and highlight, and it's always "online" everywhere you go. Finally, it's shareable. When you return from your trip you can hand it off to friends or family complete with your added learnings in the margins.

I'm happy to say that travel authors Julie and Mike Neal are back with their 2015 edition of "The Complete Walt Disney World." It is the first guidebook I recommend for beginning and experienced travelers alike. The Neals manage to cover everything you need to know with just enough detail that you come away ready for your vacation without feeling overwhelmed.

And there's news. The Neals have partnered with a new publisher, which has given them the resources to make this edition their best yet. They've added more photos, more reviews of restaurants and shops, beefed up their park coverage, and much more. My favorite additions are the short summaries of each park's attractions. The Neals sort them by rating and don't hold back when one doesn't live up to its promise. Julie and Mike are not afraid to tell it like it is.

Writing a Disney guidebook is equal parts research, adventure and organization. With an area twice the size of Manhattan to cover, a lot of planning is required to make sure everything you need to know gets included. Since 2007, the guidebook that does that best is this one, the only one that gives you "the world" in strikingly rich and colorful detail. I am certain that you will get as much use and enjoyment out of this definitive Disney handbook as I have.

— John Frost, owner, The Disney Blog (thedisneyblog.com)

Contents

Illustration © Disney

A world of its own

TWICE THE SIZE OF MANHATTAN, Walt Disney World is the world's largest collection of theme parks, water parks and resorts. It's truly a world of its own unlike anything else.

A trip to Walt Disney World is not just a way to spend time with your children, nor merely an escape from day-to-day doldrums. It's a reawakening of that free-spirited, good-natured soul who lives deep inside you—the one your spouse married, the one you want your kids to emulate. Yes it can be crowded, yes it can be expensive, yes it takes a good plan to see it all, but no other man-made vacationland so deliberately embraces creativity, optimism and a sense of wonder about the world.

Populated daily by more than 100,000 visitors as well as 57,000 employees (Disney calls them "cast members"), the 47-square-mile property is the No. 1 vacation destination on the planet. It includes four theme parks, two water parks, a sports complex, a shopping and entertainment district and 20 resort hotels.

Magic Kingdom. It's only 122 acres—just 0.5 percent of Disney property—but to many folks this park *is* Walt Disney World. A spacious version of California's Disneyland, it re-imagines the original Main Street U.S.A., Adventureland, Fantasyland, Frontierland and Tomorrowland. A family favorite, it has more than 40 attractions, including classics such as Peter Pan's Flight and Space Mountain. It's the most popular theme park in the world.

Epcot. A sort of permanent World's Fair, this 300-acre park is divided into science-themed Future World and internationally focused World Showcase. Future World attractions include simulators that offer realistic sensations of hang gliding (Soarin') and astronaut training (Mission Space). World Showcase is highlighted by its memorable entertainment, dining and shopping.

Disney's Hollywood Studios. The front of this show-biz-themed park is a tribute to Old Hollywood, with re-created 1940s-era icons

such as Hollywood Boulevard and Grauman's Chinese Theatre. The rear was originally a working studio, and still carries that theme. This 135-acre park includes two of Disney World's best thrill rides—the Twilight Zone Tower of Terror and the Rock 'n' Roller Coaster Starring Aerosmith.

Disney's Animal Kingdom. This theme park combines exotic live animal exhibits with high-quality attractions. Top stops include Expedition Everest, a roller coaster that travels backward into a mountain cave; Kilimanjaro Safaris, an exploration through a replicated African wildlife preserve aboard an open-sided truck; and Festival of the Lion King, a show with energetic acrobats, dancers, singers and stilt walkers. The centerpiece of the 500-acre park is the Tree of Life, a 145-foot-tall man-made sculpture.

Other parks and activities. On a summer morning it's hard to beat the family fun at Disney's Blizzard Beach and Typhoon Lagoon. Disney also has four championship golf courses as well as a 9-hole, two miniature golf courses and many tennis courts, and offers organized fishing, horseback riding, stock-car driving, water sports and other activities.

Downtown Disney. This 120-acre dining, entertainment and shopping district sits on the eastern edge of the property, and is currently undergoing an extensive renovation.

ESPN Wide World of Sports. This complex is 220 acres of stadiums, fieldhouses, outdoor fields and other facilities that host amateur and some professional competitions.

Resort hotels. Distant lands and forgotten eras are recalled at most of Disney's 20 hotel properties. Accommodations range from campsites to multilevel suites.

Project X. In 1964, the Walt Disney Company began secretly buying up parcels of land southwest of Orlando, using false names and dummy corporations to keep prices low. In October, 1965, the Orlando Sentinel-Star identified the buyer; a month later Walt Disney and his brother, Roy, confirmed the existence of their "Project X," a plan for a futuristic city—the Experimental Prototype Community of Tomorrow (EPCOT)—where solutions to the urban problems of the day could be explored. To help fund itself, the area would include a theme park, an East Coast version of California's Disneyland.

Walt dies. After Walt's sudden death the next year, Roy decided to go ahead with the idea, at least the theme park portion for right then, but changed the project's name from EPCOT to Walt Disney World to honor his brother. The largest private construction project in the history of the United States, it broke ground in 1969. Development was led by two military men. Former Army general Joe Potter had overseen operations at the Panama Canal and the 1964 World's Fair; former Navy admiral Joe Vallor had supervised

the building of Disneyland. Potter, Vallor and 9,000 workers moved 8 million cubic yards of dirt, built 47 miles of canals and 22 miles of levees, dredged the 406-acre Bay Lake and created a 172-acre "Seven Seas Lagoon." They also built roads, maintenance shops, a phone company, power plant, sewage plant and tree farm.

Disney World opened to the public on Oct. 1, 1971. It consisted of the Magic Kingdom, the Contemporary and Polynesian Village resorts and the Fort Wilderness Resort & Campground. Disney's Golf Resort (today's Shades of Green) was built in 1973, and the Lake Buena Vista Village (today's Downtown Disney Marketplace) opened in 1975.

EPCOT becomes Epcot. Disney executives wrestled with Walt's EPCOT idea through the early 1970s, but the vision for an experimental city just wasn't clear without its visionary. Instead, in 1976 the company announced plans for EPCOT Center, a theme park with "demonstration concepts" and an "international people-to-people exchange" located in the center of what was to be Walt Disney's city. It opened in 1982, and later became the lowercase "Epcot" in 1994.

A total vacation destination. For all that Disney created in Florida during the '70s and early '80s, it has built far more since. In 1988, when arch-rival Universal Studios announced plans to built a movie-studio theme park just down the road, Disney quickly put together

Disney-MGM Studios (today's Disney's Hollywood Studios). It opened a year later, along with the Typhoon Lagoon water park and the since-closed Pleasure Island nightclub complex. A second water park, Blizzard Beach arrived in 1995. Disney's Animal Kingdom had its grand opening in 1998. Downtown Disney's West Side and the Wide World of Sports complex arrived in 1999.

During that same period the number of hotel rooms on Disney property grew from 2,000 to 33,000. Disney's Caribbean Beach and Grand Floridian resort hotels opened in 1988. Thirteen more resorts debuted in the 1990s. They included the Yacht and Beach Club and Walt Disney World Swan and Dolphin resorts (1990), the Port Orleans French Quarter and Old Key West complexes (1991), Dixie Landings (now Port Orleans Riverside, 1992), All-Star Sports Resort and Wilderness Lodge (1994), All-Star Music and BoardWalk (1995), Coronado Springs (1997) and All-Star Movies (1999). Disney's newest hotels are Animal Kingdom Lodge (2001), Pop Century (2003), Saratoga Springs (2004) and Art of Animation (2012).

Finally, a community. Disney developed the southwest corner of its property as a residential area, complete with its own downtown, school and post office. Named Celebration, the planned community broke ground in 1996. Today 7,500 people live there; the authors of this book did for a decade.

Best bets

It's like Christmas. You plan and save and anticipate for weeks and months. You yearn for a magical time with your family, full of memories and unforgettable moments. It certainly runs up the balance on your credit cards, but when it's over you're most likely glad you did it. Yes, a vacation to Walt Disney World has a lot in common with Christmas, at least the secular American version. But how do you decorate your particular tree? Which presents do you choose? Here are the authors' Best Bets; two dozen of Disney's most seminal experiences:

Best thrill ride. A wild experience, Space Mountain fills everyone with joy. Zoom through the dark on this indoor roller coaster, which zips you past twinkling stars and shooting comets. Sound effects make your trip seem faster than it is, with whooshing noises at its corners and drops. The low-sided, one-person-wide rocket is one of the narrowest coaster vehicles ever built, barely interfering with the feeling of flying solo through the cosmos.

Best princess attraction. A dazzling musical stage show, Beauty and the Beast—Live on Stage is both touching and laugh-out-loud

funny. While romantics will swoon over the love story between Belle and her Beast, everyone will laugh at the cartoonish slapstick humor. And the music! It's comprised of some of Disney's best songs, the Howard Ashman classics "Belle," "Gaston," "Be Our Guest," "Something There," "The Mob Song" and "Beauty and the Beast." Villain Gaston is a hoot, funnier and less threatening than in the movie. When bookworm Belle and her resurrected Beast finally embrace, the happy ending makes some onlookers cry. The show plays daily at Disney's Hollywood Studios.

Best theatrical show. Energetic performers bring to life the best songs from Disney's 1994 movie "The Lion King" in the Festival of the Lion King, an in-the-round musical spectacle at Disney's Animal Kingdom. Creative costumes turn dancers into antelopes, warthogs, zebras and other beasts. Similar to a good circus, there is almost too much to look at; during the joyful finale singers belt out their numbers center stage while a human bird soars overhead, wisecracking host Timon mimes his reactions, animal dancers and stilt-walkers circle the action and four huge puppets react in each corner of the theater. In 2014, the show moved to the park's Africa area.

Best vintage ride. You'll fly over London and head off to Never Land on Peter Pan's Flight, a classic dark ride at Magic Kingdom. Dusted with pixie dust and led by Tinker Bell, you fly a pirate ship from Wendy Darling's home as you head toward and through a variety of scenes from Disney's 1953 animated film, "Peter Pan." Designed more than 50 years ago, the ride's imaginative engineering and overdose of black lights conjure an experience that still charms all ages.

Best toddler attraction. Classic Magic Kingdom boat ride It's a Small World creates a child's view of our planet, one of a million colors, patterns, shapes, sparkles, textures and twinkly lights. Nearly 300 smiling dolls sing and play music while animals with flower-shaped spots and jeweled eyes dance and spin around them. Butterflies, clowns, jugglers and magic carpets float overhead like giant crib mobiles. The gentle attraction holds nothing threatening, and its reassuring message of unity and friendship resonates with young and old alike.

Best animal attraction. Nirvana for animal lovers, Kilimanjaro Safaris is a bouncy, open-air truck ride that offers unpredictable beastly encounters as it roams through real grasslands and forests. Each "two-week" tour is different, as the scores of spectacular animals are always busy living their own lives—feeding, fighting, nursing, running, even raising babies.

Best educational attraction. A robotic President Barack Obama speaks, as do George Washington and Abraham Lincoln at Magic Kingdom's Hall of Presidents. Created as lifelike Audio-Animatronics figures, all 43 American leaders are represented as breathing, fidgeting, murmuring individuals... a mirror of our unsettled selves, the American people. Before the curtain raises on the presidents, a high-definition, ultra-widescreen film tells the illuminating tale of our country's origins.

Best fireworks. You're likely to tear up as you watch Wishes. Not the typical reaction

to a fireworks show, perhaps, but this Magic Kingdom evening extravaganza is anything but typical. Though often subtle and understated, its synchronized starbursts, music and dialogue pack an emotional punch, bringing back childhood dreams and memories. The show begins quietly—a lone shooting star arches over Cinderella Castle—and slowly builds to a spectacular finish.

Best special events. Fans of the Force will love Star Wars Weekends at Disney's Hollywood Studios. Not just because of the characters and live-action stars who appear (Mark Hamill showed up in 2014), but also because it's free-of-charge with a park ticket. For extra-cost events you can't beat Mickey's Not-So-Scary Halloween party at Magic Kingdom, which young-adult couples seem to enjoy as much as kids.

Best movie. Donald Duck finds himself in the dining hall from "Beauty and the Beast," the undersea grotto of "The Little Mermaid" and other classic Disney settings in the 3-D Mickey's PhilharMagic, a dazzling Magic Kingdom experience that all ages will love. When the duck steals a magical sorcerer's hat that Mickey Mouse needs to conduct a musician-free orchestra, the foul-minded fowl gets swept up into a long, strange trip. Don't miss his attempt to kiss Ariel, the Little Mermaid—it's electrifying.

Best scary attraction. "The next time you check into a deserted hotel on the dark side of Hollywood, make sure you know just what kind of vacancy you're filling." That's the lesson host Rod Serling teaches you at the Twilight Zone Tower of Terror, a remarkable ride at Disney's Hollywood Studios. From its abandoned, weed-filled grounds to its eerie music to its cobweb-covered lobby to its unwelcoming boiler room, the Tower of Terror is designed expressly to freak you out. And all that is before you board the creaky freight elevator for a randomly-selected series of violent plunges and sudden ascents.

Best ride at night. Magic Kingdom's "wildest ride in the wilderness," Big Thunder Mountain Railroad is even wilder at night, as its scenery is lit but its track is so pitch black that each curve and dip comes as a surprise. Crystals glow in its bat cave, and sulphur pools swirl in vivid colors. At the mining town of Tumbleweed, sharp-eyed riders will spot drunks and dance-hall dames partying upstairs at the Gold Dust Saloon.

Best character meal. It says a lot that Cinderella is *not* the most entertaining character at Cinderella's Happily Ever After Dinner, a dinner experience at the Grand Floridian hotel. Little girls love the princess, of course, but for adults the real treat is her supporting cast: regal Prince Charming proposes

to moms; squabbling stepsisters Anastasia and Drizella flirt with little boys; haughty Lady Tremaine disapproves of everything. And the buffet is delicious.

Best night spot. Located right in the middle of a huge construction project, spirited Emerald Isle restaurant and pub Raglan Road features no-cover entertainment (step-dancers and a live band) a lavish stock of Irish beers and whiskeys and sophisticated comfort food. Most decor, including four antique grand bars, was imported from Ireland. Children are welcome—and strangely, fit right in—and the menu offers something for every taste.

Best band. The exceptional Mariachi Cobre was formed in Tucson, Ariz., way back in 1971 and played with Linda Ronstadt on her Spanish-language albums. Led by trumpets, violins and exuberant vocals backed by harmonizing guitars, the band expresses the romantic soul of Mexico in a way even the most whitebread gringo can appreciate. The group plays at Epcot's Mexico pavilion.

Best improv troupe. Street performers who channel the mythical residents of a 1940s Tinseltown, the Citizens of Hollywood perform in Disney's Hollywood Studios, incorporate park guests in makeshift dating games, spelling bees and other silly setups.

They include frustrated director Alberto Dante, sassy script girl Paige Turner and dumb-blond starlet Evie Starlight.

Best Pixar attraction. You don't have to be a child to love Finding Nemo—The Musical. Playing at Disney's Animal Kingdom, the stage show taps into the bonds between fathers and sons and is a visual delight. Costumed singers act out their roles as they operate large puppets, some the size of cars.

Best water park ride. There's nothing quite like Crush 'n' Gusher, a Typhoon Lagoon water coaster that powers its riders up lifts and down dips, tunnels and many tight turns. The ride is great for couples and families, as each tube seat two, or even three people. Those with three people *fly*.

Best place to meet locals. Have the town mayor serenade you with "Happy Birthday," gossip with Hildegard Olivia Harding, learn to sing from ebullient voice teacher Victoria Trumpetto. It's all possible at Magic Kingdom's Main Street U.S.A., thanks to Citizens of Main Street, the living, breathing embodiment of the almost-real town.

Best parade. Accompanied by colorful stilt-walkers, dancers and a catchy soundtrack, the stars of some of Disney's most beloved films ride on towering floats in its Festival of Fantasy Parade, a wildly creative new procession through Magic Kingdom. Its stunning floats include a fire-breathing steampunk dragon.

Best restaurant. No, it doesn't serve roast zebra. Ignore the misconceptions about the food at Boma, a beautiful buffet restaurant at Animal Kingdom Lodge; the fare is a mix of non-exotic African dishes with traditional American comfort food. You'll have a wide variety of dishes to pick from both at breakfast and dinner. The artistic decor features hand-cut tin, hand-blown glass and thatched roofs. Servers are outstanding.

Best refurbished ride. During Disney's recent expansion of Fantasyland, the world's most adorable baby-elephant ride was moved, beautifully repainted, and doubled. Now the park's Storybook Circus area sports two Dumbo the Flying Elephants. Disney added a pool for the pachyderms to fly over and multi-colored lights that make a fountain-ringed pool underneath them glow at night. The attraction also includes a great waiting line, with its own indoor playground.

Best meet-and-greet. Audience volunteers help the heroine of "Beauty and the Beast" act out her tale as old as time in Enchanted Tales with Belle, an intimate storytelling show. Everyone who wants to participate can—including parents—and all participants meet the mademoiselle afterward. The child who is picked to play the Beast gets to dance with her, and is rewarded with a kiss on the cheek.

Best new ride. The last attraction in New Fantasyland to be completed is also its best. Everyone digs-digs-digs the Seven Dwarfs Mine Train, a smooth indoor-outdoor roller coaster at Magic Kingdom. Inside it coasts by state-of-the-art Audio-Animatronics versions of the dwarfs; outside it picks up speed and swerves around curves. It was designed to appeal to families, with a fear factor that falls somewhere between nearby kiddie coaster The Barnstormer and the ever-popular Big Thunder Mountain Railroad. An innovative ride system allows each mine cart to sway from side to side, which keeps its passengers from falling into each other. Expect a very long wait unless you have a Fastpass.

What's new

One thing that's always true at Walt Disney World: it's always been enhanced, improved or expanded. Here's a quick scan of the biggest changes over the past few years:

New Fantasyland. The largest expansion in Magic Kingdom history nearly doubled the size of Fantasyland. Disney has added a whole slew of new attractions that aren't very scary, don't have huge height minimums and aren't focused on violent storylines. Instead, its New Fantasyland focuses on calm, good-natured attractions fit for nearly any young child. The area is themed to four classic Disney movies—"Beauty and the Beast," "The Little Mermaid," "Snow White and the Seven Dwarfs" and "Dumbo," the last of which has its own Storybook Circus mini-land. New attractions include the Seven Dwarfs Mine Train roller coaster, the intimate show Enchanted Tales with Belle storytelling and character encounter; the indoor dark ride Under the Sea—Journey of the Little Mermaid and two beautiful circling hubs of the classic Dumbo the Flying Elephant. There's also Be Our Guest, a new restaurant inside the Beast's castle. Building New Fantasyland reportedly cost Disney $300 million. It was finished in 2014.

Festival of Fantasy Parade. The first completely original Magic Kingdom procession in years, the afternoon Festival of Fantasy Parade debuted in March 2014. Its floats expand on the stories told in Fantasyland, such as "The Little Mermaid," "Peter Pan," "Brave," and "Tangled"—Fantasyland has new restrooms themed to that film—and feature princesses Belle, Cinderella, Tiana and those ever-popular "Frozen" sisters Elsa and Anna. It's a beautiful spectacle, with intricate, artistic costumes and dozens upon dozens of performers. The most memorable part is the Sleeping Beauty float, a steampunk-inspired fire-breathing dragon that channels villain Maleficent's more monstrous form. The parade concludes with a cavalcade of classic Disney characters, including Mickey Mouse and Minnie Mouse riding in a hot-air balloon.

Test Track. This popular Epcot ride keeps its old track, but the rest of the attraction is unrecognizable. Now, before riding, guests design their own virtual cars using a touchscreen, tweaking their vehicle's color, shape, graphics and accessories, and choosing its strongest attribute—capability, efficiency, responsiveness or power. Guests then board

open-topped cars that travel first indoors, turning and twisting (but never falling), culminating in a zippy spin outdoors at speeds reaching 65 mph. Throughout the ride, guests are scored against each other based on their car designs. The post-show contains a number of games and activities, including screens that allow guests to create brand-new car designs, with no time limit. The attraction is conspicuously sponsored by Chevrolet.

Wilderness Explorers. Inspired by Russell's scout troop in the Pixar movie "Up," the new attraction Wilderness Explorers is a scavenger hunt focused on animals and conservation. Guests visit over 30 stations scattered throughout Disney's Animal Kingdom, earning badges (stickers) as they complete nature-themed activities. The badges are collected inside an elaborate paper handbook given to guests at the beginning of their adventure. The activities are delightfully low-tech, educational and surprisingly fun. Most teach badge-gatherers simple lessons in biology, environmental responsibility and other worthwhile topics. Wilderness Explorers was designed to be a multi-day experience; finishing all the activities takes approximately six hours.

Art of Animation. Disney World's newest hotel complex, Art of Animation is a Disney Value Resort similar to the Pop Century and All-Star resorts. It contains nearly 900 rooms and over 1,100 family suites. The huge property is divided into four areas, each themed to a different Disney animated movie: "Cars," "Finding Nemo," "The Lion King" and "The Little Mermaid." The resort's vividly colored motel-style buildings are trimmed with towering icons from those movies that hide outdoor stairwells and elevator banks. The grounds of the "Cars" area is especially well-done; life-size figures of the automotive "Cars" characters are scattered here and there, providing good photo opportunities.

Starbucks. What's that? An outside franchise on sacred Disney ground? Heresy! Some Disney loyalists are boiling mad that Disney has allowed Starbucks to sprout up inside its theme parks, but judging by the lines most visitors are delighted. The Main Street Bakery at Magic Kingdom has already been converted, as has the Fountain View at Epcot and the former L.A. Prop Cinema Shop at Disney's Hollywood Studios. Animal Kingdom's Starbucks is scheduled to open on its Discovery Island this year. Downtown Disney now has two Starbucks spots. None of these have any seating to speak of, or even a hint of Disney on their menus. Downtown Disney's West Side Starbucks does has a fun feature: a 70-inch touchscreen that makes a chalk outline of anything you draw on it.

Disney's MyMagic+ system: A whole new world

Developed by the Disney company at a cost reportedly between $800 million and $1 billion, MyMagic+ is a new, high-tech vacation management system that can help you plan and make the most of your Disney vacation. You can use it to schedule attractions days in advance, make dining reservations, buy food and merchandise, even open your hotel-room door. It consists of three things: a "MagicBand" wristband, an app called My Disney Experience, and a new Fastpass+ attraction reservation system. All three became fully operational in March 2014, and Disney has been tweaking them ever since. Based on how they worked as of August, here's a Q&A-style primer of each one:

What is a MagicBand? A MagicBand appears to be a plain rubber wristband, but it's actually a high-tech device. A radio-frequency identification (RFID) chip inside it stores an encrypted code that identifies its wearer's personal profile in a backstage Disney database, which itself stores information on the guest, such as his or her park and Fastpass+ privileges, hotel room access and credit card data. This lets the band function as a park ticket, room key and charge card. An online system lets you decide how much information to give it. (While you can use a MagicBand as a charge card, it doesn't store your credit-card information on it. A handy safety precaution requires you to provide your PIN to make a purchase that totals more than $50.)

MagicBands are available in seven colors: red, blue, green, pink, yellow, orange and gray; replacement bands are gray by default. Bands are designed to withstand both hot and cold temperatures, and are waterproof but don't float. Each has a three-year battery. The bands can be customized with trinkets called MagicBandits.

One of the most noticeable changes brought about by the addition of MagicBands is that Disney has done away with turnstiles at the entrances to its theme and water parks. Now, guests line up in front of waist-high posts called "touch points," where they get their fingerprint scanned and tap their MagicBand (or park ticket) against a sensor. When it turns green, you're good to go.

Why should I wear a MagicBand? Because it can make your Disney stay more efficient, as it replaces a lot of cards and papers that you'd have to carry otherwise. You could potentially visit a park bag-free, with nothing but your band, your smartphone and an ID. As Disney continues to add to its technology, a guest's theme-park experience will likely become more tailored to their individual tastes and preferences. Though at press time (August 2014) it wasn't possible yet, in the future Disney promises that Audio-Animatronics robots in waiting lines will greet guests by name, and live meet-and-greet characters such as Cinderella may offer unprompted greetings such as "So Maddie, I hear it's your birthday today!"

What are its drawbacks? It's not that comfortable, and more importantly, it tracks you in ways you may not care for. Disney databases will now be able to monitor which characters you meet, which souvenirs you buy, and which attractions you visit and when. At its best, this information will help the company respond to shifts in crowd patterns, sending out additional entertainment to busy areas, and beefing up its staff and adding ride vehicles to overwhelmed attractions. However it's possible—perhaps inevitable—that Disney will use the band's ability to collect personal data in other ways, in an attempt to maximize guest spending. A band isn't required to get into a park or to use

the Fastpass+ system, as Disney also offers credit-card-sized plastic tickets.

How do I get a MagicBand? MagicBands are free for Disney hotel guests and annual passholders. Other guests can buy them for $12.95 each. If you're planning to stay at a Disney hotel and reserve it at least 10 days early, Disney will ship your MagicBand(s) to you before you leave for your trip. Otherwise you'll get them when you check in. Disney ships the bands free to annual passholders upon request at 407-560-7277 or disneyworld. disney.go.com/login. Disney sells the bands in all of its theme parks, Downtown Disney and other locations, at its Magic Band Service Centers. MagicBand shipping is only available to addresses in the United States.

What if I lose it? If you misplace your MagicBand, you don't have to worry about someone else using it to get into your hotel room or make purchases under your name. As soon as you report it as missing, a Disney cast member will deactivate it. Replacement bands (always gray) are free for Disney resort guests; other pay $12.95. If you aren't able to get a replacement band right away, you can still use the My Disney Experience app to access your Disney information, including your Fastpass+ reservations.

What is My Disney Experience? My Disney Experience is a free app for iPhones, iPads and Android devices. Using it lets you

view attraction wait times and park maps, make and modify your Fastpass+ reservations, schedule restaurant reservations and over time, Disney says, many more things. To use the app properly, you create a Disney account and link your park ticket to it.

What is Fastpass+? Fastpass+ is an attraction reservation system that lets you avoid waiting in long lines for rides or getting stuck with lousy viewing spots for shows and parades, and allows you to make and modify these reservations months in advance—before you leave home. It replaces Disney's Fastpass—notice, no "plus"—which used paper tickets that could only be obtained at the ride or show they were good for on the day they were issued, and once issued couldn't be changed or modified. The new system has no paper tickets; everything is handled electronically through the MyMagic+ database. As part of the change, more than twice as many Disney attractions accept Fastpasses.

Like before, each Fastpass you reserve assigns you a window of time for you to arrive at a particular attraction. Most rides give you a one-hour window; some parades and shows require you to arrive no later than a particular time. Also like before, Disney's Fastpasses are completely free of charge.

You reserve your rides through the Disney website (disney.com), with the My Disney Experience app or at special theme-park kiosks. Your reservation data is stored in the Disney database, and accessed through your MagicBand or plastic ticket. At each participating attraction, you tap your band or ticket against a MyMagic+ Touchpoint to enter its Fastpass area.

How does it work? For each day of your visit, you can book three Fastpasses for you or your group, at your choice of any one Walt Disney World theme park. If you have a Disney resort room booked and have bought theme park tickets as part of that package, you can reserve rides and shows 60 days in advance. If not, you can do so 30 days out. Magic Kingdom and Disney's Animal Kingdom let you freely choose any attractions you want, however Epcot and Disney's Hollywood Studios divide your choices into two tiers, and restrict you to one from column A (the most popular attractions) and two from column B.

Disney hotel guests can reserve attractions for each day of their stay; other guests can schedule up to seven days of Fastpasses at a time. If you have Fastpasses reserved at one park and decide to go to a different park that day, you can cancel your reservations and rebook new ones. You can do this through the app or website, or at a MyMagic+ Service Center.

Once you use all three of your Fastpasses (or after they expire), you can reserve another ride or show for that day at Fastpass+ kiosks, including one in another park. You can then continue booking same-day Fastpasses one-at-a-time.

What are these kiosks? Walk-up touch-screens that are clustered together in many theme-park lands. If you want to tweak the times or locations of your Fastpasses while you're in a theme park, or add more rides or shows to your schedule, you can make same-day, same-park Fastpass reservations at in-park kiosks, with the hands-on assistance of a knowledgeable Disney cast member. Need to schedule other Fastpasses, for other days and other parks? MyMagic+ Service Centers can schedule those.

What if I don't show up on time? Though Disney doesn't publicize it, its 1-hour Fastpass window has a grace period. Typically, you can arrive up to 5 minutes early, or 15 minutes late, and still enter a Fastpass line. If you miss your designated Fastpass window for an attraction due to circumstances beyond your control (weather, Disney transportation issues), cast members will usually try to accommodate you. However, the later you are, the less helpful they'll be.

How do I take advantage of Fastpass+? Look through this book before you schedule your Fastpasses. Note the hourly wait times for attractions you want to experience, so you don't waste a pass on a ride or show that doesn't need one. Other tips:

• **Reserve your rides** and attractions as soon as you can, so you create theme-park days that best suit your needs. Morning reservation times usually go quickly, especially for the more popular attractions.

• **If you're part of a family** or group that's visiting the parks together, add each member to your Family & Friends list on your Disney account so that your Fastpass times will sync together. Once you've booked your group's Fastpasses, they can be changed and tweaked just like those for an individual.

• **At a park, use the Fastpass+ kiosks** when they're convenient. Doing so not only gets you the help of someone who knows what they're doing, it lets you avoid any Wi-Fi reception problems. Though it employs an innovative AT&T system, Disney's service isn't always available, especially inside buildings, remote park areas, and during heavy-use times such as right before a parade. Kiosks near park entrances tend to be the most crowded; to avoid a long wait visit one deep in the park, such as those in Magic Kingdom's Storybook Circus.

- **After you make your reservations,** use your phone to take a photo of its screen, or the screen of the computer or kiosk you used to make them. This will make it easy to remember your reservation times, and, when you show up at an attraction, serve as proof to its cast members that you do indeed have Fastpasses for it.
- **If you're a parent,** consider taking advantage of Disney's unpublicized Child Swap option, which can be used with or without a Fastpass. You'll find information on it in this book's chapter Walt Disney World A–Z, under the heading Children.

What if I don't want any of this 'magic'?
If you decide you don't feel comfortable using MyMagic+, don't worry; you aren't required to participate in it to visit Walt Disney World. However, Disney has made the system so convenient, efficient and widespread that you'll probably feel compelled to be part of it. If you don't, you'll probably have to deal with Standby lines that are longer than ever, especially at popular attractions such as the new Seven Dwarfs Mine Train roller coaster at Magic Kingdom, Soarin' at Epcot, and Toy Story Mania at Disney's Hollywood Studios.

What if I don't have a smartphone?
You need one (or a tablet) for the My Disney Experience app, but not to use MyMagic+. The system's planning and reservation tools are available at mydisneyexperience.com and can be accessed through MyMagic+ kiosks that dot all four theme parks. See the Overview pages of this book's theme park chapters for locations.

Ready… get set… plan. If you take the time to plan for your trip properly, MyMagic+ can be a useful tool. However, if you aren't familiar with the system and don't use it to reserve your Fastpasses ahead of time, you could easily find yourself spending much of your Disney vacation waiting in line—to choose among "leftover" attractions at in-park Fastpass kiosks, and then in long Standby lines for the rides and shows you most wanted to experience. Standby lines during the summer of 2014 set record levels. At one, the character meet-and-greet Princess Fairytale Hall in Magic Kingdom, parents and their "Frozen"-obsessed offspring waited in line for six hours—six hours!—to meet that movie's queen Elsa and princess Anna.

Needless to say, using MyMagic+ also makes your Disney visit much less spontaneous, and the pre-trip planning required, at up to two months in advance, may be impractical. We hope this guidebook helps.

For what it's worth, the authors go to Disney all the time (at least every other day), and don't wear MagicBands (we think they're a little dorky). But we use the Fastpass+ system every single day.

Photo © Disney

Planning your trip

With just a little bit of preparation, it's easy to put together a terrific Walt Disney World vacation. Planning your trip isn't brain surgery—all you need is this book, the Internet and a phone; a Disney telephone directory appears at the back of this book. Ideally you should put your plan together a year early. As your vacation nears, doing Disney World-focused activities with your family will help everyone look forward to it. For basic planning, here's a step-by-step strategy:

1. Decide when to go. You can have a good time at Disney any day of the year, but if you've got the flexibility, the first two weeks of December is the best time to go. It's not terribly crowded, and there's more to see and do than any other time of the year, thanks to special holiday decor and entertainment. Crowds are also light, and hotel rooms less expensive, from mid-January to Valentine's Day, early- to mid-May and between Labor Day and mid-November (but it's not all good: some attractions close during these times for maintenance, and some parks close earlier). The least crowded week of the year is the one that starts the day after Labor Day.

The worst times to visit? July and early August, when crowds are thick and the air thicker; and the week between Christmas and New Year's, when crowds are horrid and temperatures can be near freezing.

See also the chapter **Walt Disney World A-Z.**

2. Decide how long to stay. Want to see the best of everything Disney has to offer? You'll need at least a week. Each theme park takes a day or more to fully enjoy. You can easily spend a day at each water park as well. Diversions such as fishing, golf, horseback riding and water sports add variety to your trip. If you can't stay a week, three days is enough to get a decent dose of Disney.

3. Build your budget. Add up your daily expenses, including the obvious costs like the hotel and food, but also sometimes-forgotten budget items like gratuities, snacks, souvenirs and gifts for folks back home.

4. Decide where to stay. You have hundreds of choices. Disney itself operates 20 resorts, and nearly every hotel chain known to man has at least one property within 10 miles. Disney resorts are most convenient, of course, and offer other benefits such as Extra Magic Hours (additional time in the parks before or after closing time), free transportation and packaged dining and recreation options. Off-property accommodations run the gamut from very cheap (and often very poorly maintained) motels to

huge luxurious convention complexes. This book's Accommodations chapter reviews every resort on Disney property.

See also the chapter **Accommodations.**

5. Buy your airline tickets. The Orlando International Airport is 19 miles east of Walt Disney World, about a 30-minute drive. It's served by 36 airlines, including American, Delta, Frontier, Southwest, United, U.S. Airways and Air Canada. Driving to Disney? It's smack dab in the middle of Florida next to Interstate 4, 15 miles southwest of downtown Orlando, 70 miles northeast of Tampa.

See also the chapter **Walt Disney World A-Z.**

6. Decide what you want to do. Thumb through this book and check out the official Disney website disneyworld.com. If you have children, let them pick out their favorites.

7. Choose your park tickets. Disney offers a variety of options, including packages with pre-paid dining and recreation if you stay at a Disney resort hotel. Tickets are priced by the number of days they are good for; the longer you stay, the better the value.

See also the chapter **Walt Disney World A-Z.**

8. Make a plan. Check the calendar at disneyworld.com for park hours, fireworks schedules and special events. Talk with your family about having a day or two when you don't visit a park (after all, this is a *vacation*). Keep your plan flexible in case of bad weather. If you will be staying at a Disney hotel, check Extra Magic Hours at disneyworld.com.

9. Book it. Purchase your park tickets and reserve your Disney room through Disney at 407-934-7639 or disneyworld.com. Call between 7 a.m. and 10 p.m. Eastern time.

10. Reserve your restaurants. Character meals, dinner shows and key dining times for regular restaurants fill up months in advance for peak periods. The meals that book quickest are those at Cinderella's Royal Table, inside Cinderella Castle. You can book a table as early as 190 days out if you're staying at a Disney resort (407-939-3463 or at disneyworld. com). Many entertainment, sports and recreation choices require reservations, too.

11. Reserve your rides. Choose your Fastpass+ times on the first day you can, so you have the most variety to pick from. If you have already booked a room at a Disney resort hotel and have bought theme park tickets as part of that package, you can reserve Fastpasses 60 days in advance; if not, you can do so 30 days out. Be as obsessive as you can with this; key times for popular rides, shows and character greetings are often taken on the first day they are available.

See also the earlier article in this book **MyMagic+: A Whole New World.**

12. Rent a car, maybe. Disney has such an extensive transportation system that you may not need to rent a car. The company's unique Magical Express bus service shuttles Disney resort guests from the Orlando International Airport, and complimentary

boats, buses and monorails move guests around Disney World property. However, those with cars get around quicker, and have the option to visit areas outside Disney. You can rent a car from the airport or from many locations on Disney property. (The authors would absolutely rent a car. They hate riding Disney buses; they can take forever.)

See also the chapter **Walt Disney World A-Z.**

What to pack. Walt Disney World visitors often underestimate the heat and humidity inherent in Central Florida, and can be unprepared for the amount of outdoor exposure a Disney vacation requires. Therefore, they pack poorly. Here are some packing tips that recognize that Florida is indeed the Sunshine State:

For all ages. Suitcase fundamentals include T-shirts, loose-fitting cotton tops, capris and shorts with large pockets, baseball caps and swimsuits, and broken-in walking shoes (pack two pair per person, so if it rains everyone still has a dry pair). Flip-flop sandals with a strap between the toes are a bad idea; they create blisters when used this intensely. In the winter guests need clothes to layer, such as jackets, sweaters and sweatshirts, as days start off cool but warm quickly. January mornings can be below freezing at 9 a.m. but 60 degrees by noon. Temperatures at 7 p.m. should be no higher than the 50s through March. From May through August, the heat index is usually at least 105 degrees by noon. (For detailed weather data log on to weather.com, type in the ZIP code 32830 and then scroll down to the tab "Monthly.")

Other essentials include an umbrella or rain poncho, sunglasses and sunscreen.

Sun protection

Florida visitors should use a sunscreen with a high SPF rating and quality ingredients (such as No-Ad 50, above left). Aloe-based after-sun products (above right) ease pain and help repair skin.

Guests can keep their hands free by using a backpack or waist pack instead of a purse. Don't forget tickets, reservation confirmations and all the various battery chargers a modern life requires. And don't splurge on those specs—sunglasses are the No. 1 item guests lose at Disney World. Cast members find hundreds of pairs a day.

For children. You should dress your children like you dress themselves—casually and comfortably—but with more protection from the sun. Wide-brimmed hats help. Bring snacks (granola bars, raisin boxes) and, for autographs, a fat Sharpie pen (pick a thick one so furry characters can hold it easily).

Most forgotten item. The most common item Disney World visitors mistakenly leave at home—and at the end of the trip, the item they most often leave behind in their hotel rooms—is a cell phone charger.

Involving your children

Announcing the trip. "We're going to Disney World!" Letting your children know about an upcoming Disney trip can be a thrilling moment all on its own. Here are some creative ways to spring the good news:

Quiz cards. Create a quiz with questions for children to answer on Disney characters, movies or on Disney World itself. Each question is on the front of a card laid face up on a table; its answer is on the back with one letter written larger, with a thick marker. When a child answers a question correctly, he or she turns over that card. When all the cards are revealed, they spell out a message such as: "We Are Going to Disney World on Tuesday!" For help coming up with questions see this book's theme-park and character chapters.

Scavenger hunt. Create a scavenger hunt that uses clues about Disney characters or quotes from Disney movies. Make each "find" a Disney trinket that has a card attached with the next clue. The final card—announcing the trip—can be attached to a helium-filled Mickey balloon tucked inside a new suitcase. When the suitcase is opened, the balloon floats up. The child can then use the suitcase to pack for the trip.

Letter from Mickey Mouse. Mail your child a letter or postcard that appears to be from Mickey Mouse, Cinderella or another

Disney character and reads "can't wait to meet you at Disney World!" (Mickey could add "See ya real soon!").

Backpack with Walt Disney World stuff. As a present, fill a new backpack with Disney World items such as an autograph book, several Disney Dollars and a T-shirt. Your child will quickly figure out where he or she is headed.

Jigsaw puzzle. Create a personalized jigsaw puzzle that, when assembled, announces the trip. Use paint or felt-tip markers to write "We're going to Walt Disney World tomorrow!" (or "next week!" or "for Christmas!" etc.) on the pieces. Give your child the puzzle as a surprise present.

Sources for these materials. Disney items (including theme-park merchandise) for most of the above ideas are available online at disneystore.com or over the phone at 407-363-6200; choose option 3 to reach a live operator. At press time, Disney World postcards were sold only over the phone. Disney Dollars can be purchased through Walt Disney World Ticketing at 407-566-4985. Uninflated Disney Mylar balloons can be ordered online through many sources, including Amazon.com, for less than $10; the balloon can be inflated at most any florist or card shop for a token fee. Dick Blick Art Supplies (800-828-4548, dickblick.com) sells pre-cut Create-A-Puzzle kits.

Smart snacks

Nut packs, fruit and nut bars and raisin boxes are easy to stuff into a backpack or fanny pack, offer tasty and nutritious energy, and can help avoid expensive and time-consuming stops at snack stands.

Disney's best food and restaurants

THEME PARK RESTAURANTS

50's Prime Time Cafe: Retro dining with mom as your server. Hollywood Studios.

Be Our Guest: French-American dinner inside the Beast's castle. Magic Kingdom.

Biergarten: Meat-heavy German buffet with a live oompah band. Epcot.

Cinderella's Royal Table: Character meals inside Cinderella Castle. Magic Kingdom.

Coral Reef: Seafood. Dining room looks into The Seas aquarium. Epcot.

Hollywood Brown Derby: A fine-dining gem. Hollywood Studios.

La Hacienda de San Angel: Waterfront dining room. Great margaritas. Epcot.

Le Cellier: Cozy steakhouse. Epcot.

Liberty Tree Tavern: Hearty Colonial food. Magic Kingdom.

Mama Melrose's Ristorante Italiano: First-rate flatbreads and pastas; comfy ambience. Hollywood Studios.

Monsieur Paul: Gourmet French dinners with outstanding pedigrees. Epcot.

Sci-Fi Dine-In Theater Restaurant: Burgers, shakes in a simulated drive-in, tables are in classic-car replicas. Hollywood Studios.

Spice Road Table: Tasty tapas-style Mediterranean cuisine. Epcot.

Teppan Edo: Teppanyaki chefs. Epcot.

Tokyo Dining: Relaxing meals, sushi for American tastes. Epcot.

Tony's Town Square: Italian comfort food. Magic Kingdom.

Tusker House: African-flavored buffets at lunch, dinner; characters at breakfast and lunch. Disney's Animal Kingdom.

Tutto Italia Ristorante: Traditional pastas, meat and fish. Epcot.

Via Napoli: Outstanding real-Italian wood-fired pizza, rich pastas. Epcot.

Yak & Yeti: Southeast Asian cuisine in an artifact-filled eatery. Animal Kingdom.

OTHER RESTAURANTS

1900 Park Fare: Walt Disney World's best character meals, especially at dinner. Grand Floridian Resort.

Artist Point: Rustic Pacific Northwest cuisine in relaxed atmosphere. Wilderness Lodge Resort.

Beaches & Cream: Huge sundaes; tasty burgers. Yacht and Beach Club Resort.

Boma—Flavors of Africa: African-flavored buffet. Animal Kingdom Lodge.

California Grill: New American fine dining atop the Contemporary Resort.

Captain's Grille: A varied American menu offers a little of everything. Yacht and Beach Club Resort.

Cítricos: Comfortable Mediterranean dinners. Grand Floridian Resort.

Crossroads at House of Blues: Southern Creole, folk-art rooms. Downtown Disney.

Garden View Tea Room: An elegant formal lunch on flowery china. Very civilized. Grand Floridian Resort.

Grand Floridian Café: Pleasant American fare. Grand Floridian Resort.

Jiko—The Cooking Place: Fine African fusion dishes. Animal Kingdom Lodge.

Narcoossee's: Seafood; building sits over water. Grand Floridian Resort.

Portobello: Comfortable eatery features classy pasta, pizza. Downtown Disney.

Raglan Road: Irish-American comfort food; table dancers, band. Downtown Disney.

Sanaa: East African cuisine in eatery overlooking animal-filled savanna. Animal Kingdom Lodge.

Turf Club Bar & Grill: American fare in a golf-club setting. Saratoga Springs Resort.

Victoria & Albert's: Disney's ultimate gourmet dining experience requires formal dress. Grand Floridian Resort.

The Wave: Fresh healthy choices in a relaxing, though windowless, room. Contemporary Resort.

Yachtsman Steakhouse: Disney World's best steakhouse; inviting setting. Yacht and Beach Club Resort.

FAST FOOD

Columbia Harbour House: Healthy, quality meals. Magic Kingdom.

Earl of Sandwich: Inexpensive, hot, crusty-bread sandwiches; incredibly soothing tomato soup. Downtown Disney.

Flame Tree Barbecue: Scenic outdoor spot serves good chicken, ribs, pork. Best on cooler days. Animal Kingdom.

Sunshine Seasons: Grilled meats, sandwiches, fresh salads. Nothing fried. Epcot.

TREATS

Big Top Treats: Freshly prepared sweets include candy apples. Magic Kingdom.

L'Artisan Des Glaces: Artisan ice cream cones. Epcot.

Saving for your trip. Want to teach your kids the value of a dollar? A Disney trip can help. The more involved they are in budgeting for your vacation, the more they'll learn the benefits of saving and wise spending.

Countdown chain
Tick off the days before your Disney trip with the help of a countdown chain you make with your family.

Disney Fund. Once a trip is in the works, the family can create a special "Disney Fund" to help pay for the entire trip or for special parts of it such as a character meal, a backstage tour, a fireworks cruise or a horseback ride. Start with a large can (a washed coffee can will do), then cover it, decorate it and label it "Disney Fund." Put it in a visible spot in your kitchen, so it's easy for everyone to toss in extra money and spare change.

The fund can also be used for spending money for your kids. Cash can be turned into Disney Dollars or Disney gift cards.

Anticipating your trip. Like looking forward to Christmas day, anticipating a Walt Disney World vacation can be nearly as much fun as the event itself. Build your family's excitement with these ideas:

Countdown meals. Look forward to your Disney trip by creating meals and activities inspired by Disney movies and characters that you have at regular intervals (60 days before your trip, 30 days before, etc.). One of the easiest meals to make: Mickey Mouse pancakes. Other ideas: "Alice in Wonderland" tea sandwiches (ham and cheese, PB&J) with Cheshire Cat smiles (slices of melon), an unbirthday cake; a "Beauty and the Beast" dining table set with a single red rose; flying kites or feeding birds "Mary Poppins" style; "Pirates of the Caribbean" fruit swords on wooden skewers, perhaps with a treasure hunt; a "Sleeping Beauty" cake that is half blue, half pink that no one can eat unless they are wearing pajamas; a "Snow White and the Seven Dwarfs" bobbing-for-apples game, or perhaps this: you tie a string to a stem of an apple, hang it up, and have everyone take turns biting it without using their hands.

Countdown chain. "How long until Disney World?" One consequence of planning a trip to Walt Disney World with your family is hearing this question. Endlessly.

A countdown chain is a fun way to answer it, especially when your family takes on this craft project together. Here's how you do it:

Using construction paper, create a chain that has the same number of links as the number of days until your trip. Number the links consecutively on one side. Decorate the other side with glitter, markers, paint and stickers. Perhaps give each link its own theme, such as a particular character or ride. Make special links for birthdays and holidays, as well as milestones such as "One Month To Go" or "One Week To Go." Hang the chain in a conspicuous spot, such as the kitchen ceiling.

Each day tear off one of the links, perhaps at bedtime or first thing in the morning.

Remove the last link right before leaving for your trip.

Disney World movie nights. Sitting down with the family for a few Walt Disney World movie nights—watching films that form the basis of the rides and shows you're about to experience—is a great way to get in the right state of mind for a trip to the Vacation Kingdom, and will make the trip itself more fun, because you'll be more familiar with Disney's stories. In fact, many Disney attractions make little or no sense if you don't already know their characters, back stories or music. By the way, not every choice needs to be a Disney movie. Some Disney World attractions are based on films from other studios, such as "Raiders of the Lost Ark" and the "Star Wars" series.

To make your movie nights truly special, schedule them when everyone can relax together. Before a movie begins, parents and children alike should get all of their distractions out of the way—no e-mails, no chores, no homework, no texting! Set a start time, turn down the lights and make sure everyone has a comfortable seat. Schedule an intermission for bathroom runs and snack grabs.

Walt Disney World

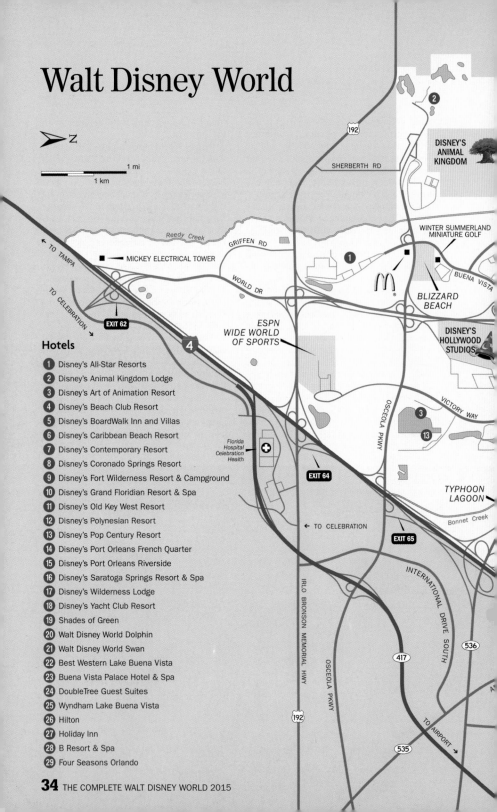

N

1 mi
1 km

TO TAMPA

TO CELEBRATION

EXIT 62

4

MICKEY ELECTRICAL TOWER

Reedy Creek

GRIFFEN RD

WORLD DR

192

SHERBERTH RD

DISNEY'S ANIMAL KINGDOM

WINTER SUMMERLAND MINIATURE GOLF

BUENA VISTA

BLIZZARD BEACH

DISNEY'S HOLLYWOOD STUDIOS

ESPN WIDE WORLD OF SPORTS

Florida Hospital Celebration Health

EXIT 64

← TO CELEBRATION

OSCEOLA PKWY

VICTORY WAY

TYPHOON LAGOON

Bonnet Creek

EXIT 65

IRLO BRONSON MEMORIAL HWY

192

OSCEOLA PKWY

INTERNATIONAL DRIVE SOUTH

536

417

535

TO AIRPORT →

Hotels

1. Disney's All-Star Resorts
2. Disney's Animal Kingdom Lodge
3. Disney's Art of Animation Resort
4. Disney's Beach Club Resort
5. Disney's BoardWalk Inn and Villas
6. Disney's Caribbean Beach Resort
7. Disney's Contemporary Resort
8. Disney's Coronado Springs Resort
9. Disney's Fort Wilderness Resort & Campground
10. Disney's Grand Floridian Resort & Spa
11. Disney's Old Key West Resort
12. Disney's Polynesian Resort
13. Disney's Pop Century Resort
14. Disney's Port Orleans French Quarter
15. Disney's Port Orleans Riverside
16. Disney's Saratoga Springs Resort & Spa
17. Disney's Wilderness Lodge
18. Disney's Yacht Club Resort
19. Shades of Green
20. Walt Disney World Dolphin
21. Walt Disney World Swan
22. Best Western Lake Buena Vista
23. Buena Vista Palace Hotel & Spa
24. DoubleTree Guest Suites
25. Wyndham Lake Buena Vista
26. Hilton
27. Holiday Inn
28. B Resort & Spa
29. Four Seasons Orlando

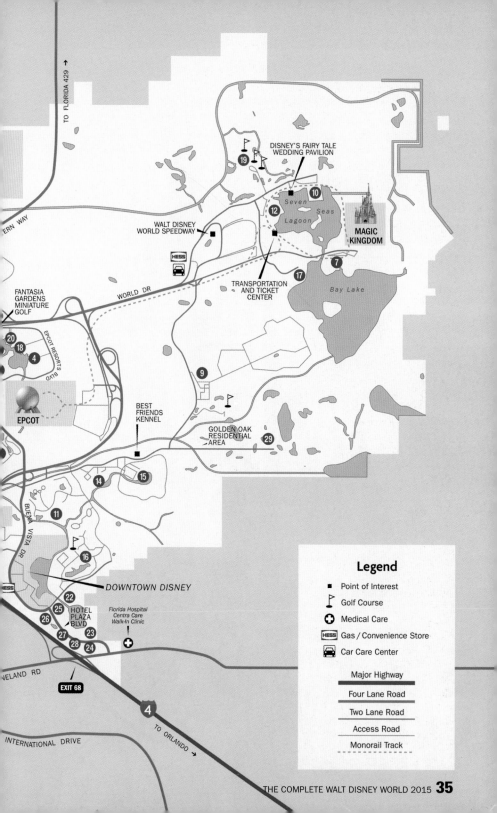

TO FLORIDA 429 →

DISNEY'S FAIRY TALE
WEDDING PAVILION

19

10

12

Seven
Seas
Lagoon

**MAGIC
KINGDOM**

WALT DISNEY
WORLD SPEEDWAY

HESS

TRANSPORTATION
AND TICKET
CENTER

7

17

Bay Lake

WORLD DR

FANTASIA
GARDENS
MINIATURE
GOLF

20

18

4

EPCOT RESORTS BLVD

9

EPCOT

BEST
FRIENDS
KENNEL

GOLDEN OAK
RESIDENTIAL
AREA

29

14

15

BUENA VISTA DR

11

16

DOWNTOWN DISNEY

22

25

26

27

23

28

24

HOTEL
PLAZA
BLVD

Florida Hospital
Centra Care
Walk-In Clinic

HESS

ERN WAY

VELAND RD

EXIT 68

4

TO ORLANDO →

INTERNATIONAL DRIVE

Legend

■ Point of Interest

⚑ Golf Course

✚ Medical Care

HESS Gas / Convenience Store

🚗 Car Care Center

Major Highway

Four Lane Road

Two Lane Road

Access Road

Monorail Track

Magic Kingdom

A place for adventure, fantasy and nostalgia; a place to celebrate "Once upon a time…" and "…happily ever after," Magic Kingdom appeals to memories and imagination, childhood dreams, the wish to be the prettiest girl at the ball. Its idealized world includes the friendliest small town ever, an achingly beautiful castle, flying elephants and pirate ships.

The first park to open at Walt Disney World, Magic Kingdom started off as a larger, more spacious version of California's Disneyland. Though Walt Disney unexpectedly died just before construction began, his brother Roy ensured that his dream park was completed. It opened October 1, 1971.

The most child-focused Disney park, Magic Kingdom is easy to navigate, with attractions placed closely together. In the 2014 TripAdvisor Travelers' Choice Awards, it was rated the third best amusement park in the United States. (First place in the survey went to Discovery Cove at nearby SeaWorld, second place to Islands of Adventure at nearby Universal Orlando, fourth place to Disney's Hollywood Studios.)

Best of the park

Lots of rides and shows. It has more than twice the attractions of other Disney World parks, everything from a century-old merry-go-round to a brand-new roller coaster.

A cornucopia of characters. More of these bonafide Disney celebrities appear here than anywhere else at Disney World. You'll find them in various parades, shows and attractions, in a street party and three character meals, and at many meet-and-greet spots.

Classic Disney movies. From Dumbo the Flying Elephant to the Seven Dwarfs Mine Train to Peter Pan's Flight, Magic Kingdom is filled with attractions inspired by Disney's legendary animated films.

Main Street USA. This slice of Americana re-creates a small town boulevard from a

century ago. Elaborately detailed from its architecture and music to the costumes of its engaging "citizens," the dreamlike lane triggers nostalgia.

The master's touch. Although he didn't live to see Walt Disney World completed, Walt Disney was deeply involved in its planning as well as in several of its attractions. Those include Carousel of Progress, The Enchanted Tiki Room, The Haunted Mansion, It's a Small World, the Jungle Cruise, PeopleMover, Peter Pan's Flight, Pirates of the Caribbean, the Prince Charming Regal Carrousel and the Walt Disney World Railroad.

Worst of the park

The crowds. Attraction capacity: 9,750. Park capacity: 60,000. You do the math. Afternoons are the worst; holidays can be jam-packed.

The inconvenience. Getting to the Magic Kingdom can be an adventure in itself, as its parking lot does not adjoin the park. Visitors coming from non-Disney hotels have to first drive or ride a bus, then board a monorail or a ferry boat to get to the park entrance.

Afternoons in Tomorrowland. Apparently the future holds little shade but lots and lots of sunny asphalt. Not good on a warm day.

Getting oriented. Magic Kingdom is divided into six distinctly themed areas:

Main Street USA. After entering the park under a train station, guests find themselves in the bustling Town Square of a (re-created) turn-of-the-century American town. A boulevard leads straight to Cinderella Castle. From there, walkways spoke out to five attraction-packed lands.

Adventureland. A mix of African jungles, Arabian nights, Caribbean architecture and South Seas landscaping, this land is home to the Jungle Cruise, Pirates of the Caribbean and several smaller adventures.

Liberty Square. Honoring America's Colonial heritage, this land's Federal and Georgian architecture brings back the time of the Revolutionary War. Its best attractions: the special-effects-laden Haunted Mansion and the seriously patriotic Hall of Presidents.

Facing page: One of the most famous landmarks in the world, Cinderella Castle faces Main Street U.S.A.

Guests enter Magic Kingdom at Town Square, which is dominated by stately City Hall. A double-decker bus loads passengers for a free trip to Cinderella Castle.

Frontierland. Twangin' banjo and fiddle music welcomes you to this fun look at 19th-century rural America. It's home to Big Thunder Mountain Railroad, Splash Mountain and a few less memorable efforts.

Fantasyland. Set behind Cinderella Castle, Magic Kingdom's largest land holds attractions ideal for young children and their families. Most are based on fairy tales or classic Disney movies. The original Fantasyland resembles a royal courtyard during a Renaissance fair. A second area, which opened in stages from 2012 through 2014, includes an Enchanted Forest section with an indoor "Little Mermaid" ride, a magical show starring Belle, a rollicking Seven Dwarfs Mine Train and a "Beauty and the Beast" restaurant. A third area contains a "Dumbo"-inspired Storybook Circus with a kiddie coaster and a double dose of the baby pachyderm.

Tomorrowland. Themed to be an intergalactic spaceport, today's version of tomorrow is a trip back to the future of the 1930s. Except for some of it, which is the 1970s as seen from the 1970s. Confusing? You betcha. Sort of sad, too. Iconic rides include the classic Space Mountain, a roller coaster in the dark.

Family matters. All four thrill rides have height minimums—40 inches for Big Thunder Mountain Railroad and Splash Mountain; 38 inches for Seven Dwarfs Mine Train; 44 inches for Space Mountain. Also, Stitch's Great Escape has a height minimum of 40 inches. Children need to be 54 inches to drive alone on Tomorrowland Speedway; 32 inches to ride as a passenger.

Except for the Speedway, all rides with height minimums have elements that could frighten children. Others include Astro Orbiter (fast, high, tilted flight); The Haunted Mansion (dark ominous atmosphere, some screams, pop-up heads); and Pirates of the Caribbean (dark, short drop, realistic cannon battle, simulated fire).

If it rains. Ducking out of the rain is pretty easy at Magic Kingdom, as stores and counter-service restaurants line most walkways. Big Thunder Mountain Railroad and the Seven Dwarfs Mine Train close when it rains, and parades, street parties, outdoor shows and fireworks can be shortened or cancelled. Eleven attractions close when lightning is in the area—Astro Orbiter, Dumbo the Flying Elephant, Jungle Cruise, Liberty Square Riverboat, Magic Carpets of Aladdin, Main Street Vehicles, Splash Mountain, Swiss Family Treehouse, Tomorrowland Speedway, Tom Sawyer Island and the Walt Disney World Railroad.

The Dapper Dans pose on the Main Street horse trolley. The barbershop quartet serenades riders a few times each morning.

Fun finds. These little things to look for are scattered throughout the park:

Main Street USA. "Well, howdy!" a statue of Goofy says every 30 seconds. It sits on a bench in front of Tony's Town Square Restaurant... The stars of 1955's "Lady and the Tramp" have put their paw prints in the sidewalk in front of the restaurant patio... A window at the Emporium identifies its proprietor as Osh Popham, the owner of the general store in the 1963 movie "Summer Magic"... A singer and dancer can be heard from two Center Street windows marked "Voice and Singing Private Lessons" and "Music and Dance Lessons, Ballet, Tap & Waltz."

Liberty Square. Streams of brown pavement symbolize sewage that often flowed down 18th-century streets... A 1987 cast of the Liberty Bell sits across from the Hall of Presidents... Two lanterns in a Hall of Presidents window facing The Haunted Mansion recall the 1860 Longfellow poem "Paul Revere's Ride."

Fantasyland. In the mosaic in the castle breezeway, stepsister Drizella's face is green with envy, stepsister Anastasia's is red with anger... Cinderella's wishing well is to the right of the castle, on a walkway that leads to Tomorrowland... Her fountain is behind the castle to the left. Thanks to a wall sketch behind it, youngsters who stand in front of the fountain see the princess wearing her crown... Luggage racks outside the Storybook Circus restroom include bags for Hyacinth Hippo from 1940's "Fantasia" and the Big Bad Wolf. One bag is stamped with the logo for Red's Amazing Juggling Unicycles, referencing Pixar's 1987 short "Red's Dream," about a red unicycle ridden by a circus clown as part of a juggling act. Another bag is stamped Melody Time brand Brass Horns 'Always in Toon,' a reference to Disney's 1948 animated feature "Melody Time." Hat boxes are from Ten Schillings and Sixpence Ltd., which refers to the number on the Mad Hatter's hat brim seen in the 1951 Disney movie "Alice in Wonderland."

Hidden Mickeys. You'll see the three-circle shape if you know where to look:

Main Street USA. Inside Tony's Town Square restaurant, as bread loaves in a basket on a server.

Adventureland. On the entrance bridge, as white flowers on the first shield on both sides of the walkway.

Liberty Square. In the Columbia Harbour House restaurant, as circular wall maps in the room across from the order counter... In Liberty Tree Tavern, as painted grapes at the top of a spice rack in the lobby, to the right of the fireplace.

Lashed together by rope, a wood sign welcomes you to Frontierland, a rural American settlement straight out of the 1800s.

Fantasyland. An impression of Oswald the Lucky Rabbit hides in the middle of the walkway across from the Enchanted Tales with Belle entrance sign, as three imbedded pebbles… On Gaston's statue in front of his tavern, the three-circle shape is formed by dark impressions in the rock below Gaston's left leg, near the water line.

Tomorrowland. In a Mickey's Star Traders mural as loops of a highway, train headlights, glass domes of the building, satellite dishes, clear domes covering a city and Mickey ears on top of two windows.

Know before you go. Need cash? A stroller? Help with MyMagic+? Read on:

ATMs. The park has five: There's one right at the entrance by the lockers, another at City Hall, one in the breezeway between Adventureland and Frontierland, one near the Pinocchio Village Haus restroom and one inside the Tomorrowland arcade.

Baby Care Center. To the left of the Crystal Palace on Main Street U.S.A., this indoor spot has changing rooms, nursing areas, a microwave and playroom. It sells diapers, formula, pacifiers and over-the-counter meds.

FastPass+ kiosks. Cast members help you book Fastpasses at walk-up touchscreens at City Hall and Town Square Theater (Main Street U.S.A.), Jungle Cruise and the Adventureland breezeway (Adventureland), Buzz Lightyear's Space Ranger Spin and Stitch's Great Escape (Tomorrowland) and Mickey's PhilharMagic and Pete's Silly Sideshow (Fantasyland).

First aid. By the Baby Care Center, nurses treat minor issues, call EMTs for serious stuff.

Guest Relations. Located at walk-up windows outside the entrance to the park on

A crowd of park guests enter Adventureland at the start of a Magic Kingdom day. This tropical area represents everywhere in the world that isn't the United States or Europe.

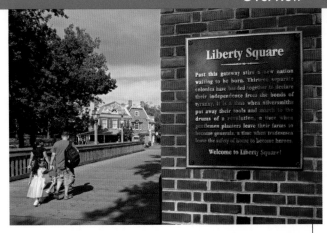

A family crosses a wooden bridge into Liberty Square, a colonial village at the dawn of America's independence. A plaque at the entrance reads "Past this gateway stirs a new nation waiting to be born."

the right, and a walk-in lobby at City Hall. Cast members answer general questions, make dining reservations, exchange currency, hand out maps and times guides for all Disney World parks, and store lost items found in the park that day.

Locker rentals. Rent them just inside the park on the right ($7 a day, $5 deposit). Lockers are adjacent.

MyMagic+ Service Center. Inside Town Square Theater, cast members answer questions about MyMagic+ services: the My Disney Experience website and app, the MagicBand ticketing system and the FastPass+ attraction-reservation service.

Package pickup. Anything you buy in the park can be sent to the park entrance for you to pick up later at no charge. Allow three hours. Packages can also be delivered to Disney hotels or shipped nationally.

Parking. $17 a day per car. Free for Disney hotel guests and annual passholders.

Stroller rentals. Just inside the park entrance on the right, the Stroller Shop has single strollers for $15 a day ($13 length of stay), doubles for $31 ($27 length of stay). Get replacements at the Trading Post in Frontierland or the Tomorrowland Arcade.

Disney transportation. Monorails go to Epcot and the Contemporary, Grand Floridian and Polynesian Resorts. Boats travel to Ft. Wilderness, Grand Floridian, Polynesian Resorts and Wilderness Lodge. Buses serve all Disney resorts and theme parks as well as Blizzard Beach; there's no direct service to Downtown Disney, Typhoon Lagoon or ESPN Wide World of Sports.

Wheelchair and scooter rentals. The Stroller Shop rents wheelchairs for $12 a day ($10 length of stay). EVCs are $50 ($20 deposit).

Fantasyland represents, for the most part, Europe. Except for its Storybook Circus area, which portrays a small American town hosting a traveling circus. The area is decorated with colorful, old-fashioned signs and posters.

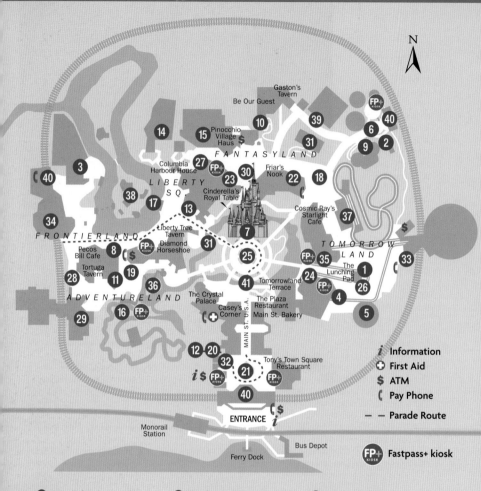

- **1** Astro Orbiter
- **2** The Barnstormer
- **3** Big Thunder Mountain RR
- **4** Buzz Lightyear's Space Ranger Spin
- **5** Carousel of Progress
- **6** Casey Jr. Splash 'n' Soak Station
- **7** Celebrate the Magic
- **8** Country Bear Jamboree
- **9** Dumbo the Flying Elephant
- **10** Enchanted Tales with Belle
- **11** The Enchanted Tiki Room
- **12** Festival of Fantasy Parade (start)
- **13** The Hall of Presidents
- **14** The Haunted Mansion
- **15** it's a small world
- **16** Jungle Cruise
- **17** Liberty Square Riverboat
- **18** Mad Tea Party
- **19** Magic Carpets of Aladdin
- **20** Main Street Electrical Parade (start)
- **21** Main Street Vehicles
- **22** The Many Adventures of Winnie the Pooh
- **23** Mickey's PhilharMagic
- **24** Monster's Inc. Laugh Floor
- **25** Move It! Shake It! Celebrate It! Street Party
- **26** The PeopleMover
- **27** Peter Pan's Flight
- **28** A Pirate's Adventure
- **29** Pirates of the Caribbean
- **30** Prince Charming Regal Carrousel
- **31** Seven Dwarfs Mine Train
- **32** Sorcerers of Magic Kingdom
- **33** Space Mountain
- **34** Splash Mountain
- **35** Stitch's Great Escape!
- **36** Swiss Family Treehouse
- **37** Tomorrowland Speedway
- **38** Tom Sawyer Island
- **39** Under the Sea
- **40** Walt Disney World Railroad
- **41** Wishes (best viewing spot)

Attractions at a Glance

Here's a quick look at the attractions at Magic Kingdom, each of which is reviewed in detail later in this chapter. Each attraction is rated from one to five stars (★) based on how well it lives up to its promise. Note: ratings are not based on the size and scope of attractions, therefore a relatively slight experience such as Enchanted Tales with Belle can have the same five-star rating as the much more elaborate Seven Dwarfs Mine Train. A checkmark (✔) indicates an author favorite. The Fastpass+ logo (FastPass+) appears if the attraction can be reserved in advance.

Five-star attractions

Big Thunder Mountain Railroad. ★★★★★ ✔ FastPass+ This outdoor roller coaster twists and turns through mountain landscapes and a mining town. No steep drops. Height minimum 40 inches. Frontierland.

Disney Festival of Fantasy Parade. ★★★★★ ✔ FastPass+ New-for-2014 daytime procession includes princess floats, Maleficent as a fire-breathing dragon. Travels Frontierland, Liberty Square, Main Street U.S.A.

Enchanted Tales with Belle. ★★★★★ ✔ FastPass+ "Beauty and the Beast" heroine retells her story with audience volunteers. Fantasyland, Enchanted Forest.

The Hall of Presidents. ★★★★★ ✔ FastPass+ Widescreen film followed by robotic presentation of all U.S. presidents. Washington and Obama speak. Liberty Square.

The Haunted Mansion. ★★★★★ ✔ FastPass+ "Doom buggies" tour ghostly retirement home. Silly spooky. Liberty Square.

It's a Small World. ★★★★★ ✔ FastPass+ Dark gentle ride starring singing dolls and whimsical animals tours world cultures. Fantasyland, Castle Courtyard.

Main Street Vehicles. ★★★★★ ✔ Horse trolleys, motorized vehicles shuttle up and down Main Street U.S.A.

Mickey's PhilharMagic. ★★★★★ ✔ FastPass+ Donald Duck stumbles through classic Disney films in this delightful 3-D movie. Fantasyland, Castle Courtyard.

Seven Dwarfs Mine Train. ★★★★★ ✔ FastPass+ Mild indoor/outdoor coaster has Audio-Animatronic dwarfs. Height minimum 38 inches. Fantasyland, Enchanted Forest.

Space Mountain. ★★★★★ ✔ FastPass+ Very dark indoor coaster simulates space flight. Unexpected drops. Height minimum 44 inches. Tomorrowland.

Wishes. ★★★★★ ✔ FastPass+ Creative fireworks show behind and beside Cinderella Castle syncs with music. Launches behind Cinderella Castle.

Four-star attractions

The Barnstormer. ★★★★ ✔ FastPass+ Kiddie coaster is fast, but not threatening. Height minimum 35 inches. Fantasyland, Storybook Circus.

Casey Jr Splash 'n' Soak Station. ★★★★ ✔ Splash zone with the "Dumbo" circus train and animals. Fantasyland, Storybook Circus.

Celebrate the Magic. ★★★★ ✔ Creative projected light show onto Cinderella Castle.

Dumbo the Flying Elephant. ★★★★ ✔ FastPass+ Two-seat baby elephants circle, with an indoor playground queue. Fantasyland, Storybook Circus.

Main Street Electrical Parade. ★★★★ ✔ FastPass+ Retro night procession has floats, characters in lights. Travels Frontierland, Liberty Square, Main Street U.S.A.

The Many Adventures of Winnie the Pooh. ★★★★ ✔ FastPass+ Indoor dark ride recalls Blustery Day. Fantasyland, Castle Courtyard.

Monsters Inc Laugh Floor. ★★★★ ✔ FastPass+ Interactive video improv show with animated characters. Tomorrowland.

Move It! Shake It! Celebrate It! Street Party. ★★★★ ✔ Interactive street party with characters, dancers and stiltwalkers. In front of Cinderella Castle.

The PeopleMover. ★★★★ ✔ Elevated indoor / outdoor tour through four buildings of Tomorrowland.

Peter Pan's Flight. ★★★★ ✔ FastPass+ Vintage dark ride has aerial views of London, Never Land. Fantasyland, Castle Courtyard.

Pirates of the Caribbean. ★★★★ ✔ FastPass+ Indoor boat ride populated with rowdy pirates. Adventureland.

Prince Charming Regal Carrousel. ★★★★ ✔ Canopy-covered antique merry-go-round. Fantasyland, Castle Courtyard.

A ride operator controls the action at Dumbo the Flying Elephant. All Disney cast members wear costumes; at Fantasyland's Storybook Circus they dress as circus emcees.

Sorcerers of the Magic Kingdom. ★★★★ ✔ Interactive video game uses embedded-RFID "spell cards" to vanquish villains throughout the park. Sign up on Main Street U.S.A.

Splash Mountain. ★★★★ FastPass+ Soggy flume ride travels indoors and outdoors, past Audio-Animatronics figures telling Brer Rabbit's story, ending in a steep splashdown. Height minimum 40 inches. Frontierland.

Walt Disney's Carousel of Progress. ★★★★ ✔ Audio-Animatronics stage show stars a robotic family through the ages extolling the joys of progress. Note: We've rated it four stars because it's such a weird historical relic. It delivered fully on its promise in 1964, now… not so much. Tomorrowland.

Three-star attractions

Astro Orbiter. ★★★ ✔ Elevated hub-and-spoke rockets circle at a 45-degree angle. Lousy long queue. Tomorrowland.

Buzz Lightyear's Space Ranger Spin. ★★★ ✔ FastPass+ Dated ride-through shooting gallery uses laser beams. Tomorrowland.

The Enchanted Tiki Room. ★★★ ✔ Vintage Audio-Animatronic revue stars robotic birds, flowers and tikis. Adventureland.

Jungle Cruise. ★★★ FastPass+ The quality of this outdoor boat ride depends on its skipper's skills as a comic. Adventureland.

Liberty Square Riverboat. ★★★ Steam-powered paddlewheeler circles Tom Sawyer Island. Liberty Square.

Mad Tea Party. ★★★ ✔ FastPass+ Outdoor spinning teacups are covered with a canopy. Fantasyland, Castle Courtyard.

Magic Carpets of Aladdin. ★★★ ✔ FastPass+ A four-seat Dumbo, with spitting camels. Adventureland.

A Pirate's Adventure. ★★★ Scavenger hunt uses treasure map to trigger hidden special effects in Adventureland.

Swiss Family Treehouse. ★★★ Climb-through improvised home of "Swiss Family Robinson." Adventureland.

Tomorrowland Speedway. ★★★ ✔ FastPass+ Old-time kiddie race cars. Tomorrowland.

Walt Disney World Railroad. ★★★ ✔ Steam train circles the park. Stations at Main Street U.S.A., Frontierland, Fantasyland.

Two-star attractions

Tom Sawyer Island. ★★ Two wooded islands have a walk-through cave, mine and calvary fort but no chance to explore off walkways. You reach them by riding a raft. Frontierland.

Under the Sea—Journey of the Little Mermaid. ★★ FastPass+ Budget-conscious slow-moving dark ride goes past scenes from Ariel's story. Fantasyland, Enchanted Forest.

One-star attractions

Country Bear Jamboree. ★ Brain-dead Audio-Animatronics stage show stars low-brow bears singing cornball songs. IQ maximum 50. Frontierland.

Stitch's Great Escape. ★ In-the-round show sort of creates the illusion of Experiment 626 skittering around you, definitely makes you forget why you liked "Lilo & Stitch." You wear a harness, and the theater goes dark. Height minimum 40 inches. Tomorrowland.

© Disney

Filled with detail and decorated to the nines, the Beast's castle holds the Be Our Guest restaurant. It's routine at lunch, outstanding at dinner.

Restaurants and food

Almost guaranteed to be both better and more expensive than you expected, the restaurants at Magic Kingdom will irritate your credit card but please your palate. At least most of them will. Below, each is rated from one to five stars (★) based on the quality of its food, service and atmosphere. A five-star eatery fully lives up to its promise; a one-star place should be avoided. A checkmark (✓) indicates an author personal favorite. The price of a typical adult dinner entree is summarized by dollar signs as follows:

$ less than $10
$$ less than $15
$$$ less than $20
$$$$ less than $25
$$$$$ more than $25

To reserve a table at any Walt Disney World restaurant call Disney at 407-939-3463.

Table service. A quick summary: The best food at Magic Kingdom is at Be Our Guest, for dinner. The best value is Liberty Tree Tavern for lunch. The author's choice has good food and value: Tony's Town Square, for lunch.

Be Our Guest. ★★★★★ ✓ $$$$$ Boasting a stunning dining hall that recalls the 1991 movie "Beauty and the Beast," this contemporary French-American restaurant is beautiful, and filled with lovely special effects. Its fast-food lunch (mostly sandwiches and salads) is only available to those who secure a Fastpass-like reservation card ahead of time. But regular reservations are taken for dinner, an enchanting table-service experience that features a creative menu, an inspired wine list and impressive service. Some dishes are prepared tableside, and the Beast himself greets guests in a side chamber. Special decor effects add charm. *Fantasyland, Enchanted Forest. Lunch 10:30 a.m.–2 p.m., $9–$13 (children $7–$8). Dinner 4 p.m.–park close, $17–$33 (children $9–$11). Seats 546 for lunch, 340 dinner.*

Cinderella's Royal Table. ★★★★ $$$$$ Snow White, Jasmine and other Disney princesses greet guests at their tables at this regal restaurant, which hides up on the second floor of Magic Kingdom's iconic Cinderella Castle. No one comes for the food; the ridiculously overpriced *prix fixe* menus offer French-American fare that's worth about half its tab. Instead, the draw here is location, location, location—your child will never forget that you ate inside this world-famous landmark—as well as the bevy of impossibly poised young women who embody their princess roles to perfection. The medieval dining hall seems authentic;

You'll almost be guaranteed a relaxing, hearty meal at Liberty Tree Tavern, which resembles a Colonial home that's been turned into a restaurant. It's ala carte at lunch, a Thanksgiving feast at dinner.

its stone walls, sky-high ceiling and stained glass windows fit for royalty. Though the experience will be too corny if you're an adult couple eating on your own, it's a magical moment for many young girls. Unlike the other princesses, Cinderella does not appear in the dining room. She's in the lobby. Note: Cinderella's Royal Table is the toughest restaurant reservation to nab in all of Disney World; its tables often book to capacity 190 days early, on the first day they're available to Disney-hotel guests. Meals are paid for at the time they're reserved. *Cinderella Castle. Hours: 8 a.m.–park close. Breakfast $50 (children $32). Lunch $58 (children $36). Dinner $67 (children $41). Prices include souvenir trinkets for children and a photo of each guest with Cinderella. Seats 184. A Disney Signature Restaurant.*

Crystal Palace. ★★ $$$$$ Even adorable Winnie the Pooh, Eeyore, Piglet and Tigger can't redeem this character buffet. It's just too crowded, overpriced, and loud. Tables are packed together, with little room between them, which makes it a chore to squeeze back and forth to the food lines, where there are decent meats and salads but salty soups and vegetables. High ceilings and marble table-tops make for a pretty decor, but amplify the noise. Characters often can't linger at your table, so when you meet one it's just for a moment. For the most time with them reserve a table for 8:05 a.m. (the first breakfast seating), 10:30 a.m. (the last) or 3:45 p.m. (the first dinner seating). *Main Street U.S.A. Breakfast 8–10:30 a.m., $29 (children $17). Lunch 11:30 a.m.–2:45 p.m. $31 (children $17). Dinner 3:45 p.m.–park close, $44 (children $21). Seats 400.*

Liberty Tree Tavern. ★★★★ ✔ $$$$$ Hearty comfort food and a cozy atmosphere make this unpretentious New England eatery a relaxing break. Resembling a large, Colonial house, it has six separate little dining rooms, which keeps its noise level low. Despite its name, no liquor flows. Best choice for lunch: the tender pot roast. Dinner is a fixed-price, family-style Thanksgiving feast. Window-side tables overlook the park's parade route. *Liberty Square. Lunch 11:30 a.m.–2:45 p.m. $12–$20 (children $9). Dinner 4 p.m.–park close. $34 (children $17). Seats 250.*

The Plaza. ★★★ ✔ $$$ The food at this Victorian café screams diner—good hamburgers, sandwiches and sundaes—but the quiet atmosphere fits a more upscale eatery. Carpeted floors, padded wrought-iron chairs and faux-marble tabletops add to the charm. Hand-dipped ice cream treats come from the adjacent parlor. *Main Street U.S.A. 11 a.m.–park close. $12–$18 (children $9). Seats 94.*

Tony's Town Square. ★★★★ ✔ $$$$ Fans of 1955's "Lady and the Tramp" may not recognize this comfortable café as the Tony's from that film—it's not overly themed—but that's about its only weakness. The menu offers generous portions of Italian comfort food; the shrimp scampi has roasted tomatoes. A lovely glass-ceiling solarium can be too sunny but there are many indoor tables; ask for one by the fountain. The authors eat lunch here often. *Main Street U.S.A. Lunch 11:30 a.m.–2:45 p.m. $13–$21 (children $9). Dinner 4:30 p.m.–park close. $18–$30 (children $9). Seats 286.*

Counter service. The top choice here: Columbia Harbour House. Stay away from Peco Bill's but embrace Tortuga Tavern, a plain but satisfying spot that hides next door.

Casey's Corner. ★★★ ✔ $ A recent refurbishment improved this little hot dog spot

Sit upstairs at Columbia Harbour House for a calm, relaxing atmosphere. Fresh, healthy food choices include veggie chili, grilled salmon and steamed broccoli.

by replacing its bleachers and low-res video screen with tables and chairs, creating a dining area that's clean and relatively peaceful. The hot dogs and fries remain the same: decent, satisfying and pricey. *Main Street U.S.A. $5–$10. 11 a.m.–park close. Seats 48 inside, 80 outside.*

Columbia Harbour House. ★★★★★ ✔ $ Focused on chicken and seafood, this fresh, healthy eatery is one of Magic Kingdom's gems. Its grilled salmon is as good as fast-food fish gets, served with moist couscous and steamed broccoli. The dinner menu includes a creamy seafood macaroni and cheese and a chicken pot pie which tastes nearly homemade, with big chunks of white meat and crisp veggies. Served all day, a hearty vegetarian chili is a steal at less than $5. The restaurant straddles the border between Liberty Square and Fantasyland; sit upstairs over the walkway to people-watch *Liberty Square. Lunch 10:30 a.m.–4 p.m. $8–$10 (children $5–$6). Dinner 4 p.m.–park close. $8–$11 (children $5–$6). Seats 593.*

Cosmic Ray's Starlight Cafe. ★★★★ ✔ $$ This sprawling spot has really improved over the past few years. Deli sandwiches are generous; ribs and rotisserie chicken come with a refreshing cucumber salad; a condiment bar is expansive. On the downside, the ordering system still requires you to wait in different lines to order different items, and the cheap Six Flags decor still features tiresome robotic lounge singer Sonny Eclipse. Avoid the midday rush and you'll find a calm atmosphere. *Tomorrowland. $8–$15 (children $5–$6). 10:30 a.m.–park close. Seats 1,162.*

Diamond Horseshoe. ★★★ $ This old-time saloon and dance hall opens as a restaurant during peak periods, with food from the kitchens of the nearby Liberty Tree Tavern. There's no drinking or dancing, but for Frontierland fast food it can't be beat. *Frontierland. $7–$9 (children $5–$7). Open seasonally. Seats 300.*

Friar's Nook. ★★ $ It's mostly mac and cheese at this outdoor fast-food window—you can get it on a hot dog, pot roast, a bacon cheeseburger or all by its lonesome, and it's always bland. For breakfast there are equally challenged French toast sticks and sausage dogs. *Fantasyland, Castle Courtyard. $7–$9. Park hours. No seating.*

Gaston's Tavern. ★★★ ✔ $ Living up to its name in ways that aren't always good, this heavily themed little spot has the mark of its buffoonish he-man owner (the villain of 1991's "Beauty and the Beast") all over it. It uses antlers in all of its decorating, serves beer (or at least a sweet slushy kids' drink that certainly looks likes beer) and has as its only entree a pork shank, which unfortunately is just a tasteless hunk of fatty meat. Fans of the film love the decor; few leave without taking a selfie or two in a fireside faux-fur chair. The authors eat here often, not for the food, but because it's the only indoor fast-food spot in the park that's open in the morning and has seats. We order a cinnamon roll, and always ask for a warm one with lots of icing. *Fantasyland, Enchanted Forest. $3–$9. Park hours. Seats 70 inside, 32 outside.*

The Lunching Pad. ★★ $ Overpriced hot dogs are the sole offerings at these sunny outdoor windows. Best is the messy Coney Island. *Tomorrowland. $8–$9. 11 a.m.–park close. Seats 83.*

Main Street Bakery. ★★★ $ Reopened in 2013 as a Starbucks, this former Disney bakery is now a part of that popular franchise.

Situated directly in the center of the Big Top Souvenirs gift shop, Big Top Treats makes mouth-watering concoctions in front of your eyes, including elaborate caramel apples, chocolate-dipped fruit.

There's certainly a Disney touch to the decor, but other than that it's the same as any other Starbucks anywhere else. Except there's no place to sit, and lines are often ridiculously long. *Main Street U.S.A. $4–$5. Park hours. No seating.*

Pecos Bill Cafe. ★ $ Expect to be disappointed by this uninspired spot, where the focus is on meat—burgers, chicken, pork, ribs, even steak—but not at all on quality. A toppings bar includes freshly grilled onions and hot cheese. Dining rooms on the right are the quietest. *Frontierland. $8–$11 (children $5–$6). 10 a.m.–park close. Seats 1,107.*

Pinocchio Village Haus. ★★ $ Located right in the middle of Fantasyland just behind Cinderella Castle, this Italian-themed spot is as unreliable as its namesake's ability to tell the truth—sometimes its generous flatbreads are full of sharp flavor; at other times they're barely cooked. Lined with murals that depict scenes from Disney's 1933 movie "Pinocchio," its Old World interior is charming as long as it's vacant; unfortunately the tables are often packed with screaming children. To avoid the ruckus, eat here very early or very late. Nab a window-side table in the far left dining room and you'll look down into the boarding area of It's a Small World *Fantasyland, Castle Courtyard. 10:30 a.m.–park close. $8–10. Seats 400.*

Tomorrowland Terrace. ★ $ This perfect outdoor location is ruined by lousy food. Its menu changes often, but most recently has included a lobster roll with no taste, ho-hum salads with no thought behind them, and pastas that were worse than those frozen ones you can buy at Walmart for $1. *Tomorrowland. $9–$10 (children $5–$6). Open seasonally. Seats 500.*

Tortuga Tavern. ★★★ ✔ $ Take advantage of the topping bar at this breezy outdoor café and no matter what you get it will be better than anything you could have gotten at the adjacent Pecos Bill Café. Best bets are the burritos, which overflow with quality ingredients and come with a side of delicate cilantro rice. Ask for a complimentary side of salsa when you order; the one from the kitchen is a pico de gallo. The best tables are those on a back patio that's sheltered by tropical foliage. Ambient fiddle music adds some life, as do signs and posters that reveal a back story: the place is run by Angelica from the "Pirates of the Caribbean" films, and she has her rules. *Adventureland. $8–$9 (children $5–$6). 11 a.m.–4 p.m. Seats 240, including 12 seats at the bar and seven umbrella-covered tables.*

Snacks. Creating temptations before your eyes, **Big Top Treats** ★★★★★ ✔ serves up concoctions that are fresher and more varied than those of the similar **Confectionery** near the park entrance. Located in Fantasyland's Storybook Circus inside Big Top Souvenirs, it often sends its bakers strolling through the store with free samples. Guests rave about the chocolate-covered bananas; the authors love the elaborate caramel apples and the caramel corn, especially when it's fresh.

Other worthwhile Magic Kingdom treats include the Dole Whip soft-serve at **Aloha Isle** ★★★ in Adventureland, the hand-dipped real ice cream at the **Plaza Ice Cream Parlor** ★★★ on Main Street U.S.A., and the waffles and funnel cakes at **Sleepy Hollow** ★★★★ in Liberty Square.

See also **Restaurant Policies** in the chapter **Walt Disney World A–Z.**

Two friends step out of Big Top Souvenirs. Decorated with old-time posters that feature obscure Disney characters, the Fantasyland Storybook Circus shop looks like a circus tent.

Shops

It's not all Mickey Mouse stuff. Many Magic Kingdom stores offer quality merchandise that goes beyond typical theme-park stuff. The best are summarized below. Stores are rated from one to five stars (★) based on the quality of their merchandise, service and atmosphere; one- and two-star stores are not listed. A checkmark (✔) indicates that the store is one of the authors' personal favorites.

Big Top Souvenirs. ★★★★★ ✔ A hidden oasis at the back of Fantasyland, this giant circus tent offers a huge variety of apparel, plush, toys and dolls; features a watch-them-make-it sweet shop right in the middle; and has a terrific atmosphere—cast members often juggle scarves, spin plates or play games with kids as they work the floor, and sometimes give away candy samples. Merchandise includes Storybook Circus souvenirs; a side station embroiders Mickey ear hats while you wait. The store's heavenly aroma, jaunty circus music and cool air-conditioning tempt you to stay forever. Disney geeks will drool over hidden tributes to obscure Disney characters such as Salty the Seal. *Storybook Circus, Fantasyland.*

Bonjour Village Gifts. ★★★ Cozy but charmless, this upscale boutique sells china, housewares and other high-end stuff themed to the 1991 Disney film "Beauty and the Beast." Stone arches and a wood-beamed ceiling add a rustic feel. *Next to Gaston's Tavern, Fantasyland.*

Castle Couture. ★★★★ Wanna-be princesses squeal over the sparkly ball gowns and costumes at this cramped little shop, and tap out their parents' credit cards as they insist on all the accessories Disney ruthlessly displays right alongside the outfits—tiaras, white gloves, plastic high heels, even faux fur stoles. Have a boy? Rest easy. There's almost nothing for princes. The store is supposedly the dressmaker's shop for the adjacent castle's royalty; sewing materials fill the top shelves. A hidden antechamber serves as a Photopass studio for little princesses, though anyone who asks can have their picture taken in it at no extra charge. A professional backdrop and overhead soft boxes help create a perfect portrait. *Directly behind Cinderella Castle, Castle Courtyard.*

The Emporium. ★★★ Though it doesn't look like it from the outside, The Emporium is one big, continuous shop that takes up half of Main Street. Inside is a huge selection of all kinds of merchandise; it's Magic Kingdom's biggest store, with a little of everything but nothing all that special. *The left side of Main Street U.S.A. as you face Cinderella Castle.*

Friends Jennifer and Jenny wear personalized Mickey Mouse and Minnie Mouse ear hats, an iconic park souvenir. You'll find them at the Chapeau on Main Street U.S.A. and at Fantasy Faire and Big Top Souvenirs in Fantasyland.

Other Main Street shops. The right side of Main Street U.S.A. holds the park's Confectionery (great for fudge, but otherwise lesser than the candy store at Big Top Souvenirs), a hat shop, an art gallery and a shop full of glass and crystal figurines, with an artisan working on the spot.

Fantasy Faire. ★★★ ✓ An angry Donald Duck glares down at you from the ceiling of this small store; maybe he's mad because a slew of parked strollers usually blocks its entrance and he hates seeing the place empty, which it often is. Underneath him are some unique Donald T-shirts (an author favorite) and impulse items, as well as Mickey Mouse ear hats. Orchestral ambient music adds to a relaxing atmosphere. *At Mickey's PhilharMagic, Fantasyland.*

Hundred Acre Goods. ★★★★ ✓ Head to this teeny shop for cute-as-a-button Pooh apparel, plush and toys for infants and preschoolers. A cute decor features giant storybook pages on the walls and ceiling; shelves appear to be dripping honey on the floor. The store is almost always crowded; Disney's Pooh ride exits into it. *At The Many Adventures of Winnie the Pooh, Fantasyland.*

Island Supply. ★★★★ ✓ Quality warm-weather junior apparel from Roxy, Quiksilver and O'Neill fill this open-air store. *Near Magic Carpets of Aladdin, Adventureland.*

Pirate's Bazaar. ★★★★ ✓ This sprawling open-air shop offers pirate booty galore, including fashion apparel, toys and a bunch of Jake and the Never Land Pirates stuff. *At exit to Pirates of the Caribbean, Adventureland.*

Sir Mickey's. ★★★★ ✓ Despite its name, this longtime menswear shop has responded to the opening of the Princess Fairytale Hall character spot next door by dumping its guy gear and going female. Nearly the entire store is filled with clothing for girls and women, most of it themed to Disney princesses, much of it unexpectedly creative. Fashion T-shirts feature haughty sketches of Ariel, Aurora and other Disney teen queens as grown women; the store's infant wear is often both adorable and classy. The holdover male decor is based on two classic cartoons: "The Brave Little Tailor" and "Mickey and the Beanstalk." Look around to see tailoring references, large vines and the "Beanstalk" giant peeking in from outside. *Directly behind Cinderella Castle, Castle Courtyard.*

Ye Olde Christmas Shoppe. ★★★★ This cute spot sells Christmas merchandise year round, with oodles of ornaments, nutcrackers, stockings and other festive gear. *Across from The Hall of Presidents, Liberty Square.*

Salon. If your little girl is into the princess look you'll be tempted to spend her college savings at the makeover salon **Bibbidi Bobbidi Boutique** ★★★★. Depending on how much you'd like to draw out of that account, she can get her hair and nails done, her cheeks and lips made up, a princess costume and sash, even a photo session. The room is a shrine to princess glamour. Elaborate tiaras sparkle in glass domes; frothy princess gowns hang on the walls as if they're works of art. Little boys can get their hair glittered and spiked; those who do get a toy sword and shield. *Girls $55–$190 and up; boys $16. Ages 3–12. 8 a.m.–7 p.m.; allow 30–60 minutes. Reservations: 407-939-7895 available 6 months in advance. Inside Cinderella Castle.*

See also **Shopping** in the chapter **Walt Disney World A–Z.**

Street performers

Casey's Corner Pianist. ★★★★
✔ A skilled musician bangs out honky tonk, ragtime, Disney tunes and requests on a white upright piano. *20-minute shows. Casey's Corner patio, Main Street U.S.A.*

Citizens of Main Street. ★★★★★
✔ A troupe of improvisational actors portray the boulevard's turn-of-the-century townsfolk, strolling the street to chat, dance, joke, sing and pose for photos. Characters include Mayor Weaver, Fire Chief Smokey Miller, voice instructor Victoria Trumpetto and socialite suffragettes Hildegard Olivia Harding and Bea Starr. Guests who are into pin trading exchange wares with Main Street Gazette reporter Scoop Sanderson. *20-minute appearances. Main Street U.S.A.*

Dapper Dans. ★★★★★ ✔ This barbershop quartet mixes their harmonically perfect repertoire with chimes, tap dancing and very corny humor. *20-minute shows. Main Street U.S.A.*

Flag Retreat. ★★ A Security Color Guard lowers the park's U.S. flag, often with a guest military vet. Sincere, but uninspired. *20-minute ceremony. 5 p.m. daily. Town Square flagpole, Main Street U.S.A.*

Frontierland Hoedown. ★★★ The Country Bears play washboard and spoons as guests square dance with friendly country-western couples. Kind of cool—if it wasn't for those stupid bears. *20-minute shows. In front of Country Bear Jamboree, Frontierland.*

Street performers immerse guests in an out-of-the-ordinary world. From top: The Main Street Trolley Parade, Mayor Weaver greets a guest, the Notorious Banjo Brothers and Bob, the Main Street Philharmonic.

Main Street Philharmonic. ★★★★
✔ 12-piece comedic brass and percussion ensemble plays Disney hits and Americana favorites. *20-minute shows. Main Street U.S.A. and Storybook Circus.*

The Main Street Trolley Parade.
★★★★ ✔ Gay '90s couples hop off a horse trolley to perform a soft-shoe pantomime—there's lots of lip-syncing, but no parade. The troupe changes its show for every season. So strange, but so Disney. *Three 5-minute shows per parade. Main Street U.S.A.*

The Notorious Banjo Brothers and Bob. ★★★★ ✔ Two banjo pickers and a tuba player perform Disney tunes, bluegrass and cowboy melodies. A park institution. *20-minute shows. Frontierland.*

Royal Majesty Makers. ★★★
A retired knight, etiquette diva, squire and lady-in-waiting Bridget conduct Knight School, deliver ball invitations and lead little dances as they bake in the Fantasyland sun. *Castle Courtyard, Fantasyland.*

Storybook Circus Giggle Gang.
★★★★★ ✔ Outstanding clown troupe performs silly skits, often with "volunteers." *20-minute shows. Storybook Circus, Fantasyland.*

Welcome Show. ★★★★ ✔ The park opens with a warm hello from a Citizen of Main Street and some very happy singers, who usher in a steam-train-full of characters, including Mickey Mouse. *Train station, entrance plaza.*

Wowzer. ★★★★ ✔ A silent clown performs impressive feats of balance and dexterity, often with the help of a child from the audience. *20-minute shows. Storybook Circus, Fantasyland.*

Whinny Horselaugh of the Storybook Circus Giggle Gang; Citizens of Main Street Bea Starr, Hildegard Olivia Harding and Victoria Trumpetto; Capt. Jack Sparrow hosts a pirate tutorial in Adventureland; the Dapper Dans.

Where to see characters

Ariel's Grotto. ★★★ FastPass+
Meet the Mermaid and her tail in this cozy indoor spot, styled like an underwater cave. *Fantasyland.*

Be Our Guest. ★★★ The "Beauty and the Beast" beast greets fans in a castle alcove after they've finished dinner. *Fantasyland.*

Captain Jack Sparrow's Pirate Tutorial. ★★★★ ✔ Comical Capt. Jack Sparrow and first mate Mack recruit a crew from youngsters in the crowd. *Across from Pirates of the Caribbean, Adventureland.*

Cinderella's Royal Table. ★★★★
Cinderella greets you in the lobby at this character meal; other princesses work the dining room. *Inside Cinderella Castle, Fantasyland.*

Crystal Palace. ★ Winnie the Pooh, Eeyore, Piglet and Tigger meet their fans at this character buffet. They're adorable; the cramped space is not. *Between Main Street U.S.A. and Adventureland.*

Disney Festival of Fantasy Parade.
★★★★★ ✔ FastPass+ Wave to Anna and Elsa ("Frozen"), Merida ("Brave"), Rapunzel and Flynn Ryder ("Tangled"), Tiana ("Princess and the Frog") and many others. *Travels through Frontierland, Liberty Square, Main Street U.S.A.*

Dream Along with Mickey. ★★★
Stage show stars Donald Duck, Goofy, Maleficent, Mickey and Minnie Mouse, many princesses, the cast of "Peter Pan." *Cinderella castle forecourt, Fantasyland.*

Enchanted Tales with Belle.
★★★★★ ✔ The heroine from

From the top: Pete's Silly Sideshow in Storybook Circus, Princess Fairytale Hall just behind the castle in Fantasyland, Town Square Theater, Lady Tremaine and daughter Drizella ham it up in Town Square.

"Beauty and the Beast" acts out her story with audience volunteers at this elaborate indoor show. *Enchanted Forest, Fantasyland.*

Fairytale Garden. ★★★★ Meet flame-tressed Merida from "Brave" in this alcove. Kids learn archery while they wait. *At the far right of the castle grounds, Fantasyland.*

Main Street Electrical Parade. ★★★ FastPass+ Nighttime parade includes Tinker Bell, Alice from "Alice in Wonderland," and Pete and Elliott from "Pete's Dragon." *Travels through Frontierland, Liberty Square, Main Street U.S.A.*

Move It! Shake It! Celebrate It! Street Party. ★★★★★ ✓ Boogie with Chip 'n Dale, Donald Duck, Frozone and Mr. Incredible from "The Incredibles," Goofy, King Louie and Baloo from "The Jungle Book" and Woody and Jessie from "Toy Story." *Travels Main Street U.S.A., stops in front of the castle.*

Pete's Silly Sideshow. ★★★★★ ✓ Classic characters as carnival performers. One line leads to Daisy Duck and Minnie Mouse; another to Donald Duck and Goofy. *Storybook Circus, Fantasyland.*

Princess Fairytale Hall. ★★★ FastPass+ Anna and Elsa draw gigantic crowds; Cinderella and Rapunzel are also on hand. *Behind Cinderella Castle, Fantasyland.*

Town Square Theater. ★★★★ FastPass+ Mickey Mouse sometimes talks to you (it's very weird); Tinker Bell always chats your ear off. *Next to Tony's Town Square, Main Street U.S.A.*

Characters also greet guests on walkways throughout the park.

See also the chapter **Characters.**

Anna and Elsa in the Festival of Fantasy Parade, Mickey Mouse ready to Move It! Shake It! Celebrate It!, Wendy and Mr. Smee at Dream Along with Mickey, Tinker Bell cracks up the author at Town Square Theater.

A steam engine pulls an open-air passenger train around Magic Kingdom. The park uses four such locomotives, all of which were built between 1916 and 1928.

Walt Disney World Railroad

Smart steam-train rides are marred by dopey details

★★★ ✔ A relaxing way to get around Magic Kingdom, this authentic narrow-gauge railroad circles the park. Antique steam locomotives pull street-trolley passenger cars down a track lined with bamboo, palms, pines and live oaks. Two or three trains run continuously, so there's rarely much of a wait.

It's a nice ride. You're always out of the sun, you get some wind in your hair and, unlike walking, you can't get lost—hop on a train at Frontierland and you will go directly to Dumbo and his circus, even if you have no idea how to get there. But it's not perfect. A hokey pre-recorded narrator drops every "G" as if he's ridin' the rails at Dollywood. Alongside the track, fake alligators and deer never have a hankerin' to move.

Tips. *When to go:* Anytime. *Where to sit:* On the right for the best views, though riders on the left sometimes spot live alligators in a canal behind Fantasyland.

Fun finds. Mutoscopes and other antique amusements line the waiting room of the Main Street station; some still work.

Fun facts. Built by Philadelphia's Baldwin Locomotive Works between 1916 and 1928, the four steam engines hauled passengers, jute, sisal and sugar cane for the United Railway of the Yucatan for decades. Acquired by Disney in 1970, they were restored in 1971. The engines take on water at the Fantasyland station every third loop. They get serviced every few hours.

Key facts. *Best for:* All ages. *Duration:* 20-minute round trip (1.5 miles). *Capacity:* 360. *Queues:* Outdoor, covered. *Operating hours:* Idle during parades, fireworks. *Weather issues:* Closed during thunderstorms. *Debuted:* 1971. *Access:* Guests may remain in wheelchairs, ECVs. No Disney strollers. *Disability services:* Handheld captioning. *Location:* Stations at Main Street U.S.A., Frontierland, Fantasyland.

Average wait times

9am	10am	11am	Noon	1pm	2pm	3pm	4pm	5pm	6pm	7pm	8pm	9pm
5m	5m	5m	5m	5m	5m	5m	5m	5m	5m	5m	5m	5m

Hitched to his Main Street trolley, 'Queasy' the Clydesdale waits for the Magic Kingdom to open. Once the trolley fills with riders, he'll pull it down a track embedded in the pavement.

Main Street Vehicles

Just hop on one of these quaint replicas and feel special

★★★★★ ✔ It's too bad they're usually out only in the mornings, because these old-fashioned vehicles are a true Disney treasure. Shuttling passengers between Town Square and Cinderella Castle, they offer complimentary old-school fun. Just hop on and off you go... no wait in line, Fastpass or extra charge required.

Riding one gives you a taste of a bygone era. The vehicles look completely authentic, with their uncushioned metal dashes, worn leather and wood benches, and their sounds only reinforce that notion. Bells ding. Engines chug. Horns honk. Horses clop. You also feel special. As you are driven down Main Street crowds part for you, and then wave.

The fleet consists of four horse trolleys, three horseless carriages, two jitneys, a miniature fire truck and a double-decker bus. The trolley runs on a track embedded in the street; its driver operates a set of reins, a brake pedal and a foot bell. The Dapper Dans barbershop quartet often hop on and sing.

Tips. *When to go:* Immediately after you enter the park. *Where to sit:* Up front, for the best view and to chat with your driver. *For families:* Ask ahead of time and your child might be able to honk a horn, ring the trolley's bell or crank the fire truck's siren.

Fun facts. Built for the Disney company, the vehicles debuted at Magic Kingdom the day it opened. They run on natural gas. License plates are dated "1915," the first year Florida issued automobile tags.

Key facts. *Best for:* Children, families, seniors. *Duration:* 3–4 minutes. *Capacity:* 6–40 depending on vehicle. *Operating hours:* Typically park open—late morning. *Weather issues:* Closed during rain. *Debuted:* 1971. *Access:* Must be ambulatory. *Location:* Main Street U.S.A.

Average wait times

9am	10am	11am	Noon	1pm	2pm	3pm	4pm	5pm	6pm	7pm	8pm	9pm
0m	0m	0m	0m	n/a	n/a	n/a	n/a	n/a	n/a	n/a	n/a	n/a

MYSTIC SPELL

RAFIKI'S WISDOM STICK

| CHARMING ATTACK **2** | CHARMING BOOST **2** | CHARMING SHIELD **2** |

56/70

This might hurt, but I just gotta
Hit you with "Hakuna matata."

Sorcerers of the Magic Kingdom players sign up on Main Street U.S.A., then search the park for hidden video screens to vanquish Disney villains using collectible "spell cards."

Magic Kingdom interactive games

Easy-to-play adventures feature high-tech effects

★★★★ ✓ **Sorcerers of the Magic Kingdom.** You play this game on hidden video screens throughout Magic Kingdom. Recruited by Merlin the Magician (from 1963's "The Sword in the Stone"), you stop Hades (from 1997's movie "Hercules") from making Magic Kingdom his summer home. You do it by casting spells on Disney villains, who appear on the screens and react to you when you hold up an RFID-embedded card, a packet of which you get when you sign up. Play the game long enough (think a full day) and you'll send Hades back to H-E-double-hockey sticks. The cards are free, and Pokémon quality. The video animation, however, is beneath Disney's standards, and some characters don't have their well-known voices.

★★★ **A Pirate's Adventure.** You trigger special effects throughout Adventureland in this game, as you use a treasure map to help Capt. Jack Sparrow lift a curse. There's never much of a line to play, and the effects are pretty cool—you may fire a cannon, or raise a sunken skeleton out of its water. But there are no cards to collect.

Tips. *Sorcerers:* Get your cards as soon as you enter the park, while it's convenient. Play the game as it fits into your attraction schedule. *A Pirate's Adventure:* Play the game during the morning or late afternoon, when the weather is relatively cool. If you get lost, touching your MagicBand to any game station will tell you where you should be.

Key facts. *Best for:* Children, Disney enthusiasts. *Duration:* Allow 5 minutes per portal or effect. *Debuted:* Sorcerers: 2012, Pirate's Adventure 2013. *Access:* Guests may remain in wheelchairs, ECVs. *Disability services:* Sorcerers: Video captioning. *Sign-up location:* Sorcerers: The firehouse on Main Street U.S.A. Pirate's Adventure: Next to Pirates of the Caribbean, Adventureland.

Average wait times

9am	10am	11am	Noon	1pm	2pm	3pm	4pm	5pm	6pm	7pm	8pm	9pm
5m	15m	15m	20m	10m	10m	5m	5m	5m	5m	5m	5m	5m

A family walks across a suspension bridge to reach the base of the Swiss Family Treehouse, an improvised home made from items scavenged from a shipwreck.

Swiss Family Treehouse

Dated but detailed walk-through home requires a tiring trek

★★★ You'll climb six stories at this outdoor attraction, a self-guided walking tour through the improvised home of a shipwrecked father, mother and three sons. Various rooms display ingenious contraptions (a water-wheel system lifts bamboo buckets, a barrel in the kitchen cools a refrigerator) but have no interactive elements. The tree's 62 steps can challenge overweight adults, but offer healthy kids an easy way to burn off energy.

Though the tree pales as an attraction based on modern standards, from a 1960s perspective it's pretty cool. Remnants of the ship are everywhere, and include its lantern, log book and captain's wheel. Ropes from the ship appear to hold the home together, while its rooms adapt found objects into everyday effects. Giant clamshells form sink basins.

Tip. *When to go:* At night, when the tree looks most realistic and you'll get a nice view of Magic Kingdom with its lights on.

Fun finds. There's a bible in the living room (one of the few seen in Disney attractions, a sticking point for some), with some brandy right above it... Wild hummingbirds and butterflies flutter among the flowers; huge bullfrogs live under the tree's bridges.

Fun facts. Based on a banyan tree—a tropical fig that grows aerial roots to support its outlying branches—the 200-ton, 60-foot-tall, 90-foot-wide *Disneyodendron eximus* ("out-of-the-ordinary Disney tree") is made of concrete, stucco and steel. Its 330,000 leaves are polyethylene, but its Spanish moss is real, as are its lush surroundings.

Key facts. *Best for:* Children, fit adults, Disney enthusiasts. *Duration:* Unlimited, allow 20 minutes. *Capacity:* 300. *Queue:* Outdoor, shaded. *Operating hours:* Park hours. *Debuted:* 1971 (Disneyland 1962). *Access:* Guests must be ambulatory to enter. *Location:* Adventureland.

Average wait times

9am	10am	11am	Noon	1pm	2pm	3pm	4pm	5pm	6pm	7pm	8pm	9pm
0m	0m	0m	0m	0m	0m	0m	0m	0m	0m	0m	0m	0m

© Disney

"If you want to take pictures go ahead," Jungle Cruise skippers tell guests as they pass a pool of playful pachyderms. "All the elephants have their trunks on."

Jungle Cruise

With the right skipper, this tropical boat ride is hilarious

★★★ **FastPass+** Elephants squirt water from their trunks, headhunters shake their spears, hungry hippos threaten to attack… and they're all fodder for jokes on this ancient outdoor boat ride, as a crazed skipper rattles off corny puns and one-liners at every turn. You tour four mighty rivers: the Amazon, Congo, Nile and Mekong. Worth your time? It depends entirely on your skipper. Some are terrific, many are not.

Tips. *When to go:* At night. The line might be shorter and the boat's spotlight adds to the fun. *Where to sit:* Ask to sit on the left for the best views, ideally next to the skipper. *For families:* Ask nicely as you board and your child may be able to "steer" the boat.

Fun finds. A sign in the queue honors the Jungle Cruise company's latest Employee of the Month: E.L. O'Fevre. Along the covered exitway, a list of missing persons includes "Ilene Dover" followed by "Ann Fellen."

Hidden Mickeys. The queue radio plays Cole Porter's 1935 hit tune "You're the Top," which includes the lyrics *"you're a Bendel bonnet, a Shakespeare sonnet, you're Mickey Mouse!"*… Three-circle Mickey shapes hide on the side of a crashed plane between and below its windows and in a temple as yellow spots on the back of a giant spider on your right.

Fun facts. The water is dyed its dark, murky color… The boats are on a track; skippers control their speed but not their course.

Key facts. *Best for:* All ages. *Duration:* 10 minutes. *Capacity:* 310. *Queue:* Outdoor, covered. *Fear factor:* The temple is dark. *Operating hours:* Park hours. *Weather issues:* Closed during thunderstorms. *Debuted:* 1971 (Disneyland 1955). *Access:* Guests may remain in wheelchairs, ECVs. *Disability services:* Assistive listening, handheld captioning. *Location:* Adventureland.

Average wait times

9am	10am	11am	Noon	1pm	2pm	3pm	4pm	5pm	6pm	7pm	8pm	9pm
5m	20m	35m	45m	40m	30m	20m	40m	65m	25m	25m	20m	30m

Couples sit side-by-side and families of four ride together on Magic Carpets of Aladdin, a carnival-style ride that circles in a tropical setting.

Magic Carpets of Aladdin

Colorful carnival ride is simple, satisfying

★★★ ✓ FastPass+ Inspired by Disney's 1992 animated feature "Aladdin," this carnival-style hub-and-spoke ride is a fun diversion. Circling around a giant genie bottle, guests fly magic carpets which climb, dip and dive at their command. It's a nice use of 90 seconds, especially early in the morning or late at night when its waiting line is short.

Just another Dumbo? Not really. Each carpet seats four, not two, so small families can ride together. The carpets ride rougher than Dumbo, too. Tall palms lend a tropical air.

Tips. *When to go:* In the evening, when lines are shorter and the weather cool. *Where to sit*: In front, so you can control the height of your carpet with a lever. The back seat controls the pitch with a "magic scarab" button, which rarely works. *While you fly:* Move the front-seat lever up and down quickly to bounce your carpet. Fly about halfway up to be in the line of fire of a spitting golden camel.

Fun finds. The carpets travel over a pool of water—little camel heads drool water into it—so as you fly you can look down at your reflection just as Aladdin and princess Jasmine do in the film (the moment in which he shows her "A Whole New World")... On the ride's genie-bottle hub, cart-wheeling images of Aladdin's pet monkey Abu recall early zoetrope animation... A second spitting golden camel targets passersby from behind the ride's sign.

Hidden Mickey. The three-circle shape is in the surrounding walkway behind the camel statue that faces the ride, on two yellow stones of a small, faded four-piece bracelet.

Key facts. *Best for:* Children, couples. *Duration:* 90 seconds. *Capacity:* 64. *Queue:* Outdoor, shaded. *Operating hours:* Park hours. *Weather issues:* Closed during thunderstorms. *Debuted:* 2001. *Access:* ECV users must transfer. *Location:* Adventureland.

Average wait times

9am	10am	11am	Noon	1pm	2pm	3pm	4pm	5pm	6pm	7pm	8pm	9pm
10m	10m	15m	30m	30m	35m	20m	25m	30m	25m	20m	15m	10m

A vintage Disney show created in 1963, The Enchanted Tiki Room was designed during the height of "Tiki culture," an American fantasy of Polynesian food, drinks and style.

Walt Disney's Enchanted Tiki Room

Singing birds, flowers, tikis are woefully dated, still enchant

★★★ ✓ "All the birds sing words and the flowers croon" in this sweet yet woefully dated musical revue, a 1960s Disney icon which stars over 200 robotic birds, flowers and tiki faces. Young children may like the show's vintage songs and corny jokes; others will yawn at its slow pace. The performance takes place in-the-round in an air-conditioned theater. You sit on a bench.

Perched above the audience, parrots and toucans sing "Let's All Sing Like the Birdies Sing," "The Hawaiian War Chant" and, of course, "The Tiki, Tiki, Tiki Room." Flowers sing from hanging baskets; tiki statues come to life in the theater's walls. Hosting the revue are four macaws—German Fritz, Mexican José, Irish Michael and French Pierre—all of which are stereotyped beyond anything that would be created today: the show begins with José waking up and complaining that "my siestas are getting *chorter* and *chorter*."

Two toucans recount how they migrated to the Tiki Room from the nearby Jungle Cruise in the show's vintage preshow, which takes place alongside the outdoor waiting area. As robotic bird Claude—voiced by Sebastian Cabot, best known as French the butler on the 1960s sitcom "Family Affair"—tells the story, his mechanical friend Clyde supplies the sounds of an elephant, lion and lurking crocodile ("Lurk! Lurk!").

Disney's first robots. Conceived by Walt Disney as a restaurant with a coffee bar in its center, the Tiki Room became a show before it debuted at California's Disneyland in 1963. Its new Audio-Animatronics technology stunned audiences, as hundreds of tiny movements in its birds, flowers, and tiki idols were synchronized to its audio, and triggered by hidden pneumatic valves that opened and closed at the perfect times—creating a life-like effect that seemed almost real.

Average wait times

9am	10am	11am	Noon	1pm	2pm	3pm	4pm	5pm	6pm	7pm	8pm	9pm
n/a	5m	5m	5m	5m	5m	5m	5m	5m	5m	5m	5m	5m

© Disney

Walt Disney poses inside Disneyland's The Enchanted Tiki Room in 1963. The attraction featured Disney's first Audio-Animatronics figures.

Hunky tuna tostada. A duplicate version opened at Walt Disney World in 1971. The Disney company redid the show in 1998, creating a shorter, sarcastic storyline starring hornbill Zazu from 1994's "The Lion King" and parrot Iago from 1992's "Aladdin" (who misinterprets a reference to *hakuna matata*). In 2011 Disney redid the attraction again, this time reverting the show back to a shorter version of its original self, but with modern lighting and remastered audio.

Tips. *When to go:* In the afternoon when other attractions have long lines, or during a rain. There's never a crowd. *Where to sit:* Halfway down on the left side of the room; the host birds will often face you. Kids may like to sit in a back corner to be near the tikis.

Fun finds. In the preshow, Claude invites you to enjoy a "Tropical Serenade," the original name of the attraction... During "Let's All Sing Like the Birdies Sing," the four host birds do impressions of vintage crooners Louis Armstrong, Maurice Chevalier, Bing Crosby and Jimmy Durante... Though modern Audio-Animatronics creatures use hydraulic oil-filled valves, the Tiki Room still uses air, as its birds and flowers are the only Disney robots that perform above their audience and theoretically could leak oil onto unsuspecting heads. Turning off and on throughout the show, the pressurized air is easy to hear.

Hidden Mickey. On the entrance doors, as 2-inch berries on a stem underneath a bird's tail, 4 feet off the ground.

Fun facts. The show's bird calls and whistles were all voiced by one man. A. Purvis Pullen was also the voice of the birds in Disney's seminal 1937 movie "Snow White and the Seven Dwarfs" as well as those in 1959's "Sleeping Beauty," Cheetah the chimpanzee in the 1930s Johnny Weissmuller Tarzan films and Bonzo the chimp in the 1951 Ronald Reagan flick "Bedtime for Bonzo." Using the stage name Dr. Horatio Q. Birdbath, he also performed with the legendary novelty band Spike Jones and His City Slickers, providing its bird calls and dog barks. Despite that resume, Pullen called his Tiki Room work "my favorite accomplishment... The one that's gonna last."

Key facts. *Best for:* Children, seniors, Disney enthusiasts. *Duration:* 13 minutes. *Capacity:* 250. *Queue:* Outdoor, shaded. *Fear factor:* A simulated thunderstorm seems real and can startle timid toddlers. *Operating hours:* Opens at 10 a.m. *Debuted:* 1971 (Disneyland 1963); updated 1998, 2011. *Health advisories:* None. *Access:* Guests may remain in wheelchairs, ECVs. *Disability services:* Audio Description, assistive listening, handheld captioning. *Location:* Adventureland.

The entrance of Disney's Pirates of the Caribbean ride recalls an actual Spanish fort—El Morro, a 16th-century fortress in San Juan, Puerto Rico.

Pirates of the Caribbean

Immersive slow boat ride has plundering, plastered pirates

★★★★ ✔ FastPass+ Drunk pirates "pillage and plunder... rifle and loot... kidnap and ravage and don't give a hoot" in this rowdy, rum-soaked attraction, a dark indoor boat ride which takes you through the robotic ransacking of a Spanish port. There's plenty to look at, as you pass dozens of vignettes and sight gags. Special effects simulate fire, lightning, wind and, best of all, splashing cannon balls. The inspiration for the "Pirates of the Caribbean" movies, the ride keeps a lightweight tone; its pirates have such caricatured features they seem straight from a cartoon. Updated in 2006, it now features Capt. Jack Sparrow and other characters from those films. Its cool, dim queue winds through a stone fort.

Aye, a tale there be. The attraction's storyline is a morality tale, told in flashback form. It begins in the present, as you pass through a watery grotto lined with pirate (and mermaid) skeletons, then goes back in time to show what led the pirates to their doom. Scenes include Capt. Barbossa attacking a Caribbean port as he and his men search for Capt. Jack, and later Jack himself lounging smugly among the town's riches, having outsmarted them all.

Historic it be. The last ride Walt Disney helped design, the attraction combines a farm boy's view of high-seas adventure with a Hollywood showman's use of theatrics. Conceived as a wax museum, the attraction became an Audio-Animatronics boat ride after the success of two Disney-designed efforts at the 1964 New York World's Fair. It drew from Carousel of Progress, with its then-revolutionary robotic characters, and It's a Small World, which debuted a water-jet system that propelled boats through scenes.

PC it be not. The ride's story is all in good fun, but even the most carefree parent may

Average wait times

9am	10am	11am	Noon	1pm	2pm	3pm	4pm	5pm	6pm	7pm	8pm	9pm
5m	5m	20m	25m	45m	30m	25m	40m	30m	30m	20m	20m	5m

© Disney

Clockwise from top left: Jailed pirates beg a dog for a key, Capt. Jack listens in as a drunken pirate reveals the location of the town's treasure, the ride's infamous bridal auction.

wonder if scenes showing torture, heavy drinking and the selling of women send the best messages to a wide-eyed child. "There is nothing politically correct about Pirates of the Caribbean," admits Imagineer Eric Jacobson. "In fact, much of it is patently offensive."

In fairness, the ride does imply the consequences of such behavior; its first scene shows that the pirates end up murdered, their bodies left behind to rot. And it's more sensitive than it used to be. A barrel that today hides Capt. Jack (see above) once contained a scared-yet-titillated young woman who was nearly naked. Holding her slip, a pirate in front of her yearned to "hoist me colors on the likes of that shy little wench. I be willin' to share, I be!"

Tips. *When to go:* Early in the morning or late at night, when lines are short. *Which line to pick:* The right one. Its sights include some chess-playing skeletons. *Where to sit:* Ask for the front row. You'll have a clear view of everything, and lots of legroom.

Fun finds. At the bridal auction, the first woman in line is beaming, happy to be sold. Referring to her portly figure as "stout-hearted and corn-fed" the auctioneer asks her to "shift yer cargo, dearie. Show 'em yer larboard side." As an impatient buxom redhead lifts her skirt, he calls "Strike yer colors you brazen wench! No need to expose

yer superstructure!"... Frustrated that the dog in front of them won't bring them a key, one jailed prisoner tells another "Hit him with the soup bone!" As the dog glances at your boat, another captive says "Rover, it's us what needs yer ruddy help, not them blasted lubbers"... Painted on the exit ramp, "shoe prints" that indicate where to step consist of a normal right shoe and peg-leg left mark.

Hidden Mickeys. In the gift shop, the three-circle shape appears as three coins among a group of coins on a scale near the ride exit, and on the left shoulder of woman in a painting on the back wall.

Fun facts. A fog screen showing the face of Blackbeard is made of microscopic water droplets held in place by columns of air... The voices of Blackbeard, Capt. Barbossa and Capt. Sparrow are those of actors Ian McShane, Geoffrey Rush and Johnny Depp; the auctioneer is voiced by Paul Frees, the Haunted Mansion's ghost host.

Key facts. *Best for:* Ages 10 and up. *Duration:* 9 minutes. *Capacity:* 330 (15 per boat). *Queue:* Indoor, air-conditioned. *Fear factor:* Dark, spooky start; cannon fire may scare toddlers. *Debuted:* 1973, revised 2006, 2012 (Disneyland 1967). *Access:* ECV and wheelchair users must transfer. *Disability services:* Handheld captioning, Audio Description. *Location:* Adventureland.

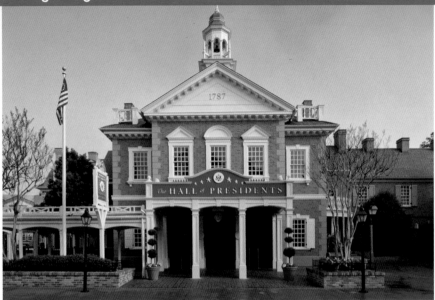

The exterior of the Hall of Presidents resembles Independence Hall in Philadelphia. The "1787" atop the building refers to the year of its Constitutional Convention.

The Hall of Presidents

A civil civics lesson with robotic commanders-in-chief

★★★★★ ✔ FastPass+ A robotic version of President Barack Obama speaks in this uplifting theatrical show, which also features Abraham Lincoln standing up to recite the Gettysburg Address and a short speech by George Washington. Every president of the United States makes an appearance. Fans of American history, parents wanting to inspire their children or perhaps just anyone longing for a return to civility in American politics should love every minute. It's really good.

The show begins with a large-format film. Starting with Washington's struggle to build a new nation, the movie scans U.S. history through the start of this century, highlighting presidents who have reached out to Americans during times of strife—Franklin Roosevelt, John F. Kennedy, Lyndon Johnson, Bill Clinton, George W. Bush.

Later, a curtain rises to show every president on stage simultaneously—43 life-sized animated figures, three-deep across the 100-foot-wide podium. Each president nods at the audience as he is introduced, and fidgets, looks around and sometimes whispers to his colleagues as the roll call continues.

Soon Washington stands to explain the importance of the oath of office, then Obama offers his thoughts on the American dream.

Updated often, exhibits in the lobby include the Eagle Scout medal earned by Gerald Ford, a roto-gauge used by FDR for his stamp-collecting hobby, and the incredibly gaudy cowboy boots George W. Bush wore to his first inauguration. A Caroline Herrera dress worn by Laura Bush hangs next to a photograph of her wearing it. Reproductions of other First Ladies' dresses show Martha Washington's tiny height and Edith Roosevelt's svelte waistline.

Tips. *When to go:* In the afternoon. Rarely crowded and providing lots of time out of

Average wait times

9am	10am	11am	Noon	1pm	2pm	3pm	4pm	5pm	6pm	7pm	8pm	9pm
10m	10m	10m	10m	10m	10m	10m	10m	10m	10m	10m	10m	10m

© Disney

A robotic President Obama speaks during The Hall of Presidents, which includes Audio-Animatronics versions of every commander-in-chief. Below, a replica of the Liberty Bell in front of the attraction; a still from its movie.

the sun, the show offers a great way to beat the heat. *Where to sit:* Front row center. The closer you are to the presidents, the more you can catch their gestures and facial expressions. *For families:* The show provides a great starting point to talk with your child about the next presidential election, and how it fits in with the attraction's premise that our president should be "one of us." Is that a good idea? Would he or she like to be president?

Fun facts. The show's widescreen projection system was invented by Ub Iwerks, the original animator of Mickey Mouse. Disney combed through the National Archives, Library of Congress, museums and private collections to acquire more than 130 historical images that appear in the film.

The Lincoln figure is a simplified remake of Disney's first Honest Abe that debuted at the Illinois pavilion at the 1964 New York World's Fair, "Great Moments with Mr. Lincoln," and didn't exactly work that well. With any spike in current, it would flail its arms, hit itself repeatedly in the head, and then slam itself down in its chair, confusing audiences who wondered if the bizarre routine was supposed to be part of the show. The

malfunction inspired a scene in a 1993 episode of "The Simpsons." In "Selma's Choice," Aunt Selma takes Bart and Lisa to the Disney World-like Duff Gardens, where every attraction is themed to Duff Beer. At the Duff Hall of Presidents, Lincoln holds up a Duff can and takes a swig, then mindlessly smashes it onto his head. Today's Lincoln uses the original World's Fair recording when the robot recites the Gettysburg address.

A Disney publicist used to mischievously tell visiting reporters that some of the show's presidents were played by real people—that since there were always a few robots out for repairs, each performance had at least one human stand-in. When he asked the late Walter Cronkite to spot the live actor, the veteran newsman just laughed. A minute later he turned back and said, "Jefferson?"

Key facts. *Best for:* Ages 8 and up, history buffs. *Duration:* 20 minutes. *Capacity:* 740. *Queue:* Indoor, air-conditioned. *Operating hours:* Sometimes opens at 10 a.m. *Debuted:* 1971, revised 2009. *Access:* Guests may stay in wheelchairs, ECVs. *Disability services:* Assistive listening, reflective captioning. *Location:* Liberty Square.

An actual paddle-driven steamboat, the Liberty Square Riverboat takes riders on a tour of Magic Kingdom's "Rivers of America," a wide waterway that circles Tom Sawyer Island.

Liberty Square Riverboat

Real paddlewheeler is interesting, but its sights are not

★★★ "Steady as she goes!" With recorded narration by an actor playing the role of author Mark Twain, this three-tiered steamship offers a taste of life on the Mississippi. Circling Tom Sawyer Island, its peaceful half-mile journey passes scenes that depict the rural America of the 1800s.

Unfortunately the sights are nothing special—a wilderness cabin, an incredibly small Native American camp and a few remarkably stoic woodland creatures. Morning voyages offer a nice diversion from thrill rides, but afternoon trips are often hot and crowded. The boat has only a handful of seats.

Despite its flaws as a ride, the boat itself offers a decent look at a forgotten aspect of American history. Though guided by an underwater rail, it is a true steam wheeler. Pumped full before each trip, a diesel boiler turns river water into steam, then pipes it to an engine which drives a large wheel as well as the electrical system. A working whistle and smokestack top the boat.

Tips. *When to go:* Just before dusk when the weather is cool and lines are long elsewhere. *Where to stand:* On mild days head to the top deck for the best view; on hot days try the covered second floor. Need to sit? A second-floor lounge has cushioned benches, as well as authentic maps, etchings, photos and a display of playing cards and poker chips. *What to notice:* The lovely wildflowers that border Tom Sawyer's Island, the respectful talk about American Indians, and as you exit, the huge sweaty steam engine and its crew on the first floor. They'll talk with you.

Key facts. *Best for:* Children, seniors. *Duration:* 13 minutes. *Capacity:* 400. *Queue:* Outdoor, covered. *Operating hours:* 10 a.m.– dusk. *Debuted:* 1971, updated 2007. *Access:* Guests may remain in wheelchairs, ECVs. *Location:* Liberty Square.

Average wait times

9am	10am	11am	Noon	1pm	2pm	3pm	4pm	5pm	6pm	7pm	8pm	9pm
n/a	15m	15m	15m	15m	15m	15m	15m	15m	15m	15m	n/a	n/a

Especially spooky at night, The Haunted Mansion grounds include a toppled garden planter, a ghostly hearse with an invisible horse and the sounds of a howling wolf.

The Haunted Mansion

A charmingly creepy tour of a ghostly retirement home

★★★★★ ✔ FastPass+ Ghosts drink, duel, fly, play music, sing, sip tea, waltz and even hitchhike in this dark indoor ride, which is never truly scary. Touring a ghostly retirement home, you creep room-by-room past its inhabitants, who are brought to life by age-old visual tricks as well as modern effects. Highlights include Madame Leota, a psychic medium who appears twice—as a head in a floating crystal ball and as an eerie tiny bride just before the end of the ride, who urges you to "Hurry back... Hurry back..."

Tips. *When to go:* At night, when lines are usually short. *Where to sit:* It doesn't matter. Your "Doom Buggy" ride vehicle rotates to line you up perfectly with every sight.

Hidden Mickeys. In the dining hall as the left-most place setting on the near side of the banquet table, and toward the end of the ride's graveyard as a silhouette at the end of the arm of the Grim Reaper.

Fun finds. An outdoor cemetery adds life to the Standby queue; when touched its stone coffins squirt water, play music and reveal secret messages. Dining hall ghosts include Marc Antony and Cleopatra on the room's chandelier.

Fun facts. The attraction's music consists of only one song: "Grim Grinning Ghosts" is performed in eight styles, including a dirge that plays as you enter. The mansion's "dust" is made from fuller's earth, an ingredient in kitty litter. You never go in the home; the entire ride takes place in a building behind it.

Key facts. *Best for:* Anyone ages 5 and up. *Duration:* 11 minutes *Capacity:* 320. *Queue:* Outdoor, mostly covered. *Fear factor:* Dark, some screams and pop-up heads. *Restraint:* Lap bar. *Debuted:* 1971, revised 2007. *Access:* Must be ambulatory. *Disability services:* Handheld captioning, Audio Description. *Location:* Liberty Square.

Average wait times

9am	10am	11am	Noon	1pm	2pm	3pm	4pm	5pm	6pm	7pm	8pm	9pm
5m	15m	20m	25m	35m	30m	30m	40m	25m	15m	15m	20m	10m

Country Bear Jamboree band the Five Bear Rugs includes (clockwise from left) "thing" player Tennessee, mouth-harpist Big Fred, jug blower Ted, fiddler Zeb and banjo player Zeke.

Country Bear Jamboree

Goofy stupid bears ain't worth seein'

★ Idiotic mechanical bears sing snippets of old-time country and cowboy songs in this indoor stage show, a corn-pone piece of Disney kitsch that somehow manages to have no appealing elements whatsoever. Devoid of wit, dated beyond reason and downright insulting to rural America, women and, yes, even bears, the show is a total waste of time. Watching it is like watching the worst rerun ever of the 1960s variety TV show "Hee Haw." And who would want to do that?

Set in the union hall of an 1880s lumber camp, the show features 18 life-sized performers. It was revised in 2013 to make it shorter.

Tips. *When to go:* Mid-afternoon, when other lines are lengthy and you're desperate to get out of the sun. *Where to sit:* In the middle of a middle row. You'll be able to see the bears' faces well, and hear them okay. *For families:* Have your kids make the silly bear faces. That will be funny.

Fun facts. Two songs come from legendary cowboy star Tex Ritter: 1950's "My Woman Ain't Pretty (But She Don't Swear None)" and 1937's "Blood On the Saddle," which in its day was known as the goriest country song of all time... The show's bear faces were designed by Marc Davis, the animator who created Cruella De Vil, Maleficent and Tinker Bell, the faces on the Pirates of the Caribbean and the animals in It's a Small World... The show was meant to be part of a never-built 1960s Disney resort in California's Sequoia National Forest, and was said to be Walt Disney's favorite attraction. Of course, he was old then.

Key facts. *Best for:* Disney enthusiasts. *Duration:* 11 minutes. *Capacity:* 380. *Queue:* Indoor, air-conditioned. *Operating hours:* 10 a.m.–park close. *Debuted:* 1971. *Access:* Guests may remain in wheelchairs, ECVs. *Disability services:* Assistive listening, reflective captioning. *Location:* Frontierland.

Average wait times

9am	10am	11am	Noon	1pm	2pm	3pm	4pm	5pm	6pm	7pm	8pm	9pm
n/a	10m	10m	10m	10m	10m	10m	10m	10m	10m	10m	10m	10m

No spell check, no problem. Tom Sawyer himself appears to have written the signs that direct guests around Tom Sawyer Island.

Tom Sawyer Island

Who knew trails, forts and caves could be so dull?

★★ Tom Sawyer would be bored to death on this small wooded island, which is meant to recall the classic 1876 novel by Mark Twain, "The Adventures of Tom Sawyer." Though children have plenty of things to walk through—a small meandering cave, a mine, a windmill and a charming watermill—they have little chance for free-spirited adventure, as they're rarely allowed off the sidewalks. Across a footbridge a second island has Fort Langhorn, a frontier outpost. Toy rifles in its watch towers can be aimed and "fired" at Big Thunder Mountain Railroad trains and the passing Liberty Square Riverboat.

Visiting the islands takes forever, as the only way on and off them is aboard a small powered raft. Counting the wait (see below), that roundtrip alone can suck up 50 minutes.

Tips. *When to go:* In the morning or about 90 minutes before dusk, when it's not so hot out. *Hidden things to do:* Play checkers at the island dock, at a landing down the left trail from it or at Fort Langhorn; cross over a bouncy barrel bridge along the right side of the island; worm your way through the "secret" escape tunnel at the back of the fort.

Fun finds. Water appears to run uphill in the mine... The mill's various creaks and groans subtly create the tune "Down By The Old Mill Stream"... The women's restroom at Fort Langhorn is labeled "Powder Room."

Fun facts. The bird trapped in the mill's cogs re-creates a scene from the landmark 1937 Disney short "The Old Mill."

Key facts. *Best for:* Children. *Duration:* Allow 1.5 hours. *Capacity:* 400. *Queue:* Outdoor, covered. *Fear factor:* Toddlers can get temporarily lost in the cave's side niches. *Operating hours:* Closes at dusk. *Weather issues:* Rafts don't operate during thunderstorms. *Debuted:* 1973. *Access:* Must be ambulatory. *Location:* Frontierland.

Average wait times

9am	10am	11am	Noon	1pm	2pm	3pm	4pm	5pm	6pm	7pm	8pm	9pm
n/a	5m	5m	15m	20m	20m	20m	15m	5m	5m	5m	n/a	n/a

Scaredy-cats can watch Splash Mountain riders take the big plunge from a stone overpass. The 52-foot drop is one of Disney World's most thrilling moments.

Splash Mountain

Elaborate log-flume ride recalls controversial Disney film

★★★★ FastPass+ You plunge 52 feet into a soaking splashdown during this half-mile flume ride, which recalls Disney's controversial 1946 film "Song of the South." A hollowed-out log takes you through bayous, swamps, a cave and a flooded mine as you witness a fox and bear's attempts to snare a wily rabbit. The ride's bright colors, many Audio-Animatronics characters and peppy music will appeal to young children; its many false drops and one big fall to thrill-seekers.

Weak versus strong. Though few guests notice it, the ride's storyline demonstrates how the weak can outwit the strong. Based on folk tales popular with slaves in the antebellum South, it portrays how tiny Brer ("brother") Rabbit is continually threatened by Brer Fox and Brer Bear, but always outsmarts them. In his final escape, the hare tricks the fox into tossing him safely back home, where he is welcomed by his friends.

Three tales in one. The attraction combines elements from three Brer Rabbit folk tales. In "Mr. Rabbit and Mr. Bear," he gets out of a rope trap by convincing the bear to switch places with him, saying he's earning a dollar a minute as a scarecrow. In "Brother Rabbit's Laughing Place," he leads the bear and fox to what he says is an ideal spot—his "laughing place." When it turns out to be a hollow tree full of stinging bees (from which only he escapes) he reminds them that it is *his* laughing place, not theirs. In "How Mr. Rabbit Was Too Sharp for Mr. Fox," Brer Rabbit escapes being cooked by the fox by urging the fox to cook him, as anything would be better than being thrown in a nearby briar patch. So the fox does just that, and the rabbit, who lives in the briar patch, gets away scot free.

'Pleasant memories of slavery.' Though the Brer Rabbit stories are not the least bit racist, the way they became widely known

Average wait times

9am	10am	11am	Noon	1pm	2pm	3pm	4pm	5pm	6pm	7pm	8pm	9pm
5m	20m	45m	35m	60m	55m	45m	70m	40m	45m	40m	30m	20m

A view from the top of Splash Mountain's Chickapin Hill, just before splashdown. Below: the Briar Patch gift shop; on the ride, Brer Fox captures Brer Rabbit by slamming a beehive over his head.

has some ugly overtones. They were first published in "The Complete Tales of Uncle Remus," an 1895 compilation in which its white author, Atlanta newspaper columnist Joel Chandler Harris, added a freed-slave narrator whom he described as having "nothing but pleasant memories of the discipline of slavery." At the time, the word "uncle" was often used as a patronizing term for an elderly black man. Disney's movie featured the Uncle Remus character, and did little to convey that being a slave caused him any grief or hardship.

Tips. *When to go:* With a Fastpass, during the hottest part of the day. *Where to sit:* The front seat for the best view and to get soaked, the back seat to stay relatively dry. *How to make sure you stay dry:* Choose the left side of the back seat, duck down before the splash and stay down until after the slosh (though this will ruin your souvenir ride photo).

Fun finds. "Fleas, flat feet and furballs" are all cured by the Critter Elixir trumpeted on a wagon past the second lift hill... At the beginning of the flooded Laughing Place, two gophers pop out of the ceiling and cheer "F... S... U!" a reference to a designer's alma

mater of Florida State University... Just before the drop, vultures above you ask "If you've finally found your laughing place, how come you're not laughing?"

Hidden Mickeys. As stacked barrels along the right side of the second lift hill... As a hanging rope in the flooded cavern, past a turtle... As a cloud to the right of the riverboat, a full figure reclining in the sky.

Fun facts. Because of the movie's racist overtones, Disney does not sell "Song of the South" on DVD, show it in theaters or on television, or sell any merchandise related to it, or even the folk tales, at Walt Disney World. The gift shop offers Thumper dolls instead.

Key facts. *Best for:* All ages. *Duration:* 12 minutes. *Capacity:* 440. *Queue:* Covered, indoor. *Fear factor:* One small drop is completely dark. The big drop can scare adults. *Restraint:* Lap bar. *Operating hours:* Park hours. *Weather issues:* Closed during thunderstorms. *Debuted:* 1992 (Disneyland 1989). *Health advisories:* Guests should be free from motion sickness; pregnancy; high blood pressure; heart, back or neck problems. *Access:* Height minimum 40 inches. Must be ambulatory. *Location:* Frontierland.

All curves all the time, Big Thunder Mountain Railroad trains jostle riders into each other. The coaster is wilder than the new Seven Dwarfs Mine Train, tamer than Space Mountain.

Big Thunder Mountain Railroad

Thrilling runaway mine train has super swerves, no scares

★★★★★ ✓ FastPass+ Full of fun, this rollicking roller coaster is ideal for those who like fast turns but not big drops. A curvy trip through a Utah desert, the "wildest ride in the wilderness" travels around and into a mountain, and passes through a flooded town and collapsing mine shaft. Sights include bubbling hot springs, spurting geysers and a dinosaur skeleton. Like many coasters, the railroad runs faster late in the day, after its track grease fully melts.

Tips. *When to go:* At night. The scenery is lit but the track is pitch black, which makes every swerve a surprise. *Where to sit:* For the wildest ride ask for the back seat.

Fun finds. Some entranceway crates are from the "Lytum & Hyde" explosives company... An empty bird cage that hangs from the queue rafters is labeled "Rosita," a reference to the long-lost Enchanted Tiki Room songbird... In Tumbleweed, a prospector on the right side of the track has washed into town while still in his bathtub.

Hidden Mickey. The three-circle shape appears on the right toward the end of the ride as three rusty gears laying on the ground.

Fun fact. The "Howdy partners!" announcer is Dallas McKennon. He's also the voice of Zeke in the Country Bear Jamboree, Ben Franklin at Epcot's American Adventure and Ripper Roo in Crash Bandicoot video games.

Key facts. *Best for:* Ages 8 and up. *Duration:* 4 minutes. *Capacity:* 150. *Queue:* Outdoor, covered. *Fear factor:* Jerky, violent turns toss riders in their seats. *Restraint:* Lap bar. *Top speed:* 36 mph. *Weather issues:* Closed during thunderstorms. *Debuted:* 1980 (Disneyland 1979). *Health advisories:* Guests should be free from motion sickness; pregnancy; high blood pressure; heart, back or neck problems. *Access:* Height minimum 40 inches. Must be ambulatory. *Location:* Frontierland.

Average wait times

9am	10am	11am	Noon	1pm	2pm	3pm	4pm	5pm	6pm	7pm	8pm	9pm
5m	20m	30m	40m	40m	50m	40m	40m	40m	30m	30m	30m	30m

One of the largest vintage merry-go-rounds still operating today, the Prince Charming Regal Carrousel features five rows of horses in five sizes. The largest steeds line the outer rim.

Prince Charming Regal Carrousel

Charming antique merry-go-round recalls forgotten era

★★★★ ✔ It's a basic pleasure, but one children today rarely get to enjoy: the fun of straddling almost life-size horse which glides up and down as it circles, a gentle breeze on your skin, the sounds of a calliope in the air. Designed to fit every member of the family, this large outdoor merry-go-round has five sizes of horses. Each horse is unique.

Tips. *When to go:* Early in the morning (you'll get on right away and can easily pick your horse) or after dark (when the ride is lit by 2,300 tiny white lights). *Where to sit:* On the outside ring for the fastest ride, on the inside ring for the slowest.

Fun finds. Disney says Cinderella's horse is the one with a golden ribbon around its tail, in the second row... The namesake of the carrousel when it was built, dignified blonde Miss Liberty adorns the side of the ride's lone chariot, clad in a robe and sandals that were originally red, white and blue; her face appears in the top rounding boards... Some horses carry medieval weapons, including a battle axe, lance, war hammer and a one-handed flail with a spiked steel ball... Eighteen hand-painted illustrations recount the story of Cinderella on the ride's inner rounding board.

Fun facts. The carousel was built in 1917 by the Philadelphia Toboggan (roller coaster) Co., a shop that sold hand-carved merry-go-rounds on the side. One of only four five-row units the company ever made, it was created for the Detroit Palace Garden Park, and spent time in Olympic Park in Maplewood, N.J.

Key facts. *Best for:* Toddlers, children, horse lovers. *Duration:* 90 seconds (4 revolutions). *Capacity:* 91 (87 horses, 1 four-seat chariot). *Queue:* Outdoor, shaded. *Restraint:* Safety belt. *Top speed:* 7 mph. *Debuted:* 1971. *Access:* Must be ambulatory. *Location:* Fantasyland, Castle Courtyard.

Average wait times

9am	10am	11am	Noon	1pm	2pm	3pm	4pm	5pm	6pm	7pm	8pm	9pm
0m	0m	0m	0m	5m	5m	5m	5m	5m	5m	0m	0m	0m

© Disney

Donald Duck finds himself in key musical moments of classic Disney films in Mickey's PhilharMagic. The 3-D movie is shown on one of the world's widest movie screens.

Mickey's PhilharMagic

Delightful 3-D tribute to Disney musicals stars Donald Duck

★★★★★ ✓ FastPass+ Donald Duck steals a smooch from the Little Mermaid, battles the brooms from "Fantasia" and causes chaos in the dining room of the Beast in this terrific 3-D movie. Action-packed yet never scary, funny but also touching, it's a treat for any age. The plot? When maestro Mickey Mouse runs late for a performance of his musician-free orchestra, Donald's attempt to replace him leads to a madcap adventure, as he gets swept into the signature moments of six musical Disney movies, all of them classics. Hidden odorizers, air guns and water misters immerse you in the action, as do innovative lighting effects and a terrific wrap-around sound system. The 3-D images are blurry compared to modern standards, but plenty bright.

Tips. *When to go:* In the afternoon when other attractions have long lines. *Where to sit:* In the middle of a back row, where the 3-D effects have the most impact.

Fun finds. Before the movie, listen as Goofy walks behind the curtain and stes on a cat ("Sorry little feller!")... As you exit, Goofy says goodbye to you in five languages ("Sigh-a-NAIR-ee!"), a reference to the last scene in the nearby attraction It's A Small World.

Hidden Mickeys. On the theater's right stage column, in the French horn tubing... As a hole that Aladdin's carpet makes in a cloud as he and Jasmine fly through it.

Fun fact. For the most part, the words spoken by Donald Duck are clips from vintage Disney cartoons, voiced by the original Donald, the late Clarence "Ducky" Nash.

Key facts. *Best for:* All ages. *Duration:* 12 minutes. *Capacity:* 450. *Queue:* Indoor, air-conditioned. *Fear factor:* Sudden images, briefly totally dark. *Debuted:* 1971. *Access:* Viewers may stay in wheelchairs, ECVs. *Disability services:* Assistive listening, reflective captioning. *Location:* Fantasyland.

Average wait times

9am	10am	11am	Noon	1pm	2pm	3pm	4pm	5pm	6pm	7pm	8pm	9pm
10m	10m	10m	10m	10m	10m	10m	10m	10m	10m	10m	10m	10m

Head to Peter Pan's Flight to fly off to Never Land in a miniature pirate galleon. Loaded with timeless charm, the classic indoor dark ride hasn't changed since it opened in 1971.

Peter Pan's Flight

Vintage flying pirate ships take you off to Never Land

★★★★ ✓ FastPass+ You'll fly over London and swoop through Never Land on this indoor dark ride, which uses an overhead track to suspend two-seat pirate ships. Designed 60 years ago and essentially unchanged since, the attraction has a throwback charm that just gets sweeter with age.

The ride depicts key moments of Disney's 1953 movie "Peter Pan." You start off in the Darling nursery, then fly over night-time London—its roads filled with moving vehicles—as you head off to Never Land. Passing the Lost Boys, Princess Tiger Lily and a trio of mermaids, you eventually sail through Capt. Hook's ship, and witness his battles with Peter and a ticking crocodile.

Tips. *When to go:* Either first thing in the morning or anytime with a Fastpass. The long lines at this attraction are legendary. *Where to look:* Up and down. You fly through the scenes, so there are sights all around you.

Fun finds. The glow from a volcano comes from visible sheets of aluminum foil... One of the mermaids looks like Ariel.

Fun facts. When the ride debuted at California's Disneyland in 1955 Peter Pan wasn't in it, as riders were supposed to be re-living his flight. Disney assumed the title of the attraction made that clear, but few riders understood... One of the oldest and best known Hidden Mickeys in Magic Kingdom, scars on a painted tree trunk next to the ride's queue turnstile used to form the three-circle shape—until a clueless Disney painter covered it up in 2013.

Key facts. *Best for:* Toddlers, children. *Duration:* 3 minutes. *Capacity:* 60. *Queue:* Indoor, covered. *Restraint:* Safety bar. *Debuted:* 1971 (Disneyland 1955). *Access:* Must be ambulatory. *Disability services:* Handheld captioning, Audio Description. *Location:* Fantasyland.

Average wait times

9am	10am	11am	Noon	1pm	2pm	3pm	4pm	5pm	6pm	7pm	8pm	9pm
5m	35m	45m	50m	35m	45m	35m	65m	40m	70m	40m	35m	35m

Two hundred and eighty-nine singing dolls populate the It's a Small World landscape, representing the cultures of Europe, Asia, Africa, Latin America and Polynesia.

it's a small world

Colorful classic boat ride offers hope of world peace

★★★★★ ✓ FastPass+ Promoting world harmony with dolls that sing in unison, this indoor boat ride takes you on a colorful, cultural trip around the globe. Abstract sets, whimsical animals and hundreds of singing dolls fill your field of vision in six huge dioramas, each of which represents a different region of the world.

"The happiest cruise that ever sailed" starts off in Europe, then crosses through Asia, Africa, Latin America and Polynesia. The finale returns to Europe, to Copenhagen's Tivoli Gardens (Walt Disney's inspiration for the look of his theme parks) where all the planet's children unite to celebrate the "world that we share" by dressing in white, singing in unison and enjoying the carnival together.

As for flaws...the dolls' lips barely move, the short song repeats ad nauseum (though in different languages and usually as an instrumental), the Latin American and South Pacific sets are skimpy compared to the others and the ride concludes with glitter-board good-byes that seem like a hasty addition to the more elaborate earlier scenes.

But get past all that and there's a lot to like:

As a ride. To infants, the ride is a wide-eyed journey filled with happy faces, funny animals, gentle music and the largest crib mobiles they've ever seen. To older children it's a place to bond with their parents, as there's no narration and lots of time to chat. ("Where are we now, mom?" "Hawaii!").

As a political statement. It's a Small World argues that you can honor diversity while still celebrating the commonality of mankind. Though the dolls speak different languages they all sing the same song, and though they wear different costumes, their faces are nearly identical.

As a piece of art. As designed by illustrator Mary Blair—she did the backgrounds for

Average wait times

9am	10am	11am	Noon	1pm	2pm	3pm	4pm	5pm	6pm	7pm	8pm	9pm
10m	10m	15m	25m	20m	25m	20m	20m	40m	15m	20m	15m	10m

© Disney

"The happiest cruise that ever sailed," It's a Small World takes guests on a celebratory tour of the globe. Stylized landscapes form a collage of color.

the Disney movies "Cinderella" (1950) and "Alice in Wonderland" (1951)—the modernist sets have a sophisticated sensibility, forming a playful pop-art collage that combines organic and geometric shapes as well as cultural motifs. For ideas, Blair tried different combinations of wallpaper cuttings, cellophane and acrylic paint.

As a piece of history. The ride was initially created for the UNICEF pavilion at the 1964 New York World's Fair. One of 50 attractions that charged a fee, It's a Small World accounted for 20 percent of paid admissions, more than any other attraction. It also inspired some political merchandise, as The Women's International League for Peace and Freedom sold It's a Small World-style dolls to help fund protests against the Vietnam War.

Tips. *When to go:* Early, late or with a Fastpass. *Where to sit:* Ask for the front row of the first boat for the best view and the most legroom. Sit on the left for the best views of Don Quixote, Cleopatra and the flower-spotted kangaroos, or on the right to get an up-close look at the French can-can girls, the yodeling Swedish bell shakers and the winking hippo. *Where to look:* Up. Lots of stuff hangs from the ceilings. *Tips for families:* Compete with your kids: Who can identify the most countries? Who can spot the most animals?

Fun finds. In the first room a pink poodle ogles the can-can girls, a crazy-eyed Don Quixote tilts at a windmill while Sancho Panza looks on in alarm, and a Swiss yodeler wields an ax... In the Middle Eastern room, one of the flying carpets has a steering wheel... In the African room, Cleopatra winks at you... In the boarding area, a giant clock comes to life every 15 minutes.

Hidden Mickey. The three-circle shape of Mickey's head appears as 6-inch purple flower petals in Africa, along a vine between the giraffes on your left.

Fun facts. Disney itself cracks jokes about the ride. Jungle Cruise skippers tell guests that children left on board their boats will be taken to It's a Small World, have their feet glued to its floor and be forced to sing its theme song "over and over for the rest of their lives." During the finale of Jim Henson's MuppetVision 3-D at Disney's Hollywood Studios, It's a Small World dolls join forces to help destroy the theater.

Key facts. *Best for:* Toddlers, children, young women, families, Disney enthusiasts. *Duration:* 11 minutes. *Capacity:* 600. *Queue:* Indoor. *Debuted:* 1971, renovated 2010 (New York World's Fair 1964, Disneyland 1966). *Access:* ECV users must transfer. *Disability services:* Handheld captioning, Audio Description. *Location:* Fantasyland.

A surreal hefflalump-and-woozle nightmare highlights The Many Adventures of Winnie the Pooh, an old-fashioned ride that includes many special effects.

The Many Adventures of Winnie the Pooh

Charming dark ride tells tale of chubby little cubby

★★★★ ✓ FastPass+ You bounce with Tigger, float in a flood and see Pooh drift off to dreamland on this dark indoor ride, which uses imaginative effects to create a memorable experience. Traveling in a four-person "Hunny Pot," you enter a storybook to witness the weather woes and hefflalump-and-woozle nightmare of the 1968 featurette "Winnie the Pooh and the Blustery Day." Hidden behind swinging doors, each scene comes as a surprise. A standby queue has an interactive playground; children swipe honey-dripping video walls to reveal hidden scenes.

Tips. *When to go:* Before 10 a.m. *Where to sit:* The front seat of your Pot has the best view. Children in back can't see over adults in front of them. *For families:* The ride gives parents a chance to talk to kids about fear. Scenes depict Pooh characters afraid of two things they should be (a windstorm and flood) and one thing they shouldn't (rumored truths).

Fun finds. A boarding-area mirror makes riders appear to disappear into the storybook... Words on the first storybook page blow off of it; words on the Floody Place page wash off.

Hidden Mickeys. There's one at the attraction's entrance, on the transom of the door to Mr. Sanders treehouse... On the ride, look for one on the radish marker in Rabbit's garden.

Key facts. *Best for:* Children. *Duration:* 3 minutes, 30 sec. *Capacity:* 48. *Queue:* Outdoor, covered. *Fear factor:* A clap of thunder and a bizarre dream sequence may startle timid toddlers. *Restraint:* Lap bar. *Debuted:* 1999. *Access:* ECV users must transfer. *Disability services:* Audio Description. *Location:* Fantasyland.

Average wait times

9am	10am	11am	Noon	1pm	2pm	3pm	4pm	5pm	6pm	7pm	8pm	9pm
5m	25m	35m	35m	30m	40m	35m	35m	35m	25m	25m	25m	20m

South Florida's Kisha and Jay Garcia spin their teacup on the Mad Tea Party. The ride is one of the few Disney World attractions in which guests totally control their experience.

Mad Tea Party

Simple spinning teacups will leave you giddy and grinning

★★★ ✔ **FastPass+** "If I had a world of my own, everything would be nonsense," says well-mannered schoolgirl Alice, in Disney's 1951 movie "Alice in Wonderland." "Nothing would be what it is because everything would be what it isn't. And contrary-wise; what it is it wouldn't be, and what it wouldn't be, it would. You see?"

You'll be as confused as she was as you leave this classic carnival ride, which puts you in an oversized teacup that spins as it circles on a floor that circles too. Most guests get dizzy, and most love it. "My favorite Disney World ride has always been the teacups," NASCAR driver Kyle Petty tells us. "From the time I was little I've loved to jump in and make people sick."

A wheel in the center of your cup lets you control how fast you spin, and which direction. Covered by a huge canopy, the Mad Tea Party operates in any weather.

Tips. *When to go:* Morning, late afternoon or evening… anytime it's not crowded. *Where to sit:* Pick a cup. Any cup. *How to get really dizzy:* Spin your teacup's wheel first one direction, then the other. *How not to get dizzy:* Don't spin the wheel. Instead, hold onto it so it doesn't spin, and stare at it as the ride itself rotates and turns. *For families:* The teacups give parents an excuse to get silly with their children. Most kids love it when their mom or dad scoots into them or playfully spins the wheel.

Fun finds. The movie's soused mouse pops out of the attraction's central teapot… The film's Japanese tea lanterns hang overhead.

Key facts. *Best for:* Children, teens, young adults, small families. *Duration:* 2 minutes. *Capacity:* 72 (18 4-person teacups). *Queue:* Outdoor, shaded. *Debuted:* 1971 (Disneyland 1955). *Access:* Must be ambulatory. *Location:* Fantasyland.

Average wait times

9am	10am	11am	Noon	1pm	2pm	3pm	4pm	5pm	6pm	7pm	8pm	9pm
5m	5m	10m	25m	20m	20m	20m	20m	15m	15m	15m	10m	5m

After re-enacting the story of how she and the Beast met and fell in love, Belle poses for photos with her castle guards—volunteer dads from the audience.

Enchanted Tales with Belle

Audience volunteers help the princess act out her story

★★★★★ ✔ **FastPass+** This wonderful attraction is Disney's ultimate character meet-and-greet, with a live show to boot. Belle, engaging and lovely in her golden gown, acts out the story of how she met the Beast with the help of eye-popping re-creations of Madame Wardrobe and Lumiere as well as audience volunteers. Ladeling a small experience with what seems like an unlimited budget, Disney has put a sincere effort into this, and created a great experience.

Tips. *When to go:* In the morning, as soon as the park opens. Disney needs at least 20 people to present a show, so you might wait a few moments if you're first in line. But you'll avoid having to wait outside and get a fresh, lively Belle. *Where to sit:* Front and center if you can. *For families:* Encourage your children to volunteer. Everybody who wants to be in the show can be, and usually they're the only ones who get a photo with Belle.

Have your own princess? In the first room of the cottage, take a photo of her in front of little Belle's height chart on the right wall.

Fun finds. A book telling the French version of the Cinderella tale lies open on a table in Belle's cottage... A book near the door to Maurice's workshop is titled "La Belle au Bois Dormant"—in other words, Sleeping Beauty... Maurice's plans for the wood-chopping machine seen in the film "Beauty and the Beast" hang on his workshop's wall.

Hidden Mickeys. The three-circle shape appears at the neckline of Belle's gown, as three yellow roses.

Key facts. *Best for:* Children, princess fans. *Duration:* 20 minutes. *Capacity:* 45. *Queue:* Unshaded outdoor line feeds indoors. *Debuted:* 2012. *Access:* Guests may remain in wheelchairs, ECVs. *Disability services:* Assistive listening, handheld captioning. *Location:* Fantasyland, Enchanted Forest.

Average wait times

9am	10am	11am	Noon	1pm	2pm	3pm	4pm	5pm	6pm	7pm	8pm	9pm
15m	30m	30m	50m	30m	40m	20m	65m	70m	20m	30m	30m	40m

All ages can enjoy the Seven Dwarfs Mine Train. The coaster's carts swing independently from side to side, creating a smooth journey that doesn't toss riders into each other.

Seven Dwarfs Mine Train

Ingenious combo of coaster and dark ride delights all

★★★★★ ✓ FastPass+ This musical indoor/outdoor coaster is ideal for families. It gives the right amount of thrills—more than Barnstormer, less than Big Thunder Mountain Railroad—making it a perfect fit for kid-friendly Fantasyland. Better still, the ride appeals to both sexes, even though it's based on a princess story, as it focuses its attention on the dwarfs rather than Snow White. She appears only at the end of the ride, and only if you're looking for her.

Tips. *When to go:* The very first thing in the morning (you'll need to be one of the first people in the park to avoid a long wait) or anytime with a Fastpass. *Where to sit:* In the front seat for the best views and the mildest ride; in back for a more thrilling experience.

Fun finds. The image of Walt Disney's first cartoon character, Oswald the Lucky Rabbit, appears in the mine, on a beam to your left past the crest of the second lift hill.

Hidden Mickeys. You'll find Mickey as a three-circle shape on the loading area on the back wall above the podium, and three times inside the mine: just to the left of Dopey (level with his head, on a support beam); as three jewels slightly to the right of Grumpy; and as a full-bodied figure atop the second lift down low on your right, across from the hidden image of Oswald, holding a pickaxe.

Key facts. *Best for:* All ages. *Duration:* 2.5 minutes. *Capacity:* 20 (4 per mine cart, 2 per row; 5 mine carts are attached together.) *Queue:* Outdoor, tree-lined path leads into an indoor queue. *Fear factor:* Tight speedy turns may frighten preschoolers, especially in the back rows. *Restraint:* Lap bar. *Weather issues:* Closed during thunderstorms. *Debuted:* 2014. *Health advisories:* Expectant mothers should not ride. *Access:* Height minimum 38 inches. Wheelchair and ECV users must transfer. *Location:* Enchanted Forest, Fantasyland.

Average wait times

9am	10am	11am	Noon	1pm	2pm	3pm	4pm	5pm	6pm	7pm	8pm	9pm
60m	90m	90m	75m	75m	75m	75m	90m	90m	120m	90m	90m	75m

© Disney

Creepy villain Ursula the Sea Witch belts out "Poor Unfortunate Souls" as a video image of Ariel appears on a crystal ball on the ride Under the Sea—Journey of the Little Mermaid.

Under the Sea— Journey of the Little Mermaid

Gut the Haunted Mansion and you're left with this

★★ **FastPass+** Pardon the pun, but this headliner has no legs to stand on. Based on Disney's charming 1989 film "The Little Mermaid," its charm-free, an unmemorable indoor dark ride that creeps past scenes from the movie that are distinctly lackluster, with uninspired hard-plastic figures, little detail and dull-as-sea-muck scene transitions. No wonder Ariel wanted to get out of this place.

On the plus side, the ride sounds great. In the "Under the Sea" scene you drift through a fish band and hear its individual instruments. Sound effects like water splashing, a breeze through trees and fireworks bursting in a night sky are crisp and clear.

Tips. *When to go:* Before 10 a.m. or after dark to beat long lines. *For families:* Play the fun crab game in the queue; it's more entertaining than the ride itself. Wave your hand and a crab responds as it sorts Ariel's collection of human gadgets and gizmos.

Fun find. A reference to the ride that used to be on this spot, an image of the Nautilus submarine from the movie "20,000 Leagues Under the Sea" hides on the left side of the queue, in the rocks along the side of a pool.

Hidden Mickeys. The three circles appear in the queue as sunlight projected on a wall past a carved figure of a ship's figurehead, from holes in a rock above it. But only once a year: on Nov. 18, Mickey Mouse's birthday.

Key facts. *Best for:* Children. *Duration:* 7 minutes. *Capacity:* 4 per clamshell. *Queue:* Indoor. *Fear factor:* Ursula may scare toddlers. *Restraint:* Lap bar. *Debuted:* 2012. *Access:* ECV users must transfer. *Disability services:* Handheld captioning, Audio Description. *Location:* Enchanted Forest, Fantasyland.

Average wait times

9am	10am	11am	Noon	1pm	2pm	3pm	4pm	5pm	6pm	7pm	8pm	9pm
5m	15m	30m	40m	40m	30m	50m	40m	30m	30m	40m	20m	10m

Appealing to riders of all ages, Dumbo the Flying Elephant puts its guests in single-bench baby pachyderms that circle slowly. The ride recalls the finale of the classic 1941 film.

Dumbo the Flying Elephant

New and improved carnival ride is better than ever

★★★★ ✔ FastPass+ Flying baby elephants become cozy ride vehicles on this classic hub-and-spoke ride. Since the attraction's move to Storybook Circus in 2012 it's gotten much better—it now has two Dumbo rides, one that moves clockwise, the other counterclockwise. Each has a pool for Dumbo to fly over and multi-colored, changing lights that, at night, make the water glow. A new queue includes an indoor playground. When there's a wait to ride Dumbo, parents sit on benches while children play. When it's time, a restaurant-style pager sounds an alert.

Couples will enjoy the ride almost as much as children; its small seat requires scootching together and sharing one big seatbelt.

Tips. *When to go:* Before 11 a.m. for the shortest lines of the day, or use a Fastpass. If you can, ride at night, when the attraction glows with brilliant lights. *For families:* Snap a pic of your children in a stationary Dumbo

between the two rides. *Other tips:* Ask for the Dumbo on the right (i.e., the one closest to the rest of the park) to get a terrific view of Magic Kingdom. The Dumbo on the left mostly just views the adjacent Barnstormer ride.

Fun finds. Flying storks deliver baby Dumbos along the top of each hub... Golden peanut images adorn the ride, almost as if the legume was an object of worship.

Key facts. *Best for:* Families, couples, Disney enthusiasts. *Duration:* 2 minutes (6 revolutions). *Capacity:* 64 (32 per Dumbo ride, in 16 2-seat vehicles); play area capacity 175. *Queue:* Indoor, includes large, elaborate play area; leads to outdoor shaded queue. *Restraint:* 2-person seatbelt. *Weather issues:* Closed during thunderstorms. *Debuted:* 1971, redone and expanded 2012 (Disneyland 1955). *Access:* Wheelchair and ECV users must transfer. *Location:* Storybook Circus, Fantasyland.

Average wait times

9am	10am	11am	Noon	1pm	2pm	3pm	4pm	5pm	6pm	7pm	8pm	9pm
10m	15m	45m	25m	30m	30m	35m	25m	45m	15m	15m	20m	15m

A family rounds a curve on The Barnstormer, a junior roller coaster themed to the stuntman adventures of "The Great Goofini."

The Barnstormer

Brief, cheerful kiddie coaster packs punch, is fun for all ages

★★★★ ✔ **FastPass+** The perfect first coaster for children, this little biplane is also fun for couples and friends. Though its turns last only 20 seconds, its planes zip around a tight track at 25 mph, about as fast as the rockets inside Space Mountain. Constantly leaning into each other, riders sit two abreast in a cozy seat.

The Great Goofini. Adding to the fun is a witty backstory. According to Disney lore, the coaster retells an aerial mishap of the Great Goofini, the stage name Goofy gave himself during his career as a circus daredevil. Taxiing a crop duster out of an abandoned barn, he climbed up into the air perfectly straight... and straight into a signal tower. Immediately losing control, he swooped and swayed back to his barn, crashing through his billboard on the way.

Tips. *When to go:* The ride is almost always deserted first thing in the morning; ride then and Disney cast members will often let you stay in your seat for multiple flights. *Where to sit:* For the wildest ride ask for the back seat (Row 8); for the best view the front seat.

Fun finds. Goofy's "Canine Cannonball" cannon, next to the Fastpass queue. Its fuse flickers now and then; one of its cannonballs is Goofy's bowling ball.

Hidden Mickey. On the right of the billboard, in the blades of an airplane propeller.

Key facts. *Best for:* Toddlers, children, couples. *Duration:* 1 minute. *Capacity:* 32 (16 per plane; 2 planes). *Queue:* Outdoor, mostly unshaded. *Fear factor:* The coaster's tight turns could scare preschoolers. *Restraint:* Lap bar. *Top speed:* 25 mph. *Track:* Steel, height 28 feet, distance 790 feet. *Weather issues:* Closed during thunderstorms. *Debuted:* 1996, revised 2012. *Health advisories:* Expectant mothers should not ride. *Access:* Height minimum 35 inches. ECV and wheelchair users must transfer. *Location:* Fantasyland, Storybook Circus.

Average wait times

9am	10am	11am	Noon	1pm	2pm	3pm	4pm	5pm	6pm	7pm	8pm	9pm
5m	5m	15m	35m	25m	35m	25m	25m	30m	25m	20m	20m	15m

A co-star of the 1940 Disney movie "Dumbo," the Casey Jr. locomotive pulled the circus train. Fantasyland's version of the train sprays water from its smokestack and animals.

Casey Jr. Splash 'n' Soak Station

Beat the heat at this jolly circus-themed splash zone

★★★★ ✓ It's more soak than splash, but that's part of the fun. Kids have a blast trying to dodge the intermittent sprays, especially if parents join in. Surrounding little locomotive Casey Jr. from Disney's 1941 film "Dumbo" are several boxcars holding faux circus animals that shoot, spit and squirt water. Oddly, the pavement is brick, not the typical squishy soft stuff water-play areas usually have. Few kids seem to have trouble with it, though.

Tips. *When to go:* Anytime. *Where to play:* If your youngsters want a light spray instead of a drench, have them play in front of the boxcar with the monkeys on top. *Other tips:* To dry off, a cart just out of range of the water sells $20 beach towels.

Fun finds. Each boxcar has a number on back that references the year each of the Disney World parks opened. The elephant car reads "71" for Magic Kingdom's 1971 opening, the monkey car "82" for Epcot in 1982, the giraffes' reads "89" for Disney's Hollywood Studios in 1989 and the camel's boxcar reads 98 for Disney's Animal Kingdom in 1998.

Fun fact. The soak station area and its adjacent restroom are designed to look like a 1940s railroad turntable and "roundhouse" storage shed—surrounded by his animal-filled boxcars waiting to be unloaded, Casey Jr. sits on a turntable, tracks from the Walt Disney World railroad leading up to it. For most of their history locomotives did not have a reverse gear, so in order to turn around an engine would pull onto a piece of track that was mounted on a circular turnabout, and be twirled around on it to the face the opposite direction.

Key facts. *Best for:* Children. *Duration:* Allow 15 minutes. *Weather issues:* Closed during thunderstorms. *Debuted:* 2012. *Access:* Guests may remain in wheelchairs, ECVs. *Location:* Storybook Circus, Fantasyland.

Average wait times

9am	10am	11am	Noon	1pm	2pm	3pm	4pm	5pm	6pm	7pm	8pm	9pm
0m	0m	0m	0m	0m	0m	0m	0m	0m	0m	0m	0m	0m

© Disney

Experiment 626 is one steamed Stitch, unhappy with his detainment at Planet Turo's Prisoner Teleport Center. When the lights go out, the mischievous alien appears to escape.

Stitch's Great Escape

Cheap, confusing theatrical show is only for Stitch fans

★ Stitch burps in your face in this in-the-round theatrical show, geared to those familiar with the early moments of the 2002 movie "Lilo & Stitch." A low-budget makeover of the attraction that preceded it (The ExtraTERRORestrial Alien Encounter), the show is confusing and dull, and relies on cheaply animated video to tell its story—one which assumes you already know that Stitch can trick DNA-tracking cannons into tracking spit—and isn't really scary. A shoulder harness locks you in your seat, not because there's some risk you'll fall out (there's not) but to project sounds and smells behind you.

The attraction has one good quality: the host of its preshow. Trying to train audience members how to guard prisoners as he chats with his wife on the phone, a sarcastic skinless robocop channels Fire Marshall Bill, Jim Carrey's character from the 1990s television series "In Living Color."

Tips. *When to go:* Whenever you're down to either this or Country Bear Jamboree, and you really hate stupid bears. *Where to stand for the preshow:* Front row center (as you leave the indoor queue, choose the door to the left); the cop will look right at you. *Where to sit:* In a back row. The 39-inch Stitch character sits high above the front rows. *How to deal with the shoulder harness:* If you've got bony shoulders, shrug them as the harness lowers over you and adjusts itself. Otherwise it will hurt. *How to hear the special sound effects:* Lean back into your seat.

Key facts. *Best for:* Stitch enthusiasts. *Duration:* 18 minutes. *Capacity:* 240 (2 120-seat theaters). *Queue:* Indoor. *Fear factor:* Ominous harnesses, dark periods scare some children. *Restraint:* Shoulder harness. *Debuted:* 2004. *Access:* Height minimum 40 inches. ECV users must transfer. *Location:* Tomorrowland.

Average wait times

9am	10am	11am	Noon	1pm	2pm	3pm	4pm	5pm	6pm	7pm	8pm	9pm
10m	10m	10m	10m	10m	10m	10m	10m	10m	10m	10m	10m	10m

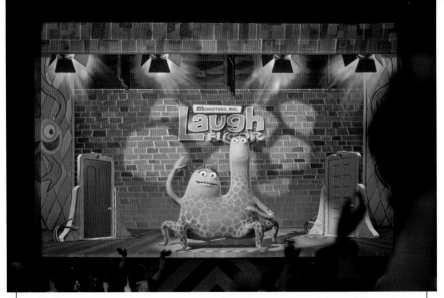

A two-headed animated monster—named Sam 'n' Ella—asks for audience volunteers during a performance of the Monsters Inc Laugh Floor, an interactive comedy show.

Monsters Inc Laugh Floor

Hilarious animated creatures interact with their audience

★★★★ ✔ FastPass+ An animated monster may pick you out of the crowd to chat with or might tell your joke during this high-tech improvisational comedy show. Three large video screens front a club-style theater, where characters from the "Monsters, Inc." world tease and talk with audience members in real time. The host is Mike Wazowski, who wants to generate electricity for his utility company by gathering laughter in bulk.

The show pulls off its magic through the use of hidden cameras, powerful animation software and talented backstage actors.

Most shows are surprisingly funny. Every one is different, as the characters base much of their humor (and anti-humor) on audience members. You can text a joke to the performers ahead of time from the waiting area.

Tips. *When to go:* In the middle of day, so you see a show with a full house. The performers feed off the audience. *How to have a character talk to you:* Wear a colorful shirt or a big hat. *How to get your texted joke read:* Make it simple and Disney-based. "Where did Captain Hook get his hook? The second-hand store!" That one worked for me.

Fun finds. As you enter the second holding room, a vending machine immediately to your left offers such treats as a Same Old Raccoon Bar and Polyvinyl Chloride Bar—the second of which, according to its wrapper, is artificially flavored... In that room's pre-show video, the first child Mike Wazowski makes laugh has a poster of Tomorrowland on his bedroom wall.

Key facts. *Best for:* All ages. *Duration:* 15 to 20 minutes. *Capacity:* 400. *Queue:* Indoor. *Operating hours:* Park open to one hour before park close. *Debuted:* 2007. *Access:* Guests may remain in wheelchairs, ECVs. *Disability services:* Reflective captioning, assistive listening. *Location:* Tomorrowland.

Average wait times

9am	10am	11am	Noon	1pm	2pm	3pm	4pm	5pm	6pm	7pm	8pm	9pm
5m	10m	10m	10m	10m	10m	10m	20m	10m	10m	10m	10m	10m

Need to get off your feet? It's easy to relax and chat with your group on the PeopleMover, a small automated train that takes you on an elevated tour of Tomorrowland.

PeopleMover

Breezy tour of Tomorrowland offers a nice way to unwind

★★★★ ✔ Zip around above Tomorrowland on this breezy and remarkably relaxing tour, as an elevated track snakes you alongside, around and through four buildings.

Tips. *When to go:* During a rain (the track is covered), at night (red lights illuminate your path) or when Space Mountain is closed (its work lights may be on). Want to go twice? Ask. *Where to sit:* Across from an empty seat so you can put your feet up. *What to do:* Take photos of each other. PeopleMover is one of the few Disney rides where you can face each other.

Fun finds. You'll pass the centerpiece of Progress City, Walt Disney's model for his Experimental Prototype City of Tomorrow, in the building that holds Stitch's Great Escape... That show's original 1971 incarnation, its host and the host of the second show there are referenced in a page asking Mr. Tom Morrow to "contact Mr. Johnson in the Control Tower to confirm your Flight to the Moon."

Hidden Mickey. In the building that holds Buzz Lightyear's Space Ranger Spin, on a belt buckle in a beauty salon.

Fun fact. While planning his dream city of EPCOT, Walt Disney thought a system of small electric trains would give people a way to get around without creating pollution or traffic. The Disney company brought the idea to life with this ride, and attempted to sell the system to cities. It bombed, selling only to the Houston airport (where it still runs today).

Key facts. *Best for:* Couples, friends. *Duration:* 10 minutes. *Capacity:* 900 (4 per car). *Queue:* Outdoor, covered. *Fear factor:* A two-minute stretch through Space Mountain is pitch dark and filled with (delighted) screams of that coaster's riders. *Top speed:* 7 mph. *Debuted:* 1975, revised 1996, 2009. *Access:* Must be ambulatory. *Disability services:* Audio Description, handheld captioning. *Location:* Tomorrowland.

Average wait times

9am	10am	11am	Noon	1pm	2pm	3pm	4pm	5pm	6pm	7pm	8pm	9pm
0m	0m	0m	0m	0m	0m	0m	0m	0m	0m	0m	0m	0m

Astro Orbiter's machine-age rockets circle high above Tomorrowland. The ride was dismantled, totally refurbished and reassembled in 2014.

Astro Orbiter

Thrilling retro rockets fly twice as fast as Dumbo

★★★ ✔ Fast, high and a little bit scary, open-air rockets twirl five stories above Tomorrowland on this hub-and-spoke ride. Perched atop the boarding station of the already-elevated PeopleMover ride, Astro Orbiter lifts you 55 feet off the ground. Guests take an elevator to reach it.

But there's more to this ride than height. Top speed is 20 mph—plenty zippy when you're in a tight circle and your rocket tilts at 45 degrees. Flying within a huge kinetic model of rings, planets and moons, riders make about 20 revolutions around a Buck Rogers-style antenna. At night the rockets' nose cones glow green, their exhaust fires red.

Unfortunately, the waiting line is usually awful. Astro Orbiter loads very slowly, and guests wait on hot asphalt with absolutely nothing to do.

Tips. *When to go:* First thing in the morning. You'll get right on and can ride two, sometimes even three times in a row. *It's a must for:* Young thrill-seekers who are too short for the roller coasters. Astro Orbiter is Walt Disney World's only thrill ride that doesn't have a height minimum.

Fun fact. Unchanged from the ride's original incarnation as space-age Star Jets, the ride's steel-mesh elevator looks just like the rocket gantries used at launchpads in early manned space missions at nearby Cape Canaveral, Fla.

Key facts. *Best for:* Children, teens, young adults, couples. *Duration:* 2 minutes. *Capacity:* 32. *Queue:* Outdoor, partially shaded. *Fear factor:* Height, angle can bother all ages. *Restraint:* Safety belt. *Top speed:* 20 mph. *Weather issues:* Runs during light rains; grounded by downpours, lightning. *Debuted:* 1971, updated 1994 (Disneyland 1955). *Access:* Must be ambulatory. *Location:* Adventureland.

Average wait times

9am	10am	11am	Noon	1pm	2pm	3pm	4pm	5pm	6pm	7pm	8pm	9pm
5m	10m	25m	40m	25m	25m	25m	40m	35m	45m	30m	35m	20m

A Rock 'Em Sock 'Em-style robot defends the home planet of the evil emperor Zurg in Buzz Lightyear's Space Ranger Spin. Riders rack up points by shooting at targets marked with "Z."

Buzz Lightyear's Space Ranger Spin

Ride-through laser-gun game is a blast if you aim well

★★★ ✔ **FastPass+** You use a laser gun to shoot at over a hundred cartoon targets at this video arcade, which turns the idea of a shooting gallery inside out: here the targets stay in one place while you move on a track. Riding in a two-seat "space cruiser," you fire at mostly silly cartoon aliens, black-lit targets that often move, light up or make noise if you hit them. A dashboard display tracks your score. Though the ride is low-tech by today's standards, children and gamers should still enjoy it. Note that despite the attraction's name, its vehicles do not spin. They swivel.

The plot—yes, there is one, even in a shooting arcade—involves an epic battle between Buzz Lightyear and the Evil Emperor Zurg.

Though it is fun, the ride does have drawbacks. Every laser light is the same color (red), which makes it tough to get feedback on your aim. Targets are not labeled with point values, so serious gamers waste a lot of shots. And instead of being rewarded by working together—as players are in the more modern Toy Story Mania arcade at Disney's Hollywood Studios—here you compete solely against each other. Whoever controls a vehicle's joystick gets a huge advantage.

Tips. *Where to sit:* On the right. You'll face the most targets. *For Buzz fans:* The space ranger often guests nearby, in front of Walt Disney's Carousel of Progress.

How to get a high score. The maximum point total possible on the ride is 999,999. Here's how your score can get close to that:
1. Call dibs on the joystick, so you can keep your vehicle facing the right targets.
2. Sit on the right side of your vehicle. That side has two-thirds of the targets.
3. Once your gun is activated, pull the trigger and hold it in for the entire ride. The flashing laser beam will help you track your aim. It will fire about once a second.

Average wait times

9am	10am	11am	Noon	1pm	2pm	3pm	4pm	5pm	6pm	7pm	8pm	9pm
5m	5m	25m	35m	40m	35m	25m	50m	45m	30m	30m	25m	20m

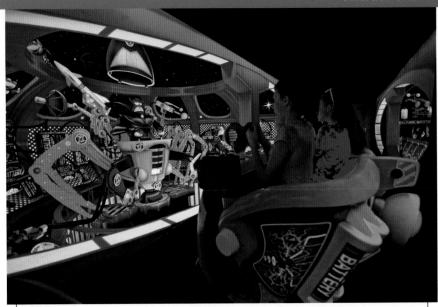

Riders in the know earn 100,000 points each time they hit the lone "Z" target at the bottom center of Zurg's space scooter. Other targets in the scene are worth far less.

4. Aim only at targets with big payoffs: As you enter Room 1, aim for the left arm of the left robot (each hit is 100,000 points).

5. As you pass that robot, turn your vehicle to the left and hit the other side of that same arm (25,000 points).

6. As you leave the first room, turn backwards and aim at the overhead claw of the other robot (100,000 points).

7. As you enter the second room, aim at the top and bottom targets of the large volcano (25,000 points).

8. As soon as you see Zurg, hit the bottom target of his space scooter (100,000 points) by firing early and late; you can't aim low enough to hit it straight on.

9. As you enter the third room, aim about six feet to either side of the top of the exit to hit an unmarked target in the middle of a rectangular plate (25,000 points).

10. If the ride stops, keep your blaster fixed on a high-value target and keep firing. You'll rack up points.

Fun finds. The ride takes place in a world of toys. Buzz gets his information from a Viewmaster; your space cruiser gets its power from a backpack of batteries... As you enter Planet Z the bendy snake from the "Toy Story" movies appears in front of you... Man-eating plant Audrey 2 from the 1986 movie "Little House of Horrors" circles

to your right... "Guards! Seize them! And their little green friends, too." Zurg orders as you cruise through his spaceship... As you exit the ride, the spaceship of Stitch flies on the first mural on your right. It's tiny.

Hidden Mickeys. A green land mass forms a Mickey profile on the planet Pollost Prime. The image appears four times: on a poster in the queue, to the left of the Viewmaster in the queue, in front of you as you fight the video version of Zurg on the ride, and to your left in the final battle scene... Another Mickey profile appears on your left as guests enter Zurg's spaceship, under the words "Initiate Battery Unload."

Fun facts. The track layout is unchanged from the ride's days as "If You Had Wings," a 1970s attraction that took passengers through a series of sets that portrayed Caribbean and Latin American countries served by Eastern Airlines. One area created the sensation of speed by combining wraparound point-of-view video clips with a slight breeze. As the ride didn't require one of the park's various "A" through "E" tickets, it was a guest favorite.

Key facts. *Best for:* Children, teens, young adults. *Duration:* 5 minutes. *Capacity:* 201. *Queue:* Indoor. *Debuted:* 1998. *Access:* ECV users must transfer. *Disability services:* Audio Description, handheld captioning. *Location:* Tomorrowland.

A fascinating relic from the 1964 World's Fair, the Carousel of Progress explores how a typical American family lives better with electricity throughout the 20th century.

Walt Disney's Carousel of Progress

A charming look at yesterday's great big beautiful tomorrow

★★★★ ✔ Disney's first Audio-Animatronics family welcomes you into their home as they live through the ever-changing 20th century in this vintage theatrical show, which demonstrates how electricity has improved everyday life. Four scenes depict the 1900s, 1920s, 1940s and 1990s. The show is way past its prime, and cries out for either an update or total restoration. But even as it is, it's a fascinating look at the optimism of the past.

A great big all-electric tomorrow. First presented at the 1964 New York World's Fair at the General Electric pavilion, the attraction used a unique circular theater in which the seating area rotated from scene to scene. In each one, the family marveled about how great things were in "today's world," thanks to electricity and GE appliances. A finale showed the family in the future at Christmas in their stylish all-electric GE Medallion home, opening presents such as a

GE portable television. To bridge the scenes, songwriters Robert and Richard Sherman ("It's a Small World") composed "There's a Great Big Beautiful Tomorrow." After the fair Disney moved the show to California's Disneyland, when its script was changed to keep pace with GE's products and marketing.

That '70s show. When the show moved to Disney World in 1975, a third version of its script tied it to the women's movement. Wife Sarah now cheerfully talked back to her husband through the ages, and demanded equal pay for wallpapering the rumpus room. An all-new finale showed John acting as the bumbling family cook. As part of the move GE insisted the show no longer focus on the future, but the present. "We're not interested in selling light bulbs tomorrow," one executive groused, "we want to sell them right now!" As a result, the show got a new theme song, "The Best Time of Your Life"

Average wait times

9am	10am	11am	Noon	1pm	2pm	3pm	4pm	5pm	6pm	7pm	8pm	9pm
5m	5m	5m	5m	5m	5m	5m	5m	5m	5m	5m	5m	5m

"We've now got gas lamps, and the latest design in cast-iron stoves," the show's father raves in the first scene. Other sets place him at a 1940s kitchenette, and his entire family at a 1990s Christmas dinner.

(*Now is the time, now is the best time…*). Disney revised the script a fourth time in 1981, to update the finale to a future with video-cassette recorders.

Lumbago and laser discs. In 1994 Disney revised the show a fifth time, bringing back its original song, peppering its 1970s script with old-time sayings—husband John knows it won't rain because "my lumbago isn't acting up"—and redoing the finale yet again, this time to show a great big beautiful 21st century—a time when "everything will be automated!" As dad fumbles with a voice-activated oven, Grandpa longs for the days before "car phones and laser discs."

Tips. *When to go:* During a hot afternoon. *Where to sit:* Second or third row center. Any farther back and the dialogue from the stage will be too faint and the background music (from the back of the room) will be too loud. *For families:* Children will like watching Rover, the family dog, who glances at the audience, wags his tail and barks.

Hidden Mickeys. In the 1940s scene, the sorcerer's hat from 1940's "Fantasia" sits near an exercise machine… Mickey items in the finale include a nutcracker on the mantel, a plush under the Christmas tree, a salt shaker on the bar, an abstract painting on the wall and at the start of a video game the son and grandma play, as engines of a spaceship.

Fun facts. The auditoriums rotate at 2 feet per second on large steel wheels and tracks, just like a railroad train car… The show's grandma also rocks in front of the Haunted Mansion ballroom fireplace… A piece of the original finale appears on the Spaceship Earth ride… As part of the move to Florida, Disney returned to using wigs made from human hair. Nylon versions had been used at Disneyland, but over time klieg lights above the father had melted his hair into what a Disney imagineer described as "a sticky pile of goo"… Carousel of Progress is the only attraction at Disney World that was touched by Walt Disney himself.

Key facts. *Best for:* Seniors, Disney history buffs. *Duration:* 21 minutes. *Capacity:* 240 per theater, six theaters. *Queue:* Outdoor, uncovered. *Debuted:* 1964 World's Fair, Walt Disney World 1975. *Access:* Guests may remain in wheelchairs, ECVs. *Disability services:* Assistive listening, handheld and activated video captioning. *Location:* Tomorrowland.

A subtle tribute to the 1968 movie "2001: A Space Odyssey," the ride's angled clapboard walls replicate those of that film's transport interior. Fastpass riders use the line at the right.

Space Mountain

Walt Disney World's first roller coaster is still its best

★★★★★ ✓ FastPass+ "Daddy, did you hear me scream?!" beamed the 6-year-old girl, hopping out of her rocket. "That! Was! Cool!" said her 10-year-old brother. The parents shared a look. "Let's ride again!" exclaimed the wife.

Open-air rockets zoom through a dark universe inside this circular building, which holds the world's oldest, and arguably still best, roller coaster in the dark. Sitting in low-slung ride vehicles that are just a single seat wide, guests hurtle through an inky abyss filled with shooting stars. Every dip, drop and turn comes as a surprise. Top speed is 28 miles per hour, plenty fast in the dark.

Have a nice flight. The ride's story begins as you enter the building and walk in to a futuristic spaceport and repair center that's orbiting above the earth. Passing the departure board, a long tunnel leads to a launch platform. Once you board a rocket, a sign urges you to "Check Invisible Oxygen Dome,"

another flashes "Have a Nice Flight" and then off you go—into a flashing blue "energizing portal" that supposedly powers your machine. Climbing a launch tower (a chain lift), you pass under a large ship that has come in for service. Then you blast off, on a journey through what an early Disney press release called "the void of the universe." As you come back to earth, you trigger a sonic boom in a red "de-energizing" tunnel.

A 2009 update made the ride darker and smoother and added video games to its standby queue. In 2010 Disney added ambient techno music and sound effects to the ride itself, as well as a few references to the 1970s.

'Where's Mr. Smee?' With astronauts Scott Carpenter, Gordon Cooper and Jim Irwin as its first passengers, Space Mountain opened on Jan. 15, 1975. Though Disney promoted it as "the nation's most breathtaking thrill ride," not every guest got the message. As

Average wait times

9am	10am	11am	Noon	1pm	2pm	3pm	4pm	5pm	6pm	7pm	8pm	9pm
10m	15m	45m	45m	70m	55m	45m	45m	55m	50m	50m	55m	30m

Space Mountain riders zoom through an "energizing portal" before their launch into space. Florida's oldest operating roller coaster, its open-air rockets are one-person wide. Waiting lines form early each morning.

they climbed in their rockets many expected something along the lines of Peter Pan's Flight, since at the time Disney didn't do roller coasters. Moments later, up came their lunches and out flew their hats, purses, eyeglasses and, more than once, false teeth. Disney's response included discreetly ironing out some of the most violent jerks and jolts.

Though it opened during a recession, Space Mountain was an instant smash. When summer came, families with teens, many of whom would have not considered a Disney vacation before, began crowding Magic Kingdom turnstiles early each morning. The recession, in Orlando at least, ended.

Tips. *Where to sit:* Ask for the front row of a front rocket for the most immersive experience, the most breeze and the most surprises—Row 1 on the boarding platform. Riders with long legs will prefer either Row 1 or 4. Request a back seat to go faster down the drops and in the turns.

Fun finds. Panels just inside the building refer to it as "Star Port Seven-Five," a nod to the attraction's opening year... Intergalactic route maps along the queue contain references to the Little Mermaid, Mickey's pet

dog and the 1937 movie "Snow White and the Seven Dwarfs"... The spaceship alongside the chain-lift is labeled MK-1, a hint that this Magic Kingdom version of Space Mountain is the original ride; similar versions have since been built in four other Disney parks.

Fun facts. The ride's blue "energizing portal" has a practical function: its flashing lights shrink your pupils, so your flight seems darker than it really is... Why do the docked ship's engine nozzles look like plastic caps of spray-paint cans? Because they are. Used by an artist on a small pre-production model, real caps were accidentally reproduced perfectly on the full-scale prop... The ride has 30 rockets, numbered 1 through 31. There is no rocket 13.

Key facts. *Best for:* Ages 9 and up. *Duration:* 2 minutes, 30 seconds. *Capacity:* 180. *Queue:* Indoor. *Fear factor:* Constant, surprising dark drops and turns. *Restraint:* Lap bar. *Top speed:* 28 mph. *Debuted:* 1975, revised 2009. *Health advisories:* Guests should be free from motion sickness; pregnancy; high blood pressure; heart, back or neck problems. *Access:* Height minimum 44 inches. Must be ambulatory. *Location:* Tomorrowland.

Two sisters prepare to take off at the start of the Tomorrowland Speedway, as an attendant gives the younger girl instructions on how to drive. Other racers wait for her to move.

Tomorrowland Speedway

Slow smelly race cars are horribly dated, surprisingly fun

★★★ ✓ FastPass+ Sounding and smelling like Harleys that desperately need tune-ups, small-scale race cars rumble down a half-mile track at this vintage attraction, children behind their wheels. Meandering past beautiful live oaks and magnolias, riders wind around five turns and under and over a bridge. Some cars are left-hand drive, some right.

Straight out of Six Flags, the ride's sunbaked waiting line is one of Disney's worst. Umbrellas offer some shade; a covered grandstand gives those not riding a way to sit down.

Tips. *When to go:* First thing in the morning when the line is short, or after dark with Fastpass when the ride is breezy. *Where to sit:* In the passenger seat if you have a child, or aren't as child-like as your companion. *Want to race?* Ask for two cars side by side. *Not riding?* Take a starting-line snapshot from a footbridge above the track, just past the boarding area.

Fun facts. Why is this old-time attraction in Tomorrowland? For a reason that could only make sense to Disney: When it opened in 1971, the track was a version of the Disneyland attraction Autopia, which, when that California ride premiered in 1955, was a simulation of the limited-access highways destined for that era's future. A 1994 redo as an alien Indy-style race confused the theme further. Today's ride has remnants of that, but officially has no futuristic theme at all.

Key facts. *Best for:* Children, couples, families. *Duration:* 5 minutes. *Capacity:* 292 (146 2-seat cars). *Queue:* Outdoor, partially shaded. *Restraint:* Lap belt. *Top speed:* 7.5 mph. *Weather issues:* Closed during thunderstorms. *Debuted:* 1971 (Disneyland 1955). Revised 2011. *Access:* Height minimum: 54 inches to take car out alone, 32 inches to ride. Must be ambulatory. *Location:* Tomorrowland.

Average wait times

9am	10am	11am	Noon	1pm	2pm	3pm	4pm	5pm	6pm	7pm	8pm	9pm
5m	20m	20m	30m	40m	30m	40m	30m	20m	20m	20m	20m	20m

Goofy dances with park visitors during the Move It! Shake It! Celebrate It! street party. The dippy dog is one of eight Disney characters who step off their floats.

Move it! Shake it! Celebrate it!

Dance with Disney characters in this lively street party

★★★★ ✓ You can dance with a Disney character in this colorful street party, which takes place a few times a day in front of Cinderella Castle. If you're not shy about dancing in public, it's an easy way to have a fun character experience.

After an energetic emcee leads the crowd in a roll-call of celebrations ("If you're having a birthday... raise your hands!"), giant gift boxes open to reveal Sebastian the crab (from 1989's "The Little Mermaid"), Lumiere (1991's "Beauty and the Beast"), the Mad Hatter (1951's "Alice in Wonderland") and Genie (1992's "Aladdin"). Then you're invited into the street to dance with characters for several songs, including a conga line when the weather is cool. Characters don't pose for pictures or sign autographs.

Tips. *When to go:* See the first or last show of the day, when the weather's cooler. *How to dance with a particular character:*

Know where they'll be ahead of time: Chip 'n Dale dance directly in front of the castle, Mr. Incredible and Frozone (2004's "The Incredibles") get down near the entrance to Tomorrowland, Goofy and Donald Duck at the back right side of the hub. King Louie and Baloo (from 1967's "The Jungle Book") dance near the Adventureland entrance, "Toy Story" stars Woody and Jessie near the walkway to Liberty Square.

Key facts. *Best for:* Toddlers, children, teens, young adults. *Duration:* 12 minutes. *Weather issues:* Cancelled during rain. The performance is shortened when the heat index rises above 105 degrees (most shows from May through August); the conga-line segment is cut. *Debuted:* 2009. *Access:* Special viewing areas for guests in wheelchairs, ECVs. *Location:* Dancers and floats parade down Main Street U.S.A., stop at Cinderella Castle hub for the show, then return.

Average wait times

9am	10am	11am	Noon	1pm	2pm	3pm	4pm	5pm	6pm	7pm	8pm	9pm
n/a	n/a	n/a	n/a	n/a	n/a	n/a	n/a	n/a	n/a	n/a	n/a	n/a

© Disney

Perched on an oyster shell, Ariel rides high above the crowd in the Disney Festival of Fantasy Parade. Peter Pan and Wendy follow, behind Skull Rock on the Jolly Roger pirate ship.

Disney Festival of Fantasy Parade

Disney's best parade has beautiful floats, costumes, music

★★★★★ ✓ FastPass+ Magic Kingdom's new parade is truly new—nothing re-used from past parades, nothing patched together. The performers wear fantastical costumes, bursting with color. Floats celebrate Disney princesses, "Tangled," "The Little Mermaid," "Peter Pan," and "Brave." The eye-popper is the "Sleeping Beauty" segment, starring the evil Malificent as a giant Steampunk-styled fire-breathing dragon. Mickey and Minnie Mouse ride a hot-air balloon in the finale. One downside: Some characters are too high in the air to effectively interact with children along the curb; a few can barely be seen.

On rainy days Disney runs an alternate procession, the brief "Rainy Day Cavalcade" with an assortment of classic characters waving from Main Street Vehicles.

Tips. *When to go:* Arrive 45 minutes early to get a great viewing spot (with a Fastpass, 15 minutes). *Where to stand:* The best spot is in front of the Emporium in Town Square, in the middle of Main Street U.S.A., facing the castle. Fastpass viewers watch from the inner side of the castle hub. Disney gives out a maximum of 350 Fastpasses for this spot.

Hidden Mickeys. As balloons in the upper left corner of the parade banner... As a blue jewel and two smaller white jewels in the center of a large snowflake above "Frozen's" Elsa... As indentations on a gear on the belly of the dragon Maleficent, and as three bolts on the elbow of its left fore-leg.

Key facts. *Best for:* Children, teens, adults. *Duration:* 12 minutes. *Fear factor:* The dragon occasionally breathes bursts of fire. *Showtime:* Daily at 3 p.m. *Weather issues:* During rain exchanged for the Rainy Day Cavalcade. *Debuted:* 2014. *Access:* Guests may remain in wheelchairs, ECVs. *Location:* Travels through Frontierland, Liberty Square, Main Street U.S.A.

Average wait times

9am	10am	11am	Noon	1pm	2pm	3pm	4pm	5pm	6pm	7pm	8pm	9pm
n/a	n/a	n/a	n/a	n/a	n/a	n/a	n/a	n/a	n/a	n/a	n/a	n/a

Inspired by the Pleasure Island sequence in Disney's 1940 movie "Pinocchio," a giant smiling head lights up like a Christmas tree in the Main Street Electrical Parade.

Main Street Electrical Parade

Light-bright retro floats, performers are cheesy, charming

★★★★ ✓ FastPass+ Shimmering with light, everything—floats, characters, twirling snails—is covered with tiny colored bulbs in this Moog-music nighttime parade, which is either wonderful, weird or wonderfully weird, depending on your point of view and perhaps how many magic mushrooms you've recently eaten. It's the one Disney parade where guests clap along to its music (the manic 1966 synthesizer ditty "Baroque Hoedown") and applaud its floats, which are themed to old Disney movies such as 1940's "Pinocchio," 1951's "Alice in Wonderland," 1954's "Peter Pan" and, since it was new at the time the procession debuted here, 1977's "Pete's Dragon."

Tips. *When to go:* Arrive 30 minutes early to get a decent viewing spot. *Where to stand:* On Main Street U.S.A. You'll see the parade with a great backdrop, and if you're leaving the park afterward you'll have just a short walk to the exit.

Fun finds. A caterpillar smokes a hookah on the "Alice in Wonderland" float... Cinderella's two stepsisters awkwardly hold their legs high in front of Prince Charming, giving him views of their bloomers as they beg to try on his glass slipper... Played by grown men, Peter Pan's Lost Boys hold each other's tails as they twirl in a circle. Not that there's anything wrong with that... Huge cigar-store Indians line the back of Pinocchio's float, a giant smirking head that's part of a decadent carnival... Saluting red-white-and-blue chorus girls high-step along the final float, a patriotic flag so brightly lit it seems straight out of Vegas.

Key facts. *Best for:* Toddlers, children, seniors, Disney enthusiasts. *Weather issues:* Cancelled during rain. *Debuted:* 1977, revised 1999, 2010 (Disneyland 1972). *Access:* Special viewing areas for guests in wheelchairs and ECVs. *Location:* Travels Main Street U.S.A., then Liberty Square, Frontierland.

Average wait times

9am	10am	11am	Noon	1pm	2pm	3pm	4pm	5pm	6pm	7pm	8pm	9pm
n/a	n/a	n/a	n/a	n/a	n/a	n/a	n/a	n/a	n/a	n/a	n/a	n/a

Unseen projectors bathe Cinderella Castle in brilliant, eye-popping light during Celebrate the Magic, bringing the building to life with moving images and video.

Celebrate the Magic

Stunning high-tech light show transforms Cinderella Castle

★★★★ ✔ Using projected animated images and video, Cinderella Castle appears to transform during this nighttime show. Some of the visuals are truly bizarre. At one point the star of the 2012 movie "Wreck it Ralph" appears on the structure, which morphs it into an 8-bit brick version of itself that Ralph proceeds to wreck until hero Fix-It Felix saves the day. Later the castle becomes Buzz Lightyear's rocket ship and appears to blast off. Disney updates the show a few times each year; the version playing in the summer of 2014 included a frosty segment from the movie "Frozen," complete with Elsa belting out the Academy Award-winning song "Let It Go." Celebrate the Magic sometimes plays twice a night, before the fireworks and then again before the nighttime parade.

Tips. *When to go:* Show up in front of the castle about 15 minutes before the show begins to get a good spot to watch it. *Where to stand:* In the center of the castle hub, no closer than the statue of Walt Disney. From this spot you'll be far enough away to see the front of the castle and its angled sides, all of which have different images and special effects projected onto them, but still be close enough to see all of the effects' details. If viewed from an angle, the projections become distorted and skewed. *For families:* Since the segment featuring Maleficent could frighten your toddlers, you may want to distract them during its appearance.

Key facts. *Best for:* All ages. *Duration:* 10 minutes. *Fear factor:* The Maleficent moment has scary music and images. *Showtimes:* Typically twice a night; once before Wishes, once before the nighttime parade. *Weather issues:* Cancelled during rain. *Debuted:* 2012 (revised often). *Access:* Guests may remain in wheelchairs, ECVs. *Location:* Projected onto the front of Cinderella Castle.

Average wait times

9am	10am	11am	Noon	1pm	2pm	3pm	4pm	5pm	6pm	7pm	8pm	9pm
n/a	n/a	n/a	n/a	n/a	n/a	n/a	n/a	n/a	n/a	n/a	n/a	n/a

Dozens of rockets and nearly 700 explosions light up the sky during Wishes, Walt Disney World's signature fireworks show. The visuals synchronize to a symphonic score.

Wishes

Synchronized fireworks are breathtaking, inspiring, touching

★★★★★ ✔ FastPass+ Tinker Bell flies from Cinderella Castle in Disney's signature fireworks show. It starts with a lone glowing star arching through the night sky. After narrator Jiminy Cricket (from 1940's "Pinocchio") talks about wishing on a star, $200,000 worth of pyro explode in sync with the voices of beloved Disney characters and the beats and rhythms of classic Disney songs.

Far more sophisticated than you might expect, Wishes paints delicate strokes as well as bold. Sometimes the sky sparkles, sometimes it flashes. The show packs an emotional punch too, as it teaches a heart-tugging lesson about believing in yourself. Parents often tear up during the finale.

Tips. *When to go:* 20 minutes before show-time. *Where to stand:* On the crest of the Main Street U.S.A. bridge, between the ice cream parlor and the castle hub. You'll be far enough away to see all the pyro, but close enough

to see all of the castle's lighting effects. *For families:* Instead of fighting the huge crowd that leaves the park right after the show, get some ice cream and ask your children about their dreams and wishes. Tell them yours.

Fun finds. Fireworks form stars during the opening verse of "When You Wish Upon a Star." Hearts appear at the end of a "Beauty and the Beast" segment; a frowning face during the villains portion.

Fun fact. Tinker Bell is sometimes a man. The role's physical requirements are only that the performer weigh no more than 105 pounds and be no taller than 5 foot 3 inches.

Key facts. *Best for:* Children, families. *Duration:* 12 minutes. *Fear factor:* Loud explosions. *Weather issues:* Cancelled for thunderstorms. *Debuted:* 2003. *Access:* Special viewing areas for guests in wheelchairs, ECVs. *Location:* The fireworks explode far behind and to the sides of the castle.

Average wait times

9am	10am	11am	Noon	1pm	2pm	3pm	4pm	5pm	6pm	7pm	8pm	9pm
n/a	n/a	n/a	n/a	n/a	n/a	n/a	n/a	n/a	n/a	n/a	n/a	n/a

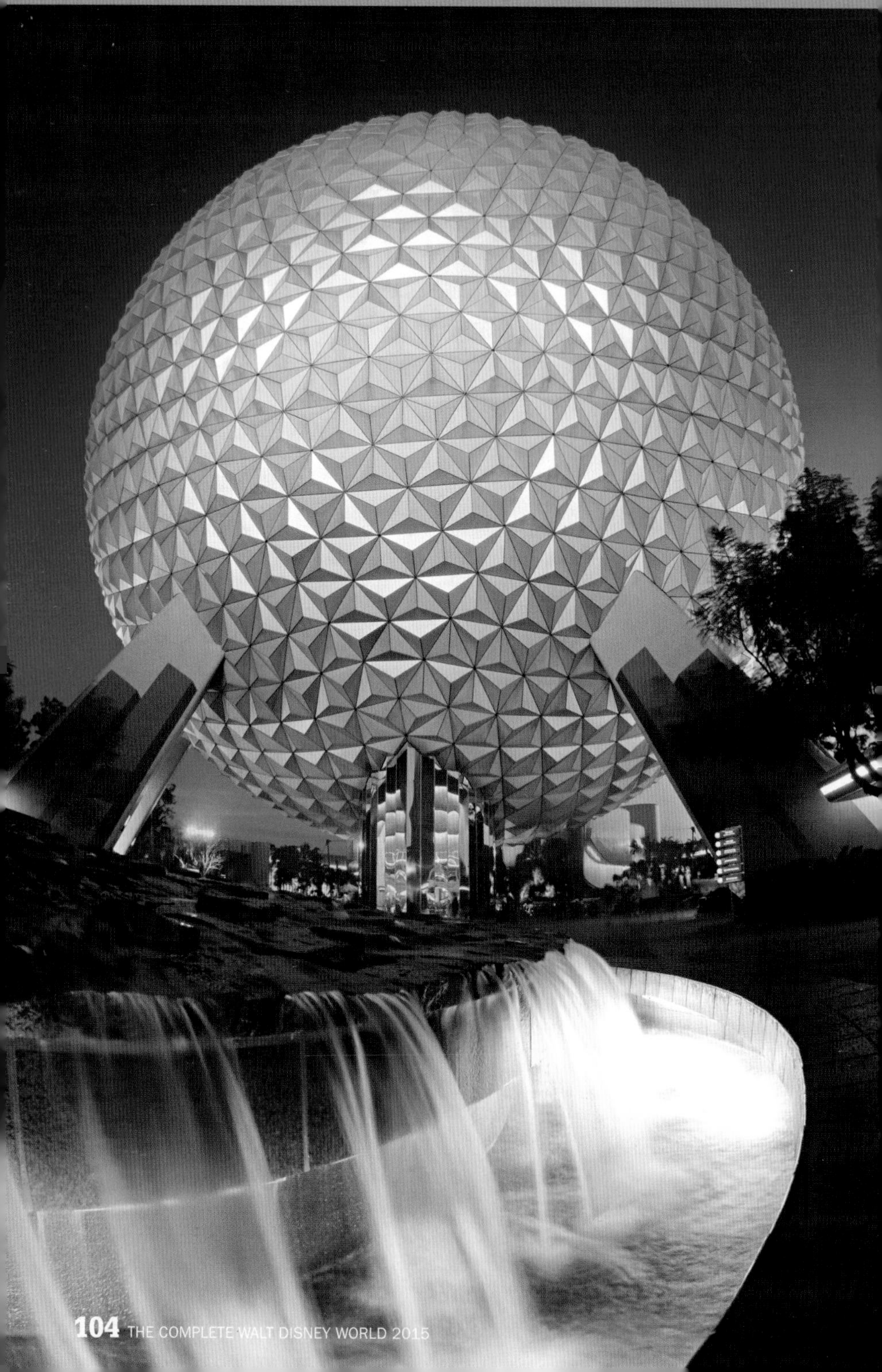

Epcot

Human achievement rules at this inspiring theme park, which celebrates science, technology and cultural diversity. Like a traditional World's Fair, Epcot's rides and shows are grouped into pavilions and focus on subjects such as communication, energy, agriculture, transportation and world cultures. Appealing most to the curious and educated, the park tends to be more interesting than thrilling.

Divided into two distinct sections—Future World and World Showcase—Epcot has a split personality. With its abundance of concrete buildings and scientific themes, Future World is a logical thinker, the nerdy corporate guy with a pocket protector. World Showcase, on the other hand, is a people person, a music-loving shopaholic with a $14 margarita in her hand. She also sleeps late; World Showcase doesn't open until 11 a.m.

Best of the park

Soarin'. You fly and glide over California's most eye-popping sites in this breathtaking ride, one of the best attractions in all of Walt Disney World.

The dolphins. A quartet of bottlenose dolphins live at The Seas pavilion. Training sessions spotlight their intelligence.

The people. Each World Showcase pavilion is staffed by natives of its country. Handpicked by Disney and flown to the United States on special one-year visas, these young friendly people love talking to guests about their homelands.

Eating and drinking around the world. Good food and drink, and lots of variety of both, set Epcot apart from all other theme parks. No other Disney spot has so many places to eat.

Unique shopping. Stores brim with wares in most World Showcase pavilions, offering goods as varied as Japanese bonsai trees to bottles of Mexican tequila to Epcot-exclusive French perfume.

Facing page: The symbol of Epcot, Spaceship Earth is a 180-foot-tall geodesic sphere. There's a ride inside it.

Worst of the park

Its impersonal future. Curiously lacking in Disney cast members, the wide walkways and public spaces in Future World are almost free of Disney smiles.

What's the matter with kids? With its emphasis on science, technology and international culture, Epcot has relatively few child-focused experiences.

Limited breakfast choices. The only table-service breakfast restaurant is a princess character meal in Norway; one fast-food spot for breakfast is inside The Land pavilion, the other in the France pavilion.

Corporate Sponsorland. Many attractions are conspicuously sponsored by corporations. Spaceship Earth has the name of its sponsor, Siemens, projected onto it as you leave the park after the fireworks display.

The walking. This is a big park. Hike out to World Showcase and you've still got 1.3 miles to go to get around it, little of which is in the shade.

Getting oriented. Epcot consists of two separate areas, which have little to do with each other. The front of the park is Future World, with six pavilions circling a central plaza. This part of Epcot contains the majority of its rides. In back is World Showcase, which holds most of the park's restaurants and shopping. Its 11 pavilions circle a lake.

The two areas keep separate hours. Future World opens at 9 a.m. and closes at 7 p.m. except for its major attractions. World Showcase opens at 11 a.m. and closes at 9 p.m.

Family matters. Four rides have height minimums—44 inches for Mission Space, 40 inches for Soarin' and Test Track, 48 inches for The Sum of All Thrills at Innoventions. Other attractions that might scare children include Ellen's Energy Adventure (loud noises, bright flashes, darkened dinosaur habitat); IllumiNations (loud explosions, fire); Journey Into Imagination... with Figment (loud noises, a sudden flash) and Maelstrom (dark, with scary faces).

A young couple walks through Innoventions Plaza toward its west breezeway, which leads to the Seas, Land and Imagination pavilions.

Every Epcot restaurant offers a children's menu, even the gourmet Monsieur Paul. The park has two character meals: Akershus Royal Banquet Hall in Norway (princesses) and Garden Grill in The Land pavilion (Mickey Mouse and his pals).

Children can make their own souvenirs in the World Showcase. Each pavilion holds a Kidcot Fun Stop, which is a spot for kids to decorate a cardboard mask with markers, and get a stamp unique to that pavilion's country. Children can choose between a mask shaped like Duffy the Disney Bear or Phineas and Ferb's pet platypus, Perry, as Agent P.

If it rains. Epcot is a mixed blessing on wet days—though it's comprised of indoor pavilions with multiple activities, those pavilions are spread out. Test Track closes when lightning is nearby. IllumiNations can get cancelled due to rain, as can all the park's outdoor concerts and street entertainment.

A closer look. In 1965, flush with success after decades in the entertainment industry, 63-year-old Walt Disney still had one dream left to explore: he wanted to find a fix for America's urban areas.

His idea: Combine corporate sponsorships with the money he had just made from the 1964 movie "Mary Poppins," and then—using all 43 square miles of land he had secretly just purchased in Florida—build an experimental city that, filled with technological advancements, would demonstrate how communities could solve their housing, pollution and transportation problems. He called the project the Experimental Prototype Community of Tomorrow. "EPCOT" for short.

The design called for a 50-acre town center enclosed in a dome, an internationally themed shopping area, a 30-story hotel and convention complex, office space, apartments, single-family homes, monorail and PeopleMover systems, an airport, underground roads for cars and trucks, even a nuclear power plant. There would be a theme park, too, a larger version of Disneyland.

On Nov. 15, 1965, Walt and his brother, Roy, held a press conference in Orlando to announce the project. "I'm very excited about it," he said, "because I've been storing these things up over the years. I like to create new things."

"We think the need is for starting from scratch on virgin land, building a community that will become a prototype for the future," Disney said in a videotaped sales pitch to potential corporate sponsors. "EPCOT will be a community of tomorrow that will never be completed, but will always be introducing and testing and demonstrating new

A wide promenade circles World Showcase Lagoon, traveling past each of that area's international pavilions. More than a mile long, it offers little shade on sunny afternoons.

materials and new systems." Monsanto was interested. General Electric, too. But little more than a year later, Walt Disney died unexpectedly. Smoking had caught up with him.

After his death, the Disney company took two of Walt's ideas—a corporate-sponsored science center and an international exposition that showcased other cultures—and reworked them into a theme park. Epcot—lowercase—opened on October 1, 1982.

Fun finds. The layout of Future World mimics the left-right division of the human brain. As you enter the park, pavilions on the left are themed to analytical, linear or engineering issues and sit within a landscape of straight-lined walkways. Those on the right cover more natural topics in a hilly, meandering, watery landscape... Voices inside a trash can talk to you inside the Electric Umbrella restaurant. Swing open the lid of the only receptacle marked "Waste Please" (it's usually sitting next to a topping bar to the left of the order counter) and you may hear a surfer dude complain *"Like, your trash just knocked off my shades!"* or a Frenchman exclaim *"Zis ees my lucky day! French fries!"*... Every 30 minutes the Innoventions fountain offers a five-minute show choreographed to music... Three Future World drinking fountains imitate submarine sounds, sing opera and offer wisecracks such as *"Hey, save some for the fish!"* when water hits their drains. One sits in front of MouseGear along the east side of the Innoventions fountain. A second is near the play fountain between Future World and the World Showcase. A third drinking fountain sits close to the restrooms behind Innoventions West... Fiber-optic lights are embedded in the sidewalks in front of the Innoventions buildings. Pinpoints of shimmering, flickering stars hide in dozens of small squares. Larger, colorful changing patterns appear in three 6-foot squares in front of Innoventions West. The lights are on all day, but most noticeable at night... Thirty-eight discoveries and inventions are honored in the rarely noticed Epcot Inventor's Circle, five concentric rings embedded into the walkway that leads from Innoventions Plaza to The Land pavilion. Inner-ring discoveries lead to outer-ring ones. For example, the inner Alphabet leads to the outer World Wide Web.

Hidden Mickeys. In Future World in the MouseGear store, as wall gauges behind the main cash registers.

Fun facts. The park has 3.5 acres of flowers and plants, 70 acres of lawns, 12,500 different trees and 100,000 shrubs... There are nearly 300 optical, motion and sound effects at

Epcot has the most restaurants of any Disney World theme park, and the most variety. The Italy pavilion's Via Napoli specializes in Neopolitan-style pizza that's cooked in wood-burning ovens.

Epcot, more than five times the number in Magic Kingdom... The construction of Epcot was the largest private construction job in U.S. history up to that point. The $1 billion project involved 7,500 people (3,000 designers and 4,500 construction workers), and the movement of 54 million cubic feet of dirt.

Know before you go. Need cash? A stroller? Help understanding your MyMagic experience? Here's where to find it:

ATMs. The park has three: There's one at the entrance on the far left, another on the bridge between Future World and World Showcase, and one near the American Adventure restrooms.

Baby Care Center. Situated at the Odyssey Center between Future World and World Showcase, this indoor spot has changing rooms, nursing areas, a microwave and a playroom. It sells diapers, formula, pacifiers and over-the-counter meds.

FastPass+ kiosks. Cast members help you book and reschedule Fastpasses at these walk-up touchscreens. You'll find them on the East and West breezeways in Future World, at Innoventions East, in the center of Innoventions Plaza and at the International Gateway, the park's back entrance.

First aid. An indoor clinic is in the Odyssey Center, next to the park's Baby Care Center. Registered nurses treat minor emergencies. They call EMTs for serious issues.

Guest Relations. Located at the entrance to the park on the far right, this office has walk-up windows outside the touchpoint scanners, a walk-in lobby inside to the left of Spaceship Earth. Cast members answer general questions, make dining reservations, exchange currency, hand out maps and times

Perry the platypus (also known as Agent P) stars in the park's interactive game Agent P's World Showcase Adventure. Guests follow clues to foil Perry's archenemy, the bumbling Dr. Doofenshmirtz.

Each World Showcase pavilion is staffed by young adults from its country, using a special visa created just for that purpose. They stay at Disney for one year, then return home.

guides for all Disney World parks, and store lost items found in the park that day.

Locker rentals. They're inside the park at the Camera Center in Future World, and also at the International Gateway in World Showcase ($7 a day, $5 deposit).

MyMagic+ Service Center. Inside the Innoventions East building, cast members answer questions about MyMagic+ services: the My Disney Experience website and app, the MagicBand ticketing system and the FastPass+ attraction-reservation service.

Package pickup. Anything you buy in the park can be sent to the main park entrance or the International Gateway entrance for you to pick up later at no charge. Allow three hours. Packages can also be delivered to Disney hotels or shipped nationally.

Parking. $17 a day per car. Free for Disney hotel guests and annual passholders.

Stroller rentals. A stroller shop at the front entrance on the left—and also at the International Gateway entrance—rents single strollers for $15 a day ($13 length of stay), doubles for $31 ($27 length of stay). Get replacements at the Germany pavilion.

Disney transportation. Boats serve Disney's Hollywood Studios and Epcot-area resorts. Monorails run to the Transportation and Ticket Center (TTC), then connect to the Contemporary, Grand Floridian, Polynesian resorts and the Magic Kingdom park. Buses serve all other Disney resorts and theme parks as well as the Blizzard Beach water park; there's no direct service to Downtown Disney, Typhoon Lagoon or ESPN Wide World of Sports.

Wheelchair and scooter rentals. Each entrance rents wheelchairs for $12 a day ($10 length of stay). EVCs are $50 ($20 deposit).

Snack stands dot Epcot's walkways. Among the most popular is the creatively named Funnel Cakes, which bakes and sells funnel cakes. Part of the American Adventure pavilion, it's at the back at the park.

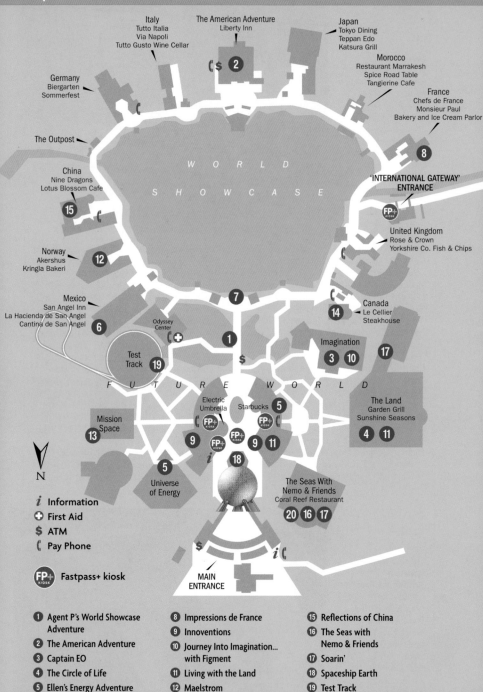

Italy
Tutto Italia
Via Napoli
Tutto Gusto Wine Cellar

The American Adventure
Liberty Inn

Japan
Tokyo Dining
Teppan Edo
Katsura Grill

Morocco
Restaurant Marrakesh
Spice Road Table
Tangierine Cafe

Germany
Biergarten
Sommerfest

France
Chefs de France
Monsieur Paul
Bakery and Ice Cream Parlor

The Outpost

China
Nine Dragons
Lotus Blossom Cafe

'INTERNATIONAL GATEWAY' ENTRANCE

WORLD SHOWCASE

United Kingdom
Rose & Crown
Yorkshire Co. Fish & Chips

Norway
Akershus
Kringla Bakeri

Mexico
San Angel Inn
La Hacienda de San Angel
Cantina de San Angel

Canada
Le Cellier
Steakhouse

Odyssey Center

Imagination

Test Track

FUTURE WORLD

The Land
Garden Grill
Sunshine Seasons

Mission Space

Electric Umbrella

Starbucks

Universe of Energy

The Seas With Nemo & Friends
Coral Reef Restaurant

N

i Information
✛ First Aid
$ ATM
(Pay Phone

FP+ Fastpass+ kiosk

MAIN ENTRANCE

1. Agent P's World Showcase Adventure
2. The American Adventure
3. Captain EO
4. The Circle of Life
5. Ellen's Energy Adventure
6. Gran Fiesta Tour
7. IllumiNations
8. Impressions de France
9. Innoventions
10. Journey Into Imagination... with Figment
11. Living with the Land
12. Maelstrom
13. Mission Space
14. O Canada!
15. Reflections of China
16. The Seas with Nemo & Friends
17. Soarin'
18. Spaceship Earth
19. Test Track
20. Turtle Talk with Crush

Attractions at a Glance

Here's a quick look at the attractions at Epcot, each of which is reviewed later in this chapter. The Fastpass+ logo (FastPass+) appears if the attraction can be reserved in advance. A checkmark (✔) indicates an author favorite.

Five-star attractions

Agent P's World Showcase Adventure. ★★★★★ ✔ Cute, funny interactive scavenger hunt triggers special effects, stars characters from "Phineas and Ferb." World Showcase.

The American Adventure. ★★★★★ ✔ Film and Audio-Animatronics figures tell the story of this country. World Showcase.

IllumiNations. ★★★★★ ✔ FastPass+ Nightly fireworks and laser show portrays an abstract history of the world. Explosions and fire may scare preschoolers. World Showcase lagoon.

The Seas with Nemo & Friends pavilion. ★★★★★ ✔ FastPass+ Calm dark ride retells story of 2003 film "Finding Nemo"; leads to marine exhibits and aquariums with dolphins, manatees and other sea life. Future World.

Soarin'. ★★★★★ ✔ FastPass+ Simulated hang-glider tour of California. Virtual and actual heights could frighten some; mostly it's very calm. The Land pavilion, Future World.

Turtle Talk with Crush. ★★★★★ ✔ FastPass+ Interactive theatrical show features real-time conversations with the animated sea turtle from the 2003 film "Finding Nemo." The Seas with Nemo & Friends pavilion, Future World.

Four-star attractions

Living with the Land. ★★★★ ✔ FastPass+ Indoor boat ride through greenhouses full of real, amazing plants, aquaculture tanks. The Land pavilion, Future World.

Mission Space. ★★★★ ✔ FastPass+ Space-flight simulator ride to Mars. The original ride ("Orange") spins in a centrifuge and is seriously intense; a milder version ("Green") is available. May bother those with claustrophobia or problems with virtual experiences. Height minimum 44 inches. Future World.

O Canada. ★★★★ ✔ Comedian Martin Short hosts humorous CircleVision 360 film about Canada. Canada pavilion, World Showcase.

Spaceship Earth. ★★★★ ✔ FastPass+ Slow-moving dark ride uses Audio-Animatronics characters to teach the history of communications. Better than it sounds. Future World.

Test Track. ★★★★ ✔ FastPass+ Guests design a virtual car, then test its capabilities against other riders' designs on an indoor/outdoor track; speed reaches 65 mph. Height minimum 40 inches. Future World.

Three-star attractions

Ellen's Energy Adventure. ★★★ Ellen DeGeneres hosts a series of wide-screen films and a slow-moving ride that present an oil-company view of energy. Future World.

Impressions de France. ★★★ Film celebrates the art, landscape and music of France. France pavilion, World Showcase.

Innoventions. ★★★ ✔ Corporate exhibits showcase innovations and new technologies. In Sum of All Thrills, guests design a virtual ride and then experience it atop a robotic arm. Height minimum for Sum of All Thrills 48 inches. Future World.

Maelstrom. ★★★ FastPass+ Indoor dark boat ride, film celebrate Norway's achievements, culture, history. Ride briefly travels backward. Norway pavilion, World Showcase.

Two-star attractions

The Circle of Life. ★★ Film uses stars of 1994's "The Lion King" to preach environmental protection. The Land pavilion, Future World.

Gran Fiesta Tour. ★★ Dark boat tour through Mexico stars Donald Duck and his amigos from the 1944 film "The Three Caballeros." Mexico pavilion, World Showcase.

Journey Into Imagination... with Figment. ★★ FastPass+ Mischievous little dragon Figment interrupts host Eric Idle's tour of the stuffy Imagination Institute. Imagination pavilion, Future World.

Reflections of China. ★★ CircleVision 360 film celebrates the culture, geography and selective history of China. China pavilion, World Showcase.

One-star attraction

Captain EO. ★ FastPass+ Woefully indulgent space adventure stars the late Michael Jackson; originally ran here 1986–1994. Imagination pavilion, Future World.

Restaurants and Food at a Glance

Epcot has a few outstanding table-service restaurants, and some surprisingly good counter choices, but the food at the park is not consistently the world standard Disney advertises it to be, and the company seems to relish overcharging for it. Below, each restaurant is rated from one to five stars (★) based on the quality of its food, service and atmosphere. A five-star eatery fully lives up to its promise; a one-star place should be avoided. A checkmark (✓) indicates that the spot is one of the authors' personal favorites. The price of a typical adult entree is summarized by dollar signs as follows:

$ less than $10
$$ less than $15
$$$ less than $20
$$$$ less than $25
$$$$$ more than $25

To reserve a table at any Walt Disney World restaurant call Disney at 407-939-3463.

Table service restaurants

Akershus Royal Banquet Hall. ★★★ $$$$$ American breakfast, American / Norwegian lunch and dinner. Character dining with three to five Disney princesses. Norway pavilion, World Showcase.

Biergarten. ★★★★ ✓ $$$$$ Meat-heavy German buffet with a live oompah band. Lunch, dinner. Germany pavilion, World Showcase.

Chefs de France. ★★★ ✓ $$$$ Traditional French cuisine, including French onion soup, quiche, creme brulee. Lunch, dinner. France pavilion, World Showcase.

Coral Reef. ★★★★★ ✓ $$$$ Seafood, also chicken, pork, steak and a vegetarian dish. Dining room views huge aquarium. Lunch, dinner. The Seas pavilion, Future World.

Garden Grill. ★★★ $$$$ American dinner served family style. Character dining with farmer Mickey Mouse, Chip 'n' Dale and Pluto. Dinner. The Land pavilion, Future World.

La Hacienda de San Angel. ★★★★ ✓ $$$$$ Modern Mexican cuisine. Dining room views World Showcase lagoon. Great specialty margaritas. Lunch, dinner. Mexico pavilion, World Showcase.

Le Cellier. ★★★★ $$$$$ Steakhouse, also fish, seafood, chicken and sandwiches. A Disney Signature Restaurant. Lunch, dinner. Canada pavilion, World Showcase.

Monsieur Paul. ★★★★★ ✓ $$$$$ Gourmet French cuisine. Dinner. France pavilion, World Showcase.

Nine Dragons. ★★ $$$$ Sadly routine chinese cuisine; could be so much better. Lunch, dinner. China pavilion, World Showcase.

Restaurant Marrakesh. ★★★ ✓ $$$$$ Traditional mild Moroccan cuisine includes lamb-shank couscous. A belly dancer entertains. Lunch, dinner. Morocco pavilion, World Showcase.

Rose & Crown Dining Room. ★★★★ ✓ $$$ British cuisine. Hearty comfort food, British beers. Lunch, dinner. United Kingdom pavilion, World Showcase.

San Angel Inn. ★★★ ✓ $$$$$ Traditional Mexican cuisine. Inside the Mexican pyramid, overlooking a "volcano." Lunch, dinner. Mexico pavilion, World Showcase.

Spice Road Table. ★★★★★ ✓ $$$$ Tasty tapas-style Mediterranean cuisine. Lunch, dinner. Morocco pavilion, World Showcase.

Teppan Edo. ★★★★ $$$$ Teppanyaki cuisine (Hibachi) in a stylish red-and-black decor. Chefs use grills set into dining tables. Lunch, dinner. Japan pavilion, World Showcase.

Tokyo Dining. ★★★★ ✓ $$$$ Nice Japanese lunches, dinners for Western palates. Very gracious servers. Japan pavilion, World Showcase.

Tutto Italia Ristorante. ★★★★★ ✓ $$$$$ Traditional Italian cuisine, with pastas, meat and fish. Lunch, dinner. Italy pavilion, World Showcase.

Via Napoli. ★★★★ ✓ $$$$ Pizzaria, by the pie or by the slice. Pasta, too. Lunch, dinner. Italy pavilion, World Showcase.

Counter service restaurants

Electric Umbrella. ★★ $$ Burgers, chicken and salads. Lunch, dinner. Innoventions Plaza, Future World.

Fife and Drum. ★ $ Turkey legs. Outdoor counter. Lunch, dinner. American Adventure pavilion, World Showcase.

Fountain View / Starbucks. ★★★ $ Typical Starbucks menu, including pastries and breakfast sandwiches; many coffee options. Breakfast, lunch, dinner. Innoventions Plaza, Future World.

Katsura Grill. ★★★★ ✓ $$ Sushi, teriyaki, udon, combos, sake. Lunch, dinner. Japan pavilion, World Showcase.

Kringla Bakeri Og Kafe. ★★★★ ✓ $$ Fresh pastries and sandwiches. Rich school bread is a favorite. Lunch, dinner. Norway pavilion, World Showcase.

La Cantina de San Angel. ★★★ ✓ $ Tacos, empanadas, tacos on the lagoon. Lunch, dinner. Mexico pavilion, World Showcase.

Les Halles Boulangerie & Patisserie. ★★★★ ✓ $ Good quiche, sandwiches, pastries. The only World Showcase counter-service spot that's open for breakfast. France pavilion, World Showcase.

Liberty Inn. ★★ $$ Burgers, hot dogs, strip steak. Kosher meal. Lunch, dinner. American Adventure pavilion, World Showcase.

Lotus Blossom Cafe. ★★ $ Egg rolls, chicken and stir-fry meals. Outdoor counter. Lunch, dinner. China pavilion, World Showcase.

Sommerfest. ★★★ $ Bratwurst, frankfurters, pretzels, beer. Outdoor counter. Lunch, dinner. Germany pavilion, World Showcase.

Sunshine Seasons. ★★★★★ ✓ $ Food court serves grilled meats, noodle dishes, pastries, salads, sandwiches, soups. Breakfast, lunch, dinner. The Land pavilion, Future World.

Tangierine Cafe. ★★★★ ✓ $$ Chicken and lamb platters, pastry counter with baklava. Lunch, dinner. Morocco pavilion, World Showcase.

Yorkshire County Fish Shop. ★★★ $ Fish and chips. Outdoor counter. Lunch, dinner. United Kingdom pavilion, World Showcase.

Notable snacks and treats

Artisan ice cream cones. ★★★★ ✓ $ At L'Artisan Des Glaces. Try the caramel with sea salt. France pavilion, World Showcase.

Shaved-ice snowcones. ★★★ ✓ $ Multiple flavors; all are good. On the promenade in front of the Japan pavilion, World Showcase.

See also **Restaurant Policies** in the chapter **Walt Disney World A–Z.**

Shops at a Glance

After Market. ★★★ Automotive merchandise, Test Track souvenirs. Test Track.

The Art of Disney. ★★★ Lithographs, oils, figurines. Future World.

Canada shops. ★★★ Maple treats, amusing moose-themed apparel. Canada pavilion.

Club Cool. ★★★ Coca-Cola items, unlimited free samples of foreign soft drinks. Innoventions Plaza, Future World.

Germany shops. ★★★★ ✓ Beer steins, Christmas merchandise, cuckoo clocks, teddy bears, a mouth-watering caramel shop. World Showcase.

Guerlain Paris. ★★★★ ✓ Cosmetics; perfume. Makeup applied on the spot. France pavilion, World Showcase.

House of Good Fortune. ★★★ Big store, lots of apparel. China pavilion, World Showcase.

Italy shops. ★★★★ ✓ Murano glass, perfumes. An artisan creates papier-mache, fabric Carnivale masks. World Showcase.

L' Esprit de la Provence. ★★★★ ✓ Kitchen items. France pavilion, World Showcase.

Mexico shops. ★★★★ ✓ Large indoor market with mucho items. World Showcase.

Mitsukoshi. ★★★★★ ✓ Sprawling store with bonsai, kimonos, sake, pearls, much more. Japan pavilion, World Showcase.

MouseGear. ★★★ ✓ The main Epcot souvenir store. Innoventions Plaza.

Morocco shops. ★★★★★ ✓ Traditional carpets, lamps, belly-dancer costumes, apparel, food, furniture. World Showcase.

Norway shops. ★★★ Sweaters, fragrance, troll dolls. World Showcase.

Parfums Givenchy. ★★★★ ✓ Everything Givenchy. France pavilion, World Showcase.

Soarin' gift counter. ★★★ Horticulture items. The Land pavilion, Future World.

United Kingdom shops. ★★★★ ✓ Soccer items, tea, Beatles gear. World Showcase.

Village Traders. ★★★ ✓ Carved wood and soapstone art from sculptor Andrew Mutiso. The Outpost, World Showcase.

See also **Shopping** in the chapter **Walt Disney World A–Z.**

Entertainers and performers

The British Revolution. ★★★ ✓ Four-piece band plays British rock hits. *United Kingdom pavilion.*

Jammitors. ★★★★★ ✓ Future World janitors take a break, transform into a percussion group. *Innoventions Plaza.*

Jeweled Dragon Acrobats. ★★ Acrobatic troupe. *China pavilion.*

Mariachi Cobre. ★★★★★ ✓ Eleven-piece band is the best one in the park. *Mexico pavilion.*

Matsuriza. ★★★★ ✓ Trio creates propulsive beats. *Japan pavilion.*

Mo' Rockin. ★★★★ Modern North African melodies with a slinky belly dancer. *Morocco pavilion.*

Off Kilter. ★★★★ ✓ Kilt-wearing Celtic band, led by a bagpiper. *Canada pavilion.*

Pub performer. ★★★★ ✓ A piano player entertains at the Rose and Crown. *United Kingdom pavilion.*

Sergio. ★★★★ ✓ Mime juggler puts child in his act. *Italy pavilion.*

Serveur Amusant. ★★★ Waiters do a balancing act. *France pavilion.*

Spirit of America Fife & Drum Corps. ★★★ A drill-team trio. *American Adventure pavilion.*

Voices of Liberty. ★★★★★ ✓ Gracious, spirited a cappella group. *American Adventure pavilion.*

World Showcase Players. ★★★★★ ✓ Funny street skits star audience "volunteers," butcher classic literature. United Kingdom pavilion.

All shows are 20 minutes.

From the top: The British Revolution in the United Kingdom pavilion; Voices of Liberty at the American Adventure; the Jammitors in Innoventions Plaza; the Serveur Amusant chef outside the France pavilion.

Where to meet characters

Epcot Character Spot. ★★★★ ✓
FastPass+ Mickey Mouse, Minnie Mouse and Goofy are inside this air-conditioned spot, which has colorful cartoon-style backdrops. *Innoventions Plaza, Future World.*

Future World walkways. ★ Daisy Duck and Pluto are often just inside the park entrance, Chip 'n Dale appear in Innoventions Plaza near the Epcot Character Spot.

At World Showcase pavilions. ★★★ *United Kingdom:* Alice in Wonderland in the tea garden, Mary Poppins on the promenade, Winnie the Pooh and Tigger (or Rabbit) in the Tin Soldier shop with a cozy room as a backdrop. *France:* Belle along the promenade left of the pavilion, Aurora along the right of the pavilion in a garden gazebo. *Morocco:* Aladdin and Jasmine indoors, with an Agrabah backdrop. *Germany:* Snow White on the left side of the pavilion. *China:* Mulan in the plaza. *Mexico:* Donald Duck to the right of the pavilion, in his Three Caballeros garb. *Showcase Plaza:* Duffy the Disney Bear, under a small gazebo with a backdrop of posters of Epcot's countries.

Garden Grill. ★★★★ ✓ Farmer Mickey Mouse, Chip 'n Dale and Pluto greet diners in this rotating restaurant. *The Land pavilion.*

Akershus Royal Banquet Hall. ★★★★ Five princesses visit your table at these character meals. Belle's always there; the others take turns. *Norway pavilion.*

See also the chapter **Characters.**

From the top: Donald Duck in his Three Caballeros garb at the Mexico pavilion; Snow White alongside the Germany pavilion; Alice at the United Kingdom pavilion, the Epcot Character Spot in Innoventions Plaza.

Micaela Neal

A Spaceship Earth scene imagines a 1960s computer room complete with its programmers. The slow-moving ride passes 22 dioramas on its trip through the history of communications.

Spaceship Earth

Slow ride through history is cooler than it sounds

★★★★ ✓ FastPass+ This huge silver sphere is more than just the park icon. It's also a ride—a trip back in time through the history of communications. Starting with prehistoric cave-dwellers and continuing through the Renaissance, Dark Ages and early uses of telegraphs, telephones and computers, nearly two dozen dioramas and twice that many Audio-Animatronic robots depict communication advances through history.

A four-seat ride vehicle spirals you slowly through each scene. At one point, you travel through a 1960s IBM computer room where two programmers watch over a huge reel-to-reel mainframe; a young female tech sports a miniskirt and giant Afro. Another scene shows a 1976 Silicon Valley garage where a young man—Steve Wozniak, maybe?—creates the first personal computer. Dame Judi Dench's calm narration emphasizes how the early moments led to the development of technology; behind her voice a 62-piece orchestra and 24-voice choir create a dramatic ambient score.

You shape your own future as the ride nears its finish. Using a touch-screen inside your ride vehicle, you first decide how you would like to live or work in the years ahead. A few seconds later you see your future on the screen, your face (which was none-too-subtly photographed at the beginning of the ride) superimposed onto an animated cartoon body.

An expansive post-show area, "Project Tomorrow" features interactive exhibits which showcase Siemens, the attraction's sponsor. In the center a giant globe-shaped screen pinpoints the hometowns of that day's Spaceship Earth passengers, while video screens show their future cartoon selves.

Tips. *When to go:* Immediately after the park opens, when you can walk right on.

Average wait times

9am	10am	11am	Noon	1pm	2pm	3pm	4pm	5pm	6pm	7pm	8pm	9pm
5m	15m	25m	35m	25m	10m	20m	25m	20m	20m	15m	15m	5m

An Audio-Animatronic figure in an ancient-Greece scene portrays an early actor at the dawn of theater. Spaceship Earth uses almost 50 animated figures to tell its story.

Epcot's Spaceship Earth exterior recalls the icons of the 1939 World's Fair (bottom left) and the 1964 World's Fair (bottom right). The 1939 "Perisphere" held a slow-moving ride in which guests took in views of the future.

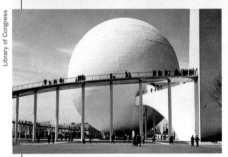

Another good time is around 8 p.m. *Where to sit:* On the left in your ride vehicle to be on the same side as the scenes that have details you want to see up close. The vignette depicting the birth of the personal computer is crammed with little details. *For families:* Have your child look up and smile at the automatic camera at the beginning of the ride, on your right. That photo will be used in a funny video you can email back home. *To hear the narration well:* Lean back in your seat. It comes from speakers behind you. *For couples:* This is the best ride in the park for those wanting to snuggle and kiss; it's dark and slow and has two-person bench seats.

Fun finds. A placard on the right of the computer room reads, "Think," the slogan of IBM founder Thomas J. Watson. It inspired the 1990s Apple slogan, "Think Different"... Nearby is a 1960s Selectric typewriter and a manual for IBM's System 360 Job Control Language used on 1964 mainframes... The radio station's call letters "WDI" refer to Walt Disney Imagineering.

Hidden Mickeys. As parchment blots made by a sleeping monk... As bottle rings on the table of the first Renaissance painter.

Fun facts. Science-fiction author Ray Bradbury ("Fahrenheit 451") helped design the attraction... The caveman is speaking a Cro-Magnon language... The cave drawings are based on images found in the Salon-Niaux cave in Ariége, France... The Egyptian hieroglyphics reproduce actual Middle Eastern drawings... The pharaoh's words come from a real letter... Guest "work" futures predict "a great big beautiful tomorrow," the theme song to Magic Kingdom's Carousel of Progress... A 180-foot-high geodesic sphere, Spaceship Earth does not drip water: a 1-inch gap between each panel flows rainwater into two interior gutters... The building weighs 16 million pounds. That's 158 million golf balls.

Key facts. *Best for:* Adults, couples, history buffs. *Duration:* 14 minutes. Allow up to 45 minutes for post-show activities. *Capacity:* 38 (2 per seat). *Queue:* Outdoor, partially covered. *Debuted:* 1982, revised 1994, 2008. *Access:* Must be ambulatory. Stops intermittently to load mobility-impaired guests. Vehicles offer a choice of narration languages—English, French, German, Japanese, Portuguese and Spanish. *Disability services:* Audio Description. *Location:* Future World.

A dad and daughter stroll past IBM's Think exhibit in Innoventions West, one of two buildings in Epcot that are filled with business presentations.

Innoventions

Corporate exhibits offer fun diversions, change often

★★★ ✓ These two buildings—Innoventions East and West—house sponsored displays with games or activities. Some are fun, but it's hard to feel like you've escaped on your vacation when a giant T. Rowe Price or Liberty Mutual logo stares you in the face.

• **Habit Heroes.** ★★ Blue Cross teaches healthy living (East).

• **Vision House.** ★★★ A tour of an energy-efficient home (East).

• **Sum of All Thrills.** ★★★★ Raytheon's physics-based exhibit is the only Innoventions ride. After designing a roller coaster, jet plane or bobsled track, you experience it virtually atop a robotic arm (East).

• **StormStruck.** ★★★ A Federal Alliance for Safe Homes exhibit combines a theatrical show with a display comparing how homes fare during a hurricane (East).

• **Test the Limits Lab.** ★ Guests swing a hammer at a TV, smash a 55-gallon drum onto a helmet and cause other havoc at this Underwriters Laboratories area (East).

• **Think.** ★★★ Guests explore 20 seven-foot touchscreens at this IBM exhibit (West).

• **The Great Piggy Bank Adventure.** ★★★ T. Rowe Price helps you set financial goals (West). Nice for older children.

• **Where's the Fire.** ★★★★ Players compete against each other to find fire hazards at this fun Liberty Mutual game. (West).

Tips. *When to go:* For Sum of all Thrills, before 11 a.m. or between 2 and 3 p.m. For the other exhibits, go anytime. *For families:* Play Where's the Fire; your family can be a team.

Key facts. *Best for:* Families. *Duration:* Presentations average 20 minutes. *Operating hours:* Park open–7 p.m. *Debuted:* 1994, revised 2009. *Access:* For Sum of all Thrills, height minimum: 48 inches. Wheelchair and ECV users must transfer. *Disability services:* Audio Description. *Location:* Future World.

Average wait times (Sum of All Thrills)

9am	10am	11am	Noon	1pm	2pm	3pm	4pm	5pm	6pm	7pm	8pm	9pm
0m	5m	10m	20m	30m	10m	10m	20m	25m	20m	n/a	n/a	n/a

Audio-Animatronics gulls outside the Seas pavilion squawk "Mine! Mine! Mine!" just as they do in "Finding Nemo." The voice is that of the movie's director, Andrew Stanton.

The Seas pavilion

Underrated pavilion displays sealife, serves seafood

★★★★★ ✓ Themed to the 2003 Pixar film "Finding Nemo," this two-story pavilion surrounds guests with marine life real and animated. Visitors enter the pavilion on "clam-mobiles"—three-seat ride vehicles which pass animated dioramas of Nemo and his pals, who appear at one point to swim in the aquarium itself.

Attraction. Children have real-time conversations with the animated sea turtle at **Turtle Talk with Crush** (★★★★★ ✓ FastPass+), using a huge video screen that resembles a viewing window into an ocean. Crush addresses kids by name ("Elizabeth, your polka-dot shell is totally cool!"), asks questions ("Austin, is that your female parental unit in the fourth row?") and reacts to responses. He also welcomes Dory the blue tang, who speaks whale perhaps a little too well. The show's queue area holds jellyfish, stingrays, eels and fish from the

Great Barrier Reef. Getting a Fastpass for the show guarantees you entry, but no special seating. *12 minutes. Capacity: 210. Indoor queue. Access: Guests may stay in wheelchairs, ECVs. Reflective captioning, assistive listening. Debuted: 2004.*

Exhibits. The Seas pavilion holds many marine creatures, some in the main aquarium, others in smaller tanks in side rooms.

• **Nemo & Friends.** ★★★★ ✓ This room displays live versions of many "Finding Nemo" stars, including clownfish, blue tangs, Moorish idols and cleaner shrimp. Tanks also hold eels, frogfish, venomous lionfish, seahorses and live coral.

• **Bruce's Shark World.** ★★★ 4 A recreation of the film's sunken submarine has interactive displays and photo props, educating kids about the threats sharks face.

• **Caribbean aquarium.** ★★★★★ ✓ On the second floor, this huge saltwater

Average wait times (Turtle Talk with Crush)

9am	10am	11am	Noon	1pm	2pm	3pm	4pm	5pm	6pm	7pm	8pm	9pm
5m	5m	15m	15m	15m	10m	10m	10m	10m	10m	10m	10m	n/a

The author's daughter with one of the pavilion's bottle-nose dolphins. Below, guests ride clam-mobiles to enter the pavilion; its attractions include Turtle Talk with Crush.

© Disney

© Disney

aquarium simulates a coral reef. It's filled with blacknose, brown and sand tiger sharks; some angelfish, cobia, snapper and tarpon; schools of lookdown; sea turtles; and a few rays. Lined with floor-to-ceiling windows, an observation tunnel extends into the tank. Divers unload food pouches while a presenter adds educational trivia at 10 a.m., 1 p.m. and 3:30 p.m. A side area holds a bachelor herd of dolphins—Rainer (born in 1986), Calvin and Kyber (1997) and Malabar (2001). Huge bars keep the mammals in their area; otherwise they "play" with the fish. Stop by the dolphin tank at 10:45 a.m., 2:15 p.m. or 4:15 p.m. to watch trainers conduct identity-matching, rhythm-identification or echolocation research.

• **Aquaculture.** ★★★ ✔ This upstairs room holds fascinating coral and cuttlefish, as well as farm-raised endangered species such as giant clams and clownfish.

• **Manatee aquarium.** ★★★★ ✔ Guests watch endangered Florida sea cows munch lettuce heads from above the surface on the second floor or through a first-floor under-water window. Docents give talks at 15 and 45 minutes after each hour.

Restaurants and food. Seafood fans will love the dimly lit **Coral Reef** (★★★★★ ✔), a hidden treasure with its own entrance. Diners look into The Seas aquarium with its 85 different tropical fish species. Non-seafood choices include chicken, pork, steak and a vegetarian dish. For an appetizer try the signature creamy lobster soup. Ask for an aquarium-front table or a booth near the tank. *Lunch, dinner. 11:30 a.m.–8:50 p.m. $19–$33 (children $9–$11). Seats 275.*

Shop. At the exit to the pavilion, a tiny walkway shop (★★) sells "Finding Nemo" souvenirs and sealife books and trinkets.

Tips. *For Turtle Talk:* Crush mostly chats with children near the screen who volunteer enthusiastically. Have your child sit on the floor in front, wear a funny hat and wave with abandon.

Fun find. As clam-mobile guests pass her by on their way into the pavilion, "Finding Nemo" sea star Peach clings to the aquarium glass as the fish around her continue to sing the theme song "Big Blue World." "Hey wait! Take me with you!" she begs. "It's a nice song but they just never stop! Never, never, ever, ever, ever!"

© Disney

Soarin' flies guests high literally and virtually. Rising 40 feet in front of a concave screen, riders appear to glide 800 feet above California sights such as the Golden Gate Bridge.

The Land pavilion

The home of Soarin', a nice boat ride and good fast food

★★★★★ ✓ There are two good attractions here, plus a movie, a character dinner and an outstanding food court.

Attractions. Most people come here for one reason—the hang-glider experience:

• **Soarin'.** ★★★★★ ✓ FastPass+ Way more than just a 5-minute film, this unique attraction uses an innovative theater to immerse you in its experience. After boarding a multi-seat hang glider, you lift up to 40 feet into an 80-foot projection dome. Your field of vision is filled with the beauty of California. The glider tilts as you travel; your legs dangle underneath. Special effects provide gentle breezes and fragrances. The overall experience is exhilarating. *5 minutes. Capacity: 174 per theater. Indoor queue. Fear factor: Gentle, but may be troubling for those who fear heights. Restraint: Seat belt. Access: Height minimum: 40 inches. Wheelchair and ECV users must transfer. Handheld captioning. Debuted: 2005.*

• **Living with the Land.** ★★★★ ✓ FastPass+ This indoor boat ride presents a subject seemingly as dull as dirt—agricultural science—in an entertaining way. A trip through four greenhouses, it's filled with weird plants and odd growing techniques. Crops include hanging bananas, coconuts and enormous nine-pound lemons and jackfruit which weigh down their branches. Many plants hang from strings, their roots exposed to the air. Others grow on overhead conveyor belts, touring their greenhouses like suits in a dry cleaner. An aquaculture hut has tanks of sturgeon, eels, even young alligators. *14 minutes. Capacity: 20 per boat. Indoor queue. Access: ECV users must transfer. Handheld captioning, Audio Description. Debuted: 1982 (as Listen to the Land); revised 1993, 2009.*

Movie. Since it stars Timon and Pumbaa from "The Lion King" you'd think **The Circle of Life** (★★) would be worthwhile. But

Average wait times (Soarin')

9am	10am	11am	Noon	1pm	2pm	3pm	4pm	5pm	6pm	7pm	8pm	9pm
5m	55m	90m	65m	50m	60m	80m	50m	60m	60m	50m	40m	20m

The Living with the Land boat ride travels through fragrant greenhouses filled with exotic plants. Boats also pass through an aquaculture hut where fish swim in elevated glass tanks.

unfortunately, it's dated, blurry and preachy. When the duo start to clear a savanna to build the "Hakuna Matata Lakeside Village," Simba tells them about a creature—man—who first lived in harmony with nature, but now often forgets that everything is part of the circle of life. Live-action scenes show smokestacks, traffic and an oil-soaked bird, but later wind turbines, electric cars and recycling. *13 minutes. Capacity: 482. Indoor queue. Access: Guests may stay in wheelchairs, ECVs. Handheld, reflective captioning; assistive listening. Debuted: 1995.*

Restaurants and food. The pavilion holds a character buffet and a fast-food spot.

• **Garden Grill.** ★★★ $$$$$ Children and adults alike will enjoy this pricey country dinner, which is served family-style. The menu includes grilled steak, turkey and fish; some food comes from the pavilion's greenhouses. As you dine, Mickey Mouse, Pluto and Chip 'n Dale mosey up to say hi. The circular dining area slowly rotates around the kitchen; its outside rim overlooks the Living with the Land dioramas. *Dinner. 4–8 p.m. $42 (children $20). Seats 150.*

• **Sunshine Seasons.** ★★★★★ ✔ $ This excellent food court serves freshly prepared grilled meats, noodles, salads, sandwiches, soups and breakfast. *9 a.m.–9 p.m. $5–$12 (children $6–$7). Seats 707.*

Shop. The incredibly small **Soarin' gift counter** (★★★) sells horticulture items, including books on hydroponics.

Tip. *For Soarin':* Ask to enter the theater at Gate B, Row 1. You'll be in the center, at the top.

Fun finds. The Soarin' entranceway resembles an airport; its theater has runway lights… Your flight is "Number 5-5-0-5," a reference to the ride's opening date of May 5, 2005.

Hidden Mickeys. As a Mickey Mouse profile in the Living with the Land queue area mural (as bubbles under the word "nature")… In the mural behind the loading area, an angled Mickey is formed by green and blue circles (near the right wall, near the floor)… On Soarin', a blue Mickey Mouse balloon shows up in the Palm Springs scene, behind a golf cart in the far lower left, and there's a small Mickey silhouette on an errant golf ball… The shape is also created by the second burst of Disneyland fireworks.

Average wait times (Living with the Land)

9am	10am	11am	Noon	1pm	2pm	3pm	4pm	5pm	6pm	7pm	8pm	9pm
5m	5m	10m	10m	10m	10m	10m	10m	10m	10m	10m	n/a	n/a

Guests choose from two versions of Disney's space-flight simulator Mission Space, the original intense adventure or a mild alternative. Crowds are often light.

Mission Space

Its G-forces makes you feel like an astronaut. Or feel sick.

★★★★ FastPass+ So intense it includes motion-sickness bags, this flight simulator offers realistic sensations of space travel. It's set in the year 2036, when you and other "future astronauts" are training for a mission to Mars. But soon after your simulator takes off, everything goes wrong.

The ride comes in two variations. The "Orange" one is a rapidly rotating centrifuge with capsules on its spokes. Its G-forces mimic those of a real rocket launch but can make you feel dizzy, nauseated or worse. A "Green" variation offers the same video experience but doesn't create G-forces, as it doesn't spin. An elaborate post-show area includes games, kiosks and a toddler play area.

Tips. *When to go:* Not around mealtime. *How not to get sick:* Stare straight at the video screen without glancing around. *Feel queasy afterward?* Splash water on yourself from a water fountain on the exit walkway.

Fun finds. The queue holds a 35-foot Gravity Wheel, a prop from the 2000 Disney live-action film "Mission to Mars." The logo for Horizons, the previous ride at this site, decorates its hub.

Hidden Mickeys. The three-circled shape appears as craters on the courtyard moon, near the Luna 8 site, and as tiles in the patio… In the queue, as Mars craters on the left and right monitors above the desks.

Key facts. *Best for:* Teens. *Duration:* 6 minutes. *Capacity:* 4 per vehicle. *Queue:* Indoor. *Fear factor:* Intense physical sensations. *Restraint:* Seat belt. *Debuted:* 2003. *Health advisories:* Guests should be free from claustrophobia; motion sickness; pregnancy; high blood pressure; heart, back or neck problems. *Access:* Height minimum 44 inches. Wheelchair and ECV users must transfer. *Disability services:* Activated video captioning. *Location:* Future World.

Average wait times

9am	10am	11am	Noon	1pm	2pm	3pm	4pm	5pm	6pm	7pm	8pm	9pm
10m	10m	15m	10m	20m	10m	15m	10m	20m	20m	15m	20m	20m

© Disney

The attraction offers a realistic simulation of what is like to be an astronaut, including the launch. This gantry-eye view appears on your video screen just before lift-off.

The entrance to Test Track, an automotive-themed ride which lets you create your car onscreen and then test its performance as you travel through a proving ground.

Test Track

You design your car (in a sense) at this exhilarating attraction

★★★★ ✔ **FastPass+** Revised in 2012, Test Track is now more than a ride. Before boarding, you customize your own concept car using a touchscreen in a "Design Studio." In the four minutes allotted, you decide your car's color, shape, graphics, accessories and strongest attribute—capability, efficiency, responsiveness or power. The way you design your car affects how well your car will score based on these four attributes. After you build your sleek silver sports sedan (or Hot-Wheels-like hot-pink bulgemobile with a giant spoiler and solar panels on its hood), you're off to the boarding area.

The car you ride in bears little resemblance to the one you've designed; all of the actual vehicles are the same. But throughout the ride video screens in your car show you how your design would perform, and how it would score against the cars of your seatmates.

The ride itself is a thrill, as your open-topped car reaches 65 mph as it travels through an automobile proving ground. With 34 turns but no drops or loops, the mile-long course is perfect for those who like speed but hate falling.

A post-show is dotted with games and activities linked to your car. They show you how your design fared against others, and use your car to create a commercial. Three screens allow you to make more designs, for as long as you want.

Tips. *When to go:* Go first thing in the morning; if you can't either use the single-rider line or a Fastpass. Using the single-rider line over-simplifies the car customization process, however. *Where to sit:* In the middle of your seat, with another rider on each side of you. You'll have far more legroom. *Tips for families:* Help your young children design their cars; it's a little complex. There

Average wait times

9am	10am	11am	Noon	1pm	2pm	3pm	4pm	5pm	6pm	7pm	8pm	9pm
5m	40m	80m	80m	30m	30m	50m	40m	40m	30m	50m	60m	50m

Guests create their custom automobiles at the "Chevrolet Design Studio," then have it tested against others in four different attributes: capability, efficiency, responsiveness and power.

is a time limit for designing, so be brisk. If you're with a friend or spouse, or have older children, don't pitch in on a design together, instead build two different cars, so you can virtually race them against each other. To get two design screens, just tell the cast member outside the design studio that each of you want to make a car (when they ask "how many?"). *About the Single Rider line:* If you use it, you won't get to design a car. Instead, you'll pick from eight pre-made vehicles.

Hidden Mickeys. In the Standby queue, the three-circle shape of Mickey Mouse appears on two photo collages on the right side of the walkway. First in a collage of designers, to the left of the drawing hand of a man wearing glasses and writing with a marker, and second in a collage which shows people drawing concept art, above a vertical white dashed line.

Fun facts. The first attraction at this location was General Motor's World of Motion, which opened with the park in 1982. The pavilion has always been sponsored by GM, even during its recent bankruptcy... With a top speed of 65 mph, Test Track is the fastest attraction at Walt Disney World.

Key facts. *Best for:* Older children, teens, car enthusiasts. *Duration:* 5 minutes for the ride. Allow 1 hour if you add every post-show experience. *Capacity:* 192 (6 per two-row car). *Queue:* Indoor. *Fear factor:* Intense for those scared by speed. *Restraint:* Seat belt. *Weather issues:* Closed during thunderstorms. *Debuted:* 1999, revised 2012. *Health advisories:* Guests should be free from motion sickness; pregnancy; high blood pressure; heart, back or neck problems. *Access:* Height minimum 40 inches. Must be ambulatory. *Location:* Future World.

Speeds reach 65 mph as riders leave the round Test Track building, go through some tight turns, then zip around the outside of the structure.

Disney's Universe of Energy pavilion holds Ellen's Energy Adventure. The elaborate oil-company presentation stars robotic dinosaurs and comedian Ellen DeGeneres.

Ellen's Energy Adventure

A lesson about energy, as taught by an oil company

★★★ An out-of-date attraction that features dinosaurs, a funny comedian and a skewed corporate picture of the 'Universe of Energy.' What is… Ellen's Energy Adventure! Based on the game show "Jeopardy," this lengthy presentation about energy is highlighted by a slow-moving tram that passes Audio-Animatronic dinosaurs. Produced back when the average price of a gallon of gasoline was $1.30, the show ignores the problems of fossil fuels. There's no mention of the Middle East, no talk of global warming, oil spills or fuel efficiency. It's laughably dated, and very much a product of its time—the 1980s and 1990s, when it was sponsored by Exxon.

Tips. *When to go:* Anytime; there is never a wait. *Where to sit:* In the pre-show, stand in the center of the room to have a proper view of the wide screens. In the ride vehicle, sit in the left-hand car, on the right side of the row, halfway back. You'll get close to the

dinosaurs and get a good view of the video screens. You'll also be able to see more of the show, since the left car leads the others. *For families:* The show's dark Big Bang section, its oil-rig segment and its explanation of fusion could frighten young children.

Fun finds. After Alex Trebek praises Ellen for her "first correct response!" her lips don't move when she yells "Freeze!"… Bill Nye's lips stay shut when, in front of a solar mirror, he says "All right."… Michael Richards, who played Kramer in "Seinfeld," makes a cameo as a caveman who discovers fire.

Key facts. *Best for:* Seniors. *Duration:* 45 minutes (new shows begin every 17 minutes). *Capacity:* 582. *Queue:* Outdoor, unshaded. *Fear factor:* The portrayal of the Big Bang is loud. *Operating hours:* Park open–7 p.m. *Debuted:* 1996. *Access:* ECV users must transfer. *Disability services:* Assistive listening, handheld captioning. *Location:* Future World.

Average wait times

9am	10am	11am	Noon	1pm	2pm	3pm	4pm	5pm	6pm	7pm	8pm	9pm
10m	10m	10m	10m	10m	10m	10m	10m	10m	10m	10m	n/a	n/a

Toward the end of the Journey Into Imagination tour of its Imagination Institute, dragon Figment diverts your vehicle and gives you a tour of his home, which is built upside down.

Imagination pavilion

This is Disney's idea of imagination?

★ This forgotten complex houses a recycled 3-D movie and an uninspired ride that only preschoolers will enjoy.

Attraction. Irritating dragon Figment—a fixture of this pavilion since it opened in 1982, and still popular among some older Disney fans—interrupts **Journey Into Imagination... with Figment** (★★ FastPass+), a slow-moving dark ride that rumor has it will be shut down soon. Figment appears as you set off on a tour of the stuffy Imagination Institute, a place where Dr. Nigel Channing (Monty Python's Eric Idle) attempts to "capture and control" imagination. Figment wrecks your tour, and arranges for the smell of skunk to spray in your face, among other mischief. The ride's final scene uses black lights and primitive cut-out flowers and graphics. *6 minutes. Capacity: Two or three per vehicle. Indoor queue. Fear factor: A dark room has the clamor of an oncoming train. Access: Guests may stay in wheelchairs, ECVs. Handheld captioning, Audio Description. Debuted: 1983, revised 1998, 2001.*

Movie. And you thought Jar Jar was bad. Developed by "Star Wars" creator George Lucas, the 1986 3-D musical film **Captain EO** (★ FastPass+) stars Michael Jackson at his most wacko. Perhaps diverting for those wearing rosy nostalgic glasses, for a typical audience the show wallows in '80s excess. *17 minutes. Capacity: 570. Indoor queue. Access: Guests may stay in wheelchairs, ECVs. Handheld, reflective captioning; assistive listening, Audio Description. Debuted: 1986, reintroduced 2010.*

Shop. The **ImageWorks store** (★★★) sells typical Disney items and Figment souvenirs. Little high-tech games make the area next to the shop the most fun spot in the pavilion.

Tips. Go anytime; crowds are rare.

Fun finds. In the attraction queue a page for Merlin Jones seeks the chimp teacher seen in Disney's 1965 live-action movie "The Monkey's Uncle"... Tennis shoes outside the ride's computer room refer to 1969's "The Computer Wore Tennis Shoes."

Hidden Mickeys. On the ride, a Mickey Mouse-eared headphone sits in the Sight Lab, on top of the left wheeled table... In Figment's bathroom the three-circled shape is made of two circular carpets and a flowered towel seat.

Bracketed by totems, the main entrance to the Canada pavilion through a native village as they approach the Hotel du Canada, Disney's version of Ottawa's Chateau Laurier.

Canada pavilion

A beautiful landscape, a funny film, tender steaks

★★★ Rockers wear kilts at this pavilion, a woodsy 3-acre salute to America's northern neighbor. It holds a movie theater, two connected shops, a pricey steakhouse and a stage for a fun Canadian band. A pretty flower garden and rolling landscape add to the pavilion's appeal. "O Canada," a travelogue starring comedian Martin Short, is an amusing film with images that circle its theater.

Restaurants and food. Canada has one lone food choice, an expensive steakhouse.

• **Le Cellier.** ★★★★ $$$$$ Ideal for big-budget diners who want comforting food, this steakhouse is one of the toughest World Showcase reservations to nab. Walk-ups may be available right at 11:30 a.m., but it's so popular (and has so few seats) that typically you need to make your reservation at least a week in advance, sometimes way before that. Alberta beef steaks are aged a perfect 28 days. Other carefully-prepared entrees include fish, seafood, chicken and sandwiches. Made with Moosehead beer, a cheddar-cheese soup makes a nice makeshift dip for the complimentary soft breadsticks. The low-ceilinged, stone-walled eatery resembles a chateau wine cellar; it's cozy and, since it has no windows, a little claustrophobic. *Lunch, dinner. 11:30 a.m.–9 p.m. $27–$49 (children $9–$15). Seats 156. A Disney Signature Restaurant.*

Shops. Two connected stores offer little authentic Canadian merchandise, though **Northwest Mercantile** (★★★) sells real maple-syrup treats and dreamcatchers, and **The Trading Post** (★★★) offers Canadian books and a silly moose-antler hat.

Movie. Fans of Martin Short will enjoy the CircleVision 360 film **O Canada** (★★★★ ✔), a travelogue in which he stars. You stand up to watch it, as the film is shown on screens that wrap completely around you. The images zoom by, surrounding you as you appear to sweep by rocky crags and waterfalls. It's like Soarin' without the ride. *14 minutes. Capacity: 600. Covered outdoor queue. Access: Guests may stay in wheelchairs, ECVs. Reflective captioning, assistive listening, Audio Description. Debuted: 1982, revised 2007, 2012.*

Entertainment. Quirky Celtic rock band **Off Kilter** (★★★★ ✔) combines guitars, a

Flower gardens channel the famed Butchart Gardens in Victoria. Below, Off Kilter's bagpiper and guitarist; a young visitor views a waterfall that recalls the Canadian Rockies.

bagpipe and laid-back humor into an irreverent show (don't be surprised to hear "Sweet Home Alabama"). At many performances a few guests get up and twirl with Deadhead joy. The band's catchy, rhythmic music reminds the author of the steerage-class band in "Titanic," with its exhilarating beat. *20-minute shows. Promenade stage.*

Architecture. The grounds are dominated by the "Hotel du Canada," a near replica of Ottawa's famed Chateau Laurier hotel. The forced-perspective French Gothic facade sits behind a flower garden that's inspired by the Butchart Gardens in Victoria. Along the promenade, a native village is represented by a log cabin, a trading post and some totems. Carved by a Tsimshian Indian in 1998, the totem on the far left shows the Raven folkbird releasing the sun, moon and stars from a carved cedar chest. Up the steps, a stone building reflects the British architecture common on the country's East Coast. The back of the pavilion recalls the Canadian Rockies; a 30-foot waterfall flows into a stream. The opening to a mine shaft—the entrance to the theater—is trimmed with shoring and Klondike equipment.

Tips. *For the movie:* Stand as close as possible to the dead center of the room, and look all around you, as the images in front of you will be different from the images behind you. If you are short, try to avoid standing next to a tall person. *For shopping:* Look for the small beanbag figure of Goofy as a lumberjack. *For a treat:* Check out the 100-percent-maple-syrup lollipops, at the Trading Post for $3.

Fun find. A fun photo spot sits along the promenade—an odd carved bird head is split in two with a hole for you to stick your face through and say "Cheese."

Fun fact. Developed in the 1950s by video engineer (and original Mickey Mouse animator) Ub Iwerks, Disney's CircleVision 360 theaters use nine projectors to display video from a nine-lens camera onto nine screens. Why nine? Because the concept only works with an odd number—each projector sits in a gap between two screens, and lines up with one screen across from it.

Hidden Mickeys. Along the entranceway, two Mickey Mouse shapes hide on the left totem, underneath its top set of hands… The shape also appears in Le Cellier, as wine-rack bottles behind the check-in counter.

Performing a street skit with wild abandon, a member of the World Showcase Players improv troupe urges his audience to get involved.

United Kingdom pavilion

A lovely pavilion, with multiple areas to explore

★★★★★ ✔ Friendly Brits serve authentic brews and sing Beatles and Rolling Stones tunes in this storybook village. Two streets are lined with shops, restaurants and lovely gardens. Stores stock everything from pub coasters and rugby balls to fine bone china and tartan sweaters. Those who enjoy Disney's British films such as 1951's "Alice in Wonderland" and 1964's "Mary Poppins" will find their favorite characters on hand, as well as Winnie the Pooh and his pals. Friendly cast members often chalk out a promenade hopscotch game at 11 a.m.

Restaurants and food. Dining options include a relaxed table-service restaurant and a fish-and-chips fast-food window.

• **Rose & Crown Dining Room.** ★★★★ ✔ $$$$ Fans of hearty food will enjoy this comfortable eatery. Good choices include deliciously creamy potato leek soup, bangers and mash and shepherd's pie. Eating indoors is relaxed and comfortable; its small shady patio is one of Disney's best outdoor dining spots. With a little luck you can be sitting on the patio during IllumiNations, and be able to sit, eat and enjoy the show. *Lunch* *12–3 p.m. $15–$27 (children $8–$11). Dinner 4 p.m.–park close. $15–$32 (children $8–$11). Seats 242, including 40 on a covered porch.*

• **Yorkshire County Fish Shop.** ★★★ $ This walk-up window has an extremely limited menu, but it's hard to find fault with its fish and chips, especially if you wash them down with a Bass ale. *Lunch, dinner. 11 a.m.–9 p.m. $9. Seats 30 outdoors.*

Shops. Half a dozen pretty little shops offer a variety of merchandise from the United Kingdom, including Beatles souvenirs, pub coasters and all sorts of tea and tea accessories. The **Crown & Crest** (★★) specializes in family name and coat of arms items as well as Guinness souvenirs. **Lords and Ladies** (★★★) stocks fine silver jewelry and "Downton Abbey" merchandise. **The Queen's Table** (★★★) sells "Keep Calm and Carry On" items. As its name suggests, **The Sportsman's Shoppe** (★★★★) stocks sports apparel; rugby, soccer and tennis shoes; balls; and sports books. **The Tea Caddy** (★★★★★ ✔) offers many varieties of Twinings tea, plus fine bone china, teapots, biscuits and British candies. Though it used to sell toys, **The Tin**

The architecture of the pavilion re-creates many facades of Olde England, including the Abbotsford estate of Sir Walter Scott (right), the thatched-roof cottage of Anne Hathaway and stately London townhouses and shops.

Soldier (★★★★ ✓) now offers Beatles, Dr. Who, Monty Python and Mr. Bean merchandise and apparel, mostly T-shirts.

Entertainment. Street skits star audience volunteers as the hilarious **World Showcase Players** (★★★★★ ✓) improv troupe butchers classic literature; "Romeo and Juliet" becomes "Romeo and Edna." *20-minute shows. Tudor Street.* Four-piece cover band **The British Revolution** (★★★★ ✓) plays hits by famed British rockers such as the Beatles, Clash, Led Zeppelin and The Who. *20-minute shows. Back green stage.* Late in the day, a **piano player** (★★★★) adds life to the Rose & Crown pub. *12 seats have a direct view.*

Architecture. Each building represents a different period in United Kingdom history. The brick turrets and medieval crenulation of the Sportsman's Shoppe mimic Henry VIII's 16th-century Hampton Court. Its whitestone side is Abbotsford, the 19th-century Scottish estate where Sir Walter Scott wrote novels. Across a street is the 16th-century thatched-roofed cottage of Anne Hathaway, the wife of William Shakespeare. Further down the street sits a half-timbered 15th-century Tudor leaning with age, a plaster

17th-century pre-Georgian, a stone 18th-century Palladian and a home built of angled bricks. Bordering the World Showcase lagoon, the Rose & Crown Pub is divided vertically into three styles—a medieval rural cottage, a 15th-century Tudor tavern and an 1890s Victorian bar.

Tips. *For a photo:* In the garden behind the Tea Caddy, a foliage arch over the walkway makes a nice frame for a photograph. *For shopping:* Quirky Monty Python and Dr. Who T-shirts make unique souvenirs. *For a treat:* Try the Cadbury dairy milk chocolate candy bar at the Tea Caddy for $3.50. Cadbury reportedly has the best chocolate around; smoother and creamier than the Hershey's brand. The bar melts quickly, as this chocolate obviously wasn't made for Florida weather; eat it fast and hold it by the wrapper.

Fun finds. Three oh-so-British red phone booths make great photo spots, but are not, alas, operational.

Hidden Mickeys. The three circles are formed by a soccer ball, a football and a racket on a sign above the Sportsman's Shoppe along the promenade.

A replica of the Pont des Arts footbridge leads from Epcot's United Kingdom pavilion to France, specifically the Paris of La Belle Époque—"the beautiful time" from 1870 to 1910.

France pavilion

Quality food, wine, treats, perfume. Even a nice travelogue.

★★★★ ✓ A good spot to get off your feet, this well-done pavilion offers a relaxing film in a cozy theater, a tempting array of pastries, a sidewalk ice cream parlor and some good restaurants. Fine perfume and wine highlight the shopping; the fragrance shops have heavenly aromas.

Restaurants and food. You name it, if it's French it's here—from a basic croissant to a bowl of award-winning black truffle soup.

• **Chefs de France.** ★★★ ✓ $$$$ Fans of traditional French food will enjoy this sophisticated café, which serves everything from sandwiches to quiche to seafood. Good appetizers include lobster bisque and French onion soup; for dessert the signature créme brulee is rich and silky. *Lunch 12–3 p.m., $13–$30 (children $8–$11). Dinner 5 p.m.–park close, $13–$35 (children $8–$10). Seats 266.*

• **Monsieur Paul.** ★★★★★ ✓ $$$$$ One of Disney's few actual gourmet restaurants, this second-floor eatery offers spot-on-French dishes and superb service. Diners rave about the food. It's named after the legendary Paul Bocuse, whose son owns the place. If it's on the menu try the black truffle

soup, which placed Bocuse in the French Legion of Honor in 1975. *Dinner 5 p.m.–park close. $39–$44 (children $13–$16). Seats 120.*

• **Halles Boulangerie & Patisserie.** ★★★★ ✓ $ The only World Showcase counter-service spot that's open before 11 o'clock; this bakery serves pastries, quiche and sandwiches. *9 a.m.–9 p.m. $7–$10. Seats 64.*

• **L'Artisan Des Glaces.** ★★★★ ✓ $ This tiny parlor scoops up artisan ice cream and sorbet. The author loves the caramel with sea salt. *Noon–9 p.m. $4–$10. Seats 24 outside.*

Shops. Small **Guerlain Paris** (★★★★ ✓) offers limited-edition fragrances, some in signature bee bottles, all very French. Cosmetics can be applied on the spot. Fragrance brands at **Plume et Palette** (★★★★) include Annick Goutal, Chanel and Dior. Tiny boutique **Parfums Givenchy** (★★★★ ✓) is the only place in the United States with the full line of Givenchy products. Each year it has a U.S. exclusive on one perfume. A cozy store that channels a homey village kitchen, **L' Esprit de la Provence** (★★★★ ✓) sells cookware, cookbooks and kitchen items. **Aux Vins de France** (★★★★ ✓) sells wines by the glass or

Impressionistic posters paper columns in front of the pavilion; the formal Monsieur Paul is the most expensive, and best, Epcot restaurant; the manager of the pavilion's street artists prepares for a summer day.

by the bottle. Skip **Souvenirs de France** (★); its faux French souvenirs come from China.

Movie. Lovely travelogue **Impressions de France** (★★★) shows off stunning visuals of France, from mountain peaks to huge castles to icons such as Notre Dame. Produced more than 30 years ago, the film has a timeless feel, with clear evocative imagery that's accompanied by classical music. What it doesn't have is a sense of humor. Early on, its stuffy narrator intones *"My Frahnce awakens with the early dawn."* Well, duh. The theater is pretty but has tight seating. Adult women larger than a size 16 won't be comfortable. *18 minutes. Average wait 9 minutes. Capacity: 325. Indoor queue. Access: Guests may stay in wheelchairs, ECVs. Reflective captioning, assistive listening. Debuted: 1982.*

Live entertainment. An "amusing server," **Serveur Amusant** (★★★) and his chef mime a balancing act with a table, five chairs and five bottles of champagne. *20-minute shows. Along the promenade.*

Architecture. You approach the Paris of La Belle Époque ("the beautiful time" from 1870 to 1910) on a replica of the Pont des Arts footbridge. Three-story facades have copper and slate mansard roofs, many with chimney pots. A rear shop is based on the Les Halles fruit and vegetable market, an 1850 iron-and-glass-ceilinged structure. Towering behind it all is the Eiffel Tower, with a period-correct tawny finish. Disney built the one-tenth-scale replica using Gustave Eiffel's blueprints.

Tips. *For shopping:* A top-seller in France, Guerlain's La Petite Robe Noire ("little black dress," $75 for 1.6 ounces) starts with a base of vanilla, patchouli, smoked tea and musk, then brings out notes of lemon, almonds, anise, roses, even raspberry macaroons and licorice. And yet it's subtle. Don't overlook the parasols on the promenade, hand-painted by the pavilion's young French artists. Little girls love them. *For a drink:* Try the wine flights at Aux Vins de France. Three two-ounce pours are $9 (champagne flights $22). *For a treat:* Get the bakery's créme brulee, top it off with a little cream and sugar, stir it up and head off to heaven.

Hidden Mickeys. In the courtyard, as circles in the metal grates... As a bush in the fleur-de-lis hedge garden... In the movie, in a second-floor window of the house in the background of the wedding reception.

A belly dancer shimmies in front of the band Mo'Rockin, which blends a violin, a Zendrum and other instruments to create hypnotic North African sound.

Morocco pavilion

To most Americans, this pavilion is a whole new world

★★★★★ ✔ This exotic pavilion features food, merchandise and music that's little-known in the West. Alongside the promenade is a cafe, a new small-plate eatery and an exhibit room; in back are open-air markets and a traditional restaurant. Created and sponsored by the Kingdom of Morocco, the pavilion is managed independently of Disney. Wafting incense will remind some baby boomers of a head shop.

Restaurants and food. The pavilion's eateries are the easiest in the World Showcase to get into, as many Epcot visitors assume their menus must be weird. They're not.

• **Restaurant Marrakesh.** ★★★ ✔ $$$$ The comfort food served at this relaxing spot uses the same ingredients as those in American cooking, and flavors are mild. Lunch includes beef and fish dishes; dinner adds sampler plates. Meat falls off the bone. A belly dancer shimmies in front of a small band (on the hour from 1–8 p.m. except for 4 p.m.). Ask to sit by the dance floor. *Lunch 12–3:30 p.m., $15–$28 (children $8). Dinner. 3:30 p.m.–8:45 p.m., $21–$45 (children $8). Seats 255.*

• **Spice Road Table.** ★★★★★ ✔ $$$$ The plates here may be small, but the food tastes huge. Served tapas-style, dishes offer flavors from not only Morocco but the entire Spice Road region, including France, Greece, Portugal, Spain and Turkey. Attentive service and huge arched windows overlooking the lagoon add to the memorable experience. *Lunch, dinner. 11 a.m.–park close, $7–$16. Seats 70 inside, 102 outside.*

• **Tangierine Café.** ★★★★ ✔ $$ The pavilion's sole fast-food option offers tasty chicken and lamb platters. A nearby pastry counter serves assorted baklava, tea, liqueur coffees and beer. *Lunch, dinner. 11 a.m.–park close, $9–$15 (children $8). Seats 100.*

Shops. Five open-air shops (★★★★★ ✔) offer handmade brass platters, rosewater, henna-dyed lambskin lamps, traditional caftans and gandouras. Belly-dancer costumes abound, for all ages.

Exhibit. Traditional accessories, jewelry and clothing are displayed in **Moroccan Style: The Art of Personal Adornment** (★★★). Heavily tiled and molded, the Gallery of Arts and History is easy to overlook from outside, it's to the left of the pavilion's front courtyard, behind closed doors.

The pavilion includes the Restaurant Marrakesh (right), the Gallery of Arts and History exhibit space (below) and a new tapas-style restaurant, Spice Road Table (below right).

© Disney

Entertainment. A skilled belly dancer fronts hypnotic group **Mo'Rockin** (★★★★ ✔), which uses a violin, Zendrum and passionate vocals to blend North African rhythms and melodies. Of course, your husband may not notice there is a band. *20-minute shows. Along the promenade.*

Architecture. Meant to evoke a desert city, buildings are made of brick, tan plaster and reddish sandstone. Like traditional Moroccan cities, the pavilion is divided into two sections, the ville nouvelle (new city) and the medina (old town). In front, the pavilion's new city recalls Casablanca and Marrakesh. It's anchored by the Koutoubia Minaret prayer tower. The medina of Fez lies in back, behind the 8th-century Bab Boujouloud Gate. On the left is the central courtyard of a traditional Moroccan home, complete with the sounds of the family. On the right is an open-air market, its bamboo roof lashed to thick beams. Restaurant Marrakesh is a Southern Moroccan fortress. Nearby is the Nejjarine Fountain. Rising above the old city is the Chellah Minaret, a 14th-century necropolis found in Morocco's capital city of Rabat.

Tips. *For the exhibit:* Once you're inside, look up. The ceiling is gorgeous. *For shopping:* Check out the aromatic bowls and boxes of thuya, made of a burled-root wood grown only in Morocco. *For a treat:* A small bakery case in the Tangierine Café holds stacks of authentic baklava. The walnut is best; almond and cashew are also good. Each serving costs $3.

Fun finds. Each of the pavilion's intricate tiled rooms has at least one tiling mistake. Moroccan artists created deliberate flaws to reflect the Muslim belief that only Allah creates perfection... Seen from across the lagoon—specifically from the promenade area to the right of the Mexico pavilion—the pavilion appears to also include a tall reddish building in the distance behind it. Actually, that's The Twilight Zone Tower of Terror at Disney's Hollywood Studios, which shares a Spanish influence.

Hidden Mickeys. As brass plates on the left door of the Souk-Al-Magreb shop... As a window in the dome of a minaret on the backdrop in Aladdin and Jasmine's indoor meet-and-greet area. Mickey is in the upper right-hand segment, next to a small ladder.

A group of friends crosses a small creek as they head to the Japan pavilion's popular Katsura Grill. Unseen by most visitors, the pavilion's back gardens are behind its pagoda.

Japan pavilion

A huge department store anchors this welcoming pavilion

★★★★★ ✔ An authentic Japanese shop highlights Epcot's friendliest exotic pavilion, which also includes three good restaurants and an exhibit. Anime, manga, Pokémon and sake aficionados will love the store. The pavilion is run by the Mitsukoshi company, Japan's oldest retail business.

Restaurants and food. Japan offers two good table-service restaurants and one equally-good counter-service spot.

• **Katsura Grill.** ★★★★ ✔ $$ The options at this fast-food eatery have improved recently, and today may be the best in the park. Teriyaki dishes are subtle and work well for all ages; the udon noodle soup is even better. *Lunch, dinner 11 a.m.–park close, $8–$13. Seats 60 inside, 34 outside.*

• **Teppan Edo.** ★★★★ $$$$ An entertaining tableside chef may juggle knives or make a "smoking Mickey train" out of onion stacks in these stunning red-and-black dining rooms. Using a hibachi grill set into the dining table, the chef's hands fly fast as they slice, dice and stir-fry. Diners choose between chicken, beef, pork, seafood or vegetables, and share their table with other guests.

Lunch, dinner 12 p.m.–park close, $18–$32 (children $9–$14). Seats 192.

• **Tokyo Dining.** ★★★★ ✔ $$$$ With good food, a calm atmosphere and great service, this is what a World Showcase restaurant is supposed to be—a non-threatening way to experience a foreign cuisine. Traditional entrees include a tender beef teriyaki and light shrimp tempura. The sushi and sashimi menu has over 50 selections. For dessert, the subtle green tea ice cream melts in your mouth. Diffused lighting, dark tables and a tile floor create a peaceful atmosphere. The friendly staff bows to diners at every opportunity. *Lunch, dinner 12 p.m.–park close, $16–$29 (children $11–$12). Seats 116.*

Shop. A 10,000-square-foot **Mitsukoshi department store** (★★★★★ ✔) overflows with merchandise. The largest area has Pokémon plush, figurines and cards; Hello Kitty items; and quirky toys. An entertaining Pick-A-Pearl station draws big crowds, as shoppers select their own oyster and get to keep whatever size pearl is discovered inside for $17. A second zone bridges Japanese and Western cultures with glass-bead jewelry,

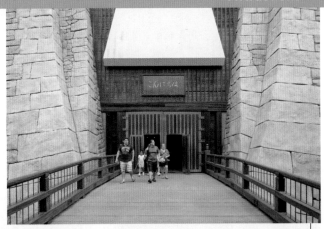

Though it looks like the 14th-century Shirasagijo castle, the rear of the pavilion is really just the exit of the Mitsukoshi store. Below, the store's entrance is less imposing; the Matsuriza drummers in front of it.

sandals, Mikimoto pearl jewelry and creative fashion apparel. Also for sale are bonsai trees, silk kimonos, lanterns, rice paper and tatami mats. In back, chopsticks, porcelain dishes, teas and sweets fill the shelves. A sake-tasting bar offers five microbrews.

Exhibit. The connection between ancient Japanese myths and modern media is explored in **Spirited Beasts: From Ancient Stories to Anime Stars** (★★★). Filled with more than 100 objects, displays showcase nine creatures from Japanese folklore that have inspired characters in video games, television shows and anime. The exhibit is located at the left rear of the pavilion, in the Bijutsu-kan Gallery.

Entertainment. Intense drumming trio **Matsuriza** (★★★★ ✔) creates propulsive beats on hand-made instruments. *20-minute shows. On the pagoda, sometimes in the plaza.*

Architecture. An 83-foot pagoda recalls the 8th-century Horyuji Temple in Nara. Its five stories represent the five elements of creation—earth, water, fire, wind and sky. A hill garden's evergreens symbolize eternal life, its rocks the longevity of the earth and its koi-filled water the brief life of animals and man. In the garden, the rustic Katsura

Grill is modeled on Kyoto's 16th-century Katsura Imperial Villa. The structure on the right houses the store and restaurants, and recalls the ceremonial Shishinden Hall of the 8th-century Gosho Imperial Palace at Kyoto.

In back, a (very shallow) 17th-century wood and stone Nijo castle houses sculptures of mounted samurai warriors. A moat fronts the Shirasagijo (White Heron) castle, a 14th-century feudal fortress.

Tips. *For the exhibit:* Look for Kappa the water sprite, an inspiration for the Pokémon character Golduck. *For shopping:* Try some sake at the little bar at the back of the store. It has many choices. *For a treat:* Each piece of sweet watermelon-flavored Botan rice candy has a melt-in-your-mouth wrapper. Each package comes with a colorful little Japanese sticker; each one is odd (for example, a smiling diva pickle wearing high-heels and lipstick). A package of eight wrapped pieces is only about $1. Other treats include a creamy Tirol green tea mochi chocolate for $3 and Sakuma strawberry ichigo milk candy for $4.

Hidden Mickeys. In the metal tree grates in the courtyard.... As the center of a koi-pond drain cover, near a bamboo fence.

The English-Georgian architecture of the American Adventure pavilion recalls the look of many colonial buildings built just before and after the Revolutionary War.

The American Adventure pavilion

Spirited entertainment, adventure-free food and shopping

★★★ Historic Americans come to life at this pavilion's attraction, which uses Audio-Animatronics figures to tell the story of the United States. Fans of Ken Burns documentaries will especially enjoy it. The area also has some exceptional live entertainment and a small exhibit.

Attraction. The **American Adventure** (★★★★★ ✔ FastPass+) Boldly honest for a Disney attraction, this warts-and-all theatrical show does the U.S. proud. combining stirring film footage with Audio-Animatronic figures. Ben Franklin and Mark Twain narrate, telling our country's story from the time of the Pilgrims through World War II, with help from icons like George Washington, Thomas Jefferson, Will Rogers and Rosie the Riveter. The only World Showcase attraction that is critical of its country, the show embraces America's triumphs and optimism but doesn't shy away from its flaws and challenges. Chatting with Franklin after the Revolutionary War, Twain says "You Founding Fathers gave us a pretty good start... [but then] a whole bunch of folks found out that 'We the People' didn't yet mean all the

people." Subsequent scenes cover slavery and Native Americans. The film, a combination of real and re-created images, pans across paintings and photos. The robots move convincingly; for a moment Franklin appears to walk. The finale highlights famous citizens who embody the curious mix of what it means to be an American. It includes Apple founder Steve Jobs and Muhammad Ali lighting the torch at the 1996 Atlanta Olympics. *30 minutes. Typically every 45 minutes starting at 11:15 a.m., last showing 9 p.m. Capacity: 1,024. Indoor lobby. Access: Guests may stay in wheelchairs, ECVs. Reflective captioning, assistive listening, Audio Description. Debuted: 1982, revised 1993, 2007.*

Restaurants and food. The pavilion houses one uninspired counter-service spot.

• **Liberty Inn.** ★★ $$ This fast-food eatery serves ho-hum burgers, chicken, hot dogs, pork sandwiches, salads, steaks and a kosher meal. *Lunch, dinner. 11 a.m.–park close. $9–$11 (children $6). Seats 710.* Better are the treats at **Funnel Cakes** (★★★), a small stand out front. For an extra-decadent touch, get one with a slab of vanilla ice cream.

Robotic versions of Benjamin Franklin and Mark Twain host the American Adventure attraction. Below, the Spirit of America Fife & Drum Corps at the entrance to the pavilion; Goofy greeting fans alongside it.

Shops. Small **Heritage Manor Gifts** (★) sells patriotic apparel and books, most of which come from China. Some fancy packaged food items are American. Out front, a wood cart sells T-shirts.

Exhibit. A disappointment, **Re-Discovering America: Family Treasures from the Kinsey Collection** (★) displays artwork and a few slave- and oppression-related artifacts from an African-American family. Included is a bill of sale for a slave sold in 1832 and a 1930 steel plaque from the American Beach Negro Ocean Playground. Narrators such as Diane Sawyer and Whoopi Goldberg intone on the five concepts the exhibit revolves around: Belief, Courage, Heritage, Hope and Imagination. Unfortunately it's all pompous and dull, as it has way too few historic items to support its display space, and its art—despite being describe as the work of "genius"—is routine. *Lobby.*

Entertainment. Led by a town crier, the **Spirit of America Fife & Drum Corps** (★★★★) performs "The Battle Hymn of the Republic," "God Bless America" and similar tunes. Children from the audience join in. *10-minute shows. In front of the pavilion.*

Spirited a cappella group **The Voices of Liberty** (★★★★★ ✔) belts out traditional favorites like "America the Beautiful," but also occasionally modern hits such as "Let It Go." *20-minute shows. In the lobby.*

Tips. *For the attraction:* Time your visit so it coincides with the a cappella singing ensemble Voices of Liberty. Sit in the center of a middle row. Note the inclusion of Lance Armstrong in the montage at the end. Talk with your children about what's wrong with that. *For shopping:* Pick up a copy of the constitution at Heritage Manor Gifts.

Fun facts. One of the few Disney buildings that uses a reversed forced perspective, the pavilion appears just three stories tall from a distance, though it actually rises seven stories—more than 70 feet—to accommodate its large theater... The structure has 110,000 hand-formed bricks, laid with an old-fashioned one-then-a-half technique... The theatrical show uses 35 Audio-Animatronic characters, including three Ben Franklins and three Mark Twains.

Hidden Mickey. As three rocks at the beginning of the first film in the show, behind and to the right of a kneeling Pilgrim woman.

A Via Napoli cook works in front of the gaping mouths of the pizzeria's three wood-burning ovens, which are named after the three active volcanoes in Italy: Etna, Vesuvio and Stromboli.

Italy pavilion

No attraction, no exhibit, but good restaurants

★★★ One of the most attractive World Showcase facades, a Venetian entrance area disguises the fact that this version of Lo Stivale ("the boot") is little more than two shops and three restaurants. Except for watching its street performer, it offers little to do but spend money. Too bad, because originally it was to include a dark gondola ride and a walk-through attraction through Roman ruins. Alas, those plans were cancelled.

Restaurants and food. The table-service choices in Italy are both a little expensive and very good. One is formal, the other relaxed. An excellent small-plate extension of the table-service restaurant sits just off its lobby.

• **Tutto Gusto Wine Cellar.** ★★★★ ✔ $$$ Located just off the lobby of Tutto Italia, this tiny spot resembles an Italian wine cellar with its brick arches, wood beams and stone walls and floors. The menu features small-plate appetizers of cheeses, mini-panini sandwiches, pasta and seafood, a handful of combination platters and nearly 200 Italian wines. It's a delectable way to get a taste of Italy without breaking the bank. *Lunch, dinner. 11:30 a.m.–9 p.m. $9–$18. Seats 96.*

• **Tutto Italia.** ★★★★★ ✔ $$$$$ Pricey yes, but you get the best Italian food on Disney property, thanks to imported pastas, delicate sauces and handmade mozzarella. Desserts are luscious. Entree salads use ingredients like asparagus, curly endive and fava beans. A young Italian wait staff is friendly; an elegant decor has dark woods, chandeliers and Roman murals. *Lunch, dinner. 11:30 a.m.–9 p.m. $27–$49 (children $9–$15). Seats 156.*

• **Via Napoli.** ★★★★ ✔ $$$$ Disney's best pizza place, this one may be the most satisfying restaurant in Epcot. Its true-Italian toppings and flavorful flaky crusts are worth every penny it charges, which is about twice as many as your neighborhood Pizza Hut. Individual pizzas are large enough to share if you add an appetizer. The authors like the classic margherita pie, but are in love with the restaurant's decadently creamy paccheri pasta. Ask to sit in the breezy main dining room. It's so relaxing you'll lose track of time. Just don't plan on any quiet conversations; the room's tile floors and open wood and plaster ceiling can create quite a noisy din. *Lunch, dinner. 11:30 a.m.–9 p.m. $19–$24*

With the 10th-century Campanile dominating its skyline, the Italy pavilion recalls the cityscape of Venice. Two freestanding columns mimic 12th-century monuments.

(children $10). Seats 400, including 24 at a community table.

Shops. Two stores offer some unique Italian merchandise. **Il Bel Cristallo** (★★★) offers an eclectic collection of Murano glass, jewelry, fragrances, and Puma sportswear. An artisan creates papier-maché, fabric Carnivale masks in front of you. **La Bottega** (★★★★ ✓) sells wine by the bottle or glass, Perugina candy and Christmas ornaments.

Entertainment. Funnyman juggler and mime **Sergio** (★★★★ ✓) pulls children into his shows, which often involve soccer balls. *20-minute shows. Central plaza.*

Architecture. The pavilion is a town square—the Piazza San Marco—surrounded by buildings that evoke Florentine, Roman and Venetian architecture. Two freestanding columns recall 12th-century monuments, one topped by the city's guardian, the winged lion of St. Mark the Evangelist, the other crowned by St. Theodore, the city's former patron saint. He's shown killing a dragon, an act that gave him the courage to declare himself a Christian. The 10th-century Campanile (bell tower) dominates the skyline, though this version is just 100 feet tall, less than a third the height of the original. Gold-leafed ringlets decorate an angel on top.

On the left of the square is a pink-and-white replica of the 14th-century Doge's (leader's) Palace. Its facade replicates many details of the original. The first two stories rest on realistic marble columns that front leaded-glass windows. The third floor is tiled and topped by marble sculptures, statues, reliefs and filigree. Adjoining the palace, a stairway and portico reflect Verona. The La Bottega shop is a Tuscany homestead. A sculpture behind it of Neptune and his dolphins recalls Bernini's 1642 fountain in Florence and Rome's Trevi Fountain.

With the World Showcase lagoon doubling as the Adriatic Sea, a waterfront area includes replicas of Venice bridges, gondolas and striped pilings.

Tips. *For Sergio:* If your child wants to be in his show, have her wear a distinctive hat or outfit, smile and catch his eye. *For shopping:* Check out the delicate Murano-glass Christmas ornaments. Each is unique. *For a treat:* Try a Baci Perugina hazelnut chocolate fortune ball ($1), sold at La Bottega. Each treat has a different fortune inside.

The Germany pavilion's quaint cobblestone plaza recalls a 16th-century village. In the center is a fountain topped with a statue of dragon-slaying St. George.

Germany pavilion

Unusual shops and lively buffet highlight this jolly pavilion

★★★★ ✔ Like its Italian pavilion, Disney's version of Germany is little more than shops and food. But in this case, it's worth a stop. Not only can you sample the foods at an outdoor cafe (with tables tucked into a recessed patio), the jolly table-service restaurant is the most fun place to eat in the World Showcase. However, there's no entertainment outside.

If you've got children, make sure you stop at the miniature outdoor train village, located to the right of the main pavilion. A walkway leads over track tunnels and alongside the little town, which has its own wee little live landscape. Four working trains roam out over the rivers and through the woods, each on its own track. During some holidays the train village is decorated for the season. At Christmastime some of the tiny trees have lights, homes have wreaths and snow sits on rooftops. For the Flower and Garden Festival the small streets have banners celebrating the event.

Restaurants and food. Germany's food choices include a lively buffet and an outdoor fast-food spot.

• **Biergarten.** ★★★★ ✔ $$$$ An oompah band rolls out a barrel full of polkas and waltzes at this boisterous Oktoberfest buffet. Musicians lead toasts and demonstrate bizarre instruments like the alpine horn. Parties smaller than eight dine at a long table with others; it's all part of the fun. The "all you care to eat" buffet features lots of sausages; cutlets of pork, chicken and other meats; a few seafood dishes; various types of potatoes and mixed vegetables; unusual salads; assorted breads; and succulent desserts. Come hungry, order beer and skip the seafood. The dining room simulates a medieval Rothenburg outdoor courtyard at night; the moon and stars glow overhead. Cheery young servers wear traditional German garb. *Lunch 12 p.m.–3:45 p.m., $23 (children $13). Dinner 4 p.m.–park close, $38 (children $18). Seats 400.*

• **Sommerfest.** ★★★ $ This outdoor stand has covered tables. Choose from hearty fare such as bratwurst, frankfurters and Reuben sandwiches. Wash it all down with beer, of course. *11 a.m.–park close. $7–$9. Seats 24.*

Shops. Eight stores and one promenade stand line a central courtyard. Masculine **Das**

A miniature locomotive chugs around its track in the pavilion's outdoor train village. Below, two wide-eyed child figures ring in the hours atop a courtyard clock; a young German cook makes caramel popcorn.

Kaufhaus (★★★) sells apparel, backpacks, soccer balls and sandals. Children's items at **Der Teddybar** (★★★★ ✔) include Steiff bears, Schleich toys, Playmobil sets, plushies, Snow White costumes and customized Engle-Puppen dolls. Christmas shop **Die Weihnachts Ecke** (★★★★ ✔) sells classic pickle ornaments and handmade Steinbach nutcrackers. Worth visiting for the aroma alone, Old World German caramel shop **Karamell-Küche** (★★★★★ ✔) is an Epcot treasure. Young German bakers make treats before your eyes. Arribas Brothers store **Kunstarbeit in Kristall** (★★★★) sells lovely crystal jewelry, personalized glassware, Swarovski crystal pins and collectible figurines. **Stein Haus** (★★★★ ✔) offers intricate beer steins. More are at **Volkskunst** (★★★★ ✔), as are Schneider cuckoo clocks, glassware, pewter and Troika watches. Egg artist Jutta Levasseur often works in a corner. **Weinkeller** (★★★★ ✔) serves wines and schnapps by the bottle or glass. On the promenade, the **Glaskunst** (★★★) stand personalizes glass figures, frames, glassware and steins.

Architecture. The outdoor plaza has some interesting detailing. Its centerpiece is a sculpture of the patron saint of soldiers, St. George, slaying a dragon during a trip to the Middle East. A clock comes to life at the top of each hour with a three-minute animated display. On the right side of the plaza, the facade of the Das Kaufhaus shop was inspired by the Kaufhaus, a 16th-century merchants' hall in the Black Forest town of Freiburg. Three statues on its second story recall the rule of the Hapsburg emperors. The rear facade combines the looks of two 12th-century castles, the Eltz and the Stahleck.

Tips. *For a treat:* For less than $5, the Karamell-Küche shop sells a big, freshly made Werther's caramel apple oatmeal cookie. Drizzled over the top with fresh Werther's caramel, it's rich, soft and easily broken apart to share. The thing is as wide as a large grapefruit. Don't want something from the bakery case? You can't go wrong with some packaged Werther's candy.

Hidden Mickeys. In the center of the crown of the left-most Hapsburg emperor statue on the second story of Das Kaufhaus… A little figurine of Mickey Mouse often hides in the train village. Usually he stands in a window of a hilltop castle.

The China pavilion's miniature Hall of Prayer for Good Harvests recalls the main building of Beijing's Temple of Heaven, a 15th-century summer retreat for emperors.

China pavilion

It's trying hard to please, but doesn't seem happy about it

★★ Global communist superpower? There's no hint of *that* China in this conflicted pavilion, which offers skilled but slow-paced entertainment, a department store determined to come up with something Americans will buy and, sadly, a pretty lame restaurant. The exhibit is worth seeing. The pavilion is run not by Disney, but rather a Chinese company—a fact which should make it special, but seems to make it mundane.

Restaurants and food. China has a restaurant and a fast-food spot; both are forgettable.

• **Nine Dragons.** ★★ $$$$ Nearly everything this tired restaurant serves lacks imagination and punch. There are some high points, including good teas and light desserts. Window tables make for good people-watching. *Lunch, dinner. 12 p.m.–9 p.m. $13–$24 (children $8–$10). Seats 300.*

• **Lotus Blossom Cafe.** ★★ $ The quick service at this fast-food spot doesn't make up for the substandard food, which is neither cheap nor flavorful. The eatery sells egg rolls, chicken and stir-fry meals. All the seating is outdoors, though covered. *Lunch, dinner. 11 a.m.–9 p.m. $7–$12 (children $7). Seats 106.*

Shop. The spacious **House of Good Fortune** (★★★) department store carries a variety of interesting merchandise. but it's been redone recently to focus on apparel, both traditional Chinese clothing and modern T-shirts. Other choices include incense, jewelry, accessories and housewares. Panda-themed clothing, toys and stuffed animals are tucked into the back of a children's area.

Movie. The most dated Epcot movie, the CircleVision 360 **Reflections of China** (★★) has faded visuals and out-of-date content: its scene of "modern" Shanghai shows a room filled with box-style personal computers. It also has a blatant exclusion of history and culture; stuff China doesn't want to acknowledge. You stand up to watch it, as it projects all around you on a circular screen; one scene was filmed by a camera hanging from a banking helicopter. *20 minutes. Capacity: 200. Indoor queue. Access: Guests may stay in wheelchairs, ECVs. Reflective captioning, assistive listening, Audio Description. Debuted: 1982, revised 2003.*

Exhibit. The terra cotta "spirit army" found in the tomb of China's first emperor

Below left: Once comprised of children, the pavilion's acrobats today consist of young adults. They often perform to less-than-attentive crowds. Below right: Village Traders, an eclectic World Showcase shop nearby.

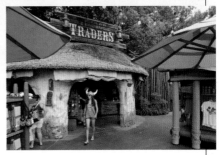

Qin Shi Huang (259–210 B.C.) is re-created at **Tomb Warriors—Guardian Spirits of Ancient China** (★★★★). The largest archeological find in the world, the actual 22-square-mile site contains 8,000 full-size statues arranged in military formations; here an army of 200 half-size reproductions offers a sense of the real thing. The exhibit also includes two dozen small tomb artifacts from the Han, Six, Sui and Tang Dynasties (through 906 A.D.). It's in the Gallery of the Whispering Willow, in the center of the pavilion.

Entertainment. The six 18- to 21-year-old adults that make up the Jeweled Dragon Acrobats (★★) perform feats of agility, balance and strength. The pace is a bit slow; sometimes it seems the performers are just warming up for a yoga class. For the most part they balance things on their heads or on their feet, and then present themselves for applause. Ta da! *20-minute shows. Courtyard.*

Architecture. The pavilion is anchored by a triple-arched gate. Behind it sits the Hall of Prayer for Good Harvests, the circular main building of Beijing's 1420 Temple of Heaven, a summer retreat for emperors. Its rotunda columns and beams allude to the cycles of nature. A floor stone is cut into nine pieces, as, in China, nine is a lucky number. The main walkway also includes facades of an elegant home, a school house and shop fronts reflecting European influences. The gallery has a formal saddle-ridge roof line. A Suzhou-style pond garden symbolizes nature's order and discipline. Keeping with Chinese custom, it appears old and unkempt. Alongside the lagoon, pockmarked boulders demonstrate a tradition of designing surprising views in landscapes by creating holes in waterside rock formations.

Tips. *For the movie:* Stand in the dead center of the room and look around, as the images in front of you will be different from those behind you. *For shopping:* Marionettes in front of the pavilion are worth a look. *For a treat:* Check out the White Rabbit creamy candy, which tastes like chewy vanilla taffy. Each mini-tootsie-roll-shaped candy has an edible inner wrapping made from a transparent sheet of rice. A $6 bag holds a few dozen individually wrapped candies.

Fun finds. Wild giant bullfrogs hide under lily pads in the pond, and sometimes poke their heads above water.

Gift shop facades at the Norway pavilion recall coastal cottages in a village square. In reality they're all the same structure, and all a front for the pavilion's single gift shop.

Norway pavilion

Because what's a trip to Disney without trolls and kjøttkake?

★★★ Beauties and beasts dominate this pavilion—pretty princesses at a Disney character meal, three-headed trolls inside a dark boat ride. Chiseled Nordic cast members greet guests at the store, restaurant and fast-food spot. The bizarre attraction includes Audio-Animatronics polar bears, trolls and a mysterious god with gleaming eyes.

Restaurants and food. Dining choices include a princess character meal and a good small fast-food spot with irresistible pastries.

• **Akershus Royal Banquet Hall.** ★★★ $$$$ Disney princesses visit your table at all three Princess Storybook Dining Experience meals in this oddball spot, which combines traditional Norwegian food with an all-princess Disney character experience. For lunch and dinner guests order a Norwegian entree (including tasty meatballs, or kjøttkake) and help themselves to a buffet of chilled Norwegian appetizers and salads. American items are also available, and make up the entire menu at breakfast. Noisy rooms have closely-packed tables. The meal price includes a photo with one of the princesses, usually, for some reason, Belle. The last

lunch and dinner seatings often have walk-up tables available. *Breakfast 8–11 a.m. $45 (children $27). Lunch 11:55 a.m.–3:30 p.m. $46 (children $28). Dinner 4:55–8:35 p.m. $51 (children $28). Seats 255.*

• **Kringla Bakeri Og Kafe.** ★★★★ ✔ $ This counter-service spot offers fresh pastries and sandwiches, all displayed in glass cases. Rich custard-filled school bread is an author favorite. *11 a.m.–9 p.m. $6–$8 (children $5). Seats 50, outdoor but shaded.*

Shops. The pavilion has just one gift shop, **The Puffin's Roost** (★★★), which sells "Frozen" merchandise, troll figurines and stylish, pricey Helly Hansen and Dale of Norway apparel. For the young, young at heart or anyone who is "drinking around the world," there are silly plastic Viking helmets—all with horns, some with braids.

Attraction. Themed to Norway's rich seafaring heritage, Maelstrom (★★★ FastPass+) offers a diverting log-flume ride and a dull film. Sailing in a dragon-headed longboat, you head up a chainlift as ancient Norse god Odin urges you to "seek the spirit of Norway." After being cursed by a three-headed troll,

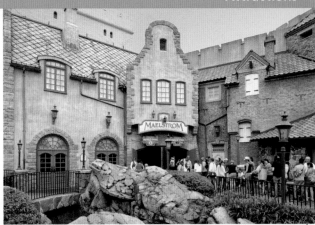

Populated with trolls, Maelstrom is one of the few World Showcase rides. As such it's nearly always crowded. Below, a troll T-shirt; a statue of a Viking outside the pavilion's tiny Stave church.

your Viking ship enters a confused chaos (a "maelstrom"), by plunging backward and nearly tipping over a waterfall. It's not quite as thrilling as it sounds, but this dark indoor ride has a quirky charm, especially for children and troll aficionados. Sit in the back row, on the right; you'll be able to look outside, down onto Akershus and the Norway plaza, when the boat nearly tips backward over the waterfall. The front row has the best views of the forward-motion half of the ride, and is most likely to splash you during the plunge. After disembarking, you have the option of watching a brief travelogue. *15 minutes. Average wait 30 minutes. Capacity: 192. Indoor queue. Fear factor: Often dark, with a few scary troll faces. Access: Wheelchair and ECV users must transfer. Assistive listening, reflective captioning. Debuted: 1988.*

Exhibit. A small museum-style exhibit inside a tiny Stave Church (see below), **Norsk Kultur: Creating the World of Frozen** (★★★) displays traditional Norwegian clothing, musical instruments, furniture and artifacts that relate to Disney's 2013 movie "Frozen." A female figure wears an outfit similar to Anna's. Some items date back to the 1200s.

Architecture. At the entrance is a replica of the 13th-century Gol Church of Hallingdal, one of Norway's Stave churches that played a key role in its movement to Christianity. Next door, the bakery has a sod roof, a traditional way to insulate homes in the Norwegian mountains. Gift shop facades recall coastal cottages. The restaurant and rear facade of the pavilion re-create Akershus, a 14th-century Oslo castle and fortress.

Tips. *For the attraction:* Skip the film. It's six dated minutes of tourism propaganda. *For shopping:* Look for the small stuffed Donald Duck dressed as a Viking. *For a treat:* Made of milk chocolate with a brittle toffee-like caramel center, luscious Daim candy bars sell for $3. Don't pass up the school bread, fresh in the bakery for $3. It's a sweet cardamom bun filled with vanilla cream custard and topped with toasted coconut and sugar crystals.

Hidden Mickeys. Three are in the mural behind Maelstrom's loading area: As Mickey ears on a Viking in the middle of a ship... As shadows on a cruise-line worker's blouse (her right pocket is Mickey's head, her clipboard ring his nose)... On the watch of a bearded construction worker wearing a hardhat.

The front of the Mexico pavilion resembles the temple of the Aztec serpent god Quetzalcoatl. Inside the building are shops, a restaurant, a ride and a tequila bar.

Mexico pavilion

The food's good... the band's great... the ride is bizarre

★★★★ ✔ It's margaritaville! Young adults in particular enjoy this pavilion's Cinco de Mayo atmosphere. Everyone likes the mariachi music, most like the shopping and tasty (if pricey) dining experiences. The bulk of the pavilion is indoors, housed in what appears to be an ancient pyramid.

Restaurants and food. Food choices includes two good restaurants.

• **La Hacienda de San Angel.** ★★★★ ✔ $$$$$ This inviting waterside spot offers modern Mexican fare and unique margaritas; its cozy hacienda-style dining rooms have oversized windows, original artwork and lovely blown-glass light fixtures. *Dinner. 4–9 p.m. $24–$50 (children $9–$10). Seats 250.*

• **San Angel Inn.** ★★★ ✔ $$$$$ Good traditional choices include tortilla soup and a steak that tastes like it's straight off a backyard grill. You dine in a faux moonlit courtyard so dark it's tough to see your menu. The backdrop is a rumbling volcano, part of the Gran Fiesta Tour ride. Down a couple of margaritas and its lava flow looks real. *Lunch, dinner. 11:30 a.m.–9 p.m. $24–$36 (children $8–$10). Seats 156.*

• **La Cantina de San Angel.** ★★★ ✔ $ Sitting lakeside along the promenade, this fast-food spot sells empanadas, nachos, tacos, churros, margaritas and beer. *Lunch, dinner. 11 a.m.–9 p.m. $8–$12 (children $8). Seats 150.*

• **La Cava del Tequila.** ★★★★★ ✔ $ This bustling little bar serves over 200 tequilas, and has varied and eclectic margaritas. It's a great escape from the Disney madness. *Noon–9 p.m. $8–$50. Seats 30.*

Shops. The large, dim Plaza de los Amigos (★★★★ ✔) sits inside the Mexican pyramid offers a huge variety of merchandise, including blankets, books, candy, crystal, glassware, ceramic piggy banks, piñatas, fleece ponchos, salsa, sombreros, Day of the Dead T-shirts and tequila. A small table in the corner holds the Animalés Fantasticos Spirits in Wood artisans and their exquisite handmade wooden animals.

Attraction. The slow-moving dark boat ride **Gran Fiesta Tour** (★★) tours the cultural history of Mexico, though it's hard to notice that, as a wacky, tacked-on video-screen overlay tells a Donald Duck story based on Disney's 1944 movie "The Three Caballeros."

The La Hacienda de San Angel restaurant sits lakeside. Below, shoppers pose in sombreros; members of Mariachi Cobre pose after a performance.

Mariachi Cobre

Needing Donald to sing with them at a concert, two of his pals—Brazilian parrot José Carioca and Mexican rooster Panchito Pistoles—search for him as he vacations in Mexico and ogles every human female he comes across. Disney fans will note that at one point Donald wears a tall stack of tottering hats, an homage to a scene in the Pirates of the Caribbean and José says "It's cho-time!" exactly like José the parrot does in the Enchanted Tiki Room. It's all in good fun, of course, but those with Mayan blood may find it offensive, and everyone will find it a confusing, bizarre mess. A duck-free Day of the Dead scene has singing dolls straight out of It's a Small World. There's rarely a wait for the ride unless a Brazilian tour group shows up. And then—!ay caramba! *8 minutes. Capacity: 250 per hour (10 per boat). Indoor queue. Access: ECV users must transfer. Handheld captioning. Debuted: 1982, revised 2007.*

Entertainment. An outstanding 11-piece group, **Mariachi Cobre** (★★★★★ ✔) is led by trumpets, violins and confident vocals, and backed by harmonizing guitars. Together for 44 years, the band has played with, and recorded with, singers Julio Iglesias and Linda Ronstadt. It has been performing at Epcot since the park opened. Three members have been with the group since it began; five more have been with it since it's park debut. *20-minute shows. Along the promenade; indoors during poor weather.*

Architecture. The pyramid facade is modeled on the Aztec temple of serpent god Quetzalcoatl. Inside the building, the portico to the "outdoor" market resembles a Mexican mayor's mansion. Surrounding facades represent the 16th-century silver mining town of Taxco. Back outside, the café looks similar to the 17th-century San Angel Inn in Mexico City, a restaurant operated by the family that runs the ones here.

Tips. *For the attraction:* Sit in the front seat for the best view and the most legroom. *For shopping:* It seems everyone poses wearing one of the huge sombreros at the pavilion's outdoor stand. *For a treat:* Indulge in Glorias, goat's milk candy with pecans. This subtle, creamy treat can get sticky once unwrapped. A package of five wrapped pieces sells for $6.

Fun find. In the Gran Fiesta Tour, when Donald Duck reaches Acapulco his swimsuit falls off. His swimsuit. *He's a duck.*

A boy signs up to play Agent P's World Showcase Adventure near the U.K. pavilion. Other sign-up locations are near the Italy and Norway pavilions and on the Odyssey Bridge.

Agent P's World Showcase Adventure

'Phineas and Ferb' fans will love this scavenger hunt

★★★★★ ✔ This interactive game uses refurbished cell phones and hidden special effects to channel the comic sensibility of "Phineas & Ferb," the Disney Channel animated series about two brothers and their pet platypus, Perry. As fans of the show know, Perry has an alter ego as a secret agent—Agent P—and a nemesis—Dr. Doofenshmirtz, a bumbling mad scientist who for years has been out to take over his tri-state area. But now he has bigger plans. Off on a vacation to Epcot and its World Showcase, now he wants to take over the world. And what's worse, Agent P can't stop him. It's up to you.

As you sign up for the game, you become a fellow agent of OWCA (the Organization Without a Cool Acronym) and are sent to a World Showcase pavilion to foil the scientist's plans. You receive clues and instructions by using a FONE (Field Operative Notifications Equipment), which reveals the characters and brings other items to life.

Fans of the show will love it. Its silliness breaks up the seriousness of World Showcase—it's by far the funniest thing at Epcot—and gives children something to do.

Where to sign up. There are four spots; one on the wide footbridge that connects Future World to the World Showcase, three others on the World Showcase walkway. The mission you get depends on where you sign up. *Odyssey Bridge:* You'll be sent to Mexico, Norway or the U.K. *United Kingdom pavilion:* The U.K., France, Japan, Mexico or Norway. *Norway pavilion:* Mexico, Norway or China. *Italy pavilion:* Germany or Japan. When you finish one mission, you can do another one.

By the way, you choose your agent name. When the author plays, she's Agent J.

Tips. *When to play:* During the summer at 11 a.m., before the weather gets too hot or rainy. *For families:* Play this with your child, with him controlling the FONE.

Fun facts. "Phineas & Ferb" creators Dan Povenmire and Jeff "Swampy" Marsh helped develop the game, and spent many days at Epcot brainstorming and scouting locations.

Key facts. *Best for:* Phineas & Ferb fans. *Length:* Each adventure takes about 25 minutes. *Capacity:* 10 FONEs per pavilion. *Hours:* 11 a.m.–8:15 p.m. *Access:* Guests may stay in wheelchairs, ECVs. *Debuted:* 2012.

A fiery ballet of chaos highlights the IllumiNations laser and fireworks spectacle. Directed to the front of the park, the symmetrical show is best viewed from World Showcase Plaza.

IllumiNations

Epcot's nightly fireworks and laser finale doesn't disappoint

★★★★★ ✔ **FastPass+** IllumiNations sets its sights high: to tell the history of planet Earth, without narration. Synchronized to a symphonic world-music score, this nightly fireworks and special-effects extravaganza uses the entire World Showcase to do that, though its messages are so abstract you have to watch closely to realize what's going on. Strobe lights flash, laser beams dance, pavilions light up and fireworks burst in a choreographed spectacle. A rotating Earth glides across the lagoon and shows moving images on its continents. It's a confusing, eye-popping experience—one that shouldn't be missed. The subtitle of the show is "Reflections of Earth."

Tips. *When to go:* Nab a spot 20 to 30 minutes before 9 p.m., when the show begins. *Where to watch it:* You'll need a Fastpass for the best viewing spot—between the two gift shops at World Showcase Plaza. Not only will you see the symmetrical show as the designers intended it, you'll also be close to Epcot's front exit, so you'll be ahead of the masses when IllumiNations ends. *For families:* Whisper to your children what appears on the globe; it can be tough for them to make out the images.

Fun facts. Two-thousand eight-hundred fireworks launch from 750 mortar tubes in 34 locations; some explode 600 feet overhead... Wrapped in more than 180,000 LEDs, the 28-foot steel globe was the world's first spherical video display... The pavilions are outlined in 26,000 feet of lights... The Morocco pavilion does not participate in the show since some of its buildings represent religious structures... The show's music supervisor was Hans Zimmer, the composer for the 1994 Disney movie "The Lion King"... Nineteen torches around the lagoon symbolize the first 19 centuries of modern history. The 20th torch, in the globe, represents the Millennium.

Key facts. *Best for:* Anyone ages 5 and up. *Duration:* 14 minutes. *Fear factor:* Loud, bright explosions and fire (the authors' daughter hated this show when she was little). *Weather issues:* Cancelled during thunderstorms. *Debuted:* 1988; revised 1997, 1999. *Access:* Guests may remain in wheelchairs, ECVs. *Location:* On and above World Showcase Lagoon.

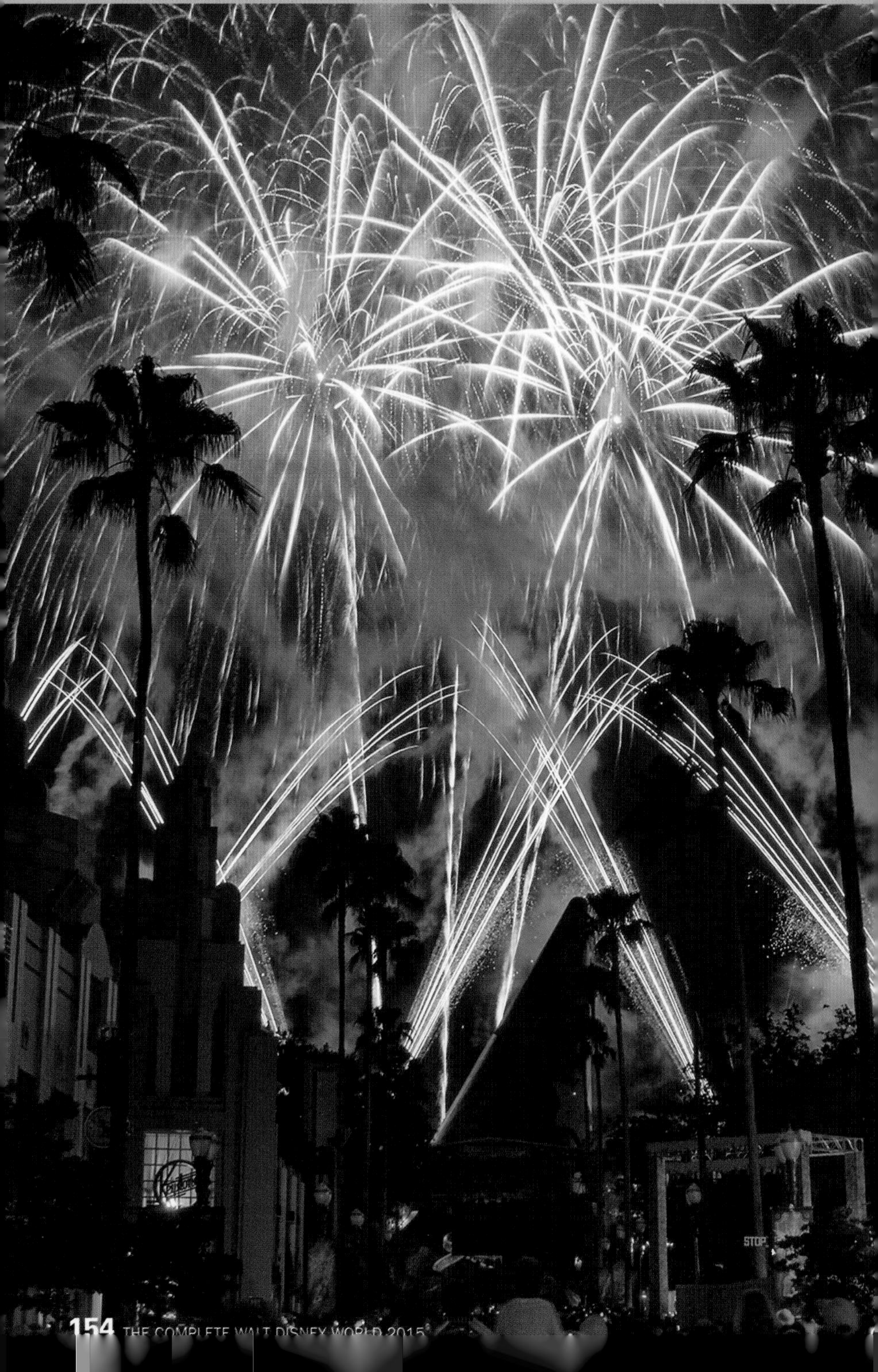

Disney's Hollywood Studios

Love movies and television? If so, you'll enjoy this theme park, Disney's love letter to show business. Chock full of attractions based on movies and television shows, it appeals to every age. Fans of old-style glamour encounter Humphrey Bogart and James Cagney at the Great Movie Ride; a 3-D Star Tours ride delights fans of the Force. Animation buffs get experiences featuring the Muppets and "Toy Story." You enter the world of television with attractions based on current Disney Channel shows as well as "The Twilight Zone." In the 2014 TripAdvisor Travelers' Choice Awards, Disney's Hollywood Studios was rated the No. 4 amusement park in the United States. That's one spot behind Magic Kingdom, one spot ahead of California's Disneyland.

Best of the park

Its exhilarating thrill rides. Fully realized and truly memorable, Rock 'n' Roller Coaster Starring Aerosmith and the Twilight Zone Tower of Terror hurl you through the dark.

Its interactivity. The park offers many opportunities to be part of the show. Children can duel Darth Vader in Star Wars: Jedi Training Academy. Go anywhere near one of the wacky Citizens of Hollywood and you might find yourself "volunteering" to be in their improvised street skits. Other attractions are interactive too. At Toy Story Mania—the most popular ride in all of Walt Disney World—you shoot targets in a virtual 3-D video game. At The Magic of Disney Animation, you sketch a Disney character and keep the result.

Its sense of humor. Many experiences are almost guaranteed to put a smile on your face. Examples include watching the strutting Gaston of Beauty and the Beast—Live on Stage, witnessing the antics of Dr. Bunsen Honeydew and Beaker at Jim Henson's MuppetVision 3-D, and being the target of a sarcastic server at the 50's Prime Time Café.

Facing page: Fireworks paint the sky at Disney's Hollywood Studios during special events. This "Frozen" one took place in 2014.

Its preschooler show. A lively gem of a puppet show, Disney Junior—Live on Stage speaks directly to young children without being condescending.

It won't wear you out. Unlike other Disney theme parks, the Studios doesn't make you spend all day on your feet. The smallest Disney theme park, it has the most sit-down shows as well as some time-consuming rides.

Worst of the park

Its limited breakfast choices. The only indoor breakfast choice is a Disney Junior character meal at Hollywood & Vine, the only outdoor hot food in the morning is an uninspired breakfast sandwich at Sunset Ranch Market. The best breakfast food is at Starring Rolls, a takeout bakery.

Its three awful attractions. Though the Studio Backlot Tour pretends there is still a working backlot at the park—recorded narration gushes "you never know who you might see!"—there isn't. Guests get an eyeload of sad, rusting movie props. Horrid pacing, distinctly un-Disney gunplay, a lack of humor and seating far from the action mar the presentation of automotive stunts at Lights, Motors, Action. And the Legend of Captain Jack Sparrow is simply a special-effects-laden promo for the various "Pirates of the Caribbean" movies; even a holographic Johnny Depp can't save it.

Its lack of rides. There's only six of them, the same number as Disney's Animal Kingdom, which at least is also a zoo. By comparison, Epcot has 10 rides; Magic Kingdom 23.

Getting oriented. Disney's Hollywood Studios is divided into five themed areas:

Animation Courtyard. Its entrance arch is modeled on the Paramount Studio gate; inside is a plaza bordered by soundstages and a former working studio of Walt Disney Animation.

Echo Lake. This picturesque spot recalls downtown Los Angeles' Echo Lake Park, where 1920's silent movie czar Mack Sennett shot many of his Keystone Comedies.

Opposite page photo © Disney

The park's mythical Sunset Boulevard glows with neon marquees, advertising the names of stores which line it. Rows of stately palms lead to the Twilight Zone Tower of Terror.

Hollywood and Sunset Boulevards. The front of the park channels Old Hollywood. Its architecture and street entertainment embody Los Angeles during the glory days of Tinseltown—the 1920s through the 1940s.

Pixar Place. Styled after Pixar's headquarters in Emeryville, Calif., this small, busy spot holds one of Walt Disney World's most popular attractions—the high-tech shooting gallery Toy Story Mania. Green Army Men patrol the street and pose for photos.

Streets of America. This former backlot area is dominated by New York Street, a 500-foot Beaux Arts thoroughfare based on the Big Apple's West 40th Street. A crossing street recalls San Francisco.

Family matters. All of the park's thrill rides have height minimums—48 inches for Rock 'n' Roller Coaster Starring Aerosmith, 40 inches for Twilight Zone Tower of Terror as well as the Star Tours motion simulator. Other attractions that may be too much for youngsters include Fantasmic, The Great Movie Ride, Voyage of the Little Mermaid and the Studio Backlot Tour.

The Animation Courtyard is the area of the park that offers the most for pre-schoolers. It includes two live shows, some hands-on activities and plenty of characters to meet indoors and out.

Every restaurant offers a children's menu. Disney Junior characters appear at Hollywood & Vine for breakfast and lunch.

If it rains. With its small size and plethora of indoor things to do, the park is easy to enjoy during a shower. There are plenty of stores and dining spots to duck into; self-guided attractions The Magic of Disney Animation and Walt Disney One Man's Dream have no restrictions on how long you stay in them. Only the Indiana Jones and Lights Motors Action stunt shows, the Studio Backlot Tour and the park's playground close due to rain. The nightime show Fantasmic is cancelled when lightning is in the area.

Fun finds. Lots of little show-biz-themed details are scattered through the park:

Echo Lake. Offices behind Keystone Clothiers include acting-and-voice studio Sights and Sounds. With the motto "We've Finished Some of Hollywood's Finest," it's run by master thespian Ewell M. Pressum, voice coach Singer B. Flatt and account executive Bill Moore; nearby are the dental offices of C. Howie Pullum, Ruth Canal and Les Payne... Crates to the left of the Min & Bill's snack stand refer to films "Casablanca," "Citizen Kane," "Gone With the Wind," "It's a Wonderful Life" and "The Producers."

Looks can be deceiving on the Streets of America, the "backlot" of the park's studios area. Detailed facades, real props and painted flats create illusions of real urban environments.

Hollywood Boulevard. Offices above an entrance to the Keystone Clothiers shop include one for tailor Justin Stitches.

Streets of America. A back corner of the Stage 1 Company Store includes the Muppet lockers and Happiness Hotel front desk from 1981's "The Great Muppet Caper." Nearly two dozen silly signs in that shop include one over a doorway that reads "Absolutely no point beyond this point."

Sunset Boulevard. An office above the Villains in Vogue store is home to the union the International Brotherhood of Second Assistant Directors (say it slowly: IBSAD), which has the motto "We're Standing Behind You." The facade is a reference to the Great Depression, when Second Assistant Director was a mercy title given to go-fers, who were often told "Get coffee and stand behind me."

Hidden Mickeys. Sharp eyes can spot the three-circle-shape of the head of Mickey Mouse throughout the park's grounds:

Echo Lake. As washers used to secure tops of coffee tables in the Tune-In Lounge.

Hollywood Boulevard. In the Cover Story store, in the black decorative molding below the second-floor windows.

Streets of America. Outside the Stage 1 Company Store as purple paint drips on a recessed light under a bronze lion head.

Inside the store, as green drips on a wood bureau shelf. Mickey's red shorts hang above the hotel desk.

Sunset Boulevard. Along the walkways, impressions along the curbs read "Mortimer & Co. Contractors 1928," a reference to Walt Disney's original name for the mouse that became Mickey, which Disney created in 1928.

Fun facts. Actual movies and television shows were once produced at the park, as at first the Disney company planned to operate it as a real television and motion picture production center as well as a tourist attraction.

Hit me Justin, one more time. In 1988, a year before the park opened to the public, the movies "Ernest Saves Christmas" and "Newsies" were filmed on the backlot. Soon, three soundstages hosted shows such as the Disney Channel's "New Mickey Mouse Club." Produced inside the building that today holds the Toy Story Mania ride, the 1989–1994 show starred youngsters Christina Aguilera, Ryan Gosling, Britney Spears and Justin Timberlake. Today's Streets of America area was used for Touchstone's 1990 Warren Beatty/Madonna vehicle "Dick Tracy." Third-party productions included Ed McMahon's "Star Search"—a talent show in which 11-year-old Timberlake and 10-year-old Spears both competed. Neither won.

The park icon is a giant version of the sorcerer's hat worn by Mickey Mouse in the 1940 movie "Fantasia." It's flanked by a pair of stylized ears and a gloved hand that tips it to one side.

Home on the what? Meanwhile, a separate animation studio (Walt Disney Feature Animation Florida) produced sequences for such classics as 1991's "Beauty and the Beast" and later complete films such as 1998's "Mulan" and 2002's "Lilo & Stitch." But after the flop of its 2004 movie "Home on the Range," Disney management decided to downsize and eventually close all the animation studio, as well as everything else. Today, no television or motion-picture work is done at the park.

Legendary marks. Aired as a two-hour special on NBC-TV, the park's 1989 Grand Opening featured appearances by many Tinseltown legends—including Lauren Bacall, George Burns, Audrey Hepburn and Bob Hope—most of whom signed their names and left their footprints in the plaza in front of the Chinese Theater.

Know before you go. Need some cash? A stroller? Help understanding MyMagic+? Here's where to find it:

ATMs. The park has two: There's one outside the entrance on the left, another inside the Toy Story Pizza Planet Arcade.

Baby Care Center. Located on your left as you enter the park, right beside the Guest Relations office, this indoor spot has changing rooms, nursing areas, a microwave and a playroom. It sells diapers, formula, pacifiers and over-the-counter meds.

FastPass+ kiosks. Cast members help you book and modify Fastpasses at these walk-up touchscreens. You'll find them at Sid Cahuenga's One-of-a-Kind shop, at the corner of Hollywood and Sunset, at Jim Henson's MuppetVision 3-D and Toy Story Mania, and on Sunset Boulevard next to The Twilight Zone Tower of Terror.

Pixar Place is modeled after the headquarters of Pixar Animation Studios in Emeryville, Calif. The park area is built from the same brick, and its entranceway has a similar overhead sign.

The park's Animation Courtyard resembles the office buildings and soundstages of a Hollywood movie studio. The central building was at one time a real Disney animation studio.

First aid. An indoor clinic is beside Guest Relations next to the Baby Care Center. Registered nurses treat minor emergencies. They call EMTs for serious issues.

Guest Relations. Located at the entrance to the park on the left, this office has walk-up windows outside the touchpoints, a walk-in lobby just inside. Cast members answer general questions, make dining reservations, exchange currency, hand out maps and times guides for all Disney World parks, and store items found in the park that day.

Locker rentals. They're inside the park at Oscar's Super Service ($7 a day, $5 deposit).

MyMagic+ Service Center. Inside Sid Cahuenga's One-of-a-Kind shop, cast members answer questions about MyMagic+ services: the My Disney Experience website and app, the MagicBand ticketing system and the FastPass+ attraction-reservation service.

Package pickup. Anything you buy in the park can be sent to the park entrance for you to pick up later at no charge; allow three hours. Packages can also be delivered to Disney hotels or shipped nationally.

Parking. $17 a day per car. Free for Disney hotel guests and annual passholders.

Stroller rentals. Oscar's Super Service rents single strollers for $15 a day ($13 length of stay), doubles for $31 ($27 length of stay). Get replacements at Tatooine Traders.

Disney transportation. Boats go to Epcot and Epcot resorts. There's direct bus service to all other Disney resorts, theme parks and Blizzard Beach; but not to ESPN Wide World of Sports, Downtown Disney or Typhoon Lagoon.

Wheelchair and scooter rentals. Available at Oscar's Super Service. Wheelchairs $12 a day, $10 a day length of stay. Four-wheel electric scooters $50 a day, $20 deposit.

Picturesque Echo Lake recalls downtown Los Angeles' Echo Lake Park, an on-location setting for many early movies and television shows. Subtle tributes to the beginnings of California show business surround the small pond.

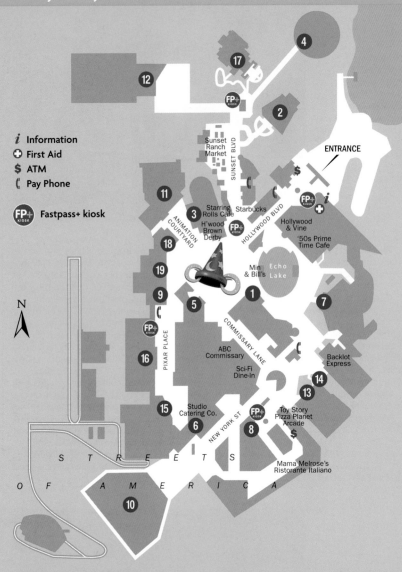

i Information

✛ First Aid

$ ATM

(Pay Phone

FP+ KIOSK Fastpass+ kiosk

Sunset Ranch Market

ENTRANCE

SUNSET BLVD

Starring Rolls Cafe

Starbucks

ANIMATION COURTYARD

H'wood Brown Derby

HOLLYWOOD BLVD

Hollywood & Vine

'50s Prime Time Cafe

Min & Bill's

Echo Lake

N

COMMISSARY LANE

PIXAR PLACE

ABC Commissary

Backlot Express

Sci-Fi Dine-In

Studio Catering Co.

Toy Story Pizza Planet Arcade

NEW YORK ST

Mama Melrose's Ristorante Italiano

S T R E E T S

O F   A M E R I C A

① The American Idol Experience

② Beauty and the Beast—Live on Stage

③ Disney Junior—Live on Stage

④ Fantasmic!

⑤ The Great Movie Ride

⑥ "Honey, I Shrunk the Kids" Playground

⑦ Indiana Jones Epic Stunt Spectacular

⑧ Jim Henson's MuppetVision 3-D

⑨ The Legend of Captain Jack Sparrow

⑩ Lights Motors Action

⑪ The Magic of Disney Animation

⑫ Rock 'n' Roller Coaster Starring Aerosmith

⑬ Star Tours

⑭ Star Wars: Jedi Training Academy

⑮ Studio Backlot Tour

⑯ Toy Story Mania

⑰ The Twilight Zone Tower of Terror

⑱ Voyage of the Little Mermaid

⑲ Walt Disney: One Man's Dream

Attractions at a Glance

There are three duds here, but there's more good than bad, including two five-star thrill rides. Here's a quick look at the attractions at Disney's Hollywood Studios, each of which is reviewed in detail later in this chapter. Each attraction is rated from one to five stars (★) based on how well it lives up to its promise. A checkmark (✔) indicates an author favorite. The Fastpass+ logo (FastPass+) appears if the attraction can be reserved in advance.

Five-star attractions

Beauty and the Beast Live on Stage. ★★★★★ ✔ FastPass+ Stage musical is fun, moving. Sunset Boulevard.

Disney Junior Live on Stage. ★★★★★ FastPass+ Lively puppet show stars Disney Junior TV characters. Disney's best preschooler attraction. Animation Courtyard.

Rock 'n' Roller Coaster Starring Aerosmith. ★★★★★ ✔ FastPass+ Dark coaster corkscrews, goes upside down, blares rock. Height minimum 48 inches. Sunset Boulevard.

Star Wars: Jedi Training Academy. ★★★★★ ✔ Children volunteer to learn light saber techniques, duel Darth Vader. Echo Lake.

The Twilight Zone Tower of Terror. ★★★★★ ✔ FastPass+ Out of control elevator falls and ascends 13 stories in an unpredictable pattern. Sudden, swift drops and lifts. Height minimum 40 inches. Sunset Boulevard.

Four-star attractions

Indiana Jones Epic Stunt Spectacular. ★★★★ FastPass+ Performers re-enact physical stunt scenes from 1981's "Raiders of the Lost Ark." Echo Lake.

Jim Henson's MuppetVision 3-D. ★★★★ ✔ FastPass+ Muppets star in this funny-but-dated 3-D movie which takes you on a tour of a 3-D lab. Streets of America.

The Magic of Disney Animation. ★★★★ ✔ Animation exhibits and activities include a short film, computer games, characters to meet, drawing lesson. Animation Courtyard.

Star Tours. ★★★★ ✔ FastPass+ Wacky thrills aboard a "Star Wars" spaceship. Flight routes vary with each ride. High-tech 3-D motion simulator can cause motion sickness. Height minimum 40 inches. Echo Lake.

Toy Story Mania. ★★★★ ✔ FastPass+ Shoot at targets and rack up a high score in this ride-through series of 3-D video games starring "Toy Story" characters. Pixar Place.

Walt Disney One Man's Dream. ★★★★ ✔ Walt Disney and Disney Company memorabilia and artifacts in a museum-style setting; a short biographical film narrated by Walt himself. To the left of Animation Courtyard.

Three-star attractions

The American Idol Experience. ★★★ ✔ FastPass+ Singing contest stars guest volunteers; audience picks winner. Echo Lake.

Fantasmic. ★★★ FastPass+ Evening spectacle stars Mickey Mouse. Characters, lasers, dancing fountains, water screens, fireworks, loud noises, bright flashes, scary villains abound. Sunset Boulevard.

The Great Movie Ride. ★★★ ✔ FastPass+ Slow indoor tram ride tours classic film scenes, which robotic characters bring to life. The newest movie depicted is from 1981. Hollywood Boulevard.

Voyage of the Little Mermaid. ★★★ FastPass+ Musical stage show tells Ariel's story with puppets, a live singer, special effects and video. Uses dated 1990s effects. Animation Courtyard.

Two-star attractions

'Honey, I Shrunk the Kids' Playground. ★★ Soft-floored outdoor play area has tunnels, oversized props; it's based on 1989's "Honey, I Shrunk the Kids" film. Streets of America.

One-star attractions

The Legend of Captain Jack Sparrow. ★ Lame special-effects show has one redeeming feature: a holographic Johnny Depp. You stand to watch it. To the right of Pixar Place.

Lights, Motors, Action Extreme Stunt Show. ★ FastPass+ Outdoor automotive stunts create faux action-movie scenes. You sit on bleachers far from the action. Loud, often boring. Streets of America.

Studio Backlot Tour. ★ Weak backlot-themed walking tour turns into feeble tram ride. Streets of America.

Decked out with old knickknacks, formica tables and vinyl chairs, seating areas at the 50's Prime Time Café recall vintage dinettes. Black-and-white televisions play old sitcom clips.

Restaurants and food

Disney's Hollywood Studios has some great table-service restaurants, but not the best fast-food choices. Below, each restaurant is rated from one to five stars (★) based on the quality of its food, service and atmosphere. A five-star eatery fully lives up to its promise; a one-star place should be avoided. A checkmark (✔) indicates that the restaurant is one of the authors' personal favorites. The price of a typical adult entree is summarized by dollar signs as follows:

$ less than $10
$$ less than $15
$$$ less than $20
$$$$ less than $25
$$$$$ more than $25

To reserve a table at any Walt Disney World restaurant call Disney at 407-939-3463.

Table service. A quick summary: The best food at Disney's Hollywood Studios is at Hollywood Brown Derby (but it's pricey), the most relaxing atmosphere is at Mama Melrose's, the most fun spot is the 50's Prime Time Cafe. The best fast food is at ABC Commissary. The author's top choices: The fried chicken at Prime Time and the Cobb salad at Brown Derby.

50's Prime Time Cafe. ★★★★★ ✔ $$$
The retro dining experience is a hoot at this unique restaurant, where servers hassle diners who don't keep their elbows off the table, finish their meals or, especially, eat their vegetables. Stage-set dinettes may remind baby boomers of grandma's house. Formica tables, sparkly vinyl chairs and black-and-white table TVs help create a surreal atmosphere. The menu is old-fashioned comfort food — fried chicken, meatloaf, pot roast. No reservations? You can order from the full menu at the bar. *Echo Lake. Lunch, dinner. 11 a.m.–park close. $13–$22 (children $9). Seats 225, 14 at the bar.*

Hollywood & Vine. ★★★ $$$ At dinner this crowded, noisy buffet serves a wide variety of meats, seafood and side dishes, some quite good. Unfortunately, it smells a little greasy, and the carpet is often spattered with the meals and muddle of those before you. For the price you can do a lot better. The experience at breakfast and lunch is very different—a character buffet that stars Disney Junior's Doc McStuffins, Handy Manny, Jake from "Jake and the Never Land Pirates" and Sofia from "Sofia the First." These popular characters not only greet their young fans, they also sing, dance and play with them, with a human host acting as emcee. Ironically, the experience is not very well known, so kids often get

Sitting inside miniature versions of old Chevy and Pontiac convertibles, diners at the Sci-Fi Dine-In Theater Restaurant chow down burgers and slurp down milkshakes.

to spend an enormous amount of time with the characters. The uninspired breakfast buffet has a standout—Mickey Mouse-shaped waffles. *Echo Lake. Breakfast 8–11:20 a.m., $27 (children $15). Lunch 11:40 a.m.–2.25 p.m. $34 (children $18). Dinner 3:30 p.m.–30 minutes before park close, $34 (children $17). Seats 468.*

Hollywood Brown Derby. ★ ★ ★ ★ ★ ✓ $$$$$ With some of the best food of any Disney restaurant, this fine-dining spot offers steaks, seafood and other American classics that are reworked to a modern, yet never trendy, standard. As a Disney Signature Restaurant, the Derby's food is consistently excellent, providing a great break from the theme-park grind. Especially good—the famous Hollywood Derby Cobb salad in all its chopped authenticity, and the light, tart grapefruit cake. The elegant eatery faithfully re-creates the 1929 second location of the famous Tinseltown landmark; to fully enjoy it take time to walk around. Check out the details — the hat-shaped brass table-side lamps, the gorgeous four-table Bamboo Room in the back corner (ask nicely when you check in and the host or hostess may let you sit there), and especially all the celebrity caricatures on the walls. Those in black frames are re-creations of portraits of Derby diners that once hung on the walls of the original restaurant. Those in gold frames are of singers and musicians of the era who had million-selling recordings. *Hollywood Boulevard. Lunch, dinner. 11:30 a.m.–park close. $16–$43 (children $6–$14). Seats 224, 40 in the outdoor lounge.*

Mama Melrose's Ristorante Italiano. ★ ★ ★ ★ ✓ $$$$ Traditional Italian cuisine gets a California twist at this comfortable eatery, which is hidden in a back corner of the park. It's so relaxing you may need a nap afterward. Mama's is best for families and couples who need a break and want comfort food. The signature dish is chicken alla parmigiana; other choices include seasonal pastas, brick-oven flatbreads, even a steak. Portions are generous. Resembling a converted warehouse, the dining room has open ceilings strung with Christmas lights, brick walls covered with Californian and Italian pop-culture relics, and wood floors. Mismatched light fixtures add to the eclectic look. *Streets of America. Lunch, dinner. Noon-one hour before park closing. $13–$30 (children $9). Seats 250.*

Sci-Fi Dine-In Theater Restaurant. ★ ★ ★ ★ $$$$ This "starlit" indoor dining room channels a 1950s drive-in theater, with a huge silver screen that shows trailers from kitschy sci-fi flicks, newsreels, intermission bumpers and odd space-age cartoons. Sound comes from actual drive-in speakers mounted to booths; some servers roller skate. Diners sit two abreast in booths hidden inside miniature versions of old Chevy and Pontiac convertibles. The dining area is certainly unique; where else can you watch trailers for such forgotten shlock as "The Cat Woman from Mars"? Unfortunately, the concept here is more fun than the experience. Younger diners may be bored, the tight row seating makes it tough for families to talk, and Disney tempts you to fork over the dough with a pricey menu that overhypes its food. If you go, stick to the hamburgers and milkshakes, and if you want to sit in a car be sure to ask for one when you check in. Otherwise you may get a plain-Jane patio table at the back at the room. *Streets of America. Lunch, dinner. 11 a.m.–park close. $13–$30 (children $9). Seats 252.*

The outdoor snack bar Min & Bill's Dockside Diner appears to be a boat floating on palm-lined Echo Lake. It's an homage to the 1930 Academy Award-winning film "Min and Bill."

Counter service. The park's fast-food spots do not match up to the quality of the table service restaurants. The top choice is the ABC Commissary. Avoid Toy Story Pizza Planet Arcade and Backlot Express.

ABC Commissary. ★★★ ✔ $ Live palms, cushioned booths and chairs, unobtrusive lighting and soft carpet make the ABC Commissary the park's most comfortable counter-service restaurant—at least when it's not crowded. The only downside: Ceiling-mounted televisions play annoying ABC-TV promos on a short loop, over and over, ad infinitum. The food ranges from fine but forgettable burgers and sandwiches to a mediocre fried seafood platter to very good salads. The star is the couscous, quinoa & arugula salad with salmon, which has a light vinegary dressing and a large portion of perfectly cooked fish. Outside seating provides nice people-watching, although in the summer even a covered umbrella is too warm to be comfortable. *Commissary Lane. Lunch, dinner. 11 a.m.–park close. $9–$11 (children $6). Seats 562 indoors, 128 outdoors at umbrella-covered tables.*

Backlot Express. ★ $ This faux prop warehouse offers lackluster burgers, hot dogs, grilled sandwiches and salads. None of the choices match up to the quality of the food at the ABC Commissary. Open ceilings and concrete floors add to the "warehouse" feel of the place, which almost always has at least a few empty tables. The condiment and self-serve fountain drink areas are sticky and not very well maintained. Real Hollywood clutter crowds the walls and corners—thousands of authentic movie and television props, gadgets and trivial-but-fascinating down-and-dirty junk (for example, call sheets from the "Cheers" television series and Bennie the Cab stunt car from 1988's "Who Framed Roger Rabbit). Outside seating is mostly under umbrellas; several tables offer good viewing of the adjacent Jedi Training Academy shows. *Echo Lake. Lunch, dinner. 11 a.m.–8 p.m. $6–$11 (children $6). Seats 330 indoors, 270 outdoors, mostly covered.*

Min & Bill's Dockside Diner. ★★ $ You'll swear this outdoor counter-service spot is a boat. There it is, apparently floating on Echo Lake. Disney can't make its mind up on the menu. At press time Min & Bill's offers meat-heavy fare: a frankfurter in a pretzel roll, an Italian sandwich in French bread, a pork shank and a turkey leg. *Echo Lake. Lunch, dinner. 10 a.m.–park close. $8–$12. Seats 140.*

Starbucks. ★★ $ Newly opened in 2014, this Starbucks has the same menu as every other Starbucks you've ever been to; there's nothing Disney about it. Breakfast sandwiches and pastries are good, but coffee is

The comfortable ABC Commissary has the look of a movie set commissary—a backstage spot that provides meals to a studio's actors and crew members.

the star. *Hollywood Boulevard. Breakfast, lunch, dinner. Park hours. $4–$5. No seating.*

Starring Rolls Cafe. ★ ★ ★ ✔ $$$ Laughably small, this combination bakery and sandwich shop is packed during meal times, with a line spilling out the door. Seating is outdoors, mostly under umbrellas. The cafe is recessed down a few steps, so a small wall separates diners from passersby. Breakfast offers fresh pastries, bagels and muffins. Lunch is either a generous ham or turkey sandwich from the kitchens of the adjacent Brown Derby or fresh sushi from the Japan pavilion in Epcot. The excellent food can be trumped by the problem of having to eat outdoors; the Florida weather doesn't always cooperate. *At the corner of Hollywood and Sunset Boulevards. Breakfast, 9–11:30 a.m., $3–$6. Lunch, 11:30 a.m.–4 p.m., $6–$11 (children $5). Seats 60, mostly covered.*

Studio Catering Co. ★ $ The only thing commendable about this outdoor covered concrete patio is its good grilled vegetable sandwich—pressed flat and crusty like a Cuban sandwich. Everything else is uninspired and problematic. The menu changes often, but recently its sandwiches and salads are forgettable. The tables and chairs are metal and uncomfortable; the chairs have seats that angle back, forcing you to sit on an incline. The tables and condiment stations always seem a little sticky and messy. It's the closest spot to Toy Story Mania to sit down and eat. If you must go, get that grilled veggie sandwich. *Streets of America. Lunch, dinner. 11:30 a.m.–7 p.m. $7–$10 (children $5–$6). Seats 498 (328 covered).*

Sunset Ranch Market. ★ ★ ★ ✔ $ Sitting alongside bustling Sunset Boulevard, the outdoor food court Sunset Ranch Market can be a pleasant spot to people-watch. Delighted screams from the nearby Twilight Zone Tower of Terror fill the air. The market's food ranges from nondescript burgers and turkey legs to tasty barbecue and hand-dipped ice cream. One of the food stands sells breakfast bagel sandwiches. *Sunset Boulevard. Breakfast (only at Fairfax Faire), lunch, dinner. Park open–park close. $8–$15 (children $5–$6). Seats 400.*

Toy Story Pizza Planet Arcade. ★ ★ $ The pizza is ho-hum at this combination arcade and pizza parlor; the pies are bland and haphazardly cooked. Side salads come drenched in Caesar dressing. Kids choose from a mini chicken sub or a cheese pizza the size of a hockey puck. None of the offerings are as good as mall food. Another downer: the noise. Open ceilings and tile floors add to the din from the arcade. Sit on the second floor away from the railing for the quietest experience, or if you want to charge your phone; there are plenty of outlets. The last disappointment—the place looks nothing like the Pizza Planet from "Toy Story." *Streets of America. Lunch, dinner. 11 a.m.–90 minutes before park close. $8–$11 (children $6). Seats 472 indoors; 112 outdoors, mostly covered.*

Snacks. Re-creating the atmosphere of a small bookshop café, the **Writer's Stop** ★ ★ ★ ★ ✔ offers freshly baked goods, coffee and frozen drinks. Try the cream-cheese-filled carrot cake cookie for an indulgent treat. A tiny spot next to the Sci-Fi Dine-In, it has four small tables. In Echo Lake, **Peevy's Polar Pipeline** ★ ★ ★ serves up frozen soft drinks behind the Keystone Clothiers shop.

See also **Restaurant Policies** in the chapter **Walt Disney World A–Z.**

Despite its marquee, Legends of Hollywood is just a routine gift shop with nothing for the film fan. Its Streamline Moderne facade recalls a Los Angeles movie theater from the 1930s.

Shops

Stores at Disney's Hollywood Studios offer a good variety of apparel, and merchandise themed to movies or television shows. The best are summarized below. Stores are rated from one to five stars (★) based on the quality of their merchandise, service and atmosphere; one- and two-star stores are not listed. A checkmark (✔) indicates that the store is one of the authors' personal favorites.

Adrian & Edith's Head to Toe. ★★★ It will only take 10 or 15 minutes to personalize a Mickey Mouse ear hat at this small shop. Choose from dozens of styles, including some for newlyweds and graduates. The basic embroidery uses black, gold or dark pink thread; a fancier version offers more color choices and your choice of typefaces. Towels can be personalized, too. Formerly a candy shop, the store has the black and white tile common in Disney confectioneries. Tailoring and sewing equipment line upper shelves. *Next to Starbucks, Hollywood Boulevard.*

Animation Gallery. ★★★★ ✔ This store's walls and shelves are covered with original art and prints, along with figurines, Walt Disney World Collectibles (coins, medallions, gold-plated tickets), Precious Moments works, Disney by Britto artwork and posters.

A Disney artist draws and paints before your eyes; when he's done you can buy the results. Light classical versions of Disney songs fill the air. *At the exit to The Magic of Disney Animation, Animation Courtyard.*

Gem Creations. ★★★ ✔ Every piece of jewelry is unique at this tiny shaded open-air stand. The artist is local—not a Disney employee. Handcrafted necklaces sell for $12 to $14; bracelets $4 to $5. *Near the Indiana Jones theater, Echo Lake.*

In Character. ★★★ This open-air shop offers Disney princess costumes and accessories, but not for every princess. Belle's stuff is at Once Upon a Time (see below). At press time, Anna and Elsa costumes were only available at Sir Mickey's in Magic Kingdom. *Next to the Voyage of the Little Mermaid attraction, Animation Courtyard.*

It's a Wonderful Shop. ★★★ Oddly, this Christmas shop doesn't have a Christmas theme. Instead, it looks like a prop warehouse, with all sorts of gewgaws on the walls. Merchandise includes ornaments, stockings and nutcrackers. A snowman in front of the store makes a good spot for a Christmas-in-July photo. *Between Toy Story Pizza Planet and Mama Melrose's, Streets of America.*

Keystone Clothiers. ★★★★ ✔ Men, women and juniors will find fashionable apparel and accessories in this upscale

The exit to the Star Tours ride, the Tatooine Traders gift shop holds a plethora of Star Wars merchandise. The home of Anakin and Luke Skywalker, the desert planet of Tatooine appears in nearly every Star Wars movie.

boutique. Its selection of hats and shoes is especially stylish. *Across from Starbucks, Hollywood Boulevard.*

Once Upon a Time. ★★★★ This children's shop has stylish kids' apparel, Belle costumes and accessories, casual shoes, costume jewelry, plush and toys. An homage to Hollywood's Carthay Circle theater, its interior has an ornate arched ceiling and maroon velvet drapes. The radio broadcast of the 1937 premiere of "Snow White and the Seven Dwarfs" at the Carthay Circle fills the air. *Next to the Beauty and the Beast Theater, Sunset Boulevard.*

Rock Around the Shop. ★★★★★ ✔ Slash as a Mickey Mouse doll? Guitar-shaped purses? Guitar-pick earrings? This Rock 'n' Roller Coaster shop has 'em, as well as Aerosmith items and a surprising variety of fashionable shirts for juniors. Wood floors, open ceilings and exposed lighting recall a backstage area, as do display stands that look like instrument cases and trunks. *At the exit to Rock 'n' Roller Coaster Starring Aerosmith, Sunset Boulevard.*

Stage 1 Company Store. ★★★★ ✔ This faux prop storage room was originally a Muppet shop, and the back half still is—though Phineas and Ferb items have also crept in, as those characters meet fans right outside. The front is a children's shop, with infantwear, children's wear and costumes that will transform your little girl into Minnie Mouse or Tinker Bell. *Outside Jim Henson's MuppetVision 3-D, Streets of America.*

Sweet Spells. ★★★ ✔ Bakers create candies, caramel apples and cookies in front of you at this small confectionery, which also sells packaged treats. Wall art features the Evil Queen, Maleficent, Jafar, Cruella de Vil,

Scar and Ursula, as the shop shares its space with Villains in Vogue (see below). *At the corner of Hollywood and Sunset Boulevards.*

Tatooine Traders. ★★★★★ ✔ Drool you will over this store's "Star Wars" stuff—from its "Build Your Own Lightsaber" station to its Yoda backpacks to its Droid Factory to its Stormtrooper helmets. Star Tours souvenirs include toy Starspeeders and action figures. *At the exit to Star Tours, Echo Lake.*

Tower Gifts. ★★★★★ ✔ Looking like the gift shop of an old ritzy hotel—it's the exit of the Hollywood Tower Hotel, AKA The Twilight Zone Tower of Terror—Tower Gifts has fancy carpet, plaster walls with arches and elaborate ironwork. Keeping with its theme, it offers items from the hotel: door hangers, room key chains, front-desk bells, bathrobes, towels, mugs and glassware, all with the Hollywood Tower Hotel logo. Very cool. And then off in a corner is merchandise related to the 1993 movie "The Nightmare Before Christmas" and the Magic Kingdom ride The Haunted Mansion. Apparently because at Disney, spooky is as spooky sells. *At the exit to Twilight Zone Tower of Terror, Sunset Boulevard.*

Villains in Vogue. ★★★ This Art Deco Disney Villains store is packed with even more Nightmare Before Christmas items (have these Disney folks even watched that movie?) as well as stuff themed to Maleficent, Lotso, and from the classic 1951 movie "Alice in Wonderland," the Cheshire Cat and Queen of Hearts. And then off in a corner are... Vinylmation figurines! Apparently because at Disney, anything is as anything sells. *Next to Sunset Ranch Market, Sunset Boulevard.*

See also **Shopping** in the chapter **Walt Disney World A–Z.**

Micaela Neal

Street performers

Citizens of Hollywood. ★★★★★

✔ Impersonating showbiz stereotypes with unfettered glee, this improvisational troupe roams the park's Old Hollywood area as the living, breathing residents of a 1940s Tinseltown. The cast includes directors, divas, heartthrobs, has-beens, wannabes, starlets, inept public works employees, super sly card shark Jack Diamond, even a "caterer to the stars." Most skits include audience "volunteers." To be chosen as one, wear something colorful, then stand in front, smile, and make eye contact with the performers. If you see sassy script girl Paige Turner, tell her Oliver says hi. *20- to 30-minute shows. Random spots on Hollywood and Sunset Boulevards.*

Mulch, Sweat and Shears. ★★★★★

✔ Driving its pickup truck and trailer onto the Streets of America a few times each day, landscape crew Mulch, Sweat and Shears transforms itself into a humorous live rock band ready to "Rake 'n' Roll." Tapping into their engine's battery for a power source, wannabe comedian and ladies man Morris Mulch and his group crank out a set of classic tunes and medleys, grabbing audience members (always female) to join them on cow bells and air guitars. Because of their Disney location, the band changes some of its songs' lyrics. A line from the Eagles' 1977 hit "Life in the Fast Lane" becomes "They had one thing in common, they were good… at sports!" *30-minute shows. Streets of America, also Hollywood Boulevard.*

Citizens of Hollywood frustrated director Alberto Dante, caterer and wannabe ventriloquist Ben Appetit, vain screen queen Dara Vamp, star-struck script girl Paige Turner with cordial cowboy star Beau Wrangler.

Where to meet characters

The Magic of Disney Animation.
★★★★★ ✓ "Fantasia" sorcerer's apprentice Mickey Mouse stands in front of a backdrop of the Animation Courtyard archway. Minnie Mouse is in Mickey's queue. Mr. Incredible and Frozone from "The Incredibles" pose in front of their logo; Ralph and Vanellope from "Wreck-It Ralph" are in front of the Sugar Rush grandstands. Indoor. *Animation Courtyard.*

Monsters Inc Open House. ★★★
Mike Wazowski and Sulley from the "Monsters, Inc" movies stand in front of a closet door attached to laugh canisters. *Studio Backlot Tour exitway, Streets of America.*

Play 'n Dine at Hollywood & Vine.
★★★★★ Preschoolers dance and sing with Disney Junior's Doc McStuffins, Handy Manny, Sofia the First and Neverland pirate Jake at this buffet. Bland food, but outstanding experience. *Next to 50's Prime Time Cafe, Echo Lake.*

Team McQueen Headquarters.
★★ Meet Lightning McQueen and Mater from the "Cars" movies in this open-air tent. The backdrop shows flames shooting from Lightning's exhaust. *Next to Mama Melrose's, Streets of America.*

Woody's Picture Shootin' Corral.
★★★ Woody and Buzz Lightyear stand in front of a backdrop of Andy's bed. Indoor. *Across from Toy Story Mania, Pixar Place.*

Characters also greet guests on walkways throughout the park.

See also the chapter **Characters.**

"Wreck-It Ralph" stars in the Magic of Disney Animation; Phineas and Ferb's spot is outside Mama Melrose's; "Monsters, Inc." stars appear near the Studio Backlot Tour; Woody's Picture Shootin' Corral is in Pixar Place.

Audio-Animatronics robots depict Humphrey Bogart bidding goodbye to Ingrid Bergman in "Casablanca," one of many vintage films brought to life on The Great Movie Ride.

The Great Movie Ride

Pleasant tribute to classic films is starting to show its age

★★★★ ✔ FastPass+ Gene Kelly "Singin' in the Rain," Humphrey Bogart reminding Ingrid Bergman that "we'll always have Paris," all those nearly naked showgirls twirling on that tiered Tower of Beauty in "Footlight Parade"—OK, so you may not recognize everything you pass, but even so, this indoor tram-trip down Hollywood's memory lane is still worth your time. A robotic tribute to Tinseltown, it takes you through soundstage sets that depict nearly every type of movie, with actors represented by robotic figures who sing, swing, fly, cower, sneer and threaten. Issues include special effects that never quite all work, and the fact that all of the ride's movies were made before 1981—before anyone under the age of 34 was born.

The entrance facade is a full-scale reproduction of Grauman's Chinese Theatre, the famous Hollywood landmark. Like its inspiration, the Disney building's plaza is filled with real celebrity imprints. A queue room shows clips from the trailers of films portrayed on the ride—a sort of "coming attractions."

Tips. *When to go:* Before 11 a.m. or after dusk to avoid long lines. *Where to sit:* Ask the boarding attendant for the second row of the first car of your tram, right behind the tram operator. When your tram is hijacked, the villain will be right there with you, and may even talk to you ("What are you lookin' at?").

Key facts. *Best for:* Seniors, movie buffs. *Duration:* 22 minutes. *Capacity:* 560. *Queue:* Indoor. *Fear factor:* An encounter with a live performer brings faux gunshots and sometimes real fire, the "Alien" creature menaces your tram. The Wicked Witch threatens your tram and looks real from a distance. *Debuted:* 1989. *Access:* ECV users can stay in their vehicle. *Disability services:* Assistive listening, handheld captioning. *Location:* Hollywood Boulevard.

Average wait times

9am	10am	11am	Noon	1pm	2pm	3pm	4pm	5pm	6pm	7pm	8pm	9pm
5m	15m	30m	25m	15m	15m	15m	15m	15m	5m	20m	20m	5m

Three contestants await an audience vote during a performance of The American Idol Experience. The park attraction has sent many rising stars onto the television show.

The American Idol Experience

You call the shots at this entertaining singing contest

★★★★ ✔ FastPass+ Spontaneous, warts-and-all reality. It's rare at Disney, but common at this live talent show, which pits singers against each other. Though the best performers almost always win, the shows take unexpected twists and turns, as over-confident singers often flub lyrics or sing off-key and on-stage judges ad-lib critiques that are sometimes too harsh. Meanwhile, wallflowers sometimes belt out tunes that earn standing ovations.

Just like on television, an entertaining emcee hosts, and singers compete on a flashy stage as roaming camera operators circle around them. Each show's winner is chosen by an audience vote. Winners compete against each other in an evening finale; the winner of that gets to be first in line at an upcoming audition for the television show.

Note: The American Idol Experience closed at press time.

Tips. *Which show to see:* The finale. It's twice as long and has the best singers. Use a Fastpass. *How to avoid a crowd:* See the first show of the day. The talent may be iffy, but you can usually show up at the last minute and still get a good seat. *How to be in the show:* Anyone age 14 or older can compete, as long as they go through a backstage audition. Nearly everyone who tries out makes it. Auditions are held daily from 9 a.m. to 2 p.m.; the audition entrance is behind the theater on Commissary Way. For questions call the show at 407-939-4365.

Key facts. *Best for:* Teens and adults. *Duration:* 20–25 minutes, finale 45 minutes. *Capacity:* 1,040. *Queue:* Outdoor, covered. *Showtimes:* Scheduled performances; five or six shows daily, finale at 7 p.m. *Debuted:* 2009. *Access:* Guests may remain in wheelchairs, ECVs. *Disability services:* Assistive listening. *Location:* Echo Lake.

Average wait times

9am	10am	11am	Noon	1pm	2pm	3pm	4pm	5pm	6pm	7pm	8pm	9pm
---	---	---	n/a	n/a	n/a	n/a	n/a	n/a	n/a	n/a	---	---

Indiana Jones battles an Egyptian bad guy in the Indiana Jones Epic Stunt Spectacular, a display of physical stunts that retells the story of the 1981 movie "Raiders of the Lost Ark."

Indiana Jones Epic Stunt Spectacular

Witty, fast-paced special-effects show is visibly dated

★★★ ✔ FastPass+ Basically unchanged since its debut in 1989, this outdoor stage show is still entertaining and often funny, especially if you've never seen it before. Fireballs, gunshots, spears, swords, a great big boulder and a muscle-bound Nazi threaten Indiana Jones and his girlfriend Marion, as Disney actors re-create physical stunts from the 1981 movie "Raiders of the Lost Ark." Between scenes you'll learn how backdrops can be quickly set up and dismantled, how heavy-looking props can be feather-light, and how stunt actors fake a punch. For flavor, Disney pretends the show is a real film shoot. Mock cameramen peer through mock cameras; a fake director barks out fake directions. The show may close soon.

Tips. *Which show to see:* Either the first one or the last, when crowds are typically light and it's easy to get a good seat. The best show is at dusk, when fiery explosions pop against the sky. Avoid afternoon shows in the summer, when the poorly ventilated seating area can feel like a sweatbox. *Where to sit:* Front row center. The left side of the theater is set aside for Fastpass holders, who enter the theater early. *How to be in the show:* A few minutes before the show begins, a "casting director" chooses a handful of adults to be "extras" in the show. If you're seated close to the front, and jump up, wave and scream with wild abandon, you'll likely get picked.

Key facts. *Best for:* Adults, seniors. *Duration:* 30 minutes. *Capacity:* 2,000. *Queue:* Outdoor, covered. *Fear factor:* Fire, simulated gunfire and explosions may upset young children. *Showtimes:* Scheduled performances, typically starting at 11:30 a.m. *Weather issues:* Canceled during rain. *Debuted:* 1989. *Access:* Guests may remain in wheelchairs, ECVs. *Disability services:* Assistive listening, handheld captioning, Audio Description. *Location:* Echo Lake.

Average wait times

9am	10am	11am	Noon	1pm	2pm	3pm	4pm	5pm	6pm	7pm	8pm	9pm
---	---	n/a	n/a	n/a	n/a	n/a	n/a	n/a	n/a	n/a	---	---

© Disney

A podrace through the desert canyons of Tatooine is one of many possible journeys on Star Tours, a 3-D motion simulator that varies its flight with every ride.

Star Tours

High-tech simulator offers thrilling, randomized adventures

★★★★ ✔ **FastPass+** Taking off on a tourist trip where everything goes wrong, you'll be immersed in the Star Wars universe by this 3-D motion simulator, which Disney and George Lucas redid a few years ago with lots of love, care and technical expertise. Even the waiting line is loads of fun.

You'll want to go on it multiple times, as its scenes and destinations change with each flight. You might head to Tatooine, Coruscant, Naboo, or even a Death Star, may be stopped by Darth Vader or receive a hologrammed message from Princess Leia ("Help me, Star Tours, you're my only hope!")

Tips. *When to go:* Early using the standby queue, again after lunch. *Where to sit:* For the best 3-D experience and to avoid nausea, ask for the middle of a center row. Avoid the front row; the visuals may be skewed. *For families:* Kids can climb on a Speeder bike across from the ride entrance. It's perfect for a snapshot.

How to understand the ride: Watch the video in the boarding area; it sets up the plot.

Fun finds. The queue rooms are filled with references to the "Star Wars" films, especially in the comments of the security droids.

Hidden Mickeys. Outside the attraction, as greenish-white moss high on a tree trunk just below the Ewok village platform.

Key facts. *Best for:* Children, teens, adults. *Duration:* 7 minutes. *Capacity:* 240 (six 40-seat simulators). *Queue:* Indoor. *Fear factor:* Skittish children may be startled by some effects. *Restraint:* Seat belt. *Debuted:* 1989 (Disneyland 1987), redone 2011. *Health advisories:* Riders should be free from motion sickness; pregnancy; high blood pressure; heart, back or neck problems. *Access:* Height minimum 40 inches. Wheelchair, ECV users must transfer. *Disability services:* Assistive listening, handheld captioning. *Location:* Echo Lake.

Average wait times

9am	10am	11am	Noon	1pm	2pm	3pm	4pm	5pm	6pm	7pm	8pm	9pm
10m	10m	20m	20m	10m	10m	10m	10m	10m	10m	10m	10m	10m

Guided by a wise Jedi Master, younglings from the audience use "training" light sabers to duel Darth Vader. Stormtroopers keep a close watch for potential troublemakers.

Star Wars: Jedi Training Academy

Enjoy this show you will, even if padawans you have not

★★★★★ ✓ Adorable and surprisingly funny, this outdoor stage show teaches children how to be Jedi knights. Donning brown robes, young Padawans pledge the Jedi oath, learn light saber techniques, then duel Darth Vader (or, on peak days, maybe Darth Maul). The host is a wise-cracking Jedi Master, who makes the show a delight for the audience. You stand to watch it, on the pavement between the Star Tours ride and the Backlot Express restaurant.

About 15 children can be in each show. Sign up your kids in advance by stopping by the registration station, which is next to the exit of The American Idol Experience. There's no charge to sign up, but you must have your children with you, and time slots are first-come, first-serve. On busy days the best times get taken before 10 a.m., and the entire day's worth of shows can fill up before noon. Children ages 4 to 12 can participate.

Tips. *When to go:* On hot days either early in the morning or late in the afternoon. Neither the stage nor viewing area is shaded. *Where to stand:* In front of the center of the stage. Most of the show plays to this spot, and the kids face it as they pose for a photo.

Fun finds. Notice how seriously the stormtroopers guard the children, as if the youngsters were an actual threat.

Key facts. *Best for:* Families. *Duration:* 30 minutes. *Capacity:* 15 children per show. *Queue:* Outdoor, unshaded. *Showtimes:* Scheduled performances; 13 to 15 shows daily. *Weather issues:* Cancelled during rain. *Debuted:* 2007. *Access:* Audience members may remain in wheelchairs, ECVs. Deaf children and children in wheelchairs may be in the show; participants must be able to follow instructions independently and hold a lightweight plastic light saber. *Sign-up location:* ABC Sound Studio. *Location:* Echo Lake.

Average wait times

9am	10am	11am	Noon	1pm	2pm	3pm	4pm	5pm	6pm	7pm	8pm	9pm
---	n/a	n/a	n/a	n/a	n/a	n/a	n/a	n/a	n/a	n/a	---	---

© Disney

Though Kermit says his show "will not stoop to any cheap 3-D tricks," Fozzie Bear soon guides a remote-control cream pie over its audience. The pie ends up, of course, on Fozzie's face.

Jim Henson's MuppetVision 3-D

Silly 3-D film entertains, despite two weak characters

★★★★ ✓ FastPass+ Chaos reigns as Kermit the Frog attempts to demonstrate the latest invention of Dr. Bunsen Honeydew in this 3-D movie, which showcases the inspired humor and attention to detail of the late Jim Henson. Miss Piggy stars in two musical numbers, both of which go haywire. In the process, guests get squirted with water, showered with bubbles and caught in a crossfire of cannonballs.

Though it also features two of Henson's least known, and least appealing, characters — Bean Bunny and Waldo C. Graphic — the attraction has a timeless charm. Digitally restored in 2010, both the film and its witty pre-show video are bright and clear. The pre-show takes place in a prop warehouse that's filled with real Muppet memorabilia.

Tips. *When to go:* In the middle of the day, when the lines are long at other attractions, and the cool theater will feel especially refreshing. *Where to sit:* In the center of a middle or back row. The film will be in great focus, and the 3-D effects will really pop. Avoid the first few rows. The film will seem blurry as the red and green images separate when viewed too closely, and some effects won't make sense without an audience in front of you. *For families:* Don't be afraid that your young children could be startled by the 3-D effects. Unlike some 3-D films, this one uses the technology to make you smile, not jump.

Key facts. *Best for:* Anyone ages 5 and up. *Duration:* 25 minutes including pre-show. *Capacity:* 584. *Queue:* Indoor, air-conditioned; also rarely used shaded outdoor area. *Fear factor:* The film has no startling or frightening images. *Debuted:* 1991, restored 2010. *Access:* Guests may remain in wheelchairs, ECVs. *Disability services:* Assistive listening, reflective and activated video captioning, Audio Description. *Location:* Streets of America.

Average wait times

9am	10am	11am	Noon	1pm	2pm	3pm	4pm	5pm	6pm	7pm	8pm	9pm
5m	5m	5m	5m	5m	5m	5m	5m	5m	5m	5m	5m	5m

A car jumps through fire in the finale of the Lights, Motors, Action! stunt show. Other high points include tightly choreographed chase scenes involving multiple cars and motorcycles.

Lights, Motors, Action

Loud automotive stunt show isn't worth your time

★ **FastPass+** Cars and motorcycles fly through the air—for a few seconds—in this loud outdoor stage show, as stunt drivers demonstrate how Hollywood chase scenes are created. Little boys will like it, as will fans of the 2002 movie "The Bourne Identity," from which much of the show is obviously inspired. Unfortunately you sit far from the action, and there are boring delays between each stunt. "Cars" star Lightning McQueen (a real car) appears during a silly bit with his friend Mater, who pops up on a video screen.

Tips. *When to go:* See the first show of the day, especially during the summer. Later shows often get rained out. Arrive about 30 minutes before showtime to get a decent seat. *Where to sit:* If you have a choice, take a center seat about 10 rows up. *For families:* Skip this one. It'll take over an hour of your time, and there's a good chance your kids will be fussy and bored during the bulk of the show. If you

do go, talk to your children about the gunplay in this show. It's casual, deadly and not played for laughs, and that deserves a conversation.

Fun finds. A background shop is the Cafe Fracas, the "restaurant of the noisy rumpus."

Hidden Mickeys. The shape is formed by a gear and two circular belts in a window of a motorcycle shop. A full-figure Mickey appears in the window of the Antiquites Brocante ("Secondhand Antiques") shop.

Key facts. *Best for:* Young boys. *Duration:* 33 minutes. *Capacity:* 5,000. *Queue:* Outdoor, shaded. *Fear factor:* Loud, with fire and simulated gunplay. At one point, a man appears to catch fire. *Showtimes:* Scheduled performances. Two to three shows daily. *Weather issues:* Cancelled during rain. *Debuted:* 2005, Disneyland Paris 2002. *Access:* Guests may remain in wheelchairs, ECVs. *Disability services:* Assistive listening. *Location:* Streets of America.

Average wait times

9am	10am	11am	Noon	1pm	2pm	3pm	4pm	5pm	6pm	7pm	8pm	9pm
---	n/a	n/a	n/a	n/a	n/a	n/a	n/a	n/a	---	---	---	---

Girls race around a huge can of Play-Doh in the "Honey, I Shrunk the Kids" playground. A cushy ground makes falls relatively painless. Other props include a huge, sneezing dog.

'Honey, I Shrunk the Kids' Playground

Small, dated play area has 'shrunken' decor that kids love

★★ Too cramped, too small, and too sweaty on hot days, this outdoor play space is nevertheless fun for young children, as it lets them pretend they're the size of bugs, wandering in a suburban backyard. Towering blades of grass shade climb-through ant tunnels and super-sized plants, insects and toys. Unfortunately, it's all packed into just a sliver of space, and is never updated. The playground is based on Disney's 1989 movie "Honey, I Shrunk the Kids," but children don't have to know the film's plot to enjoy it.

On most days the area stays pretty cool. Electric fans create a breeze, water areas spray and mist guests and, unlike the asphalt and concrete walkways everywhere else in the park, the playground's cushy floor doesn't retain heat. Water fountains are scattered throughout.

Tips. *When to go:* Late in the afternoon, ideally about a hour before sunset. Your children will be ready to burn off some energy. Use your morning for attractions that will be impossibly crowded later. *Other tips:* Photograph your kids with some of the props: a giant spiderweb, atop fiddlehead ferns, posing with a huge ant. Because of its many nooks and crannies, the playground makes it tough to keep track of your children. There's only one exit, however, and it's always monitored by a Disney cast member.

Fun finds. As you enter, look to your left for a leaky garden hose, which squirts water on unsuspecting heads. On the back wall a nose of a huge dog sniffs you, then sneezes.

Key facts. *Best for:* Young children. *Duration:* Allow 30 minutes. *Capacity:* 240, including parents. *Operating hours:* Park open–dusk. *Weather issues:* Closed during rain. *Debuted:* 1990. *Access:* Guests may remain in wheelchairs, ECVs. *Location:* Just off New York Street, Streets of America.

Average wait times

9am	10am	11am	Noon	1pm	2pm	3pm	4pm	5pm	6pm	7pm	8pm	9pm
0m	0m	0m	0m	0m	0m	0m	0m	0m	0m	0m	0m	0m

© Disney

An earthquake, fire and flood strike at the same time when your trams stop at Catastrophe Canyon, a display of old-fashioned special effects on the Studio Backlot Tour.

Studio Backlot Tour

Dated special-effects tour bores, insults, misleads

★ Though the Disney company shut down its Florida studio and its backlot years ago, it left this tram ride in place, which now does little more than circle a backstage parking lot. A dated pre-show features a pre-CGI water-effects presentation; a staged prop room has dusty set pieces, mostly from movies and television shows that few people remember (i.e., the sitcom "Dinosaurs"). It's not all bleak: the tram does pass a working costume and set shop (now used for Disney World purposes) and Walt Disney's personal jet from the 1960s, and it still stops at corny "Catastrophe Canyon," a fake disaster set that's at least still functioning.

The ride's best part is its exit, a museum-quality exhibit of props and memorabilia from classic movies. Most compelling is the "Titanic" display, which contains the safe from Cal's room, the ax Rose used to free Jack, his split handcuffs, Rose's dragonfly hair comb, Jack's art portfolio and pencil case and a life boat. The exhibit changes often; it's sponsored by the American Film Institute.

Tips. *When to go:* In the afternoon, when the line is short. *How to be in the pre-show:* Go first thing in the morning and tell a cast member at the ride's entrance. You'll play a Pearl Harbor seaman, and insult any vets in the crowd. *To see only the AFI exhibit:* Enter it from the sidewalk used for the ride's exit.

Key facts. *Best for:* Seniors. *Duration:* 30–40 minutes. *Capacity:* 1,000 per hour. *Queue:* Outdoor, covered. *Fear factor:* The pre-show has fake gunfire and torpedoes; Catastrophe Canyon has real fireballs and a brief flood. *Operating hours:* Park open–dusk. *Weather issues:* Closed during thunderstorms. *Debuted:* 1989, last revision 2011. *Access:* Guests may remain in wheelchairs, ECVs. *Disability services:* Closed captioning, hand-held captioning. *Location:* Streets of America.

Average wait times

9am	10am	11am	Noon	1pm	2pm	3pm	4pm	5pm	6pm	7pm	8pm	9pm
---	0m	20m	20m	20m	10m	20m	10m	10m	10m	20m	---	---

© Disney

A live host chats with Jake the Never Land Pirate during Disney Junior Live on Stage. The puppet show features stars from other Disney Junior shows too, including "Sofia the First."

Disney Junior Live on Stage

Disney World's best preschooler attraction delights families

★★★★★ FastPass+ In this lively puppet show, Mickey Mouse and other Disney Junior stars teach children how to solve everyday problems as the young audience bounces, dances and sings along. Updated in 2013, the current version features characters from "Mickey Mouse Clubhouse," "Doc McStuffins," "Jake and the Never Land Pirates" and "Sofia the First." The plot? When Mickey and his friends want to throw Minnie Mouse a surprise birthday party, they decide to hear stories from the other shows to get ideas, all of which involve teamwork.

Production values are the equal of any Disney show. The puppets have articulated faces, the sound is crisp, and hundreds of tiny overhead spotlights ensure everything is lit. Human host Casey addresses her young audience as equals, and bounces into the crowd to meet children face-to-face. A flat, carpeted floor makes it easy for kids to participate.

Tips. *When to go:* See the first show of the day. The crowd will be smallest of the day, and both the performers and the young crowd will be fresh. People with Fastpasses enter the theater first, and get the primo spots. *Where to sit:* In the middle of the theater, where young ones are close to the stage but can still see onto it. *Need a bathroom?* Doors at the far right of the theater lead to the restrooms of the Hollywood Brown Derby.

Fun facts. The stage has a hidden sliding walkway that allows the host to magically walk on the same floor as the puppets.

Key facts. *Best for:* Young children. *Duration:* 22 minutes. *Capacity:* 600. *Queue:* Outdoor, shaded. *Operating hours:* Eight to 12 scheduled performances daily. *Debuted:* 2001, last revision 2013. *Access:* Guests may remain in wheelchairs, ECVs. *Disability services:* Assistive listening; handheld and reflective captioning. *Location:* Animation Courtyard.

Average wait times

9am	10am	11am	Noon	1pm	2pm	3pm	4pm	5pm	6pm	7pm	8pm	9pm
n/a	n/a	n/a	n/a	n/a	n/a	n/a	n/a	---	---	---	---	---

© Disney

Guests learn how to draw Disney characters such as Tinker Bell with the help of a Disney animator in a 20-minute lesson inside The Magic of Disney Animation.

The Magic of Disney Animation

An engaging collection of games, exhibits and characters

★★★★ ✔ You'll learn how Disney develops an animated character, meet a few and then draw one yourself in this building, which contains a hodgepodge of exhibits and activities focused on Disney and Pixar animation. The highlight is an Animation Academy drawing lesson. Paper and pencil in front of you (but no eraser), you'll draw a particular Disney character as a live host provides step-by-step instructions. Best of all, you keep your sketch. Meet-and-greet characters include Mickey and Minnie Mouse, the stars of the film "The Incredibles" and Ralph and Vanellope from "Wreck-It Ralph."

Kiosks offer short video games for children, while display cases focus more on adult interests. One along the exitway holds the Oscar statuette Disney won for creating Mickey Mouse (1932) as well as the Oscar it received for the infamous Donald Duck World War II short "Der Fuehrer's Face" (1943).

Tips. *When to go:* Before 5 p.m. if you want to meet a character. *For families:* At the drawing lesson have your child do a sketch of a character, then get it signed by that character later in your visit.

Fun facts. The building is the former East Coast home of Disney Feature Animation, which created the movies "Mulan" (1998), "Lilo & Stitch" (2002), "Brother Bear" (2003) and "Home on the Range" (2004).

Key facts. *Best for:* Budding artists. *Duration:* Allow 45 minutes. *Capacity:* Animation Academy 50. *Queue:* Outdoor, covered. *Operating hours:* Animation Academy classes typically start at 10:30 a.m., and are offered every 30 minutes. *Debuted:* 1989, latest revision 2012. *Access:* Guests may remain in wheelchairs, ECVs. Lap boards available for drawing. *Disability services:* Reflective, video captioning, Audio Description. *Location:* Animation Courtyard.

Average wait times

9am	10am	11am	Noon	1pm	2pm	3pm	4pm	5pm	6pm	7pm	8pm	9pm
0m	5m	5m	10m	10m	10m	10m	10m	5m	5m	0m	0m	0m

"I want more!" Gadgets and gizmos aplenty, whosits and whatsits galore aren't enough for teenage Ariel in the stage show "Voyage of The Little Mermaid."

Voyage of the Little Mermaid

Stage show has talented singer, lively puppets, grainy video

★★★ ✓ **FastPass+** Sweet but not sappy, this indoor stage show tells an abridged version of Disney's 1989 movie "The Little Mermaid" with live performers, puppets and video clips. A misty high-tech theater creates the sensation of being underwater, as you watch a rollicking blacklight rendition of "Under the Sea," a Broadway-quality Ariel longing to be "Part of Your World" and Ursula the Sea Witch singing "Poor Unfortunate Souls." At the end the mermaid grows her gams and hugs her honey. The only downer: an abundance of large-screen video that is distinctly low-res.

Tips. *When to go:* Before noon or after dark. First thing in the morning the theater is usually only half full. *Where to sit:* In the center, two-thirds back from the stage. You'll see many cool effects on the theater's ceiling and walls. *For families:* Don't sit in the front three rows; small children can't see onto the elevated stage.

Fun find. A wooden replica of P.T. Barnum's 1842 "FeeJee Mermaid" hides in the waiting room above the theater's right entrance door as one of Ariel's treasures. Half dead monkey, half dried fish tail, Barnum's version "proved" that mermaids exist.

Fun fact. One of the show's original Ariels was Leanza Cornett, who went on to become the 1992 Miss Florida, the 1993 Miss America and a popular host of many television shows.

Key facts. *Best for:* Children, Ariel fans. *Duration:* 17 minutes. *Capacity:* 600. *Queue:* Outdoor, shaded; air-conditioned waiting room. *Fear factor:* Little ones are often scared by Ursula, a 12-foot-tall robotic octopus with glowing eyes. *Showtimes:* Continuous performances; shows typically start within an hour of park opening. *Debuted:* 1992. *Access:* Guests may remain in wheelchairs, ECVs. *Disability services:* Assistive listening, reflective captioning. *Location:* Animation Courtyard.

Average wait times

9am	10am	11am	Noon	1pm	2pm	3pm	4pm	5pm	6pm	7pm	8pm	9pm
0m	20m	25m	25m	30m	25m	20m	25m	25m	15m	20m	15m	10m

Just a few inches tall, a model boat awaits guests in the 1954 hand-built concept diorama for Disney's Jungle Cruise ride. The piece is often on display at Walt Disney: One Man's Dream.

Walt Disney: One Man's Dream

Biographical gallery has interesting artifacts adults will enjoy

★★★ There's not much for young children inside this serious multimedia gallery, but plenty for adults, especially those with an interest in history. A salute to the life and dreams of Walt Disney, it combines a straightforward short film with interesting memorabilia exhibits, the most unique of which include the wooden diorama he built in 1949 to test ideas for multiple-room theme-park attractions and his original Abraham Lincoln robot from the 1964 New York World's Fair, shown skinless except for its head and hands.

Also worth a look are a re-creation of his 1960 office, tabletop attraction models and a simulated television studio that shows Disney filming a video he used to interest investors in his ultimate dream of the Experimental Prototype Community of Tomorrow— the Florida project his successors developed as Walt Disney World.

Tips. *When to go:* During the hottest part of the day, when this calm, cool spot is especially refreshing. One Man's Dream is busiest during a sudden rain, when passersby duck inside. *For families:* Check out Walt's second-grade school desk; children will like how he carved his initials in it. *For young adults:* Watch the movie. Walt's own voice tells his story, which is surprisingly honest and moving.

Key facts. *Best for:* Adults, history buffs, Disney enthusiasts. *Duration:* Allow 35 minutes total, the movie is 16 minutes. *Capacity:* 200. *Operating hours:* Park hours; the movie plays continuously. *Debuted:* 2001, revised 2010. *Access:* Guests may remain in wheelchairs, ECVs. *Disability services:* Assistive listening, reflective and handheld captioning, Audio Description. *Location:* Behind the Great Movie Ride, just to the left of the Animation Courtyard.

Average wait times

9am	10am	11am	Noon	1pm	2pm	3pm	4pm	5pm	6pm	7pm	8pm	9pm
n/a	n/a	n/a	n/a	n/a	n/a	n/a	n/a	n/a	n/a	n/a	n/a	n/a

© Disney

The soundstage building that holds The Legend of Captain Jack Sparrow sports a large mural featuring the talking skull from the attraction.

The Legend of Captain Jack Sparrow

Dull video-effects demo has contrived 'interaction'

★ Even Johnny Depp can't save this lame special effects presentation, which makes you stand in a room and "interact" with pre-recorded video. Supposedly you're there to help ward off the dangers of the Caribbean, but actually all you do is watch an elaborate promo piece for Disney's "Pirates of the Caribbean" franchise. Just when all seems lost — the giant kraken is poised to kill, murderous mermaids are ready to attack, Davy Jones vows to send you to his locker, your inner goddess is about to cut loose with an embarrassing "Why is this so dull!" scream—you (and a few dozen or so other guests) save the day by stomping your feet, raising your arms, or doing some other remarkably easy and childish activity that anyone can do, and few visitors bother with.

The best effect by far is an impressive appearance by Captain Jack himself, a synchronized series of sounds, video projections and separate supporting shadows that could trick that inner goddess of yours into believing Johnny Depp himself is actually in the room with you. Alas, he's not.

Say it with me: Aargh.

Cynics will note that you never do learn of any "legend" of Captain Jack Sparrow.

Tips. *When to go:* Early to avoid a long wait on outdoor pavement. *Where to stand:* Up front for the best view.

Key facts. *Best for:* Johnny Depp fans. *Duration:* 8 minutes. *Capacity:* 200. *Queue:* Outdoor, covered. *Fear factor:* Young children may be frightened by the dark, as well as by a creepy talking skull on a wall, simulated gunfire and many threatening video moments. *Debuted:* 2012. *Access:* Guests may remain in wheelchairs, ECVs. *Disability services:* Handheld captioning, Audio Description. *Location:* Next to Walt Disney: One Man's Dream.

Average wait times

9am	10am	11am	Noon	1pm	2pm	3pm	4pm	5pm	6pm	7pm	8pm	9pm
0m	25m	30m	30m	35m	30m	25m	30m	30m	20m	25m	20m	10m

Riders wear 3-D glasses as they travel through Toy Story Mania, a series of virtual shooting arcades. The game take place in the "Toy Story" world, under Andy's bed.

Toy Story Mania

Quick 3-D midway games are easy to play, tough to master

★★★★ ✓ **FastPass+** It's not worth waiting in line for hours on end, but this series of virtual midway games is certainly fun. You don 3-D glasses and then sit side-by-side with a partner in a moving vehicle, stopping in front of each game for about 45 seconds. Using what appears to be a pull-string toy cannon, you'll pitch baseballs at flying plates, shoot darts at dinosaur balloons, even hurl eggs at scurrying animals. Although firing the cannon exhausts your hand, the games are easy to play and rewarding whether you score high or low. When you hit an object, the illusion is often enhanced by a real blast of air or spritz of water. The games are hosted by an assortment of "Toy Story" characters, including Woody and Buzz Lightyear.

The standby queue winds past a huge robotic Mr. Potato Head, who interacts with people in line thanks to a wealth of phrases pre-recorded by the voice of the character, comedian Don Rickles. He occasionally sings a song, or takes off his hat or ear.

Tips. *When to go:* Immediately after the park opens; anytime with a Fastpass. *For families:* A small child can ride on your lap as long as his or her legs fit under the lap bar.

Hidden Mickey. In the boarding area on a wall mural, as frames on the box this "toy"—a "Toy Story Midway Games Playset"—came in.

Key facts. *Best for:* Children, teenagers, adults. *Duration:* 7 minutes (game play 5 minutes). *Capacity:* 108 (2 per vehicle). *Queue:* Indoor, overflows into uncovered outdoor area. *Restraint:* Lap bar. *Debuted:* 2008, revised 2010. *Health advisory:* Vehicles move in a jerky, funhouse fashion. *Access:* Offline loading area for disabled guests, into vehicles equipped with guns that have buttons as well as pull strings. ECV users must transfer. *Disability services:* Closed captioning. *Location:* Pixar Place.

Average wait times

9am	10am	11am	Noon	1pm	2pm	3pm	4pm	5pm	6pm	7pm	8pm	9pm
30m	75m	80m	80m	60m	55m	65m	65m	65m	50m	50m	65m	45m

You've got a friend in... your partner!

BY MICAELA NEAL There are three keys to getting a high score on Toy Story Mania: Shoot constantly (your cannon can fire six objects per second), know where the high-value targets are, and... teamwork! To get a top score, work together with the person sitting next to you. That way, the two of you can hit multiple targets simultaneously, which will reveal hidden levels of the game.

GAME BOOTH	HIGH-VALUE INITIAL TARGETS	HOW TO REVEAL BONUS TARGETS
HAMM AND EGGS	❶ In the doorway of the barn is a 500-point horse. ❷ The green ducks in the lake are also 500 points. ❸ A 500-point squirrel runs up both the left and right edges of the screen. ❹ Three gophers repeatedly pop up along the bottom. The brown gophers are worth 500 points; the gray ones 1000 points. ❺ The animals in the tree are 1000 points each. A 1000-point goat peers out of the barn window. A 1000-point mouse skitters along the barn's roof.	❶ Hit the mouse (see Tip No. 5 at left) and the barn will rotate to reveal its interior, which is filled with 2000-point rats. Hit every barn rat and more rats appear in the grass as 1000-point targets. ❷ Hit the fox on top of the henhouse (in the bottom left corner of the screen) and three hens will scurry out. The first is worth 1000 points; the second is worth 2000 points; the third 1000 points. ❸ Hit the 500-point donkey that walks along the hills and the animal will turn and run the other way as a 2000-point target.
REX AND TRIXIE'S DINO DARTS	❶ 500-point targets are in the lava streams of the volcano, on dinosaur eggs at the bottom left, held by two red dinosaurs at the bottom center and tied onto a blue stegosaurus and red raptors in the back. ❷ A blue dinosaur on the right chews 1000-point targets, others are tied to a pink brontosaurus in the background. ❸ Pterodactyls hang from the sky with 500- and 1000-point targets.	**Team up with your partner** to hit the lava flows until the volcano erupts. Then hit the two meteors on the left and right of the volcano three times each (the last two meteors, worth 500 points each, must be hit within one second of each other). This will cause three large comets (spheres formed by 1000-point balloons) to crash into the screen.
GREEN ARMY MEN SHOOT CAMP	❶ Helicopters hover with plates worth 1000 points. Other 1000-point plates appear within the mass of plates, while more are carried by trucks along the bottom. ❷ Airplanes tow plates worth 2000 points. Others are tossed up on either side of the mountain.	**Team up with your partner** to simultaneously hit the two 2000-point plates that are tossed up from the sides of the mountain (see note at left) at the same time. Doing so will open the mountain and reveal a tank that shoots plates toward you worth 5000 points each.
BUZZ LIGHTYEAR'S FLYING TOSSERS	❶ Meteors near the sides of the screen are 500 points. ❷ Rockets are 1000 points. ❸ Jetpack aliens are worth 2000 points. ❹ Aliens at the top corners of the screen are 5000 points.	**Team up with your partner** to simultaneously hoop all of the aliens in the large central rocket to launch the rocket and reveal a huge robot. When the robot's mouth opens, toss rings into it to score—if you reveal the robot early enough—up to 2000 points per toss.
WOODY'S ROOTIN' TOOTIN' SHOOTIN' GALLERY	All initial targets are worth 100 points each.	❶ Each 100-point target triggers a series of bonus targets worth up to 1000 points each. ❷ As your vehicle moves from screen 1 to 2 (or from screen 2 to the Woody's Bonus Roundup screen), hit two 100-point or 500-point targets close together to reveal a 2000-point target.
WOODY'S BONUS ROUNDUP	The second-to-last mine cart on each track is always worth 2000 points.	❶ Hit 1000-point targets above the carts by two bats to awake them and reveal 5000-point targets. ❷ Hit all of the carts on a track and the last one will be worth 5000 points. ❸ The final target is worth 2000 points if you hit it often enough.

A colorful stage musical, Beauty and the Beast Live on Stage retells Disney's version of the famous fairy tale. Above, spoons-turned-chefs welcome Belle to dinner in "Be Our Guest."

Beauty and the Beast Live on Stage

Timeless stage show is as lovely as ever despite its age

★★★★★ ✓ FastPass+ As good as ever after more than two decades of performances, this lavish stage show re-creates the spirit of Disney's 1991 movie by focusing on its musical numbers. Choreographed productions of "Belle," "Gaston," "Be Our Guest," "Something There," "The Mob Song" and the title song, "Beauty and the Beast," are thoroughly entertaining, as they form a condensed account of the tale as old as time. While Belle and villain Gaston sing live, other characters rely on pre-recorded audio from the film. Like the movie, the show manages to be both funny and touching, and is a visual delight. Colorful costumes and creative lighting lend a true theatrical feel.

The supporting cast is a delight by itself. Portraying villagers and castle attendants, unheralded performers faint, fight, jump, kick, swoon, twirl and waltz, often with skill usually seen only in Broadway performances.

Outside the theater, 30 television stars have left handprints in an entrance plaza. "Star Trek's" Scotty, James Doohon, added "Beam Me Up." "Jeopardy" host Alex Trebek wrote "Who is Alex Trebek?" (Similar handprints of movie stars are in the plaza of The Great Movie Ride.)

Tips. *When to go:* See the first show of the day; it's generally the least crowded. During the summer avoid shows after noon; the theater is covered but otherwise open to heat, humidity and blowing rain. *Where to sit:* As close to front-row center as you can. This means getting a Fastpass, as this area is set aside for Fastpass holders until right before the show starts. You'll see every expression on the performers' faces, details such as the sequins on the ball gowns, and be able to fully enjoy the show's many symmetrical dance numbers. *While you wait:* There's no pre-show, but unlike most Disney theaters,

Average wait times

9am	10am	11am	Noon	1pm	2pm	3pm	4pm	5pm	6pm	7pm	8pm	9pm
---	n/a	n/a	n/a	n/a	n/a	n/a	n/a	n/a	n/a	---	---	---

At right, village girls dismiss the "most peculiar mademoiselle." Below, Gaston explains how "it's not right for a woman to read" and later villagers rally to "kill the beast!" as they prepare to storm the castle.

this one allows you to bring in food, and return and come back to your seat as often as you wish before showtime. If you get there early enough, and if someone in your group can hold your seat, consider leaving to take a restroom break, or even to bring back food. Decent barbecue and hand-scooped ice cream is sold at the Sunset Ranch Market, which is right out in front. *For families:* Talk with your children afterward about the strong message of the story, which is that what matters about a person is what they are like inside, not how they look. *For birthday girls:* If you have a little girl celebrating a birthday, she may be able to get a velvety faux rose presented to her by Belle and the prince at the end of the show. Talk with a cast member at the show entrance ahead of time, preferably in the morning, to set this up.

Fun finds. Keep an eye on Gaston, especially during the "Belle" and "Gaston" songs. He struts onstage, makes the village girls swoon and admires himself in any reflection he can find. After the finale, when the whole cast comes onstage to bow, he stays perfectly in character, often flexing his biceps as he winks and flashes the "call me" sign at female members of the crowd... The show begins with a pun: a ringing bell... The Theater of the Stars stage arch resembles the one at the famous Hollywood Bowl in Los Angeles. It lights up during some of the songs.

Fun fact. "The Mob Song" includes a quote from Shakespeare. As he rallies villagers to kill the Beast, Gaston commands "Screw your courage to the sticking place," the phrase Lady MacBeth uses to urge her husband to kill Duncan.

Key facts. *Best for:* Anyone ages 5 and up. *Duration:* 25 minutes. *Capacity:* 1,500. *Queue:* Outdoor, unshaded. *Fear factor:* Little ones may be disturbed during the ominous "Mob Song" and just afterward when Gaston stabs the Beast. The violence is not graphic. *Showtimes:* Scheduled performances; five or six shows daily, typically starting at either 10:15 a.m. or 11:30 a.m. *Weather issues:* If it's raining, bring your umbrella or poncho if you plan to get there early. The waiting area is simply a sidewalk. *Debuted:* 1991, latest revision 2001. *Access:* Guests may remain in wheelchairs, ECVs. *Disability services:* Assistive listening, Audio Description. *Location:* Sunset Boulevard.

An upside-down vintage Cadillac—mounted on a headstock of an electric guitar—tops off the entrance gate to G-Force Records and Rock 'n' Roller Coaster Starring Aerosmith.

Rock 'n' Roller Coaster Starring Aerosmith

Thrilling dark coaster highlighted by rocketing launch

★★★★★ ✓ FastPass+ You'll be livin' it up while you're upside down on this indoor roller coaster, which features an intense launch, two inversions and the music of Aerosmith. The seminal rock band is the focus of the attraction's storyline, appears in both a pre-show and post-show video, and created a custom soundtrack for the ride by redoing some of its biggest hits to give them a roller-coaster theme— "Love in an Elevator" becomes "Love in a Roller Coaster." The idea is that you're touring a Hollywood music company ("G Force Records"), meet Aerosmith as it's finishing up a new take on one of its classic songs ("Walk This Way"), and get backstage passes to one of the band's concert. Trouble is, the show's about to start, so the only way to see it is to take a really fast car—a vintage Cadillac convertible.

The resulting ride through a Los Angeles night is a half mile of twists and turns. The most intense moment is at the very beginning, when Aerosmith lead singer Steven Tyler screams out a countdown to a rubber-burning start that rockets you from 0 to 57 mph in just 2.8 seconds.

The trip slows a little after that, but anybody who enjoys thrill rides will still love it.

Tips. *When to go:* During the first hour; you'll be able to ride it again before the hour's up. Later, use the single-rider line or get a Fastpass. Note: the single-rider line is often closed. *Where to sit:* For the most intense launch, ask for the front row. It will only add a couple of minutes to your wait, and it's worth it for its great view and most surprising ride (front-row passengers never know what scenery is coming up, as it lights

Average wait times

9am	10am	11am	Noon	1pm	2pm	3pm	4pm	5pm	6pm	7pm	8pm	9pm
5m	20m	70m	70m	40m	40m	40m	30m	30m	30m	50m	40m	40m

A 40-foot guitar graces the ride's entrance facade. Below, the lobby's rotunda uses guitar necks as its columns. Leaving the building through a back door, riders board their "stretch limos" in a dingy parking garage.

up just before they get to it). Riders with long legs should ask for an odd-numbered row; those seats have far more legroom. Guests who use the single-rider line are not allowed to choose their seat. *For families:* Your child shouldn't be afraid to ride; the coaster starts fast but is always very smooth. Though children may have no idea who Aerosmith is, that won't diminish their fun. The thrills stand on their own. *Other tips:* In the pre-show room, stand to the left to be first in line when the door opens.

Fun finds. Put your ear to the doors in the queue marked "Studio A" or "Studio B" and you will hear Aerosmith rehearsing. Limo license plates sport messages such as 2FAST4U and H8TRFFC.

Hidden Mickeys. As cables on the floor of the recording studio.

Fun facts. Unlike most roller coasters, Rock 'n' Roller Coaster doesn't start off with a lift hill and doesn't rely on gravity for its power. Instead it starts flat, its trip powered by a linear-induction system imbedded in its track. Vehicles move by being quickly pushed away from, and pulled to, a sequential series of electromagnets. A similar, if more

basic, system powers Magic Kingdom's PeopleMover ride… You experience 4.5 G just after the launch as you enter the first inversion, more force than astronauts experienced on Space Shuttle launches.

When Disney chose Aerosmith as the band for the attraction, initially the company couldn't reach frontmen Steven Tyler and Joe Perry. Unbeknownst to Disney, the two were vacationing with their families at the time… at Walt Disney World.

Key facts. *Best for:* Children, teenagers, adults. *Duration:* 1 minute 22 seconds. *Capacity:* 120; five 24-seat vehicles seated two across. *Queue:* Indoor, air-conditioned; overflows into shaded outdoor area. *Single-rider line:* Often available. *Fear factor:* Very fast start, darkness, speed. *Restraint:* Shoulder harness. *Top speed:* 57 mph. *Track:* Standard steel, 3,403 feet, maximum height 80 feet. *Debuted:* 1999. *Health advisories:* Guests should be free from motion sickness; pregnancy; high blood pressure; heart, back or neck problems. *Access:* Height minimum 48 inches. Wheelchair and ECV users must transfer. *Location:* Next to The Twilight Zone Tower of Terror, Sunset Boulevard.

Guests enter The Tower of Terror through the grounds of the Hollywood Tower Hotel. Supposedly abandoned since 1939, the hotel has a "Keep Out" sign on its gate.

The Twilight Zone Tower of Terror

Disney's best thrill ride randomizes drops, psychs you out

★★★★★ ✓ **FastPass+** You plummet and soar over and over again, up and down 130 feet aboard a pitch-black freight elevator in this fully realized thrill ride. Both the falls and lifts are unpredictable, as the sequence is randomly selected by a computer. Loaded with special effects and superb detailing, the ride appeals to nearly everyone except those with an intense fear of falling.

But it's way more than a drop tower—the entire attraction works as one seamless experience, all of it designed to freak you out. It's set in what appears to be an abandoned hotel, covered in cobwebs and stuffed with strange artifacts from episodes of the 1960s television series "The Twilight Zone." The queue snakes through a spooky library and an unwelcoming basement boiler room. The rusty elevator creaks as its doors shut. And the ride itself is filled with creepy images and just the right amount of perfectly timed… silence.

'In tonight's episode…' Meant to recall the eerie style of "The Twilight Zone," the attraction is even more fun if you know its story. According to Disney lore, the extravagant 12-story Hollywood Tower Hotel opened in 1917 as a gathering place for Tinseltown elite. Two decades later, on Oct. 31, 1939, the hotel hosted a Halloween party in its rooftop lounge. At precisely 8:05 p.m. a huge lightning bolt hit the building, dematerializing two elevator shafts and the wings they supported. Among the victims were five people in an elevator: a child actress with her nanny, a young Hollywood couple and a bellhop.

The hotel stood deserted for decades, but now has mysteriously reopened, just in time for your visit. As you arrive to check in, a bellhop asks you to wait in the library, where as the power goes out a black-and-white television somehow comes on—and shows the beginning of a "Twilight Zone" episode.

Average wait times

9am	10am	11am	Noon	1pm	2pm	3pm	4pm	5pm	6pm	7pm	8pm	9pm
10m	20m	30m	30m	30m	30m	20m	20m	20m	10m	30m	10m	20m

According to Disney lore, the Hollywood Tower Hotel lost its front wings during a lightning strike, and has been closed ever since.

© Disney

Riders sit in a falling hotel service elevator on The Twlight Zone Tower of Terror. Then they're jerked up again, and fall a second time, a third, maybe even a fourth. Each ride has an unpredictable pattern.

As host Rod Serling describes a "somewhat unique" story about a maintenance service elevator, he adds, "we invite you, if you dare, to step aboard, because in tonight's episode, you are the star."

Boarding the hotel's service elevator, you travel past strange images as you journey to a mysterious 13th floor. After your elevator cab unexpectedly moves forward, its doors slam shut and soon it is tossed—violently—up, down—down, up—up, up, down.

Every ride is different. Occasionally other doors open, revealing the open sky and the theme park down below. Sometimes those five victims from 1939 appear again. Sometimes there's rain, or an odd smell. After about a minute the madness stops, and you calmly arrive… in the hotel basement.

Tips. *When to go:* First thing in the morning, or at night. *Where to sit:* For the most unobstructed view of all the special effects, ask to sit in the center of your elevator's front row. As you line up at the boarding area, that's the last spot in Row 2. *For families:* If your child is a little uneasy about riding but still wants to go, have her sit at the end of one of the rows (in the boarding area, the first spot in any of the six rows). She'll be against a wall and have a handle to hold onto.

Fun find. As you exit the attraction, look back at the gift shop's windows. They're still decorated for 1939's Halloween.

Hidden Mickey. The little girl in the library video holds a 1930s Mickey Mouse doll.

Key facts. *Best for:* Teenagers, adults. *Duration:* 4 minutes. *Capacity:* 84 (four 21-seat elevators). *Queue:* Indoor, air-conditioned; overflows into shaded outdoor queue. *Fear factor:* This is one scary ride. Although its ascents and drops are smooth, Disney's mind games are intense, especially for younger riders who have never been in such a believable artificial environment. When the elevator cab stops moving, gets dark and quiet and then JUST SITS THERE for a moment, even some adults find the tension hard to bear. *Restraint:* Seat belt. *Debuted:* 1994, last revision 2002. *Health advisories:* Guests should be free from motion sickness; pregnancy; high blood pressure; heart, back or neck problems. *Access:* Height minimum 40 inches. Wheelchair and ECV users must transfer. *Disability services:* Handheld captioning. *Location:* Sunset Boulevard.

Mickey Mouse wields a magical sword in the evening spectacle Fantasmic. Using a variety of scenes and many Disney characters, the multimedia show tells a story of good versus evil.

Fantasmic

Kitschy spectacle offers an eye-popping way to cap your day

★★★ **FastPass+** Held in a large open-air amphitheater, this lavish, confusing evening spectacle includes boats, cannons, characters, fireworks, fountains, laser beams, music, smoke, water screens and before you can say "great balls of fire!" one of those, too. It tells a story of good versus evil, as Mickey Mouse has a dream that turns into a nightmare. Most action takes place on a 60-foot-tall mountain that's ringed by a narrow lagoon.

Highlights include flowers and animals that dance to "I Just Can't Wait to be King" (from 1994's "The Lion King"), Englishmen who "dig up Virginia" for Gov. Ratcliffe (1995's "Pocahontas"), a fiery dragon that ignites the lagoon with its breath (1959's "Sleeping Beauty") and a now-you-see-him, now-you-don't, now-you-do-again Mickey farewell.

Fantasmic usually plays only a few times a week, but often twice a night. During busy periods the first show often fills to capacity.

A snack bar sells hot dogs and other snacks. Souvenir hawkers roam the stands.

Tips. *When to go:* If there are two shows, see the second one; it will be much less crowded. You can arrive about 30 minutes early and still get a good seat. If you go to the first show, arrive an hour early. *Where to sit:* As close to front row center as possible. Note that the front few rows often get misted with water. If you get a FastPass you'll be guaranteed a seat just left of center.

Key facts. *Best for:* Disney enthusiasts. *Duration:* 25 minutes. *Capacity:* 9,900 (6,900 seats). *Queue:* Outdoor, uncovered. *Fear factor:* Loud noises, bright flashes, scary villains, fiery water. *Weather issues:* Cancelled during rain. *Debuted:* 1998 (Disneyland 1992). *Access:* Guests may remain in wheelchairs, ECVs. *Disability services:* Assistive listening, reflective captioning. *Location:* Sunset Boulevard.

Average wait times

9am	10am	11am	Noon	1pm	2pm	3pm	4pm	5pm	6pm	7pm	8pm	9pm
n/a	n/a	n/a	n/a	n/a	n/a	n/a	n/a	n/a	n/a	n/a	n/a	n/a

Disney's Animal Kingdom

Nature lovers will adore this sophisticated theme park. Themed to animals and their environments, its attractions include a roller coaster through the Himalayas, stage shows based on two of Disney's best animal-themed movies, and a truck ride into a wildlife savanna. The park is also a zoo, with 250 species of exotic animals displayed in lush natural habitats. Many are either endangered or the biggest, smallest or most colorful of their kind.

The only Disney World theme park that's less than 25 years old, Animal Kingdom has no wide expanses of concrete, cheesy fast-food spots, aging restrooms or embarrassingly dated attractions. In the 2014 TripAdvisor Travelers' Choice Awards, it was rated the sixth best amusement park in the United States, one spot behind California's Disneyland, one spot ahead of Orlando's SeaWorld.

Accredited by the Association of Zoos and Aquariums, the park conducts animal research and breeds endangered species. It's the most popular zoo in the United States.

Best of the park

Kilimanjaro Safaris. A giraffe—or a rhino, or an ostrich—may come right up to your truck on this open-air ride, as you meander through 110 acres of simulated African habitat brimming with free-roaming animals.

The gorillas. Just 10 feet away from their human onlookers, two groups of gorillas look at you with eyes and expressions that are oh-so-human. One's a family, with a massive silverback, motherly females and wrestling youngsters; the other is a lively bachelor troupe.

The slower pace. The self-guided nature of the park's many animal attractions slows down your day and invites you to relax.

The shows. Festival of the Lion King invigorates you with acrobatic acts, a fire dancer,

Facing page: Disney's Animal Kingdom celebrates the beauty, magnificence and importance of the animal world.

wildly creative costumes and great music. Finding Nemo: The Musical re-imagines the beloved Pixar film in song, using huge puppets and live singers.

The coaster. With an unexpected backward plunge followed by an 80-foot drop, Expedition Everest takes you into and out of the Himalayan mountain range as you encounter an angry Yeti.

Worst of the park

The walking. It's a half-mile from the front of Animal Kingdom to the back of it, and a half-mile from the left side of the park to the right. Attractions are often far apart, with large gaps of open space between them. Altogether the park covers 500 acres, five times that of Magic Kingdom.

The heat. Since the park has few indoor attractions, you spend a lot of time outside. This can be challenging between April and October, when the weather is especially hot and humid.

The lack of rides. There are six, the same as Disney's Hollywood Studios. Epcot has 10, Magic Kingdom 23.

The lack of table-service restaurants. There are only three, and one of those is outside the front gate. Hollywood Studios has five, Magic Kingdom six, Epcot 17.

Getting oriented. Animal Kingdom is divided into six themed areas:

Oasis. With shady walkways that connect the park's entrance gate to its central hub, this tropical strip is bordered by fascinating creatures in natural habitats.

Discovery Island. The hub of the park is a lush circle wrapped by a river. It surrounds its icon, the huge Tree of Life, which is covered with interwoven animal carvings. Discovery Island is home to most of the park's restaurants and shops, each of which decorated in a creative, colorful Caribbean theme.

Africa. The largest section of Animal Kingdom, Africa is home to the mythical East African port town of Harambe. Appearing worn and weathered from decades of rain

Animal Kingdom's Discovery River meanders through the park. Above, a footbridge connects the land of Asia (left) to Discovery Island.

and sand storms, it represents an old gold and ivory trading post struggling to establish a new economy based on ecotourism.

Asia. Also wrestling with economic and environmental issues, this land is comprised of the kingdom of Anandapur and its mountainside village of Serka Zong.

DinoLand U.S.A. This tongue-in-cheek land's Dino Institute pokes fun at the stuffiness of 1970s scientists, while its adjacent DinoRama takes on tacky roadside tourist traps and traveling carnivals.

Rafiki's Planet Watch. A train takes you from Africa to this conservation-oriented land, which includes the park's working veterinary facility, animal- and nature-focused exhibits and a petting zoo.

If it rains. With its large size and many outdoor attractions, Disney's Animal Kingdom makes it tough to ignore the weather. No ride or show closes due to rain alone, but the Flights of Wonder bird show can be changed and shortened. Roller coasters Expedition Everest and Primeval Whirl temporarily close when lightning is in the area, as does The Boneyard playground, Kali River Rapids, TriceraTop Spin and the walking trails in Africa and Asia. Ironically, Kilimanjaro Safaris trips are actually better in the rain, as its savanna animals are usually more active.

Family matters. All of the park's thrill rides have height minimums—40 inches for Dinosaur, 44 inches for Expedition Everest, 38 inches for Kali River Rapids and 48 inches for Primeval Whirl. The park offers one character meal, available for breakfast and lunch: Donald's Safari Dining at Africa's Tusker House, with Donald Duck, Daisy Duck, Mickey Mouse and Goofy. Wilderness Explorers offers hands-on activities that are especially fun for kids, who can earn badges at 31 stations spread throughout the park.

Fun finds. Disney really paid attention to detail in this park, creating environments filled with extra touches. Some examples:

Africa. The sounds of residents of a boarding house sometimes can be heard behind the back door of the Tusker House restaurant. Sometimes there's knocking on a door: a landlady trying to collect back rent.

Asia. Each Anandapur business displays a tax license featuring the fictional kingdom's king and queen. The bigger the license, the more taxes that business pays.

DinoLand U.S.A. To the right of the gift shop Chester & Hester's Dinosaur Treasures, two baby dinosaurs hide underneath the Cementosaurus folk-art sculpture. One is hatching. Four hanging signs above the Dinosaur Treasures entrance read, from

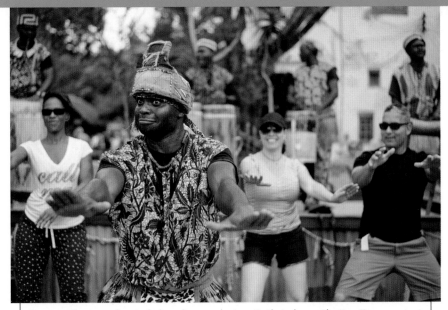

Street performers often include audience volunteers in their shows. The Tam Tam Drummers of Harambe teach guests African dances, usually without saying a word.

one direction, "When in Florida... Be sure to... Visit... Epcot." Ambient music includes bone-themed country songs (played on radio station "W-BONE") such as "I Like Bananas Because They Have No Bones," a 1935 ditty by the Hoosier Hot Shots. Archeological and dinosaur references abound in the Restaurantosaurus fast-food eatery. Among the best: The shapes formed by greasy hand prints on the walls of the Quonset hut; the cans of Sinclair Litholine Multi-Purpose Grease and Dynoil ("keep your old dinosaur running") on the shelves of that room; the song titles in the Hip Joint rec room juke box (such as "Dust in the Wind"); posters in that room for bands Dinosaur Jr. and T Rex; and the ambient music, which includes the 1988 Was Not Was hit "Walk the Dinosaur."

Hidden Mickeys. The iconic three-circle head-and-ears silhouette of Mickey Mouse can be found throughout the park:

Africa. In Harambe, as a large shape of gray pavement behind the Fruit Market. As a drain cover (marked with a "D") and two ear-shaped pebble groupings, to the left of the main entrance to Mombasa Marketplace, across from Tusker House. As another drain cover (this one with the letter "S") and two pebble groupings in front of Tamu Tamu Refreshments, facing Discovery Island.

DinoLand U.S.A. As cracks in the asphalt parking lot next to the Cementosaurus, to the right of Dinosaur Treasures. On a Steamboat Willie cast member pin on the right of the fourth back hump on the Cementosaurus. As small black scales on the back of the hadrosaur at the start of the Cretaceous Trail.

Discovery Island. In the Pizzafari restaurant, as an orange firefly in the nocturnal room, to the left of a large tiger, behind a frog.

Know before you go. Need cash? A stroller? Help understanding your MyMagic MagicBand Fastpass+ Disney Guest Tracking Experience? Here's where to find it:

ATMs. The park has two: There's one right at the entrance on the right, another outside the Dinosaur Treasures gift shop.

Baby Care Center. Situated behind the Creature Comforts store on Discovery Island (just before the bridge to Africa), this indoor spot has changing rooms, nursing areas, a microwave and a playroom. It sells diapers, formula, pacifiers and over-the-counter meds.

FastPass+ kiosks. Trained cast members help you book and reschedule Fastpasses at these walk-up touchscreens. Look for them on Discovery Island at the Island Mercantile and Disney Outfitters shops, in Africa at the entrance to the Kilimanjaro Safaris ride and in Asia at the entrance to Kali River Rapids.

© Disney

Animal Kingdom is currently undertaking the largest expansion in its history, scheduled to be complete in 2017. A nighttime spectacle, "Rivers of Light" (above) promises live music, floating lanterns and water screens. Replacing the park's Camp Minnie Mickey land, a new area (below) will bring to life the world of Pandora seen in the 2009 movie "Avatar."

© Disney

© Disney

The towering Tree of Life serves as the park's icon. A fantastical African baobab, it symbolizes the grandeur of nature and embodies the idea that all life is interconnected.

First aid. An indoor clinic is behind the Creature Comforts shop next to the Baby Care Center. Registered nurses treat minor emergencies. They call EMTs for serious issues.

Guest Relations. Located at the entrance to the park on the left, this office has walk-up windows outside the gate, a walk-in lobby just inside. Cast members answer general questions, make dining reservations, exchange currency, hand out maps and times guides for all Disney World parks, and store items found in the park that day.

Locker rentals. They're inside the park next to Guest Relations ($7 a day, $5 deposit).

MyMagic+ Service Center. Inside the Creature Comforts shop, cast members answer questions about MyMagic+ services: the My Disney Experience website and app, the MagicBand ticketing system and the FastPass+ attraction-reservation service.

Package pickup. Anything you buy in the park can be sent to the park entrance for you to pick up later at no charge. Allow three hours. Packages can also be delivered to Disney hotels or shipped nationally.

Parking. $17 a day per car. Free for Disney hotel guests and annual passholders.

Stroller rentals. Just inside the park entrance on the right, Garden Gate Gifts rents single strollers for $15 a day ($13 length of stay), doubles for $31 ($27 length of stay). Get replacements at Mombasa Marketplace.

Disney transportation. Buses serve all Disney resorts and theme parks and Blizzard Beach; but there's no direct service to Downtown Disney, Typhoon Lagoon or ESPN Wide World of Sports.

Wheelchair and scooter rentals. Garden Gate Gifts rents wheelchairs for $12 a day ($10 length of stay). EVCs are $50 ($20 deposit).

Micaela Neal

Animals stand, sit or perch only a few feet from guests at natural habitats throughout the park. This scarlet macaw makes the Oasis its home.

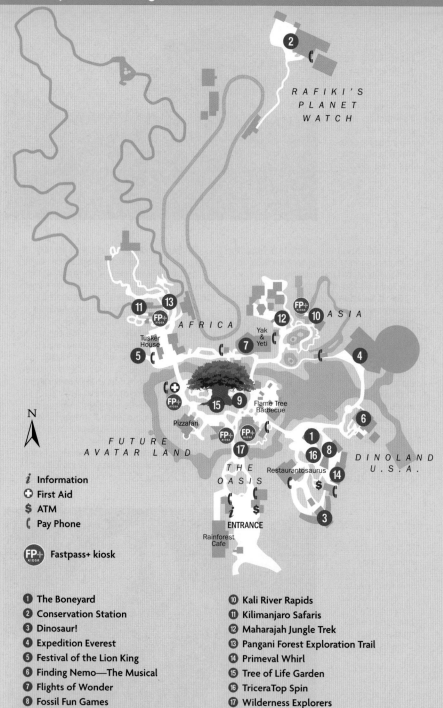

RAFIKI'S
PLANET
WATCH

AFRICA

ASIA

Tusker House

Yak & Yeti

Flame Tree Barbecue

Pizzafari

FUTURE AVATAR LAND

DINOLAND U.S.A.

Restaurantosaurus

THE OASIS

ENTRANCE

Rainforest Cafe

N

i Information
✚ First Aid
$ ATM
(Pay Phone

FP+ KIOSK Fastpass+ kiosk

1 The Boneyard
2 Conservation Station
3 Dinosaur!
4 Expedition Everest
5 Festival of the Lion King
6 Finding Nemo—The Musical
7 Flights of Wonder
8 Fossil Fun Games
9 It's Tough to Be a Bug!

10 Kali River Rapids
11 Kilimanjaro Safaris
12 Maharajah Jungle Trek
13 Pangani Forest Exploration Trail
14 Primeval Whirl
15 Tree of Life Garden
16 TriceraTop Spin
17 Wilderness Explorers

Attractions at a Glance

There aren't many rides, but there's plenty to do, including seeing two terrific live shows. Here's a quick look at the attractions at Disney's Animal Kingdom, each of which is reviewed in detail later in this chapter. The Fastpass+ logo (FastPass+) appears if the attraction can be reserved in advance. A checkmark (✓) indicates an author favorite.

Five-star attractions

The Boneyard. ★★★★★ Dig-site playground has climbing zone, slides, sand pit and tunnels. Kids can trigger dinosaur roars and other special effects. DinoLand U.S.A.

Expedition Everest. ★★★★★ ✓ FastPass+ This indoor-outdoor roller coaster is a runaway train which speeds into and out of a mountain, goes backward and zooms past an angry yeti. Smooth ride, high lift, one curving steep drop. Height minimum 44 inches. Asia.

Festival of the Lion King. ★★★★★ ✓ FastPass+ Rousing in-the-round musical revue includes acrobats, fire-baton twirler, flying ballerina, many stilt walkers and talented live singers. Based on the 1994 film "The Lion King." Africa.

Finding Nemo—The Musical. ★★★★★ ✓ FastPass+ Broadway-quality stage musical retells 2003's "Finding Nemo" with huge puppets and live singers. Dory is a hoot. DinoLand U.S.A.

Kilimanjaro Safaris. ★★★★★ ✓ FastPass+ Bouncy open-air truck wanders 100-acre African forest and savanna; passes elephants, giraffes, lions, rhinos and many other rare species, all of which appear to be roaming freely. New species include addax and springbok antelope, zebra. Africa.

Maharajah Jungle Trek. ★★★★★ ✓ Pathway around and through a crumbling palace passes bats, tigers and other Asian animals, meanders through an Asian aviary. Asia.

Pangani Forest Exploration Trail. ★★★★★ ✓ Shady walkway roams past unusual African species. Includes a beautiful aviary and large gorilla habitat. Other animals include okapi, meerkats, monkeys. Africa.

Wilderness Explorers. ★★★★★ ✓ Earn badges in this series of nature-themed activities, based on Russell's scouting experiences in the 2009 movie "Up." Earnest docents help you out. Very well done; includes an elaborate booklet. Park-wide.

Four-star attractions

Dinosaur. ★★★★ ✓ FastPass+ You search for dinos in an open-vehicle on this dark jerky ride, and barely miss a meteor shower. An intense, loud experience. Threatening dinosaurs chase you. Height minimum 40 inches. DinoLand U.S.A.

Flights of Wonder. ★★★★ ✓ Bird show presents conservation message in a humorous, lightweight way. Includes about 20 species; some fly over the audience. Asia.

Primeval Whirl. ★★★★ FastPass+ Kitschy spinning roller coaster takes you back in time, as cartoon-cutout dinosaurs warn "The End is Near." Jerky, with one slight-but-steep drop. Height minimum 48 inches. DinoLand U.S.A.

Tree of Life Garden. ★★★★ Narrow pathways wind through a lush tropical garden, alongside massive Tree of Life roots and waterfalls, past kangaroos and other exotic creatures. Discovery Island.

Three-star attractions

Conservation Station. ★★★ ✓ Animal-care facility has exhibits, presentations, veterinary center with viewable procedures. Petting zoo holds domesticated animals, mostly free-roaming, brushes provided. Inconvenient, accessible only by train. Rafiki's Planet Watch.

Fossil Fun Games. ★★★ ✓ Winners of these midway games get stuffed-animal prizes. $4 to $5 per game. DinoLand U.S.A.

Kali River Rapids. ★★★ FastPass+ Jerky, wet raft ride travels down a threatened rainforest river; riders often get soaked. Height minimum 38 inches. Asia.

TriceraTop Spin. ★★★ Dumbo with four-seat dinosaurs, cheesy roadside carnival theme. DinoLand U.S.A.

Two-star attraction

It's Tough to Be a Bug. ★★ Playfully sadistic 3-D movie displays insect survival skills. Stars characters from 1989's "A Bug's Life." Intense for preschoolers. Discovery Island.

From out front the Tusker House appears to be a ramshackle hotel. A sign directs diners to the entrance, which is in back. At right: the main dining room at Yak & Yeti.

Restaurants and food

Animal Kingdom has the fewest restaurants of any Walt Disney World theme park, but there is much to like. The fast-food spots in particular have a lot to recommend them. Below, each restaurant is rated from one to five stars (★) based on the quality of its food, service and atmosphere. A five-star eatery fully lives up to its promise. A checkmark (✔) indicates one of the authors' personal favorites. The price of a typical adult entree is summarized by dollar signs as follows:

$ less than $10
$$ less than $15
$$$ less than $20
$$$$ less than $25
$$$$$ more than $25

To reserve a table at a Disney restaurant call Disney at 407-939-3463.

Table service. A quick summary: The best food is at Yak & Yeti, for lunch or dinner. The best fast food is at Flame Tree Barbecue. The author's choice: Yak & Yeti's mahi mahi, with fried won tons for dessert.

Rainforest Cafe. ★★★ $$$$ The atmosphere is the draw at this kid-friendly spot, where robotic elephants and gorillas come to life in a dense faux jungle. Huge aquariums hold exotic fish. Delivered by friendly servers, the food is fine, portions are generous. But it's all overpriced, because here you're paying not just for a hamburger, but also a hooting chimp. *Entrance plaza. Breakfast 8:30–10 a.m., $9–$15 (children $5–$7). Lunch, dinner 10 a.m.–park close, $12–$42 (children $7–$9). Seats 985 plus 72 at the bar. Run by Landry's. Direct reservations at 407-938-9100.*

Tusker House. ★★★★ $$$$$ Quality vegetarian dishes highlight this varied, well-prepared, overpriced buffet. Standouts at dinner include couscous, hummus, tabbouleh and salads; carving station meats and desserts are also good. The "Safari Orientation Centre" of the mythical Harambe Village, the dining area is lined with real African artifacts, faux maps and notices. Breakfast and lunch are character meals with Donald Duck, Daisy Duck, Mickey Mouse and Goofy; breakfast is American fare. *Africa. Breakfast 8–10:30 a.m. $29 (children $17); lunch 11:30 a.m.–3:30 p.m. $30 (children $17); optional photo package. Dinner 4 p.m.–park close. $35 (children $18). Seats 1,206. Outdoor bar seats 256.*

Yak & Yeti. ★★★★★ ✔ $$$$ Cool couples and families love the tasty Southeast Asian cuisine at this interesting restaurant, the only place inside Animal Kingdom where servers bring you your food. Crispy Mahi Mahi doesn't taste a bit fishy; its sweet and sour sauce is the

Opposite page photo: © Schussler Creative

Carts and snack stands line the walkways of Disney's Animal Kingdom. The popcorn, nuts and other warm items are made on site, and good when they're fresh.

best I've had. For an appetizer try the mild Ahi tuna, served with hot dipping sauce and sweet slaw. As for desserts, order the pineapple and cream cheese wontons—two honey-sauced skewers which you dip into vanilla ice cream—then resist the urge to lick your plate like a dog. Infused with flavor, mango iced tea is a perfect accompaniment. Other good food choices: pork egg rolls, seafood curry, baby back ribs and a Kobe beef burger. Kids pick from a mini burger, vegetable lo mein, chicken tenders or an egg roll. The food is worth its price, thanks in part to the generous portions. Service is at least as good as at Disney spots. Relaxed dining areas offer lots to look at; a plethora of authentic Asian artifacts decorate the walls and ceilings. Chairs, drapes and light fixtures are charmingly mismatched. You can usually be seated immediately without a reservation before 11:30 a.m. Ask to sit upstairs by the windows, overlooking the walkway below. *Asia. Lunch and dinner 11 a.m.–park close. $18–$27 (children $9). Seats 250, 8 at the bar. Run by Landry's. Direct reservations at 407-824-9384.*

Counter service. The top picks here: Flame Tree Barbecue (outside) and Pizzafari (inside). A basic walk-up window, Tamu Tamu has some tasty choices too.

Flame Tree Barbecue. ★★★★★ ✔ $$ This outdoor restaurant specializes in smoked meats: chicken, ribs and pork. Each has the flavor you hope for: that savory taste that tells you it's straight out of an outdoor smoker. Chicken, ribs and pork are all so tender they nearly fall off their bones. Sides include delicious barbecue baked beans. Overall prices are a touch higher than the park's other fast-food spots but this place is

still a relative value—you get more and better food, and if the weather's right a wonderful atmosphere. Looking for a bargain? Get the combo chicken and rib meal, $15 but big enough for two. Want all-white-meat chicken? Whenever we've asked it's no extra charge. On the downside, the weather's often not right, and on a hot or muggy day even Flame Tree's shaded waterfront tables—complete with nice views of the Expedition Everest mountain-scape—won't keep you from lusting after some air-conditioning. Also, of course, it's messy. Unlimited moist towelettes help. The children's offers only non-messy choices—a chicken sandwich, baked drumstick, hot dog or PB&J. Wherever you sit, note the subtle predator-and-prey theme. *Next to the entrance to DinoLand U.S.A., Discovery Island. $9-$15, kids meals $5-$6. Lunch, dinner 11 a.m.–park close. Seats 500 outside, mostly shaded from the sun and rain.*

Pizzafari. ★★★★ ✔ $ Yes! A Disney-run pizza spot that cares about its pizza! The individual pies here are head and shoulders better than those in other Disney parks, with evidence of actual herbs and spices and preparation that included something more than just a microwave oven, perhaps even a wood-burning oven. Other choices aren't bad either—a hot Italian deli sandwich and a Caesar salad with chicken. The sprawling eatery has several different dining rooms, each themed to a different type of animal. Beautiful murals, floor mosaics and ceiling art add to a clean, cool, relaxing feel that makes it tempting to stay here for hours. In fact, the authors often do just that. See that middle-aged couple, or that sweet college girl over in the corner, pounding away at their

What at first glance is an authentic Southeast Asian bus — complete with a flat tire — is actually an ice-cream stand. It sits alongside the walkway to Expedition Everest in Disney's Asian village of Anandapur.

iPhones and laptop? That's us! *On the walkway to Africa, Discovery Island. Breakfast: park open–10:30 a.m. Lunch, dinner: 10:30 a.m.–one hour before park close. $9–$10, kids $5–$6. Seats 680.*

Restaurantosaurus. ★★★ $ Tucked into a corner of DinoLand U.S.A., this place has a lavishly wacko theme — it's an old fishing lodge that's been converted into the dorm of the graduate students who work at the nearby Dinosaur Institute—i.e., the Dinosaur ride. Unfortunately, the food is also dorm-like: bland cheeseburgers, mac and cheese and such that make no impression on you at all. At least soda refills are free—that's unusual at Disney World—and there's a nice self-serve fixings station with grilled onions and mushrooms and that collegiate staple: runny gooey yummy fake cheese. Kids meals are pricey compared to similar spots, but the regular menu is priced correctly if this is the kind of food you want. *Near TriceraTop Spin, DinoLand U.S.A. $9–$10, kids $7, 11 a.m.–park close. Seats 750, including 104 outside in mostly shady seating.*

Tamu Tamu. ★★★★ ✔ $ This shady outdoor window couldn't be more unassuming; you'll have to look twice to find it. At press time, its sophisticated choices included a slow-cooked beef sandwich with a minty yogurt sauce, a quinoa salad, a roasted chicken salad made with spiced meat and dried fruit, and a fresh fruit salad served in half a pineapple. Want an adult treat? Try the Dole Whip-like pineapple soft serve topped with a pour of either dark or coconut rum. It's not real ice cream, but you won't care. Kids "Snack Packs" are collections of pre-packaged items such as yogurt, carrot sticks and goldfish crackers served with a drink. You'll have to look three times to find the seating area—it's behind the window, in a patio-like setting that is covered but not protected from the rain. Tables often have vegetation on them courtesy of the surrounding trees. *Across from Tusker House, Africa. $9, kids Snack Pack $5. 10:30 a.m.–one hour before park close. Seats 92 in outdoor covered seating.*

Yak & Yeti Local Food Cafés. ★★ $ Next to Yak & Yeti, these walk-up windows offer Asian-themed food court staples, none of which compare to what the restaurant serves. Nearby tables seem to be an afterthought. In the afternoon DJ Anaan may be playing his driving pop music right next to you, which helps takes your mind off the fact that you've picked the wrong place to eat. *In front of Yak & Yeti, Asia. $9–$11, kids $5. 10:30 a.m.–one hour before park close. Seats 350 in outdoor covered seating.*

Snacks. The park has lots of little snack stands and carts serving up all the basics—popcorn, ice cream, gigantic turkey legs. Want something more memorable? Africa's **Kusafiri Coffee Shop and Bakery** ★★★★ ✔ serves freshly baked pastries, desserts, coffee and hot chocolate from a window adjacent to Tusker House. There's also the Amarula Schokoleti—hot chocolate with Amarula. Right in front of it is a stand selling fresh fruit. A very nice tea stand, the **Royal Anandapur Tea Co.** ★★★★★ ✔ offers a wider variety of hot individually brewed teas than you'd expect, as well as specialty and iced coffees and pastries. It's in Asia, across from the Yak &Yeti Restaurant.

See also **Food and Restaurants** in the chapter **Walt Disney World A–Z.**

Africa's Mombasa Marketplace sells distinctly non-Disney and non-brand items such as bamboo plants, Kenyan batik caftans, hand-carved figurines and henna body artistry.

Shops

You can go wild shopping at Disney's Animal Kingdom. The park is filled with merchandise you won't find anywhere else at Disney, sometimes anywhere else in the United States. The best shops are summarized below. Stores are rated from one to five stars (★) based on the quality of their merchandise, service and atmosphere; one- and two-star stores are not listed. A checkmark (✔) indicates that the store is one of the authors' personal favorites.

Bhaktapur Market. ★★★ Amazingly cramped, this small, open-air boutique sells authentic merchandise from Asia, much of it interesting kitsch. Run by the adjacent Yak & Yeti Restaurant, it's also stocked with Yak & Yeti souvenirs. *In front of Yak & Yeti, Asia.*

Chester & Hester's Dinosaur Treasures. ★★★★ This uber-themed children's store appears to be a rural gas station that's been turned into a tacky souvenir stand run by amateur fossil hunters. The ceiling and walls abound with hundreds of cheap plastic dinosaurs, arranged in bizarre yet creative ways. None of that, unfortunately, is for sale, but underneath it is plenty of standard Disney games, novelty hats, plush, sundries, toys and Vinylmation figurines. There's plenty

of "Star Wars" and "Toy Story" stuff. You can even pick up some bulk penny candy — for $3.25 for a quarter pound. *Across from Primeval Whirl, DinoLand U.S.A.*

Creature Comforts. ★★★ Princess Atta from "A Bug's Life" sits on a leaf throne in the center of this children's store, which offers books, plush, toys and apparel, including Pocahontas and Sofia the First costumes. The decor features striped and spotted animals. The shop also serves as the park's My Magic+ Service Center. It stays open up to an hour after park closing. *Near entrance to Africa, Discovery Island.*

The Dino Institute Gift Shop. ★★★★ Resembling a museum gift shop, this classy store is decorated with fossils and paintings of dinosaur skeletons lit with track lighting. A giant sea turtle skeleton hangs from the ceiling. Dinosaur souvenirs and toys dominate the store, from apparel to plush, books to puppets. Check out the toy remote-control Time Rover from the ride. You can also purchase a souvenir ride photo. *At the exit to the Dinosaur ride, DinoLand U.S.A.*

Disney Outfitters. ★★★★ ✔ This calm spot with its wood shelving, carved wooden animal statues and tile floors provides an appropriate setting for its high-end merchandise. Dooney & Bourke and Vera Bradley bags get their own featured displays, and

Animal- and nature-themed merchandise abounds in the park. Harambe's Mombasa Marketplace sells this glass-beaded lion figurine.

you'll also find fashionable apparel for men, women, juniors, children and infants. Fine artwork is worth a look. The shop stays open up to an hour after park closing. *Across from Flame Tree Barbecue, Discovery Island.*

Mandala Gifts. ★★★★ ✓ This teeny open-air store sells junior fashion apparel and accessories, much of nature-themed and little of it having anything to do with Disney. Included are sundresses, short-shorts, scarves, costume jewelry and a good selection of cute straw hats. *In front of Yak & Yeti Restaurant, Asia.*

Mombasa Marketplace. ★★★★★ ✓ For a real taste of Africa, check out this eclectic shop. Merchandise includes African books and cookbooks, bamboo plants and braided "money trees," batik caftans made in Kenya, beaded animal figurines, musical instruments and serious safari hats. The store's dark woods, plaster walls and authentic African table displays transport you to a different place. Artist Larry Dotson sells prints of Animal Kingdom scenes. Outside the shop an African artist carves figurines, canes and other works. There's a henna artist, too. *Across from Tusker House, Africa.*

Island Mercantile. ★★★★ Like a grab bag, Island Mercantile has a little of everything—everything you can find everywhere else at Walt Disney World. It's this park's version of The Emporium at Magic Kingdom or MouseGear at Epcot, though it's much smaller and has a way-more-interesting decor. Hanging from the ceiling are charming brightly painted wooden birds and butterflies designed to look like airplanes; nearby are beavers designed to be saws. Beyond the typical merchandise, the shop also carries a wide range of Animal Kingdom-themed

apparel, backpacks, hats and souvenirs as well as toy binoculars and Expedition Everest T-shirts. Island Mercantile stays open up to an hour after park closing. *Next to the Oasis bridge, Discovery Island.*

Rainforest Cafe Gift Shop. ★★★ This sprawling store sells mostly Rainforest Cafe items, but look closely and you'll find some stylish fashion apparel for women and juniors. A giant aquarium sits in the middle of the store. Every now and then, robotic animals roar and hoot. The shop opens an hour before the park does, and stays open two hours after it closes. *Inside Rainforest Cafe, park entrance.*

Serka Zong Bazaar. ★★★★ ✓ The high shelves of this big shop are jam-packed with gobs of authentic Asian artifacts and mountaineering gear. A huge clawed yeti figure rises from the center of the store. Merchandise includes Expedition Everest souvenirs (don't miss the adorable yeti plush and knit hats) and ride photos, as well as prayer flags from Tibet and an interesting selection of Mt. Everest books. Check out the lovely Christmas ornaments created from air cylinders left behind on Mt. Everest. *At the exit to Expedition Everest, Asia.*

Ziwani Traders. ★★★ Fans of "The Lion King" will like this shop's merchandise inspired by the film, including CDs, DVDs, pins, puzzles, Simba plush and original oil paintings that sell for up to $5,500. Decorated like a trading post and outfitting shop, the store's high shelves and ceiling are lined with authentic safari gear such as heavy-duty backpacks, canteens and lanterns. *Adjacent to Mombasa Marketplace, Africa.*

See also **Shopping** in the chapter **Walt Disney World A–Z.**

Street performers

Burudika. ★★★★★ ✔ An outstanding Afropop band performs engaging rhythmic music that's subtly complex. 30-minute shows. *In front of Tusker House, Africa.*

Chakranadi. ★★★★★ ✔ A sitar-and-tabla duo perform haunting instrumentals. 20-minute shows. *In front of Flights of Wonder, Asia.*

DiVine. ★★★★ ✔ Covered in realistic leaves, fruit, flowers and vines, this sinuous stilt-walker blends into the foliage. Many visitors walk right past her. 20-minute shows. *On the walkway between Africa and Asia.*

DJ Anaan. ★★★★ ✔ A DJ on a small platform spins catchy Asian pop tunes while two young women in colorful saris dance and encourage onlookers to dance with them. The scene will remind you of the dancefest finale of "Slumdog Millionaire." 20-minute shows. *Near Yak & Yeti Restaurant, Asia.*

Gi-Tar Dan. ★★★★ This funny-man guitarist sings catchy animal songs to and with children, often weaving their names into the lyrics. 20-minute shows. *Outside the Conservation Station building, Rafiki's Planet Watch.*

Tam Tam Drummers of Harambe. ★★★★★ ✔ Fun, rousing native percussion quintet gives guests of all ages quick lessons in hip-shaking West African dances. About a dozen delighted volunteers follow the leader's whistled cues. Shows are unshaded from the sun. 15-minute shows. *On a small stage in front of Tusker House, Africa.*

Animal Kingdom's street performers immerse visitors in world culture. From top: the Tam Tam Drummers of Harambe, the Chakranadi sitar player, African band Burudika, the graceful dancers of DJ Anaan.

Where to meet characters

Adventurers Outpost. ★★★★
✔ **FastPass+** Dressed in safari gear, Mickey Mouse and Minnie Mouse pose in front of a giant park map. Actual photos of Mickey and Minnie in Africa, Nepal, Tibet and the Himalayas in those outfits decorate the queue. *Discovery Island. Formerly the Beastly Bazaar shop.*

Rafiki's Planet Watch. ★★★ Rafiki greets guests inside Conservation Station with no backdrop; Chip 'n Dale are outside. *Conservation Station, Rafiki's Planet Watch.*

Tusker House. ★★★★ ✔ Donald Duck hosts breakfast and lunch at this African-flavored buffet. Joining him are Daisy Duck, Goofy and Mickey Mouse. *Africa.*

Canine Pals. ★★★★ ✔ Under a covered roof, Goofy and Pluto pose in front of a giant postcard. *Across from the TriceraTop Spin ride, DinoLand U.S.A.*

Duckasaurus Donald. ★★ Donald Duck with his own creation. *On the Cretaceous Trail, DinoLand U.S.A.*

Wilderness Explorers Club House.
★★★★★ ✔ Meet Dug and Russell in this gazebo. The backdrop has the Wilderness Explorers logo and Club House signs. While you're there bark into a Bark-O-Lator and then learn what you just "said" in dog language. There's one at the entrance to the queue, one inside it. *Near the entrance to It's Tough To Be a Bug, Discovery Island.*

Characters also greet guests on walkways throughout the park.

See also the chapter **Characters.**

Mickey and Minnie Mouse greet guests at Adventurers Outpost, Pluto and Goofy strike a pose and Donald Duck signs an autograph in DinoLand U.S.A., the author woofs into a Bark-O-Lator at the Wilderness Explorers Club House.

Reached via a winding tropical walkway, the indoor theater for It's Tough to Be a Bug is tucked inside the base of the icon of Disney's Animal Kingdom, the Tree of Life.

It's Tough to Be a Bug!

Witty 3-D film suffers from dated tech, frightening effects

★★ **FastPass+** "It was awesome!" said the 8-year-old girl, leaving the theater with her parents. "I hated it!" said the 7-year-old boy next to her, crying to his parents. Different children have different reactions to this sadistic 3-D movie, which demonstrates how insects defend themselves by pretending to torture its audience. Special effects make it seem like guests are sprayed with acid and attacked by poison quills. Two characters from the 1998 movie "A Bug's Life" appear in the theater as robotic figures—mild-mannered ant Flik (the host) and grasshopper villain Hopper. Once state-of-the-art, the show is blurry compared to modern 3-D efforts.

Tips. *When to go:* Anytime. A Fastpass guarantees you a seat, but there are no seats set aside for Fastpass holders, and they don't enter the theater early. *Where to sit:* In the center of a back row. Lean back to feel all the effects.

Fun finds. Outside the lobby a plaque honors Dr. Jane Goodall's work with chimpanzees. Lobby posters and ambient music recall supposed previous shows such as "Beauty and the Bees" and "Little Shop of Hoppers." The theater is an anthill; its projection booth a wasp nest. As the show ends, fireflies swarm to exit signs.

Hidden Mickey. As spots on a root in the lobby, to the left of the handicapped entrance.

Fun facts. Character voices include those of Dave Foley (Flik), Cheech Marin (Chili the tarantula) and Kevin Spacey (Hopper).

Key facts. *Best for:* Older kids. *Duration:* 8 minutes. *Capacity:* 430. *Queue:* Outdoor, shaded. *Fear factor:* Intense, with darkness, fog, cartoonish menacing bugs. *Debuted:* 1998. *Access:* Guests may stay in wheelchairs, ECVs. *Disability services:* Assistive listening, reflective captioning, Audio Description. *Location:* Discovery Island.

Average wait times

9am	10am	11am	Noon	1pm	2pm	3pm	4pm	5pm	6pm	7pm	8pm	9pm
5m	5m	5m	10m	5m	5m	5m	5m	5m	5m	5m	n/a	n/a

A carved crocodilian emerges from an oversized root in the Tree of Life garden. Pathways pass habitats of kangaroos, Galapagos tortoises and other exotic creatures.

Tree of Life Garden

Beautiful tropical area has hidden walkways, exotic animals

★★★★ The centerpiece of Disney's Animal Kingdom, this remarkable garden combines a lush landscape, exotic wildlife and massive man-made icon. Surrounding the iconic Tree of Life, tropical hills are dotted with streams, grottos and waterfalls. Two walking paths wind through them, offering close-up views of unusual creatures. The trails are tough to find and therefore rarely crowded; once you discover one you'll have its idyllic views and peaceful environment almost all to yourself.

Garden path. This spot directly in front of the Tree offers a good view of a variety of creatures. Flamingos and whistling ducks hang out in a pond to the left, near a cotton-top tamarin habitat. Next to that is a shady otter habitat with an underwater viewing area.

Front trail. So hidden few guests notice it, a trail off the park's walkway to Africa leads to an up-close look at the kangaroo enclosure. The narrow path weaves through the huge roots of the Tree and past a waterfall. It connects to the walkway to Africa (on the right, just past the Pizzafari restaurant) and the walkway to Asia (on the left, behind the Wilderness Explorers Club House).

Back trail. Running alongside the park's Discovery River, this trail leads from its Africa gate to its Asia gate, snaking past parrot, porcupine, stork and tortoise habitats.

Tips. *When to go:* Early in the morning to see the animals at their liveliest. *For families:* Small children may have a hard time seeing the kangaroos. Their viewing spot sits behind a concrete wall that's about 4 feet tall.

Key facts. *Best for:* All ages. *Duration:* Allow 20 minutes. *Specs:* Garden path plus two trails (1,680 feet), nine viewing areas, 15 species. *Debuted:* 1998. *Access:* Guests may remain in wheelchairs, ECVs. *Location:* Discovery Island.

See also **Animal Guide.**

Average wait times

9am	10am	11am	Noon	1pm	2pm	3pm	4pm	5pm	6pm	7pm	8pm	9pm
0m	0m	0m	0m	0m	0m	0m	0m	0m	0m	0m	n/a	n/a

A "troop leader" teaches a brother and sister the "W" sign of the Wilderness Explorers, preparing them for a day that will take them throughout Disney's Animal Kingdom.

Wilderness Explorers

All ages will enjoy this hands-on scavenger hunt

★★★★★ ✓ You start off learning the Wilderness Explorer call: "The wilderness must be explored! Caw! Caw! Roar!" Then you go off to earn badges—stickers—at 31 stations scattered throughout the park by completing activities that teach you fascinating things about animals, nature and world cultures. Yes it can take forever—in fact, Disney assumes you'll take more than one day to complete everything—but assuming you've got that time there's no rush, and if you've got a child interested in these subjects it's a terrific bonding experience.

It's all wonderfully low-tech. You'll find no video screens. You don't carry a hand-held gizmo. There are zero special effects—nothing you do changes the environment. Instead, Disney hands you a surprisingly nice handbook (a wonderful free souvenir) and you and your child discover, sketch, explore and occasionally talk to real live people.

If you like to help your child earn scouting awards you'll love it, though so will nature lovers of any age. Even earning just a few badges is a great way to enhance your day. Wilderness Explorers is based on Russell's troop in the 2009 Pixar movie "Up."

Tip. *How to do it:* Get your handbook as soon as you enter the park, and earn your badges as you take in whatever rides, shows and animal exhibits you were already planning to see. For example, as you view the Pangani Forest animals you can earn a Ham Radio Badge, a Hiking Badge, a Birding Badge, a Tracking Badge and a Gorilla Badge.

Key facts. *Best for:* Families. *Duration:* Allow 20 minutes per badge. *Operating hours:* Park open–6 p.m. *Weather issues:* Closed during thunderstorms. *Debuted:* 2014. *Access:* Guests may remain in wheelchairs, ECVs. *Location:* Sign-up spot is on the bridge between the Oasis and Discovery Island.

Average wait times

9am	10am	11am	Noon	1pm	2pm	3pm	4pm	5pm	6pm	7pm	8pm	9pm
0m	0m	0m	0m	0m	0m	0m	0m	0m	0m	0m	n/a	n/a

Micaela Neal

Creatively costumed Festival of the Lion King dancers channel wild animals as they dance and twirl directly in front of audience members.

Festival of the Lion King

In-the-round musical spectacle is Disney's best show

★★★★★ ✓ FastPass+ Fans of Disney's 1994 movie "The Lion King" will love this rousing musical spectacle. Filled with energized renditions of the best songs from the film, it combines the pageantry of a parade, the wit of a Catskills comedy revue and the emotions of a gospel revival. The show is presented in-the-round in an air-conditioned theater.

It begins with an evocative take on the film's opening scene, as animal-costumed dancers create an abstract sunrise to "The Circle of Life." Four lead singers bring in nearly four dozen additional performers, including Timon, the revue's wisecracking emcee. Parade floats roll in too; on one is Simba, on another Pumbaa.

From then on, singers, dancers, acrobats, stilt-walkers and giant puppets fill your field of vision. Acrobats fly through the air, a fire-baton twirler performs to "Be Prepared," a ballerina soars overhead to "Can You Feel the Love Tonight?" A twirling finale becomes a kaleidoscopic circle of life.

Tips. *When to go:* Anytime, but with a Fastpass. You'll enter the theater before the rest of the audience and easily get a good seat. *Where to sit:* As close to the front as you can, as the performers come right up to the crowd. *For families:* Since the bleachers are shallow, small children often can't see if someone tall sits in front of them.

Key facts. *Best for:* Children, teens, adults, seniors. *Duration:* 28 minutes. *Capacity:* 1,375. *Queue:* Indoor waiting area spills into outdoor, covered line. *Showtimes:* Scheduled performances typically every hour starting at 10 a.m. *Weather issues:* During a rain, the audience is held in the theater until the floats move backstage. *Debuted:* 1998. *Access:* Guests may remain in wheelchairs, ECVs. *Disability services:* Assistive listening, handheld captioning. *Location:* Africa.

Average wait times

9am	10am	11am	Noon	1pm	2pm	3pm	4pm	5pm	6pm	7pm	8pm	9pm
n/a	n/a	n/a	n/a	n/a	n/a	n/a	n/a	n/a	n/a	n/a	n/a	n/a

All photos: Micaela Neal

The Festival of the Lion King: A closer look

Floats. The show's floats were originally part of a 1990s parade at California's Disneyland—the Lion King Celebration parade.

Music. Musical numbers include "Be Prepared," "Can You Feel the Love Tonight?," "Hakuna Matata," "I Just Can't Wait to Be King" and "The Lion Sleeps Tonight." The Tumble Monkey acrobats perform to a zippy medley that combines swing standards (Benny Goodman's "Sing Sing Sing," Duke Ellington's "Caravan," Kay Kyser's "Playmates") with snippets of 1895's "The Streets of Cairo" (AKA "They Don't Wear Pants in the Southern Part of France") and the 1923 ditty "Yes! We Have No Bananas" (the No. 1 song in the United States for five weeks). As the fire-baton twirler takes the stage, Timon protests that he wouldn't be able to do his Songs of the South Seas Medley by scatting a few bars of the "Hawaiian War Chant," an ancient love song made famous by everyone from Tommy Dorsey to Spike Jones to Walt Disney (with his Enchanted Tiki Room) to the University of Michigan marching band.

Puppets. Though many audience members don't realize it, Simba, Pumbaa and the other animals on the show's floats are puppets, their mouths and arms controlled by performers hidden inside them. The giraffe sings along to the show's songs and nods at audience members, Pumbaa often waves his tiny front legs at Timon or at

A stilt walker greets audience members at the start of the show, singer Kibibi sings "The Circle of Life," a fire-baton twirler performs during "Be Prepared," a Tumble Monkey acrobat hangs from a trapeze.

children who wave at him. The puppets were designed by Michael Curry, who won a Tony Award for his work on the Broadway version of "The Lion King." Curry also created the puppets seen in Finding Nemo—The Musical, the park's old Mickey's Jammin' Jungle parade, Fantasmic at Disney's Hollywood Studios, and Epcot's lamented Tapestry of Nations parade.

Fun finds. Timon is a show all by himself. As his float enters the theater and heads to a corner, the frustrated meerkat looks at the performer holding the float's remote-control device and says "Slow down! I'm supposed to be center stage!" He cracks up watching the Tumble Monkeys, trembles during "Be Prepared" and swoons throughout "Can You Feel the Love Tonight?" After the show a backstage microphone picks up his aside, "Could somebody hose down those Tumble Monkeys? They're starting to smell a little gamey."

Fun facts. Although today one of Disney World's longest-running live shows, The Festival of the Lion King was originally meant to be temporary, a pieced-together placeholder for an area of Animal Kingdom that was designed as a "Beastly Kingdom" but never fully created. Audience popularity kept the show going for decades, until it became a permanent part of the park in 2014... Fifty cast members perform in the show... The Tarzan yells, cow's moo and other odd sounds in the Tumble Monkeys music are cues for the acrobats... Since its debut the show has only had one minor change: a new Timon costume that lets the meerkat move his mouth and blink his eyes. It debuted in 2009.

Dressed as a bird, a ballerina soars in the air during "Can You Feel the Love Tonight?," a girl from the audience learns to roar like a lion, Timon kisses a fan, a performer in an abstract giraffe costume dances in front of the crowd.

Open-sided safari trucks wind through a re-created savanna where free-roaming African animals forage for food. Giraffes often feed directly in the path of the trucks.

Kilimanjaro Safaris

Disney's largest attraction makes you forget you're in Florida

★★★★★ ✔ FastPass+ One of the best zoological attractions in the United States, this open-air truck ride takes you through a seamless re-creation of African jungles and savannas that are filled with free-roaming wildlife. There are no visible fences, and many animals can come up to your vehicle. Creatures include crocodiles, elephants, giraffes, hippos, lions, rhinos and warthogs and many species of antelope. Rutted roads, creaky bridges and blind corners lend a sense of adventure.

The ride appears to be a trip through an African wildlife preserve, an effort by Disney's village of Harambe to replace its timbering economy with eco-tourism. Though drivers say the journey will take two weeks and cover 800 square miles, it's actually a 22-minute trip through about 100 acres.

Disney veterans may notice that the ride no longer has a storyline. There's no Big Red or Little Red elephants, the driver no longer speaks to a game warden in an overhead plane, the poachers have packed up and left. Instead, all of the emphasis now is on the animals themselves.

Some of the ride's animals have changed recently too. Springboks have been added to the savannah, along with zebra and addax. Thompson's gazelle and scimitar horned oryx are now only at Animal Kingdom Lodge. There are no longer impala (they didn't take well to the climate) or male greater kudu with impressive, spiraling horns. After one male kudu jumped a fence, all the other guys were deported. Now there are only females.

Tips. *When to go:* First thing in the morning through the standby line, when crowds are light and the animals are feeding. Another good time: during a shower, especially after a hot morning or afternoon. The animals will be especially active; elephants

Average wait times

9am	10am	11am	Noon	1pm	2pm	3pm	4pm	5pm	6pm	7pm	8pm	9pm
5m	30m	20m	40m	20m	40m	40m	60m	40m	30m	10m	n/a	n/a

A safari truck cruises by a flock of flamingos. Below, a white rhino crosses the road. Animals always have the right-of-way; trucks are sometimes forced to stop and wait for them to move.

Micaela Neal

Micaela Neal

sometimes play in their pool when it rains. *Where to sit:* On the left of the truck for the best views, in front for the smoothest ride, in back to take photos because you can turn around and shoot behind you. Hold on tight to your camera, though—the back of the truck gets really bouncy. *For families:* Ask for the front row, and sit your child close to the driver for the most immersive experience. If your child asks the driver questions (especially about the animals), the driver will often speak directly with your child. Ask the cast member in the boarding area (the one who asks "How many?") to sit in the row you prefer; he or she will almost always be happy to accommodate you. Fastpass holders get no special seating.

Fun finds. Posters for Big Red still appear in the queue. "Prehistoric" drawings appear on a gate past the flamingos and on rocks to the right as you pass the lions.

Hidden Mickeys. Just beyond the clay pits past a baobab tree, as a puffy spot between a split branch, opposite the main elephant area; as the flamingo island; and just past that island but before the next gate, as an indentation in a boulder on the right.

Fun facts. Disney created the "muddy" road by coloring concrete to look like soil, then while it was still wet rolling truck tires through it and tossing in dirt, stones and twigs... There's a reason your driver says the termite mounds are "as hard as concrete." A pile of ostrich eggs is equally tough to crack... The acacia trees are actually Southern live oaks with their lower branches removed... The first baobab tree on the route isn't a tree at all. It's a storage shed... Kilimanjaro Safaris has the largest collection of Nile hippos and African elephants in North America... It's the largest Disney attraction in the world. The entire Magic Kingdom would fit inside it... The first hippo pool contains all males; the second females.

Key facts. *Best for:* Children, adults, animal lovers. *Duration:* 22 minutes. *Capacity:* Max 4,320 guests per hour (36 per truck). *Queue:* Outdoor, covered. *Operating hours:* Park open–dusk. *Debuted:* 1998, revised 2013. *Health advisories:* Expectant moms should not ride. *Access:* ECV users must transfer. *Disability services:* Assistive listening, hand-held captioning. *Location:* Africa.

See also **Animal Guide.**

Meaning "place of enchantment" in Swahili, Pangani lives up to its name. The self-guided walking tour wanders through lush jungles as it passes gorillas, hippos, meerkats and more.

Pangani Forest Exploration Trail

Enchanting walking trail passes gorillas, meerkats, hippos

★★★★★ ✓ Streams and waterfalls flow through the grounds of this self-guided tour of African animals, including gorillas, hippos and meerkats. The trail is shady, and benches are scattered throughout.

Presented as a series of research areas, the area has a scientific theme. A replica research station features naked mole rats, interactive displays and child-level cages and tanks that hold creatures kids find fascinating: plate-sized giant African bull-frogs, hissing cockroaches and dung beetles. Exhibits shed light on subjects as diverse as bushmeat hunting and baobab trees. One display recalls the African fable "When The Hippo Was Hairy." A 40-foot glass wall lets you view hippos underwater.

A suspension bridge and viewing island divide two large gorilla habitats. One holds a family (a silverback, two moms and four youngsters); the other a bachelor troupe.

Tips. *When to go:* In the morning. The hippo water is clear, the gorillas are active. *For families:* Skip the bushmeat exhibit (just past the colobus monkeys) if you have young kids; it shows animals killed for their meat. *What else to do:* Talk with the docents; they are full of fascinating stories.

Hidden Mickeys. In the research station on a backpack to the left of the naked mole rats, and as the "O" in the word "Asepco" and two paper-reinforcement rings on a box of soap on a small ledge behind the desk lamp.

Key facts. *Best for:* All ages. *Duration:* Allow 30–45 minutes. *Specs:* One trail (2,100 feet), nine viewing areas, 10 species plus aviary, indoor exhibits. *Operating hours:* Park open–dusk. *Weather issues:* Closed during thunderstorms. *Debuted:* 1998. *Access:* Guests may remain in wheelchairs, ECVs. *Disability services:* Audio Description. *Location:* Africa.

See also **Animal Guide.**

Average wait times

9am	10am	11am	Noon	1pm	2pm	3pm	4pm	5pm	6pm	7pm	8pm	9pm
0m	0m	0m	0m	0m	0m	0m	0m	0m	0m	0m	n/a	n/a

Julie Neal

Animals are examined and sometimes operated on in front of guests at Conservation Station's veterinary care center. The procedures only take place in the morning.

Conservation Station

Isolated, engaging area has petting zoo, educational exhibits

★★★ ✔ This theme-free air-conditioned pavilion houses straightforward exhibits, a veterinary care center and a few character-greeting spots. A petting zoo sits next to it. The area is inconveniently located and much of what it offers can also be seen at a good zoo. Animal lovers, however, will find it fascinating. For what it is, it's well done.

You can watch animals undergo medical procedures each morning, typically until noon. Vets explain what's going on, while overhead cameras offer up-close views. About three animals are treated daily.

To get to the area you take a "Wildlife Express" train from the park's Africa area. Despite its name the train offers no wildlife views, just a few backstage pens used to house Kilimanjaro Safaris animals.

Tips. *When to go:* Arrive before 10 a.m. to see a procedure. *For families:* If you have young kids skip the video "Sharing the Planet." It shows a poached tiger, injured manatees and wolves being hunted. *For couples:* Lovebirds will enjoy the Song of the Rainforest exhibit. You enter a small booth, close the door and sit side-by-side on a bench. With a push of a button the lights go out and an audio show begins. It lasts six minutes.

Hidden Mickeys. As overlapping circles in tree grates. Throughout the entrance mural and the Song of the Rainforest display. As orange spots on the outdoor-stage wall. Often as a pattern on a sheared sheep.

Key facts. *Best for:* Children, adults, animal lovers. *Duration:* Allow 1.5 hours. *Specs:* 49 species. *Operating hours:* 9:30 a.m.–dusk. *Weather issues:* Train closed during thunderstorms. *Debuted:* 1998. *Access:* Guests may remain in wheelchairs, ECVs. ECV users must transfer to a wheelchair to enter the petting zoo. *Location:* Rafiki's Planet Watch.

See also **Animal Guide.**

Average wait times

9am	10am	11am	Noon	1pm	2pm	3pm	4pm	5pm	6pm	7pm	8pm	9pm
n/a	10m	10m	10m	10m	10m	10m	10m	10m	10m	n/a	n/a	n/a

A crow returns a stolen dollar to an audience volunteer during a performance of Flights of Wonder. The bird show takes place in an outdoor theater with a shaded seating area.

Flights of Wonder

Educational, comedic show with flying birds, green message

★★★★ ✔ Birds fly inches over your head in this entertaining live show. It demonstrates natural bird behaviors as it promotes the intrinsic value of these animals and the need to protect them from the abuses of man. Altogether you'll see about 20 birds, including a bald eagle.

Though the subject is serious, the presentation is anything but. Just as it gets started, it's interrupted by a loony lost tour guide who wanders up on stage, flag in hand, in search of his group. You soon learn that he suffers from FOB — "fear of birds." As he faces his fears, you witness various up-close-and-personal flight demonstrations. The grassy natural stage features a backdrop of a crumbling stone building set in a shady grove.

A brief preshow in front of the theater features a great horned owl. When the show is over, handlers bring out a bird or two for a brief meet-and-greet session.

Tips. *When to go:* All shows are good. *Where to sit:* In the center, at the end of a front row. Birds will fly over your head (arrive 20 minutes early to be among the first people in the theater). *For families:* Want your child to be in the show? Sit in the second row in the center and have her wave wildly when the trainer asks for volunteers. Since the seating area is flat, small children should sit close to the stage to be able to see.

Key facts. *Best for:* Children, adults, animal lovers. *Duration:* 25 minutes. *Capacity:* 1,150. *Queue:* Outdoor, shady. *Showtimes:* Scheduled performances mid-morning through mid-afternoon. *Weather issues:* Changed and shortened during rain, cancelled during lightning and thunderstorms. *Debuted:* 1998. *Access:* Guests may remain in wheelchairs, ECVs. *Disability services:* Assistive listening. *Location:* Asia.

See also **Animal Guide.**

Average wait times

9am	10am	11am	Noon	1pm	2pm	3pm	4pm	5pm	6pm	7pm	8pm	9pm
n/a	n/a	n/a	n/a	n/a	n/a	n/a	n/a	n/a	n/a	n/a	n/a	n/a

Churning waters splash guests on Kali River Rapids. The turbulent raft ride carries a conservation message, as key scenes depict the clear-cutting and burning of a rainforest.

Kali River Rapids

Wet, exhilarating raft ride condemns rainforest destruction

★★★ FastPass+ This raft ride takes you down a turbulent jungle river that has many twists and turns and a 25-foot drop. Erupting springs, spraying water jugs and squirting statues ensure you get wet, maybe soaked. Each raft holds 12 people; nearby lockers (free to use for a short time) keep valuables dry.

The ride carries a strong conservation message, as it depicts the process of deforestation. Though it begins in a lush jungle, at the river's headwaters it shows the illegal operations of a logging business. In its never-ending quest to harvest tropical hardwoods, the company has clear-cut a pristine section of a rainforest, setting ablaze any wood that doesn't have commercial value.

Tips. *When to go:* In the heat of mid-afternoon when you'll welcome getting soaked, with a Fastpass so you can skip the long line. *For families:* Talk to your children about the ecological issues raised in this attraction. Deforestation and habitat loss are worthwhile topics, especially when you are surrounded by the species being threatened.

Fun finds. A queue building, Mr. Panika's Shop sells "Antiks Made to Order." King of Pop Michael Jackson is among the raft riders in a mural in the last queue room; he's at the top right of a raft with his hands raised. On the exitway, buttons on a footbridge shoot sprays of water on unsuspecting riders.

Key facts. *Best for:* Children, teens. *Duration:* 6 minutes. *Capacity:* 240 (20 12-person rafts). *Queue:* Outdoor, shaded. *Fear factor:* Bumpy, splashy, one steep drop *Restraint:* Seat belt. *Weather issues:* Closed during thunderstorms. *Debuted:* 1999. *Health advisories:* Guests should be free from motion sickness; pregnancy; high blood pressure; heart, back or neck problems. *Access:* Height minimum 38 inches. ECV users must transfer. *Location:* Asia.

Average wait times

9am	10am	11am	Noon	1pm	2pm	3pm	4pm	5pm	6pm	7pm	8pm	9pm
0m	5m	5m	30m	50m	80m	60m	60m	40m	30m	10m	n/a	n/a

Guests walk through the overrun grounds of a mythical ancient hunting lodge on this lovely trail, past a Komodo dragon, giant bats and playful tigers.

Maharajah Jungle Trek

Exotic trail has captivating bats, tigers, a Komodo dragon

★★★★★ ✔ Tigers, giant fruit bats and other exotic Asian animals line this shady winding walkway. Other animals include a Komodo dragon (the world's largest living lizard) and some unusual deer and cattle. A lush aviary is filled with beautiful birds. Docents are stationed at key viewing spots. Large overhead fans help keep you cool in the bat pavilion, the attraction's only indoor area. Some children are afraid of the bats, but there is no need to be. They're *fruit* bats.

The circular walkway winds through the ruins of a mythical hunting lodge, which, in one of Disney's more inspired architectural efforts, has been taken over by the forces of nature. Trees have taken root within towers, bursting their seams from within. Birds have moved into the grand ballroom, which has lost its roof. Eventually, the story goes, the lodge was donated to the local village, which uses it today as a wildlife refuge.

Tips. *When to go:* First thing in the morning (the bats are fed at 9:15 a.m., and the rest of the animals are alert and lively) or during a light shower (the tigers get playful). Avoid hot afternoons; the animals hide. *For families:* Kids will like spotting the shed antlers in the habitat just past the tigers. Eli, a male deer, gets new ones every four months.

Hidden Mickeys. At the second tiger viewing area, in the first mural on the right as swirls of water under a tiger. As a maharajah's earring in the first mural on your left.

Key facts. *Best for:* All ages. *Duration:* Allow 30 minutes. *Specs:* One trail (1,500 feet), seven viewing areas, 14 species plus aviary. *Operating hours:* Park open–dusk. *Weather issues:* Closed during thunderstorms. *Debuted:* 1998. *Access:* Guests may remain in wheelchairs, ECVs. *Disability services:* Audio Description. *Location:* Asia. See also **Animal Guide**.

Average wait times

9am	10am	11am	Noon	1pm	2pm	3pm	4pm	5pm	6pm	7pm	8pm	9pm
0m	0m	0m	0m	0m	0m	0m	0m	0m	0m	0m	n/a	n/a

Colorful prayer flags decorate the entrance to the Expedition Everest roller coaster. Its tea trains climb 200 feet to reach the top of Disney's "Forbidden Mountain."

Expedition Everest

Thrilling mountain coaster goes backward, angers Yeti

★★★★★ ✔ **FastPass+** This smooth high-speed roller coaster climbs forward, zooms backward in the dark and takes some steep sweeping turns. What appears to be an old tea train zips you around, into and through a snow-capped mountain and narrowly escapes a snarling beast. Though you don't go upside down, your 4,000-foot journey climbs 200 feet, stops twice, takes an 80-foot drop and hits 60 miles per hour. It's a rush.

A monster myth. The coaster is even more fun if you know its story, which—if you look for it—is told in the standby queue.

The tale starts in the 1920s, as tea plantations begin to flourish along the mountains of Disney's mythical Asian kingdom of Anandapur. A steam train line is established to carry the tea to villages, where it is shipped to distant markets. Soon, however, strange track snaps appear, which cause a series of accidents and force the trains to shut down. Locals blame the British, claiming their attempts to reach the summit of nearby Mt. Everest has angered the Yeti, a creature they say guards the mountains.

But today the rail line has reopened. Despite local protests and warnings, a bohemian American (known only as Bob) has restored the old tea trains for his Himalayan Escapes Tours and Expeditions, a new business which makes it easy for trekkers to get to Everest quickly. You are on his first train. What could possibly go wrong?

Tips. *When to go:* At dusk or at night if you can, when the mountain is lit in eerie oranges and purples. *Where to sit:* Right in the front seat for the best view and mildest ride; in back for the wildest experience. *How to save time:* Use the single-rider line if you arrive during a busy time, don't have a Fastpass, don't mind riding by yourself and don't care where you sit. You'll get on right away.

Average wait times

9am	10am	11am	Noon	1pm	2pm	3pm	4pm	5pm	6pm	7pm	8pm	9pm
10m	15m	20m	35m	25m	35m	25m	20m	20m	15m	10m	n/a	n/a

The Expedition Everest coaster starts with a trip up a high mountain range and ends with an encounter with a Yeti. The ride is one of only a few at Disney with a single-rider entrance.

Hidden Mickeys. In the queue, as a hat on a Yeti doll, bottle caps in a display of patches, a dent and two holes in a museum's tea kettle, and on the left wall after the museum (with a sorcerer's hat) as wood stains in a photo.

Fun facts. Yetis are not real; scientists agree there is no credible evidence they exist. The Yeti legend, however, certainly exists. For centuries, Himalayans have told stories about a humanoid monster that fiercely guards the area around Mt. Everest. Reports increased in the 20th century, when Westerners began seeing an "Abominable Snowman." Interest peaked in 1960, when Sir Edmund Hillary's fact-finding trip to the peak brought trip-wire and time-lapse cameras, but found nothing.

The villain of 1964's stop-motion classic "Rudolph the Red-Nosed Reindeer" is a Yeti named Bumbles. The 2001 Disney/Pixar film "Monsters, Inc." includes an Abominable Snowman voiced by John Ratzenberger.

Key facts. *Best for:* Children, teens, thrill seekers. *Duration:* 3 minutes. *Capacity:* 34 passengers per car (five cars of six passengers each, last car seats four, seated two across) *Queue:* Indoor, outdoor queue is mostly covered. *Fear factor:* High lift, often dark, threatening monster, one steep drop. *Restraint:* Lap bar. *Top speed:* 60 mph. *Weather issues:* Closed during thunderstorms. *Debuted:* 2006. *Health advisories:* Guests should be free from motion sickness; pregnancy; high blood pressure; heart, back or neck problems. *Access:* Height minimum 44 inches. Wheelchair and ECV users must transfer. *Location:* Asia.

Julie Neal

Nine out of ten riders agree: Expedition Everest's 80-foot drop is a highlight of their Animal Kingdom day. At top, the ride appears to come to an end as it reaches the top of a mountain.

An angry carnotaurus threatens guests on Dinosaur. A hidden hydraulic system on the ride's "Time Rover" simulates the pitch, roll and yaw of a slippery trip through a primeval forest.

Dinosaur!

A carnotaurus stalks you in this bumpy, dark, exhilarating ride

★★★★ ✓ **FastPass+** Ferocious dinosaurs chase you in this tense dark ride. As your vehicle (a motion simulator that moves on a track) careens through a primeval forest, asteroids rain from the sky, raptors threaten you and a carnotaurus tries to hunt you down. Air and smoke cannons, strobe lights and loud sounds ratchet up the thrills.

The adventure begins at the stuffy Dino Institute Discovery Center, a 1970s-style museum. After a multimedia show explains that an asteroid shower wiped out dinosaurs long ago, the director announces that—thanks to a new time-traveling vehicle—you can safely travel back to that time yourself. But when her sneaky assistant reprograms your ride, all heck breaks loose. The attraction is based on the 2000 movie "Dinosaur."

Tips. *When to go:* Early, late or with a Fastpass. *Where to sit:* Ask for the front seat for the best view and most legroom.

Fun finds. A cast of the largest and most complete T-Rex fossil ever found (Sue, South Dakota, 1990) stands in front of the ride. In the boarding area, red, yellow and white pipes are marked with the chemical makeups of ketchup, mustard and mayonnaise—a nod to McDonald's, the ride's original sponsor.

Hidden Mickey. In a mural in the first lobby, as marks on a tree trunk.

Key facts. *Best for:* Older children, teens, adults. *Duration:* 3 minutes, 30 seconds. *Capacity:* 144 per hour. *Queue:* Indoor. *Fear factor:* Intense, loud, jerky, dark. And scary. *Restraint:* Seat belt. *Debuted:* 1998. *Health advisories:* Guests should be free from motion sickness; pregnancy; high blood pressure; heart, back or neck problems. *Access:* Height minimum 40 inches. Wheelchair and ECV users must transfer. *Disability services:* Assistive listening, video captioning. *Location:* DinoLand U.S.A.

Average wait times

9am	10am	11am	Noon	1pm	2pm	3pm	4pm	5pm	6pm	7pm	8pm	9pm
5m	10m	20m	20m	20m	20m	30m	20m	20m	15m	10m	n/a	n/a

© Disney

© Disney

"Time machines" spin as they zig-zag down a narrow track on Primeval Whirl. The throwback roller coaster is the signature ride of Dino-Rama, Animal Kingdom's cheesy carnival.

Primeval Whirl

Cheap-thrill spinning coaster parodies the Dinosaur ride

★★★★ **FastPass+** A kitschy timetrip back to the days when dinosaurs became extinct, this quirky roller coaster combines the thrills of an old-school Wild Mouse with the spins of a Disney tea cup. Riders often feel like they are about to fall off its narrow track, as its wide cars whip around turns as they build speed.

According to Disney lore, Primeval Whirl is the work of local low-brows Chester and Hester, who wanted a time-travel ride for their Dino-Rama carnival that was similar to that offered by the nearby Dino Institute. Each candy-colored car features the fins and chrome of a 1950s automobile and the huge reflectors of an old bicycle. On its dash sits an alarm clock, a clock radio and an egg timer.

Lining the course are cartoon clocks, spinning vortices, dinosaur cut-outs warning "The End is Near" and eventually, meteors.

Tips. *When to go:* Very early or late, so you don't have a long wait. *How to spin fast:*

Put the heaviest person in your group at one side. *For families:* If you have a child who's nervous about roller coasters, have them sit in the middle. *For couples:* The seats fit four, but are divided in the middle, leaving two cozy couple spots. You are jerked and thrown together throughout the ride. *Feel queasy?* Stare at the orange radio box in the center of the dash to keep your dizziness at bay.

Key facts. *Best for:* Children, teens. *Duration:* 2 minutes, 30 seconds. *Capacity:* 104 on two tracks (four per car). *Queue:* Outdoor, covered. *Fear factor:* Jerky, spins, one steep drop. *Restraint:* Lap bar. *Top speed:* 29 mph. *Weather issues:* Closed during thunderstorms. *Debuted:* 2002. *Health advisories:* Guests should be free from motion sickness; pregnancy; high blood pressure; heart, back or neck problems. *Access:* Height minimum 48 inches. Wheelchair and ECV users must transfer. *Location:* DinoLand U.S.A.

Average wait times

9am	10am	11am	Noon	1pm	2pm	3pm	4pm	5pm	6pm	7pm	8pm	9pm
5m	20m	20m	30m	30m	20m	20m	20m	20m	20m	10m	n/a	n/a

TriceraTop Spin may not have the classic charm of Dumbo the Flying Elephant, but it does seat four and there's rarely a long line. A covered queue area has fans to keep guests cool.

TriceraTop Spin

A dino Dumbo, perfect for young families

★★★ Circling around a colorful spinning-top tin toy, you and up to three other passengers ride in a chubby triceratops that climbs, dips and dives at your command. Eye candy includes playful dinosaurs that pop out of the top, flying cartoon comets that circle around it and, at night, white light bulbs that line the ride's hub and spokes. Manic banjo and fiddle music adds a wacky cornpone touch.

Though the ride lacks the charm of Magic Kingdom's Dumbo the Flying Elephant, it's easier to enjoy. There's never a long wait; in fact there's often no wait at all. And since each vehicle seats four, small families can ride together.

Many Disney purists dismiss the ride as too cheesy. But younger children will love it, and after all, cheesy is the point of the whole DinoRama area.

Tips. *When to go:* Anytime except the hottest part of the day, when the asphalt "parking lot" of this faux roadside carnival reflects just too much heat. *Where to sit:* In the front seat for the most legroom, in back to control the height of your dino. *For families:* TriceraTop Spin is the only ride at Disney's Animal Kingdom that is completely toddler friendly, with nothing scary and no height minimum. *For couples:* Don't ride this unless you're in the mood to touch each other; the cozy seats force riders to squeeze together.

Fun fact. The vehicles circle every 13 seconds. That's the same speed as Dumbo and Aladdin's Magic Carpets in Magic Kingdom, half the pace of the rockets at that park's Astro Orbiter.

Key facts. *Best for:* Children. *Duration:* 1 minute, 30 seconds. *Capacity:* 64 (four per car, seated two across). *Queue:* Outdoor, covered. *Weather issues:* Closed during thunderstorms. *Debuted:* 2001. *Access:* ECV users must transfer. *Location:* DinoLand U.S.A.

Average wait times

9am	10am	11am	Noon	1pm	2pm	3pm	4pm	5pm	6pm	7pm	8pm	9pm
0m	0m	0m	0m	5m	5m	20m	10m	10m	5m	5m	n/a	n/a

Part of a tongue-in-cheek "Dino-Rama" carnival, Disney's Fossil Fun midway games are often deserted late in the day. Behind them is the Primeval Whirl roller coaster.

Fossil Fun Games

Inexpensive, fair midway games that children can beat

★★★ ✔ These whimsical midway games reward winners with prizes. Compared to actual carnival games, they're easy.

Three of the games are designed specifically for children: the watergun Fossil Fueler, the ball-rolling racing derby Mammoth Marathon and the mallet-strike game Whac-A-Pachycephalosaur ("Whacky Packy" for short). Two others—a ball toss and basketball throw—require serious skill to win.

Tips. *Fossil Fueler:* To shoot straight, use your free hand to cradle the barrel of your gun. *Mammoth Marathon:* Ask for a practice ball before the race begins. Roll your balls slowly. *Whac-A-Pachycephalosaur:* Wait until you see a dino head pop up before you swing at it; don't try to anticipate.

Key facts. *Best for:* Families. *Duration:* 1 minute. *Cost:* \$3–4. *Players:* 1–10. *Weather issues:* Closed during thunderstorms. *Debuted:* 2002. *Access:* Players may remain in wheelchairs, ECVs. *Location:* DinoLand U.S.A.

Average wait times

9am	10am	11am	Noon	1pm	2pm	3pm	4pm	5pm	6pm	7pm	8pm	9pm
0m	0m	0m	0m	0m	0m	0m	0m	0m	0m	0m	n/a	n/a

The Boneyard play area entertains elementary-age kids with a towering maze of nets, slides and tunnels; preschoolers play in a fossil-filled sandy pit.

The Boneyard

Disney's best playground is themed to an archaeological dig

★★★★★ Geared for toddlers through elementary-school kids, this large outdoor playground is themed to be a dinosaur dig site. Two distinct areas are connected by an overhead footbridge. Highlights include a three-story tower of nets and slides and a sandy pit where kids dig for mammoth bones.

Extras include a maze of walk-through tunnels, walls embedded with dinosaur skeletons, climb-on bones and rocks, steep net and rope-climbing ramps and waterfalls sized just right to drench a young head. Mesh canopies filter the sun, and the flooring is a spongy material that stays cool and won't harm tumbling youngsters.

The playground offers plenty of spots for parents to get off their feet. Overhead fans keep things breezy. An abundance of nooks and crannies makes it easy to lose sight of your child, but there's only one exit, and its gate is always monitored.

Tips. *When to go:* Anytime. *Where to sit:* There are many places for parents to sit and relax, including multiple picnic tables and a ledge that surrounds the sandy dig area.

Fun finds. Notes sound when kids bang a "xylobone" embedded in a wall near a Jeep. Nearby, dinosaur tracks trigger loud roars when kids step on them.

Hidden Mickeys. Near the entrance as a large stain under a drinking fountain; as a quarter and two pennies on a table in a fenced-off area on the second level, by the slides; as a fan and two hardhats in a fenced-off area at the back of the mammoth-bone pit.

Key facts. *Best for:* Children. *Duration:* Allow 15–30 minutes. *Capacity:* 500. *Operating hours:* May open 1 hour after park open. *Weather issues:* Closed during thunderstorms. *Debuted:* 1998. *Access:* Guests may remain in wheelchairs, ECVs. *Location:* DinoLand U.S.A.

Average wait times

9am	10am	11am	Noon	1pm	2pm	3pm	4pm	5pm	6pm	7pm	8pm	9pm
0m	0m	0m	0m	0m	0m	0m	0m	0m	0m	0m	n/a	n/a

When curious clownfish Nemo (left) defies his overprotective father in "Finding Nemo—The Musical," each takes off on a journey that teaches them to understand each other.

Finding Nemo—The Musical

The movie as a song-and-dance puppet show. And it works.

★★★★★ ✓ **FastPass+** Shimmying sharks, body-surfing turtles and a bicycle-riding stingray star in this colorful, whimsical stage show, which re-creates the 2003 Pixar movie "Finding Nemo" as a musical. Nine songs tell the story with help from acrobats, dancers and huge mechanical puppets. Broadway-quality but for its length, the show is funny, touching and a visual treat.

Main characters are represented by live performers, who act out their roles while operating large puppet versions of themselves. Other characters are portrayed with a variety of puppetry styles, including bunraku, a Japanese form in which one huge puppet is operated by multiple puppeteers.

The production takes place in the enclosed Theater in the Wild.

Tips. *When to go:* Get a Fastpass for this show; holders get to enter the theater 20 to 30 minutes before non-Fastpass holders, and take all the good seats. If you can't, arrive at least 30 minutes early; the last show of the day is usually the least crowded. Food is allowed in line but not inside the theater. *Where to sit:* In the middle of the auditorium to see the full spectacle, or along the center catwalk to be immersed in it.

Fun find. Before the show begins, Nemo swims back and forth through oversized bubbles on the sides of the stage.

Hidden Mickey. As three blue bubbles, two lit and one drawn, at the bottom left of the stage wall.

Key facts. *Best for:* Children, teens, adults, seniors. *Duration:* 30 minutes. *Capacity:* 1,500. *Queue:* Outdoor, uncovered. *Operating hours:* Scheduled performances mid-morning to mid-afternoon. *Debuted:* 2007. *Access:* Guests may remain in wheelchairs, ECVs. *Disability services:* Reflective captioning. *Location:* DinoLand U.S.A.

Average wait times

9am	10am	11am	Noon	1pm	2pm	3pm	4pm	5pm	6pm	7pm	8pm	9pm
n/a	n/a	n/a	n/a	n/a	n/a	n/a	n/a	n/a	n/a	n/a	n/a	n/a

Micaela Neal

A male silverback western lowland gorilla relaxes in his Pangani Forest Exploration Trail habitat. He shares the beautiful spot with the rest of his family.

Animal guide

By **Micaela Neal** Sure it's a theme park, but Disney's Animal Kingdom is also a zoo, the most popular one in the United States. Exotic animals are everywhere, often roaming freely in natural habitats. On the following pages, the location of each animal is abbreviated as follows:

AF = Affection Section
AS = Asia landscape
CS = Conservation Station
DI = Discovery Island
DL = DinoLand U.S.A. landscape
FL = Flights of Wonder
KS = Kilimanjaro Safaris
MJ = Maharajah Jungle Trek
OA = Oasis
PF = Pangani Forest Exploration Trail

Anteater. The 9-foot-long **southern giant anteater** (OA) is the world's largest anteater; its 2-foot-long tongue can lick up 30,000 ants a day. It has the largest claws of any mammal, and uses its huge bushy tail as a blanket.

Antelope. Domesticated by Egyptians as early as 2500 BC, the **addax** (KS) is critically endangered today. It has spiraling horns that grow up to 2 feet long, and tracks rainfall to find grazing spots... The **blackbuck** (MJ) can run 50 miles per hour. In Hindu mythology, it transports moon goddess Chandrama. Males have ringed, spiraling horns; females smooth curved ones... Chocolate-brown with a purplish sheen, the **bontebok** (KS) is extinct in the wild. Like the blackbuck, both sexes have horns... Topped with twisting 5-foot horns, clashing **greater kudu** (KS) males can get stuck together and starve to death. Their horns are used to make Jewish shofars, blown at Rosh Hashanah... The 2,000-pound, 6-foot-tall **Patterson's eland** (KS) is the world's largest antelope, and is farmed like cattle in South Africa. Its sweet milk takes months rather than days to expire... Only older male **sable antelopes** (KS) are black ("sable"); females and young are reddish-brown. Its scimitar-shaped horns can kill lions. Adults rest in a ring around their young, horns out... The national animal of South Africa, the **springbok** (KS) can run 60 miles per hour and leap 13 feet. It's the most common prey of lions, making up 70 percent of caught meals... Despite its name, the shaggy **waterbuck** (KS) doesn't spend much time in water; it just hides there to escape predators. Its coat is water-repellant... The 8-foot-tall **western bongo** (KS) is the largest forest antelope. The name "bongo"—Swahili for "thirteen"—comes from the 13 white stripes on its sides. Its shyness earns it the nickname "Ghost of the

The King of Beasts overlooks the Kilimanjaro Safaris savanna. He and his pride are separated from the attraction's trucks by a deep pit hidden between large rocks in the landscaping.

Forest"... The odd **white-bearded wildebeest** (KS) looks like a striped, hairy horse with a cow's horns. It was the partial inspiration for the Beast's face in Disney's 1991 movie "Beauty and the Beast." Herds of wildebeest migrate annually in the world's largest wildlife movement... The **yellow-backed duiker** (KS, PF) has a yellow patch on its rump that erects when alarmed. Duikers ("divers" in Afrikaans) are named for their habit of diving into underbrush when startled.

Bats. With a 6-foot wingspan, the **Malayan flying fox** (MJ) is the world's largest bat. It can eat its body weight in fruit and vegetation daily... With only a few hundred of its kind left in the wild, the **Rodrigues fruit bat** (MJ) struggles to survive on the Indian Ocean's tiny Rodrigues Island.

Beetles. The **dung beetle** (PF) rolls dung into balls. It was sacred to ancient Egyptians; they compared it to the god of the rising sun, who rolled the sun across the sky... The carnivorous but also edible **predaceous diving beetle** (CS) is served roasted and salted in Mexico, often with tacos... The iridescent, multicolored **rainbow scarab** (CS) is a North American dung beetle. The male has a curved, black horn.

Centipede. The carnivorous, 8-inch-long **giant desert centipede** (CS) has a painful, venomous "bite" that is actually a pinch.

Cockroach. The **Madagascar hissing cockroach** (PF, CS) hisses by forcing air through its abdomen breathing pores. Its docile nature makes it a common stand-in for more familiar species in films and television.

Cows. With horns 28 inches around, the **Ankole cow** (KS) has the world's largest horn circumference. Hollow and full of blood vessels, its horns keep it cool... A shy ox, the **banteng** (MJ) was the first endangered species to be successfully cloned... Descended from original Spanish stock left in the southern United States in the early 16th century, the rare **Pineywoods cow** (AF) has since bred without interference along the Gulf Coast.

Cricket. Named for its humped back, the **camel cricket** (CS) doesn't chirp, and in most places is considered a household pest.

Crocodilians. Growing up to 16 feet long, the **American alligator** (CS presentations) has 80 teeth, but usually won't eat animals larger than raccoons. Chirping, yellow-striped young grow to be solid gray-black. Adults bellow, unique for crocodilians... The **American crocodile** (DL) can grow to 18 feet and 2,000 pounds. A 2009 cold spell killed off 150 American crocs in Florida, including Wilma, a famous female on Sanibel Island, the author's hometown... The second largest crocodile at 20 feet long and 2,200 pounds, the **Nile crocodile** (KS) is the most prolific

THE COMPLETE WALT DISNEY WORLD 2015 **233**

An elephant and her calf roam the Kilimanjaro Safaris grasslands. When Disney started its elephant breeding program, it "baby-proofed" the habitat by planting more trees for shade.

predator of humans among wild animals, and kills hundreds to thousands yearly. It can also take on giraffes, young hippos and elephants, and even lions.

Deer. Hunted throughout history for its hide, meat, and impressive antlers, only a few thousand **Eld's deer** (MJ) remain in a 15-square-mile Indian marsh. Its wide, spreadable hooves are perfect for wetland living... The small, exotic **Reeve's muntjac** (OA) is known as the "barking deer" for its danger-signaling call. Males have short antlers and large canine teeth for injuring enemies.

Donkey. According to Christian lore, Mary rode a **Sicilian miniature donkey** (AF) the night Jesus was born. A cross-shaped stripe lays over its back and shoulders. Brother and sister Jack and Jill have been at Animal Kingdom since the park opened in 1998.

Elephant. At 20 feet long and 14,000 pounds, the **African elephant** (KS) is the largest living land animal. Unlike Asian elephants, both sexes have tusks. Its vocalizations include low-frequency rumbles inaudible to people. It lives in matriarchal groups. During mating, the entire herd takes part in a noisy "mating pandemonium"— females and calves mill, circle, wave their trunks, and trumpet up to an hour.

Felines. The largest African predator, the **African lion** (KS) can run 37 miles per hour and leap 40 feet. Its roar can be heard five miles away. It's the most social big cat, forming prides of five to ten individuals; the females hunt while the dominant male defends the pride. It spends 20 hours each day sleeping... The endangered, 660-pound **Asian tiger** (MJ) is the world's largest cat. Its unique stripe pattern is on both its fur and its skin. It can walk silently, leap 30 feet, and drag 3,000 pounds. A group of tigers is called an "ambush"... Able to accelerate from 0 to 70 miles per hour in three seconds—the same rate as the Rock 'n' Roller Coaster at Disney's Hollywood Studios—the **cheetah** (KS) is the world's fastest land animal. It hunts by day, primarily by sight. While chasing prey, its long tail helps it balance and its doglike semi-retractable claws provide traction.

Fish. The **African cichlid** (PF) protects its young by hiding them in its mouth. It keeps water clear by feeding on hippo waste... Using primitive lungs, the eel-like **African lungfish** (PF) can breathe air. It uses its long, fleshy fins to plod through mud. Its ancestors developed true limbs and evolved into early land animals... At up to 10 feet long and 650 pounds, the **Paroon shark-catfish** (DI) is the largest scaleless freshwater fish. It has a shark-like dorsal fin... The chubby, herbivorous **tambaqui** (DI) looks like, and sometimes confused with, the smaller carnivorous piranha.

An Asian tiger slinks through its territory along the Maharajah Jungle Trek. Its habitat includes small rolling hills, dense grasses and shrubs, trees, a fountain and a pool.

Frogs and toads. The plump **African bullfrog** (PF, CS) resembles "Star Wars" character Jabba the Hutt. It eats anything it can swallow, and has a painful bite... The largest native toad in the United States, the **Colorado river toad** (CS) is also the archetypal "psychedelic toad"—its venom contains potent hallucinogens and is illegal to possess... The world's most poisonous vertebrate, the **golden poison dart frog** (CS) has enough toxin to kill two bull elephants, or up to 20 humans. It appears to vibrate when it calls. Like all poison dart frogs, it loses its toxicity in captivity due to changes in its diet. Native South American people use poison from dart frogs to coat the tips of blow darts, hence the frogs' "poison dart" names... Named for the pattern on its back, the **hourglass tree frog** (CS) is the only vertebrate capable of laying eggs both on land and in water... The endangered **Puerto Rican crested toad** (CS) was thought to be extinct until 1967... The flat, aquatic **Surinam toad** (CS) looks like a mottled brown leaf. Its odd face has a triangular head and beady eyes, but no tongue or teeth. Young toads develop in pockets on a mother's back; 60-100 emerge as miniature adults.

Giraffes. The tallest land animal and the largest giraffe subspecies, the **Masai giraffe** (KS) is distinguished by jagged, irregular spots. Its strong kick can crush a lion's skull... The most common giraffe in captivity, the **reticulated giraffe** (KS) is distinguished by clear spots separated by a netlike ("reticulated") grid of white lines. Males fight by violently slamming their necks into one another.

Goats. The long flobby ears of the **Anglo-Nubian goat** (AF) earn it the nickname "Rabbit Goat"... With less than 300 remaining in the wild, the rare **Arapawa goat** (AF) descends from two goats released on Arapawa Island by Captain James Cook in 1773. Its face has distinctive black-striped markings. Males have wide, sweeping horns; females have short curved ones... The gentle **Nigerian dwarf goat** (AF) can be trained to use a leash. Its milk is used for cheese and making soap.

Gorilla. At up to 450 pounds, the **Western lowland gorilla** (PF) is the largest and most powerful primate. It's also the most populous gorilla species. A mature male has a silver back and is twice the size of a female. The gorilla has human-like fingernails and fingerprints. It's intelligent, able to learn sign language and can make and use tools. A herbivore, it's the least aggressive primate; its iconic chest-beating is just a display.

Hedgehog. The nocturnal **South African hedgehog** (CS presentations) rolls into a ball when threatened, exposing only its spiny back. Hedgehogs fight by butting heads.

Above left, the vegetarian Rodriguez fruit bat is harmless to man. Above right, a slender-tailed meerkat on sentry duty keeps an eye on its human spectators.

Hedgehog tenrec. Despite looking like a hedgehog, the Madagascar-dwelling **hedgehog tenrec** (PF, CS presentations) is most closely related to two other equally-strange creatures: the golden mole and the elephant shrew. Unlike true hedgehogs, it's active during the day.

Hippopotamus. The most aggressive African animal, the **Nile hippopotamus** (KS, PF) grows up to 15 feet long and 8,000 pounds. It can outrun man and hold its breath for 12 minutes. During the day it rests underwater; at night it grazes on land. Its skin oozes a pinkish, moisturizing oil that acts as a sunscreen. The hippo's closest relatives are dolphins and whales.

Kangaroos. The largest marsupial and Australian mammal, the **red kangaroo** (DI) stands 7 feet and can jump 30 feet. It's farmed for its meat, which is eaten by people around the world, and for its hide, which makes the world's lightest, strongest leather... A nocturnal 'roo relative, the timid **swamp wallaby** (OA) defensively kicks and scratches the faces of predators. It can drink salt water when fresh isn't available... The least common kangaroo in United States zoos, the **Western grey kangaroo** (DI) has a face like a donkey. When threatened, it growls like a dog.

Katydid. At up to 6 inches with a 10-inch wingspan, the **Malaysian giant katydid** (CS) is the world's largest katydid. It's bright green, camouflaged to look like a leaf.

Lemurs. One of five subspecies of the brown lemur, the **collared lemur** (DI) is distinguished by its reddish beard and orange eyes. It salivates on poisonous millipedes and rolls them between its hands before eating them, to remove toxins... The distinctive, golden-eyed **ring-tailed lemur** (DI) uses its tail as a flag to signal its location and warn of danger. Females are dominant.

Lizards. The slender **black tree monitor** (CS) uses its semi-prehensile tail for stabilization while climbing trees; its tail is two-thirds its full length. It can sense movement 800 feet away... The 4-foot **caiman lizard** (CS) is named for the raised scutes on its back that resemble those of the crocodilian caiman. Its scales are lime green; the more colorful male has a red head. Snails make up most of its diet... The colorful **emerald tree monitor** (MJ) is one of the few social monitor lizards. It removes the legs of stick insects before swallowing the bodies... At 10 feet long and 250 pounds, the **Komodo dragon** (MJ) is the world's largest lizard. Its venom, combined with 57 types of dangerous bacteria that thrive in its mouth, makes its bite deadly. A tenacious predator, it hunts monkeys, horses, smaller Komodo dragons and other animals; in 20 minutes

Micaela Neal

Micaela Neal

The okapi (above right) is the closest relative to the Masai giraffe (above left). It appears to have the giraffe's body, face and ossicones, and the rear of a Grant's zebra (top right).

it can swallow a goat whole. It will eat dead animals too; it can smell them from six miles away. Sometimes, it digs up human bodies from graves and devours them. Intelligent and curious, it plays by sticking its head into boxes and shoes... A foot-long desert herbivore, the **ornate spiny-tailed lizard** (PF) has a turtle-like head and an armored tail. A gland around its nose excretes salt... Named for the horn-like scales on its nose, the 3-foot-long **rhinoceros iguana** (OA) lays some of the largest lizard eggs. A group of iguanas is called a "mess."

Mantids. Camouflaged to look like a brown, decaying leaf, the **Malaysian dead-leaf mantis** (CS) displays colorful wings when threatened... Named for its slender, violin-shaped prothorax, the **violin mantis** (CS) hunts flying insects.

Meerkat. A type of mongoose, the **slender-tailed meerkat** (PF) can kill striking cobras. It lives in multifamily burrows that divide duties among individuals; sentry duty is shared by rotating guards. A famous fictional meerkat is Timon, of "Lion King" fame.

Monkeys. The **Angolan black & white colobus monkey** (PF) is named "colobus"—from the Greek word for "mutilated"—because it has no thumbs... With a distinctive puffy crest of fur on its head, the endangered **cotton-top tamarin** (DI, CS) lives in family groups and

mates for life. Its sophisticated communication sounds like chirping... Named for its resemblance to German emperor Wilhelm II, the **emperor tamarin** (CS) sports a long, white, regal mustache... Endangered due to habitat destruction and illegal pet trading, the **golden lion tamarin** (CS) is named for its long, mane-like golden fur... The male **mandrill** (KS) is the largest and most colorful monkey; the more times he has mated, the more vividly colored he becomes. The mandrill is non-aggressive and social; it bares its massive canine teeth as a greeting, not a threat. It beats its hands against the ground when upset. Disney's famous mandrill is Rafiki, the wise shaman in "The Lion King"... The largest, loudest gibbon species, the **siamang** (AS) inflates its throat sac and produces a "hoot" that reaches 113 decibels, nearly as loud as jet aircraft at 100 yards... The territorial call of the **white-cheeked gibbon** (AS) is a crescendo of siren-like "whoops." Males and juveniles are black with white cheeks; females and newborns are blond.

Newt. The armored skull of the **emperor newt** (CS) looks like an emperor's crown. By expanding its rib cage, it triggers a release of poison from orange glands on its body. One newt has enough toxin to kill 7,500 mice.

Okapi. With a giraffe's body, face and ossicones mixed with a zebra's striped rear, the

Young male blackbucks spar in their habitat along the Maharajah Jungle Trek. Many Animal Kingdom creatures display similar natural behaviors, in full view of park visitors.

forest-dwelling **okapi** (KS, PF) is the nearest giraffe relative. It sleeps only five minutes a day. This elusive creature was not identified as a species until 1900.

Otter. The world's smallest otter, the **Asian small-clawed otter** (DI) catches prey using its dexterous, non-webbed front paws, unlike other otters. It can stay underwater up to eight minutes at a time. Very social and playful, it loves to play tag and tug-of-war, and can juggle pebbles.

Pigs. With a name meaning "pig-deer," the male **babirusa** (OA) has strange, antler-like tusks that grow up through his muzzle and curl back toward his face. Genetically the animal is closer to a hippo than a pig... With less than 200 left in the wild, the **guinea hog** (AF) is unique to North America. The breed was brought to the United States on slave ships. Thomas Jefferson owned some guinea

hogs in 1804... With a name meaning "fat and round," the **kunekune pig** (AF) (pronounced "cooney cooney") is the world's smallest and most sociable pig. A popular pet, it's as smart as a dog... The only grassland pig, the **warthog** (KS), is named for the male's warty facial growths. It defends itself with sharp 6-inch lower tusks and curved 2-foot upper tusks. Pumbaa from "The Lion King" is a warthog.

Rhinoceros. Actually gray, the **black rhinoceros** (KS) has a triangular upper lip used for grasping leaves and a horn up to 4 feet long. It can charge at 35 miles per hour... The largest, most social, and most numerous rhino species, the **white rhinoceros** (KS) weighs up to 5,000 pounds. Its name is a mistranslation of the Afrikaans "wijt" ("wide"), a reference to its broad, grazing mouth.

Rodents. The largest, heaviest African rodent, the **African crested porcupine** (DI)

An infant western lowland gorilla explores its Pangani Forest Exploration Trail habitat. Baby animals are commonplace at Animal Kingdom. Its most recent gorilla was born in August, 2014.

A diminutive Pineywoods cow contemplates approaching guests at the Affection Section petting zoo. The area keeps its larger animals behind fences, but lets smaller ones roam freely among visitors.

has a crest formed by erect quills; others rise when alarmed. It doesn't shoot its quills; though their barbed tips imbed themselves easily in flesh... The **four-striped grass mouse** (PF) builds a burrow system with runways leading to its regular feeding grounds... Neither a mole nor a rat, the pink, blind **naked mole rat** (PF) is related to the guinea pig. Teeth on the outside of its mouth allow it to dig without swallowing dirt. It is the only mammal that organizes itself into ant-like colonies led by a queen... The long-legged **Patagonian cavy** (OA) looks like a small deer that has the head of a rabbit. It can run 28 miles per hour and leap six feet.

Salamanders. The endangered, aquatic **axolotl** (CS) (pronounced ACK-suh-LAH-tuhl) can't breathe air. Despite being cute as a button, it was a staple in the diet of Aztecs... The colored glands of the well-known **European fire salamander** (CS) exude samandarin, a neurotoxin that causes muscle convulsions, hypertension and hyperventilation... With no hind legs, the eel-like **greater siren** (CS) is the most primitive living salamander. It intimidates predators with duckling-like cheeps... At 4 feet long, the aquatic, snake-like **two-toed amphiuma** (CS) is the longest salamander in the United States. It has two rows of razor sharp teeth, and a savage bite.

Scorpions. The aggressive **desert hairy scorpion** (CS) is the largest North American scorpion. It digs to find water... The tropical, docile **emperor scorpion** (PF, CS) is one of the largest scorpions, up to 8 inches long.

Sheep. The rare **babydoll sheep** (AF) originated in the United States in the 1980s. The two-foot-tall adult has fine wool in the class of cashmere... The oldest North American

A timid South African hedgehog sits in the glove of a Conservation Station handler. Daily presentations include a variety of small creatures, most of which guests are allowed to touch.

Micaela Neal

Clockwise from upper left: An Angolan black & white colobus monkey, a cotton-top tamarin, a colorful male mandrill, a ring-tailed lemur.

sheep breed, the **Gulf Coast native sheep** (AF) was brought to the United States by Spanish colonists in the 1500s. It's now indigenous to portions of all Gulf Coast states… A breed of hair sheep, the **Katahdin sheep** (AF) has a woolless, smooth coat that doesn't need to be sheared.

Skinks. Named for its bright, curled tongue that startles predators, the **blue-tongued skink** (CS) stores food and water in its tail… The largest skink species, the tree-dwelling **prehensile-tailed skink** (CS) uses its tail to maneuver from branch to branch.

Snakes. Named for its tendency to curl into a ball when frightened, the **ball python** (CS presentations) is revered by the Nigerian Igbo people. If one is accidentally killed, the community will build it a coffin and have a

funeral… The **desert rosy boa** (CS) is one of few boas native to the United States. It moves with a slow, caterpillar-like motion… The large, angular snout of the **green tree python** (CS) has heat-sensing pits. The yellow hatchling turns green and nocturnal as an adult; the change may be overnight or take months… The **Kenyan sand boa** (PF) spends 80 percent of its life buried; it suffocates prey by dragging it under the sand. Its diet includes naked mole rats… The largest snake in Puerto Rico, the **Puerto Rican boa** (CS) hangs down in front of cave entrances to catch flying bats.

Stick Insects. Camouflaged to look like a prickly twig, the **giant spiny stick insect** (CS) travels in groups at night… Ten inches long and quite aggressive, the female **Malayan**

Clockwise from upper left: A red kangaroo, a bontebok, a pair of Ankole cattle, a Patagonian cavy, a crouching cheetah, a banteng ox.

jungle nymph (CS) lays the largest eggs in the insect world. She snaps her spiny back legs together like scissors.

Tarantulas. The burrow of the **Arizona blond tarantula** (CS) goes two feet straight down... The third largest tarantula, the **Brazilian salmon pink tarantula** (CS) is also known (correctly) as the "birdeater"... The aggressive **brown baboon tarantula** (CS) rears up and strikes down repeatedly when provoked. It is eaten by baboons... The agile **Indian ornamental tarantula** (CS) can catch flying insects in midair... A **Mexican red rump tarantula** (CS) stars in the 1955 sci-fi movie "Tarantula," in which a giant one terrorizes a desert... The bite of the **Mombasa starburst tarantula** (PF) can put you in the emergency room.

Tortoises and turtles. The primitive **Asian brown tortoise** (DL) provides more parental care than any other tortoise... The third-largest tortoise, the **African spurred tortoise** (KS queue) is named for its spurred back legs. It's regarded by some African cultures as a mediator between men and gods... The male **Eastern box turtle** (CS) has red eyes; the female has brown eyes... The tiny **Egyptian tortoise** (CS) is only 5 inches long... At 5 feet long, the **Galapagos tortoise** (DI) is the world's largest tortoise. It lives 150 years. Males "fight" by opening their mouths and stretching their necks; the highest stretch wins... The endangered **gopher tortoise** (CS) digs deep burrows that it shares with other animals. These burrows can be 50 feet long and 10 feet deep. It lives

Clockwise from upper left: A Nile hippopotamus, a brilliant male caiman lizard, a Komodo dragon, a dark gray American crocodile, a pale gray Nile crocodile, an axolotl salamander.

in the southeast United States, including on Disney property... The flat, pliable shell of the **pancake tortoise** (PF) lets it squeeze into tight openings. When threatened, it doesn't withdraw into its shell; instead it dashes for cover... The **South American yellow-footed tortoise** (CS) makes a sound like a baby cooing... Named for the web-like pattern on its shell, the **spider tortoise** (PF) is critically endangered.

Zebras. Black with white stripes, the **Grant's zebra** (KS) is the most abundant zebra. It "barks" instead of neighs. Members of a herd sleep in turns, so some members are always alert... White with black stripes, the **Grevy's zebra** (PF) is the rarest and largest zebra; it's twice the size of the Grant's zebra. It brays like a donkey. A herd's foals are left in male-led "kindergartens" while their mothers get water. It was used in circuses in ancient Rome.

Birds. Animal Kingdom has more than 140 species of exotic birds on display. Most make their home in the aviaries of the Pangani Forest Exploration Trail and the Maharajah Jungle Trek, though you'll also find them in the Oasis entrance area, along the Discovery Island trails, and beside the queue and in the habitats of the Kilimanjaro Safaris ride.

Barbet. Named for the thick bristles under its bill, the **bearded barbet** (PF) has a call that's a growling *scrawk*.

Cormorant. A skilled fisher, the **white-breasted cormorant** (KS) is also known by its unusual mating ritual—it courts by wrapping

Clockwise from upper left: A male babirusa, a white-bearded wildebeest antelope, a warthog, a white rhinoceros, a rhinoceros iguana, a Galapagos tortoise, a black rhinoceros.

its neck around a potential mate. A group of cormorants is called a "gulp."

Crow. The intelligent **pied crow** (FW) drops stones onto ostrich eggs to crack them open. This African bird is a popular pet in the United States, since native corvids are illegal to own.

Doves and pigeons. Rare in zoos, the fig-eating **African green pigeon** (PF) also likes carrion and dried antelope blood...

All photos: Micaela Neal

Top: A close relative to the extinct dodo, the Nicobar pigeon has long hackles around its head that look like dreadlocks. Above, a green-winged dove (left) and an African green pigeon.

The **Bartlett's bleeding-heart dove** (MJ) is named for the crimson patch on its breast, which looks like a bloody wound... Common in rainforests, the male **green-winged dove** (MJ) courts females by dancing and bobbing his head... A close relative to the extinct dodo, the **Nicobar pigeon** (MJ) has long hackles around its head that look like dreadlocks... The male **pied imperial pigeon** (MJ) displays by inflating his neck and hopping in place... The world's largest pigeon, the turkey-sized **Victoria crowned pigeon** (MJ) is named after Queen Victoria. It has an unusual booming call, and sports a lacy white-tipped crest.

Ducks. Actually a misnamed duck, the **African pygmy goose** (PF) is the smallest African waterfowl. Its favorite food is water lilies... The hot-headed **common**

shelduck (OA) honks like a goose... A mother **Mandarin duck** (MJ) coaxes her ducklings to jump to the ground from their tree hollow nest; she then leads the youngsters to water. A pair of Mandarin ducks are a traditional wedding gift in Korea... Used as a "guard dog" in its native Tibet, the **ruddy shelduck** (MJ) is large, loud and aggressive.

Eagles and hawks. The national symbol of the United States since 1782, the **bald eagle** (FW) is named using an older usage of the word "bald," which means "white headed." Its high-pitched chirps are often replaced by the more impressive cries of the red-tailed hawk in movies and television shows, most ridiculously in the tongue-in-cheek opening credits of the Comedy Central program "The Cobert Report." Some wild bald eagles nest

Left: A West African crowned crane. Top: A turkey-sized Victoria crowned pigeon. Above: A Mandarin duck.

near Disney property... Unlike other birds of prey, the **Harris hawk** (FW) hunts in coordinated groups, earning it the nickname "the wolf of the sky." It nests in saguaro cacti.

Goose. One of highest-flying birds, the **bar-headed goose** (MJ) migrates seasonally over the Himalayas.

Hoopoe. A relative of kingfishers, the **green wood hoopoe** (PF) climbs trees like a woodpecker.

Hornbill. Named for its loud call, the **trumpeter hornbill** (FW) sounds like a crying human child.

Junglefowl. The colorful **green junglefowl** (MJ) is metallic green, but many other colors too. Some of its feathers are bronze, and its comb and wattles are pastel blue, pink and purple.

Kingfisher. Using its large red and black bill, the **blue-breasted kingfisher** (PF) excavates nests in termite mounds.

Ostrich. At 8 feet tall, the **common ostrich** (KS) is the world's largest bird. Capable of reaching 45 miles per hour when it runs, it is the fastest two-legged land animal; kicks from its strong legs can kill a lion. Contrary to popular belief, an ostrich doesn't "hide" by sticking its head in sand; it just lays its head on the ground.

Owls. Named for the "horns" on its head (which are really just tufts of feathers), the **great horned owl** (FW) has golden eyes that are among the largest and most powerful in the animal kingdom... The rainforest-dwelling **spectacled owl** (FW postshow) sometimes hunts sloths. The female screams like a steam-whistle.

Partridge. The small, rotund **crested wood partridge** (MJ) uses its feet to probe for insects and seeds.

Parrots. Capable of associating human words with their meanings, the intelligent **African gray parrot** (FW) develops a large vocabulary and an individual personality over its 50- to 70-year lifespan... The second largest macaw, the **green-winged macaw** (DI, FW) is twice the size of the similar-looking scarlet macaw... Named for its olive-green feathers that resemble Spanish army fatigues, the **military macaw** (OA) eats clay from riverbanks for nutrients... Only the male **plum-headed parakeet** (MJ) has a purple head; the female's is gray. The bird likes to mimic electronic tones... Better known as the "galah"—derogatory Australian slang for "loud-mouthed idiot"—the **rose-breasted cockatoo** (FW) has a puffy pink crest... The national bird of Honduras, the noisy **scarlet**

Micaela Neal

Micaela Neal

Top: The bearded barbet has a thick bristle "beard" under its beak. Above, a green-winged macaw (left) and two red-fronted macaws.

macaw (OA, FW) has the longest tail feathers of any macaw.

Peafowl. Unlike those of the more iconic Indian peafowl, the sexes of the **Java green peafowl** (MJ) look similar, though only the male has a 6-foot tail. The bird is also known as the dragonbird because it hunts venomous snakes.

Pelican. Social, group-hunting **pink-backed pelicans** (KS) will reuse the same nests for years, until they collapse.

Pheasant. One of the largest pheasants, the male **great argus pheasant** (MJ) is over 6 feet long. It is named after the mythological Argus, the Greek hundred-eyed giant, for the eye-like pattern on its flight feathers.

Seriema. An odd, terrestrial bird of prey, the **red-legged seriema** (FW) has long legs and can run up to 15 miles per hour. It kills its prey by slamming it repeatedly against the ground.

Songbirds. The **black-collared starling** (MJ) feeds by blindly probing dense vegetation with an open bill... The **chestnut-breasted malkoha** (MJ) is a large cuckoo that—unlike most cuckoos—builds its own nest and raises its own young... The male **fairy bluebird** (MJ) is iridescent blue and black; its call is a liquid, two-note *glue-it*... The usually timid **hooded pitta** (MJ) displays excitement by bowing, bobbing its head, flicking its wings and fanning its tail... Known for its acrobatic somersaults, the **racquet-tailed roller** (PF) is named for its teardrop-tipped double tail streamers... One of the first recordings of birdsong was

Right: The pink-backed pelican feeds in groups by herding fish. Females reuse their nests for years until they fall apart. Below, a black swan and a black-necked swan.

All photos: Micaela Neal

of a **Shama thrush** (MJ), in 1889 on an Edison wax cylinder.

Swans. With the longest neck of any swan, the **black swan** (OA) has a loud, bugle-like call. It is featured on the flag and coat of arms of Western Australia… The **black-necked swan** (OA) is the largest South American waterfowl. Parents piggyback their young to keep them warm and safe from predators.

Toucan. With a huge bill making up a third of its length, the **toco toucan** (FW preshow) is the world's largest toucan. Sacred to South American natives, it's seen as a conduit between the living and spirit worlds.

Turacos. The world's largest turaco, the **great blue turaco** (PF) has tail feathers that are prized for making good luck talismans… The **white-bellied go-away bird** (PF) is named for its call, which sounds like *g'away.*

Wading birds: cranes. Distinguished by its halo-like golden crown and red-and-white face patch, the **East African crowned crane** (FW) stomps the ground to kick up insects… The world's tallest flying bird, the **Sarus crane** (MJ) is 6 feet tall and has an 8-foot wingspan. It's revered and considered a symbol of marital fidelity in India… Unlike

the East African crowned crane, which has a white cheek with a red top, the **West African crowned crane** (DI, KS queue) has a red cheek with a white top. It trumpets loudly at sunrise… With only 5,000 left in the wild, the **white-naped crane** (MJ) is the only crane with pink legs.

Wading birds: flamingos. A flamingo gets its pink color from its diet. It feeds by holding its head upside-down in the water to filter out food. A group of them is called a "flamboyance"… The world's largest and palest flamingo, the **greater flamingo** (KS) can live up to 75 years… The smallest, pinkest and most numerous flamingo, the **lesser flamingo** (DI) performs ritualized group displays of marching, head-flagging and wing salutes.

Wading birds: spoonbills. Disney often lets its spoonbills breed and raise their young in front of guests… When courting, the white **African spoonbill** (OA) clacks its bill… Often mistaken for a flamingo from a distance, the **roseate spoonbill** (OA) has vivid pink plumage that's tinged with red and orange.

Wading birds: storks. Named for Turkish Governor Bey El-Arnaut Abdim, the small **Abdim's stork** (DL) is seen as a harbinger

All photos: Micaela Neal

Top: A male taveta golden weaver builds a nest. Above, an East African crowned crane and great blue turaco. Right (clockwise): A lesser flamingo, roseate spoonbill, painted stork, lappet-faced vulture, white stork, and African jacana.

of rain and good luck to native Africans... Though a young **painted stork** (DI) can loudly call to attract its parents, by 18 months it is practically voiceless. A threatened chick disgorges its food and plays dead... Named for its bill, which is topped with a yellow saddle-like growth, the **saddle-billed stork** (DI, KS) is depicted in Egyptian hieroglyphics... The legend of storks bringing human babies to homes comes from the migration of the **white stork** (DI) from Africa to Germany every spring, a common time for human births. The bird nests on German chimneys.

Other wading birds. The oversized feet of the **African jacana** (PF) allow it to walk on water plants. Females are dominant, which is rare for birds... The neon-yellow-billed

black crake (PF) pecks parasites off of hippos and warthogs... Named after the German "hammerkopf" ("hammerhead") because of its odd-shaped head, the **hammerkop stork** (PF) is actually not a stork at all, and is more closely related to pelicans. It builds tree nests up to 4 feet across, which are strong enough to support a man's weight... Named for its distinctive yellow mask, the **masked plover** (MJ) has a small yellow claw hidden in each wing; a false myth says the claws inject venom. The bird sleeps for only a few minutes each day.

Vultures. The foul-smelling nest of the colorful **king vulture** (FW) wards off predators. In the Mayan calendar it represents the 13th day of the month... The most powerful, aggressive and widespread African vulture,

the **lappet-faced vulture** (DI) will eat live prey, unlike other vultures. Skin folds called lappets hang off its bare head.

 Weavers. The male **taveta golden weaver** (PF) builds an oval nest over water; the female chooses her mate based on how impressed she is by his nest-building... The **white-headed buffalo weaver** (PF) is named for its tendency to follow African buffalo and eat the insects it disturbs.

Water Parks

Giggles, laughs and squeals fill the air at Blizzard Beach and Typhoon Lagoon, Walt Disney World's two water parks. Close your eyes and you'll notice a unique serenade of happy people enjoying life. Why? Because it's just so much fun to play in water, especially when you're with family or friends.

The United States has more than a thousand water parks, but few offer such an immersive experience as these two. Plastic culverts appear to be streams and rivers, their steel supports hidden under forested hills. An offbeat mix of pop songs fills the air. Everywhere you look is spic-and-span, and everywhere you go is family oriented.

How do the parks compare? Sunny and spacious, Blizzard Beach has longer and faster slides with many height minimums, a better preteen spot and a wackier theme. Shady and intimate, Typhoon Lagoon offers bigger waves, a better toddler spot and a wider variety of attractions, only two of which have height minimums.

Best reasons to go

You bond. Whether it's a multi-person tube slide, a side-by-side mat race or simply a makeshift Monkey in the Middle game in a pool, Disney's water parks offer many ways for you to interact with your partner, children or friends.

You chill. Disney's lazy rivers let you drift away in dappled shade, and there's hardly ever a wait.

You thrill. The scariest attraction in all of Walt Disney World is Summit Plummet at Blizzard Beach. The most fun? For many, it's the wave pool at Typhoon Lagoon.

You do. Unlike the passive "here we are now entertain us" attractions common in theme parks, water-park experiences often demand you get off your rear end and actually do something. Such as swim, slide, splash, snorkel or surf.

Facing page: The authors' daughter soaks up the sun in front of Melt-Away Bay at Disney's Blizzard Beach water park.

Worst aspects of the parks

The food. Except for some creative snacks, the food at Disney water parks is overpriced and uninspired.

The lines. If you don't plan your day right, long waits for the water slides can definitely put a damper on your fun.

The stairs. Tummy not toned? Butt not buff? You'll be huffin' and puffin' as you climb Disney's many hot, sunny stairways.

Planning your day. Regardless of whether you visit Blizzard Beach or Typhoon Lagoon, be prepared for a day that wears you out. Though both parks are smaller than any Disney theme park and require less walking, their attractions are much more physical. Queue lines often wind up stairs, sometimes in direct sun. What's more, you'll be outside all day. At either park, the only indoor spots are the restrooms and the gift shop.

Cooler days can be more enjoyable than you might think. Except for the 70-degree pools of Typhoon Lagoon's Shark Reef, all of Disney's water-park water is heated to 80 degrees.

Tickets. As of August 2014, an adult ticket to either park costs $53. Children ages 3–9 pay $45. Those under 3 are admitted free.

If you already have a ticket to a Disney theme park, you can use it to get into a water park by upgrading it with what Disney calls the Water Park Fun & More option. Allowing you unlimited visits to both water parks for the duration of your theme-park ticket, it adds $55 to the cost of a one-day Magic Kingdom ticket, $60 to a longer Magic Kingdom ticket, and $60 to any other theme-park ticket regardless of length.

Water park annual passes cost $104 for adults, $85 for children. Most prices are discounted for Florida residents and members of the military.

See also **Tickets** in **Walt Disney World A–Z**

What to bring with you. We say travel light—just a cap or hat, wallet or purse, sunscreen and swimsuit (Disney does not allow suits with rivets, buckles or exposed metal; or string-back or thong suits). Consider

Despite their family focus, Disney's water parks are a haven for teenagers. Blizzard Beach offers thrilling slides; Typhoon Lagoon has the largest surf pool in the United States.

rash guards to protect skin from burns and scrapes, especially for children. A towel is a must, but you can rent one for $2. Want to bring more? Disney will let you haul in a cooler, food, small toys, strollers, towels and wheelchairs, but not alcohol, boogie boards, glass containers, tubes or water toys.

How to avoid the crowd. The two most popular water parks in the world, Blizzard Beach and Typhoon Lagoon each attract about 8,000 visitors a day. Such a crowd often makes empty beach chairs tough to find, and creates lines for water slides that are just ridiculous. At a theme park few people would wait in line 40 minutes for a 10-second ride, but at a water park people do it every day. To avoid that crowd, follow these four steps:

First, arrive at your park before it opens. In other words, on the day you visit your water park, get there 45 minutes before it officially opens, which is typically 9 or 10 a.m. This gives you time to park, walk to the entrance, scan your ticket or MagicBand, and rent a locker and towels at a relaxed pace, while still staying ahead of the masses (at both water parks, the entrance usually opens 15 minutes early).

Snare your chairs, then do the slides. You'll have your choice of beach chairs, including those right up next to the pool and others back in the shade. Waiting lines at the slides will be short or nonexistent, and you'll do them all before noon.

Do playgrounds, pools and rivers after lunch. They get crowded on busy days, but never have lines.

If there's a storm, wait it out. Most guests will leave, unaware that in Florida a thunderstorm usually lasts no more than an hour, and is almost always followed by a clear sky. Once it appears you'll have your park almost all to yourself.

Sitting down. Each park has hundreds of beach chairs and their use is complimentary. But those in good spots get taken very early.

Want to pay for a spot? You can. Both parks rent reserved covered patios or decks, but they cost a pretty penny—$325 a day for up to 6 guests ($175 after 2 p.m.) with additional guests (up to 10) $25 each. For that you get 6 cushioned chairs including 2 lounge chairs, a table, a cooler stocked with water, a locker rental, towels, refillable soft-drink mugs and an attendant who stops by every 20 minutes. The best spot at Blizzard Beach is patio No. 4, a secluded, shady alcove near the chairlift, preteen area and toddler zone. The best spots at Typhoon Lagoon are cabanas No. 2, which is very shady, next to a large strangler fig and overlooks that park's lazy river; and No. 3, a wood deck under a large umbrella that sits on the bank of the river

Several slides let guests race against each other. Regardless of skill or strategy, the heaviest rider usually wins at Toboggan Racers at Disney's Blizzard Beach.

and has a nice view of the surf pool. Though way overpriced, these spots can be handy for families with very young or elderly members. They often sell out in the summer. To reserve one call 407-939-7529 up to 90 days in advance.

For $55 you can reserve a much smaller spot—two lounge chairs, a small table and a beach umbrella. These usually aren't conveniently located, and offer no real views.

Drinking up. Addicted to caffeine? Disney sells a refillable soft-drink mug at both water parks for $10.75. It's good for just one day, but can be renewed for another day for $6.50. Want alcohol? Both parks sell beer and mixed drinks, but with no all-you-can-drink option.

Seasonal closures. Both parks close for annual maintenance. Typhoon Lagoon usually shuts down in November and December, Blizzard Beach in January and February.

What if it rains? If lightning is within five miles of a Disney water park it will close its rides and clear its pools. The attractions reopen afterward.

Rain checks. If the attractions are closed for 30 minutes or more, a guest who has been inside a park less than four hours can get a rain check good for a future entry anytime within the next year; all members of that party then have to leave. Rain checks are issued from the park's Guest Relations stand

or any ticket booth. Disney will not issue a rain check if the park entry was with a previous rain check.

Family matters. Almost nowhere offers a better place for families to bond than a Walt Disney World water park. There are, however, a few issues parents should be aware of.

Age restriction. Visitors under the age of 14 must be accompanied by an older guest to enter either park.

Life jackets. Disney offers use of standard life jackets at no charge. The parks do permit guests to bring in water wings, even though those swimming aids are easy to puncture.

Lost children. Easy to identify by their distinctive uniforms and name tags, water park staffers and life guards ("cast members") take lost children to marked areas (usually picnic tables) at the front of each park. To avoid losing their children, some families arrange before their visit to meet in a specific spot at a specific time just in case family members lose track of each other.

Rafts and toys. Neither water park allows guests to bring in rafts or other air-filled toys. The parks provide rafts, tubes and mats at rides that are designed for them.

Swim diapers. Infants and toddlers who are not potty-trained are required to wear plastic swim diapers. Gift shops sell them.

Summit Plummet rises high above Melt-Away Bay, a swimming pool that appears to be created by streams of melting snow. Bobbing waves wash through it.

Blizzard Beach

Sunny park has many thrilling slides, inspired preteen spot

A towering ski jump, snow-covered ski slopes and a mountainside chairlift create the illusion that this whimsical water park is a melting ski resort. But hiding within it is a hot-weather haven, an assortment of pools and slides that the whole family can love. Carved from a forest of stately pines, Blizzard Beach is within walking distance of Disney's Coronado Springs Resort, about a mile from Disney's Animal Kingdom theme park. Disney's Winter Summerland miniature golf course sits in front of it. The second-most-popular water park in the world, Blizzard Beach attracts nearly 2 million guests a year.

Attractions. Blizzard Beach has two intense body slides, two tube slides and two mat slides. There's also a bobbing wave pool, a family raft ride, a lazy river, a toddler area and a great preteen spot. Below, each attraction is rated from one to five stars (★) based on how well it lives up to its promise. A checkmark (✓) indicates an author favorite.

Cross Country Creek. ★★★★ ✓ Lined with evergreens, this shady floating stream circles the park as it flows under bridges, over springs, past a squirting snowmaking machine and through a cave with dripping water that's icy cold. Seven entry points offer complimentary tubes. Want a souvenir photo of you and your group? Photopass photographers stand in the water. *25 minutes (roundtrip). 3,000 feet, 15-feet wide, 2.5-feet deep, maximum speed 2 mph. Fear factor: None.*

Downhill Double Dipper. ★★★ You'll drop down a short tunnel, drop down again, then shoot through a curtain of water... all as you race against someone next to you in these steep, enclosed tube slides. Alpine cowbells cheer you on as you leave the gate; a finish-line scoreboard flashes your time. Thrill-seeking youngsters love it. Pull up on your tube handles just before the catch pool to fly across the water. *6 seconds. 230 feet, 50-foot drop, maximum speed 25 mph. Fear factor: You feel out of control. Height minimum: 48 inches.*

Melt-Away Bay. ★★★ ✓ Nestled against the base of Mt. Gushmore, a 90-foot snow-capped peak, this swimming pool appears to be created by streams of melting snow.

Riders are timed as they race each other on Downhill Double Dipper, Walt Disney World's scariest tube ride. Cowbells sound as the competitors leave the starting gate.

Bobbing waves wash through the pool for 45 minutes of every hour; a sandy sunbathing beach lines one side. The pool's shallow beachside entry makes it easy for young children to enter it. *Unlimited time. 1 acre. Fear factor: None.*

Runoff Rapids. ★★★★ ✔ Banked curves make riders feel like bobsledders on these three banked tube slides. Two open slides allow two-person tubes; an enclosed one-person slide is inside a dark plastic pipe that's lit by pin lights, which gives it a Space Mountain effect. Reached by a back-of-the-park climb up 127 steps, Runoff Rapids is worth every huff and puff. *600 feet. Fear factor: Enclosed tube may feel claustrophobic.*

Ski Patrol Training Camp. ★★★★★ ✔ This inventive collection of experiences is a gem. At Fahrenheit Drop, kids hold on to a sliding T-bar that drops them into an 8-foot pool. The ride has two bars, which move over the water at different heights. At the Thin Ice Training Course, overhead rope grids help kids hang on as they walk over slippery floating "icebergs." As for tube slides, Snow Falls has wide ones for the timid, Cool Runners has short bumpy ones. A short enclosed body slide, Frozen Pipe Springs plops riders out a few inches above its pool. Children can see each ride before choosing it. *Unlimited time. Fear factor: None.*

Slush Gusher. ★★★★ ✔ Looking like a gully covered in slushy snow, this steep body slide starts off slow but gives fully grown riders some airtime off its second drop; the heavier the rider, the wilder the flight. A viewing area at the end has covered bleachers. Visible from most of the park, Slush Gusher is easy for children to evaluate ("I am definitely doing that!") before they get in line. *2 drops. 11–13 seconds. 250 feet, 90-foot drop, maximum speed 50 mph. Fear factor: Scary after the second drop. Height minimum 48 inches.*

Snow Stormers. ★★★★ ✔ You lie face-first and speed down S-curves on these fast high-banked mat slides, three side-by-side courses that make it easy for family or friends to race each other. To win your race, keep your elbows on your mat and your feet up. As you careen up corners water splashing in your face makes it tough to see; a horizontal line on the wall helps you keep your bearings. *15–20 seconds. 350 feet. Fear factor: Fast, disorienting.*

Summit Plummet. ★★★★★ ✔ The scariest ride in all of Walt Disney World, this very steep 12-story body slide is Disney's true tower of terror. Lying down at the top of what looks like a ski jump, you cross your arms and feet then push yourself over the edge. The sky and scenery blur as you fall; the

Though her boyfriend backed out moments earlier, a teen girl braves Summit Plummet.

A rider gets airborne on Slush Gusher, a body slide that looks like a snowy gully.

water around you roars as you splash down. The impact can send much of your swimsuit where the sun never shines; wear a T-shirt or rash guard to avoid stinging your skin.

One of the tallest and fastest slides in the United States, Summit Plummet has no exit stairway; those who chicken out at the last second squeeze back down the crowded entrance steps in what cast members privately refer to as the "walk of shame." The launch tower rises only 30 feet above Mt. Gushmore and just 120 feet over the park, but it seems much taller. The fall is so intense even some of its designers don't care for it. During its construction, Disney Imagineer Kathy Rogers "made the mistake of going up the stairs and looking down. I thought, 'There's no way I'd put my body in there!' I did it once and said, 'Done!'"

It's easy to determine if Summit Plummet is a ride you can handle, as it's viewable from throughout the park. Is your child going, but you're not? There's an observation deck and viewing area at the end of the slide; a display shows rider speeds. *9–10 seconds. 360 feet, 66-degree 120-ft drop, maximum speed 60 mph. Fear factor: All of it. Height minimum: 48 inches.*

Teamboat Springs. ★★★★★ ✔ Nowhere else at Disney do so many families have such a good time together—all ages laugh and smile on this, the world's longest family raft ride. Sitting in a raft the size of a plastic kiddie pool, up to 8 people slide down a high-banked course together, spinning on tight curves which toss them up on steep walls. Thirty holes in each raft's bottom edge make sure derrieres get soaked; a 200-foot ride-out area passes under a dilapidated roof that's dripping cold water. There's often a minimum of four riders per tube, so smaller groups sometimes ride together. *2 minutes. 1,200 feet. Fear factor: Rough ride; unavoidable water sprays.*

Tikes Peak. ★★ Gentle slides, rideable baby alligators and an ankle-deep squirting "ice" pond highlight this unshaded preschooler playground. Though much of it is paved concrete, there is a fountain play area, a little waterfall and a scattering of sand boxes, as well as lawn chairs, chaise lounges and picnic tables. Still, there are few ways for parents and children to spend time together. Children should wear water shoes; the pavement can get very hot. *Unlimited time. Fear factor: None. Height maximum: 48 inches for slides.*

A chairlift makes it easy for guests to reach the top of the park's Mt. Gushmore.

Tubers take it easy on Cross Country Creek, a shady stream that circles Blizzard Beach.

Toboggan Racers. ★★★★ ✔ Inspired by amusement-park gunnysack slides, this straight, 8-lane mat slide races guests down its two dips face first. Since multiple riders go at once, whole families and large groups of friends can compete against each other. More joyful than scary, Toboggan Racers is fun for all ages. To go really fast, push off the starting line quickly then slightly lift the front of your mat so it doesn't plow in the water. Regardless of technique, the heaviest rider usually wins. *10–20 seconds. 250 feet. Fear factor: None.*

Characters. Goofy often greets guests next to the park's Lottawatta Lodge fast-food spot and sometimes wanders nearby walkways. He's usually out for 30 minutes at a time. Expect the shortest lines late in the afternoon.

Food. Three Blizzard Beach fast-food spots and two seasonal ones offer hamburgers, hot dogs, sandwiches, salads and personal pizzas ($8–10). Snack stands sell hot mini donuts, cotton candy, funnel cakes, ice cream treats, nachos and snow cones. Other spots have coffee, tea, pastries, beer and rum drinks.

Have a sweet tooth? If they're fresh, get the hot mini-donuts. Disney will let you bring a cooler and food into the park, but not glass containers or alcohol.

Shopping. Located in the park's Alpine Village entrance area, the Beach Haus stocks a good selection of beachwear and swimwear from Billabong, Oakley, O'Neill, Quiksilver, Roxy and Speedo. Across from the park's changing rooms, the Shade Shack sells beach towels and sundries while North Pearl offers Japanese akoya pearls in their oysters (5–10 millimeters, $16), pearl settings and pearl jewelry.

Fun finds. Barrels of "Instant Snow" (from the Joe Blow Snow Co.) line the walkways to Slush Gusher, Summit Plummet and Teamboat Springs; authentic snow-making equipment (from the Sunshine State Snow Making Co.) sits alongside Cross Country Creek and the queue for Toboggan Racers... A beach chair with an umbrella and a skier with a leg cast are depicted in the "ancient" drawings inside the Cross Country Creek cave; the Northern Lights shine through the cave's ceiling.

A preschooler plays on a squirting alligator at Tikes Peak, the park's kiddie spot.

A girl hangs in there on the Thin Ice Training Course at the Ski Patrol Training Camp.

Key facts. *ATM:* At the Guest Relations kiosk at the park entrance. *Cooler policy:* Coolers with up to two wheels are allowed. Blizzard Beach does not store medication coolers. *First aid:* To the right of the Beach Haus gift shop, in the Alpine Village entrance area. *Guest Relations:* A kiosk just outside the park entrance. *Life jacket use:*

Complimentary. At Snowless Joe's, Alpine Village. *Lockers:* Rented at the Beach Haus and Snowless Joe's in Alpine Village ($8–$10 per day plus $5 deposit; stands typically open 15 minutes before the stated park opening time). Lockers are located next to Snowless Joe's, near the Ski Patrol Training Camp, and alongside the Downhill Double Dipper. *Lost*

Blizzard Beach average wait times

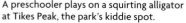

ATTRACTION	9A	10A	11A	Noon	1P	2P	3P	4P	5P	6P	7P	8P
Chair lift	0	5	10	20	25	25	20	15	15	10	10	5
Downhill Double Dipper	0	5	5	10	10	15	20	15	10	15	5	5
Fahrenheit Drop	0	5	5	5	5	5	10	10	10	5	5	5
Runoff Rapids	0	0	10	15	15	15	15	15	15	15	15	5
Slush Gusher	0	5	15	20	25	20	25	10	15	20	10	5
Snow Stormers	0	0	10	10	15	15	15	15	15	15	15	5
Summit Plummet	0	5	20	30	40	35	35	20	30	25	20	10
Teamboat Springs	0	5	10	20	30	25	25	10	20	15	10	5
Thin Ice Training Camp	0	5	5	5	5	5	10	10	10	5	5	5
Toboggan Racers	0	5	5	10	10	10	15	10	10	15	5	5

Wait times: averages of random days, summers 2011–14

A raft the size of a kiddie pool spins riders down curves and up banks at Teamboat Springs, a raft ride that's 1,200-feet long. Below, two teens compete on Toboggan Racers; the park closed to new visitors on a busy summer day.

children: Taken to a marked, staffed table in Alpine Village, on the walkway between the changing rooms and Lottawatta Lodge food spot. There's sometimes a sandwich board there that reads "Lost Children." *Lost and Found:* At the Guest Relations kiosk, outside the park entrance. *Parking:* Free. *Phone number:* 407-560-3400. *Strollers and wheelchairs:* Allowed but not available for rent. The park's sandy areas are tough to wheel through. *Towel rentals:* At the Beach Haus and Snowless Joe's, Alpine Village ($2 each). *Disney transportation:* Disney buses shuttle guests to Blizzard Beach from all Disney-owned hotels, the Walt Disney World Swan and Dolphin and Disney's Animal Kingdom theme park. Officially there is no service from Blizzard Beach to other parks or Downtown Disney, but all buses that stop at Animal Kingdom also stop at Blizzard Beach.

Let's build a ski resort. Disney's history books tell of a freak winter snowstorm that hit central Florida in the mid-1990s. And of how, mesmerized by the snow, the company's "imagineers" had a brainstorm—"Let's build a ski resort!"

Just a few days later, they had done just that. They built a small mountain and topped it with a ski jump as well as bobsled, slalom and sledding runs. And they had finished things off with an adjacent Alpine Village, complete with a hotel and—of course—a large gift shop.

When the snow stopped they realized the foolishness of their efforts—they were, you know, in the Sunshine State—but before the imagineers could go drown their sorrows they spotted a lone alligator, still blue from the cold, which had somehow strapped on a pair of skis and was careening down their ski jump. Flying wildly through the air, this giddy "Ice Gator" landed on their restrooms, crashed into their gift shop, and emerged with a smile.

Watching him, the imagineers realized that their failed ski resort would make a great water park. They quickly reconfigured the ski jump as a body slide, redid the ski runs into mat and tube slides, and turned a convenient creek into a lazy river.

Naming its new creation Blizzard Beach, Disney opened it to the public. On April Fools Day, 1995.

Before the waves begin, the Typhoon Lagoon surf pool is a calm, peaceful spot perfect for anyone wanting to take an easy dip in the water...

Typhoon Lagoon

Laid-back shady park has something for everyone

With an atmosphere that's one part Hawaii and two parts "Gilligan's Island," Typhoon Lagoon is a shady, silly escape. Thorough landscaping immerses guests in a tropical environment. Located along the eastern side of Disney World property, the 61-acre park is located across the street from Downtown Disney, within easy access of Interstate 4. Typhoon Lagoon is the most popular water park in the world, drawing more than 2 million visitors a year.

Attractions. Typhoon Lagoon features a signature surf pool that's the largest in the United States, a saltwater-snorkeling experience and a terrific water playground for toddlers. Below, each attraction is rated from one to five stars (★) based on how well it lives up to its promise. A checkmark (✓) indicates an author favorite.

Bay Slides. ★★ These two short children's body slides are in the calm left corner of the surf pool, an area called Blustery Bay. One slide is uncovered with a few gentle bumps; the other has a 4-foot tunnel. Though kids disappear on the walkway up to the slides parents have no need for concern; the path is just 10 steps and leads only to the slides. *10 seconds. 35 feet, maximum speed 7 mph. Fear factor: None. Height maximum: 60 inches.*

Castaway Creek. ★★★★★ ✓ Lined with palms, this shady lazy river circles the surf pool. Expect to get misted, drizzled on and, as you float into a cave, maybe completely drenched. Shoreline sights include three crashed boats and the Ketchakiddee Creek playground; the Mt. Mayday Trail suspension bridge crosses high above you. The creek splits in two for a short distance. There's never a wait, though the creek gets crowded on summer afternoons. *25 minutes (round trip). 2,100 feet, 15-feet wide, 3-feet deep, maximum speed 2 mph. Seven entry points. Complimentary tube use. Some tubes hold two people. Fear factor: None.*

Crush 'n' Gusher. ★★★★★ ✓ Powered by water jets as well as gravity, these three flumes have both lifts and dips, just like roller coasters. Each offers a different experience: The wildest one, Pineapple Plunger has three short tunnels and two peaks. Coconut Crusher has three tunnels of various lengths.

... but once its waves start with a mighty "WHUMPH," the pool becomes chaotic, and ideal for guests who long to be hit by walls of rushing water.

A slightly longer track, Banana Blaster includes one long and two medium-length tunnels, but only has two-person rafts.

To stay in control, push your feet down into the front of your tube. For a wilder time, lift your feet up. Riding Pineapple Plunger? Lean back to catch some air. Ride together if there are no more than three people in your group; in general the more people on a tube, the faster and more fun it is.

Crush 'n' Gusher is meant to be the hurricane-ravaged remains of the (say it slowly) Tropical Amity fruit-packing plant. The flumes are the plant's spillways, which cleaned fruit before it was shipped. Aptly named Hideaway Bay, the attraction's 5-acre setting is tucked behind Typhoon Lagoon's main locker area. Besides the flume rides, it includes a shallow gradual-entry swimming pool lined with beach chairs and chaise lounges—a perfect place for parents and toddlers to play. *30 seconds. 420 feet, maximum speed 18 mph. 2- and 3-person tubes. Covered queue. Fear factor: Chaotic, disorienting; few visual reference points. Height minimum 48 inches.*

Gangplank Falls. ★★ Though it doesn't last long, this big-tube slide has its moments, as riders go under waterfalls and through a small cave. The rafts hold four, maybe five people. To make Gangplank Falls worthwhile,

ride it early or late in the day, when there's little or no wait. *30 seconds. 300 feet, average speed 7 mph. 4-person rafts. Fear factor: Rough ride; unavoidable water sprays.*

Humunga Kowabunga. ★★ Did Bart Simpson name these three identical enclosed body slides? Maybe so; they are his type of thing: short, steep, straight dark drops. A shady viewing area lets Homer and Marge types watch others whoosh into the run-out lanes. *7 seconds. 214 feet, 60-degree 50-foot drop, maximum speed 30 mph. Fear factor: Scary but brief. Height minimum 48 inches.*

Keelhaul Falls. ★★★ Tubes slowly build speed on this short gentle C-curve, the park's tamest full-size tube slide. Heavier guests glide up the side of the slide just before it ends. *50 seconds. 400 feet, average speed 6 mph. Fear factor: None.*

Ketchakiddee Creek. ★★★★★ ✔ This large and elaborate geyser-and-volcano area is a kiddie water park all its own. For tiny tots a 100-foot palm-lined tube slide has three little dips; a surrounding area offers bubbly small fountains and ankle-deep streams and pools. More adventurous toddlers hurl themselves down two slip 'n' slides (cushy 20-foot mats with 20-degree drops) while older kids battle each other at the S.S. Squirt, an oversized sand sculpture with swiveling water cannons. Nearby water hoses shake, shimmy

Orlando's Rathbun family relaxes under the lush landscaping of Castaway Creek, a palm-lined stream that takes floaters on a tropical journey around the park.

and squirt atop a 12-foot-tall Blow Me Down boiler. The area has shady chairs and picnic tables; many families build sandcastles. Crowds often pack Ketchakiddee Creek in the afternoon, as Disney doesn't enforce its posted rule that children who play here be shorter than 48 inches. *Unlimited time. 18 activity spots. Fear factor: None. Height maximum 48 inches for slides.*

Mayday Falls. ★ A triple vortex, this swervy "white water" tube slide triple vortex can spin you around, but it's not as much fun as it should be. Since its water is just an inch or two deep and its bottom is rippled concrete, the ride pounds your rear end like some sadistic fitness machine. There's one small waterfall. *30 seconds. 460 feet, average speed 10 mph. Fear factor: Rough ride.*

Mount Mayday Trail. ★★★ Hidden at the back of the park, this fern-and-hibiscus-lined scenic walkway goes over a suspension bridge high above Castaway Creek, then winds up Mount Mayday to the impaled Miss Tilly shrimp boat. There's nothing to do, but it is pretty. Tiny streams splash over the walkway, which begins at the entrance to the Gangplank Falls tube slide (look for the sign) and ends at the top of the Humunga Kowabunga body slide. The trail is usually vacant even on the most crowded days, as few visitors know it's here. *Fear factor: None.*

Shark Reef. ★★★★★ ✔ You look down on tropical fish as you swim over an artificial reef in this chilly saltwater snorkeling pool. Sights include "smiling" rainbow parrotfish, Dory-esque blue tangs, rays and (quite passive) little leopard and bonnethead sharks. Hold still as you float to have the fish come close to you. For the most time above the reef take the scenic route, in the uncrowded water away from the overturned tanker. A resting area sits in the middle of the pool. Want to watch someone else snorkel? Do it underwater, through the windows of a real capsized tanker. *Unlimited, though swimmers are not allowed to reverse their course. Fear factor: Cold saltwater. Complimentary use of masks, snorkels, life vests, changing areas and outdoor showers.*

An optional Supplied Air Snorkeling experience (Reef Adventure, ★★★★★ ✔) includes use of an air tank, regulator, flippers and instruction and usually takes place away from the crowd. It's run by the National Association of Underwater Instructors. Fees go to a conservation program. *30 minutes. Ages 5 and up, $20. Late April to late August).*

Storm Slides. ★★★★ Winding down a steep wooded hill, these shady, high-banked body slides are long and curvy. Each of the three offers a different experience: Jib Jammer is totally open to the sky; Rudder

Shark Reef snorkelers swim and float in a crystal-clear, cold saltwater pool past a (real) overturned tanker. The water is filled with fish, rays and small passive sharks.

Buster has a small tunnel; Stern Burner includes a longer, dark tunnel. Don't want to ride? You can wait for those who do on unshaded bleachers at the catch pool. *25 seconds. 300 feet, maximum speed 20 mph. Fear factor: May frighten young children.*

Surf Pool. ★★★★★ ✔ Body-surfable waves sweep down this large pool, making it a popular teen hangout as well as a fun spot for families. Few people body surf but many gather to be knocked around by the waves, the height of the which varies throughout the day. A chalkboard in the front of the pool shows the daily schedule. *Unlimited time. Waves 2–6 feet. Fear factor: Waves intimidate, can topple you even in shallow areas. Young children should stay with parents.*

The 2.5-acre area resembles a tropical cove, with a real sandy beach, bubbling "tide pools" and an artificial sand bar about 50 feet "offshore." The 115-by-395-foot wave pool is the largest in North America in terms of guest capacity, water volume and wave height. Waves are created in the closed-off deep end of the pool, as 12 backstage collection chambers repeatedly push 80,000 gallons of water through two underwater doors.

Surfing lessons are often held in the pool early in the morning, before the park opens. For more information see this book's chapter Walt Disney World A–Z.

Characters. Lilo and Stitch (from the 2002 movie "Lilo & Stitch") greet parkgoers until 4 p.m. in front of the Singapore Sal's gift shop. They do not appear together, but rather alternate for 20 minutes at a time. Expect the shortest lines after 3 p.m.

Food. Typhoon Lagoon fast-food spots sell fish, hamburgers, hot dogs, small pizzas, salads, sandwiches, fried shrimp and turkey legs ($7-$11). The Leaning Palms fast-food counter has the greatest variety.

Snack stands have cotton candy, funnel cakes, hot mini donuts, nachos, pretzels, smoothies and faux ice cream. The hot mini-donuts are an indulgent treat. Other stands offer coffee, tea and pastries; a converted scooter truck serves beer and mixed drinks. Try the truck's frozen mango margarita, made with Patrón Silver.

The park has two picnic areas, though you can set up a meal virtually anywhere. Disney will let you bring a cooler and food into the park, but not glass containers or alcohol.

Shopping. Located near the park entrance, Singapore Sal's gift shop has beach towels, sundries, swimwear and a good selection of young-adult apparel from Billabong, Oakley, O'Neill, Quiksilver and Roxy (the authors' daughter shops here for her college

New Jersey's Amanda Mathus, 14, braces for the splash on the Stern Burner Storm Slide.

Dads join in water-cannon fun at the Ketchakiddee Creek children's area.

clothes). At Shark Reef, a Pearl Factory stand sells Japanese akoya pearls in their oysters (5–10mm, $16), pearl settings and jewelry.

Fun finds. Nautical flags hanging above the park entrance spell out "WELCOME TO TYPHOON LAGOON." Discreetly hanging to their right, other flags spell out "PIRANHA IN POOL"... Feel sadistic? In front of the Happy Landings snack bar, the props of outboard motors waiting to being serviced can be aimed at passing floaters on Castaway Creek, and can squirt them with water... Long-forgotten Typhoon Lagoon mascot Lagoona Gator lives in the Board Room, a shack in front of the surf pool. Look inside to find a poster for the movie "Bikini Beach Blanket Muscle Party Bingo," a flyer for a concert by The Beach Gators ("So cold blooded, they're hot!").

Key facts. *ATM:* At Singapore Sal's gift shop, near the park entrance. *Cooler policy:* Coolers with up to two wheels are allowed.

Typhoon Lagoon average wait times

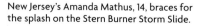

ATTRACTION	9A	10A	11A	Noon	1P	2P	3P	4P	5P	6P	7P	8P
Crush 'N Gusher	0	5	10	10	10	10	15	15	15	10	10	5
Gangplank Falls	0	5	20	30	40	35	35	20	30	25	20	10
Humunga Kowabunga	0	0	5	5	5	10	15	15	15	10	5	5
Keelhaul Falls	0	0	10	10	10	15	15	15	15	15	15	5
Mayday Falls	0	0	10	15	15	15	15	15	15	15	15	5
Shark Reef	0	0	10	10	10	10	15	10	15	10	5	5
Storm Slides	0	5	5	10	10	10	15	10	10	15	5	5

Wait times: averages of random days, summers 2011–14

At right, a young boy enjoys the Mayday Falls tube ride. Below, Keelhaul Falls is the park's tamest full-size tube slide, while the family-style Gangplank Falls has rafts that hold up to five people.

Typhoon Lagoon does not store medication coolers. *First aid:* Behind the Leaning Palms fast-food restaurant. *Guest Relations:* A kiosk just outside the park entrance. *Life jacket use:* Complimentary. At Singapore Sal's and High 'N Dry Towels, both near the park entrance. *Lockers:* Rented at Singapore Sal's near the park entrance ($8–$10 per day plus $5 deposit), which typically opens 15 minutes before the official park opening time. Most lockers are nearby; some are at Shark Reef. *Lost children:* Taken to Safe Harbor, a staffed area outside of Singapore Sal's gift shop, near the park entrance. There's sometimes a sandwich board there that reads "Lost Children." *Lost and Found:* At the Guest Relations kiosk, outside the park entrance. *Parking:* Free. *Phone number:* 407-560-7223. *Strollers and wheelchairs:* Allowed but not available for rent. The park's sandy areas are tough to wheel through. *Towel rentals:* At Singapore Sal's, near the park entrance ($2 each). *Disney transportation:* Disney buses shuttle guests to Typhoon Lagoon from all Disney resort hotels. Before 10 a.m. the buses drop off guests at Typhoon Lagoon and then continue to Downtown Disney; after 10 a.m. they stop first at Downtown Disney. There is no direct bus service between Typhoon Lagoon and any Disney theme park.

A topsy-turvy tropical playground. According to Disney lore, the Placid Palms resort was built on Florida's volcanic Atlantic coastline, in a tranquil Florida valley alongside a Florida mountain. *Right.* Anyway, over the years the valley experienced a few tremors and rumblings but overall remained, well, placid. Then in 1955, Hurricane Connie struck the Placid Palms head-on. The storm impaled a shrimp boat on the volcano, destroyed an adjacent fruit processing plant, blew in crates of fireworks from a nearby island (where at the time a Mr. Merriweather Pleasure put on a nightly fireworks show) and cut off the harbor from the Atlantic, trapping saltwater fish at a reef. Despite these setbacks, Placid Palm managers remained totally cool. Grabbing some sign paint, they renamed their place the Leaning Palms and re-opened it as a topsy-turvy playground: a water park.

Typhoon Lagoon opened on June 1, 1989.

Downtown Disney

This lakeside commercial center offers unusual dining, entertainment and shopping. Located near the northeast corner of Disney property along Village Lake, the 120-acre strip is divided into three sections:

Marketplace. Originally called the Walt Disney World Shopping Village, this open-air shopping mall has been a Disney fixture since the 1970s. Rough-hewn buildings are covered in cedar-shake shingles.

Pleasure Island. Built in 1989 as a night-club district, this central area has been largely vacant for years.

West Side. This strip of land is home to many creative restaurants and some unusual entertainment venues.

At the moment all of Downtown Disney is a mess, as a massive construction project is transforming it into Disney Springs, a more unified area with twice as many shops and restaurants. The work will continue throughout 2015.

Best of Downtown Disney. The lively atmosphere at night, which includes lots of street performers and musicians. The many quality places to eat, and the unusual shops. The authors go to movies here all the time

Worst of Downtown Disney. The parking. You'll swear there isn't any, as through 2015 most of the lots are closed for the construction of parking garages. Also bad: the heat. There's lots of it during sunny afternoons, as there's little shade.

Author's picks. The authors of this book head to Downtown Disney about once a week. For what it's worth, here's where we go: **Where we eat.** *Breakfast:* At Wolfgang Puck Express. *Lunch:* At Earl of Sandwich; a sandwich and a cup of tomato soup; or at the House of Blues Crossroads restaurant. *Dinner:* For a real "date night" dinner (or a nice night out with our college-age daughter) we go to Raglan Road and sit in front of

the stage. For lesser meals you'll find us at the Wolfgang Puck sushi bar if there's no wait (there often isn't for just two people), Splitsville (on off nights when we can sit up on the balcony) or at a Disney food truck.

Where we drink. Outside on the patio at House of Blues, because of the live music. And inside at Paradise 37, because of the tasty appetizers.

What we buy. Cornbread mix at the House of Blues store, spice blends at Mickey's Pantry, wonderful soaps at Basin. Our daughter buys eclectic Vinymation figures at D Street, clothes at Tren-D and Curl, purses at the Cirque du Soleil shop.

What we do. Mainly see movies on the Fork & Screen side of the AMC Theater; occasionally bowling at Splitsville, every year we see La Nouba. If my husband would dance, we'd go to Bongos.

Know before you go. Besides the parking problem, here's what else you should know:

ATMs. The Marketplace has three ATMs: near the Tren-D store, next to the Ghirardelli chocolate shop and inside the World of Disney. The West Side area has two ATMs: at the House of Blues Company Store and near the Characters in Flight balloon.

First aid. At the Marketplace, aspirin, Band-Aids and similar items are sold at World of Disney and the stroller and wheel-chair rental store. In the West Side you'll find them at the DisneyQuest Emporium and the Cirque du Soleil box office.

Guest Relations. At the Marketplace adjacent to Arribas Brothers, 8:30 a.m.–11 p.m. Sunday–Thursday, to 11:30 p.m. Friday and Saturday. At the West Side at the DisneyQuest Emporium 9 a.m.–11:45 p.m.

Mailbox. In the Marketplace, next to the fountain in front of World of Disney.

Parking. Free. If you can find a spot.

Stroller rentals. At the Marketplace next to the Once Upon a Toy shop; at the West Side at the DisneyQuest Emporium (single $15 day, double $31 day, plus $100 deposit).

Transportation. Boats shuttle you from one end of Downtown Disney to the other, and to and from Old Key West, Port Orleans and Saratoga Springs (10:30 a.m.–11:30 p.m.).

Facing page: There's no other store like Tren-D. Downtown Disney's chic junior boutique sells apparel and accessories.

A second-story Splitsville bar and dining area overlooks the walkway of Downtown Disney's West Side. Other elevated guest areas are planned for nearby spots.

Disney buses serve all Disney resorts (noon–midnight at the Marketplace, 8 a.m.–2 a.m. at Pleasure Island). Valet parking is $20 a day.

Wheelchair and scooter rentals. At the Marketplace next to the store Once Upon a Toy; at the West Side at the DisneyQuest Emporium. Wheelchairs are $12 day, ECVs are $50 day. Each requires a $100 deposit.

Entertainment

Here's a quick review of the entertainment at Downtown Disney. Each is rated from one to five stars (★) based on how well it lives up to its promise. A checkmark (✔) indicates an author favorite.

AMC 24 Theater. ★★★ ✔ This huge movie theater is divided into two areas. One is a traditional multiplex. The other area—the Fork & Screen Dine-In Theaters section—is more like a restaurant, with full menus, waitresses and large, comfortable seats you can reserve in advance. Multiplex: Auditorium No. 1 offers an Enhanced Theater Experience, with a 20 percent larger floor-to-ceiling screen, 12-channel audio and ultra-high resolution digital projection. Self-service concession area is awkward and creates delays. *Fork & Screen: Six auditoriums serve moviegoers at tables and offer advanced reserved seating (18 years or older or accompanied by someone 21 years or older; servers on-call). Multiplex: $7 before noon; Adults $9.75 (children 2–12 $8.50) noon–4 p.m.; Adults $11.75 (children 2–12 $8.50) after 4 p.m.; seniors 60+ $10.75, $7 on Tuesdays. Digital 3-D movies $5 additional; in ETX auditorium $5 additional; in ETX 3-D auditorium $6 additional. Fork & Screen: Adults $10 (children 2–12 $10), seniors $10 before noon; Adults $13 (children 2–12 $11), Sr. $12 noon–4 p.m.; Adults $15 to $19 (children 2–12 $11), seniors $14 after 4 p.m., seniors $10 on Tuesdays. Both: Annual/Seasonal Passholders get $2 off adult evening admission price after 6 p.m. Hours vary. 24 theaters, 18 with stadium seating, 2 3-story auditoriums with balconies. THX Surround Sound, Sony Dynamic Digital Sound. Listening devices available. Guests may remain in wheelchairs, ECVs. Seats 5,390. Tiny bar. AMC movie listings: 888-262-4386. Local box office: 407-827-1308. West Side.*

Bongos Cuban Cafe. ★★★ Dance to a traditional Latin band on Friday and Saturday nights at this Cuban restaurant created by pop star Gloria Estefan and her husband, Emilio. *All ages. 11:30 p.m.–2 a.m. Seats 560. No cover. Info: 407-828-0999. West Side.*

Characters in Flight. ★★★★ ✔ The world's largest tethered helium gas balloon silently lifts a 30-person gondola 400 feet in the air. On a clear day you can see 10 miles. A certified pilot rides along. *Adults $18 (children*

A performer prepares herself to go onstage at Cirque du Soleil's La Nouba. The show's cast comes from around the world, though many are natives of Canada.

3–9 $12). Between 8:30 a.m. and 10 a.m. all tickets $10. 8:30 a.m.–midnight. 9-minute rides (2 minute ascent, 5 minutes at 400 feet, 2 minute descent). Flights, times subject to change due to weather. Capacity: winds 0–3 mph: up to 30; 3–12 mph up to 20; 12–22 mph up to 10; over 22 mph does not fly. Access: Guests may stay in wheelchairs, ECV users must transfer to a wheelchair. Children under 12 must fly with adult. Weather refunds day of purchase only. West Side.

DisneyQuest. ★★ Virtual reality experiences highlight this five-story arcade, which was state-of-the-art when it opened in 1998. Today it has a retro appeal, as some floors are filled with early arcade games such as PacMan and Donkey Kong. Admission includes unlimited experiences. Evening crowds pack popular games; the complex is least crowded on fair-weather afternoons.

Aladdin's Magic Carpet Ride. A virtual reality hunt through the alleys of Agrabah for a magic lamp. Second floor.

Animation Academy. 30-minute class teaches how to draw Disney characters. Printouts $5, $12 with pen. Second floor.

Buzz Lightyear's AstroBlaster. Cannon-firing bumper cars. Third floor.

CyberSpace Mountain. Design a roller coaster, then "ride" it in a motion simulator. DVD of your ride: $12. Second floor.

Mighty Ducks Pinball Slam. Guests stand on a giant joystick and steer themselves among other guests on a huge screen in this life-sized pinball game. Third floor.

Pirates of the Caribbean Battle for Buccaneer Gold. The best DisneyQuest game, this virtual boat ride puts a crew of four into a 3-D pirate battle. First floor.

Replay Zone. Classic games such as Asteroids, Centipede, Donkey Kong, Frogger, Pac-Man, Space Invaders and Tron. Third, fourth, fifth floors.

Ride the Comix. Guests don virtual reality helmets to battle supervillains. Fourth and fifth floors.

Sid's Create-a-Toy. Make a toy from mismatched parts. Buy it for $10. Second floor.

Virtual Jungle Cruise. Guests row a raft down a prehistoric river past dinosaurs. First floor.

Adults $45, children $39. Sunday–Thursday 11:30 a.m.–10 p.m., Friday–Saturday to 11 p.m. Height minimums: 51 inches for CyberSpace Mountain, Buzz Lightyear's AstroBlaster; 48 inches for Mighty Ducks Pinball Slam; 35 inches for Pirates of the Caribbean. Children under 10 must be accompanied by an adult. No strollers. Complimentary coat check. 2 counter cafes. 3,689 capacity. 407-828-4600. West Side.

House of Blues Music Hall. ★★★★ This two-story venue books a range of

An AMC movie complex is split into two sections. Its Dine-In Theatres offer reserved seating, large comfortable chairs, a full dining and drinking menu, and a wait staff that's always just a push of a button away.

acts; blues and rock dominate. A folk-art decor, hardwood floors and quality sound and lights add to the experience. An adjacent restaurant offers acoustic acts on its outdoor bar from 6–11 p.m., a plugged-in show Thursday–Saturday 10:30 p.m. to 2 a.m. *$8–$95. Showtimes typically 7–9:30 p.m. General admission; restaurant diners get priority. Doors open 1 hour before showtime weekdays, 90 minutes early on weekends. All ages. Capacity 2,000 (tables and stools seat 150, standing room 1,850). 407-934-2583 or hob. com. West Side.*

Kiddie rides. ★★★ A small mini-train and antique carousel offer rides for children. Adults can join in, too. $2 token, sold at a vending machine that takes cash or a credit card. *Monday–Friday 10 a.m.–11 p.m., Saturday–Sunday 10 a.m.–11:30 p.m. Marketplace.*

La Nouba. ★★★★★ ✓ Blending the traditions of a European circus with modern acrobatics, dance and street entertainment, this invigorating Cirque du Soleil spectacle fills its audience with delight. Costumes, choreography, music and stagecraft are all world-class. Movie buffs will find references to 1997's "The Fifth Element" in La Nouba's odd music and warbling diva, and influences of 1998's "Dark City" in its looming cityscapes and unexpected moving floors. Art lovers will note homages to Calder and Matisse. Designed specifically for a Disney audience, the show's purpose is to "wake up the innocence in your heart." You'll be surprised how well it succeeds. Front-row center is Row A, Section 103, Seat 6. The highest prices are in the "Golden Circle," Rows E and F, Section 103, Seats 1 through 20. Tickets go on sale six months in advance. *Adults $75–$162 (children $64–$137). Tuesday–Saturday 6 p.m., 9 p.m.*

Arrive 30 minutes early. Box office opens 11 a.m.–11 p.m. Tuesday–Saturday, 11 a.m.–9 p.m. Sunday–Monday. 90-minute show, no intermission. Best ages 4+. Snack stand. Seats 1,671. Tickets available 6 months in advance at 407-939-7600, cirquedusoleil.com or at the box office. West Side.

Raglan Road. ★★★★★ ✓ Authentic Irish musicians and dancers put on a unique show in this dyed-in-the-wool Emerald Isle pub. The Main Stage features three-piece house band Creel, which starts off its show with jigs and reels; a later rock set gets rowdy. Other bands include The Raglan Rebels, The Brayzen Heads and The West Coast Trio. Dancers perform in front of the band as well as atop a parson's pulpit in the middle of the room. Guests looking for a cheerful, lively atmosphere—that welcomes children—will not be disappointed. The outdoor Patio Stage offers music every evening. *No cover. Main Stage band plays 4 p.m.–1:30 a.m. Monday–Thursday, 7:30 p.m.–1:30 a.m. Friday–Saturday, noon–4 p.m. and 7:30 p.m.–1:30 a.m. Sunday. Irish table dancers on the hour every hour from 5–10 p.m. The Rollicking Raglan Brunch Irish Dance Show Sundays noon–4 p.m. All ages. Seats 600. Direct reservations: 407-938-0300. Pleasure Island.*

Splitsville. ★★★ This comfortable, hip but family-friendly two-story bowling alley also offers dining, billiards and five bars. A live musician often entertains on an outside patio. Its 30 lanes have electronic scoring. Shoe rentals are included in prices. *No cover. Prices: $12 per person ($7 children 9 and under) Monday–Friday 10:30 a.m.–12:30 p.m.; $15 12:30–4 p.m.; $20 4 p.m.–close; Saturday–Sunday all day. Hours: Monday–Wednesday 10:30 a.m.–1 a.m.,*

Car Masters Weekend takes place each year around Father's Day. The event lines Downtown Disney walkways with dozens of unique and antique automobiles.

© Disney

Thursday–Friday 10:30 a.m.–2 a.m., Saturday 10 a.m.–2 a.m., Sunday 10 a.m.–1 a.m. Phone 407-938-7467. West Side.

Restaurants and food

What sets Downtown Disney restaurants apart from those at other Walt Disney World spots is mainly one thing: none of them are run by the Disney company. And overall that's good, because it adds variety to your Disney experience—for example no where else at Disney will you find Irish or Southern Creole food. Below, each Downtown Disney eatery is rated from one to five stars (★) based on the quality of its food, service and atmosphere. A five-star spot fully lives up to its promise. A checkmark (✓) indicates that the place is one of the authors' favorites. The price of a typical adult dinner entree is summarized by dollar signs as follows:

$ less than $10
$$ less than $15
$$$ less than $20
$$$$ less than $25
$$$$$ more than $25

Table service. The authors' picks? Raglan Road, Portobello and Crossroads at the House of Blues. Appetizers only? Paradiso 37.

Bongos Cuban Cafe. ★★ $$$$ Impressive resume, a fun decor, forgettable food. Created by singer Gloria Estefan—you do remember the Miami Sound Machine, right?—this whimsical Cuban restaurant is dominated by a three-story adobe pineapple. Ask to sit in the pineapple or outside on the second-story patio. An outside bar serves sandwiches, desserts and drinks. *West Side. Lunch, dinner. 11 a.m.–11 p.m. $18–$42 (children $6–$8). Open*

until midnight Friday and Saturday. Seats 560, including 60 outside and 87 at bar. No reservations. 407-828-0999.

Crossroads at House of Blues. ★★★★ ✓ $$$ With spicy jambalaya, flavorful cornbread and walls and ceilings covered with folk art, this funky down-home Southern Creole eatery is a perfect antidote to too much Disney. Live free music plays late some evenings in the dining area; a concert hall sits next door. *West Side. Lunch, dinner. 11:30 a.m.–11 p.m. Sunday–Monday, 11:30 a.m.–midnight Tuesday–Wednesday, 11:30 a.m.–1:30 a.m. Thursday–Saturday. $12–$29 (children $7). Seats 578, including 158 at outside tables and 36 at outdoor bar. No reservations. Gospel brunch with live music Sunday 10:30 a.m., 1 p.m., in Music Hall, 250 seats. Adults $34 (children $17). Info: 407-934-2583.*

Fulton's Crab House. ★★ $$$$$ OK for lunch, too expensive for dinner, this white-tablecloth seafood spot offers lots of crab dishes as well as lobster, shrimp and steaks. It looks just like an old paddlewheeler. Ask to sit on the lake side of the semicircular Constellation Room on the second deck; its ceiling glows blue at night. *Pleasure Island. Lunch 11:30 a.m.–3:30 p.m., dinner 4 –11 p.m., $29–$59 (children $8–$14). Seats 660, including 24 outside. Direct reservations: 407-934-2628.*

Paradiso 37. ★★★ ✓ $$$$ This little Miami-infused lakefront eatery is a good alternative to the more touristy restaurants nearby. Its menu represents the 37 countries of the Americas. A bar offers 37 tequilas at $8–$50 a glass. World music thumps day and night. *Pleasure Island. Lunch, dinner. Sunday–Wednesday 11:30 a.m.–midnight, Thursday–Saturday 11:30 a.m.–1 a.m. $14–$38*

A glowing blue ice cave is among the dining options at T-REX, a dinosaur-themed restaurant that's decorated with authentic casts of dinosaur skeletons. A main dining room has robotic dinos that roar to life.

(children $8). Seats 250, 100 outside, 20 stools at bar. Live entertainment nightly: 6–11:30 p.m. Sunday–Thursday, 6–12:30 a.m. Friday and Saturday. Direct reservations: 407-934-3700.

Planet Hollywood. ★★★ $$$ Surprise! The food is actually pretty good inside this kitschy planet-shaped monument to movie stars, the flagship Planet Hollywood and most popular in the world. A haven for the star-struck, it's filled with memorabilia, most notably the blue gingham dress Judy Garland wore in 1939's "The Wizard of Oz." Fresh, inventive choices include the restaurant's signature Chicken Crunch appetizer, a recipe from co-founder Demi Moore that's secretly coated in crushed Cap'n Crunch. *West Side. Lunch, dinner. 11 a.m.–midnight (summer 11 a.m.–2 a.m.). $14–$30 (children $8). Seats 720. Info: 407-827-7827.*

Portobello. ★★★★ ✔ $$$$ Italian-food lovers will appreciate this comfortable eatery. Pasta dishes dominate the menu; other offerings include pizzas from the wood-burning oven and, for dinner, chicken, fish or steak. *Pleasure Island. Lunch 11:30 a.m.–3:45 p.m. $9–$19. Dinner 4–11 p.m. $10–$29 (children $5–$11). Seats 414, including 86 outside. Direct reservations: 407-934-8888.*

Raglan Road. ★★★★★ ✔ $$$$ Run by Irish proprietors, this pretension-free pub and restaurant offers sophisticated comfort food. Tops are tender meats, creamy soups and sinful bread pudding. The antique decor includes two 130-year-old bars from Ireland with traditional leaded-glass dividers. A live band and Irish table dancers entertain every night but Sunday. *Pleasure Island. Lunch 11 a.m.–3 p.m. $15–$26. Dinner 3–11 p.m. $15–$29 (children $7–$14). Live band, table*

step-dancers evenings Monday–Saturday. Two outdoor bars. Children welcome. Seats 600, including 300 outside. Direct reservations: 407-938-0300

Rainforest Café. ★★ $$$$ The atmosphere is the draw at kid-friendly Rainforest Café, where robotic animals come to life every 22 minutes in a dense faux jungle inside the dining room. The food is fine if routine. The food is overpriced, but you're paying for the monkeys as well as the meatballs. *Marketplace. Lunch, dinner. 11:30 a.m.–11 p.m. Sunday–Thursday, till midnight Friday, Saturday. $13–$30 (children $7). Seats 575. Direct reservations: 407-827-8500. No same-day reservations.*

Splitsville Luxury Lanes. ★★★ $$$ You don't have to bowl to eat at this upscale bowling alley. Choose from good individual pizzas, a dozen types of sushi, decadent sliders and other bar favorites. The second-floor balcony is great for people-watching. *West Side. Monday–Wednesday 10:30 a.m.–1 a.m., Thursday–Friday 10:30 a.m.–2 a.m., Saturday 10 a.m.–2 a.m., Sunday 10 a.m.–1 a.m. $12–$25 (children $7). Seats 450, including 50 outside.*

T-REX. ★★★ $$$$ Young dino fans will love this big, brash, loud take on its sister restaurant, Rainforest Café. A "meteor shower" hits every 22 minutes, with accompanying loud dino roars. Dining areas include an active volcano, a glowing blue ice cave, and a sea-life spot with saltwater fish tanks. The best bet on the huge, varied menu—blackened fish tacos. A free fossil dig site for kids provides a slot for shoes and a place to wash up. *Marketplace. Lunch, dinner. 11 a.m.–11 p.m. Sunday–Thursday, till midnight Friday, Saturday. $15–$35 (children $7–$8). Seats 626, including 26 at bar. Direct reservations: 407-828-8739.*

Four food trucks serve items inspired by various Magic Kingdoms throughout the world, Epcot's World Showcase, Animal Kingdom and Hollywood Studios. They're based in a small park in Downtown Disney's West Side.

© Disney

Wolfgang Puck Grand Café. ★★★ $$$$ This loud eatery often has slow service. Signature California fusion dishes (i.e. crusted chicken, pumpkin ravioli, veal weinerschnitzel) are mild yet flavorful. Some sushi bar selections are quite good. *West Side. Lunch 11:30 a.m.–4 p.m. $13–$29. Dinner Sunday–Monday 4–10:30 p.m., Tuesday–Thursday till 11 p.m., Friday, Saturday till 11:30 p.m. $13–$29 (children $8–$9). Weekend lunch serves dinner menu. Takeout window. Private room for groups. Seats 586, including 30 at sushi bar. Direct reservations: 407-938-9653.*

Wolfgang Puck Dining Room. ★★★ $$$$$ This white-tablecloth spot blends flavors into sophisticated entrees. Prices and quality are higher than at the more boisterous Café downstairs. The room features orange walls dominated by a gigantic ornamental hookah, though sadly, no giant ornamental caterpillar. *West Side. Dinner 6–9 p.m. Sunday–Thursday, 6–10 p.m. Friday–Saturday. $25–$45 (children $10–$16). Seats 120. Direct reservations: 407-938-9653.*

Counter service. The top choice here: Earl of Sandwich. It's legendary among locals.

Cookes of Dublin. ★★★★ ✔ $ This unassuming eatery has a surprisingly large menu, offering fish and chips, a hand-battered beef burger and Irish sausages, with deep-fried "Doh Bar" candy bars for dessert. It's part of the Raglan Road enterprise. *Pleasure Island. Lunch, dinner. 11 a.m.–11 p.m. Seats 20, with additional stand-up bar tables.*

Earl of Sandwich. ★★★★★ ✔ $ Tasty hot sandwiches make this fast-food spot a long-time favorite (it's the original restaurant in the chain). The crusty bread is baked all day; beef is roasted every morning. The best

deal: the $3.50 cup of steaming hot, creamy-orange tomato soup. Morning fare includes a breakfast BLT. Owned by the ancestors of John Montagu, the fourth Earl of Sandwich. *Marketplace. Breakfast 8:30–10:30 a.m. $2–$5. Lunch, dinner 10:30 a.m.–11 p.m. $5–$6 (children $4). Seats 190 including 65 outside.*

Ghirardelli Soda Fountain. ★★★ ✔ $ A bustling parlor with luscious ice cream treats. Hot fudge sauce is made daily. *Marketplace. 10:30 a.m.–11 p.m. Sunday–Thursday, 10:30 a.m.–midnight Friday–Saturday. $7–$10. Seats 88, including 22 outside.*

The Smokehouse at House of Blues. ★★★ $ Located in the former House of Blues box office, this new fast-food barbecue window has limited but tasty choices, including pulled-meat and brisket sandwiches (all on the small side), a smoked turkey leg and excellent St. Louis-style ribs. The messy food is served in small cardboard boxes, with side dishes (cole slaw or baked beans) in small plastic cups. An expanded outdoor patio has uncovered seating; live music plays during the late afternoons and evenings. *West Side. 11:30 a.m.–10 p.m. $7–$13. Seats 88 outside.*

Wolfgang Puck Express. ★★★★ ✔ $$ offers an imaginative mix of pasta, pizza, salads, sandwiches and soups, including signature Crispy Cornflake French Toast and silky butternut squash soup. *Marketplace. Breakfast 9–11 a.m. $9–$15. Lunch, dinner. 11 a.m.–11 p.m. $9–$18 (children $7). Seats 184, including 96 outside.*

Snacks. Downtown Disney's best snacks are the hot, soft treats at **Wetzel's Pretzels** ★★★ ✔ which also offers fresh-squeezed lemonade and Haagen-Dazs ice cream. Wetzel's primary stand is on the West Side across

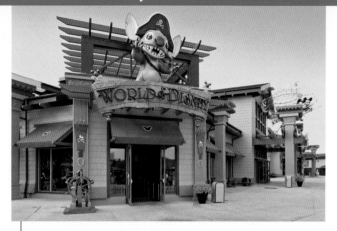

Originally meant to resemble a European shopping village, the Marketplace suffered an ugly update in the 1990s, its once natural wood shingles and trim painted garish shades of orange, red and green.

from Cirque du Soleil, a smaller one is in the Marketplace. Yearning for a good cup of Joe? A new West Side **Starbucks** ★★★★ has it.

See also **Restaurant Policies** in the chapter **Walt Disney World A–Z**.

Shops

Downtown Disney has a surprising variety of stores, as many are not owned by the Disney company and therefore offer items you won't find anywhere else at Walt Disney World. Even some of the Disney shops are unique. For the listings below stores are rated from one to five stars (★) based on the quality of their merchandise, service and atmosphere; only four- and five-star spots are shown. A checkmark (✓) indicates the shop is an author favorite.

Arribas Brothers. ★★★★ Hand-cut crystal, hand-blown glass. Engraving. Artisans work in front of guests. *Marketplace.*

The Art of Disney. ★★★★ Animation cels, attraction posters, Lenox china figurines, lithographs, oil paintings, plates, vases and quality art pieces. *Marketplace.*

Basin. ★★★★★ ✓ The aroma is intoxicating inside this lovely store, which offers items for the "shower, tub, sink and soul." Sinks let you to try your choice of salt and sugar scrubs, which make your hands feel softer than they've ever felt before. Shelves teem with all-natural massage and shampoo bars, bath bombs, body butters and lotions. Fresh soaps come in an amazing array of scents, colors and designs. *Marketplace.*

Cirque du Soleil Boutique. ★★★★★ ✓ Stunning Cirque-branded circus caps, fashion apparel, figurines, masks, purses, scarves. La Nouba souvenirs. *West Side.*

Curl by Sammy Duvall. ★★★★ ✓ Junior and adult beachwear, fashion apparel, hats, jewelry, purses, shoes, sunglasses, swimwear. Billabong, Hurley, Oakley, Roxy brands. *West Side.*

Disney's Days of Christmas. ★★★★ Huge holiday shop has ornaments, figurines. Mickey-eared Santa hats, stockings. Embroidery, engraving. *Marketplace.*

D Street. ★★★★★ ✓ Vinylmation collectible figures. Quirky Star Wars, Marvel T-shirts, accessories. *West Side.*

Fit2Run, The Runner's Superstore. ★★★★ Men's and women's running-themed apparel, shoes, strollers. *West Side.*

Ghirardelli. ★★★★ Candy, cocoa, fudge sauce, hot-chocolate mix. Free chocolate samples. *Marketplace.*

Goofy's Candy Company. ★★★★★ ✓ Custom and create-your-own apples, cookies, other treats. Coffees, smoothies. *Marketplace.*

House of Blues Company Store. ★★★★★ ✓ This laid-back little shop sells an eclectic collection of merchandise that at first glance seems to have little in common with itself. But the blues CDs, cornbread mix, folk art, hot sauce and incense all share an attribute— a through-the-roof quotient of cool. Funky skull-head T-shirts fit right in. *West Side.*

Hoypoloi Gallery. ★★★★ This little art gallery has interesting home accents, including unusual clocks, figurines, fountains, lamps, paintings, pottery. *West Side.*

The LEGO Store. ★★★★★ Part store, part playground, this huge, always crowded shop boasts the world's largest Pick-A-Brick wall, with 320 bins of Lego bricks sorted by color and size. There's a huge variety of Lego collections, priced as little as $6. Indoor-outdoor play areas include tracks for kids

© Disney

When Downtown DIsney finishes its transformation into Disney Springs, it will have a significantly different look, that of a Florida waterfront town of a hundred years ago. Disney plans to have the work done in 2016.

to race vehicles they build. Giant creations make good photo backdrops. *Marketplace.*

Marketplace Co-Op. ★★★★ ✔ Six boutiques make up this new spot, which opened in 2014: Beautifully Disney has women's cosmetics and fragrances. Cherry Tree Lane stocks sophisticated women's accessories such as bags, jewelry, scarves, shoes. Disney Centerpiece sells unique Disney-themed home furnishings, housewares. D-Tech on Demand offers personalized electronic accessories. The Trophy Room sells sports apparel and collectibles. Zoey and Pickles has girl's apparel and accessories. *Marketplace.*

Mickey's Pantry. ★★★★★ ✔ Mickey Mouse-styled housewares. Non-Disney cookware, food, tableware, wine. The Spice and Tea Exchange sells unique blends of salts, sugars, spices and teas. *Marketplace.*

Pop Gallery. ★★★★ Signed paintings, three-dimensional wall hangings, wild glass sculptures. Small champagne bar. *West Side.*

Shop for Ireland. ★★★★ Irish apparel, cookbooks, infantwear, mugs, music. At Raglan Road. *Pleasure Island.*

Something Silver. ★★★★ Sterling jewelry from designers Jordan Schlanger, Kit Heath. *West Side.*

T-REX Dino-Store. ★★★★ Dinosaur-themed children's apparel, toys. Build-A-Bear Workshop Build-A-Dino area. Outdoor "sand" play pit has faux fossils, sluice. *Marketplace.*

Tren-D. ★★★★★ ✔ Junior apparel from Disney, Billabong, Hurley, Roxy. *Marketplace.*

United World of Soccer. ★★★★ Cleats and other sports gear, jerseys. *West Side.*

World of Disney. ★★★★ Department store has areas for Girls, Ladies and Juniors, Boys, Men, Infants, Hats and T-shirts, Housewares, Home Decor, Jewelry and Pins,

Candy and Snacks, Souvenirs. Includes a Bibbidi Bobbidi Boutique salon (girls $55–$190 and up; boys $16. Ages 3–12. Allow 30–60 minutes. Reservations 407-939-7895 available six months in advance). *Marketplace.*

Disney Springs

Throughout 2015 Disney is expanding and updating Downtown Disney, so much so that the complex will be getting a new name—Disney Springs. Disney representatives say the revamped area will have significantly more shopping, dining and entertainment "amid beautiful open-air promenades, meandering springs and waterfront charm, with the same focus on storytelling and attention to detail that goes into our theme parks." The number of shops, restaurants and other venues will double, to more than 150. Only a few of them will be Disney venues. "There are a couple of Disney concepts," says Tom Staggs, chairman of Walt Disney Parks and Resorts, "perhaps one in food, a couple in retail."

Meant to resemble a small Florida waterfront town of a hundred years ago, Disney Springs will consist of four interconnected "neighborhoods": an adult-oriented Town Center, a new lakefront restaurant area, The Landing; an upgraded yet still family-focused Marketplace; and an upgraded West Side entertainment district with elevated spaces above its walkways.

Also new: Two parking garages, two pedestrian bridges over a widened Buena Vista Drive, and a new Disney highway that will connect the complex directly to Interstate 4—and therefore probably make it more popular than ever.

Disney plans to finish the work in 2016.

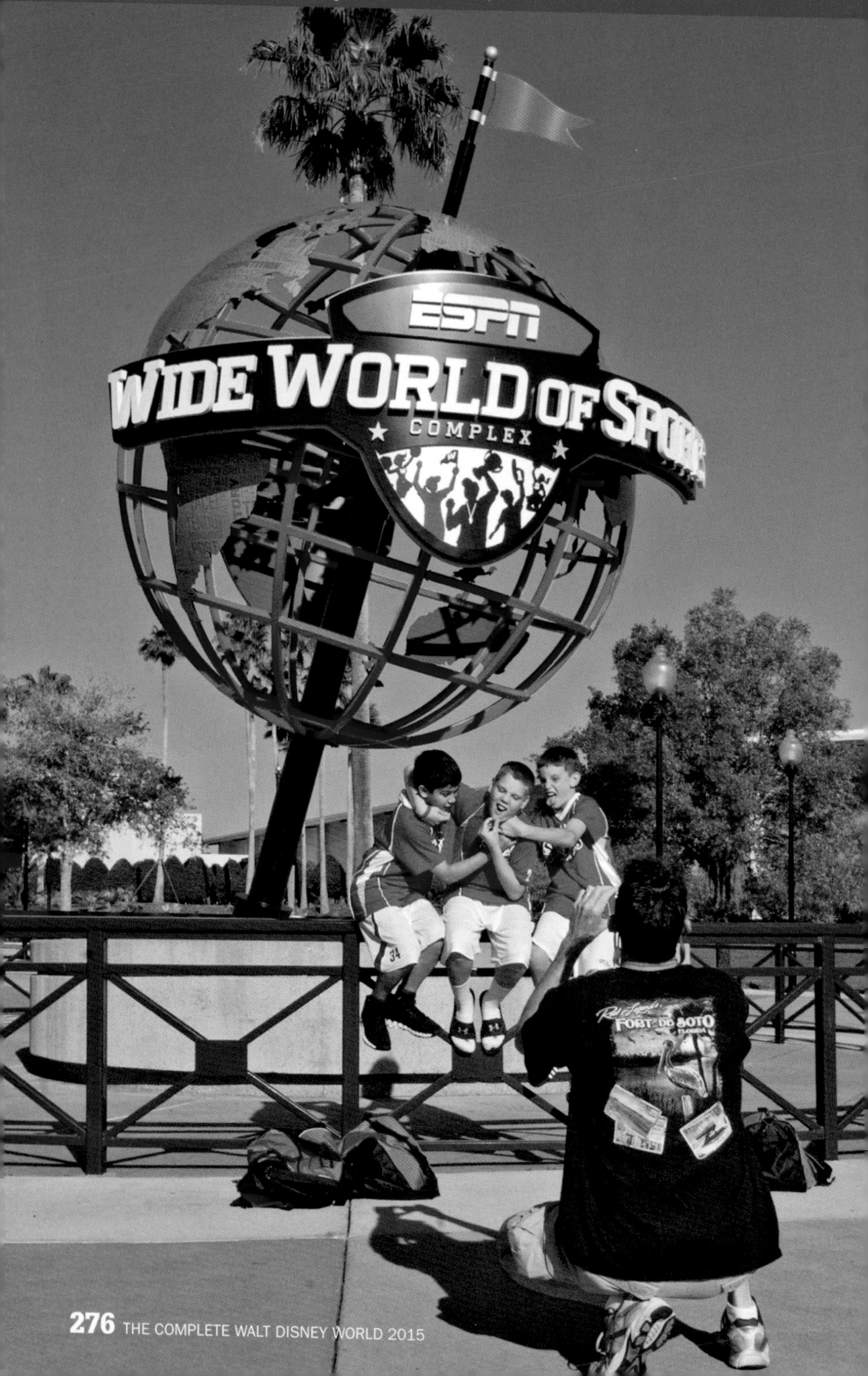
ESPN
WIDE WORLD OF SPORTS
COMPLEX

ESPN Wide World of Sports

One of the few places on Disney property that is not a tourist spot, the ESPN Wide World of Sports complex (700 S Victory Lane, Lake Buena Vista FL 34747. 407-828-3267, live operator 407-939-1500, youth group information 407-939-4263; espnwwos.com) is one of the largest amateur sports centers in the United States. The 220-acre facility hosts hundreds of events each year, including the Spring Training camp of the Atlanta Braves Major League Baseball club. It attracts two million visitors annually—about the same number as the Hawaiian island of Maui.

The complex includes a baseball stadium, two field houses, 29 outdoor fields, a tennis center and a track-and-field area. Built in 1996, it features "Florida Picturesque" architecture. Offset by blue and green accents, pastel yellow buildings have Spanish towers, archways and roofing. Landscaped with palms and hardwoods, the left side of the complex—the main baseball, softball and tennis area—has shady walkways.

Broadcast coverage. Designed to make amateur athletes feel like they've made it to the big time, the area is infused with the broadcasting style of ESPN, a Disney-owned network. Lining walkways, video kiosks show highlights of games played, a Bottom Line ticker of game results, interviews with players and coaches and local weather. Roving reporters and robotic cameras capture the action at most events; about a dozen highlight and interview clips are produced daily. Guests staying at Disney hotels can view the coverage on their in-room televisions.

Family and friends who aren't at Disney can follow athletes on various ESPN networks. Broadband channel ESPN3.com airs 200 hours of coverage a year. ESPNU airs collegiate events. The main network sometimes shows highlights from the complex in its Top Plays of the Day. Coverage is also posted on ESPN YouTube channels.

A Broadcast Center coordinates coverage. ESPN staffers mix footage from field reporters, remote cameras, a 20-zone audio system and an in-house studio. Major events are covered with up to seven cameras, two more than most ESPN college-football telecasts. Also serving as an ESPN distribution hub (one of five in the United States), the center is the anchor point to more fiber-optic cable than Cowboys Stadium in Dallas.

ESPN Innovation Lab. Headquartered in a small building between the Tennis Center and Hess Convertible Fields 7 and 9, ESPN staffers develop broadcast technologies by using the sports complex as a testing ground. So far the results have included Ball Track, a Doppler-radar system that can continuously update the distance and height of a baseball in flight; the ESPN Snap Zoom, a freeze-frame technology for football plays that zooms in on an area to provide more insight on the action; and the EA Virtual Playbook application, which allows studio analysts to bring to life key match-ups, formations and game action with multi-dimensional animation. The lab is closed to the public.

Venues

Consisting of eight distinct venues, the complex has an array of courts and fields.

Baseball Quadraplex. For baseball this is Disney's nicest place to play. It features four manicured fields, a half field for infield drills and various bullpens, batting tunnels and pitching machines. Center fields have batter's-eye backdrops. Field 3 has lights. A separate pitching area has 10 enclosed bullpens. The quad is used by pros during Atlanta Braves Spring Training, Gulf Coast League and Fall Instructional League seasons. *340-foot right- and left-field lines, 385-foot power alleys, 400-foot center field. Fields 2, 4 and 5 have small covered infield bleachers, Field 3 has small covered bleachers behind home plate. No concession stand. Restrooms, pay phones, souvenir kiosk.*

Champion Stadium. This double-decker ballpark hosts amateur competitions as well as Atlanta Braves Spring Training games. Most seats are in direct sun; a few are under a balcony. Wide concourses create a pleasant atmosphere, but the stadium lacks the

Facing page: "Now let's try a silly one." Teammates pose at the entrance to the ESPN Wide World of Sports complex.

The multi-sport Jostens Center is one of two field houses. It can hold two inline hockey rinks, six basketball courts or a dozen volleyball courts. The larger HP Field House is nearby.

intimate feel found at other Florida Spring Training sites. Concession stands offer sandwiches, hot dogs, snacks, soft drinks, and beer. A general-admission grass berm beyond left field seats 2,000. *340-foot right- and left-field lines, 385-foot power alleys, 400-foot center field. 9,500 seats, 80 percent behind infield. Four sky boxes; two open-air suites with patios. Concession stands, carts, restrooms throughout. Gift shop.*

Hess Sports Fields—Baseball. Four large diamonds (Fields 21–24) sit at the far right of the complex. A lack of landscaping creates a hot, sunny environment for spectators. All fields have lights and bullpens, with batting tunnels nearby. *355-foot maximum right- and left-field lines, 489-foot maximum center field. Small 3-row infield bleachers may be tented. No concession stand, snack tents may be set up. Soft-drink machine. Restrooms nearby.*

Hess Sports Fields—Convertible Fields. Spread throughout the complex, these 13 huge rectangles can host football, lacrosse, soccer and similar sports. Features vary. *Specs:* Next to the Baseball Quadraplex, Fields 7 and 9 lack scoreboards, though Field 7 has a coaching tower. Behind the HP Field House, Fields 16 and 17 include lights for night play, as do adjacent Fields 18 and 19. Next to the Jostens Center, Field 20 has no scoreboard. Note: Because of their proximity to the complex entrance plaza, Fields 19 and 20 have ambient music: a soundtrack of upbeat pop tunes. Most fields are crowned with 1-degree slopes. *Fields 7 and 9 lack spectator seating; share a concession stand, restrooms. Field 16 has a small shaded bleacher area. Fields 17 and 18 have large sections of covered stadium seats; has concession stands and restrooms nearby. Field 19 lacks spectator seating; has concession stands and restrooms nearby. Field 20 has no spectator amenities.*

HP Field House. With high arches and trusses reminiscent of a 1950s field house, the main arena at this 165,000-square-foot facility can host a variety of multi-court events. Two auxiliary courts sit upstairs. The bottom floor has locker rooms, a workout area and pro memorabilia cases. *Next to Champion Stadium. 5,500 stadium seats; top row 35 feet high. Auxiliary courts have 6-row bleachers. Concession stands sell sandwiches, hot dogs, snacks, soft drinks, no beer. Wetzel's Pretzels stand at auxiliary courts. Restrooms, pay phones. No gift shop. Back patio overlooks Hess Field 17.*

Jostens Center. This indoor arena has all of its competition area in one space. It can be divided into two inline hockey rinks, six basketball courts or a dozen volleyball courts. Locker rooms are available. *5-row bleachers line two sides. Concession stand, Wetzel's*

The main arena of the HP Field House holds 5,500 spectators. With the highest row of seats only 35 feet above the court, everyone gets a close view of the action.

Pretzels stand on second level. Restrooms on both levels. Adjacent to souvenir shop, ESPN Wide World of Sports Grill.

Diamondplex Softball Complex. Six fields can accommodate fast-pitch softball, slow-pitch softball or youth baseball. A central tower at the main quad has a concession stand, as well as areas for scorekeepers and officials. All fields have lights and bullpens, with batting tunnels nearby. *Fields 10 and 11 maximum dimensions: 275-foot right-, left- and center-field lines. Quad fields (12, 13, 14 and 15) maximum dimensions: 305-foot right-, left- and center-field lines. Fields 10 and 11 have small covered bleachers behind home plates. Quad fields have small covered infield bleachers. Concession stand sells sandwiches, hot dogs, snacks, soft drinks, beer. Restrooms, pay phones. Souvenir kiosk nearby.*

Tennis Center. These 10 clay courts, which include a stadium court, once hosted the U.S. Men's Clay Court Championships. All courts are in direct sun; seven have lights. *Stadium court elevated bleachers seat 1,000. No amenities, though food and souvenir carts may be set up for events. The back side of the adjacent ESPN Innovation Lab has a concession stand that, if open, sells sandwiches, hot dogs, snacks and soft drinks; nearby are soft-drink machines, restrooms, pay phones.*

New Balance Track and Field Complex. This 400-meter polyurethane area meets the standards of the International Association of Athletics Federations, the sport's governing body. It has nine 48-inch lanes, double straightaways, three shot-put rings, two discus/hammer rings, a javelin runway, two high-jump pits, two interior horizontal-jump runways and two pole-vault zones. An adaptable cross-country course is adjacent. *Large covered bleachers. No concession stand. Adjacent restrooms.*

Events

The complex hosts more than 300 amateur events a year, which include 11,000 individual games and contests and athletes from more than 70 countries. Many are sponsored by the Amateur Athletic Union (AAU) (407-934-7200, aausports.org), which has its headquarters nearby. Signature events include:

Disney Spring Training. A pre-season warm-up for high-school and college teams, this spring festival includes baseball, softball, lacrosse, and track and field. Typically 150 to 200 teams participate.

Cheerleading World Championships. The Super Bowl of cheerleading, this April event usually includes more than 8,500 cheerleaders; 100 teams from 40 countries.

Fans await the start of an Atlanta Braves Spring Training game. The Braves take on other Grapefruit League teams at Disney's Champion Stadium each February and March.

AAU Boys National Basketball Championships. High-school players compete in this July showcase. Participants have included NBA stars Lebron James, Dwight Howard, Chris Paul and Dwyane Wade.

Old Spice Classic. A NCAA Division I basketball tournament, this bracket-format event features 12 games over three days in November. Each team competes in one game per day.

Pop Warner Super Bowl. After advancing through regional competitions, 64 youth football teams compete in these December championships. Four divisions consist of Jr. Pee Wees (ages 8–11 years), Pee Wees (9–12 years), Jr. Midgets (10–13 years) and Midgets (11–15 years).

Pop Warner National Cheer & Dance Championships. Held during the Pop Warner Super Bowl, this December event brings together about 500 cheer and dance squads. Teams compete in the same age ranges as the football players as well as by squad size (Small and Large) and three skill categories (Novice, Intermediate and Advanced).

Disney's Soccer Showcase. A series of three top-level national events, this huge fall festival typically features more than 600 teams (about 10,000 athletes) in divisions from U11 to U18. Athletes in divisions U15 through U18 first compete in a September

Qualifier. The top two finishers in each group advance to the main event in December; winners are guaranteed a spot in the top flight. For divisions U11 through U14, Disney's Junior Soccer Showcase offers national competition over Thanksgiving weekend. The Showcase is open to state-cup or higher level teams. About 800 college coaches attend.

Braves Spring Training

After two weeks of workouts, the Atlanta Braves play a 15- or 16-game Spring Training schedule at Champion Stadium in late February and March. Grapefruit League competitors include the New York Yankees, Boston Red Sox and St. Louis Cardinals. Disney characters often appear during the games; afterward, children can run the bases.

Tickets (ranging from $15 for general admission lawn seats to $52 for lower-level reserved seats; $3 additional day of game; group tickets and multi-game packages available) are sold at Ticketmaster (800-745-3000; ticketmaster.com) and the complex box office (prerecorded 407-828-3267; live voice 407-939-1500 or 407-939-4263) starting the first week in January. Games against the most popular teams sell out.

Open to all visitors at no additional charge, Braves workouts and practices take

© Disney

Fans cheer on the Orlando City Major League Soccer team at a recent Walt Disney World Pro Soccer Classic. The team currently plays its home games at the ESPN complex, on Field 17. It will move to an Orlando soon.

place in the stadium and at the Baseball Quadraplex. Major league players leave at the end of March; minor leaguers (the "Baby Braves") stay through April. Except for autograph hounds the workouts draw few fans.

Policies and resources

Admission. Though courts and fields are open only to participating groups, the public is welcome as spectators. Admission for amateur events is $16.50 for ages 10 and above, $11.50 for ages 3–9. Length-of-event tickets are often available. Walt Disney World annual passholders get in free. Professional events are ticketed separately.

ATM. There's one, outside the gates by the ESPN Clubhouse store. A portable ATM is set up in Champion Stadium for Braves games.

Coolers. Each guest may bring in one cooler of up to one gallon for personal use. A coach can bring in one cooler of up to five gallons for team use. No coolers are allowed in the Jostens Center.

Credentials. Athlete and coach credentials are distributed to teams at registration. To get them, each team must have paid its tournament entry fee and submitted waivers for each athlete and coach. A coach can pick up credentials for an entire team. Credentials provide admission to specific areas on specific dates.

Driving directions. *From the north:* Take the Florida Turnpike to Interstate 4, head west to Osceola Parkway West (exit 65). Turn left at stoplight onto Victory Way. *From the southwest:* Take Interstate 4 east to Osceola Parkway West (exit 65). Turn left at stoplight onto Victory Way. *From the southeast:* Take the Florida Turnpike north to Exit 249

(Osceola Parkway West), go about 10 miles, turn left onto Victory Way.

Equipment drop off. For some events (including those at the Softball Complex) teams can drop off equipment at a spot alongside the parking lot, where it's loaded onto a motorized cart and taken to the appropriate venue. A team representative must accompany it. Teams themselves must walk to their fields.

Family matters. Parents wanting to watch their child compete will find shaded bleachers at most outdoor venues, and either bleachers or stadium seats at most indoor spots. Nursing mothers will find the best indoor options to be various nooks and crannies in the HP Field House and Jostens Center, or, on uncrowded days, a back table at the ESPN Wide World of Sports Grill (although none of these three spots allow strollers). Moms might find it tough to nurse in Champion Stadium; the baseball park has few private spots beyond restrooms, especially out of the heat.

First Aid. During events, trainers in marked tents aid injured athletes. Non-athletes needing over-the-counter pain medications, bandages or other basic supplies should contact a Disney cast member. The entrance gift shop sells these items.

Food. Concession stands dot the grounds; temporary carts offer snacks and beverages on event days. Guests can place advance orders for boxed meals, bulk beverages and snacks to be delivered to particular fields; items range from $8 sandwiches to $20 pizzas. Officially only visitors with special dietary needs (i.e., medical conditions, religious doctrines) may bring food into the complex, however this rule is often

The Wide World of Sports Welcome Center offers event schedules, books Disney restaurants and provides general Walt Disney World information. Below, the ESPN Clubhouse Shop and the ESPN Innovation Lab.

not enforced. No glass bottles or alcoholic beverages can be brought into the complex, though many concession stands sell beer.

The complex has one restaurant:

ESPN Wide World of Sports Grill. ★ ★ ★
✔ $ This American fast-food spot has you order at a counter but delivers your food to your table. The menu has chicken wings, individual pizzas, salads and sandwiches; best bets are the roast beef and blackened fish sandwiches. Soft drinks are refillable. A photo prop looks like a "SportsCenter" set. Seven huge high-def screens show sports channels as well as events within the complex. More TVs are at the separate bar, which serves liquor as well as beer and wine. *Across from Champion Stadium, next to the Jostens Center. 10:30 a.m.–7 p.m.; on slow days will close early or have limited menu. Lunch, dinner: $8–$13, Seats 350, 48 in bar.*

Getting around. This place is huge! Larger than most Disney theme parks, the 220-acre complex requires a lot of walking to get around, especially to reach its back areas. The hike from the parking lot to the Softball Complex is seven-tenths of a mile, which at a leisurely pace takes about 15 minutes.

Lockers, equipment storage, showers. The complex has no public lockers or storage. The HP Field House and the Jostens Center have team locker rooms with showers.

Parking. General parking is free; valet parking is available for some events for $10 to $20, depending on the event. The small parking lot often fills to capacity; overflow parking is available on grassy areas behind it and on the median of Victory Way, the road that leads to the complex. Late arrivals for Spring Training games may walk almost a mile to Champion Stadium.

Park tickets. The Welcome Center sells all types of Walt Disney World theme-park tickets, including one option that's offered nowhere else: Specially priced tickets that are available only to visitors to the ESPN Wide World of Sports complex. A "1-Day After 2 p.m." ticket provides admission to any one Disney World theme park for $74; a similar "1-Day After 1 p.m." for water parks is $32. DisneyQuest tickets are $27. The tickets are valid only on the day of purchase. (Prices as of June 2014.)

See also **Tickets** in the chapter **Walt Disney World A–Z.**

An on-site ESPN production center mixes feeds from field reporters as well as 42 robotic cameras to generate coverage of events. Results appear on video displays throughout the grounds.

Pets. Except for service animals, no animals are allowed on the grounds.

Restrooms. Facilities are available at, or near, all competition venues.

Shops. The ESPN Clubhouse Shop offers ESPN, sports-team and complex apparel and other merchandise, as well as a small selection of collapsible chairs, sunglasses and umbrellas. The shop has two locations: at the complex entrance and inside Champion Stadium. Next to the ESPN Wide World of Sports Grill, a Custom Tee Center booth customizes event T-shirts. Souvenir kiosks are often set up at event venues.

Strollers. Strollers are allowed in most areas of the complex, but prohibited inside the HP Field House, Jostens Center and ESPN Wide World of Sports Grill. Stroller parking is available outside of those venues. The complex does not rent strollers.

Transportation. Complimentary bus service is available from Disney's All-Star Resort, Caribbean Beach Resort and Pop Century Resort. Buses run from one hour prior to the complex opening to 11 p.m. or closing time (whichever is later) on days when events are taking place, as well as every Thursday through Monday from 5 p.m. to 11 p.m. These buses arrive on the hour and the half-hour. Buses may not be able to accommodate all teams and equipment. Note: Disney buses no longer run between the complex and Disney's Hollywood Studios.

Welcome Center. Located between the HP Field House and Jostens Center, a small Welcome Center offers event schedules and provides general Disney World information. It also sells theme-park, water-park, DisneyQuest and La Nouba tickets; makes Disney dining reservations and helps with transportation issues.

Wheelchair rentals. No wheelchairs are available for rent, though a limited number of complimentary wheelchairs is available at the Welcome Center, for use only at the complex. A photo I.D. is required.

Wi-Fi. Free though unreliable, Disney Wi-Fi is available throughout the complex.

Weather. When lightning or other severe weather threatens, Disney halts all outdoor ESPN events at least temporarily. The Weather Channel web site (weather.com) offers current Walt Disney World conditions and forecasts.

Accommodations

As the most popular vacation destination on the planet, Walt Disney World has no shortage of places to stay. Disney itself owns and operates 20 resort hotels on its property—combined, they have enough rooms to hold 126,000 people—and other companies manage more than a dozen. This chapter reviews them all, and hopefully helps you determine the right place to stay for your particular needs.

Disney resort hotels. It's not just the theme parks that are magical. The themed architecture, decor, swimming pools, lush landscaping and, in many cases, quality restaurants at a Disney resort hotel immerse you in a unique vacation experience. Their reputation as clean, family environments is well-deserved. Fancier spots offer a variety of recreation options and sometimes character meals, where guests can meet Mickey Mouse and other beloved stars in person. Disney divides its 20 resorts into four categories, which group the properties by price, amenities, and, in most cases, the number of people that their guest rooms will accommodate.

Disney Value Resorts. (Disney's All-Star, Art of Animation and Pop Century resorts). With rack rates starting as low as $96 a night, these huge motel-like complexes have the least expensive Disney rooms. Most sleep four, have double beds, and are relatively small at 260 square feet. All-Star Movies also offers 520-square-feet family suites that sleep up to six; Art of Animation has over 1,100 more. Amenities are limited, but do include swimming pools, playgrounds and food courts. Luggage service is hourly. Parking lots are near lodging buildings. Note: the $96 rate is for up to two adults and two children; Disney charges $10 more for each additional adult.

Oddly, the Value resorts are the only Disney hotels that have obvious Disney themes; at all three many buildings are trimmed with gigantic statues and other huge props that recall Disney movies. All

Disney's least expensive rooms are at its Value Resorts—the Art of Animation, Pop Century and (at left) All-Star complexes.

properties are popular with large youth groups, especially the All-Star complex.

Disney Moderate Resorts. (Disney's Caribbean Beach, Coronado Springs, Fort Wilderness and Port Orleans resorts). With rack rates starting at $182 a night ($15 per night for each additional adult), these large complexes offer distinctive geographical themes, more elaborate swimming pools and, in most cases, a table-service restaurant. Most rooms are 314 square feet and come with two queen beds; some at Disney's Port Orleans Riverside Resort sleep five thanks to trundle beds; Fort Wilderness cabins sleep six. Amenities include on-site recreation options. Parking lots are near lodging buildings.

Disney Deluxe Resorts. (Disney's fanciest regular hotels: Disney's Animal Kingdom Lodge, BoardWalk Inn, Contemporary, Grand Floridian, Polynesian Village, Wilderness Lodge and Disney's Yacht and Beach Club resorts). Serious architecture, lush landscaping and a wealth of amenities distinguish Disney's top-of-the-line resort hotels. Rack rates start at $319 a night, with a $25 surcharge for each additional adult. Most rooms sleep five, and vary in size from 340 to 476 square feet. Amenities include fine restaurants, elaborate swimming pools, on-site recreation, full room service, club levels, fitness centers and valet parking. Restrooms in public areas offer cloth towels and hand lotion. Located in front of large resort entrance areas, parking lots are away from lodging buildings; non-valet spots can require a short hike to get to.

Disney Deluxe Villas. (Disney's Old Key West Resort, Disney's Saratoga Springs Resort, also sections of Disney's Animal Kingdom Lodge Resort, Disney's Beach Club Resort, Disney's BoardWalk Inn Resort, Disney's Contemporary Resort, Disney's Polynesian Village Resort and Disney's Wilderness Lodge Resort). These Disney Vacation Club (DVC) timeshare units are often available nightly; rack rates start at $367. Units vary from studios to multi-story suites that can sleep 12; all but studios have kitchens. DVC buildings are usually adjacent to Deluxe Resorts and share most of their amenities, though DVCs often have their own swimming pools. Distinct resorts all their

© Disney

Top-of-the-line Disney Deluxe Villas—timeshare properties such as Bay Lake Tower that are often available nightly—have ample amenities and spacious suites, with prices to match.

own, Old Key West and Saratoga Springs have amenities similar to Deluxe Resorts.

Other groupings. Disney occasionally groups its resort hotels geographically. Some highway signs on Disney property refer to the hotels in this fashion: *Animal Kingdom Area Resorts:* All-Star, Animal Kingdom, Art of Animation, Coronado Springs and Pop Century (even though, in reality, Art of Animation and Pop Century are closer to Downtown Disney than they are to Animal Kingdom). *Downtown Disney Area Resorts:* Old Key West, Port Orleans, Saratoga Springs. *Epcot Area Resorts:* BoardWalk, Caribbean Beach (though Caribbean Beach is closer to Disney's Hollywood Studios than the entrance of Epcot) and Yacht and Beach Club. *Magic Kingdom Area Resorts:* Contemporary, Grand Floridian, Polynesian Village, Wilderness Lodge and Fort Wilderness.

Benefits of Disney-owned hotels.

Staying anywhere on Disney property is certainly convenient—it's easy to get to a theme park early in the morning, and to return to your hotel for a midday break. Benefits of staying at a Disney-owed hotel include:

Extra Magic Hours. Each day, one of the four Walt Disney World theme parks has extended hours, opening one hour early, or staying open up to three hours late for Disney

resort guests with theme-park tickets. Water parks also participate. These Extra Magic Hours offer you uncrowded time in the parks and make it easier to plan out your vacation.

Complimentary transportation. Disney boats, buses and monorails take you to all theme and water parks as well as Downtown Disney at no additional charge. In some cases, it takes just a few minutes to get from your hotel room to a theme park.

Magical Express. This complimentary bus service shuttles guests between the Orlando International Airport and Disney-owned resort hotels. In most cases users can bypass baggage claim, as Disney itself picks up luggage from the airlines and delivers the bags to its hotels. In addition, many guests can check their baggage for the return flight at their Disney resort. Magical Express is only available to guests using certain commercial airlines and staying at Disney resort hotels.

MagicBand. This wristband acts as a room key, theme-park ticket and charge card. Each Disney resort guest, including each child, gets one either at check-in, or with their reservation packet beforehand.

Package delivery. Anything a Disney resort guest buys at a Disney theme park can be delivered to their resort free of charge.

Guaranteed admission. If they have tickets, Disney resort guests are guaranteed

Right in the middle are the authors' favorites, the Disney Moderate Resorts. These relaxed, affordable complexes include Caribbean Beach (right), Coronado Springs and Port Orleans.

entry into Disney theme parks, even, in most cases, when those parks are officially filled to capacity. Visiting at Christmas, the Fourth of July or another peak period? This matters.

Special deals. Disney resort guests can prepay for their meals through the Disney Dining Plan and get preferred tee times and discounts at Disney's four golf courses.

See also the chapter **Walt Disney World A–Z**.

About the following reviews. Resorts are rated from one to five stars (★) for quality and value. Restaurants are also rated by stars, based on the quality of their food, service and atmosphere—a five-star eatery fully lives up to its promise; a one-star place should be avoided. A checkmark (✓) indicates that the hotel or restaurant is one of the authors' personal favorites. Also for restaurants, the price of a typical adult dinner entree is summarized by dollar signs:

$ less than $10
$$ less than $15
$$$ less than $20
$$$$ less than $25
$$$$$ more than $25

To reserve a table at any Walt Disney World restaurant call Disney at 407-939-3463.

The reviews refer to each hotel without the word "Disney's" in front of it or the word "Resort" afterward, even though both words are included in their official names and on TripAdvisor and other online booking sites (thus, Disney's Contemporary Resort is listed as simply "Contemporary"). Room rates shown do not include resort tax (13.5 percent at All-Star Resorts; 12.5 percent at all other hotels). All Disney hotel addresses are in the city of Lake Buena Vista, Florida, ZIP code 32830.

All-Star

★★ Cramped rooms, bad food and cheap decor make these three adjacent Disney Value Resorts poor places to stay; they're really little more than basic budget motels overlaid with a bunch of garish superficial theming. However, the pools are nice for the price, with fountains and children's activities. Youth groups such as marching bands and soccer teams often stay here. Built to compete with the rash of discount motels on nearby U.S. 192 (most of which have since fallen into disrepair), each hotel is laid out like a typical motel complex, but on a giant scale. A central building holds the registration area, food court and bus station, and fronts the main pool. Boldly decorated three-story lodging buildings spread out from there, with parking lots nearby. Each lodging building is coated with bright paint; stairwells and elevator entrances are hidden by larger-than-life icons—either Disney film characters (All-Star Movies), musical instruments (Music) or sports gear (Sports). Landscaping is sparse, though native pine trees cover much of the grounds.

Highs. Good rates; child-friendly Disney theme; McDonald's adjacent; large swimming pools; All-Star Music has family suites that sleep up to six.

Lows. No table-service dining; garish theming; unshaded bus stops; lodging elevators are not air-conditioned; small guest rooms; crowded food courts and bus stops, especially in the morning.

Restaurants and food. Each resort has a food court, bakery, convenience store and small bar open to its main pool. Room service (pizza, salads, desserts) is 4 p.m. to midnight.

A huge jukebox decorates the Rock Inn lodging building at the All-Star Music Resort. Giant candy-colored guitars and musical notes complete the look.

- **End Zone Food Court.** ★ $$ Very lame American fare in a cheap atmosphere. If you have a car, drive down to McDonald's instead. *Breakfast, lunch, dinner. 6:30 a.m.–11 p.m. Seats 500. All-Star Sports.*
- **Intermission Food Court.** ★ $$ Same as above. *Breakfast, lunch, dinner. 6:30 a.m.–11 p.m. Seats 500. All-Star Music.*
- **World Premiere Food Court.** ★★★ $$ The best All-Star spot by far. *Breakfast, lunch, dinner. 6:30 a.m.–11 p.m. Seats 500. All-Star Movies.*

Rooms. Modestly decorated rooms in "star" themes have cheery colors and honey woods. *260 square feet. Sleep 4. Two double beds. Accessed by outdoor walkways. All-Star Music has family suites: 520 square feet. Sleep 6. 1 king bed, 1 sleeper-sofa double bed, 2 single beds convert from chair and ottoman, kitchenette, 2 full baths.*

Swimming pools. Each All-Star complex has two themed pools, one with a kiddie pool behind its central hall and a second nestled within its lodging buildings. No pool has a slide, but central ones have fountains that shoot water over swimmers' heads. All-Star Movie's "Fantasia" pool is themed to that film; the smaller "Mighty Ducks" Duck Pond pool resembles a hockey rink. All-Star Music's Calypso Pool is guitar shaped; a smaller Piano Pool has a cushy keyboard deck. All-Star Sport's Surfboard pool looks like a beach; its smaller Grand Slam pool resembles a baseball diamond.

Key facts. *Rates:* Rack room rates $96–$216, discount rooms from $77. Suites $239–$442, discount as low as $194. *Hotel type:* Disney Value resort with clustered multistory lodging buildings. *Location:* Southwest Disney property, near Animal Kingdom. *Distance to (in miles):* Magic Kingdom 5, Epcot 5, Hollywood Studios 3, Animal Kingdom 1, Blizzard Beach 1, Typhoon Lagoon 4, Downtown Disney 4, ESPN Wide World of Sports 3. *Addresses:* Movies 1901 W Buena Vista Drive, Music 1801 W Buena Vista Drive, Sports 1701 W Buena Vista Drive, all zip codes 32830. *Size:* 5,740 rooms, 298 suites, 246 acres. *Amenities:* Each resort has a food court, two swimming pools and one kiddie pool. Arcade, jogging trail, playground. Laundromat, laundry service. Shop with groceries. *Children's programs:* Organized activities are posted on a poolside board each morning. *Transportation:* Disney buses shuttle guests to theme parks, water parks and Downtown Disney. *Built:* Sports, Music 1994; Movies 1999. *Check In:* 3 p.m. *Check Out:* 11 a.m. *Phone:* Movies 407-939-7000. Music 407-939-6000. Sports 407-939-5000. *Fax:* Movies 407-939-7111. Music 407-939-7222. Sports 407-939-7333.

A Paul Bunyan-sized megaphone disguises a stairwell at the All-Star Sports Resort. None of the architecture at the three All-Star properties could be described as "subtle."

Animal Kingdom Lodge

★★★★★ ✔ A giraffe may wander behind your balcony at this African-themed complex. With many guest rooms overlooking wildlife savannas, it consists of two distinct spots—the original Animal Kingdom Lodge, now called Jambo House, and Kidani Village, a newer timeshare complex that's right next door.

At Jambo House, 19 interconnected lodging buildings arc into a 33-acre savanna, home to non-aggressive African animals. Kidani Village is surrounded on three sides by a similar 13-acre savanna, though its interior areas are less elaborate.

Which one to pick? Jambo House. It's a fully realized resort with comfortable rooms, first-class dining and a good swimming pool. Not at all like a village, Kidani Village is one long building—over a half mile in length—with a parking garage underneath. Its guests take a bus to Jambo House to eat breakfast, and its lunch and dinner restaurant, though excellent, serves an African/Indian cuisine that may not be everyone's cup of tea. Small children will love its swimming pool area, though, which has a winding slide and a water-park-like kiddie play zone.

Highs. Roaming wildlife, superb restaurants, all rooms are easily accessible, good pools, child-care center onsite, Kidani's larger suites are stunning.

Lows. Pricey. Distant location. Most standard rooms sleep four, not five.

Restaurants and food. Animal Kingdom Lodge has a buffet and two table-service restaurants. All are terrific. Room service is available from 6 a.m. to midnight.

• **Boma—Flavors of Africa.** ★★★★★ ✔ $$$$$ This lavish African / American buffet combines American comfort food with non-threatening African options (best are the roasted meats, breakfast oatmeal-like pap, grilled tomatoes and dinner soups). The buffet area resembles an outdoor market, with each serving station in its own hut or "makeshift" stand. Several seating areas sit under abstract thatched ceilings with hand-cut glass and tin fixtures. Servers are extraordinarily friendly and prompt. *Breakfast 7:30–11 a.m. Dinner 4:30–9:30 p.m. Seats 400. Jambo House.*

• **Jiko—The Cooking Place.** ★★★★ ✔ $$$$$ Sophisticated, relaxing and romantic, this jewel specializes in African flavor fusions: cherries with goat cheese, roasted sweet potatoes with spiced yogurt. The South African wine selection is the largest in the United States. Hanging from the ceiling are sculpted kanu birds, flying over diners to bring them good luck. Representing a sunset, the back wall slowly changes color. *Dinner. 5:30–10 p.m. Seats 300. Jambo House. A Disney Signature Restaurant.*

• **Sanaa.** ★★★★★ ✔ $$$$ Serving tasty Indian-inspired East African cuisine with dishes both spicy and mild, this colorful dining room comes with an added bonus: guests near window seats watch exotic animals roam a savanna. The bread service is a must, as is a chai cream dessert. A stylized decor recalls an African marketplace; lights that resemble ripe fruit hang from abstract acacia trees. *Lunch 11:30 a.m.–3 p.m. Dinner 5–9 p.m. Seats 124, 24 in lounge. Kidani Village.*

• **The Mara.** ★★★★ ✔ $$ Spacious and relaxed, this fast-food spot at Jambo House offers American/African options including good fresh soups. A small store has fruit, snacks, South African wines. Cartoons play

Exotic chandeliers top the lobby of Jambo House at Animal Kingdom Lodge. At the far end, a floor-to-ceiling window overlooks the resort's wildlife-filled savanna.

Some of the most high-end places to stay in all of Disney World, two-story Kidani Village Grand Villas can cost upwards of $3,000 a night. Balconies offer sweeping savanna views.

on televisions. *Breakfast, lunch, dinner. 7 a.m.–11:30 p.m. Bakery 6 a.m.–11:30 p.m. Seats 250).*

Rooms. Rooms have multicolored fabrics and dark wood furniture handcrafted in Africa. Ground-level rooms have patios; others have balconies which extend 4 feet. Most overlook wildlife savannas, though some face the pool or parking lot. Club level available. Jambo House suites are at prime locations at the end of animal trails. Some have pool tables. Kidani Village has 492 villas; Jambo House has 109. *340 square feet. Sleep 4. Two queen beds, or one queen plus bunk beds, small refrigerator. Suites: 1-, 2- and 3-bedroom units sleep up to 9. Villas: Studio, 1-, 2- and 3-bedroom units sleep up to 12.*

Swimming pools. Open 24 hours a day, the large Jambo House pool has a 67-foot water slide and a "zero-entry" gradual ramp. A kiddie pool, two hot tubs and a shady playground are nearby. The Kidani Village pool complex has a 4,200-square-foot interactive play area.

Key facts. *Rates:* Rack room rates $319–$654, discount rooms from $199. Suites $928–$2339, discounted as low as $652. Villas $444–$748, discounted to $325. *Hotel type:* Disney Deluxe resort hotel with main lodge, secondary lodge curving around wild animal savannas. *Location:* Southwest corner of Disney property, near Disney's Animal

Kingdom. *Distance to (in miles):* Magic Kingdom 6, Epcot 5, Hollywood Studios 3, Animal Kingdom less than 1, Blizzard Beach less than 1, Typhoon Lagoon 5, Downtown Disney 5, ESPN Wide World of Sports 9. *Address:* 2901 Osceola Parkway 32830. *Size:* 762 rooms, 19 suites, 708 villas, 74 acres. *Amenities:* Jambo House has two restaurants, fast-food cafe, two lounges; Kidani Village has one restaurant. Each section has a pool with slide, hot tubs, kiddie pool, play area. Animal viewing (24 hours), arcade, children's programs, night-vision animal spotting, playground, poolside crafts. Sunrise truck ride through Disney's Animal Kingdom habitat; sunset ride into resort savannas (both extra charge). Business center. Laundromat, laundry service, massages, shops. *Kidani Village:* BBQ pavilion; basketball, shuffleboard, tennis courts. Kidani Village Community Hall has games, activities. *Children's programs:* Many organized activities (daily, some with small fee) including African cultural activities, arts and crafts and pool games. *Transportation:* Disney buses shuttle guests to theme parks, water parks and Downtown Disney, as well as between Jambo House and Kidani Village. *Built:* Jambo House 2001, Kidani Village 2009. *Check In:* 3 p.m. *Check Out:* 11 a.m. *Phone:* 407-938-3000. *Fax:* 407-938-4799.

© Disney

The "Cars" section of the Art of Animation resort recalls the landscapes and small family businesses that once flourished along Route 66. Lodging buildings hold small suites.

Art of Animation

★★★ ✔ This Disney Value complex is much like the one next door—though it has its own entrance, it uses the land and some of the buildings originally meant to be a second phase of the Pop Century resort. As a result, it's landscaped and decorated in much the same fashion, with brightly colored motel-style buildings that are trimmed with gigantic icons that hide outdoor stairwells and elevator banks. A central building holds its registration area, food court and bus station, and fronts the main swimming pool. Parking lots surround the complex on three sides; in back is a large retention pond and a footbridge to Pop Century.

Art of Animation is divided into four sections, each of which is based on a popular Disney animated movie—"Cars," "Finding Nemo," "The Lion King" (all family suites) and "The Little Mermaid" (standard rooms). Many families will love the look of the resort—it's a strong dose of Disney, but it's way more tasteful than the other Value spots. The "Cars" area is especially well done. Rooms, however, are small, and even the suites have cheap furnishings.

Highs. Affordable rates, nicer and newer than other Value resorts, it's the closest hotel to the ESPN Wide World of Sports complex.

Lows. Small standard rooms, no table-service restaurant, in-your-face decor, lodging elevators are not air-conditioned.

Restaurants and food. There's no table-service restaurant, but there is a good food court, as well as a bakery, convenience store and small pool bar. Room service (pizza, salads, desserts) is available 4 p.m. to midnight.

• **Landscape of Flavors Food Court.** ★★★ ✔ $$ The food at this attractive spot includes choices that go beyond standard food-court fare. Lunch and dinner menus have Mongolian barbecue; treats include smoothies and hand-scooped gelato. *Breakfast, lunch, dinner. 6 a.m.–midnight. Seats 650.*

Rooms. Art of Animation rooms have vivid color schemes and are boldly decorated with cartoon characters; furniture is painted in a vibrant mix of bright, flat colors. Carpet in "Finding Nemo" rooms recalls waving seagrass; "The Lion King" decor uses browns and greens; "The Little Mermaid" furnishings use a seashell pattern; the "Cars" rooms have a yellow-gold Southwest coloring with large logos from that movie's various locales. Suites feature dining tables that convert into double beds. *260 square feet. Sleep 6. 1 queen bed, 1 sleeper-sofa double bed, 1 double-size table bed, kitchenette, 2 full baths.*

Swimming pools. The resort has three swimming pools, all with adjacent kiddie

Surrounded by a morning fog, Rafiki welcomes guests into the Lion King section of the resort. Though its suites have kitchenettes, many early risers make the short walk to the food court for coffee and doughnuts.

pools. The Finding Nemo pool—the largest one at Walt Disney World that's not in a water park—adds a kiddie splash zone and pool bar.

Key facts. *Rates:* Rack room rates $118–$221, discount rooms from $110. Suites $298–$511, discounted as low as $249. *Hotel type:* Disney Value resort with clustered, multistory lodging buildings. *Location:* Close to Interstate 4, near Hollywood Studios and ESPN Wide World of Sports. *Distance to (in miles):* Magic Kingdom 6, Epcot 5, Hollywood Studios 3, Animal Kingdom 4, Blizzard Beach 4, Typhoon Lagoon 2, Downtown Disney 3, ESPN Wide World of Sports 2. *Address:* 1850 Century Drive 32830. *Size:* 864 rooms, 1120 suites, 65 acres. *Amenities:* One food court. Three themed swimming pools with adjacent kiddie pools. Arcade, beach, playgrounds. Laundromat, laundry service. Shop with groceries. *Children's programs:* Pool activities. *Transportation:* Disney buses shuttle guests to theme parks, water parks and Downtown Disney. *Built:* 2012. *Check In:* 3 p.m. *Check Out:* 11 a.m. *Phone:* 407-938-7000. *Fax:* 407-938-7070.

BoardWalk Inn and Villas

★★★★★ ✔ Disney cut no corners when it built this Deluxe Resort, a re-creation of the golden days of Atlantic City. A wide lakeside promenade is lined with quaint shops, interesting restaurants, an Atlantic Dance Hall and dueling-piano bar, Jellyrolls. The pools are small, but have a fun amusement-park theme. The location is terrific: within walking distance of Disney's Hollywood Studios as well as the back entrance to Epcot.

Surrounded by water on three sides, the property includes a hotel, timeshare units and a conference center. The boardwalk level holds restaurants, shops and entertainment venues; rooms, suites and villas rise behind. Most rooms spread out among two semicircular arcs of interconnected buildings. Some overlook the lake, though most face landscaped areas or pools. The BoardWalk has the look of a community that has grown over time. "Newer" structures appear unrelated to their neighbors; mom-and-pop shops have tucked themselves into residential buildings.

Highs. Great dining variety, quality; within walking distance to Epcot, Hollywood Studios; evening entertainment on boardwalk; lovely setting on a lake.

Lows. Lodging buildings are far from the parking lot, no restaurants are within the hotel interior, there's no Disney transportation to the main entrance of Epcot.

Restaurants and food. A variety of good dining choices—all on the resort's boardwalk—includes a Disney Signature seafood eatery, a micro-brewery and good sandwich spots. Room service is available 24 hours a day at the Inn; 6 a.m. to midnight at the Villas.

Big River Grille & Brewing Works. ★★★ ✔ $$$ Sporting Disney World's only micro brewery, this classy little franchise also offers down-to-earth food and free Wi-Fi. The food—grilled meats, seafood, pasta, sandwiches—and the prices are reasonable. Small gunmetal tables make it noisy when crowded. It serves dinner later (to 11 p.m.) than most Disney restaurants. Equipped with two televisions, the small bar can be a less-crowded sports-bar alternative to the nearby ESPN Club. *Lunch, dinner. 11:30 a.m.–11 p.m. Seats 190, including 90 outside.*

• **ESPN Club.** ★★★ $$ This casual, noisy eatery combines a sports bar with a second

A whirlpool bubbles in the master bathroom of a one-bedroom villa at Disney's BoardWalk Resort. Panels open up to a relaxed pastel bedroom.

A family pedals a rented surrey down the lakefront promenade of Disney's BoardWalk Resort. The curved wooden walkway is lined with restaurants and snack shops.

room that hosts radio talk shows. It has 123 television monitors. Weekends can be packed. Basic bar chow includes burgers, hot dogs, ribs, salmon and steaks. *Lunch, dinner. 11:30 a.m.–11 p.m. Seats 450.*

• **Flying Fish Cafe.** ★★★ $$$$ Cramped, crowded, bright and loud, the poor atmosphere at this pricey seafood nightspot interferes with its quality food. A show kitchen boosts the noise. Sit in the back for the calmest experience. Good bets include the calamari, crab cakes, scallops and steak. A six-course prix fixe Chef's Wine Tasting Dinner is available. *Dinner. 5:30–10 p.m. Seats 193. A Disney Signature Restaurant.*

• **Trattoria al Forno.** This traditional Italian eatery is scheduled to open for the start of 2015, replacing Cat Cora's Kouzzina. It will serve seasonal risottos, Neapolitan-style pizza and an extensive Italian wine list.

• **BoardWalk Bakery.** ★★★ ✔ $ Pick up fresh-baked pastries and treats at this walkin spot, as well as hot breakfast sandwiches and cold lunch sandwiches. *Breakfast, lunch, dinner. 6:30 a.m.–varies. No seating.*

• **Seashore Sweets.** ★★★★ ✔ $ Handscooped ice cream, fudge, packaged candy. Walls lined with portraits of every Miss America. *10:30 a.m.–11 p.m. No seating.*

Rooms. Colorful period decor creates an immersive experience. Beds have plush mattresses on wood frames. Bathrooms have marble sinks. A club level is available. Two-story garden suites have individual front lawns with white picket fences. Timeshare villas are often available for nightly rentals. *Standard room 385 square feet. Sleep 5. Two queen beds, sleeper sofa, small refrigerator. Suites sleep 4–9. Villas sleep 4–12, in studio, 1-, 2- and 3-bedroom units.*

Swimming pools. The Luna Park swimming pool area features a 200-foot red slide that looks like a 1920s wooden roller coaster, with small dips and sweeping turns and, at its exit, becomes the mouth of a giant clown head. Nearby is a kiddie pool, playground and sunny hot tub. Two quiet pools are somewhat shady—the Villas one is nicely landscaped with a large grill; the Inn has a lesser version of the same thing: smaller pool, fewer trees, no grill.

Key facts. *Rates:* Rack room rates $411–$750, discount rooms from $256. Suites $830–$2905, discounted as low as $554. Villas $554–$1341, discounted to $256. *Hotel type:* Disney Deluxe resort hotel with interconnected, multistory lodging. *Location:* Centrally located on Disney property between Hollywood Studios and Epcot. *Distance to (in miles):* Magic Kingdom 4, Epcot less than 1 mile, Hollywood Studios less than 1 mile, Animal Kingdom 4, Blizzard Beach

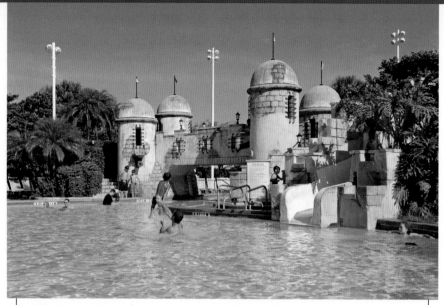

Children play at the main swimming pool at Disney's Caribbean Beach Resort, which flows through a stone fort that's tucked into a tropical landscape.

2, Typhoon Lagoon 2, Downtown Disney 2, ESPN Wide World of Sports 4. *Address:* 2101 N. Epcot Resorts Blvd. 32830. *Size:* 378 rooms, 20 suites, 533 villas, 45 acres. *Amenities:* Four restaurants, bakery, ice cream parlor, snack shops, lounge. Three pools. Main pool has a clown-faced slide, kiddie pool, playground. Arcade, BBQ grill, bike and surrey rentals, fitness center, lighted tennis courts. Two nightclubs. Laundromat, laundry service. Shop with groceries. Conference center (9,600 square feet, ballroom, 14 breakout rooms). Business center. *Children's programs:* Organized activities (daily, some have a small fee) include arts and crafts, pool games. *Transportation:* Boats go to Epcot, Hollywood Studios. Disney buses shuttle guests to other theme parks, water parks and Downtown Disney. When the boats can't operate (during lightning), buses take guests to Epcot, Hollywood Studios. *Built:* 1996. *Check In:* 3 p.m. (Villas 4 p.m.). *Check Out:* 11 a.m. *Phone:* 407-939-5100. *Fax:* 407-939-5150.

Caribbean Beach

★★★ ✔ Disney's second largest hotel complex, this 200-acre resort is landscaped with palms and native pines. Wrapped around a 42-acre man-made lake, colorful metal-roofed lodging buildings cluster into six self-contained "villages," each of which has its own parking area. Footbridges over the lake lead to a one-acre island, Caribbean Cay, a flowery spot dotted with benches and hammocks. A dining, shopping and recreation center, Old Port Royale, is centrally located. Check-in counters and the main concierge center are at the Custom House, a building along the entranceway far from other areas. A nice mix of value and convenience, Caribbean Beach is a good choice for families who want a resort-hotel experience but don't want to bust their bank account. Rooms are comfortable, though their decor is sort of cheap, especially in pirate-theme rooms.

Highs. Decent rates, convenient driving distance to all theme parks, many rooms are near parking lots, tropical landscaping lends a distinct vacation feel. All of this adds up to a package that overcomes its flaws.

Lows. Dining facilities are weak and too small, especially at breakfast; many lodging buildings are far from bus stops; superficial Caribbean theming; childish room decor.

Restaurants and food. A small restaurant is open only for dinner; a food court serves all three meals. Room service (pizza, salads, desserts) is available from 4 to 11:30 p.m.

• **Shutters.** ★★ $$$$ With pre-made food that can be served within a minute of ordering, this overpriced American/Caribbean

Standard rooms at the Caribbean Beach resort have bright and cheery "Finding Nemo" decor; other rooms have a less-subtle pirate theme.

eatery is in the lower tier of Disney's resort restaurants. The steak, chicken, ribs, pasta and seafood are a step up from frozen food. The small room is well-staffed. A bland but pleasant decor includes big tables and wide padded chairs. *Dinner. 5–10 p.m. Seats 132.*

• **Centertown Food Court.** ★★ $ Don't get your hopes up; uninspired American fare fills this faux outdoor market. Its walls look like tropical buildings, complete with balconies, shuttered windows and thatched roofs. A blue ceiling mimics a sky. A small food store next door sells fruit and snacks. *Breakfast, lunch, dinner. 11:30 a.m.–11 p.m. Seats 500.*

Rooms. All guest rooms are specifically themed. Most have a bright decor with "Finding Nemo" trim. Some have a strong pirate theme, with molded-plastic beds that resemble ships, dressers that look like old crates and skull-and-sword drapes that close off bathroom vanities. *314 square feet. Sleep 4. Two double beds, small refrigerator. Accessed by outdoor walkways.*

Swimming pools. The main pool sits in in a stone fort. Cannons spray swimmers; a small slide has a 90-degree turn. Nearby is a kiddie pool, hot tub and a small water playground with mini-slides, fountains and a barrel that dumps water from above. Calm basic pools sit within each lodging area.

Key facts. *Rates:* Rack room rates $182–$367. discount rooms from $136. *Hotel type:* Disney Moderate Resort with clustered, multistory lodging buildings. *Location:* Centrally located on Disney property, near Hollywood Studios. *Distance to (in miles):* Magic Kingdom 5, Epcot 4, Hollywood Studios 3, Animal Kingdom 5, Blizzard Beach 3, Typhoon Lagoon 1, Downtown Disney 2, ESPN Wide World of Sports 3. *Address:* 900 Cayman Way 32830. Size: 2,112 rooms, 200 acres. *Amenities:* Restaurant, food court. Central pool with slide, kiddie pool, hot tub. Each lodging area has a basic pool; the Barbados, Jamaica, Trinidad, Old Port Royale areas have playgrounds. Arcade, beach, bike rentals, boat rentals, guided fishing trips, hammocks, picnic area, sand volleyball court, surrey rentals, walking trail. Laundromat, laundry service. Shop with groceries. *Children's programs:* Pontoon-boat adventure; complimentary arts and crafts, beach and pool activities. *Transportation:* Disney buses shuttle guests to theme parks, water parks, Downtown Disney and ESPN Wide World of Sports. A separate shuttle circles within the resort. *Built:* 1988. *Check In:* 3 p.m. *Check Out:* 11 a.m. *Phone:* 407-934-1000. *Fax:* 407-934-3288.

Contemporary

★★★★ One of Walt Disney World's original resort hotels, this 1971 property is on the monorail route and a lake, has comfortable rooms and a character meal, but overall it fails to deliver a magical Disney experience. An abundance of glass, carpet and sprayed plain concrete lends an impersonal feel to most of its public areas, while its restaurants are pricey and its pools plain. However, it does have a lot to offer. It includes a distinctive 15-story A-frame main building, a garden-wing annex, a large convention center and Bay Lake Tower, a crescent-shaped timeshare tower. It's the only hotel from which guests can walk to Magic Kingdom, and the only one with an indoor monorail station. It also has the most extensive water recreation of any Disney hotel complex.

The main swimming pool at Disney's Contemporary Resort features a 17-foot-high spiraling slide. It sits behind the resort's signature 15-story A-frame.

As for being contemporary, each guest room has its own computer as well as a modern Asian theme, but the rest of the resort seems more like a coldhearted office complex straight out of the 1970s. Ceilings are often acoustical tile. A restricted Disney Vacation Club property, Bay Lake Tower certainly looks modern, though its interior areas feel like they belong in a cheaper spot. It has its own recreation area and a rooftop lounge with a fireworks-viewing deck.

Highs. On the monorail route, within walking distance to Magic Kingdom, big comfortable rooms, great recreation, lakeside.

Lows. Corporate feel, pricey dining, poor counter-service eatery, plain pools.

Restaurants and food. The resort has three restaurants; all are pricey. Room service is available 24 hours.

• **California Grill.** ★★★★★ ✔ $$$$$ Superb fare is matched by a stunning view atop the resort's A-frame. Its New American menu has many vegetarian options, exquisite sushi and an extensive wine list. Guests can watch Magic Kingdom's fireworks show from inside or on rooftop walkways, with the show's music audible. A stylish decor uses honey woodwork. *Dinner 5:30–10 p.m. Seats 156. A Disney Signature Restaurant.*

• **Chef Mickey's.** ★★ $$$$$ This popular character meal features Mickey Mouse as a chef, his pals Minnie Mouse, Donald Duck, Goofy and Pluto as cooks. Unfortunately, dining rooms often each have only one character at a time, who during busy periods has to spend time among 100 guests. Huge buffets include PB&J pizzas for breakfast, good meats and salmon for dinner. *Breakfast 7–11:30 a.m. Dinner 5–9:30 p.m. Seats 405.*

• **The Wave.** ★★★★ ✔ $$$$ This upscale American eatery serves fresh, healthy food. Its menu emphasizes sustainability, local produce and organic ingredients. Highlights include intense dessert flights and Southern hemisphere wines. The open dining room has a sophisticated decor but no windows. Typically uncrowded, the Wave is a relaxing way to escape theme-park frenzy. *Breakfast , lunch and dinner. 7:30–11 a.m, noon–2 p.m, 5:30–10 p.m. Lounge noon–midnight. Seats 222 plus 100 in the lounge.*

• **The Contempo Cafe.** ★ $$ Though it has a great location in the middle of the A-frame atrium, this fast-food spot offers little to recommend it. Its food is uneven, its electronic ordering system irritating. *Breakfast, lunch, dinner. 6 a.m.–10 p.m. Seats 112.*

Rooms. Most rooms have an Asian-styled decor with tan fabrics and dark woods; a Club level is available. A concierge lounge has seasonal and organic foods; yoga sessions and spa treatments are available. *Standard*

Spacious standard guest rooms at the Contemporary have a modern Asian decor of browns, greens and yellows with dark woods. Rooms in the A-frame have balconies with glorious views.

rooms 394 square feet. Sleep 5. Two queen beds, daybed, small refrigerator. Suites: Sleep 4–8. Villas: Studio, 1-, 2- and 3-bedroom units sleep up to 12.

Swimming pools. The main swimming pool has a 17-foot-high spiraling slide, a large central fountain and a row of smaller sprays. A second pool sits next to the lake. It's round, and gets deeper in its center. Cabana tents are available for rent (407-939-7529; 407-824-2464 same-day). Nearby are a beach volleyball court and a kiddie pool area with a splash pad and fun water cannons. A Bay Lake Tower pool includes a "zero-entry" side and a 20-foot-high spiraling slide wrapped in a glass block. A hot tub, Mickey Mouse-shaped kids fountain, shuffleboard and bocce ball courts and a barbecue pavilion with shaded picnic tables are nearby.

Key facts. *Rates:* Rack room rates $378–$1071, discount rooms from $269. Suites $1199–$3674, discounted as low as $895. Villas $492–$3555, discounted to $470. *Hotel type:* Disney Deluxe resort hotel with two towers and a separate 3-story DVC wing. *Location:* Northwest corner of Disney property, near Magic Kingdom. *Distance to (in miles):* Magic Kingdom less than 1, Epcot 4, Hollywood Studios 4, Animal Kingdom 7, Blizzard Beach 5, Typhoon Lagoon 6, Downtown Disney 7, ESPN Wide World of Sports 7. *Address:* 4600 N. World Drive 32830. *Size:* 632 rooms, 23 suites, 295 villas, 55 acres. *Amenities:* Three restaurants, fast-food cafe, snack shops, lounges. Two pools, kiddie pool. Private Bay Lake Tower complex has Community Center with video, board games. Arcades; beach; boat rentals; evening beach campfire with movie; guided fishing trips; tennis, beach volleyball courts; water sports. Fitness center, hair salon, laundromat, laundry service. Convention center (120,000 square feet, 4 ballrooms, 1,600 square foot stage, 33 breakout rooms). Business center. *Children's programs:* Arts and crafts, beach and pool activities. *Transportation:* Monorail goes to Magic Kingdom, Epcot; Grand Floridian, Polynesian Village resorts. Boats travel to Wilderness Lodge, Fort Wilderness resorts. Disney buses shuttle guests to Hollywood Studios, Animal Kingdom, water parks and Downtown Disney. *Built:* 1971. *Check In:* 3 p.m. (Bay Lake Tower 4 p.m.). *Check Out:* 11 a.m. *Phone:* 407-824-1000. *Fax:* 407-824-3539.

Coronado Springs

★★★ ✔ This sprawling Spanish Colonial convention complex offers a quality place to stay at a decent price, even if you're not there on business. It consists of an amenities and convention center and three distinct lodging areas, all of which circle outward around a 15-acre lake. Rooms and suites are grouped into an urban-styled Casitas area near the convention center; a Ranchos section that has an American Southwest landscape of sagebrush, cactus and gravel; and a Cabanas area decorated like Mexico's Gulf Coast. Swimming pools are excellent, and include a large central one with many features. Dining options are poor, but there's a decent McDonald's down the street. The resort has little Disney atmosphere, but its tropical landscaping is well-maintained. It's Disney's only mid-priced convention property.

Highs. Family-friendly despite convention location, many rooms near parking lots, fun themed pool, close to McDonald's, 22-person hot tub is one of Disney's largest.

Disney's Coronado Springs Resort was designed to reflect the Spanish-Colonial heritage of Mexico. Lodging buildings sit among palms and low hedges.

Lows. Dining facilities limited, weak food court, lodging buildings distant. Guests using Disney's Magical Express service have a long walk from the bus depot.

Restaurants and food. The Disney touch is absent at the Coronado's dining choices, which are run by an outside company. Room service is available 7 a.m. to 11 p.m.

• **Maya Grill.** ★★★ $$$$ Breakfast dishes at this American-Latin eatery include a Kobe brunch burger and Huevos Rancheros. Dinners come with delicious breads and a chimichurri dipping sauce. Meats and Tex Mex platters dominate entrees; the filet mignon and pork belly enchiladas stand out. An open kitchen has a wood-burning oven. *Breakfast 7–11 a.m. Dinner 5–10 p.m. Seats 220.*

• **Pepper Market Court.** ★★ $$ The American/Mexican dishes offered here are mall-quality at best, but the atmosphere is nice. There's an automatic 10 percent service charge, though you get your food yourself. *Breakfast 6–10:30 a.m. Lunch, dinner 11 a.m.–11 p.m. Seats 420.*

• **Café Rix.** ★★ $ This small spot serves pastries, sandwiches, gelato. *Breakfast, lunch, dinner 6:30 a.m.–midnight. Seats 50.*

Rooms. Rooms have comfortable beds and calm decors; most are close to parking lots but a long walk from many amenities. A modern Mexican decor combines dark woods with blue, green and yellow fabrics. Club-level rooms have DVD players. *314 square feet. Sleep 4. Two queen beds, small refrigerator. Accessed by outdoor walkways.*

Swimming pools. With old-fashioned swing sets, treasures buried in the sand and a sneaky spitting jaguar next to a winding swimming-pool slide, children may never realize they're at a convention hotel if they hang out at the resort's first-rate recreation area. Adjacent to the Ranchos lodging buildings, it includes a large swimming pool, kiddie fountain pool, huge hot tub, sand volleyball court and indoor arcade. Smaller quiet pools are located in each lodging area.

Key facts. *Rates:* Rack rates $187–$335, discount rooms from $140. *Hotel type:* Disney Moderate Resort with clustered, multistory lodging buildings in three separate themed areas. *Location:* Next to Disney World's Western Way entrance, near Hollywood Studios. *Distance to (in miles):* Magic Kingdom 4, Epcot 3, Hollywood Studios less than 1, Animal Kingdom 2, Blizzard Beach less than 1, Typhoon Lagoon 3, Downtown Disney 4, ESPN Wide World of Sports 5. *Address:* 1000 W. Buena Vista Drive 32830. *Size:* 1,877 rooms, 44 suites, 125 acres. *Amenities:* Restaurant, food court, fast-food cafe, lounge. Large outdoor recreation complex with swimming pool, children's programs, playground,

Coronado Springs rooms have a modern Mexican decor that combines dark woods with turquoise and orange accents. Beds have blue, green and white fabrics.

sand volleyball court, large hot tub. Three smaller pools in lodging areas. Arcades; beach; bike, boat, surrey rentals; fitness center, guided fishing trips, hammocks. Hair salon, laundromat, laundry service. Shop with groceries. Convention center (220,000 square feet, ballroom, exhibit hall, 45 breakout rooms). Business center. *Children's programs:* Organized activities (daily, some have small fee) include arts and crafts, pool games. *Transportation:* Disney buses shuttle guests to theme parks, water parks and Downtown Disney. *Built:* 1997. *Check In:* 3 p.m. *Check Out:* 11 a.m. *Phone:* 407-939-1000. *Fax:* 407-939-1001.

Fort Wilderness

★★★★ ✓ Just about everything you'd hope a campground to be except three or four times as expensive, Fort Wilderness is a huge swath of wooded land with a wide range of recreation options, relaxed dining choices and decent swimming pools. Campsites are decent but pricey; cabins are chintzy for the price. Still, the resort offers a unique family-friendly experience many guests treasure. You certainly feel removed from civilization.

Highs. Relaxed wooded setting, wide variety of outdoor recreation, only Disney campsite, pets welcome in some spots.

Lows. Inconvenient; many areas are far from bus stops, dining, shops; cheap cabins; complicated transportation.

Getting around. Fort Wilderness is tucked into a thick pine forest and, in some areas, the remains of a drained cypress wetland. Lined with creek-like canals, it sits on a 450-acre natural lake. Its registration building and riding stables are at its entrance. From there, three roads branch off into 28 loops, each of

which is lined with either cabins or campsites. In back, a commercial "Settlement" area includes a restaurant, general store, music hall and marina, from which boats ferry guests to Magic Kingdom. But like all of the resort's guest areas, the Settlement has no parking lot. Though buses shuttle guests around the complex, many guests rent electric carts ($59 a day) to get around.

RV sites. The center of the resort is filled with campsites for recreational vehicles (picnic table, outdoor grill; concrete pad) with full hook-up (water, electric and sewer). Usually the choice of large RV owners, "preferred" sites sit closest to the Settlement and include cable-television and Internet service. All sites are near air-conditioned comfort stations with private showers, ice dispensers, laundromats and vending machines.

Tent sites. Partial hook-up tent sites (water, electric, level pads) line the sides of the property. Groups of 20 or more can reserve the tents-only Creekside Meadow. If you don't have a tent, Disney will rent you one for $32 a night.

Cabins. Worn cabins are located in the front of the resort; some sit in the drained swamp. *504 square feet. Sleep 6. Living room w/ Murphy bed, kitchen, bath, bedroom w/ one double and two bunk beds, deck, picnic table, outdoor grill. Air conditioning, vaulted ceilings, daily housekeeping.*

Pets. Fort Wilderness takes pets ($5 a day) at some campsites. Leashed dogs are allowed on carts; dogs can run free at a dog park.

Restaurants and food. Dining choices include a buffet restaurant and two dinner shows. The resort does not offer room service.

• **Hoop-Dee-Doo Musical Revue.** ★★★ $$$$$ This rootin' tootin' dinner show has been

© Disney

Fort Wilderness has full hook-ups for recreational vehicles. Some spots are on small lakes and ponds, others are nestled in pine forests.

performed 35,000 times since 1974. Children often think it's the funniest show ever; they love the six exuberant performers and the rat-a-tat jokes. The songs and skits aren't showstopping—expect a lot of "So, where're you from?"—but it's all so silly you can't help but have fun. Vittles include all-you-can-eat pails of fried chicken and ribs with lots of "fixin's" and, if you want, unlimited draft beer and wine. *2-hour shows at 5, 7:15, 9:30 p.m. Tuesday–Saturday. Pioneer Hall. Seats 360.*

• **Mickey's Backyard Barbecue.** ★★★ $$$$$ Hosted by Tumbleweed Will (a friend of the authors) and Cyclone Sally and with Mickey Mouse, Minnie Mouse, Goofy and Chip 'n Dale on hand to dance with its diners, this old-fashioned country show is especially fun for children. Held in a large outdoor pavilion, it includes a live country band, a trick roper and a big ol' dollop of patriotism. A so-so buffet offers pork ribs, chicken, corn on the cob, watermelon and beer. Diners share long tables. Arrive early; it's first-come first-seated, and the first group in sits right next to the dance floor. *2-hour shows at 6:30 p.m. Thursday, Saturday except during January, February. The Settlement. Seats 300.*

• **Trail's End Restaurant.** ★★ $$$$ The price is a step up from what you might expect at this Cracker Barrel-esque eatery, but so is the food. The potatoes are creamy, the vegetables actually have flavor. Breakfast and dinner are buffets with fried chicken and other comfort food; lunch is a la carte. Friendly servers add to a down-home ambience. A separate take-out counter offers sandwiches, salads, pizzas; there's a tiny bar. *Breakfast, lunch and dinner 7:30 a.m–2 p.m, 4:30 p.m.–9:30 p.m. Take-out service noon–2 p.m. The Settlement. Seats 192, 6 at bar.*

Swimming pools. The main swimming pool at Fort Wilderness has a water slide, hot tub and children's splash zone. A smaller quiet pool sits in the cabin area.

Key facts. *Rates:* RV sites $68–$129. Campsites $49–$154. Rack cabin rates $330–$562, discount cabins from $235. Hotel type: Disney Moderate resort with campsites and cabins. *Location:* Northwest corner of Disney property, southeast of Magic Kingdom. *Distance to (in miles):* Magic Kingdom 2, Epcot 4, Hollywood Studios 4, Animal Kingdom 6, Blizzard Beach 4, Typhoon Lagoon 6, Downtown Disney 6, ESPN Wide World of Sports 6. *Address:* 3520 N. Ft. Wilderness Trail 32830. *Size:* 784 campsites, 409 cabins, 740 acres. *Amenities:* One buffet restaurant, two dinner shows, lounge. Central pool with a slide, nearby kiddie pool with splash zone, hot tub. Smaller pool near cabins. Arcade, archery instruction, beach, bike rentals, dog park, golf cart rentals, picnic areas,

Cabins at Fort Wilderness have wood-paneled interiors. Bedrooms have one double bed and two bunk beds.

playgrounds, Segway tour, stable, surrey rentals, walking trail, watercraft rentals. Basketball, horseshoes, tennis, tetherball, volleyball courts. Cane-pole fishing, guided fishing trips. Carriage, wagon, trail, pony rides. Laundromat. Two stores with groceries, camping supplies. *Children's programs:* Complimentary arts and crafts, pool activities, campfire / movie with characters. *Transportation:* Boats take guests to Magic Kingdom. Disney buses shuttle guests to all Disney parks and Downtown Disney. A separate shuttle bus circles within the resort. *Built:* 1971. *Check In:* 3 p.m. *Check Out:* 11 a.m. *Phone:* 407-824-2900. *Fax:* 407-824-3508.

Grand Floridian

★★★★★ The signature Walt Disney World resort, the Grand Floridian lives up to its promise, even if its formal nature seems out of place next door to the world's most popular theme park. Its rooms are comfortable, its refined atmosphere grand. Genteel lodging buildings are surrounded by canary palms, Southern magnolias and formal gardens. Compared to the nearby Polynesian Village, the Grand Floridian is more beautiful but less charming, has better and more varied food choices but smaller rooms. There are two pools, one calm, one lively.

With its gabled roofs, clapboard siding and miles of moldings, scrolls and turnposts, the Grand Floridian brings the Victorian era back to life. Topped with three stained-glass domes, the five-story atrium lobby features a grand pianist and retro orchestra for entertainment. Other amenities include monorail access, a lovely little conference center and a spa. Disney's Wedding Chapel is adjacent.

Highs. On the Magic Kingdom monorail loop, big beautiful rooms, great dining options, lakeside, wedding pavilion, unique children's programs.

Lows. Very expensive, more formal than fun, self-parking area is a hike away.

Restaurants and food. Options include three high-roller restaurants and two relative bargains, including Disney World's best character-meal breakfast and dinner. Room service is available 24 hours a day.

• **1900 Park Fare.** ★★★★★ ✔ $$$$$ These joyous character meals are the best at Disney World. Breakfast, which stars Mary Poppins, Winnie the Pooh and Alice in Wonderland, serves standard American fare and a standout lobster Benedict. At dinner, everyone's favorite princess—Cinderella—is on hand, but also her fascinating family; bickering stepsisters Anastasia and Drizella usually steal the show. Varied buffet choices are delicious. The elegant dining room has a turn-of-the-century amusement park theme. *Breakfast 8–11:30 a.m. Dinner 4:30–8:30 p.m. Seats 270.*

• **Cítricos.** ★★★★ ✔ $$$$$ Lit with a soft yellow glow, this overlooked gem doesn't have Narcoossee's view or the over-the-top glam of Victoria & Albert's, but does offer imaginative, market-fresh dishes in what might be the most comfortable setting of any Disney Signature restaurant. The Mediterranean menu excels in seafood and seasonal soups. Tall windows overlook the main pool and marina. The pace is so relaxing you'll stay forever. *Dinner. 5:30–10 p.m. Seats 190. A Disney Signature Restaurant.*

• **Grand Floridian Café.** ★★★★ ✔ $$$$ This pleasant American spot is the best general-purpose restaurant on the Magic Kingdom monorail loop. Best bets include

The Grand Floridian recalls fabled Florida seaside resorts of the late 19th century, as well as California's Hotel del Coronado. A white-sand beach lines the South Seas Lagoon.

the fluffy citrus pancakes for breakfast, the tuna niçoise salad at lunch, and the steak and pasta dishes for dinner. Floral wallpaper and thick carpeting heighten the calm, comfortable atmosphere. *Breakfast, lunch and dinner. 7 a.m.–2 p.m.; 5–9 p.m. Seats 326.*

• **Narcoossee's.** ★★★★★ ✓ $$$$$ Though expensive, this pretension-free spot is one of the best seafood restaurants at Walt Disney World, though its wood floors and peaked ceilings make its dining room noisy. The circular building sits over the Seven Seas Lagoon; the view of Magic Kingdom's fireworks show includes reflections in the water. Ask for a windowside table. *Dinner. 5:30–10 p.m. Seats 270. A Disney Signature Restaurant.*

• **Victoria & Albert's.** ★★★★★ $$$$$ For an evening to remember this expensive gourmet restaurant is worth it—you may have the best meal you've ever had. Dining here is like having "Top Chef" winners cook just for you, as a seven-course dinner is created to match your personal tastes. A four-hour Chef's Table option includes more courses, a kitchen tour and a chat with cooks. Service is exemplary. *Dinner. Two seatings. Formal dress. Jackets required for men; loaners available. No children under age 10. Seats 90, including 10 at Chef's Table.*

• **Garden View Tea Room.** ★★★★ $$ This tiny, elegant indoor spot overlooks lovely outdoor gardens. English-style delicate tea sandwiches, scones, tarts, hot teas and specialty coffees are served on flowery china. Many choices have three courses. *Lunch. 2–6 p.m. Seats 80.*

• **Gasparilla Grill and Games.** ★★ $ Fast-food diners get good food but sit in a noisy 24-hour arcade. *Seats 150.*

Rooms. Situated in four detached buildings, rooms have a Victorian decor with light woods and fabrics, ceiling fans and marble-topped sinks. Each room has live plants and special touches such as iPod docks in clock radios. A club level is available. *Standard rooms: 440 square feet. Sleep 5. Two queen beds, some daybeds, small refrigerator. Suites: Sleep 2–8.*

Swimming pools. A calm swimming pool sits in a central courtyard, surrounded by a kiddie pool and hot tub. A second beachside pool, however, is the family favorite. It has a swerving 181-foot slide that takes 12 seconds to travel, as well as a 20-foot waterfall, a "zero-entry" side welcomes wheelchair guests. Cabanas are available for rent (407-939-7529 in advance, 407-824-2464 same-day). A fountain play area keeps little ones entertained.

Key facts. *Rates:* Rack room rates $540–$1528, discount rooms from $342. Suites $1412–$3127, discounted as low as $915. Villas

Light woods and a yellow-blue-and-green color scheme add charm to Grand Floridian guest rooms. Accommodations on top floors have slanted gabled ceilings.

The small marina at Disney's Old Key West Resort offers guided fishing trips and rents boats. Resort guests can also rent bicycles.

$554–$2053, discounted to $449. *Hotel type:* Disney Deluxe resort hotel with clustered, multistory lodging buildings. *Location:* Northwest corner of Disney property, near Magic Kingdom. *Distance to (in miles):* Magic Kingdom less than 1, Epcot 4, Hollywood Studios 4, Animal Kingdom 7, Blizzard Beach 5, Typhoon Lagoon 7, Downtown Disney 7, ESPN Wide World of Sports 7. *Address:* 4401 Grand Floridian Way 32830. *Size:* 842 rooms, 25 suites, 40 acres. *Amenities:* Six restaurants, snack bar, tea room, lounges. Two swimming pools, hot tub; main pool has long slide with waterfall. Kiddie pool, splash zone; children's programs. Arcade, beach, boat rentals, guided fishing trips, tea parties, tennis courts and clinics, walking trail. Child-care center, hair salon, laundromat, laundry service, spa. Shop with groceries. Convention center (40,000 square feet, 2 ballrooms, 16 breakout rooms). Business center. *Children's programs:* Pontoon-boat adventure; complimentary pool activities. Child-care facility onsite. *Transportation:* Monorail goes to Magic Kingdom, Epcot; Contemporary, Polynesian resorts. Boats travel to Wilderness Lodge, Fort Wilderness resorts. Disney buses shuttle guests to Hollywood Studios, Animal Kingdom, water parks and Downtown Disney. Built: 1988. *Check In:* 3 p.m. *Check Out:* 11 a.m. *Phone:* 407-824-3000. *Fax:* 407-824-3186.

Old Key West

★★★★ Sunshine State residents will feel right at home amid this resort's Olde Florida facades, swaying fronds and falling pine needles. The relaxing and spacious villas offer views of the woods, a canal or the Lake Buena Vista golf course. Inspired by Florida's tropical Victorian architecture, building exteriors combine tin roofs with clapboard siding, shuttered windows and gingerbread accents. Two- and three-story lodging buildings cluster into small groups along three roadways. A central Hospitality House contains a registration area, restaurant, gift shop, community hall, fitness center and marina.

Like other Disney Vacation Club timeshare resorts, it offers nightly rentals as owner bookings permit. Old Key West Resort was Disney's first timeshare property.

Highs. Spacious villas with expansive closet space, a good restaurant, parking within steps of each villa cluster, palm-filled tropical landscaping that lends a distinct vacation feel to non-Floridians.

Lows. Pools are small, simple and few for a property this size; limited dining options don't include an indoor fast-food spot; location is distant to all theme parks except Epcot; lack of indoor common areas; distant villa clusters make it tough to get around without a car.

A decorative lighthouse stands among palms near the main Old Key West swimming pool at Conch Flat Community Hall.

Restaurants and food. Small Olivia's Café is the lone restaurant; the only other option is an outdoor snack bar. Room service (pizza, salads, sandwiches, desserts) is available from 4 p.m. to midnight.

• **Olivia's Cafe.** ★★★ ✓ $$$$ Jimmy Buffett would feel at home in this Keys-inspired eatery. The menu is a nice mix of standard American fare and regional recipes that use lots of shrimp and conch, with tropical accents such as mango glaze. Breakfast in particular has unusual choices such as a shrimp and conch Benedict. Dinner offers more traditional fare. A homey decor includes a tin ceiling and mismatched padded chairs. *Breakfast, lunch, dinner. 7:30 a.m.–10 p.m. Seats 156, including 22 outside.*

• **Good's Food To Go.** ★★ ✓ $ This outdoor counter offers burgers, hot dogs, salads and sandwiches. *Lunch, dinner. 11:30 a.m.–10 p.m. No seating.*

Rooms. Most villas have a tropical peach and turquoise color scheme with upholstered furniture. Light woods look weathered. The villas have hardwood floors and granite countertops. The resort is notable for its roomy accommodations—bedrooms so big that, even with two queen beds, they still look empty. Each villa has a balcony overlooking a private courtyard. Grand Villas have the largest living areas of any Disney World timeshare units. *Studios 376 square feet; sleep 4. 1-bedroom 942 square feet; sleep 4. 2-bedroom 1,333 square feet; sleep 8. 2-story 3 bedroom 2,202 square feet; sleep 12. Accessed by outdoor walkways.*

Swimming pools. The main swimming pool, at Conch Flat Community Hall, has a water slide designed to look like a giant sandcastle. A faux lighthouse stands nearby, along with a kiddie pool, playground and hot tub. Three quiet pools sit among the villages.

Key facts. *Rates:* Rack $367–$1119, discounted to $229. *Hotel type:* Disney Deluxe Villas resort with clustered, multistory lodging buildings. *Location:* In the eastern part of Disney property, between Downtown Disney and Port Orleans French Quarter. *Distance to (in miles):* Magic Kingdom 4, Epcot 2, Hollywood Studios 3, Animal Kingdom 5, Blizzard Beach 4, Typhoon Lagoon 2, Downtown Disney 2, ESPN Wide World of Sports 3. *Address:* 1510 N. Cove Road 32830. *Size:* 761 villas, 74 acres. *Amenities:* Restaurant, fast-food window, lounge. Four pools, each with a hot tub. The main pool has a giant sandcastle slide with nearby kiddie pool. Arcades, bike rentals, boat rentals, Community Center, DVD rentals, fitness center, guided fishing trips, marina, playground, surrey rentals. Basketball, shuffleboard, volleyball courts; 3 tennis courts, 2 lighted. Laundromat, laundry service. Shop with groceries. *Children's programs:* Arts and crafts, pool activities, sandcastle building. *Transportation:* Boats go to Downtown Disney; Old Key West, Port Orleans French Quarter and Riverside, and Saratoga Springs resorts. Disney buses shuttle guests to all theme parks, water parks and Downtown Disney. A separate shuttle circles within the resort. *Built:* 1991. *Check In:* 4 p.m. *Check Out:* 11 a.m. *Phone:* 407-827-7700. *Fax:* 407-827-7710.

Polynesian Village

★★★★★ ✓ Disney World's original family resort, the Polynesian offers the definitive Disney vacation: a room at a themed, world-of-its-own hotel with an easy monorail trip over

Lifeguards and other hotel staff on a palm-lined walkway near one of the lodging buildings at Disney's Polynesian Village Resort.

to Magic Kingdom. The 12-building complex is themed to the South Seas, with many palms, waterfalls and torch-lit walkways. High in quality but not overtly luxurious, the resort has a distinctive laid-back attitude. It also has a unique claim to fame: it's where, in 1974, John Lennon signed the legal documents that officially dissolved The Beatles.

A central building has restaurants, shops and a monorail station. Lodging buildings are spacious. Complimentary activities include hula dancing (lobby, Tuesday–Saturday, 3:45 p.m.) and hula lessons with friendly resort icon Auntie Kaui (lobby, Saturday, 11 a.m.). An evening torch-lighting ceremony features a fire-baton twirler. Later, a musician often entertains in the lobby.

The resort is being transformed in 2015, as it reverts to its original name (restoring the word "Village"), adds timeshare units, gets updated infrastructure and an even more lighthearted theme. These changes will reduce its room count from 853 to about 500.

Highs. On the monorail loop, beautiful rooms, lakeside with beach, good sushi bar, Kona coffee, relaxed child-friendly ambience, child-friendly eateries, unique activities, tropical landscaping, fun swimming pool.

Lows. The large resort is very spread out in a confusing fashion. Construction barriers, cranes and crews through 2015.

Restaurants and food. A fun character meal and a nice little sushi bar highlight the dining choices. The mid-priced Kona Café offers quality food and a decent value. Room service is available 6:30 a.m. to midnight.

• **Kona Café.** ★★★ ✓ $$$$ The best value of all the restaurants on the monorail loop, this one-time coffee shop offers imaginative Pan-Pacific American meals, most of them served with complimentary pineapple-juice bread. Highlights include generous seafood dishes and, for breakfast, macadamia-pineapple pancakes. Tables and booths sit in a subdued, carpeted decor open to the hotel lobby. Kona coffee is available. *Breakfast, lunch, dinner. 7:30 a.m.–3 p.m., 5–10 p.m. Seats 163.*

• **'Ohana.** ★★★ $$$$ Highlighted by fresh coconut-pineapple bread, breakfast is one of Disney's most popular character meals. Every hour Lilo, Stitch and Mickey Mouse lead kids in a maraca-shaking parade. Carnivores, come hungry for dinner, when skewers of Polynesian-flavored meats and seafood are grilled over a fire and continually delivered to your table. Kids participate in coconut races and hula contests. *Breakfast, dinner. Credit card required for breakfast reservations, $10 per person no-show fee. 7:30–11 a.m, 5–10 p.m. Seats 300.*

• **Spirit of Aloha.** ★★★ $$$$$ A dancing, drumming and musical tour of Hawaii, New

Comfortable and spacious Polynesian Village Resort standard guest rooms feature dark woods, tall headboards and exotic-print fabrics.

Zealand, Samoa, Tahiti and Togo, this venerable dinner show features skimpy traditional costumes and lots of moving bodies. The story of a native girl returning to her roots has a corny first half with sitcom-style skits. Later, children are invited onstage to learn the hula. The meal is an all-you-can-eat feast of uninspired pork ribs and chicken. Service is perfunctory. If you go, splurge for the front-of-the-house seats; if you sit in back you may have a hard time hearing. *Dinner. Prepaid only. Two-hour shows Tuesday–Saturday at 5:15, 8 p.m. Seats 420.*

• **Captain Cook's Snack Co.** ★★★ $$ Standard American fast food plus flatbread, stir-fry dishes, packaged sushi, Dole Whip soft-serve ice cream. *Breakfast, lunch, dinner. 6:30 a.m.–11 p.m. Seats 150.*

• **Kona Island.** ★★★★ ✔ $$$ In the morning this little stand next to Kona Café serves pastries; in the afternoon it transforms into a creative sushi bar with alcoholic beverages. *6:30 a.m.–4 p.m. 6–10 p.m. Seats 16.*

Rooms. Hand-carved furniture, batik-print fabrics and dim lighting create a unique decor. A club level is available. *415 square feet. Sleep 5. Two queen beds, some daybeds, small refrigerator. Suites: Sleep up to 9.*

Swimming pools. Closed for renovations through the spring of 2015, the Nanea swimming pool is directly behind the hotel lobby, nestled against a simulated volcano,. Kids love standing underneath its waterfall, taking repeat trips down its slide—a slippery two-story tunnel with squirting water and eerie colored lights—and listening closely to hear the pool's underwater music. A "zero-entry" gradual ramp provides access for disabled guests. During the time the pool is closed for construction, hotel guests get

complimentary passes and direct bus service to the Blizzard Beach water park.

Tucked in to a lodging area, the hotel's smaller East pool is less crowded. Hidden behind its lounge chairs are six shady open huts, each with its own table and ceiling fan.

Remodeling and expansion. Besides the redone pool complex, other changes include:

• **Timeshare units.** The rooms in three existing lodging buildings (Rapa Nui, Tahiti and Tokelau) are being converted into Disney Vacation Club villas. Twenty more DVC units are being built behind the hotel, extending out over the South Seas Lagoon.

• **Lobbies.** The motor lobby will have larger and safer bus lanes, and the parking lot will be redone with more palms. The indoor lobby will have more open space, as its iconic waterfall garden will be replaced with a series of much smaller planters.

• **Bar.** Located in the resort's main Great Ceremonial House where an arcade used to be, Trader Sam's Grog Grotto promises an experience somewhat like that of the old Adventurer's Club at Downtown Disney's Pleasure Island. Supposedly owned by the "head salesman" seen on the Jungle Cruise ride in Magic Kingdom's Adventureland, it will be decorated with items collected by Sam and sent to him by globe-trotting friends, and will feature animated elements that may include Uh-Oa, the evil "tiki goddess of disaster" who appeared in the Enchanted Tiki Room show when it was "under new management." A large outdoor seating area will overlook the marina, and have its own bar. A witty staff will serve tiki cocktails and Polynesian-themed small plates.

• **Child care center.** Opened in 2014, new Club Disney offers children ages 3 to 12

A huge statue of a Mickey Mouse rotary phone overlooks an oversize foosball field in a 1970s Pop Century courtyard. Behind them, giant letters spell out "What's Your Handle?"

dress-up fun, crafts and storytelling experiences. A whimsical decor is inspired by Disney Little Golden Book art.

Key facts. *Rates:* Rack room rates $482–$1212, discount rooms from $300. *Suites* $652–$1586, discounts as low as $557. *Hotel type:* Disney Deluxe resort hotel with main lodge, multistory lodging buildings. *Location:* Northwest corner of Disney property, near Magic Kingdom. *Distance to (in miles):* Magic Kingdom 1, Epcot 4, Hollywood Studios 4, Animal Kingdom 6, Blizzard Beach 5, Typhoon Lagoon 6, Downtown Disney 6, ESPN Wide World of Sports 7. *Address:* 600 Seven Seas Drive 32830. *Size:* About 500 rooms when renovated plus about 300 villas and suites, 39 acres. *Amenities:* Two restaurants, character meal, dinner show, snack shop, sushi bar, lounge. Two swimming pools; main pool (currently undergoing renovation) has a two-story slide and waterfall. Kiddie splash zone, children's programs, playground, hot tubs. Arcade, beach, boat rentals, campfire, guided fishing trips, hula dancing and lessons, surrey rentals, 1.5-mile-long walking trail. Child-care center, laundromat, laundry service. *Children's programs:* Complimentary arts and crafts, beach and pool activities. Child-care facility onsite. *Transportation:* Monorail goes to Magic Kingdom, Epcot; Contemporary, Grand Floridian resorts. Boats travel to Magic Kingdom. Disney buses shuttle guests to Hollywood Studios, Animal Kingdom, water parks and Downtown Disney. *Built:* 1971. *Check In:* 3 p.m. *Check Out:* 11 a.m. *Phone:* 407-824-2000. *Fax:* 407-824-3174.

Pop Century

★★★ ✔ Children will know they are someplace special if you stay at this Disney Value Resort. Though meant to appeal to nostalgic adults, it looks—at least to young eyes—like a kid designed it. Poster-paint buildings feature towering props of toys and cartoon characters. Everywhere you turn is a spirit of playful tackiness. Close to the ESPN Wide World of Sports complex, Pop Century is popular with youth athletic groups.

Grouped into five sections, the lodging area is a collection of four-story motel buildings, each decorated to illustrate a particular decade of American popular culture, from the 1950s to the 1990s. Lodging areas are adorned with gigantic props such as 41-foot Rubik's Cubes and 65-foot bowling pins; buildings are topped with catchphrases such as "Flower Power" and "Do the Funky Chicken." A central complex holds a food court, arcade and gift shop. Out front is the bus station, in back the main swimming pool.

A gigantic bowling pin disguises a stairwell in the 1950s section of the Pop Century resort. Stairways in other sections are hidden by such things as huge yo-yos and Rubiks cubes.

Highs. Decent dining, large colorful swimming pools and a fun theme make this the best Disney budget resort. Good rates, good food court, covered bus stops, non-stop bus routes to nearly all destinations.

Lows. No real restaurant; childish theming; lodging elevators aren't air-conditioned; small guest rooms; long lines at food courts and bus stops, especially in the morning.

Restaurants and food. A nice food court serves all three meals, and has a bakery, convenience store and small bar open to the main pool. Room service (pizza, salads, desserts) is available 4 p.m. to midnight.

• **Everything Pop! Food Court.** ★★★ ✔ $$ This relaxing spot offers standard American fare plus tasty salads and flatbreads. The bakery is also good. The carpeted dining area has many comfortable booths, and vintage Top 40 ambient music. *Breakfast, lunch, dinner. 6:30 a.m.–midnight. Seats 650.*

Rooms. Basic rooms are cheaply decorated. A curtain hangs between the main area and the bathroom vanity. Those in the 1960s section ($10 surcharge) are closest to the bus stand, food court and lobby. 1950s rooms (no extra charge) are almost as close. *260 square feet. Sleep 4. Two double beds. Accessed by outdoor walkways.*

Swimming pools. The resort has three themed pools, each with an adjacent kiddie pool. The 1960s Hippy Dippy pool has four giant metal flowers that spray swimmers; the kiddie pool has a flower shower. The 1950s pool is shaped like a bowling pin. A 1990s computer pool (a rectangle) has a spongy keyboard deck. A Goofy water-jet fountain sits between the 1960s and 1970s areas.

Key facts. *Rates:* Rack $106–$236, discount rooms from $85. *Hotel type:* Disney Value resort hotel with clustered, multi-story lodging buildings. *Location:* Close to Interstate 4, near Hollywood Studios and ESPN Wide World of Sports. *Distance to (in miles):* Magic Kingdom 6, Epcot 5, Hollywood Studios 3, Animal Kingdom 4, Blizzard Beach 4, Typhoon Lagoon 2, Downtown Disney 3, ESPN Wide World of Sports 2. *Address:* 1050 Century Drive 32830. *Size:* 2,880 rooms, 177 acres. *Amenities:* Food court. Three themed swimming pools with kiddie pools. Arcade, beach, playground, Memory Lane walking trail IDs yearly events 1950 to 1999. Laundromat, laundry service. Shop with groceries. *Children's programs:* Pool activities. Organized children's activities are posted on a poolside board each morning. Kids can join food court cast members as they do the Twist at 8 a.m., march to the Mickey Mouse theme at 2 p.m. and do the Hustle at 6 p.m. daily. *Transportation:* Disney buses shuttle guests to theme parks, water parks and Downtown Disney. *Built:* 2003. *Check In:* 3 p.m. *Check Out:* 11 a.m. *Phone:* 407-938-4000. *Fax:* 407-938-4040.

Port Orleans

Disney's Port Orleans complex encompasses two side-by-side resorts, and they're quite different. Representing New Orleans, the small Port Orleans French Quarter (★★★) has relatively few amenities, no restaurant and none of its rooms sleep more than 4 people. Representing the plantation country of the Old South, the sprawling Port Orleans Riverside (★★★★ ✔) has many amenities, a restaurant and rooms that sleep five. Yet they're often both available at bargain rates, because they're both off the beaten path, in an area of Disney World few guests ever see.

Mansard roofs and wrought-iron railings trim lodging buildings at the Port Orleans French Quarter Resort, the smaller sister in the Port Orleans complex.

As for landscaping, Port Orleans French Quarter has narrow, tree-lined walkways, lots of wrought-iron railings and some intimate gardens. The pool area is themed to a Mardi Gras parade; the food court looks like a warehouse for Mardi Gras parade props.

Set within shady hardwoods, Port Orleans Riverside's Magnolia Bend area has four distinct sections, each with a trim lawn and parking lot. Buildings recall Southern plantations with white columns and sweeping entrances. A smaller Alligator Bayou area has faux-rustic lodging buildings, with walkways that meander through an unkempt landscape of palmettos, pines and pine needles.

Highs. *French Quarter:* Rooms are close to fast food and the pool, hot fresh beignets, easy to get around. *Riverside:* Great pools, some rooms sleep 5, lovely grounds.

Lows. *French Quarter:* Sub-standard food court, no restaurant, grounds are a little shabby for Disney, superficial theming. *Riverside:* Getting to your room can be quite a hike if you don't have a car.

Restaurants and food. Riverside has a dinner restaurant. Both resorts have food courts. Room service (pizza, salads, desserts) is available 4 p.m. to midnight.

• **Boatwright's Dining Hall.** ★★★ ✓ $$$$ This underrated Southern-American eatery serves fish, a grilled meat, pasta and a vegetarian dish—all with down-home side dishes. Recipes are delicate. A 46-foot boat hangs above the dining room; ship-building tools adorn walls. The back room has a fireplace. Faux-wood tables sit on tile floors. *Dinner 5–10 p.m. Seats 206. Riverside.*

• **The Sassagoula Floatworks & Food Factory.** ★ $ Themed as a Mardi Gras float warehouse, this small eatery is, for the most part, below mall quality. Its made-to-order beignets, however, are mouth-watering. *Breakfast, lunch, dinner. 6 a.m.–midnight. Seats 550. French Quarter.*

• **Riverside Mill.** ★★★ $ Resembling a cotton mill, this spacious spot has a water wheel with working gears. It serves fine standard American fare. *Breakfast, lunch, dinner. 6 a.m.–midnight. Seats 550. Riverside.*

Rooms. French Quarter rooms have cherry woods, purple and gold bedspreads and gold carpet. Riverside rooms vary; those in its Magnolia Bend area have cherry woods and tapestries while those in Alligator Bayou have a backwoods feel with hickory furnishings and quilted bedspreads. These rooms sleep five, thanks to their trundle beds. Riverside also offers 512 Royal Guest Rooms, decorated with Disney characters, themed fabrics and headboards embedded with fiber-optic lights that simulate fireworks. *314 square feet. Most sleep 4, Alligator*

Standard guest rooms in the Magnolia Bend area of Port Orleans Riverside feature a cool blue-and-green color scheme with cherry woods.

Bend rooms sleep 5. Two queen beds, small refrigerator. Accessed by outdoor walkways.

Swimming pools. A huge dragon winds through, and forms the slide of, the French Quarter's Doubloon Lagoon pool; an alligator jazz band dances through its grounds. At Riverside, an Ol' Man Island recreation area includes a pool with the most waterfalls of any Disney hotel swimming spot; a swerving slide dribbles water on those who go down it. Peaceful quiet pools sit between the Riverside lodging sections.

Key facts. *Rates:* Rack $182–$372, discounts as low as $147. *Hotel type:* Disney Moderate resort hotels with clustered, multistory lodging buildings. *Location:* Northeast on Disney property, near Downtown Disney. *Distance to (in miles):* Magic Kingdom 4, Epcot 2, Hollywood Studios 4, Animal Kingdom 6, Blizzard Beach 4, Typhoon Lagoon 2, Downtown Disney 2, ESPN Wide World of Sports 4. *Address:* French Quarter 2201 Orleans Drive 32830; Riverside 1251 Riverside Drive 32830. *Size:* French Quarter 1,008 rooms, 90 acres; Riverside 2,048 rooms, 235 acres. *Amenities:* French Quarter: Food court, lounge. Central swimming pool with slide, hot tub, kiddie pool. Riverside: Restaurant (dinner only), food court, lounge. Large outdoor recreation complex with swimming pool, slide, kiddie pool, hot tub; five basic pools in lodging areas. Bike, boat, surrey rentals; guided fishing trips, cane-pole fishing. Carriage rides (same-day reservations available at 407-824-2832). *Both complexes:* Arcade, playground. Laundromat, laundry service. Shop with groceries. *Children's programs:* Pontoon-boat adventure; complimentary pool activities. *Transportation:* Boats take guests to Downtown Disney; Old Key West, Saratoga Springs resorts and between Port Orleans French Quarter and Riverside. Disney buses shuttle guests to theme parks, water parks and Downtown Disney. *Built:* French Quarter 1991, Riverside 1992. *Check In:* 3 p.m. *Check Out:* 11 a.m. *Phone:* French Quarter 407-934-5000; Riverside 407-934-6000. *Fax:* French Quarter 407-934-5353; Riverside 407-934-5777.

Saratoga Springs

★★★★ This equestrian-themed condo complex is the only Disney-owned resort with a golf course. It offers tranquil grounds, good food, a full-service spa and upscale suites. A Disney Vacation Club timeshare complex, Saratoga Springs offers nightly rentals as owner bookings permit. Despite its name, there are no springs, no horses except in the decor and nothing very New York. Lodging buildings cluster into five sections that horseshoe around a recreation center.

Located behind Downtown Disney on the grounds of the former Disney Institute, Saratoga Springs is as far away as you can get from a theme park and still be at a Disney resort. Thematically unrelated but considered part of Saratoga Springs, a separate Treehouse Villas area is nestled into a pine forest; its 60 stand-alone octagons are elevated 10 feet off the ground.

Highs. Tranquil, upscale comfortable villas, many adjacent to parking lots; lush landscaping; great fitness center and spa; direct golf-course access.

Lows. Theme, decor will be of little interest to many children; far from theme parks; no room service; main pool is small, crowded.

Restaurants and food. There's a masculine steak restaurant, a nice food court

An open ceiling and huge window highlight the living room of a three-bedroom villa at Disney's Saratoga Springs complex. Its masculine interiors are unusual for a Disney resort.

Parking lots are close and convenient to lodging buildings at the Saratoga Springs resort, though they also make it resemble a suburban condo complex.

and a counter-service grill at The Paddock pool. Saratoga Springs has no room service; grocery delivery is available.

• **Turf Club Bar & Grill.** ★★★★ ✔ $$$ Great American food at decent prices makes this cozy country-club-style retreat worth seeking out. Lunch attracts golfers; this overlooked gem sits above the pro shop of the Lake Buena Vista golf course. Dinner has steaks that are worth the price. While waiting for a table, guests can shoot billiards or watch sports at the adjacent bar. An outdoor balcony overlooks the golf course, a small lake and Downtown Disney. *Lunch, dinner. Noon–9 p.m. Seats 146, including 52 outside.*

• **Artist's Palette.** ★★★ ✔ $ This pleasant food court offers above-average flatbreads and a nice dining area with padded booths. Drawing easels are set up for children. A store sells fruit, snacks and limited groceries. *Lunch, dinner. 11 a.m.–11 p.m. Seats 112.*

Rooms. Every Saratoga Springs villa features large, masculine furniture; all have dining tables and chairs and kitchen facilities. Larger units have whirlpool tubs. Three-bedroom Grand Villas feature two-story living rooms with huge windows. Rustic-chic Treehouse Villas have cathedral ceilings and granite countertops. *Studios 365 square feet; sleep 4. 1-bedroom 714 square feet; sleep 4. 2-bedroom 1,075 square feet; sleep 8. 3–bedroom 2,113 square feet; sleep 9–12. Accessed by outdoor walkways.*

Swimming pools. The main pool has a 126-foot slide between cascading waterfalls, an interactive fountain area and a "zero-entry" gradual ramp. It often shows Disney movies at night; guests float while they watch. Nearby is a kiddie pool, playground and two hot tubs. The Paddock lodging area has a

feature pool, with a water slide, splash zone and "zero-entry" gradual ramp. The other two lodging areas have quiet pools, each with a hot tub and barbecue area.

Key facts. *Rates:* Rack $367–$1287, discounted rates from $229. *Hotel type:* Disney Deluxe Villas resort with clustered, multistory lodging buildings. *Location:* In the eastern part of Disney property, north of Downtown Disney. *Distance to (in miles):* Magic Kingdom 5, Epcot 3, Hollywood Studios 4, Animal Kingdom 6, Blizzard Beach 4, Typhoon Lagoon 2, Downtown Disney 2, ESPN Wide World of Sports 4. *Address:* 1960 Broadway 32830. *Size:* 828 villas, 65 acres. *Amenities:* Restaurant, food court, lounge. Four pools, each with a hot tub. The main pool has a short slide, kiddie pool, children's programs, sand volleyball court, two playgrounds. Paddock lodging area has second feature pool, hot tub, children's splash zone. Two smaller pools in lodging area, hot tub, BBQ area. Arcades, bike rentals, Community Center, fitness center, guided fishing trips, surrey rentals. Basketball, shuffleboard courts, full-service spa, two lighted tennis courts, two walking trails. Lake Buena Vista 18-hole golf course. Laundromat, laundry service. Shop with groceries. *Children's programs:* Arts and crafts, pool activities. *Transportation:* Boats go to Downtown Disney; Old Key West, Port Orleans French Quarter and Riverside resorts. Disney buses go to all theme parks, water parks and Downtown Disney. A separate shuttle circles within the resort. Treehouse Villas guests transfer at bus stops in either The Springs or The Grandstand parking lots. *Built:* 2004. *Check In:* 4 p.m. *Check Out:* 11 a.m. *Phone:* 407-827-1100. *Fax:* 407-827-1151.

Guests relax in the main swimming area at Wilderness Lodge, a resort that channels the look of historic park service lodges of the American West.

Wilderness Lodge

★★★★ ✓ A dead ringer for one of those rustic park service lodges in the American West, this secluded resort is nestled in a forest along 450-acre Bay Lake. The four-building complex consists of a central eight-story lodge and three guest wings, one of which is a five-story Disney Vacation Club timeshare property. The lobby features a three-sided stone fireplace, the layers of which illustrate the geological history of the Grand Canyon. The fourth-floor indoor balcony has cozy sitting areas and front and back porches. The fifth floor has a small back balcony. A simulated indoor hot spring in the lobby creates a stream that appears to flow outside and into the swimming pool.

Highs. Stunning lobby; quality dining and amenities; comfortable, easily accessible rooms; pleasant boat ride to Magic Kingdom; nice pool; quiet atmosphere; great views; child-care facility; convenient self-parking.

Lows. Room decor suffers from a mismatched, somewhat chintzy cowboy theme; most rooms sleep 4 (rooms at most other Disney hotels at this price point sleep 5).

Restaurants and food. Wilderness Lodge has two terrific restaurants—one rowdy, one elegant. Room service is available 7 a.m. to 11 a.m. and 4 p.m. to midnight.

• **Artist Point.** ★★★★ ✓ $$$$$ Foodies will love this rustic Pacific Northwest restaurant which offers fine meals in a relaxed atmosphere. Inspired dishes include cedar plank-roasted salmon, grilled buffalo and Artist Point cobbler, featuring house-made black raspberry ice cream. The waitstaff is knowledgeable and pleasant. The L-shaped dining room mixes landscape murals with blond and cherry woods and a soaring ceiling. Large windows offer views of the courtyard and pool. *Dinner 5:30–9:30 p.m. Seats 225. A Disney Signature Restaurant.*

• **Whispering Canyon Cafe.** ★★★ ✓ $$$$ "Let's hand over the menus; no free souvenirs at Disney World." Brusque, loud servers keep the one-liners coming at this tasty barbecue spot. Signature all-you-can-eat skillets are overpriced, but many good choices are not. The comedic wait staff doesn't let its schtick interfere with its service. The cowboy decor is bold yet tasteful. *Breakfast, lunch, dinner. 7:30 a.m.–2:30 p.m, 5–10 p.m. Seats 281.*

• **Roaring Fork Snacks.** ★★ $$ This noisy fast-food eatery serves grilled foods, pizza, salads and sandwiches. *Breakfast, lunch, dinner. 6 a.m.–11 p.m. Seats 250.*

Rooms. Decorated with Native American and wildlife motifs, rooms have vibrant quilts, plaid drapes, Mission-style furniture and handcrafted embellishments; colors

The Wilderness Lodge lobby is dominated by a three-sided stone fireplace, the layers of which subtly portray the geological history of the Grand Canyon.

Guests stroll through the expansive back lawn of the Yacht Club, a nautical-themed compound that evokes the 19th-century summer homes of Martha's Vineyard and Nantucket.

and patterns clash. Beds have padded headboards topped with carved upper panels. A club level is available. *344 square feet. Sleep 4. Two queen beds, small refrigerator. Villas: Studio, 1- and 2-bedroom units sleep 4 to 8.*

Swimming pools. Portrayed as part of a mountain stream, a large swimming pool features a curving slide that sprays riders with mist. Nearby are two tubs (one hot, one cold), a kiddie pool and a geyser that erupts hourly. The Villas area has a smaller quiet pool with four bubbling "springs" and a 15-person whirlpool.

Key facts. *Rates:* Rack room rates $325–$609, discount rooms from $202. Suites $688–$792, discounted as low as $515. Villas $420–$1489, discounted to $299. *Hotel type:* Disney Deluxe resort hotel with main lodge with two wings; condominium-style villas. *Location:* Northwest corner of Disney property, southeast of Magic Kingdom. *Distance to (in miles):* Magic Kingdom 1, Epcot 3, Hollywood Studios 4, Animal Kingdom 6, Blizzard Beach 5, Typhoon Lagoon 5, Downtown Disney 5, ESPN Wide World of Sports 7. *Address:* 901 Timberland Drive 32830. *Size:* 701 rooms, 27 suites, 136 villas, 65 acres. *Amenities:* Three restaurants, snack bar, lounge. Two pools (one with a slide), three hot tubs, kiddie pool. Arcade, beach, bike and surrey rentals, fitness

center, guided fishing trips, lobby tour, trail to Fort Wilderness. Community Center. Child-care center, laundromat, laundry service. *Children's programs:* Organized free activities, 2:30–4 p.m. Campfire, movie at night at main pool. *Transportation:* Boats take guests to Magic Kingdom and the Contemporary, Fort Wilderness resorts. Buses shuttle guests to Disney theme parks, water parks and Downtown Disney. *Built:* 1994. *Check In:* 3 p.m. (Villas 4 p.m.). *Check Out:* 11 a.m. *Phone:* 407-824-3200, Villas 407-938-4300. *Fax:* 407-824-3232.

Yacht and Beach Club

★★★★★ ✔ These side-by-side Deluxe resorts share Disney World's best hotel swimming complex. They also have a lovely lakeside setting, comfortable rooms that are easy to get to and good food at all price levels.

The hotels have distinctive styles. The oyster-gray Yacht Club has a clapboard exterior reminiscent of formal oceanfront hotels common in New England in the 19th century. Inside, it's the look of old money—gold-fringed drapes, oak floors, antique chandeliers and lots of brass. Cast members dress in navy blue blazers. Behind the Yacht Club is a lighthouse marina.

By comparison, the pale-blue-and-white Beach Club strikes a more whimsical look,

With features much like those of a water park, Stormalong Bay includes a meandering central pool, a lazy river, a shallow sandbar inlet, a long water slide through a pirate ship and many fountains and waterfalls.

with stick-style buildings that recall wooden seaside cottages. Inside it's nouveau riche, straight out of *Coastal Living* magazine. Crisp colors and natural French limestone floors open up its lobby, which is furnished in a white-wicker seashell motif. Cast members wear pastel knickers and dresses. Behind the Beach Club is a white-sand beach.

The complex is adjacent to Epcot's back entrance; the Beach Club is right next to it.

Highs. Within walking distance to Epcot and Hollywood Studios as well as evening entertainment at the BoardWalk; lovely lakeside setting; best Disney swimming complex; good food at all price levels.

Lows. Expensive, no fair-weather transportation to the front of Epcot.

Restaurants and food. The Yacht and Beach Club Resort offerings include an excellent steakhouse, a fun soda shop and a good character meal. Fast-food items are sold in gift shops. Room service is available 24 hours.

• **Beaches & Cream.** ★★★★ ✔ $$ Gigantic sundaes are the draw at this old fashioned soda shop, which also serves good burgers and sandwiches. The claim to fame is the ridiculously huge $29 Kitchen Sink sundae that's served, literally, in a kitchen sink-shaped dish. It's a tiny spot, with just three booths, six small tables and bar seating. A tin ceiling has a tray center with elaborate moldings. Guests can choose songs for free from a classic jukebox. *Lunch, dinner. 11 a.m.–11 p.m. Take-out counter. Seats 48. Beach Club.*

• **Cape May Café.** ★★★ ✔ $$$$$ This relaxed restaurant offers the only Disney-operated character meal not in a theme park or on the monorail loop. Small parties can often get in without reservations. Characters are Donald Duck, Goofy and Minnie Mouse,

breakfast items include Mickey-Mouse-face waffles. Though billed as a clambake, the dinner's standout item is a carved-to-order top sirloin. Subdued lighting and seagull sounds make the Cape May a pleasant place to recover at the end of a day. *Breakfast 7:30–11:30 a.m. Dinner 5–9 p.m. Seats 235. Beach Club.*

• **Captain's Grille.** ★★★★ ✔ $$$$ This grade-A American restaurant makes a sincere effort to be a destination eatery, although it gets ignored by sitting next to the outstanding Yachtsman Steakhouse. Despite its nautical name, its cuisine is not focused on seafood. Choices also include beef, chicken, pork and a vegetarian option. Portions are generous, dishes distinctive. Decor is inspired by 1930s New England, with good lighting, padded chairs and gleaming brass. *Breakfast buffet 7:30–11:30 a.m. Lunch 11:30 a.m.–2 p.m. Dinner 5–9 p.m. Seats 280. Yacht Club.*

• **Yachtsman Steakhouse.** ★★★★★ ✔ $$$$$ Disney World's best steakhouse hits the trifecta—exceptional food, attentive service and a warm, inviting atmosphere. Generous portions of grain-fed beef steaks are of the highest quality. Those in the know rave about the desserts. The simple, elegant dining room has honey-colored wood, leather and brass. A glass-walled room lets you see your steak being prepared. Half of the restaurant is on a wood floor; the other half is carpeted. *Dinner 5:30–10 p.m. Seats 286. Yacht Club. A Disney Signature Restaurant.*

• **The Beach Club Marketplace.** ★★★ $ This little general store offers pastries, salads, sandwiches and soups; a small area sells fruit and snacks. *Breakfast, lunch, dinner. 7 a.m.–10 p.m. Seats 48 on tables outside in hallway and on a nearby patio. Beach Club.*

Beach Club Villa stuido kitchens have colorful cabinets, granite countertops, glass-panel cabinet doors and open shelves. The studio units sleep four people.

Rooms. Rooms have nautical motifs, with ceiling fans and white furniture. A club level is available. Suites share the salty theme, as do Beach Club timeshare villas, which are often available for nightly rentals. *381 square feet. Sleep 5. Two queen beds, some daybeds, small refrigerator. Suites: Sleep 4–8. Villas: Studio, 1- and 2-bedroom units sleep 4–8.*

Swimming pools. Themed to look like a Nantucket lagoon, 3-acre Stormalong Bay is a miniature water park. It includes a meandering central pool, lazy river, shallow inlet with a real sandbar, a shady hot tub and an assortment of fountains, waterfalls and bridges. A spiral staircase on a life-sized simulated shipwreck leads to a 300-foot slide. Starting off in a dark tunnel (the inside of the ship's fallen mast), enters daylight at a rocky outcropping. Riders get showered by two waterfalls before splashing into the central pool. A large kiddie pool has overhead sprinklers and a sandy play spot; a second kiddie pool on the pirate ship has a tiny slide.

Key facts. *Rates:* Rack room rates $400–$887, discount rooms from $249. Suites $735–$2444, discounted as low as $649. Villas $411–$1469, discounted to $269. *Hotel type:* Disney Deluxe resort hotel with adjoining multistory lodging buildings. *Location:* Centrally located on Disney property, next to the back entrance of Epcot. *Distance to (in miles):* Magic Kingdom 5, Epcot (by car) 4, Hollywood Studios 2, Animal Kingdom 5, Blizzard Beach 3, Typhoon Lagoon 3, Downtown Disney 3, ESPN Wide World of Sports 5. *Address:* Beach Club: 1800 Epcot Resorts Blvd. Yacht Club: 1700 Epcot Resorts Blvd. 32830. *Size:* 1,197 rooms, 112 suites, 208 villas, 30 acres. *Amenities:* Five restaurants, lounges. Sprawling outdoor recreation swimming complex, children's programs, playground, hot tubs. Sand volleyball, croquet, tennis courts. Arcades, beach, boat rentals, boat rides, child-care center, Community Center, guided fishing trips, walking trail. Hair salon, laundromat, laundry service. Shop with groceries. Conference center (73,000 square feet, 2 ballrooms, banquet space for 3,000, 21 breakout rooms), business center. *Children's programs:* Pontoon-boat adventure; complimentary arts and crafts, beach and pool activities. Child-care facility onsite. *Transportation:* Boats take guests to Epcot, Hollywood Studios. Disney buses shuttle guests to Magic Kingdom, Animal Kingdom, water parks and Downtown Disney. When lightning is in the area, buses take guests to Epcot and Hollywood Studios. *Built:* 1990. *Check In:* 3 p.m. *Check Out:* 11 a.m. *Phone:* Beach Club: 407-934-8000. Villas: 407-934-2175. Yacht Club: 407-934-7000. *Fax:* Beach Club: 407-934-3850. Yacht Club: 407-934-3450.

Non-Disney hotels

★★★★ **B Resort & Spa.** Refurbished with a modern style for 2014, formerly the Royal Plaza. Standard rooms are largest of any Downtown Disney hotel. Some kitchenettes, wet bars, bunk beds. In the Downtown Disney strip of hotels. *Rack rates $99-$180, discounted to $90. Suites $172–$190, discounted to $149. $20 per day per room resort fee added. Rooms sleep 5, 2 double beds, pillow-top mattresses, sleeper sofa. Suites sleep 4–5. 394 rooms, 23 acres. 17 stories. 1905 Hotel Plaza Blvd. 32830. Restaurant, mini-mart. Swimming pool. Fitness center. Full-service spa. Business center, laundromat, meeting*

© Starwood

Designed by architect Michael Graves, the Walt Disney World Swan has a distinctively playful look. It and sister resort the Dolphin create the signature property of the Starwood company.

rooms. Check in: 4 p.m. Check out: 11 a.m. Phone: 407-828-2828.

★★★ **Best Western Lake Buena Vista.** A Downtown Disney hotel. *Rack rates $79–$139, discounted to $66. 321 rooms, 4 suites, 12 acres. 2000 Hotel Plaza Blvd. 32830. Rooms and suites sleep 4–5, 2 queen beds, balconies or patios. Cherry-walnut furniture, granite counter tops, Italian tile bathrooms. 2 restaurants, snack bar, Pizza Hut Express. Swimming pool, kiddie pool. Arcade, child-care service, fitness center, playground, tennis courts. Business center, car-rental counter, cyber cafe, laundromat. Garden gazebo. Lakefront. Check in: 3 p.m. Check out: 11 a.m. Phone: 407-828-2424. Fax: 407-827-6390.*

★★★★ **Buena Vista Palace and Spa.** A Downtown Disney hotel. *Rack rates $79–$159, discounted to $74. Suites $139–$499, discounted to $109. 890 rooms, 124 suites, 27 acres. 27 stories. 1900 Buena Vista Dr. 32830. Rooms sleep 4, 2 queen beds, balconies or patios, refrigerator. Suite sleep 4–8. Ergonomic Herman Miller chairs. Two restaurants including Disney character breakfast on Sundays, mini-mart. Three swimming pools (one partially covered), hot tub. Arcade, fitness center, playground, sauna, full-service spa (407-827-3200). Basketball, tennis, volleyball courts. Business center, car-rental counter, convention center, cyber cafe, laundromat, laundry services, salon. Check in: 4 p.m. Check out: 11 a.m. Phone: 407-827-2727. Fax: 407-827-3136.*

★★★ **Doubletree Guest Suites.** This Downtown Disney hotel is the only all-suite hotel on Disney property. *Rack rates $105–$409, discounted to $99. 229 suites, 7 acres. 7 stories. 2305 Hotel Plaza Blvd. 32830. Suites: Sleep 6, 1 or 2 bedrooms, Sweet Dreams bedding, microwave, refrigerator, 2 TVs, black-and-white bathroom TV-radio. 1 restaurant, mini-mart. Swimming pool, kiddie pool, hot tub. Fitness center, playground, pool table, tennis courts. Business center, car-rental counter, child-care service, laundromat, laundry services, meeting rooms. Check in: 4 p.m. Check out: 11 a.m. Phone: 407-934-1000. Fax: 407-934-1015.*

★★★★★ **Four Seasons Orlando.** Located within Disney's uber-luxe Golden Oak residential community, the brand-new Four Seasons features Spanish Revival architecture and lush grounds with mature oak trees, live oaks, cypress stands and nearly a thousand palms. The resort has its own golf course, the Tom Fazio-designed Tranquilo, and borders a lake that's a wildlife haven.

Each room has contemporary white furnishings accented with orange or teal, with a spacious furnished balcony. Bathrooms have marble tubs, in-mirror televisions and Bose surround-sound audio. *500 square feet. Sleep 4. King bed with queen-size sleeper sofa or two double beds. Suites sleep two to four.*

Explorer Island, an elaborate swimming area, covers five acres. It includes a family pool, a lazy river with a rapids section that meanders around a dilapidated mansion, a climbing wall, two water slides and a splash zone with water cannons. *Rack room rates $545–$750, discounted as low as $479. Suites $650–$12000, discounted to $545. Southeast of Magic Kingdom, beyond Fort Wilderness. 10100 Dream Tree Blvd., Golden Oak FL 32836. 375 rooms, 68 suites, 26.5 acres. Four*

Boasting the largest standard guest rooms of any Downtown Disney hotel, the new B Resort & Spa sports a clean, modern look. Redone in 2014, the hotel was formerly the Royal Plaza.

restaurants, lounges. Beach volleyball, climbing wall. Outdoor movie nights. Arcade, basketball, fitness center, 3 Har-Tru tennis courts. Massage services, sauna, steam room, full-service spa with 18 treatment rooms, yoga. Golf course with pro shop, golf instruction, driving range, putting green, club rental and on-site restaurant. Child-care facility and teen center onsite. Buses shuttle to Magic Kingdom twice an hour, other Disney parks once an hour. Built 2014. Check In: 4 p.m. Check Out: noon. Phone: 407-313-7777. Fax: 407-313-8500.

★★★ **Hilton.** The most upscale Downtown Disney hotel, and the only one that offers Disney's Extra Magic Hours benefit. *Rack rates $89–$330 discounted to $79. Suites $149–$330, discounted to $119. 704 rooms, 110 suites, 23 acres. 10 stories. 1751 Hotel Plaza Blvd. 32830. Rooms: Sleep 4, 2 double beds, mini-bar, MP3 clock-radio. Suites: Sleep 4–6. Club level. 7 restaurants including Benihana, Disney character breakfast buffet Sunday (no reservations); mini-mart. 2 swimming pools, kiddie pool with spray area. Arcade, fitness center, golf pro shop, pool table. Business center, car-rental counter, child-care services, concierge, cyber cafe, laundromat, salon. Check in: 3 p.m. Check out: 11 a.m. Phone: 407-827-4000. Fax: 407-827-3890.*

★★★ **Holiday Inn.** A Downtown Disney hotel. *Rack rates $95–$190 discounted to $89. 323 rooms, 1 suite, 10 acres. 14 stories. 1805 Hotel Plaza Blvd. 32830. Rooms: Sleep 4 to 5, 2 queen beds, sleeper sofa, pillow-top mattresses, small refrigerator, work desk. Restaurant, Kids Eat Free program (2–12 yrs). "Zero-entry" swimming pool with whirlpool. Business center, health club,*

laundromat, meeting rooms. Business center, fitness center, laundromat, laundry services. Check in: 4 p.m. Check out: 11 a.m. Phone: 407-828-8888. Fax: 407-827-4623.

★★★★ **Shades of Green.** This relaxed resort is the only Armed Forces Recreation Center in the continental United States. Comparable in scope to a Disney Deluxe Resort, it has large rooms, full-service restaurants and a great location, though it lacks themed architecture or memorable decor. Close to Magic Kingdom, Shades of Green sits directly across from the Polynesian Village Resort and next to Disney's Palm, Magnolia and Oak Trail golf courses. About 750,000 military guests stay here annually. Huge and comfortable, rooms feature light oak woods. Exclusively for use by active and retired members of the U.S. military and their accompanying families and friends. Rates based on rank; the higher the rank, the higher the bill. *Rooms: 455 square feet. Sleep 5. Two queen beds, small refrigerator, daybed, balcony or patio. Suites sleep 6 to 8.*

★★★★ **Walt Disney World Swan and Dolphin.** Giant swan statues, huge fish figurines, a towering triangular roof—the architecture of these adjacent convention resorts is one-of-a-kind. They're the signature properties of Starwood Hotels, the company that includes the Sheraton and Westin chains. The two hotels have different personalities—the Swan is quiet, serious and intimate, the Dolphin (with twice as many rooms and the largest convention center at Disney) boisterous, boozy and impersonal.

Designed by Michael Graves—an accomplished architect who is nevertheless best

Hotels outside Walt Disney World include large convention complexes such as the Marriott World Center, just a mile away.

known for his line of housewares sold at Target stores—the Swan and Dolphin feature playful "entertainment" architecture with details that include enormous statues and fountains. Seen together, abstract designs on the buildings define the Dolphin as a tropical mountain surrounded by huge banana palms. Its waterfall splashes into the lagoon and onto the Swan, a huge sand dune. Interiors were redone a decade ago to tone down Grave's very 1990s theme; the resulting decor is generically sophisticated.

Featuring comfortable "heavenly" beds with pillow-top mattresses and goose-down comforters, rooms have pale woods, muted floral carpeting, pastel drapes and maple bureaus with frosted glass accents. Club level available. *360 square feet. Sleep 5. Dolphin rooms have two double beds, Swan rooms two queens. Suites sleep five to ten.*

An elaborate swimming area (5 pools, 5 hot tubs, kiddie pool) arcs between the resorts. A meandering Grotto pool has a waterfall and slide. Tiny waterfalls splash near a volleyball net that extends over a narrow area. A Disney movie plays at the pool every Saturday night in the summer. The area also includes a spring pool and two lap pools. A circus-themed beach area has two volleyball nets, a basketball court and a boat-like playground piece with covered slides. Children will enjoy finding the statue of a seal that sprays water out of its nose.

Rack room rates $299–$594, discount rooms from $149. Suites $390–$1440, discouned to $190. Dolphin 1500 Epcot Resorts Blvd., Swan 1300 Epcot Resorts Blvd., both 32830. 2,265 rooms, 191 suites, 87 acres. Nine restaurants, lounges. Elaborate swimming area with 5 swimming pools (2 are lap pools), 5 hot tubs, kiddie pool and play area, playground, basketball court, sand volleyball court. Arcades, beach, pedal-boat rentals, fitness centers, 4 tennis courts. Hair salon, laundromat, laundry service, massage services, full-service spa. Disney's Fantasia Gardens miniature golf across street. Disney World's largest convention center (254,000 square feet, 9,600-square-foot ballroom, 3 other ballrooms, exhibit hall, 84 breakout rooms). Business centers. Child-care facility onsite. Disney boats take guests to Epcot and Disney's Hollywood Studios. Disney buses shuttle to Magic Kingdom, Animal Kingdom, water parks and Downtown Disney. When the boats can't operate (during lightning), buses take their place. Built 1990. Check In: 3 p.m. Check Out: 11 a.m. Dolphin 407-934-4000, Swan 407-934-4499. Fax: Dolphin 407-934-4884, Swan 407-934-4710.*

★★★ **Wyndham Lake Buena Vista.** A favorite of British guests, this Downtown Disney hotel used to be the Regal Sun, before that it was The Grosvenor. *Rack rates $71–$148, discounted to $64. Suites $425–$523, discounted to $349. 619 rooms, 7 suites, 13 acres. 19 stories. 1850 Hotel Plaza Blvd. 32830. Rooms: Sleep 4, 2 queen beds, flat-screen TV, MP3 clock-radio. Suites: Sleep 4–6. Restaurant; English pub; Disney character breakfast Tuesday, Thursday, Sat. 2 swimming pools, kiddie pool, water playground for children. Fitness center, playground. Basketball, shuffleboard, tennis, volleyball courts. Business center, car-rental counter, currency exchange, laundromat, laundry services, meeting rooms. Check in: 3 p.m. Check out: 11 a.m. Phone: 407-828-4444. Fax: 407-828-8192.*

Characters

Although some fantasy-free adults may not see them as such, the Disney walk-around characters are *real* to many visitors, especially children—that's not a sweaty young woman in a fur suit, *that's Pluto!!!* Dozens of Disney stars appear in shows and parades and personally greet guests at theme parks, water parks and resort hotels.

Character types. Disney has two types of walk-around characters, "face" and "fur." Face characters, such as Cinderella, appear in a costume that shows the face of the performer, who talks to and interacts with guests in character. Fur characters, such as Pluto, appear in a complete costume that includes an oversized head. Most of them don't speak, and interact with guests purely through mime. However, fur character Mickey Mouse does speak at Town Square Theater in Magic Kingdom. His mouth moves and when you talk to him, he often talks back.

Meet-and-greet lines. Most characters pose for photos and, in most cases, sign autographs at designated locations, many of which draw long lines. Guests with autograph books should bring a pen or, better, a Sharpie marker. Some characters don't sign because of costume limitations. It's fine to hug, kiss or pat characters, but not to give them gifts. A PhotoPass photographer is often on hand, although guests are welcome to take photos themselves, or have the PhotoPass photographer take a photo for them with their camera or phone.

How to help your child interact. Though face characters rarely intimidate children, the fur folks, with their cartoonishly large heads, sometimes do. To help your child feel comfortable, talk with her beforehand so she knows what to expect. For meet-and-greet lines, buy her an autograph book to give her something to focus on besides the face-to-fur encounter. When it's her turn don't push her; the characters are patient and are trained to be sweet. Approach a character from the front. Fur characters in particular often cannot see guests standing behind or beside them.

Character meals. A handful of Disney buffet and table-service restaurants offer "character meals," in which an assortment of characters come up to each table to greet guests as they eat. Each theme park has at least one character-meal restaurant, as do many Disney resort hotels.

How to find a character. Though the following Character Guide lists the official locations of characters, they often show up other places. To learn where, ask any Disney cast member. They can usually find out.

Character guide. More than 70 Disney characters greet guests at Disney World parks and resort hotels. Here's a list of the ones who appear most often, and where you're most likely to find them:

Aladdin. Arab "street rat," star of 1992's "Aladdin." Wins love of princess Jasmine after learning to be true to himself. *Magic Kingdom: At Magic Carpets of Aladdin, Adventureland. Epcot: Morocco pavilion.*

Alice. Star of 1951's "Alice in Wonderland." Curious, proper British girl dreams of nonsensical Wonderland. The park character has confided to the authors that many young girls confuse her name, thinking it's "Allison Wonderland." *Magic Kingdom: Mad Tea Party, Fantasyland. Epcot: Tea garden, U.K. pavilion; Akershus Royal Banquet Hall meals (often), Norway pavilion. Grand Floridian Resort: 1900 Park Fare breakfast.*

Anastasia and Drizella. Squabbling stepsisters to Cinderella in 1950's "Cinderella," daughters of Lady Tremaine. Redhead Anastasia is spiteful and graceless; brunette Drizella disorganized. *Magic Kingdom: Great wall, Fantasyland. Grand Floridian Resort: 1900 Park Fare dinner.*

Anna and Elsa. Loving sisters in 2014's hit "Frozen." Redheaded younger Anna is the optimistic, fearless, awkward princess of Arendelle. Older platinum blonde Queen Elsa is more quiet and reserved, and can magically conjure snow and ice. Anna wears her blue embroidered dress; Elsa her silver and blue gown. *Magic Kingdom: Princess Fairytale Hall, Fantasyland.*

Facing page: Cinderella's stepmother Lady Tremaine reluctantly greets guests in Magic Kingdom and at the Grand Floridian Resort.

Micaela Neal

Mickey Mouse is one busy bee; he appears in every theme park and at several hotels.

Minnie Mouse in her signature red-and-white ensemble at Epcot's Character Spot.

Ariel. Rebellious redheaded teen mermaid, star of 1989's "The Little Mermaid." "Sick of swimmin,'" loves all things human. Falls in love with Prince Eric. Best friend is a fish, Flounder. Wears a seashell bikini top as mermaid, a turquoise gown as a human (though it's pink in the film). *Magic Kingdom: Ariel's Grotto, Fantasyland; Cinderella's Royal Table breakfast, lunch (often), Cinderella Castle. Epcot: Akershus Royal Banquet Hall meals (often), Norway pavilion.*

Aurora. Blameless blond princess of 1959's "Sleeping Beauty" awakened from Maleficent's cursed coma by Prince Phillip's kiss. Also known as Briar Rose. Pink gown. *Magic Kingdom: Town Square, Main Street U.S.A.; Cinderella's Royal Table breakfast, lunch (often), Cinderella Castle. Epcot: France pavilion fragrance garden; Akershus Royal Banquet Hall meals (often), Norway pavilion.*

Baloo. Happy-go-lucky, lazy bear in 1967's "Jungle Book" teaches "man-cub" Mowgli how to relax, live in wild. Loves to scratch back on trees, eat fruit. *Magic Kingdom: Move It! Shake It! Celebrate It! Street Party, Cinderella Castle hub. Disney's Animal Kingdom: Upcountry Landing, on trail off Asia-Africa walkway.*

Beast. Selfish prince is transformed by sorceress into a hideous creature in 1991's "Beauty and the Beast." Has face of wildebeest; tusks of boar; mane of lion; body of bear; legs, tail of wolf. Transforms back into prince after learning to be kind and earning love of Belle. *Magic Kingdom: Be Our Guest at dinnertime to greet diners.*

Belle. Heroine of 1991's "Beauty and the Beast," in which the brunette bookworm falls in love with beastly captor. Stands up for herself. Wears golden gown or modest blue dress with a white apron. *Magic Kingdom: Enchanted Tales with Belle, Fantasyland; Cinderella's Royal Table, Cinderella Castle. Epcot: France pavilion promenade; Akershus Royal Banquet Hall meals (often), Norway pavilion. Disney's Hollywood Studios: Sorcerer's Hat, Hollywood Blvd.*

Buzz Lightyear. Confident "Toy Story" space ranger is Woody's best friend. *Magic Kingdom: Alongside Carousel of Progress, Tomorrowland. Disney's Hollywood Studios: Woody's Picture Shootin' Corral, Pixar Place.*

Chip 'n Dale. Playful, fast-talking chipmunks from 1940s–1950s cartoons. Smarter, sneakier Chip has small black nose that resembles chocolate "chip." Goofier Dale

Micaela Neal

Micaela Neal

Cinderella greets guests in Magic Kingdom, Epcot and at the Grand Floridian Resort.

Sassy Tinker Bell shares Magic Kingdom's Town Square Theater with Mickey Mouse.

has large red nose, two separated buck teeth. *Magic Kingdom: Rivers of America Crossing, Liberty Square; Move It! Shake It! Celebrate It! Street Party, Cinderella Castle hub. Epcot: On walkway behind Innoventions West. Garden Grill dinner, The Land pavilion. Disney's Hollywood Studios: Sorcerer's Hat, Hollywood Blvd. Disney's Animal Kingdom: Conservation Station courtyard, Rafiki's Planet Watch. Fort Wilderness Resort: Mickey's Backyard Barbecue dinner show, Chip 'n Dale's Campfire Sing-A-Long.*

Cinderella. The definitive rags-to-riches heroine, upbeat strawberry-blonde saved by Prince Charming from life of stepmother servitude in 1950's "Cinderella." Friend to animals, especially Gus, Jaq and other castle mice. Lives in Cinderella Castle with her prince; wears light blue gown at Disney though in the movie it's white. *Magic Kingdom: Princess Fairytale Hall; Cinderella's Royal Table, Cinderella Castle. Epcot: Akershus Royal Banquet Hall meals (often), Norway pavilion. Grand Floridian Resort: 1900 Park Fare dinner.*

Country Bears. The stars of the infamous Magic Kingdom attraction Country Bear Jamboree. *Square-dance with guests during the Frontierland Hoedown street show. Magic Kingdom, outside the show, Frontierland.*

Daisy Duck. Donald Duck's impatient, sassy girlfriend from 1940s–1950s cartoons. Likes shopping, flowers. Best friend of Minnie Mouse. *Magic Kingdom: Pete's Silly Sideshow, Storybook Circus, Fantasyland. Epcot: Entrance Plaza. Disney's Hollywood Studios: Sorcerer's Hat, Hollywood Blvd. Disney's Animal Kingdom: Discovery Island Landing, Discovery Island; Donald's Safari Breakfast and Lunch, Tusker House, Africa.*

Doc McStuffins. The star of the Disney Junior show "Doc McStuffins," 7-year-old African-American girl pretends she's a doctor like her mom, "cures" her toys. *Disney's Hollywood Studios: Play 'N Dine character meals, Echo Lake.*

Donald Duck. He's rude, he's crude, he doesn't wear pants. He shouts, pouts and loses his temper at the drop of a pin. He likes to be mean. Yet who doesn't love Donald Duck, a character who responds to life the way we want to, but rarely dare? Created in 1934 as a foil for Mickey Mouse, Donald soon emerged as Disney's most popular star. The "duck with all the bad luck" is known for his "hopping mad" boxing stance,

© Disney

Micaela Neal

The only place to meet Ariel as a mermaid is Ariel's Grotto in Magic Kingdom.

Cute but way overconfident, Gaston checks out the ladies at the park's Gaston's Tavern.

a leaning, jumping posture with one arm straight, the other twirling like a windmill. *Magic Kingdom: Pete's Silly Sideshow, Storybook Circus, Fantasyland; Move It! Shake It! Celebrate It! Street Party, Cinderella Castle hub. Epcot: Mexico pavilion (in garb from 1944's "The Three Caballeros"). Disney's Hollywood Studios: Sorcerer's Hat, Hollywood Blvd. Disney's Animal Kingdom: On the Cretaceous Trail, DinoLand U.S.A.; Donald's Safari Breakfast and Lunch, Tusker House, Africa. Beach Club Resort: Cape May Café breakfast. Contemporary Resort: Chef Mickey's meals.*

Duffy the Disney Bear. According to Disney Merchandise lore—yes, there is such a thing—the teddy bear Minnie Mouse made for Mickey to take on his travels. Named for duffel bag Mickey uses to carry him. Has no cartoon or film credits. *Epcot: World Showcase Friendship Ambassador Gazebo, in front of the Disney Traders East gift shop.*

Eeyore. Gloomy plush donkey from 1960s "Winnie the Pooh" shorts used to create the 1977 movie "The Many Adventures of Winnie the Pooh." Speaks in depressed monotone. Devoted to friends. His tail—tied with a pink bow—often falls off. *Magic Kingdom: Crystal*

Palace meals, Main Street U.S.A.; The Many Adventures of Winnie the Pooh, Fantasyland.

Esmerelda. Beautiful gypsy of 1996 movie "The Hunchback of Notre Dame" helps Quasimodo gain confidence to escape evil master Frollo. Musical free spirit, loves soldier Phoebus. *Epcot: Akershus Royal Banquet Hall meals (often), Norway pavilion.*

Fairy Godmother. This absent-minded fairy helps Cinderella go to the ball in 1950's "Cinderella." Rotund, grandmotherly, uses wand to make magic with a "Bibbidi, bobbidi boo!" *Magic Kingdom: Cinderella Castle fountain, Fantasyland.*

Frozone. Superhero name of Lucius Best, a confident speed-skater and best friend to Mr. Incredible in 2004's "The Incredibles." Can freeze moisture in air, make snow. *Magic Kingdom: Move It! Shake It! Celebrate It! Street Party, Cinderella Castle hub. Disney's Hollywood Studios: The Magic of Disney Animation, Animation Courtyard.*

Gaston. Vain, flirty he-man villain of 1991's "Beauty and the Beast" often flexes his biceps, stares at his own reflection. *Magic Kingdom: Outside Gaston's Tavern, Fantasyland.*

Genie. Witty, fast-talking blue genie in 1992's "Aladdin" channels his voice talent,

Copper-haired Merida from "Brave" poses in Magic Kingdom's Fairytale Garden.

Snow White greets a young fan with equally black hair in Magic Kingdom's Town Square.

the late great Robin Williams. Reshapes body. Grants Aladdin three wishes. *Magic Kingdom: Magic Carpets of Aladdin, Adventureland.*

Goofy. Good-hearted country simpleton appeals to your inner idiot. Clumsy and gullible, has hard time concentrating. Has bad posture, ill-fitting clothes, big stomach yet always mugs for camera (just like, ahem, many husbands). Has many physical characteristics of a dog; was first known as Dippy Dog in 1930s cartoons. Later hosted series of "How To" cartoon sports parodies; in 1950s was oddly transformed into suburban everyman, the sometimes earless George Geef. *Magic Kingdom: Pete's Silly Sideshow, Storybook Circus, Fantasyland; Move It! Shake It! Celebrate It! Street Party, Cinderella Castle hub. Epcot: Character Spot, Innoventions Plaza. Disney's Hollywood Studios: Sorcerer's Hat, Hollywood Blvd. Disney's Animal Kingdom: DinoLand U.S.A. Service Station; Donald's Safari Breakfast and Lunch, Tusker House, Africa. Beach Club Resort: Cape May Cafe breakfast. Contemporary Resort: Chef Mickey's meals. Fort Wilderness Resort: Mickey's Backyard Barbecue dinner show. Blizzard Beach: On the walkway that circles the park.*

Green Army Men. Molded-plastic "Toy Story" soldiers have green mesh over faces; don't speak. Humorously mime guard duties. *Disney's Hollywood Studios: Pixar Place.*

Handy Manny. Star of Disney Junior TV show "Handy Manny," bilingual Hispanic handyman Manny Garcia uses talking tools. *Disney's Hollywood Studios: Play 'N Dine character meals, Echo Lake.*

Jake. Fearless, enthusiastic leader of the Never Land Pirates, from Disney Junior's "Jake and the Never Land Pirates." *Disney's Hollywood Studios: Animation Courtyard. Play 'N Dine character meals, Echo Lake.*

Jasmine. Spirited 16-year-old princess in 1992's "Aladdin." Long black ponytail. Wears aqua bedlah with pouffy pants. Has pet tiger. *Magic Kingdom: Magic Carpets of Aladdin, Adventureland; Cinderella's Royal Table breakfast, lunch (often), Cinderella Castle. Epcot: Morocco pavilion; Akershus Royal Banquet Hall meals (often), Norway pavilion.*

Jessie. Plucky yodeling "Toy Story" cowgirl. Woody's exuberant friend; has crush on Buzz Lightyear. *Magic Kingdom: Splash Mountain exit courtyard, Frontierland; Move It! Shake It! Celebrate It! Street Party, Cinderella Castle hub.*

"Beauty and the Beast" heroine Belle occasionally strolls through the promenade of Epcot's France pavilion, delighting guests who recognize her, confusing those who don't.

King Louie. Orangutan from 1967's "Jungle Book" plays practical jokes, kidnaps boy Mowgli to learn about fire and therefore learn to be like a human. *Magic Kingdom: Move It! Shake It! Celebrate It! Street Party, Cinderella Castle hub. Disney's Animal Kingdom: Upcountry Landing, on trail off Asia-Africa walkway.*

Lady Tremaine. Imperious, belittling step-mom in 1950's "Cinderella" treats Cinderella as servant. Mother of Anastasia, Drizella. *Magic Kingdom: Outside Cinderella Castle, Fantasyland. Grand Floridian Resort: 1900 Park Fare dinner.*

Lightning McQueen. Hotshot star of "Cars" movies. Was arrogant; now big-hearted, loyal. Best friends with 'Mater. *Disney's Hollywood Studios: Team McQueen Headquarters, Streets of America.*

Lilo. Lonely 7-year-old Hawaiian orphan of 2002's "Lilo & Stitch." Loves Elvis Presley, surfing. Adopts alien as pet, names it Stitch. Lives with older sister, Nani. *Disney's Hollywood Studios: Sorcerer's Hat, Hollywood Blvd. Polynesian Village Resort: 'Ohana breakfast. Typhoon Lagoon: Near High 'N Dry Towels.*

Mad Hatter. Manic milliner confuses Alice during "unbirthday" party in 1951's "Alice in Wonderland." Lisps; channels voice actor Ed Wynn. Tall green hat bears "10/6" (ten shillings, six pence) price tag. *Magic*

Kingdom: Mad Tea Party, Fantasyland. Grand Floridian Resort: 1900 Park Fare breakfast; Wonderland Tea Party.

Marie. White French kitten in 1970's "The Aristocats" thinks girls are better than boys; bosses two brothers. Wears pink bows. Often very glad to meet you. *Magic Kingdom: Town Square, Main Street U.S.A. Epcot: France pavilion (sporadically).*

Mary Poppins. Magical nanny teaches uptight family to enjoy everyday life in 1964's "Mary Poppins." Proper, kind, thinks for herself, flies with umbrella. *Magic Kingdom: Town Square, Main Street U.S.A. Epcot: Tea garden, U.K. pavilion. Grand Floridian Resort: 1900 Park Fare breakfast.*

'Mater. Rusty good ol' boy tow truck in 2006 film "Cars." Prankster, Lightning McQueen sidekick. *Disney's Hollywood Studios: Team McQueen Headquarters, Streets of America.*

Merida. Flame-tressed Scottish princess determined to be in charge of her own fate in 2012's "Brave." Loves archery. Wears dark green gown. *Magic Kingdom: Fairytale Garden, Fantasyland.*

Mickey Mouse. Based in part on silent-film star Charlie Chaplin, debuted in 1928 as underdog who dreamed big. Looks are based on his predecessor, Oswald the Lucky Rabbit. Originally named "Mortimer" Mouse. His optimistic attitude was perfect antidote

Mary Poppins poses for a practically perfect iPad photo at Epcot's United Kingdom pavilion. She also appears in the Magic Kingdom and at a breakfast in the Grand Floridian resort.

to 1930s Great Depression; at many theaters, the name "Mickey Mouse" would be in larger letters on marquee than stars of feature. In 1933 received 800,000 fan letters (more than any live-action Hollywood star); President Roosevelt later began showing Mickey cartoons at the White House. Happy-go-lucky, said to be Walt Disney's alter ego. World's most recognized and celebrated cartoon character, Americana pop-culture icon, corporate symbol. During World War II symbolized can-do spirit of U.S. Banned in Nazi Germany in 1933, the Soviet Union in 1936, Yugoslavia in 1937, Italy in 1938; in 1960s was embraced by counterculture as symbol of mischievous rebellion. *Magic Kingdom: Town Square Theater. Epcot: Character Spot, Innoventions Plaza; Garden Grill dinner, The Land pavilion. Disney's Hollywood Studios: The Magic of Disney Animation, Animation Courtyard (as Sorcerer's Apprentice). Disney's Animal Kingdom: Adventurers Outpost, Discovery Island; Donald's Safari Breakfast and Lunch, Tusker House, Africa. Contemporary Resort: Chef Mickey's meals. Fort Wilderness Resort: Mickey's Backyard Barbecue dinner show. Polynesian Village Resort: 'Ohana breakfast.*

Mike Wazowski. One-eyed green monster likes to get laughs in "Monsters, Inc." films. Emotional, overconfident; Sulley's best friend, roommate. *Disney's Hollywood Studios: Streets of America, at exit to Studio Backlot Tour.*

Minnie Mouse. Mickey Mouse's girlfriend. Flatters, swoons over her main squeeze. Quick-witted; energetic; loves animals, cooking and gardening. Can play harmonica, guitar, piano. In early cartoons she has a temper: slaps Mickey after he forces her to kiss him in 1928's "Plane Crazy" then jumps out of their open-cockpit airplane; smashes a lamp on Mickey's head when he pulls her nose in 1930's "The Cactus Kid"; when she mistakenly thinks Mickey has given her a bone for a present in 1933's "Puppy Love" kicks him out of her house and sobs "I hate him! I hate all men!" Has old flame (suave, tap-dancing Mortimer) in the 1936 cartoon "Mickey's Rival"; has children in 1933's "Mickey's Steam Roller." As portrayed in 1928 cartoon "The Gallopin' Gaucho," Mickey and Minnie first meet in an Argentine bar. When Minnie, a flirty tavern dancer, bats her eyes at Mickey, a cigarette-smoking outlaw(!), he watches her dance, chugs a beer, then grabs her for a dramatic tango. Later, he rescues her from a kidnapper. Walt Disney originally voiced both Mickey and Minnie Mouse. *Magic Kingdom: Pete's Silly Sideshow, Storybook Circus, Fantasyland. Epcot: Character Spot, Innoventions Plaza. Disney's Hollywood Studios: The Magic of*

Micaela Neal

Jasmine surprises Aladdin with a smooch. The sweethearts greet guests together in Magic Kingdom's Adventureland and at Epcot's Morocco pavilion.

Disney Animation, Animation Courtyard. Disney's Animal Kingdom: Adventurers Outpost, Discovery Island; Donald's Safari Breakfast and Lunch, Tusker House, Africa. Beach Club Resort: Cape May Cafe breakfast. Contemporary Resort: Chef Mickey's meals. Fort Wilderness Resort: Mickey's Backyard Barbecue dinner show.

Mister Incredible. Frustrated claims adjuster, super-strong Bob Parr is devoted dad, husband, superhero who misses his glory days in 2004 Pixar movie "The Incredibles." *Magic Kingdom: Move It! Shake It! Celebrate It! Street Party, Cinderella Castle hub. Disney's Hollywood Studios: The Magic of Disney Animation, Animation Courtyard.*

Mulan. Star of 1998's "Mulan"; brave Chinese girl pretends to be boy, joins army to take frail father's place. Quick-witted, strong, saves China. *Epcot: China pavilion formal gardens; Akershus Royal Banquet Hall (often), Norway pavilion.*

Peter Pan. Confident preteen boy of 1953's "Peter Pan" vows to never grow up. Loves adventure, fights pirates, flies with pixie pal Tinker Bell. *Magic Kingdom: Near Pirates of the Caribbean, Adventureland.*

Phineas and Ferb. Stepbrothers Phineas Flynn and Ferb Fletcher concoct imaginative projects over their summer vacation in the Disney Channel animated "Phineas and Ferb." Talkative optimist Phineas has eyes outside his head; quiet brainiac Ferb has a tree-trunk body and green hair. Pet platypus Perry sometimes appears at Disney. *Disney's Hollywood Studios: Near Mama Melrose's Ristorante Italiano, Streets of America.*

Piglet. Stuffed pig faithful to Pooh in 1977's "The Many Adventures of Winnie the Pooh."

Small, shy, fearful. *Magic Kingdom: Crystal Palace meals, Main Street U.S.A.; The Many Adventures of Winnie the Pooh, Fantasyland.*

Pinocchio. Wooden marionette boy given life by Blue Fairy in 1940's "Pinocchio." Naively led astray; nose grows when lying. Best friend Jiminy Cricket is his conscience. *Magic Kingdom: Town Square, Main Street U.S.A. Disney's Hollywood Studios: Sorcerer's Hat, Hollywood Blvd.*

Pluto. Pet dog of Mickey Mouse; gangly yellow hound is only Disney Fab Five character who doesn't walk upright (except, of course, at theme parks). Licks, sniffs, romps and runs in a fashion recognizable to dog lovers everywhere. Wears collar with nametag. Always thinking, known for his vivid expressions. First appeared in 1930 cartoon "The Chain Gang" as an unnamed bloodhound, then briefly was Minnie's pet, named Rover. He has spoken two lines total: in 1931 short "Mickey Steps Out" did an impersonation of Al Jolson's famous moment in 1927 talkie "The Jazz Singer," kneeling to proclaim "Mammy!" In 1931's "The Moose Hunt," Pluto looked into Mickey's eyes and whispered "Kiss me!" Named for the now-demoted planet. *Magic Kingdom: Town Square, Main Street U.S.A. Epcot: Entrance Plaza; Garden Grill dinner, The Land pavilion. Disney's Hollywood Studios: Sorcerer's Hat, Hollywood Blvd. Disney's Animal Kingdom: DinoLand U.S.A. Service Station. Contemporary Resort: Chef Mickey's meals. Polynesian Village Resort: 'Ohana breakfast.*

Pocahontas. Brave, noble Native American teen loves nature, animals (especially raccoon best friend Meeko), English captain John Smith in 1995's "Pocahontas." Spreads

Phineas Flynn (left) and Ferb Fletcher (right) meet their fans at Disney's Hollywood Studios. The stepbrothers star in the popular Disney Channel series "Phineas and Ferb."

message of preserving, honoring nature. Long straight black hair. *Disney's Hollywood Studios: Sorcerer's Hat, Hollywood Blvd. Disney's Animal Kingdom: Discovery Island Trail (by Galapagos tortoise).*

Queen of Hearts. Stout, foul-tempered monarch of Wonderland in 1951's "Alice in Wonderland." Mean, vain, quick to command "Off with their heads!" *Disney's Hollywood Studios: Sorcerer's Hat, Hollywood Blvd.*

Rabbit. Meticulous, practical gardener friend of Winnie the Pooh. *Epcot: The Toy Soldier, U.K. pavilion.*

Rafiki. Wise shaman mandrill (with a baboon's tail) advises Simba's father Mufasa in 1994's "The Lion King." Carries gourd-topped walking stick; lives in baobab tree. *Disney's Animal Kingdom: Conservation Station, Rafiki's Planet Watch.*

Ralph, Vanellope von Schweetz. Main stars of the 2012 movie "Wreck-It Ralph" are video-game characters. Ralph is a disgruntled 8-bit "bad guy" with a heart of gold; Vanellope is an 8-year-old glitch kart-racer from candy-themed game Sugar Rush. *Disney's Hollywood Studios: The Magic of Disney Animation, Animation Courtyard.*

Rapunzel. Spunky artistic teen princess with 70 feet of golden hair, star of 2010's "Tangled." Locked in tower for years, seeks escape with help from charming, handsome bandit Flynn Rider. Magical hair has healing powers. Wears purple gown. *Magic Kingdom: Princess Fairytale Hall, Fantasyland.*

Russell and Dug. Stars of 2009's "Up," Wilderness Explorer scout Russell is a young boy intent on earning badges; dog Dug can talk but has trouble paying attention because—squirrel! *Disney's Animal Kingdom: Dug & Russell's Wilderness Explorers Club House, near the entrance to It's Tough to Be a Bug, Discovery Island.*

Snow White. Gentle young princess whose jealous stepmother repeatedly tries to kill her because of her beauty in 1937's "Snow White and the Seven Dwarfs." Befriends, mothers seven dwarfs; saved from death by "love's first kiss" from a prince. White skin, raven-black hair. Has the most colorful princess gown; yellow skirt, white collar, blue bodice with red trim. *Magic Kingdom: Town Square Theater porch, Main Street U.S.A.; Cinderella's Royal Table meals (often), Cinderella Castle. Epcot: Germany pavilion wishing well; Akershus Royal Banquet Hall meals (often), Norway pavilion.*

Sofia the First. Wide-eyed young girl learning how to live like a princess, from the Disney Channel show "Sofia the First." *Disney's Hollywood Studios: Animation Courtyard. Play 'N Dine character meals, Echo Lake.*

Stitch. Mischievous alien in 2002's "Lilo & Stitch," known initially only as Experiment 626. Escapes from space prison to Hawaii, where he is adopted , named, by Lilo. Loving but has bad-boy behavior; picks nose, burps. *Magic Kingdom: Carousel of Progress, Tomorrowland. Disney's Hollywood Studios: Sorcerer's Hat, Hollywood Blvd. Typhoon Lagoon: Near High 'N Dry Towels. Polynesian Village Resort: 'Ohana breakfast.*

Sulley. Calm, good-natured giant monster James P. Sullivan in "Monsters, Inc." movies. Has blue fur, purple spots, horns. One-eyed Mike Wazowski is best friend, roommate. *Disney's Hollywood Studios: Streets of America, at exit to Studio Backlot Tour.*

Tiana

Mr. Incredible

Fairy Godmother

Tiana and Prince Naveen. Stars of 2009's "The Princess and the Frog." Disney's first African-American princess, Tiana is an aspiring New Orleans restaurant owner who falls in love with funny, carefree, jazz-loving Prince Naveen. In a twist on the classic fairytale, when she kissed the frog prince she was turned into a frog herself. Tiana wears a pale green gown inspired by bayou elements. *Magic Kingdom: Tiana's Garden Glen, behind Ye Olde Christmas Shoppe, Liberty Square.*

Tigger. Ebullient, optimistic stuffed toy tiger in 1977's "The Many Adventures of Winnie the Pooh" loves to bounce. Tells Pooh false rumors about honey-stealing "hefflalumps and woozles." Proud to be "onliest" tigger in the Hundred-Acre Wood. *Magic*

Kingdom: Crystal Palace meals, Main Street U.S.A.; The Many Adventures of Winnie the Pooh, Fantasyland. Epcot: The Toy Soldier, U.K. pavilion. Grand Floridian Resort: 1900 Park Fare character breakfast.

Tinker Bell. Feisty, jealous pixie loyal to Peter Pan in 1953's "Peter Pan," jealous of Wendy. Jingles when moving; flies using magic pixie dust. Has talent for fixing things, hence "tinker" name. Dresses in bright green leaves. *Magic Kingdom: Town Square Theater, Main Street U.S.A.*

Tweedledee, Tweedledum. Plump twin brothers in 1951's "Alice in Wonderland" dress identically. Always odd, sometimes menacing. Finish each other's sentences. *Disney's Hollywood Studios: Sorcerer's Hat, Hollywood Blvd.*

Frozone

Wendy

White Rabbit

Mulan

Donald Duck

Buzz Lightyear

All photos Micaela Neal

Wendy. In 1953's "Peter Pan," the eldest Darling child is growing out of childhood, is caring, sensible. Wears nightgown. Loves to tell stories. Close to Peter Pan; object of Tinker Bell's jealousy. *Magic Kingdom: Near Pirates of the Caribbean, Adventureland.*

White Rabbit. Nervous, worried rabbit continually declares that he's late in 1951's "Alice in Wonderland." Carries giant watch; wears waistcoat, glasses. Alice follows him down rabbit hole to Wonderland. *Magic Kingdom: Mad Tea Party, Fantasyland.*

Winnie the Pooh. Gentle, lovable stuffed bear in 1977's "The Many Adventures of Winnie the Pooh." Loves honey; fears heffalumps, woozles will steal it. Best friends Christopher Robin, Piglet. *Magic Kingdom: Crystal Palace meals, Main Street U.S.A.;* *The Many Adventures of Winnie the Pooh, Fantasyland. Epcot: The Toy Soldier, U.K. pavilion. Grand Floridian Resort: 1900 Park Fare breakfast.*

Woody. Practical, good-natured, old-fashioned cowboy sheriff doll in Pixar's "Toy Story" trilogy. Favorite toy of his owner Andy, a boy growing out of childhood. Has pull-string on back. Best friends with former rival Buzz Lightyear. Girlfriend is Bo Peep, a porcelain lamp base. Named for Woody Strode, an actor who appeared in 1939's "Stagecoach" and other classic Westerns. *Magic Kingdom: Splash Mountain exit courtyard, Frontierland; Move It! Shake It! Celebrate It! Street Party, Cinderella Castle hub. Disney's Hollywood Studios: Woody's Picture Shootin' Corral, Pixar Place.*

Lilo

Woody

Rafiki

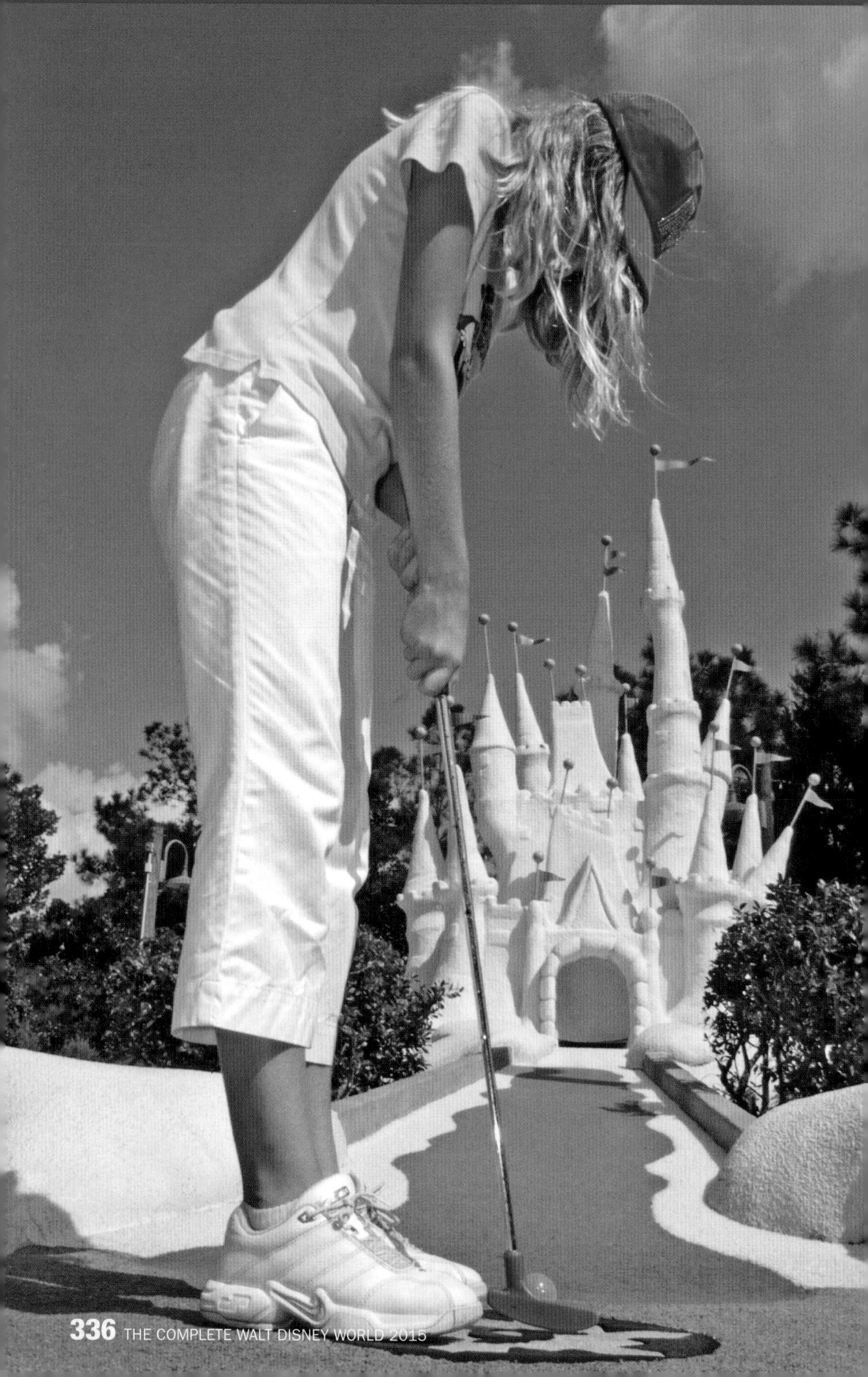

Walt Disney World A–Z

Airports. Orlando has two main commercial airports. Most U.S. airlines fly into the huge Orlando International Airport, while some international carriers use the smaller Orlando Sanford International airport.

Orlando International. Located 19 miles to the east of Walt Disney World, Orlando International Airport is one of the busiest airports in the United States. It handles 35 million passengers a year, an average of 97,000 people a day. At just over 23 square miles, it's the third largest airport in the country behind Denver and Dallas.

Orlando International's hub-and-spoke layout features a large central terminal that's connected by elevated trains to four remote concourses. The terminal is divided into two sides ("A" and "B") and has two lobbies. The east end is topped with a Hyatt Regency hotel that wraps around a tall atrium; the west end is overlooked by a Chili's Too restaurant.

The airport "MCO" IATA code refers to its former life (1940–1976) as McCoy Air Force Base, a Strategic Air Command installation. During the 1962 Cuban Missile Crisis, McCoy was the primary forward operating base for U.S. U-2 reconnaissance aircraft. Today's terminal opened in 1981; the last gate opened in 2000 (One Jeff Fuqua Blvd., Orlando, 32827; 407-825-2001; orlandoairports.net).

Arrivals and departures. Real-time information is available over the phone and on the airport's home page (orlandoairports. net). Arriving and departing flights: 407-825-8463.

Cabs and shuttles. Mears Transportation (407-423-5566) will take you to Walt Disney World by taxi ($55–$65), 4-person town car ($80–$90), 8-person van ($80–$90) or shuttle bus ($22 one-way per adult, $17 one-way child; $36 round-trip per adult, $27 round-trip child).

See also **Transportation.**

Chapel. Open to all faiths, the airport chapel is just past the west security checkpoint (Gates 1–59). Any passenger with a boarding pass is welcome. Catholic mass is held Sundays at 8:15 a.m. and noon.

Checking in. The Greater Orlando Aviation Authority says to arrive two hours before a domestic departure; three hours before an international one.

Child ID cards. In general children under age 18 are not required to have photo identification for U.S. domestic flights. Airlines have more specific requirements.

Getting to Disney. The simplest route (25 minutes) is to take the airport's South Exit road 4 miles to Florida 417 (a toll road), go west 13 miles to Osceola Parkway (Exit 3), then head west again 2 miles.

Highway tolls. Two toll booths sit between Disney and the airport on Florida 417; each requires a toll of $1.25, cash only. Vehicles enrolled in Florida's SunPass/E-Pass program are charged automatically and don't have to stop.

Internet access. Complimentary Wi-Fi is available in all public areas. Several kiosks offer wired connections.

Lost and found. You'll find this office (7 a.m.–10 p.m., 407-825-2111) in Terminal B, across from the food court.

Magical Express. This Disney service will handle your bags for you and shuttle you to your Disney resort at no charge.

See also **Magical Express.**

Operating hours. The airport is open 24 hours a day. Each airline within it sets its own hours of operation.

Paging. This system (407-825-2000) lets you page airport visitors at no charge.

Parking. Parking lots ($10–$25 daily, 407-825-8463; orlandoairports.net/ops/parking) accept cash, credit cards and SunPass/E-Pass transponders. Valet parking services can include auto detailing.

Rental cars. The airport is the largest rental car facility in the world. Most car rental companies are located in a parking garage adjacent to the terminal. Rental counters are on both sides of the terminal on the Ground Transportation level.

See also **Transportation.**

Restaurants and food. The airport has many fast-food spots. The main terminal has a food court with 10 quick-service

Facing page: A snowy Cinderella Castle creates an obstacle on the Winter Summerland miniature golf course

© Greater Orlando Aviation Authority

The Orlando International Airport is located 19 miles from Walt Disney World. The third-largest airport in the United States, the facility covers 23 square miles and features a Hyatt Hotel in the center of its terminal.

counters (including McDonald's and Carvel Ice Cream) and each of the four concourses has at least seven more. The airport has five table-service restaurants, three in the terminal (Chili's Too, Fox Sports Grill, Romano's Macaroni Grill) and two in the Hyatt (Hemisphere, a steak and seafood spot; and McCoy's Bar and Grill, which serves pizza, pasta and sushi).

Shopping. The airport has 30 stores in its main terminal, including shops from the Kennedy Space Center, SeaWorld, Universal Studios and, of course, Walt Disney World. Located in both terminal lobbies, two Disney stores stock popular Disney World merchandise, sell theme-park tickets and ship items purchased on Disney property. Disney's EarPort (407-825-2339) is in the East hall; The Magic of Disney (407-825-2370) is in the West.

Orlando Sanford International. Forty-eight miles from Disney, this airport (IATA code "SFB") serves 5,000 passengers a day. It began as a World War II Naval Air Station (1200 Red Cleveland Blvd., Sanford 32773; 407-322-7771; orlandosanfordairport.com).

Major airlines: Primarily British carriers, they include Allegiant (702-505-8888), ArkeFly (855-808-4015), Icelandair (800-223-5500), Monarch (44-0-1582-398-036), SST (407-288-8820), Thomas Cook (44-0-870-750-0512) and Thomson (44-0-871-231-4691). **Getting to Disney:** The simplest route (50 minutes): Head south on Florida 417 (a toll road) 16 miles to Florida 408, go west 8 miles to Interstate 4, then south 16 miles.

Alcohol. Guests cannot bring alcoholic beverages into any Walt Disney World theme or water park, though those of legal age can

carry open containers of purchased alcoholic beverages (drinks served in restaurants cannot be taken elsewhere). All Disney theme parks serve alcohol, though the Magic Kingdom only offers it on the dinner menu of its Be Our Guest restaurant. There are no liquor stores on Disney property, though hotels and theme-park gift shops sell beer, wine and liquor. It is illegal to carry open containers of alcohol in a car or public area in Central Florida. The legal age to purchase and consume alcohol in Florida is 21.

AA meetings. Friends of Bill W. Orlando (Alcoholics Anonymous) meet daily (3 p.m. Monday–Saturday, 10 a.m. Sunday) at the Orlando Vista Hotel (407-239-4646, 12490 Apopka Vineland Rd., 32836) in a small room between its restaurant and lounge. Catering to travelers, the group provides rides from anywhere in the Disney area and has welcomed more than 10,000 visitors since 1992. Orlando Lynx bus No. 50 serves the hotel from Disney's Transportation and Ticket Center and Downtown Disney ($2 fare).

Birthdays. Walt Disney World offers many ways to help celebrate a birthday.

Balloons and buttons. Concierge staff at Disney hotels can often have balloons delivered to a room or a restaurant. Available free at theme-park Guest Relations locations, personalized Happy Birthday buttons cue cast members to recognize celebrants.

Cakes. All Disney table-service restaurants except Victoria & Albert's offer 6-inch birthday cakes with no advance notice ($21, chocolate or vanilla, serves 5). Plan ahead and Disney's Cake Hotline will let you choose your filling, icing and personalized decorations (407-827-2253, cakes $32 and up, 48 hrs.

Located in both terminal lobbies of the Orlando airport, two Disney stores stock popular Walt Disney World merchandise. The shops also sell theme-park tickets and will ship any item bought on Disney property.

notice). Most hotel restaurants offer Mickey Mouse-shaped cakes through room service or guest services ($48, serves 12).

Cruises. You can watch Magic Kingdom's Wishes fireworks or Epcot's IllumiNations from a pontoon boat. One-hour trips include snacks and drinks ($275 for up to 8 people on 21-foot boat; $325 for up to 10 people on 25-foot boat. $25 additional for decorative banner and balloons). Cakes are available through Disney's Cake Hotline (see above). Reservations available 180 days in advance at 407-827-2253; 2-day cancellation policy.

Flowers and gifts. Disney Floral & Gifts (407-827-3505, disneyflorist.com) delivers adult and child arrangements, baskets and other presents throughout Disney property.

Goodie bags. Standard bags contain a party hat, game, coloring book and crayons; deluxe bags add a magnet activity set and Mickey-shaped straw (407-939-3463).

Goofy telephone call. Goofy will call your Disney hotel room with a free birthday greeting (407-824-2222).

Parties. At Downtown Disney, the Goofy's Candy Company store offers kids celebrations themed to Goofy or Cinderella. They include balloons, favors, treats, drinks and games, and extra goodies for the birthday child. ($350 for up to 12 guests; $25 for additional guests up to 20. Ages 3 and up. 90 minutes. Reservations available 90 days in advance at 407-939-2329.)

Room decorations. Disney Floral & Gifts will decorate your Disney room in a personalized birthday theme (407-827-3505).

Children. As you might guess, Walt Disney World offers many special services for kids.

Baby Care Centers. Located in each theme park, these quiet, air-conditioned spots are

Airlines serving the Orlando International Airport

The airport handles 800 flights a day, most of which come from 36 airlines:

Aer Lingus	800 474-7424
AeroGal	00571 414 71 85
AeroMexico	800 237-6639
Air Canada	800 247-2262
Air Transat	877 872-6728
AirTran	800 247-8726
Alaska Airlines	800 252-7522
American Airlines	800 433-7300
Avianca Airlines	800 284-2622
Bahamas Air	800 222-4262
British Airways	800 247-9297
CanJet Select Airlines	800 809-7777
Caribbean Airlines	800 920-4225
Copa Airlines	800 359-2672
Delta Airlines	800 221-1212
Frontier Airlines	800 432-1359
GOL	55 11 5504 4410
JetBlue Airways	800 538-2583
Lufthansa	800 645-3880
Magni Charters	800 201-1404
Miami Air Intl	305 871-3300
Norwegian Airlines	800 357-4159
Silver Airways	800 229-9990
Southwest Airlines	800 435-9792
Spirit Airlines	800 772-7117
Sun Country Airlines	800 359-6786
Sunwing Airlines	800 761-1711
TACA Airlines	800 400-8222
TAM Airlines	888 235-9826
Thomas Cook	0844 879 8407
United Airlines	800 241-6522
U.S. Airways	800 428-4322
Virgin America	877 359-8474
Virgin Atlantic	800 862-8621
Volaris	866 988-3527
West Jet	800 538-5696

A face painter transforms a girl into a tiger at Disney's Animal Kingdom. Other designs at that park include lions, monkeys and dinosaurs. Prices range from $12 to $18. The process takes about 10 minutes.

designed for parents with infants or toddlers. They have private nursing rooms with rocking chairs; changing rooms with tables and unisex bathrooms; feeding areas with high chairs and kitchens with microwaves, ovens and sinks; lounges with televisions, chairs and sofas; and playrooms. The centers sell baby food, diapers, formula, juice, pacifiers and over-the-counter medications.

Magic Kingdom's Baby Care Center is next to the Crystal Palace restaurant. Epcot's is in the Odyssey Center building, between Test Track and the World Showcase. The Hollywood Studios Baby Care Center is next to that park's Guest Relations office; the one at Animal Kingdom is tucked behind the Creature Comforts store on Discovery Island.

Babysitters. Disney works with two in-room childcare providers. Kids Nite Out (407-828-0920, kidsniteout.com) supplies babysitting and childcare for kids ages 6 weeks to 12 years, including those with special needs. Caregivers bring toys, activities, books, games and arts and crafts. Rates start at $16 per hour with a 4-hour minimum, plus a $10 transportation fee. All About Kids (407-812-9300, all-about-kids.com) offers child-sitting services; rates start at $14 per hour with a 4-hour minimum plus a $12 transportation fee.

Childcare centers. Five Disney-owned hotels offer an evening childcare center: Disney's Animal Kingdom Lodge, Beach Club, Grand Floridian, Polynesian and Wilderness Lodge. Each has a secure room staffed by adults and stocked with arts and crafts, books, games, toys and videos ($11.50 per hour per child, 2-hour minimum, includes dinner 6–8 p.m. Children must be toilet trained, no pull-ups, 4–12 years old. 4 p.m. [sometimes 4:30 p.m.] to midnight. 407-939-3463. Reservations

required). At the Walt Disney World Dolphin is the similar Camp Dolphin ($10 per hour per child, 2-hour minimum, includes dinner 6:30–7:30 p.m. Ages 4–12, must be toilet trained, no pull-ups. 5:30 p.m.–midnight. 407-934-4241. Reservations required).

Child swap. This complimentary, unpublicized service allows you and your spouse to enjoy a ride even if you have a child who can't (or doesn't want to) ride who you don't want to leave unattended. To use it, tell a cast member at the ride's entrance of your situation, then you or your spouse gets in line while the other waits with your child and gets a Fastpass-like ticket to ride later. If the attraction does not offer Fastpasses you, your spouse and your child wait in line together. You ride while your spouse stays with your child, then your spouse rides.

Discounts for children. Disney offers reduced prices for children ages 3 to 9 for park tickets, food and dining plans and paid-recreation options. Older children are charged adult rates. Those younger than age 3 are admitted free into Disney theme and water parks. Children are also charged less for restaurant meals, the Disney Dining Plan and some sports and recreation options.

See also **Disney Dining Plan, Tickets** and **Sports and Recreation.**

Equipment rentals. Disney has the basics, such as cribs, rollaway beds and strollers. Outside companies rent those items and more, and often handle delivery and pickup.

Cribs and rollaway beds: Disney resorts offer free use of Pack 'n Play Playard cribs; request one when you make a reservation. Rollaway beds typically incur an extra fee ($20 to $30). All About Kids (800-728-6506, 407-812-9300, all-about-kids.com) and

Riders of the Seven Dwarfs Mine Train roller coaster must be at least 38 inches tall—the shortest height minimum of any coaster at Disney. A sign in front of the attraction serves as a measuring tool.

Baby's Away (888-376-0084, 407-334-0232, babysaway.com) rent standard cribs.

Strollers: You can rent strollers at each theme park and at Downtown Disney (see theme-park and Downtown Disney chapters for locations). Single strollers rent for $15 a day; double strollers $31 a day. For multiple-day rentals, consider a length-of-stay stroller rental. You pay once, wait in line less and save some money ($2 a day for single strollers, $4 a day for doubles). Made of molded plastic, Disney's strollers are not designed for infants. For an infant stroller, contact Baby's Away (407-334-0232), Kingdom Strollers (407-674-1866), Magic Strollers (866-866-6177) or Orlando Stroller Rentals (800-281-0884).

Other equipment: Baby's Away and All About Kids rent car seats, high chairs, playpens and the like. Most local car-rental companies offer infant or child safety seats ($7–$15 per day) with advance notice. See also **Rental Cars** under **Transportation**

Face art. Scattered throughout Disney are artisans offering personalized creations.

Caricaturists: These artists offer their services in all theme and water parks, at most Disney-owned hotels and at Downtown Disney. Finished portraits come with storage tubes. Prices range from $18 to $99, based on the number of people in the work and whether it includes color.

Face painters: Children (and adults) can get their faces painted for $12 to $18 at all Disney World theme parks, Downtown Disney and on the boardwalk at Disney's BoardWalk Resort. Some park stands offer themed designs, for example animal styles at Disney's Animal Kingdom or Star Wars makeup at Disney's Hollywood Studios.

Height minimums

Magic Kingdom
The Barnstormer	40 in.
Big Thunder Mountain Railroad	40 in.
Seven Dwarfs Mine Train	38 in.
Space Mountain	44 in.
Splash Mountain	40 in.
Stitch's Great Escape	40 in.
Tomorrowland Speedway, solo	54 in.
To ride as a passenger	32 in.

Epcot
Mission Space	44 in.
Soarin'	40 in.
Sum of All Thrills (Innoventions)	48 in.
Test Track	40 in.

Disney's Hollywood Studios
Rock 'n' Roller Coaster	48 in.
Star Tours	40 in.
The Twilight Zone Tower of Terror	40 in.

Disney's Animal Kingdom
Dinosaur	40 in.
Expedition Everest	44 in.
Kali River Rapids	38 in.
Primeval Whirl	48 in.

Blizzard Beach
Chairlift	32 in.
Downhill Double Dipper	48 in.
Slush Gusher	48 in.
Summit Plummet	48 in.

Typhoon Lagoon
Crush 'n' Gusher	48 in.
Humunga Kowabunga	48 in.

DisneyQuest
Buzz Lightyear's AstroBlaster	51 in.
CyberSpace Mountain	51 in.
Mighty Ducks Pinball Slam	48 in.
Pirates of the Caribbean: Battle for Buccaneer Gold	35 in.

Six Walt Disney World resort hotels have business facilities, such as the Conference Center at Disney's Yacht Club. Business guests often get discounts or special deals on room rates, golf and park tickets.

Silhouette artists: Artists cut profiles of children or adults out of paper in Magic Kingdom (on Main Street U.S.A. and in Liberty Square), Epcot (at the France pavilion) and at Downtown Disney (in the The Marketplace). Prices start at $9.

Infant care. Diaper-changing stations are in men's and women's restrooms throughout Disney World. Moms can nurse babies anywhere on Disney property without hassle.

Lost children. Lose your child? Tell the closest Disney cast member. They'll instantly spread the news throughout the park, and advise you on what to do next. Typically cast members who encounter lost children take them to the park's Baby Care Center. Some parents introduce their children to a cast member first thing when they arrive at a theme park, and point out the worker's distinctive name tag. Other parents use a permanent marker to write their cell-phone number on the child's arm.

Makeover salons. Disney offers two distinct types of fantasy salons:

Bibbidi Bobbidi Boutiques: Little girls turn into princesses and pop stars at these female-focused salons, located at Magic Kingdom inside Cinderella Castle and at Downtown Disney in the World of Disney store. Four packages are available: Coach ($55 for a hairstyle, shimmering makeup, sash and purse), Crown ($60, adds nail polish to the Coach package), Courtyard ($95, adds a sparkling Bibbidi Bobbidi Boutique T-shirt and tutu to the Crown package) and Castle ($195 and up, adds a costume and photo session with prints to the Courtyard package). There's a Knight Package for boys ($19 for hair gel, hair confetti and a toy sword and shield). Ages

3 and up. Reservations can be made up to 180 days in advance: 407-939-7895.

Pirates League: This Magic Kingdom salon transforms adults and children into swashbucklers, swashbucklerettes and mermaids. Packages ($30–$75) include facial effects, a reversible bandana, a false earring and eye patch, a sword, a temporary tattoo, a pirate coin necklace, an official pirate name and a personalized oath. Costumes, headwear and photo packages are also available. Participants can join an Adventureland Pirate Parade daily at 4 p.m. (Ages 3 and up. At the exit of Pirates of the Caribbean. Reservations up to 180 days in advance: 407-939-2739.)

Restaurants. Most Disney eateries offer kids' menus and high chairs. Only one excludes children: Victoria & Albert's at the Grand Floridian. Expense-account spots outside Disney often aren't child-friendly.

Convention facilities. Six Disney hotels — the Disney-owned BoardWalk, Contemporary, Coronado Springs, Grand Floridian and Yacht Club and Starwood's Walt Disney World Swan and Dolphin—have convention and conference centers (the largest convention facility is at the Dolphin; its Atlantic Hall consumes 60,000 square feet). Attendees get discounted room rates, deals on golf (20 percent off greens fees; free golf club rentals, range balls and transportation) and theme-park tickets.

See also **Tickets.**

Crowd patterns. In general Disney's theme parks are the most crowded whenever schools in the United States are not in session. During peak periods the wait times at major attractions can exceed three hours,

Walt Disney World's largest convention facility, the Walt Disney World Swan and Dolphin Resort has a quarter-million square feet of meeting and exhibit space. Its Atlantic Hall consumes 60,000 square feet.

© Starwood Resorts

and reservations for popular Fastpass+ times and restaurants are often booked solid at least a month in advance.

Least crowded times of year. The day after Labor Day (the slowest day of the year) until Epcot's Food & Wine Festival and mid-January through the first week in February.

Most crowded times of year. The week between Christmas Day through New Year's Day and Independence Day weekend; also the Spring Break period (typically from the third week of March through the third week of April), holiday weekends, Presidents' week, Marathon Weekend.

Least crowded time of day. First two hours of the day; last hour of the evening.

Most crowded time of day. Afternoons.

At Disney's water parks, typically the hotter the weather, the larger the crowd.

Disability services. Disney offers a variety of services for guests with hearing, mobility, visual or other disabilities.

Disability Access Card. A replacement for Disney's old Guest Assistance Card as well as its former heavily abused policy that guests in wheelchairs and scooters always bypass waiting lines, this small folded card is for guests who are unable to withstand extended waits at attractions due to a disability. At each ride or show, showing the card lets a guest schedule a return time comparable to that attraction's current wait time, and if the guest runs late it's OK. At least that's the official policy. In reality, cast members at an attraction often have the ability to let a DAS Card holder enter it immediately through its Fastpass+ line, at their discretion—which lets them treat more seriously impaired guests with more compassion.

The card is available at Guest Relations locations. A doctor's note isn't required, but users must have their photos taken. The card is valid for up to 14 days.

Cognitive services. Disney publishes a complimentary pamphlet—Disney's Guide for Guests with Cognitive Disabilities—that's filled with tips. It's available online (at disneyworld.disney.go.com/guest-services/guests-with-disabilities) and in person at Guest Relations locations.

Hearing services. Disney's Handheld Device (yes, that's the name) is a wireless gadget roughly the size of a smart phone. It amplifies the audio at some stationary attractions, turns on captions on some pre-show video screens (single-button activators are also available for this), and displays captions at narrated moving attractions. Available at each park's Guest Relations location, Disney's Handheld Device costs nothing to borrow but requires a $25 daily deposit.

Reflective captioning: At many theatrical attractions, cast members can supply handheld acrylic panels that reflect captions from an LED display on a back wall.

Guest Assistance Packets: Available at many attractions, each packet consists of a three-ring binder which holds a script of the ride or show, a flashlight, a pen and a small pad of paper for cast members to use to communicate with any guest who has trouble hearing.

Sign language: Live interpreters typically translate live shows at Magic Kingdom on Mondays and Thursdays, Epcot on Tuesdays and Fridays, Disney's Hollywood Studios on Sundays and Wednesdays and Disney's Animal Kingdom on Saturdays. Cast members with sign language abilities

Disney's Handheld Device (that's the actual name) combines assistive listening, Audio Description, handheld captioning and closed captioning activation into one unit. The device is slightly larger than a smart phone.

wear identifying pins. For a schedule of interpreted shows call 407-824-4321.

TTY telephones: Pay phones with amplified handsets and Text Typewriters are located throughout the parks.

Mobility services. Disney rents mobility scooters (which the company calls "Electric Conveyance Vehicles," or ECVs) and wheelchairs. Both are available on a first-come, first-served, same-day basis (no reservations are accepted) and neither requires any proof of need. Disney's wheelchairs and ECVs may not be transferred from park to park, but the deposit ticket from a first rental will let you rent additional wheelchairs or ECVs on the same day at other Disney theme parks.

Mobility scooters: Disney rents ECVs for $70 a day which includes a $20 deposit. Arrive early to rent one; popular with obese as well as disabled guests, they sell out quickly. The maximum weight allowed is 450 pounds. You may bring your own mobility scooter into any park.

Wheelchairs: Disney rents wheelchairs for $12 a day ($10 for multiple-day rentals). The maximum weight is 350 pounds. Identified by blue flags, parking-lot wheelchairs are free to use. Personal wheelchairs can be used anywhere on Disney property.

Rental locations: Magic Kingdom rents wheelchairs at the Wheelchair Rental Shop at the park entrance, and offers replacements at Buzz Lightyear's Space Ranger Spin, Castle Couture and the Frontierland Trading Post. Epcot has rentals at its front and back entrances; replacements at the Germany pavilion's Karamelle-Kuche shop. Disney's Hollywood Studios rents chairs at Oscar's Super Service just inside its gate, and has replacements at the Tatooine Traders and Writer's Stop shops. Disney's Animal Kingdom has rentals at Garden Gate Gifts and replacements at the Creature Comforts and Mombasa Marketplace stores. Downtown Disney rents chairs at its Stroller Shop next to the Once Upon a Toy store and DisneyQuest Emporium—Downtown Disney chair rentals require a $100 deposit. All wheelchair shops also rent ECVs.

Strollers as wheelchairs: Disabled children in strollers can get wheelchair benefits if their parents pick up a special tag at any Guest Relations location.

Transferring: Some park attractions require wheelchair and ECV users to transfer to a ride vehicle. Disney cast members are not allowed to lift guests.

Off-property rental companies: You cannot reserve a wheelchair or ECV in advance from Disney, but you can from outside companies—such as Apple Scooter (800-701-1971), Best Price Mobility (866-866-3434), Buena Vista Scooter Rentals (866-484-4797), CARE Scooter Rentals (800-741-2282) or Scooterbug (800-726-8284).

Zero-entry pools: Some Disney resort hotels have zero-entry swimming pools, one side of which gradually slopes into the water and allows guests in appropriate wheelchairs to roll into the water. Nine Disney hotels have pools with this feature: the Art of Animation, Caribbean Beach, Contemporary (behind Bay Lake Tower), Grand Floridian, Polynesian, Saratoga Springs and Yacht and Beach Club resorts, and the Jambo House and Kidani Village areas of Animal Kingdom Lodge.

Visual services. Visually impaired guests can take advantage of four Disney resources:

The Big Blue swimming pool at Disney's Art of Animation Resort has a "zero-entry" gradual slope that allows guests in appropriate wheelchairs to roll into the water. Altogether nine Disney hotels have zero-entry pools.

Audio Description: Disney's Handheld Device provides audio descriptions of some attractions (see previous page).

Audiotape guides and tours: Audiotape guides orient guests to a theme park. Tape tours offer routes, provide distances between attractions and recommend stopping spots. Free at Guest Relations locations with a $25 deposit.

Braille maps: Each park has a stationary Braille map with raised graphics to highlight landmarks and attractions.

Handheld braille guides: Each theme park has handheld braille guides which provide descriptions of attractions, restaurants and shops. Free at Guest Relations locations with a $25 deposit.

Parking. Each theme park has a designated handicapped parking area. Courtesy trams do not serve this area, as they do not accommodate wheelchairs or ECVs.

Restrooms. All Disney restrooms have wheelchair-accessible stalls. Companion restrooms are throughout Disney property.

Service animals. Trained and leashed (or harnessed) service animals are welcome throughout Disney property, and can go on most attractions with their owners. Each park has designated potty break spots. If you have a service animal, you will most likely enter attractions through an alternate entrance, usually the Fastpass+ entrance.

Transportation. Most Disney buses and all monorail trains can accommodate wheelchairs and mobility scooters. Buses use a 30-by-48-inch lift; monorail trains use portable ramps. Some ferry boats accept chairs and scooters depending on water conditions.

Printed park disability guides. For each of its theme parks Disney publishes

a complimentary Guide for Guests with Disabilities, which has in-depth information and a detailed map. All Guest Relations locations distribute all four guides.

Disney Dining Plan. Disney hotel guests and Disney Vacation Club members can add this prepaid meal plan (which can include recreation options) to their park-ticket purchase. Over a hundred restaurants participate. Five packages are available:

Basic Plan. Provides a table-service meal, a fast food ("quick-service") meal and a snack per each nightly stay and a refillable drink mug for use at your resort.

Deluxe Plan. Provides three daily table-service (or fast food) meals, two snacks and a refillable drink mug.

Quick-Service Plan. Provides two fast food meals and one snack per day, again with a refillable drink mug.

Premium Plan. Provides three daily table-service (or fast food) meals, two snacks and a refillable drink mug for use at your resort. Other perks include unlimited use of many recreation options, vouchers to La Nouba and the Richard Petty Junior Ride-Along Experience, unlimited use of child-care facilities and select theme-park tours. Requires purchase of at least a one-day park ticket. Buy it six months early to cherry-pick your recreation times.

Platinum Plan. Same as the Premium Plan except with still more extras, such as an itinerary planning service, a spa treatment and a fireworks cruise.

How the plans work. You can use Disney Dining Plan meal and snack credits in any combination during your stay. For example, you can eat all table-service meals one day,

The crowd walking down Magic Kingdom's Main Street U.S.A. is relatively light on Extra Magic Hour mornings, when guests typically find little or no waits for rides and shows for at least an hour

all fast-food meals the next, and nothing but snacks the day after that. If one person in your party uses up his or her plan, others can continue to use theirs. Disney defines a breakfast meal as one entree and one beverage; or a combo meal and a beverage or juice. Lunch and dinner are defined as one entree, one dessert and one beverage; or a combo meal, dessert and beverage.

To use the plan, present your MagicBand to a cashier or server. Food usage is tracked electronically; balances are available on each food receipt. Nearly every Disney-owned restaurant participates in the Dining Plan, as do snack locations such as food carts and sweet shops. Tips are not included; neither are alcoholic beverages, some bottled drinks, souvenir mugs, or snacks and beverages from recreation-rental counters.

Key conditions. Each Disney Dining Plan has four key conditions:

It is sold per party, not per person. If one person in your group buys a Dining Plan, everyone else in your group must too. The only exception: children under age 3. They can eat from an adult's plate.

Kids are kids. When their parents are using a Dining Plan, children 3–9 must order from a kid's menu when one is available. Likewise, those children over 9 years of age must order from adult menus.

Some restaurants take two credits. These include all Disney Signature restaurants, dinner shows and Cinderella's Royal Table at Magic Kingdom. Room-service meals at Disney Deluxe Resorts charge two credits, too.

Leftover credits have no value. Just like those famous magical accoutrements of Cinderella, unused Dining Plan meals and snacks expire at midnight on your checkout date.

Getting your money's worth. If you take advantage of it, the Dining Plan will give you great food and memorable meals. Handle it poorly, however, and your magical vacation can include a frustrating waste of time and resources. Here are four keys to getting the most for your money:

Don't overestimate your hunger. When determining which plan to purchase, keep in mind that it's tough to eat enough food to justify three table-service meals a day. It's also difficult to dine at more than one Signature restaurant a day, as each takes awhile to fully experience.

Use your credits efficiently. Except for those at Signature restaurants, the plan considers nearly all table-service meals equal. In most cases, dining with a princess, Mickey Mouse or Lilo and Stitch at an all-you-can-eat feast uses no more credits than getting a hamburger and fries at Magic Kingdom's Plaza Restaurant.

Know where the deals are. Though your plans will charge you the same amount— one credit—for most meals, some restaurants give you more for it. Great breakfast buffets include Boma at Animal Kingdom Lodge and the 1900 Park Fare character meal at the Grand Floridian Resort. For lunch, try Coral Reef at Epcot or Sanaa at Disney's Animal Kingdom Lodge. For dinner, consider Boma, 1900 Park Fare or Raglan Road at Downtown Disney. Good quick-service choices include Sunshine Seasons at The Land pavilion and Earl of Sandwich at Downtown Disney.

Make your reservations way early. Disney restaurants book to capacity sometimes

Whole Foods offers free delivery to Disney hotels. Seven miles away off Interstate 4, the tempting 'Whole Paycheck' store includes a ready-to-eat department with salads, sandwiches and soups.

months early, especially for the most popular dining times. Make reservations as early as possible to ensure you can dine at places, and times, that best suit your needs.

Extra Magic Hours. Each day at least one Disney theme or water park opens an hour early, or stays open two hours late, for those guests staying at Disney-owned resorts, the Walt Disney World Swan and Dolphin, Shades of Green or the Downtown Disney Hilton. Residents of the Golden Oak subdivision also qualify. To take advantage of an extra morning hour, simply arrive at the designated park's entrance with a valid park ticket or MagicBand wristband. During evening hours, scan your MagicBand at each attraction. Note: On a day when a park offers an Extra Magic Hour in the morning, that park will be more crowded than usual during regular hours.

Floral services. Disney Floral & Gifts (407-939-4438, 8 a.m.–6 p.m. daily, disneyflorist.com) sells floral arrangements, gift baskets, balloons, fruit, liquor and plants, each with as much, or little, Disney theming as desired. Delivery is available at Disney theme parks, resorts and Downtown Disney. A Disney Dream Makers division can decorate your room before arrival or for special occasions; the new Star Tours Adventure Pack includes a light saber and other "Star Wars"-inspired goodies. The Disney Event Group has arrangements for business gatherings (407-939-7129, disneymeetings.com); Disney's wedding planners help with bridal displays (407-939-4610, disneyweddings.com).

Groceries. Many Disney resorts have shops that offer groceries. Stores in resorts that

offer suites and kitchen facilities have the best variety. Outside of Disney, many supermarkets are just a few miles away:

Gooding's supermarket. Close to Disney in the Crossroads Shopping Center; prices are 20–25 percent higher than Publix.

Publix supermarkets. Three locations are near Walt Disney World; at the Celebration shopping center Water Tower Place (29 Blake Boulevard; 321-939-3100), at 2915 Vineland Road (407-396-7525) and at 7640 W. Sand Lake Road (407-226-3315). Publix has decent prices, a wide variety of two-for-one items and, at Celebration, a spot to sit down to eat.

Whole Foods. A short drive from Disney property at Interstate 4 and Sand Lake Road; this pricey market offers quality natural and organic groceries. Its produce department has more than 75 locally grown types of fruits and vegetables. An indoor-outdoor dining area offers a convenient spot to chow down on to-go items (8003 Turkey Lake Road, Orlando 32819; 407-355-7100).

Winn-Dixie supermarket. Two locations are near Disney, at 11957 S. Apopka-Vineland Road (407-465-8600) and 7840 W. Irlo Bronson Highway (U.S. 192) (407-397-2210).

Grocery delivery services. Two companies deliver groceries to Disney hotels. Note: The Walt Disney World Swan and Dolphin does not allow grocery deliveries.

Gardengrocer.com. This national delivery service offers 4,700 products. Local categories include "park essentials," baby care, natural and organic fresh produce and household products (866-855-4350, gardengrocer.com, minimum order $40, delivery fee $12, orders over $200 delivered free).

Whole Foods. The Orlando Whole Foods Market offers delivery to Walt Disney

Some fast-food spots near Disney offer free Wi-Fi service. Among the best: the Celebration Chick-fil-A, located just across Interstate 4 on U.S. 192.

World, though it does not have an on-line ordering system (407-355-7100, no minimum order, delivery fee $30. 48 hours notice required).

Gasoline stations. Three Hess stations sit on Disney property, all open 24 hours with self-serve gasoline and a convenience store. Prices are not inflated; in fact, a gallon of gas is often a nickel or dime per gallon cheaper inside Disney property than outside it.

Magic Kingdom. On the parking-lot exit road, next to the AAA Car Care Center (1000 W. Car Care Drive, 32801; 407-938-0143).

Disney's Hollywood Studios. Corner of Buena Vista Drive and Epcot Resorts Boulevard. Car wash available (300 East Buena Vista Drive, 32801; 407-938-0151).

Downtown Disney. Directly across the street, under a towering sign that reads "Gas" (1475 Buena Vista Drive, 32801; 407-938-0160).

For Orlando-area gasoline prices over the past 48 hours see orlandoairports.net/transport/gas_prices.htm.

Gay and lesbian travelers. Gay adults of all ages come to Walt Disney World during the first week in June for Gay Days (407-896-8431, gaydays.com); many wear red shirts in a sign of celebration and solidarity. Disney does not sponsor the event. GayCities Orlando (orlando.gaycities.com) and Gay Orlando (gayorlando.com) have lists of LGBT-friendly Orlando accommodations, bars and restaurants.

Guest Relations. Each Disney theme and water park — and Downtown Disney — has at least one Guest Relations office. Disney staffers make dining reservations, upgrade park tickets, sell annual passes, check on lost items (for items lost the same day) and provide answers to general questions. Free guidemaps and Times Guides for all the Disney World parks are available. Disabled guests can pick up park-specific guides for guests with disabilities, get a DAS card and/or borrow Disney's Handheld Device. International visitors can pick up complimentary Attraction Translation Devices and guidemaps in German, Japanese, Spanish and Portuguese as well as exchange currency. Many staffers are multilingual.

Each theme park has a walk-up Guest Relations window outside its entrance, and at least one location inside. Magic Kingdom's Guest Relations spot is at City Hall. Epcot has an indoor office to the left of Spaceship Earth. Guest Relations at Disney's Hollywood Studios sits beside Sid Cahuenga's shop. Disney's Animal Kingdom's location is just inside the entrance on the left.

Downtown Disney has two Guest Relations offices. The Marketplace office is adjacent to the Arribas Brothers shop. The West Side location is at the DisneyQuest gift shop.

Highways. Two major limited-access highways border Walt Disney World.

Interstate 4. The main drag through Central Florida, Interstate 4 runs along the southeastern edge of Disney, connecting it to Orlando (18 miles northeast) and Tampa (53 miles southwest). Technically the highway runs east to west, but through the Orlando area it often aligns more north and south.

Florida 429. This toll road runs along the southwestern edge of Disney property, and makes for a handy shortcut for those coming from the north on Florida's Turnpike. Taking it saves about a half-hour compared

Three Hess stations sit on Disney World property—near Magic Kingdom, outside Hollywood Studios (right) and across from Downtown Disney. Gas prices are—surprise!— lower than most spots outside of Disney.

to continuing on the turnpike into Orlando, and gives you a drive through farmland and orange groves instead of congested urbania. To use Florida 429, take the turnpike south to Exit 267A, then head southeast on 429 11 miles to Exit 8, which leads to Disney's Western Way entrance. Tolls vary from $1.25 to $1.50. At Mile Marker 13 you can glimpse, way off to your left, Cinderella Castle, Space Mountain, the Contemporary Resort, Spaceship Earth and the Walt Disney World Dolphin Resort.

Holidays. Disney is especially busy during holiday periods—the days that surround Martin Luther King Jr. Day, Presidents Day, Good Friday, Easter, Memorial Day, Independence Day, Thanksgiving and the week between Christmas and New Year's Day.

Crowds. Airline seats and hotels book early. Theme parks are packed.

Costs. Room rates will be at their most expensive, as will many places to eat. Disney often temporarily increases prices for dining at its buffet restaurants during these times (typically $4 for adults, $2 for children) and charges a premium for its dining plan.

Hours. Disney theme parks have extended hours, and are often open late into the night.

Festivities. Depending on the holiday, Disney schedules additional activities and entertainment, and decorates the entrances to its theme parks and hotel lobbies.

Restrictions. Seasonal annual passes often cannot be used during holiday periods. On peak days, neither can the Tables in Wonderland restaurant discount card.

International travelers. Wireless "Ears to the World" headsets ($100 deposit) provide translation of Disney attraction audio into French, German, Japanese, Portuguese or Spanish. Other Disney services include multilingual theme-park guidemaps, restaurant menus and tours. Multilingual cast members have nametags with gold badges.

Internet access. Walt Disney World offers free Wi-Fi in all its theme parks, water parks and hotels, as well as at Downtown Disney and the ESPN Wide World of Sports complex.

Theme parks, water parks, Downtown Disney. You can access Disney's free wireless network under the name "Public Space Guest WiFi (Disney)." Covered carriers include AT&T, MetroPCS, Sprint, T-Mobile and Verizon. Expect service to be spotty.

Hotels. Disney hotels offer complimentary in-room wireless Internet access. You can access the free network under the name "In-Room Guest WiFi (Disney)." For in-room wired high-speed access, each room comes with a Local Area Network (LAN) cable to attach to a laptop. Most common areas will also have free Wi-Fi, including arcades, bus stops, convention areas, the main pool, the lobby, bus stops and restaurants.

Many non-Disney resorts also offer in-room wired access; some do so free of charge.

Business centers. Internet-connected computers ($10 for 15 minutes or $40 an hour; $1 per page to print. 9 a.m.–4 p.m.) are available at Disney's Animal Kingdom Lodge, Beach Club, Contemporary, Coronado Springs, Grand Floridian and Yacht Club resorts.

ESPN Wide World of Sports. This complex offers free Wi-Fi throughout its grounds, although it can be unreliable.

Outside Disney. Wireless Internet access is available free of charge in all public areas of the Orlando International Airport. Several

Arriving Magical Express guests check in at a Welcome Center at the Orlando International Airport, located on Level 1 of the B side of the main terminal.

kiosks offer wired Internet connections in addition to standard dial service provided via RJ-11 jacks in pay phones.

The Osceola County Public Library has free Internet access; the closest branch to Disney is the West Osceola branch in Celebration (1134 Celebration Boulevard, 34747, 407-742-8888, Mon–Sat 10 a.m.–7 p.m.). For a list of free-Wi-Fi businesses check wififreespot.com or openwifispots.com.

Lockers. You can rent a multi-use, key-operated locker to store belongings at each theme park, inside the entrance. You pay $7 a day plus a $5 deposit, for a locker 11 inches tall by 9 inches wide by 16 inches deep. For a larger locker (17.5 inches tall by 12 inches wide by 16 inches deep), you pay $9 a day. When visiting more than one park in one day, return your locker key to get your deposit back, then present your receipt (and another deposit) at any subsequent park to get a locker there at no additional charge.

You can rent single-use, coin-operated lockers at the bus information booths at Epcot, Disney's Hollywood Studios and Disney's Animal Kingdom. You pay $1; and must use quarters.

Lost and found. At Disney theme parks, water parks and Downtown Disney, you can check on items lost that same day at Guest Relations. Disney hotels have internal lost and found offices; you should check with the concierge desk. ESPN Wide World of Sports holds lost items at its Welcome Center.

After one day items move to the Theme Park Lost and Found office (407-824-4245, 9 a.m.–7 p.m. daily, shipping at no charge), located at the former Magic Kingdom kennel

next to the Transportation and Ticket Center. It keeps most items 30 days. Cameras, credit cards, prescription eyeglasses, purses and wallets are kept 90 days; hats, strollers and sunglasses just one week.

If you've lost your purse and it had, say, a wallet and iPhone inside, ask Lost and Found for all three items. Sometimes only one item is found, or is still stored inside another. (Magic Kingdom 407-824-4521, Epcot 407-560-6646, Disney's Hollywood Studios 407-560-3720, Disney's Animal Kingdom 407-938-2785, Blizzard Beach 407-560-5408, Typhoon Lagoon 407-560-6296, Downtown Disney 407-828-3150, ESPN Wide World of Sports 407-541-5600.)

Magical Express. This bus transportation and luggage delivery service is complimentary if you are staying at a Walt Disney World resort. To be more speciic, if you are bound for a Disney-owned hotel traveling via commercial airline to the Orlando International Airport you can skip the airport's baggage claim area and take a shuttle bus to your hotel, where your bags then "magically" appear. When it's time to return home, if you are traveling on a participating airline you can check your bags for your flight at your hotel. Then you simply board a bus back to the airport. If you are planning to spend your entire vacation at Disney World, Magical Express makes traveling to Walt Disney World cheaper, and eliminates the need to rent a car. The service carries over 2.2 million passengers a year.

Eligibility. You can use the service if you are staying at any Disney-owned resort. Guests of the Walt Disney World Swan and Dolphin, Shades of Green and Downtown Disney hotels are not eligible.

Magical Express buses transport Disney hotel guests to and from the Orlando International Airport. The free service delivers luggage to resorts directly from the airlines, so guests who use it bypass Baggage Claim.

Booking. You can reserve the service when booking your Disney hotel accommodations, or anytime at least 10 days before your trip at 866-599-0951.

Arrivals. Upon landing, go directly to the Magical Express Welcome Center (on Level 1 at the B side of the terminal) to check in and board your shuttle bus. Luggage is delivered to your hotel within three hours after resort check-in for flights arriving between 5 a.m. and 10 p.m. daily. For later arrivals you collect your luggage at baggage claim, bring it to the Welcome Center yourself and carry it into the resort with you. International guests always claim their own baggage.

Departures. As your vacation draws to a close, you'll receive a Magical Express Transportation Notice advising you of the time you are scheduled for a bus ride back to the airport. With some airlines—Airtran, Alaska Airlines, American Airlines, Delta Air Lines, JetBlue, Southwest, United and US Air—you can check your bags and get boarding passes at your hotel, eliminating those chores at the airport. You will need to stop by your hotel's Resort Airline Check-In Desk three hours prior to your flight time. You'll need to show a valid government-issued photo I.D. and your Disney MagicBand.

Maps. Though the maps in this book should suffice for many planning needs, larger, more detailed ones are available free from Disney.

Customized maps. You can create free customized maps of all Disney World theme parks at customizedmaps.disney.go.com. Choices include a map of the entire property. The full-color maps can be printed, or Disney will mail 14-by-20-inch copies free of charge. Allow two to four weeks for delivery.

For Disney hotel guests. If you are making a reservation to stay at a Disney-owned hotel, you can request a map of the grounds. It shows lodging areas with room numbers, restaurants, shops, pools, smoking areas, recreation locations and transportation. Also available: a set of Disney's theme-park guide maps that are distributed in the parks.

Medical services. If you need medical care at Disney World, it's close at hand; either right on Disney property or just a few minutes away. Every theme and water park has a first aid station manned by registered nurses who can handle minor medical incidents and contact the proper emergency personnel for more serious matters. Disney resort hotels can arrange in-room appointments and prescription deliveries. Doctors, dentists and a major hospital are all within 5 miles.

Automated External Defibrillators. Walt Disney World has installed 700 Automated External Defibrillators (AEDs) throughout its property. Designed to aid a person suffering from cardiac arrest, an AED is easy to use even without training. When the device is used, it automatically calls 911 and gives responders its location.

Dental services. The Celebration Dental Group provides standard and emergency care (Florida Hospital at Celebration Health, 400 Celebration Place, Celebration 34747; 407-566-2222).

Equipment rentals. Outside companies rent portable commodes, crutches, nebulizers, oxygen, scooters (electric conveyance vehicles), walkers and wheelchairs. Contact Apria Healthcare (407-291-2229 or 800-338-1640, after hours 407-297-0100, apria.com), Care Medical Equipment (407-856-2273 or

Disney's Reedy Creek Fire Department provides free EMT and paramedic treatment to Disney guests. The department has four fire stations, including this one near Downtown Disney.

800-741-2282, caremedicalequipment.com), Turner Drugs (407-828-8125, turnerdrug.com) or Walker Mobility (407-518-6000 or 800-726-6837, walkermobility.com).

See also **Pharmacies**

Hospital. Florida Hospital at Celebration Health is just three miles from Walt Disney World, across Interstate 4 (400 Celebration Place, Celebration 34747; 407-303-4000, emergencies 407-303-4034).

In-room care. For non-emergency appointments contact Centra Care (407-238-2000), Doctors on Call (407-399-3627) or EastCoast Medical (407-648-5252).

Paramedics. Available on Disney property through Disney's Reedy Creek Emergency Services (407-560-1990 via Disney Security).

Pharmacy. Turner Drugs (just across Interstate 4 from Disney at 1530 Celebration Boulevard, Celebration 34747; Monday–Friday 9 a.m.–7 p.m., Saturday–Sunday 9 a.m.–5 p.m.; 407-828-8125, fax 407-828-8027; turnerdrug. com) delivers prescription and over-the-counter medications to the concierge desks of all Disney resort hotels; drivers ask the desk to notify recipients immediately. Through an arrangement with Disney, Turner Drugs will charge an order to a guest's Disney room account (deliveries $5, Monday–Friday 8 a.m.–9 p.m., Saturday–Sunday 8 a.m.–7 p.m.).

Vision services. The closest optometrist to Disney is Celebration Eye Care, which is five miles away (741 Front Street, Celebration 34747; 407-566-2020; celebrationeyecare.com).

Walk-in clinics. No appointment is necessary for Family Medicine of Celebration, which focuses on children. It's staffed with pediatric physicians and has a separate waiting room for children and their families. The lobby in its building has a combination drug and convenience store. A small playground sits outside (1530 Celebration Boulevard, Celebration 34747. Monday, Tuesday, Friday 8 a.m.–5 p.m.; Wednesday 7 a.m.–7 p.m.; Thursday 8 a.m.–4 p.m.; 407-566-0404; familymedicinecelebration.com).

Florida Hospital's Centra Care Walk-In Urgent Care Clinic offers free transportation from Walt Disney World to its location near Downtown Disney (12500 S. Apopka Vineland Road, Orlando 32836. 8 a.m.–midnight. Monday–Friday, 8 a.m.–8 p.m. Saturday–Sunday. 407-934-2273. Book appointments online at centracare.org).

Money. Nearly every restaurant, snack stand and shop at Disney accepts credit and debit cards as well as cash. You'll need cash for tips, highway tolls, pressed-coin machines, single-use lockers, some taxi and limo services and parking fees at Disney theme parks.

ATMs. Chase Bank automated teller machines are located in each Disney theme and water park, at Downtown Disney, at the ESPN Wide World of Sports complex and at all Disney resort hotels. The machines accept cards from the Cirrus and Plus systems. Withdrawals using out-of-state cards, or cards from a bank other than Chase, incur surcharges of $1.50 to $2.50.

Magic Kingdom. ATMs are located by the lockers at the main entrance, City Hall, the Adventureland / Frontierland breezeway, near the Pinocchio Village Haus restrooms and at the Tomorrowland Arcade.

Epcot. Both entrances have ATMs, as well as at the American Adventure restrooms and the Future World bridge.

Disney's Hollywood Studios. ATMs are located outside the entranceway, outside the

Every Disney theme park has a Baby Care Center with a First Aid station. Registered nurses handle minor medical incidents. Reedy Creek paramedics arrive for more serious matters.

Keystone Clothiers shop and inside the Toy Story Pizza Planet Arcade.

Disney's Animal Kingdom. At the entrance and outside the Dinosaur Treasures gift shop.

Downtown Disney. The Marketplace has ATMs near the Tren-D store, next to the Ghirardelli shop and inside the World of Disney. On the West Side, an ATM sits outside the House of Blues Company Store.

Banks. Many banks nearby Walt Disney World offer full services.

Bank of America. In the Disney-developed town of Celebration, 5 miles from Disney World (700 Celebration Ave., Celebration 34747; Monday–Thursday 9 a.m.–5 p.m., Friday 9 a.m.–6 p.m., Saturday 9 a.m.–1 p.m.; 321-939-7677).

SunTrust. Across from Downtown Disney (1675 E Buena Vista Dr, Lake Buena Vista 32830; Monday–Thursday 8 a.m.–5 p.m., Friday 8 a.m.–6 p.m.; 407-828-6103). Two SunTrust banks are in Celebration, across Interstate 4 from Disney World: downtown (650 Celebration Ave, Celebration 34747; Monday–Thursday 9 a.m.–4 p.m., Friday 9 a.m.–6 p.m.; 407-566-2265) and in the Water Tower Shoppes along U.S. 192 (74 Blake Blvd, Celebration 34747; Monday–Thursday 9 a.m.–4 p.m., Friday 9 a.m.–6 p.m.; 321-939-3970).

Wells Fargo. Near International Drive, 6 miles from Disney (7740 W Sand Lake Rd, Orlando 32819; Monday–Friday 8 a.m.–6 p.m., Saturday 9 a.m.–2 p.m.; 407-649-5800).

Credit and debit cards. Disney accepts American Express, Diners Club, Discover, Japan Credit Bureau (JCB), MasterCard and Visa cards, even at snack stands.

Currency exchange. Foreign currency can be exchanged for U.S. dollars at the Orlando International Airport, main bank branches, theme park Guest Relations locations and Disney resort hotel concierge desks.

Disney Dollars. This whimsical scrip is accepted at all Disney World theme parks and Disney-owned resorts and gift shops. Popular as on-property currency as well as souvenirs, the dollars are sold at Guest Relations locations, Disney hotel concierge desks and the World of Disney store at Downtown Disney. Denominations are $1, $5 and $10; the exchange rate is always $1 for $1. Disney issues new designs nearly every year.

Gift cards. Disney gift cards can be used for purchases throughout Walt Disney World. The cards have no fees and don't expire, and can be ordered online in $25 increments up to $150 plus denominations of $200, $250, $300 and $500. Choose from hundreds of designs, or personalize a card using a photograph. Disney Dollars purchases are not eligible (disneygiftcard.com).

Gratuities. Tips often will be refused by Disney concierge staff and other cast members; guests can express appreciation for cast-member service by emailing wdw.guest.communications@disney.com; comments can boost a career. Gratuities are accepted by Magical Express bus drivers, housekeeping staff, restaurant servers, valets, and the non-Disney concierge staff at the Walt Disney World Swan and Dolphin Resort and Downtown Disney hotels. An 18 percent tip is automatically added to the bill on room-service orders at Disney hotels, with use of a Tables in Wonderland discount card, for restaurant parties of six or more and at prepaid eateries and dinner shows. Gratuities are not automatically included in the Disney Dining Plan, so please tip accordingly.

Shuttle trams transport visitors from theme-park parking lots. The vehicles have their own roadways. Distinctive driver shades and large rear-view mirrors have earned them the nickname "Flying Nuns."

Rental cars. Renting a car requires a major credit card or debit card with major-credit-card backing. Using a debit card will require a deposit (usually $200–$300) that will be credited back to the user's account a week or so after the car is returned.

Traveler's checks. Nearly any Disney expense can be paid for with a traveler's check. SunTrust Bank is the closest full-service bank that sells, replaces and redeems traveler's checks. For refunds on lost or stolen checks call American Express (800-992-3404). Instead of traveler's checks, Thomas Cook now sells Prepaid Currency Cards (800-287-7362).

Wire transfers. The Downtown Disney SunTrust Bank (see above) handles wire transfers. Winn-Dixie (7840 W. Irlo Bronson Hwy; 8 a.m.–10 p.m. daily; 407-397-2210) offers Western Union (800-325-6000) transfers.

Obese visitors. Guests of nearly all shapes and sizes can experience just about all Walt Disney World has to offer with no problem, as long as they heed Disney's medical advisories and use common sense.

Bench seats. On some attractions an obese person should take a bench seat alone to fit comfortably. To make this easy, when a cast member at the loading area asks how many are in your party, say "1" and then the number of the rest of your party, such as "and 3."

Getting around. Probably the biggest challenge for an overweight guest is handling all the walking at Disney. The typical theme-park guest easily ends up walking miles a day, which can be tough for anyone who isn't fit. Therefore have a good plan, pace yourself and take breaks. Disney rents Electric Conveyance Vehicles (ECVs) and extra-wide wheelchairs at its theme parks and at Downtown Disney. EVCs often sell out early on crowded days.

Lap-bar rides. Many rides have lap-bar restraints a guest controls by pulling down until the lap bar fits snugly. When two people share a restraint, an obese person should not share a seat with a small or skinny person. The lap bar will stop and lock based on the large tummy, leaving the smaller person relatively unrestrained.

Recreation. *Epcot's DiveQuest:* Disney supplies wetsuits for guests scuba diving at the Seas with Nemo & Friends; wetsuits are available up to size 5X. *Horseback riding:* The weight limit at Fort Wilderness Resort is 250 pounds. *Parasailing:* Guests taking flight at Disney's Contemporary Resort should weigh no more than 330 pounds.

Restaurants. Many Disney eateries use chairs with armrests, which can prove problematic for obese guests. Hostesses can usually supply chairs without arms.

Seatbelt rides. Pull the seat belt out all the way before sitting down. Hold it out while you sit, then fasten the buckle. Ask a family member to help attach the buckle if needed. Disney cast members aren't allowed to help anyone who struggles to buckle belts.

Shopping. Many shops sell large-sized Disney T-shirts, up to 3X. The three stores with the most variety are the Emporium at Magic Kingdom, MouseGear at Epcot and World of Disney at Downtown Disney. These stores commonly stock T-shirts, sweatshirts and jackets in sizes up to 4X and sometimes 5X. For details contact Disney Merchandise at 800-328-0368.

Spas. The Grand Floridian and Saratoga Springs spas supply robes in sizes up to 5X.

A dog "VIP Suite" at the Best Friends Pet Care Resort, a third-party kennel at Disney. The 226-square-foot space includes an elevated bed, a flat-screen TV that shows movies such as "Lady and the Tramp," and a small outdoor patio.

Theater seats. For attractions with arm-rests, obese guests may find it easier to sit on the front edge of a seat and then slide back, or sit sideways and then turn to squeeze in. Some theaters have narrow seats; the narrowest are those at Epcot's France pavilion.

Water parks. The weight limit to ride the Blizzard Beach chair lift is 375 pounds.

The independent website allearsnet.com has a terrific section for obese guests. Search "WDW at Large" and "At Large" trip reports.

Parking. Disney charges a fee for most visitors to park at its theme parks. Daily rates are $17 for cars, motorcycles or taxis; $18 for campers; $21 for buses and tractor-trailers. The fee allows self-parking at all four park lots for that day. Disney resort hotel guests and annual passholders don't pay to park. If you are a Tables in Wonderland cardholder you can park free, too; you receive a parking refund at a Guest Relations location with a table-service dining receipt.

Except for Magic Kingdom, all theme-park parking is just outside the main entrance to its park. At Magic Kingdom, the lot is located at the Transportation and Ticket Center; after parking guests then take either a monorail or a ferry to the Magic Kingdom, which is a mile away.

Parking is free at Disney water parks and Downtown Disney. Most parking is complimentary at the ESPN Wide World of Sports complex, though premium spots may cost $5.

Hotel parking. Disney-owned resort hotels offer complimentary parking if you are staying there or coming to shop or dine. Shades of Green charges $5 for parking, the Walt Disney World Swan and Dolphin Resort charges $16 for overnight self-parking, $26 for overnight valet parking, $10 per exit for day self-parking, $15 per exit for day valet parking. Valet parking is offered at all Disney Deluxe Resorts and Downtown Disney; the fee is $20 daily, not including gratuity. You can use your hangtag to valet park at any other Disney resort (except for gratuity) for no additional charge. Valet parking is complimentary for Tables in Wonderland cardholders with dining reservations and guests with a current handicap license plate or tag.

Pets. Bringing Spot or Fluffy with you to Disney? You have a few options for pet care.

At Disney resorts. Campers at Disney's Fort Wilderness Resort & Campground may keep their pet with them for $5 per day at select locations. Other Disney resort hotels permit service animals, but not pets.

Best Friends Pet Care Kennel. Located on Disney property across from the Port Orleans Resorts, this 50,000-square-foot facility is well maintained and lets dog owners spend time with their pet unleashed in a grassy backyard that has a water-play area. Billing itself as a "luxury pet resort," Best Friends refers to many of its 200-plus spaces as "suites" and "condos" since they are divided into multiple spaces, even though many are no larger than a cage. Some spots include controlled access to small outdoor areas. Dog facilities also include 14 "vacation villas" (6-feet by 7-foot rooms with raised bedding and flat-screen televisions) and four larger rooms marketed as "VIP suites." All dogs and cats must be at least 4 months old.

Birds are housed in an area with hamsters, guinea pigs, rabbits, ferrets and other pocket pets (owners supply cages, supplies and food). No primates or venomous pets are allowed.

Disney PhotoPass photographers take posed pictures of guests throughout Disney property without the guests making any commitment to buy them. Guests pay only for images they choose.

Optional services include daytime boarding; activities such as nature walks, grooming and playgroups; and pampering such as ice-cream treats and bedtime stories. (Dogs: overnight $41–$89, daycare $34–$89; optional services $5–$22. Cats: overnight $28–$40, daycare $26–$35; optional services $3–$8. Small animals: overnight $11–$25. Across from Disney's Port Orleans Resort at 2510 Bonnet Creek Parkway, Lake Buena Vista 32830; 407-209-3126; wdw.bestfriendspetcare.com).

Bass Pet Resort. Check out this quality kennel for a less-expensive alternative to Best Friends. It's where the authors board their dog. (Dogs: overnight $23 and up, daycare $14 and up. Cats: overnight $13 and up. A short drive from Disney property off Highway 192 at 1043 S Bass Rd, Kissimmee 34746; 407-396-6031; www.basspetmotel.com).

Laws. It's illegal to leave a pet in a car in Florida with the windows up; the heat makes it dangerous for the animal, as temperatures can rise to unbearable degrees quickly.

Photography. Whether it's one in your phone or a fancy DSLR, a camera can capture spontaneous moments that create treasured memories. Consider giving your children their own cameras and perhaps bringing waterproof models for swimming pools and water parks. Whatever shots you snap, take turns being the photographer; if mom takes all the pictures none will include mom.

Nikon picture spots. Disney partnered with Nikon when Kodak filed for bankruptcy in 2012. Now all its theme-park "Picture Spots" have Nikon's name and logo. These locations offer photogenic, iconic backdrops for your shot, such as Magic Kingdom's Cinderella Castle or Epcot's Spaceship Earth.

Photographic services. Disney offers various photo services in its parks, hotels, restaurants and at Downtown Disney:

Makeover salons. Some packages at the Bibbidi Bobbidi Boutique salons and Pirates League include photos (407-939-7895). See also **Children**

PhotoPass. With this service Disney photographers take shots of your group throughout Disney World, but you pay for only those images you choose, if any. Photographers are stationed many places, including most theme-park icons and character spots, ready to link images of your group to a free credit-card-size PhotoPass card or to your MagicBand. You can view and purchase each shot at park Camera Centers or online, up to 45 days from when it was taken.

PhotoPass is not a replacement for taking your own photos, as photographers shoot only posed shots at specific locations. Besides, any Disney cast member will always take a photo of your group with your own camera free of charge (a courtesy that Disney does not publicize). If you do use the PhotoPass service, write down your card's 16-digit ID number and save it—if you lose your card you won't lose track of your images (single downloads $15, Memory Maker unlimited photo package $149 if arranged in advance, Archive Disc $169; 407-560-4300; disneyphotopass.com).

Disney Fine Art Photography & Video. Disney offers professional-quality packaged portrait sessions. Guests choose locations, themes and wardrobe, then pose at picturesque settings. Sessions last 20 minutes to an hour, and include a disc with 60 to 100 images. (Sessions: $150–$350; print packages: $75–$285; book up to 30 days in advance; 407-934-4004; disneyeventphotography.com/portraits).

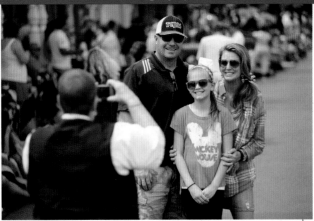

Any Disney cast member will take your photo with your camera free of charge. Here, a Guest Relations staffer takes a shot of a family as it waits for a Magic Kingdom parade.

Restaurant souvenir photos. Diners at the following locations can purchase photos taken tableside or before entering the dining area: Chef Mickey's (Contemporary Resort), Cinderella's Royal Table (Cinderella Castle, Magic Kingdom, photo charges included in meal price), Hoop-Dee-Doo Revue Dinner Show and Mickey's Backyard Barbecue (Fort Wilderness Resort & Campground), 'Ohana (Polynesian Resort), Planet Hollywood (Downtown Disney), Princess Storybook Dining (Akershus, Norway pavilion, Epcot, photo charges included in meal price), Spirit of Aloha Dinner Show (Polynesian Resort).

Thrill-ride souvenirs. On some rides an automated camera takes a photo of you on the attraction then an exitway gift shop offers it to you either as a print or digital download. Prints are approximately $20; digital images are included on the Memory Maker package and the Disney PhotoPass Archive Disc (see above). *Magic Kingdom:* Buzz Lightyear's Space Ranger Spin, Space Mountain, Splash Mountain. *Epcot:* Test Track. *Disney's Hollywood Studios:* Rock 'n' Roller Coaster Starring Aerosmith, The Twilight Zone Tower of Terror. *Disney's Animal Kingdom:* Dinosaur, Expedition Everest.

Pin trading. In 1999 Disney World began the tradition of collectible-pin trading. Many visitors exchange pins with each other, but most trading is between guests and cast members who wear pin-filled lanyards; those with green lanyards only trade with kids. Each park sells pins, which range from $8 to $35.

Postal services. Access to the U.S. Postal Service is available throughout Walt Disney World and the surrounding area.

Sending mail. *Magic Kingdom:* Station Break, Main Street U.S.A. train station. Guests can drop stamped mail in old-fashioned Main Street letter boxes (postmarks read "Lake Buena Vista" not "Walt Disney World"). *Epcot:* Camera Center, Spaceship Earth, Future World; also in front of the American Adventure pavilion in the World Showcase. *Disney's Hollywood Studios:* Oscar's Super Service, entrance plaza. *Disney's Animal Kingdom:* Garden Gate Gifts, entrance plaza. *Nearby U.S. Post Offices:* Celebration: 610 Market Street, downtown, 407-566-1145, 9 a.m.–4 p.m., Saturday 8:30 a.m.–2 p.m. Full-service facility. See other area post offices at 800-275-8777, usps.com.

Stamps. *Magic Kingdom:* Newsstand, entrance plaza. *Epcot:* Camera Center, under Spaceship Earth. *Disney's Hollywood Studios:* Oscar's Super Service, entrance plaza. *Disney's Animal Kingdom:* Garden Gate Gifts, entrance plaza. *Disney hotels:* Main gift shops. *Downtown Disney:* Guest Services, Marketplace. *Outside Disney:* U.S. Post Offices (see above).

Receiving mail. *Disney resort hotels:* You can receive letters, packages and postcards if you are staying at any Disney resort. Mail should include your arrival date if the item will be received before you check-in. *Non-Disney hotels:* Nearly all convention hotels in the area accept mail for guests, as do some other properties. Contact the particular hotel. *General Delivery:* You can receive mail care of General Delivery at most major post offices. You must first complete an application in person and show two forms of ID and a temporary local address. The application is valid for 30 days. Mail is held for up to 15 days.

See also **Shipping.**

Most of Disney's most popular attractions have indoor waiting lines, which are heavily decorated, such as this one for Toy Story Mania. Some have interactive elements.

Pregnant visitors. If you are an expectant mom, Walt Disney World can be a fun and safe place. Although roller coasters are off limits, there are numerous character greetings, fireworks, parades, shows, swimming pools and gentle rides that are easy for moms-to-be to enjoy. Of course, you should check with your doctor first, heed Disney's advisories and use common sense.

Attractions to avoid. You should consider avoiding rides that have sudden stops or drops, rough motion, spinning or require significant exertion. At Magic Kingdom, avoid Astro Orbiter, The Barnstormer, Big Thunder Mountain Railroad, Mad Tea Party, Seven Dwarfs Mine Train, Space Mountain, Splash Mountain, Swiss Family Treehouse (lots of steps) and Tomorrowland Speedway. At Epcot, skip Mission Space, Sum of all Thrills (an Innoventions exhibit) and Test Track. At Disney's Hollywood Studios stay away from Rock 'n' Roller Coaster, Star Tours and Twilight Zone Tower of Terror. At Disney's Animal Kingdom, avoid Dinosaur, Expedition Everest, Kali River Rapids, Primeval Whirl and Kilimanjaro Safaris (the bumpy ride is smoothest for those who sit in the front row). At Disney's water parks, don't ride any slides, and stay out of Typhoon Lagoon's wave pool when the big waves are in effect.

Water. It's important for everyone to stay hydrated while outdoors in Florida, but even more vital for expectant moms. You can bring water into Disney World theme parks (though not in glass containers or rolling coolers) and get free ice water (on request) from any counter-service restaurant. Water fountains dot each park.

Snacks. To ward off morning sickness, carry some light snacks, such as granola bars, crackers or fruit. It's fine to bring in food to a theme park as long as there are no glass containers. Each park has a variety of snack stands, some of which sell fresh fruit.

Baby Care Centers. All theme parks have Baby Care Centers which serve pregnant guests. Quiet air-conditioned spots offer a relaxing way to get off your swollen feet.

See also **Children's Services.**

Disney resort hotels. Staying at a hotel on Disney property—especially one on the monorail loop—will make it more convenient for you to return to your room for an afternoon rest. Housekeeping can provide extra pillows for additional support. Many Disney resorts have great swimming pools, a fact which can be especially important if you are pregnant; the buoyancy of the water can help take strain off your aching back.

Shopping. A few park stores carry unique (and usually high quality) infant apparel and other merchandise. *Magic Kingdom:* The Emporium, Hundred Acre Goods. *Epcot:* MouseGear, Showcase Station East Port. World Showcase has some hard-to-find goodies such as Steiff teddy bears (Germany pavilion) and puffin plushies (Norway pavilion). *Disney's Hollywood Studios:* L.A. Cinema Storage, Stage 1 Co. Store. *Disney's Animal Kingdom:* Creature Comforts.

Queues. One of the big down sides to Walt Disney World is that you commonly have to wait in line for attractions. This is because the number of people who can experience its rides and shows at any one time is far less than the number of people Disney allows in its theme parks. For example, the total capacity of the rides and shows at Magic Kingdom is about 9,750, though on average that park

When attraction lines get long, they often extend down nearby walkways with no protection from the weather and nothing for guests to do. Lines for the new Seven Dwarfs Mine Train can force guests to wait outside for more than an hour.

contains about 30,000 guests and can hold at least twice that many.

Wait times. A sign at each attraction displays its current wait time. At many rides, an easy way to avoid that wait is to use Disney's Fastpass+ reservation system, which is completely free of charge. In this book's theme-park chapters, the average wait time for each attraction appears at the bottom of that attraction's page.

See also **Children's Services;** also **Fastpass+** in this book's opening, **A World of Its Own.**

Single Rider lines. Three attractions have a third entrance. If you don't mind experiencing a ride by yourself, this Single Rider line is an easy way to lessen the time you have to wait. During peak periods, using it can cut your wait time by at least 30 minutes. You'll find a Single Rider line at Test Track in Epcot; Rock 'n' Roller Coaster Starring Aerosmith at Disney's Hollywood Studios; and Expedition Everest at Disney's Animal Kingdom. There's also one at the Blizzard Beach chair lift, which offers a speedy way up to that water park's main body and mat slides.

How they work. When ride operators can't fill a vehicle from the regular line without breaking up a group, they take a guest from a Single Rider line. Groups can wait in that line together but will be split up. Riders cannot specify where they sit.

Quinceañera celebrations. Walt Disney World offers Latina families ways to celebrate their daughters turning 15 with Quinceañera parties. Prices vary (321-939-4555).

Refurbishments and rehabs. For operational updates call 407-824-4321 or check online at disneyworld.com.

Restaurant policies. Disney-operated restaurants share many policies and procedures.

Children's meals. Available throughout Disney theme parks and hotels, Disney Kids' Picks meals come with unsweetened applesauce, baby carrots or fresh fruit (your choice of two) and a beverage of low-fat milk, juice or water (french fries, a cookie and soft drinks can be substituted). Less than 35 percent of a Kids' Picks meal's calories come from fat.

Discounts. The Tables in Wonderland discount card ($75–$100 annually, available to annual passholders and Florida residents only, 407-566-5858, weekdays 9 a.m. to 5 p.m.) saves its holder and up to nine guests 20 percent off food and beverage during non-holiday periods at most Disney table-service restaurants, Value Resort food courts and some other spots. An 18 percent gratuity is added.

Annual passholders typically save 10–20 percent off lunch or dinner at these locations: *Magic Kingdom:* Tomorrowland Terrace. *Epcot:* Biergarten, Nine Dragons, Restaurant Marrakesh, San Angel Inn, Teppan Edo, Tokyo Dining, Tutto Italia. *Disney's Hollywood Studios:* Disney's Hollywood & Vine. *Disney's Animal Kingdom:* Rainforest Café, Yak & Yeti. *Downtown Disney:* Ghirardelli Soda Fountain, House of Blues, Paradiso 37, Planet Hollywood, Portobello Trattoria, Rainforest Café, T-REX Café, Wolfgang Puck Café. *Disney resorts:* Sanaa (Animal Kingdom Lodge), ESPN Club (BoardWalk), The Wave (Contemporary), Trail's End (Fort Wilderness), Grand Floridian Café (Grand Floridian), Olivia's Café (Old Key West), Turf Club (Saratoga Springs), Whispering Canyon Café (Wilderness Lodge) and Captain's Grille (Yacht & Beach Club). *Other locations:* Sand Trap Bar and Grill (Osprey Ridge Golf Club).

Known as the "World's Largest Orange," Eli's Orange World sells and ships fresh Florida citrus. It's just a few miles south of Walt Disney World on U.S. 192.

The Disney World website (disneyworld.com) often offers dining deals under a "Special Offers" link on its home page.

Dress codes. Most Disney restaurants have a casual dress code equal to that of the theme parks. With the exceptions of Cinderella's Royal Table, the Hollywood Brown Derby and Le Cellier, all Disney Signature Restaurants have a business casual dress code. For men, that means jeans, dress shorts, dress slacks or trousers; and a shirt with a collar or T-shirt underneath. Women are required to wear jeans, dress shorts or a skirt with a blouse or sweater, or a dress. Not permitted: Cut-offs, men's caps or hats, swimsuits, swimsuit cover-ups, tank tops or torn clothing. Victoria & Albert's requires jackets for men and dresses or dressy pants suits for women.

Gastric-bypass surgery guests. These guests can present a weight-loss-surgery card (issued by their doctor or hospital) to a server to pay the child price for an adult meal at buffets, or to possibly order from a kids menu at non-buffet meals.

Gratuities. Disney adds an automatic 18 percent gratuity to dining bills for parties of 8 or more. In general, tip 15–20 percent for good service; 10 percent for mediocre.

Reservations. Having a dining reservation is often a must at Disney, even for restaurants in your hotel. The best eateries often book to capacity far in advance, especially for popular dining times. During peak periods many don't accept walk-up diners regardless of how long a guest is willing to wait.

Reservations can be made up to 180 days in advance (190 days for Disney resort guests) at 407-939-3463 or at disneyworld.com as well as at most restaurant check-in counters and resort concierge desks. Dinner shows and dining at Cinderella's Royal Table require payment up front; refunds are possible if bookings are cancelled 24 hours in advance. Other Disney character meals and Disney Signature restaurants charge a $10 per person cancellation fee if the reservation isn't cancelled 24 hours in advance. Reservations for parties of 13 or more always require a credit card.

Plan to arrive at least 5 minutes before your reservation time. Your party will be seated at the next available table that can accommodate it. Most Disney restaurants will hold your reservation for 15 minutes.

Cinderella's Royal Table inside Magic Kingdom's Cinderella Castle is the toughest reservation to nab. It often books in full on the first day of availability. Other hot spots: California Grill and Chef Mickey's (Contemporary Resort), Le Cellier (Epcot) and Victoria & Albert's (Grand Floridian Resort). The most popular reservation time is 7 to 8 p.m. To eat during that hour book your table at least a week early, especially for a party of six or more.

Special diets. No-sugar, low-fat, low-sodium, vegetarian or vegan diets can be met at table-service restaurants by telling a reservation clerk, host or server. Dinner shows need 24 hours notice.

With three days notice, Disney restaurants accommodate dietary needs such as allergies to gluten or wheat, shellfish, soy, lactose or milk, peanuts, tree nuts, fish or eggs. Many counter-service restaurants offer gluten-free, low-fat and vegetarian options. No Disney restaurant serves food with added trans fats or partially hydrogenated oils.

Glatt kosher meals are available at most full-service restaurants with 24 hours notice

The upscale Mall of Millenia includes Ann Taylor, Apple, Bloomingdale's, Gap, Juicy Couture and other stores. It's 16 miles from Disney just off Interstate 4.

Tom Hurst, tomhurstphoto.com

at 407-939-3463. Requests require a credit-card guarantee and have a 24-hour cancellation policy. Kosher fast-food is always available—without notice—at Cosmic Ray's Starlight Café (Magic Kingdom), Liberty Inn (Epcot), ABC Commissary (Hollywood Studios), Pizzafari (Animal Kingdom) and the food courts at the All-Star, Caribbean Beach, Pop Century and Port Orleans Riverside resorts. Disney's kosher food is prepared in Miami.

Shipping. You can ship items either from Disney or from nearby shipping centers.

At Disney hotels. Ask the front desk or concierge for instructions. Some resorts have a business center or desk with shipping supplies. Expect to pay a handling fee.

Shipping luggage to a hotel can often be cheaper than checking it as airline baggage. Send packages in enough time so they arrive a couple of days early; use FedEx or UPS for the most reliable service. To be sure the hotel will hold your package until your arrival, address the shipping label as follows:

Guest's name (same as on reservation)
c/o Name of hotel
Hold for guest arrival on (date)
Reservation (number)
Hotel street address
City, FL Zip Code

At Disney theme parks. Package Pickup at each theme park can deliver purchases made in that park to any Disney-owned resort hotel or, via UPS or FedEx, any domestic or international address.

At Downtown Disney. Stores can deliver purchases to Disney resorts or ship them elsewhere via UPS or FedEx.

Key FedEx and UPS locations. FedEx and UPS offices dot the area between the Orlando International Airport and Walt Disney World. Here are three:

Closest FedEx to Disney. Near Downtown Disney, open 24 hours (12181 South Apopka Vineland 32836; 407-465-0085).

FedEx with latest hours. At the Orlando International Airport, open to 8:30 p.m. Monday–Friday (10445 Tradeport Drive 32827; 855-596-6421).

Closest UPS Store to Disney. Behind the Orlando Premium Outlet Mall, 8 a.m.–7 p.m. Monday–Friday, 9 a.m.–5 p.m. Saturday, noon–5 p.m. Sunday (8131 Vineland Avenue 32821; 407-465-1700).

See also **Postal Services.**

Shopping. Walt Disney World has hundreds of stores, selling everything from hand-rolled cigars to the largest selection of Mickey Mouse merchandise in the world. Non-Disney apparel is sold at Downtown Disney, Disney Deluxe resorts, Epcot's World Showcase and at water parks. Ralph Lauren men's dress shirts are sold at the Commander's Porter shop at Disney's Grand Floridian Resort (9 a.m.–10 p.m.). To order Disney merchandise over the phone call 800-328-0368, online visit disneystore.com.

Disney return policy. Disney-owned stores will accept returns on merchandise within 90 days of purchase with a valid receipt. Items that cannot be returned include those marked "as is" or "all sales final," original artwork, fine jewelry and special orders. If you return an item without a receipt you'll receive credit based on the item's selling price at the time of the return. Some stores on Disney property—including many in Epcot's World Showcase and at Downtown Disney—are not run by Disney;

Micaela Neal

A storm trooper escorts a girl and her brother down one of the Streets of America during a Star Wars weekend at Disney's Hollywood Studios. The springtime events draw devoted Star Wars fans.

return policies at these shops vary. In most cases, Disney Stores across the U.S. accept returns of items bought at Disney-owned Disney World stores with a valid receipt.

Nearby retailers. *Apple Store:* Mall at Millenia, 4200 Conroy Road 32839; 16 miles from Disney, 407-241-5400. *Barnes & Noble:* 7900 West Sand Lake Road 32819, 7 miles from Disney. 407-345-0900. *Best Buy:* 4155 Millenia Boulevard 32839; 16 miles from Disney. 407-248-2439. *Eli's Orange World:* 5395 W. Irlo Bronson Memorial Highway (U.S. 192) 34746; 3 miles from Disney. 800-531-3182. *Orlando Premium Outlet Mall:* 8200 Vineland Avenue 32821 at I-4 exit 68; 5 miles from Disney. 407-238-7787. *Target:* 4750 Millenia Plaza Way 32839; 16 miles from Disney. 407-541-0019.

Smoking. Florida law requires that all restaurants in the state be smoke-free. Smoking is allowed in freestanding bars that earn less than 10 percent of their income from food.

Disney theme parks have designated smoking areas. All Disney hotel rooms, balconies and patios are smoke-free (a $250–$500 "room recovery fee" is charged to guests who smoke); smoking is permitted at Fort Wilderness campsites and on cabin porches. All shops are non-smoking except Downtown Disney's cigar shop. No tobacco products are sold in the parks, but are available (but not displayed) at hotel gift shops and Downtown Disney. Hess stations sell them openly.

Spas. Disney has three full-service spas. All offer aromatherapy, boutique products, exercise facilities, facials, manicures and pedicures, massages and both adult, couple and child services. Robes and slippers are provided for body treatments.

Mandara Spa. Located at the Walt Disney World Dolphin, this Asian-inspired spa has two indoor gardens. Signature services include cellulite reduction treatments and stone therapies (407-934-4772).

Senses Spa. Located at the Grand Floridian hotel, this spa offers a massage followed by a cocoon-like body wrap, an age-defying lavender facial and a pedicure with a hot stone massage that uses honey lavender botanical oils. A second Senses at Disney's Saratoga Springs offers bamboo fusion massages, blueberry facials and a pedicure with a blueberry sugar scrub, hydrating masque and warm paraffin treatment (407-939-7727).

Special events. Disney holds unique parties, weekends and festivals year-round.

Epcot International Flower & Garden Festival. Disney's most elaborate one-park event, this 75-day garden party includes seminars, demonstrations and celebrity guest speakers, as well as character topiaries, a butterfly house with a live caterpillar and chrysalis exhibit and 30 million flowers. Themed weekends celebrate art, insects and Mother's Day. Weekend concerts feature 1960s and 1970s "Flower Power" acts. Vendor booths line walkways. *March 4–May 17. Included in park admission. 407-934-7639.*

St. Patrick's Day. Special events mark this Irish holiday at two Disney locations: the Raglan Road restaurant at Downtown Disney and the United Kingdom pavilion at Epcot's World Showcase. *March 17. Epcot events included in park admission.*

Easter Weekend. Outfitted in colorful homemade gowns, the Azalea Trail Maids from Mobile, Alabama, greet guests at Magic Kingdom and lead its Easter Day parade. At

© Disney

Character topiaries dot the walkways of Epcot during that park's International Flower and Garden Festival. Thirty million flowers decorate both Future World and the World Showcase.

Epcot, children hunt for Easter eggs. Some Disney hotels offer egg decorating, egg hunts and characters in Easter costumes. *April 4–5. Park events included in park admission.*

Star Wars Weekends. This Hollywood Studios fan-fest includes celebrity motorcades, Q&A and autograph sessions (Mark Hamill appeared in 2014), roving characters and unique merchandise. Some guests wear costumes. Get there when the park opens to take advantage of all the activities and be greeted at the entrance by wisecracking stormtroopers. *May 17–June 7. Included in park admission. Details at 407-827-2799.*

Gay Days. Tens of thousands of gay adults congregate at Disney during the first week in June; many wear red shirts in solidarity. Groups gather at each park on a particular day. Disney does not sponsor the event but subtly condones it; in 2014 its bakery cases offered rainbow-colored cupcakes. *June 2–8. Details at gaydays.com or 407-896-8431.*

Car Masters Weekend. The Central Florida Muscle Car Network displays more than 100 classic and exotic vehicles at this Downtown Disney event. Cars compete in a judged show; visitors vote for People's Choice and Kid's Choice winners. Guests can meet "Cars" stars Lightning McQueen and Mater. "Cars" movie marathons, DJ dance parties, face painting. *Early June. No charge.*

Sounds Like Summer Concert Series. Cover bands perform tunes from Elton John, The Supremes, others. Three shows nightly at Epcot's America Gardens amphitheater. *June–August. Included in park admission.*

Independence Day Weekend. A spectacular Magic Kingdom fireworks show surrounds guests watching from Main Street U.S.A. Disney's Hollywood Studios has

fireworks too. Historic characters share their stories at Epcot's American Adventure pavilion. *July 3–5. Included in park admission.*

Night of Joy. Live concerts by many Contemporary Christian artists highlight this Magic Kingdom event. Most rides are open. *Early September. $59 one night; $108 two nights. Details at nightofjoy.com.*

Epcot International Food & Wine Festival. This two-month festival celebrates international food and drink. More than two dozen World Showcase booths sell small portions of ethnic and regional dishes. Each booth typically offers three food items and an alcoholic beverage. Events include cooking demonstrations, pricey dinners and wine seminars. Free "Eat to the Beat" concerts feature vintage pop acts such as Rick Springfield and Wilson Phillips. *Sept. 19–Nov. 10. Included in park admission. Details at disneyworld. com/foodandwine or 407-939-3378.*

Festival of the Masters. This Downtown Disney open-air festival features over 100 artists, each of whom has won a primary award at a juried art show within the past three years. Self-taught creators are at the adjacent House of Blues folk-art festival. Cirque du Soleil artists perform in front of their theater each afternoon. Chalk artists cover 6,000 square feet at the Marketplace. Held annually since 1975. *Details at festivalofthe-masters.com. November 7–9. No charge.*

New Year's Eve. Magic Kingdom, Epcot and Disney's Hollywood Studios ring in the new year with special fireworks, complimentary party hats and noise makers. Downtown Disney has special-ticket events at DisneyQuest and Splitsville. Many restaurants have special menus. *December 30-31. Park events included in regular admission.*

© Disney

Mickey's Not-So-Scary Halloween Party

One of Walt Disney World's most festive events, Mickey's Not-So-Scary Halloween Party is perfect for children, teens, young adults… people of any age who can appreciate clean campy fun. Focused on Disney themes such as "The Nightmare Before Christmas" and The Haunted Mansion, the Magic Kingdom bash includes a lively parade, a spooky fireworks show, two joyous dance parties and many fun character meet-and-greets. Dressed as candy makers, cast members hand out candy throughout the park.

Attendance is limited to no more than 25,000 people—a third of Magic Kingdom's capacity. Though most of the park's rides are open, few of them have long lines, and nothing is very crowded except the first parade and some of the character-greeting spots, as many characters are wearing Halloween costumes themselves or aren't seen at other times of the year.

Dates. The parties are held several nights a week throughout September and October. Each one runs from 7 p.m. until midnight.

Tickets. Adults $62–$77, children ages 3–9 $57–$72 (parties closest to Halloween cost more), children under age 3 admitted free of charge. Nontransferable, nonrefundable. $6 advance-purchase discount often available, small discounts for annual passholders and Disney Vacation Club timeshare owners. Not included in any other

A jack-o'-lantern leader of the Main Street marching band, the party's exclusive Boo To You Halloween parade, Cruella de Vil performs in a stage show at Cinderella Castle, a ghostly cast member at the Haunted Mansion

Disney ticket. Available at 407-939-5277, disneyworld.com, Walt Disney World Guest Relations, Guest Services and Ticketing locations. Prices here are for 2014.

Tips. If you go to one of the parties there are four key things you should know:

When to buy your tickets. Early. Especially for a party on a weekend night in October. Those sell out.

What to wear. A costume. Many people do, adults as well as children. Young adults and families often go all out. Many outfits are homemade and elaborate; some are bizarre. Once the author spotted a group of younger men dressed as masculine versions of Disney princesses, then a group of older men who had transformed themselves into dolls from It's a Small World.

When to arrive. At 4 p.m, as early as your ticket will let you in. You'll have three extra hours to explore Magic Kingdom at no extra charge. Some partygoers come early just to get in line to meet popular characters such as Jack and Sally or the Seven Dwarfs, each of whose lines start to form about 5:30 p.m. Once the party begins, the wait to meet these stars can be two or three hours.

How long to stay. Until midnight. The party really picks up after the fireworks show, as much of the crowd leaves. Lines for rides then dwindle down to nothing, and good viewing spots for the second parade are easy to find even right before it starts. During the last hour of the party, cast members handing out candy get more generous and the character dance parties get more fun, as teens and young adults show up as well as families.

Friends dressed as Giselle and Raggedy Ann with the park's Anastasia, the Evil Queen with friends and apple, two women as pirate Pluto and Mickey, a family dressed as participants in Spain's Running of the Bulls

Christmas

Even the most diehard Scrooge will warm up to Disney in November and December. Most theme parks offers special entertainment, and elaborate holiday decor seems to be everywhere.

Magic Kingdom. Hands down this park has the most Christmas spirit; its Main Street U.S.A. decorations are so iconically American you'll swear they're straight from your childhood. Santa Claus appears just inside the entrance. At night, Cinderella Castle glows from what appear to be thousands of icicles.

Epcot. Forget Future World— Disney never knows what to do with the idea of Christmas in the future, so it never does anything— the holiday mood at Epcot is all at World Showcase. Each pavilion has at least one holiday storyteller; most are excellent. The American Adventure pavilion also hosts the Candlelight Processional, a first-rate retelling of the birth of Jesus.

Disney's Hollywood Studios. The front of the park relives an Old Hollywood Christmas, with tinsel-heavy decorations and witty Citizens of Hollywood sketches. The back holds Disney World's best Christmas attraction, the Osborne Family Spectacle of Dancing Lights.

Disney's Animal Kingdom. There's not much spirit here, though some characters wear seasonal outfits.

Mickey's Very Merry Christmas Party. On many evenings Magic Kingdom hosts this festive "hard-ticket event," which is worth its extra cost. There's a lot to see and do, including exclusive shows and parades, a Christmas-themed

At Magic Kingdom: Main Street U.S.A., Mickey and Minnie star in a "Celebrate the Season" stage show, toy soldiers march in the park's Christmas parade, tap-dancing singers perform in a morning trolley show

fireworks display, two character dance parties and over two dozen character meet-and-greets. Many regular park attractions are also open, and Disney hands out complimentary hot chocolate and cookies throughout the park. Attendance is limited to 25,000 people.

Dates. November 7 through December 16 (for 2014). Each party runs from 7 p.m. until midnight.

Tickets. Adults $67–$71, children ages 3–9 $62–$66 (parties closest to Christmas cost more) for tickets bought in advance, children under age 3 admitted free (prices for 2014). Same-day tickets up to $9 more. Nontransferable, nonrefundable. Small discounts for annual passholders and Disney Vacation Club members. Not included in any other Disney ticket. Available at 407-939-5277; disneyworld.com; Guest Relations, Guest Services and Ticketing locations.

Tips. *When to buy your tickets:* Early. Many parties sell out, sometimes even the first one. *When to arrive:* At 4 p.m. Your party ticket is good at that time, so you'll have three hours to explore the park before the party starts. *How long to stay:* Until midnight. During the last two hours of the party, the lines for its attractions, characters, and complimentary hot chocolate and cookies nearly go away, but the dance parties get more crowded, and therefore more fun. *When to ride Jingle Cruise:* Late, after its lines die down. It's very popular, especially right at 7 p.m.

Note: For the last two weeks in December the party's fireworks, parade and shows become part of the standard Magic Kingdom day, so you can see them without paying extra. But the crowds are awful, so it's harder to enjoy yourself.

Snow falls in Magic Kingdom during Mickey's Very Merry Christmas Party, Neil Patrick Harris hosts an Epcot Candlelight Processional, the Osborne Lights at Hollywood Studios, Santa Goofy at Animal Kingdom

© Disney

For Father's Day your hubby *may* want a new tie... or just might prefer taking a Ferrari, Lamborghini or other exotic car out for a few loops around the Walt Disney World Speedway. Women love getting behind these wheels too.

Sports and recreation. The best choices here: The free campfire and movie at Fort Wilderness, DiveQuest scuba diving, the Winter Summerland miniature golf course, the surfing lessons at Typhoon Lagoon and parasailing behind the Contemporary resort.

Archery. Fort Wilderness offers archery lessons followed by target practice. Children's bows are small; special left-handed bows are available; arrows have rounded tips. Check in at the Bike Barn ($39, 90 minutes, Thursday–Saturday 2:45 p.m. Ages 7 and up. 10 students per class. Reservations taken 90 days in advance at 407-939-7529).

Bicycle and surrey rentals. Nine Disney hotels rent bikes and/or multi-seat surreys: BoardWalk, Caribbean Beach, Coronado Springs, Fort Wilderness, Old Key West, Port Orleans, Saratoga Springs, Wilderness Lodge and Yacht and Beach Club (bikes only) (bicycles: $9 hour, $18 day; surreys $20–$22, 30 minutes).

Boat charters. The Pirates and Pals Fireworks Voyage views Magic Kingdom's Wishes from a pontoon boat hosted by a pirate storyteller. Characters greet you afterward ($59 adults, $34 children 3–9. Friday–Monday, nightly over holidays. Contemporary Resort marina. 407-939-7529). You can charter your own guided pontoon boat to Wishes or IllumiNations with up to 9 friends ($275–$325. 1 hour. Snacks. *Wishes:* Contemporary, Grand Floridian, Polynesian, Wilderness Lodge marinas. *Illuminations:* Yacht Club dock. 407-939-7529) or charter the Grand 1, a 52-foot Sea Ray yacht that cruises Seven Seas Lagoon and Bay Lake ($744 for 1 hour, $1,116 for 90 minutes, $1,488 for 2 hours, up to 18 people. Includes captain, deckhand. Food, butler optional. Grand Floridian marina. 407-824-2682).

Boat rentals. Disney World has the world's largest fleet of rental boats. Boats vary by marina; call 407-939-7529 for details.

Two-seat canoes and kayaks. $6.50 per 30 minutes, $11 per hour.

Two-seat outboards. Sea Raycers. $32 per 30 minutes, $45 per hour. Ages 12–15 may drive with a licensed driver. Minimum height 60 inches. Maximum weight 320 pounds per boat.

Center-console outboards. 17-foot Boston Whaler Montauks, $45 per 30 minutes. Each boat holds up to 6 passengers.

Pedal boats. $6.50 per 30 minutes. The Swan and Dolphin Resort has swan boats at twice the price; $12–$14 per 30 minutes.

Personal watercraft. 3-seat Sea-Doos. Non-guided rides $80 per 30 minutes, $135 per hour. 1-hour morning group rides into Seven Seas Lagoon $135. Maximum 3 riders per vehicle, maximum combined weight 400 pounds. Sammy Duvall's Watersports Centre, Disney's Contemporary Resort.

Pontoon boats. 21-foot SunTrackers, $45 per 30 minutes. 10 passengers maximum.

Sailboats. 12-foot Sunfish $20 per hour, 13-foot Hobie Cats $25 per hour. Operator must be 16 with valid driver's license; renters must be 18. 407-939-0754.

Campfires. Held at a small outdoor amphitheater at Fort Wilderness, Chip 'n Dale's Campfire Sing-a-Long includes a marshmallow roast, 30-minute sing-a-long with the chipmunks (sit on the benches to meet one) and a movie. A snack bar sells s'mores kits, marshmallows and sticks (Free. Schedule: 407-824-2727). Port Orleans Riverside offers a campfire sing-a-long (no movie) seasonally. Other campfire activities are held seasonally at 11 other resorts—Animal Kingdom Lodge Jambo House, Animal Kingdom Lodge

Is your child a fan of the "Cars" movies? If so, here's a perfect birthday present: a "Junior Ride Along" in a real NASCAR-style vehicle that looks like a "Cars" character. It's at the speedway's Richard Petty Driving Experience.

Kidani Village, the Beach Club, BoardWalk, Caribbean Beach, Contemporary, Coronado Springs, Old Key West, Polynesian, Port Orleans French Quarter, Saratoga Springs and Wilderness Lodge.

Carriage and wagon rides. Available at the Fort Wilderness, Port Orleans Riverside and Saratoga Springs resorts, horse-drawn carriages hold four adults or a small family ($45 per carriage. 25 minutes. 5:30–10 p.m., those under 18 must ride with adult; reservations accepted 90 days in advance at 407-939-7529; same-day bookings at 407-824-2832). Fort Wilderness has 32-passenger wagons ($8 adults, $5 children 3–9, under 3 free. 45 minutes. 7 and 9:30 p.m. Firework-view rides available. Pioneer Hall. Children under 11 must ride with adult. Walk-ups only. Group rides with 24 hours notice: 407-824-2734).

Diving and snorkeling. Guests scuba dive in a 5.7-million-gallon saltwater aquarium as part of Disney's DiveQuest experience, held at Epcot's The Seas pavilion. The tank has more than 65 species, including sharks, rays and sea turtles. ($175, 40 minutes in water, 3-hour experience. Includes gear, lockers, showers, mini tour. Park admission not required. Optional video. Up to 12 divers per group. Ages 10 and up; those under 12 must dive with adult. Open-water certification required. 407-939-8687).

The Epcot Seas Aqua Tour puts you in the tank with scuba-assisted snorkel (SAS) equipment ($140, 30 minutes in water, 2.5 hours total. Includes instruction. Park admission not required. Ages 10 and up; under 18 must dive with adult. 407-939-8687). Proceeds from the experiences go to the Disney Worldwide Conservation Fund.

Dolphins in Depth. You'll spend 30 minutes in knee-deep water with Epcot's bottlenose dolphins, learn about their anatomy and behavior and watch biologists do research. Individual instruction; interaction not guaranteed. Proceeds go to the Disney Wildlife Conservation Fund ($194, 3 hours. Includes T-shirt, photo with dolphin, refreshments, use of wetsuit. No swimming. Park admission not required. Ages 13 and up. Those under 18 must be with adult. 407-939-8687).

Exotic car driving. Take six laps around the Walt Disney World Speedway in your choice of a Ferrari, Lamborghini or other exotic sports car at the Exotic Driving Experience, an offshoot of the Richard Petty Driving Experience. An instructor rides with you. Cars available in July 2014 were an Audi R8, two Ferraris (a 430 Scuderia and a 458 Italia), two Lamborghini Gallardos (an LP560-4 and an LP570-4 Superleggera), a Nissan GT-R and a Porsche 997S ($199–$439 depending on vehicle, $39 release fee, minimum age 18, reservations required at 800-237-3889). Don't want to drive? Ride shotgun around the track twice with a pro driver ($99, minimum age 14, no reservations).

Fishing. Catching a fish is almost a certainty at Walt Disney World, as all fishing areas are stocked (with bass, bluegill and catfish), all fish must be released and only a handful of anglers are fishing at any one time.

Guided excursions. Guests routinely catch largemouth bass weighing 2 to 8 pounds on these guided pontoon-boat trips. Most trips catch five to 10 fish; guests average a few fish per hour. Bay Lake and Seven Seas Lagoon are teeming with bass; the largest fish (up to 14 pounds) are in the Crescent and Village lakes ($235–$270 2 hours, $455 4 hours, additional hours $110. Up to 5 guests. Includes bait (shiners additional), guide, equipment,

Mickey and Minnie Mouse cheer on the winner of a recent Princess Half Marathon. Walt Disney World holds many races throughout the year. Most of them wind through its theme parks.

refreshments, digital camera. No license required. Trips on Bay Lake, Seven Seas Lagoon, Crescent Lake, Village Lake and the Coronado Resort's Lago Dorado. Leaves early and mid-morning, early afternoon 407-939-2277. Reservations taken 2 weeks in advance).

Shoreline fishing. At the Fort Wilderness and Port Orleans Riverside resorts (cane poles $4 30 minutes, $9 day, 4–6 pole package $14 30 minutes, $28 a day. Rods $6 30 minutes, $12.50 a day. Bait included. No license required. 7 a.m.–3 p.m. Fort Wilderness: 407-824-2900, Riverside: 407-934-6000).

Golf. Grouped into three facilities, Walt Disney World's five golf courses offer different experiences. There's the long course, the short course, the flat course, the water course, and the child-friendly 9-hole. Home to alligators, deer, egrets, herons, otters and the occasional bald eagle, each course is designated as a wildlife sanctuary by the Audubon Cooperative Sanctuary System. All but the Lake Buena Vista course roam away from civilization. Greens have ultra-dwarf TifEagle Bermuda grass, which offers a true, fast roll. All Disney courses are run by Arnold Palmer Golf Management.

The best months to play are September, April and May, when the weather is nice and good tee times are easy to book. Build extra time into your round, as the pace may be slower than you expect.

Lake Buena Vista course. Disney's least forgiving course has narrow, tree-lined fairways and small greens. Play demands accuracy on tee shots and approaches. Errant shots can hit windows. Signature hole No. 7 has an island green; No. 18 is a 438-yard dogleg to the right. Ten holes have water hazards. You tee off at Disney's Saratoga Springs Resort then weave through Old Key West's lodging areas (Yardage: 5,204–6,802. Par: 72. Course rating: 68.6–73.0. Slope rating: 122–133. Designer: Joe Lee. Year open: 1972. At the Saratoga Springs Resort).

Magnolia course. How's that shoulder turn? It needs to be efficient on this long-game course, a rolling terrain amid more than 1,500 magnolia trees. The Magnolia has elevated tees and greens and 97 bunkers, the most of any Disney course. Greens are quick. Host to the final round of a PGA Tour stop for four decades, it's tested most top-name pros (Yardage: 5,232–7,516. Par: 72. Course rating: 69.4–76.5. Slope rating: 125–140. Designer: Joe Lee. Year open: 1971. Across from Disney's Polynesian Village Resort).

Oak Trail course. A walking course, the 9-hole Oak Trail is nice for a quick nine, getting some practice, or introducing a child to the sport. With small greens and two good par 5s, the course requires accuracy with short irons. The longest hole, the 517-yard No. 5, has a double dogleg. Water hazards cross three fairways. Most greens and tees are elevated. The scorecard lists separate pars for children 11 and under and for those over 12. Golf shoes must be spikeless; tennis shoes are permitted (Yardage: 2,532–2,913. Par: 36. Course rating: 64.6–68.2. Slope rating: 107–123. Designer: Ron Garl. Year open: 1980. Next to Shades of Green, across from Disney's Polynesian Village Resort).

Osprey Ridge course. Set within beautiful rolling terrain, this challenging course winds through dense vegetation, oak forests and moss hammocks. More than 70 bunkers, mounds and a meandering ridge provide obstacles, banking and elevation changes. Some tees and greens are 20 feet above

Children roast marshmallows at a Chip 'n Dale campfire at the Fort Wilderness resort

The authors' daughter about to release a fish she caught on the Seven Seas Lagoon

their fairways. The course often has swirling winds. One bit of relief: fairway waste bunkers have hard sand, so you can play out of one with a more-normal swing (Yardage: 5,402–7,101. Par: 72. Course rating: 69.5–74.4. Slope rating: 123–131. Designer: Tom Fazio. Year open: 1992. Just east of Fort Wilderness).

Palm course. Pretty palms. Ugly hazards. This course has both. Water hazards line seven holes and cross six. Shorter and tighter than the nearby Magnolia, the Palm course has a few long par 4s and a couple of par 5s that can be reached in two using a fairway wood. The large, elevated greens can be maneuvered with good lag putting. Save a sprinkle of pixie dust for hole No. 18; a long par 4 that was rated as high as fourth toughest hole on the PGA Tour. The Palm is rated one of Golf Digest's Top 25 Resort Courses (Yardage: 5,311–6,957. Par: 72. Course rating: 69.5–73.9. Slope rating: 126–138. Designer: Joe Lee. Year open: 1971. Next to Shades of Green, across from Disney's Polynesian Village Resort).

Golf fees and policies. Greens fees: 18-hole courses $55–$195 cart included; 9-hole Oak Trail course $38, $20 for under 18. Proper golf attire required. 18-hole courses have putting greens, driving ranges. Free transportation from Disney-owned resorts. Reservations available 90 days in advance for Disney resort guests, 60 days other players. Cancellations require 48 hours notice. $50 Florida resident Annual Golf Membership saves up to 60 percent on greens fees after 10 a.m. for a member and up to three guests. Additional summer savings. Golf equipment is available for rent, including TaylorMade clubs for men and women ($15–$50). Adidas shoe rental $10 per pair; free for resort guests. Range balls $7 per basket. Oak Trail pull carts $6. 407-939-4653, disneygolf.com.

Golf lessons. Choose from 30-minute tune-ups, 1-hour lessons, half-day or full-day golf schools, video analysis, group lessons, on-course playing lessons, and Callaway and TaylorMade club fittings ($50–$150, 45-minute lesson for a single golfer $75, $50 ages 17 and under. Palm/Magnolia facility. PGA pros give lessons. All ages, skill levels. Individual lessons, clinics: 407-454-5096. Florida-resident Annual Golf Membership saves 20 percent).

Horseback riding. Guides lead small groups down shady pine and palmetto trails at the Fort Wilderness Resort & Campground. Excursions start at the Tri-Circle D Livery at the resort's entrance. Early

Anyone age 12 or older can dive by themselves (or with others, as here the authors' daughter with her friend Samia Islam) into the aquarium inside The Seas pavilion at Epcot, assuming of course she has her open-water certification.

birds see wildlife such as snakes and deer ($46, 45 minutes. Daily starting at 8:30 a.m. Ages 9 and up. Height minimum 48 inches. Maximum weight 250 pounds. Closed-toe shoes required; no sandals or flip-flops. No trotting. Required reservations can be made 30 days in advance at 407-939-7529). Smaller children can take a short pony ride at the resort's petting farm; a parent walks the pony along a path ($5, cash only. Ages 2 and up. Maximum height 45 inches. Maximum weight 80 pounds. 10 a.m.–5 p.m. daily. 407-824-2788).

Marathons. A pair of running events—a 26.2-mile full marathon and a 13.1-mile half marathon—highlight Disney's Marathon Weekend (January 7–11). The full route goes through all four theme parks. Typically more than 30,000 athletes compete. Some runners dress as princesses in the Princess Half Marathon (February 19–22) which winds through Magic Kingdom and Epcot. Other races are also scheduled. Details at rundisney.com or 407-938-3398.

Miniature golf. Two themed complexes on Disney property make it easy to take a break from theme-park activities ($14 adults, $12 children. 10 a.m.–11 p.m. Last tee time 30 minutes before close. Second rounds half-price if same day or next day. In-person same-day reservations accepted. 407-939-7529).

Fantasia Gardens. Across the street from the Walt Disney World Swan and Dolphin, this two-course complex (407-560-4753) is busy at night, when tee-time waits can be an hour. Splashing brooms and dancing-ostrich topiaries line a Gardens course themed to Disney's 1940 movie "Fantasia." A Fairways course replicates real links with long fairways, sandy bunkers, roughs and undulating hills. The Gardens course closes at 10:30 p.m.

Winter Summerland. Next to Blizzard Beach, these two courses (407-560-7161) are often deserted at night. Themed to the activities of elves who, as the story goes, vacation here (Santa bought them the course as a respite from their duties at the North Pole), the courses are dotted with tiny elf trailers and Christmas decor. Getting a hole-in-one is easy, as greens often funnel into cups.

Stock car driving. The engine rumbles with power... you tremble with excitement... then zoom! You put pedal to metal and tear down a race track at over 100 mph in a 630-horsepower stock car. Held at the Walt Disney World Speedway, the Richard Petty Driving Experience gets started with a training session. Then, wearing a driving suit, fire cap and helmet, you climb through the window of a stock car, pop on a steering wheel, strap in and take off. With your car almost always in a turn, you drive with your instructor in the seat beside you. NASCAR-style vehicles have tube frames, huge V-8s, 4-speed manual transmissions and product logos plastered everywhere. The doors don't open; that's why you climb in. Also available: no-training-required 3-lap ride-alongs with a professional driver, with speeds up to 150 mph, for both adults and children ages 6 to 13. Junior ride-alongs take place in one of the two new cars styled to look like the vehicles in the 2006 Disney movie "Cars," Aiken Axler or Sage VanDerSpin. (Drives $449–$2599 for 8–50 laps. Ride-along trips $99 adults, $59 children. 9 a.m.–4 p.m.; gates open at 7:30 a.m.. Drives 3–4 hours, 10–15 minutes driving car. Rides 30 minutes–1 hour, 3 minutes in car. Gift cards available. Drives require reservations, include training. Rides don't require reservations. Adjacent to the Magic

A young woman stands up on her second try while learning to surf early one morning in the Typhoon Lagoon surf pool. Lessons are held just after sunrise, before the park opens to regular guests.

Kingdom parking lot. Must be 18 or older to drive, 6 or older to ride, at least 48 inches tall. One-day Safe Driving Program in May for ages 15 to 25: $329–$399. Spectators welcome. 800-237-3889, 1800bepetty.com).

Surfing lessons. Know how to swim? In good shape? If so, then you are almost guaranteed to learn how to ride the crest of a wave at the Craig Carroll Surfing School. It holds instruction at dawn in the surf pool of Typhoon Lagoon, before the water park opens to the public. Conducted on dry land, a step-by-step introduction teaches you the basics, then you get in the surf pool and attempt to ride wave after wave after wave. After each try, Carroll critiques you from the lifeguard stand and an instructor in the water gives additional advice. Waves average about 5 feet for adults; half that for children.

About 70 percent of all students succeed; females tend to do better. "Girls don't think as hard about it, and try to do exactly what you say," Carroll explains. "Boys tend to think it's a macho thing." ($165. Must be 8 yrs or older, strong swimmer. Most students have never surfed. Days, hours vary with season. 2.5-hour lesson includes 30 minutes on land, 2 hours in water. Surfboards provided. Spectators permitted. Maximum 12 students per class; sessions sell out quickly. Reservations accepted 90 days in advance at 407-939-7873).

Tennis. Disney has 34 lighted courts for recreational use, all at hotels. Use is complimentary for hotel guests, from 8 a.m. to 10 p.m. on a first-come, first-served basis. Courts are at Bay Lake Tower at Disney's Contemporary Resort, Kidani Village at Disney's Animal Kingdom Lodge, BoardWalk Inn and Villas, Old Key West Resort, Saratoga Springs Resort, the Yacht and Beach Club Resorts

and the Walt Disney World Swan and Dolphin. Group and private lessons available at Bay Lake Tower, Kidani Village, BoardWalk, Saratoga Springs and the Yacht and Beach Club Resorts ($90 per hour, 321-228-1146).

Water sports. At Disney's Contemporary Resort at Sammy Duvall's Watersports Centre (407-939-0754). A legendary skier himself, Duvall has won 80 pro championships.

Parasailing. Soaring hundreds of feet above the 450-acre Bay Lake beneath an open parachute, you get a birds-eye view of Walt Disney World. You don't get wet; you take off and land on the boat (single riders $95 for 8–10 minutes at 450 feet; $130 for 10–12 minutes at 600 feet. Tandem riders $170 for 8–10 minutes at 450 feet; $195 for 10–12 minutes at 600 feet. Weight per flight 130–330 pounds).

Other water sports. Kneeboard, wakeboard or go tubing or water-skiing behind a MasterCraft inboard. Friendly instructors are patient, especially with kids (per boat: $85 30 minutes., $165 1 hour, $135 per additional hour; water-skiing approximately $20 additional. Up to 5 skiers. Includes equipment, driver, instruction. Extra charge if picked up from Fort Wilderness, Grand Floridian, Polynesian or Wilderness Lodge).

Taxes. Two types of taxes are relevant to most Disney visitors:

Hotel taxes. All area hotels charge both sales tax and a 6-percent resort tax on rooms.

Sales taxes. Nearly all of Walt Disney World sits in Orange County, where the sales tax rate is 6.5 percent. A portion of Disney property is in Osceola County, which has a sales tax of 7 percent. This area includes Disney's All-Star Resorts and the ESPN Wide World of Sports complex.

A tongue-in-cheek policy sign at the Big Thunder Mountain Railroad roller coaster. Drinking alcohol is actually encouraged at most Disney parks, though often only in restaurants. And whistling is almost always OK.

Telephone services. Although no cell-phone towers stand on Disney property, recent technology from AT&T has greatly enhanced the network experience at the resort. Miniature concealed antennas both indoors and out have greatly boosted cellular coverage. The distributed-antenna system (DAS) is the largest network of its kind in a single location in the world. All Disney parks can still have weak cell-phone service on their most crowded days; reception can be especially spotty before or after parades or fireworks, when usage is at its peak. A particularly bad area is The Seas pavilion in Epcot.

Cell-phone stores. Good locations relatively close to Walt Disney World include:

AT&T. Across from Celebration Avenue on U.S. 192. (6081 West Irlo Bronson Memorial Highway 34747; 407-396-2888. 10 a.m.–9 p.m. Monday–Thursday, 10 a.m.–7 p.m. Friday, 10 a.m.–9 p.m. Saturday, noon–6 p.m. Sunday), 4 miles from Disney.

Sprint. Next to WalMart on a service road alongside Interstate 4 (8910 Turkey Lake Road 32819; 407-351-5155; 10 a.m.–8 p.m. Monday–Friday, 10 a.m.–7 p.m. Saturday, noon–5 p.m. Sunday), 7 miles from Disney.

Verizon Wireless. Near North John Young Parkway at 1340 West Osceola Parkway #101 34741; 407-343-0516; 9 a.m.–9 p.m. Monday–Saturday, 11 a.m.–6 p.m. Sunday, 12 miles from Disney.

Disabled guests. Telecommunications Devices for the Deaf (TDD) are available at Guest Relations offices in the theme parks and Downtown Disney. Many pay phones are equipped with amplifying headsets.

Local calls. Callers must include the area code—"407" for all Disney numbers—in all local calls. It is not necessary to dial "1" first.

Hotels. Area hotels often add a hefty service charge on telephone calls made from a room phone. Check the telephone information card near the room phone for a list of all the costs involved.

Pay phones. Pay telephones are still found in all Walt Disney World theme parks, Downtown Disney and Disney hotels. Local calls, including all calls within Disney property, cost 50 cents.

Prepaid phone cards. Private prepaid phone cards are sold at Disney World gift shops and Guest Relations offices. Outside Disney they're available at convenience stores, supermarkets and pharmacies.

Theme park policies. Walt Disney World has specific policies regarding park closures, dress codes, and what you can—and can't—bring into a theme park, though they aren't heavily publicized and enforcement can vary.

Park closures. During peak periods the parks can fill to capacity and close to additional guests, even to those who have valid tickets. Closures for capacity typically occur only on obviously busy times such as Independence Day and the week between Christmas Eve and New Year's Eve. Disney closes its parks in five distinct phases:

Phase 1. The park stays open to any additional guest who has already purchased a park pass, though Disney stops ticket sales at that location.

Phase 2. Open to only those additional guests who have multi-day park passes or are staying at a Disney-owned resort.

Phase 3. Open to only those additional guests who are using the last day of a multi-day park pass or are staying at a Disney-owned resort.

Despite the "Mary Poppins" song, you can't "Feed the Birds"—or any other animals—on Disney property. Not the exotic wildlife at Animal Kingdom, nor the native Florida creatures that freely roam common areas.

Phase 4. Open to only those additional guests who are staying at a Disney resort.

Phase 5. No additional entry available; the park is at capacity.

Before employing the steps above, occasionally the Magic Kingdom will first close its parking lot to new cars, then stop using Disney transportation (monorail, buses, boats) to shuttle in new guests.

If you are already in a Disney theme park when it closes for capacity, you are not asked to leave. To learn if a Disney theme park is currently closed, call 407-824-2222.

Dress codes. As family-oriented spots, the Disney parks have long had a policy of refusing, or revoking, admission to anyone who its managers deem is inappropriately dressed, especially if another guest complains and the offender refuses suggestions to comply. In the case of an offensive T-shirt, a wearer may simply be asked to turn it inside-out. Other unacceptable attire includes clothing that is too transparent, excessively torn or exposes inappropriate portions of the body (i.e., string bikini tops), and adult clothing that can be viewed as a costume (though costumes are allowed during some special events such as Mickey's Not-So-Scary Halloween Party). Children under age 10 can wear costumes at Disney any day of the year. All visitors must wear shirts and shoes. Women may wear bikini tops if they're covered by other clothing. Guests in formal wedding attire are "discouraged" from entering the parks.

Items allowed in theme parks. You can bring a lot into a Disney World theme park:

Coolers. Those that don't have wheels and are smaller than 24 inches long by 15 inches wide by 18 inches high are OK. (This isn't true at Disney's Animal Kingdom theme park, however, which prohibits all coolers except for those needed for medications.)

Food. You are welcome to bring in any snacks, foods or beverages (except alcoholic) that do not require heating and are not in glass containers.

Medications. You can bring in any necessary medications. Medication coolers may be stored in a locker or at Guest Relations.

Umbrellas. Most any umbrella is allowed.

Items not allowed in theme parks. Just *have* to bring that folding chair? Sorry. Other prohibited items include alcoholic beverages, glass containers (excluding baby food jars and perfume bottles), oversized items (strollers larger than 36-by-51 inches; backpacks or coolers larger than 24-by-15-by-18 inches), pets (service animals are OK), pulled items such as children's wagons, weapons, or wheeled items (inline skates, skateboards, shoes with built-in wheels, wheeled backpacks and coolers) except ECVs, strollers and wheelchairs.

At Disney's Animal Kingdom. For the safety of the wildlife, balloons, coolers and plastic drink lids and plastic straws (even those little straws that come attached to juice boxes) are not permitted.

Operating hours. Park operating hours vary throughout the year; the hours listed below are the most common:

Magic Kingdom. The world's most popular theme park is typically open 9 a.m.–10 p.m. It can, however, open as early as 7 a.m. and close as late as 4 a.m. Magic Kingdom's operating hours have the greatest variance of any Disney World theme park.

Epcot. 9 a.m.–9 p.m. Future World is open 9 a.m.–9 p.m., though some minor

© Disney

Disney has replaced its paper tickets with plastic MagicBands, which also function as room keys, charge cards, Photopass cards and Fastpass tickets. For more on MagicBands see the first section of this book, "A World of Its Own."

attractions may close at 7 p.m. World Showcase is open 11 a.m.–9 p.m.
Disney's Hollywood Studios. 9 a.m.–7 p.m.
Disney's Animal Kingdom. 9 a.m.–5 p.m.
Water parks. 10 a.m.–5 p.m.
For more information call 407-824-4321 or see disneyworld.disney.go.com/calendars.

Tickets. Though Disney World's unconventional Magic Your Way ticketing concept is promoted as a way to let you create a ticket that matches your particular needs, it's also so complicated that, at first glance, it can seem impossible to understand. In a nutshell, Disney's plan lets you tailor tickets to include from one to 10 days of theme-park visits, and then add options such as the ability to visit more than one park a day or spend time at Disney's water parks. Other possible add-ons include a pre-paid dining plan (the Disney Dining Plan), itself with various options including recreation activities. To further complicate matters, Disney offers annual passes, and Florida residents get benefits like discounted tickets and the option of payment for passes in monthly increments.

Single-day tickets. A single-day ticket to Magic Kingdom costs $99 for adults, $93 for children ages 3 to 9. A single-day ticket to Epcot, Disney's Hollywood Studios or Disney's Animal Kingdom costs $5 less.

Multi-day tickets. Multi-day tickets for adults start at $91.33 a day for three days, which adds up to $274; the child's price is $255. For four days, it's $73.50 a day for adults ($294 total); $68.50 for children ($274 total). The more days the ticket includes, the cheaper it is on a per-day basis.

For more ticket prices or to buy tickets from the Disney company, go to disneyworld.

disney.go.com/tickets or call 407-934-7639, from 7 a.m. to 10 p.m. Eastern time.

Base tickets and options. The basic theme-park ticket—the "base ticket"—provides admission to one Disney theme park per day, and is good for up to 10 days. The days the ticket is used do not need to be consecutive, but it expires 14 days after its first use. Base tickets have three options:

Park Hopper. This option lets you visit more than one theme park in the same day. The price ranges from $35 to $60, depending on the number of days on your ticket. Practical benefits include the ability to go to one park during the day then another at night to see its fireworks show, sample parks during a short visit and easily revisit favorite attractions. A downside: as of August 2014 Disney's Fastpass+ policies made it difficult to book Fastpasses at a second park during a single day.
See also the opening segment of this book, **A World of Its Own.**

Water Park Fun & More. This adds admission to Disney World's two water parks, DisneyQuest, the ESPN Wide World of Sports complex and/or rounds of golf at Disney's 9-hole Oak Trail golf course or Disney's two miniature golf courses. The Water Parks Fun & More price is $55 for a one-day Magic Kingdom ticket; $60 for any other ticket. The number of admissions it provides varies by how long the base ticket is good for. Regardless of how long you stay, if you use this option at least twice during your visit it pays for itself.

No Expiration. This add-on ($41–$346) means unused days on your ticket never expire. You can add the option anytime within 14 days of first use. The cost is

© Disney

Like trains? Disney's Magic Behind Our Steam Trains tour provides an upclose, backstage view of the Magic Kingdom's vintage locomotives.

based on the number of days your ticket was originally valid.

See also **Disney Dining Plan.**

Theme-park annual passes. An annual pass ($645) includes admission to the four theme parks, plus free theme-park parking and discounts on dining, entertainment and merchandise. A Premium option ($768) adds admission to water parks, DisneyQuest and the ESPN Wide World of Sports complex. Seasonal passes are available. Florida residents, members of the U.S. military and Disney Vacation Club members pay less.

Monthly payments. Floridians can buy annual passes and pay for them monthly, without interest, with a down payment of $106. The down payment and first monthly payment are made at the time of purchase.

Discounts and upgrades. Disney offers discounts for Florida residents and members of the U.S. military. Purchased tickets can always be upgraded, but not downgraded.

Water park tickets. The basic ticket provides admission to either Blizzard Beach or Typhoon Lagoon, and is good for 1 day. The price is $54 for an adult, $46 for a child. For unlimited admission for both Blizzard Beach and Typhoon Lagoon for one year, the price is $106 for an adult, $87 for a child. A 1-day ticket can be upgraded toward the purchase of a water-park annual pass on the same day.

DisneyQuest tickets. A basic ticket provides admission for 1 day: $46 for an adult, $40 for a child. For unlimited admission for one year the price is $92 for an adult, $73 for a child. A ticket can be upgraded toward the purchase of an annual pass on the same day.

For unlimited admission to DisneyQuest and both water parks for one year, Disney charges $134 for an adult, $104 for a child.

Tours. Organized tours offer a closer look at Walt Disney World. Unless indicated below, tours are for guests ages 16 and older. Those that go backstage do not allow photography. Photo IDs are required. To book a tour listed below (except a VIP tour) call 407-939-8687.

Backstage Magic. View backstage creative and technical operations at all four theme parks ($249, lunch included, park admission not required. 7 hours. Monday–Friday).

Backstage Safari. Tours the animal hospital, elephant barn and other facilities at Disney's Animal Kingdom. One of the authors' favorite tours. ($72, park admission required. 3 hours. Monday, Wednesday–Friday).

Behind the Seeds. A backstage look at the greenhouses at Epcot's The Land pavilion ($20 adults, $16 children 3–9, park admission required. 1 hour. Daily. All ages).

BoardWalk Ballyhoo Guided Tour. A guide walks you through Disney's BoardWalk Inn and Villas, explaining its architecture and history (Complimentary. 45 minutes. 9 a.m. Wednesday–Saturday. All ages).

Disney's Family Magic Tour. This Magic Kingdom scavenger hunt captures a dastardly villain; it's a skip (literally) through the park ($34, park admission required. 2 hours. Daily. All ages, best for ages 4 to 10).

ESPN Wide World of Sports Guided Tour. An inside look at the athletic complex. (On busy days. Complimentary. 1 hour. All ages).

Holiday D-Lights. Tours the backstage decorations shop, Magic Kingdom's Main Street U.S.A., Osborne Dancing Lights at Disney's Hollywood Studios; includes seats for Epcot's Candlelight Processional, light buffet ($209, no park admission required. 4.5 to 5 hours. Monday, Wednesday. 4 p.m. Offered only in late November–December).

Disney monorail trains run through the Contemporary Resort; they also stop at the Grand Floridian and Polynesian Village hotels, Magic Kingdom, Epcot and the Transportation and Ticket Center.

Keys to the Kingdom. Guides discuss Magic Kingdom's history, philosophies; travels into Magic Kingdom's underground Utilidor areas. Walt Disney World's most popular tour ($79, includes lunch, park admission required. 5 hours. Daily).

The Magic Behind Our Steam Trains. Shows how Magic Kingdom's antique steam trains are prepped for daily operation; also discusses Walt Disney's love of trains. Another author favorite ($54, park admission required. 3 hours. Monday–Thursday, Saturday. Ages 10 and up).

UnDISCOVERed Future World. You'll learn of Walt Disney's planned Experimental Prototype Community of Tomorrow, visit all of Epcot's Future World pavilions and go backstage ($64, park admission required. 4 hours. Monday, Wednesday, Friday).

The Ultimate Day for Young Families. Designed for families with children under age 10, this "VIP Tour Experience" gives you a tour of a dozen of Disney's best family-friendly attractions ($299. 6–7 hours. Tuesday, Friday, Sunday; 8:15 a.m. Park admission required, guests under 18 must be accompanied by an adult. Table-service lunch included).

The Ultimate Day of Thrills. Another "VIP Tour Experience," this one takes you on 11 Disney thrill rides, including Expedition Everest, Space Mountain and the Twilight Zone Tower of Terror ($299. 6–7 hours. Tuesday, Friday, Sunday; 8:15 a.m. Minimum height 48 inches, park admission required, guests under 18 must be accompanied by an adult. Table-service lunch included).

VIP Tours. Your group gets its own guide, who uses your custom itinerary ($315–$380 per hour, minimum 6 hours, park admission required. Daily. All ages. 407-560-4033).

Walt Disney: From Marceline to the Magic Kingdom. Explores how Walt was motivated to achieve his dreams. Stops at Magic Kingdom attractions that had their start at the 1964 World's Fair ($30, park admission required. 3 hours, Monday, Wednesday, Thursday, Friday).

Wild Africa Trek. Small groups take guided treks through the forest and savanna of the Kilimanjaro Safaris at Disney's Animal Kingdom. Includes winding remote pathways, life-line lean over a cliff to watch hippos as they are fed lettuce, swaying footbridge high over Nile crocodiles, memorable open-air truck ride through the savanna area, stop at covered viewing area stocked with fresh appetizers. (Price varies by season; approximately $190 to $250 per person, park admission required. 3 hours. Multiple times daily. Ages 8 and up. Maximum of 12 guests per trek. Includes photographer.)

Wilderness Back Trail Adventure. You'll ride a rugged Segway X2 (a two-wheeled self-balancing electric vehicle) down shady Fort Wilderness trails ($95. 2 hours. Tuesday–Saturday; 8:30, 11:30 a.m. Minimum weight 100 pounds, maximum 250. Same-day walk-up reservations at Fort Wilderness marina).

Yuletide Fantasy. This tour explores the winter holiday decorations of Magic Kingdom, Epcot and a few Walt Disney World resorts ($89, offered only in late November–December, park admission not required. 3 hours. Monday–Saturday).

Transportation. Though many guests get around Disney's 47-square-mile property in cars, there are many other options.

Disney buses. A huge fleet of diesel buses connects Disney's resorts with all theme and

More than 300 Disney buses provide direct service from every Disney-owned hotel to every Disney theme park. Buses also serve the water parks, Downtown Disney and the ESPN Wide World of Sports Complex.

water parks and Downtown Disney, and also between some parks. Buses typically arrive every 20 to 30 minutes, from one hour before park opening until one hour after closing.

Though the buses run from theme park to theme park, and from any theme park to Blizzard Beach, they do not go from all theme parks to Downtown Disney or Typhoon Lagoon, and serve ESPN Wide World of Sports only from Disney's All-Star, Caribbean Beach and Pop Century resorts. There is also no official bus service between resort hotels, though hotels in the same area often share the same buses.

Except during thunderstorms, buses do not run from the Epcot resorts (BoardWalk, Yacht and Beach Club, Walt Disney World Swan and Dolphin) to Epcot or Disney's Hollywood Studios. Guests at those resorts travel to those parks via ferry boat or on foot. Guests enter Epcot through the park's rear International Gateway entrance into World Showcase.

Disney monorails. These electric trains connect Disney's Transportation and Ticket Center (TTC) with Magic Kingdom and the Contemporary, Grand Floridian and Polynesian resorts. A separate line runs to Epcot. Operating hours vary.

Disney boats. Ferries connect Magic Kingdom with the TTC and the hotels on Seven Seas Lagoon and Bay Lake; Epcot and Hollywood Studios with hotels in between those parks; and Downtown Disney with Port Orleans, Old Key West and Saratoga Springs.

For transportation details call 407-939-7433.

Rental cars. Orlando is the largest rental-car market in the world. At the Orlando International Airport most major rental companies have their cars in an adjacent parking garage. Rental-car counters are located on the Ground Transportation Level (Level 1) of each side of the terminal.

If you're already at Disney, the most convenient place to rent a car may be Disney's Car Care Center at the exit of the Magic Kingdom parking lot. A counter (407-824-3470) offers Alamo and National vehicles and provides shuttle service to guests at all Disney hotels. Satellite desks are at the Walt Disney World Dolphin (407-934-4930) and the Buena Vista Palace (407-827-6363). Four other hotels on Disney property have car-rental counters: the Downtown Disney Hilton (Avis, 407-827-2847), Doubletree Guest Suites (Budget, 407-827-6089), Wyndham (Dollar, 407-583-8000) and Shades of Green (Hertz, 407-938-0600).

You'll pay a 6 percent sales tax, a $2.05 daily "road impact fee" and a 10 percent surcharge to the Greater Orlando Aviation Authority.

Taxicabs and town cars. Taxicabs, town cars and other vehicles are available for travel around Disney and the surrounding area. Mears Transportation—the largest transportation operator in the area, and the only contracted provider for Disney—has the most choices (24-hour reservations 407-423-5566, taxicab mearstransportation.com; vehicles with child seats available on request).

Taxis. Mears taxis (pickup 407-422-2222 or 407-699-9999), operate under the Yellow Cab, Checker Cab and City Cab brands. Transportation within Disney property should cost $15–$30; the fare for traveling between the Orlando International Airport and Disney is typically $65–$75. For groups of 5 to 8 people, vans charge $90–$100. Non-Mears "gypsy" cabs lurk in the area, and may have unpredictable rates and may take only cash.

Town cars. Many upscale resorts in the area have Mears town cars available 24

The largest rental-car facility in the world, the Orlando International Airport rents 6,000 vehicles a day. Rental-car companies are located in a parking garage.

hours a day. Airport service includes a driver who will meet a guest at baggage claim, and transportation in a luxury sedan to the guest's resort; the fare to Disney is typically $90–$100 for up to four passengers.

Airport shuttle service. Mears offers group transportation from the Orlando International Airport to Disney-area resorts. Passengers wait on a bus or van at the airport until the vehicle is full. On the return trip, shuttle passengers are picked up three to four hours before their flight times. Fares: One-way: $22 adult, $17 child. Round trip: $36 adult, $27 child. Children under 3 ride free.

Vehicle charters. Mears has 55-passenger buses, 25-passenger mini-buses, 11-passenger vans and 8-passenger limos. For current fares see mearstransportation.com.

Weather. Florida's subtropical climate creates mild winters but summers that are hot and humid. Between May and August Disney guests can get exhausted with little effort, as the sun rises almost straight up in the sky. Temperatures in that direct heat usually are about 12 degrees warmer than those in the shade, and can easily reach 100 degrees. Afternoon heat indexes usually exceed 105 degrees. Brief afternoon thunderstorms are common. Overall, July is the hottest month at Disney, January the coolest. August is the wettest month, December the driest.

Current forecast. The Weather Channel provides a specific current forecast for Walt Disney World. Visit weather.com and search for "Disney World." There's also one available by phone, from the independent Disney Weather Hotline at 407-824-4104.

Hurricanes. Though hurricanes often strike the Florida coast, the risk of one hitting Disney is relatively low, as the resort sits in the middle of the state. Since the power of a hurricane is generated by being over water, its intensity lessens upon landfall and usually dissipates quickly. Three hurricanes, however, came close to Walt Disney World in 2004. Disney closed its theme parks, water parks and golf courses for those storms, but kept its hotels open.

Florida's hurricane season is June through November. Disney allows you to cancel hotel reservations without penalty whenever the National Hurricane Center issues a hurricane warning for the Orlando area (or a guest's place of residence) within seven days of your scheduled arrival date. If you're at Disney when a hurricane approaches, take it seriously and follow Disney's advice.

Rain gear. Disney sells clear plastic ponchos throughout its property; children and adult sizes cost about $8.50. Umbrellas are

Walt Disney World weather

Month	Avg high	Avg low	Rain
Jan	72	48	2.4 in.
Feb	73	49	2.7 in.
Mar	77	53	3.3 in.
April	82	58	3.0 in.
May	87	64	3.8 in.
June	90	70	6.0 in.
July	93	72	6.6 in.
Aug	92	72	7.3 in.
Sept	90	71	6.0 in.
Oct	84	65	3.2 in.
Nov	79	57	2.4 in.
Dec	73	50	2.2 in.

A typical summer afternoon at Disney, as an afternoon rain douses Fantasyland. Rains usually last about an hour, and skies clear afterward.

also available. Small collapsible ones go for about $15; large golf umbrellas are $43.

Weather refunds. There are no refunds for bad weather. Disney theme parks stay open, rain or shine; water parks offer rain checks in some circumstances.

See also **Water parks.**

Weddings. Up to a dozen couples tie the knot at Walt Disney World every day. And no wonder—Disney has unrivaled facilities for a family gathering, good year-round weather and a one-stop Fairy Tale Weddings division. Most weddings are performed at Disney's Wedding Pavilion next to the Grand Floridian Resort and Spa. Several hotels—including the BoardWalk, Polynesian Village, Wilderness Lodge and Yacht Club—also host ceremonies.

Planning. Named after funnyman Martin Short's wedding planner in Disney's 1991 movie "Father of the Bride," Franck's Bridal Studio can arrange accommodations, cakes, flowers, music, photography and rehearsal dinners. The facility is next to the wedding pavilion.

Costs. Disney offers three wedding packages, which vary based on the number of guests and level of services. The average Disney wedding costs $31,000 and includes 100 people. Prices start at $2,495.

For more information call 321-939-4610 or go online to disneyweddings.com.

Honeymoons. Disney planning services includes an on-line registry (407-939-7776, disneyhoneymoonregistry.com), which lets couples create a wish list for their trip and have family and friends contribute. More honeymoon help is available at 800-370-6009 or online at disneyhoneymoons.com.

Wi-Fi. Disney provides complimentary wireless Internet access throughout its property, though it is often slow on crowded days and reception can be poor. For answers to technical issues, call Disney for assistance at 407-827-2732.

See also **Internet access.**

Youth groups. Disney World offers various activities and competitions for youth groups of 10 or more. Participants get discounted group rates for both accommodations and theme-park tickets. Opportunities include:

Disney Performing Arts OnStage. This audition-based program invites community groups and middle- and high-school students to perform at Disney year round. Instrumental and vocal groups participate, as do dance ensembles (instrumental groups 866-242-3617, vocal 866-578-4823, dance 866-578-4827). Optional performance workshops are available (866-578-4830).

Festival Disney. Held each spring, this educational experience is open to middle-school, junior- and senior-high school concert bands, jazz ensembles, marching bands, orchestras, vocal ensembles, show choirs and auxiliary units. No audition is required; directors choose either competitive or non-competitive adjudication options. Performances take place at Disney's Saratoga Springs Resort, Disney's Hollywood Studios and Downtown Disney (877-939-6884).

Disney Youth Education Series (YES). These programs give elementary through high school students real-world learning experiences at Disney theme parks. Hands-on courses focus on Leadership & Careers, Arts & Humanities, Physical Sciences and Natural Sciences.

Telephone directory

Area Code 407 unless indicated

AIRPORTS

Orlando International 825-2001
  Arrivals, departures, directions, parking 825-8463
  Disney's EarPort store (East hall) 825-2339
  The Magic of Disney store (West hall) 825-2370
  Lost and Found..825-2111
  Paging 825-2000
Orlando Sanford International...............322-7771

AUTOMOBILE RENTALS

Alamo National toll-free 800 327-9633
  AAA Car Care Center 824-3470
  Buena Vista Palace 827-6363
Avis National toll-free.............................800 831-2847
  Downtown Disney Hilton...............................827-2847
Budget National toll-free.........................800 527-0700
  Doubletree Guest Suites.................................827-6089
Dollar National toll-free..........................800 800-4000
  Wyndham 583-8000
Enterprise National toll-free 800 325-8007
E-Z National toll-free...............................800 277-5171
Firefly Orlando Int'l Airport...........................859-8733
Hertz National toll-free 800 654-3131
  Shades of Green..938-0600
L & M National toll-free 800 277-5171
  Orlando Int'l Airport 888-0515
National National toll-free 800 227-7368
Thrifty National toll-free.........................800 367-2277
  Walt Disney World Dolphin............................934-4930

AUTOMOBILE SERVICES

AAA Car Care Center 824-0976
  After hours 824-4777
AAA Emergency Road Service........800 222-4357
Pep Boys Celebration...............................321 939-2581

BANKING SERVICES

Bank of America Celebration..............321 939-7677
Suntrust Downtown Disney 828-6103
  Celebration Downtown 566-2265
  Celebration Water Tower Place 321 939-3970
Traveler's Checks American Exp........800 992-3404
  Thomas Cook Prepaid Currency Card....800 287-7362
Wells Fargo Orlando....................................649-5800
Western Union transfers Winn-Dixie........397-2210

BUSINESS SERVICES

Disney Institute..566-2620
Disney Professional Seminars................824-7997

CHILDCARE SERVICES

All About Kids...812-9300

Baby's Away Equipment rental......................334-0232
Kid's Nite Out..828-0920
Orlando Stroller Rentals.................800 281-0884

CONVENTION PLANNING

Disney convention centers.............321 939-7129
Gaylord Palms Resort.................................586-0000
Marriott World Center 238-8888
Orlando Convention Center 685-9800
Walt Disney World Swan and Dolphin...934-4290

DISABILITY SERVICES

Sign-language show schedule...............824-4321
  Special requests 939-7807
TDD numbers Disney information...............827-5141
Disney hotel reservations 939-7670
Disney Vacation Club.................................566-3320

EDUCATIONAL SERVICES

Epcot Discovery Center For teachers 824-4321
Youth Education Series 877 343-5387

EMPLOYMENT

Disney College Program U.S. students.....828-3091
  International students 828-2850
Walt Disney World JobLine....................828-1000

ENTERTAINMENT

AMC theater Downtown Disney 827-1308
  Movie listings 888 262-4386
Atlanta Braves Spring Training
  Box office 939-4263
  Ticketmaster 800 745-3000
Atlantic Dance Hall BoardWalk Resort.......939-2444
Chip 'n Dale's Campfire Movie schedule..824-2727
Cirque du Soleil La Nouba Box office.......939-7600
House of Blues Box office............................934-2583
Jellyrolls BoardWalk Resort 560-8770
Raglan Road Downtown Disney 938-0300
Star Wars Weekends 938-3398

FLORISTS

Disney Floral & Gifts 827-3505
  Disney Dream Makers 939-4438
  Convention services..827-1266
  Wedding services...................................321 939-4610

GASOLINE STATIONS

Hess Express Downtown Disney 938-0160
  Epcot Resort Area...938-0151
  Magic Kingdom...938-0143

GENERAL INFORMATION

Poison Control Center.....................800 222-1222

Beach Club Villas.. 934-2175
Sandcastle Club childcare center 934-6290
Yacht Club 934-7000
Periwig's Beauty Salon 934-3260
Ship Shape Health Club.................................. 934-3256
Lost and found.. 934-1493
Doubletree Guest Suites Dwntwn Disney .. 934-1000
Car rental (Budget).. 827-6089
Gaylord Palms W Osceola Parkway 586-0000
Hilton Bonnet Creek.................................... 597-3600
Downtown Disney 827-4000
Car rental (Avis).. 827-2847
Holiday Inn Downtown Disney...................... 828-8888
Hyatt Regency Grand Cypress 239-1234
Marriott World Center World Center Dr.... 239-4200
Nickelodeon Suites Continental Gateway .. 387-5437
Shades of Green.. 824-3600
Car rental (Hertz).. 938-0600
Waldorf Astoria Bonnet Creek 597-5500
Walt Disney World Swan & Dolphin...... 934-4000
Car rental (Alamo/National).......................... 934-4930
Camp Dolphin childcare center...................... 934-4000
Mandara Spa 934-4772
The Salon.. 934-4772
Wyndham Downtown Disney........................ 828-4444
Car rental (Dollar).. 583-8000

KENNEL
Best Friends Pet Care Center 877 493-9738

LOST AND FOUND
Disney Central Lost and Found.............. 824-4245
Disney parks Animal Kingdom...................... 938-2785
Disney's Blizzard Beach.............................. 560-5408
Epcot.. 560-6646
Magic Kingdom.. 824-4521
Disney's Typhoon Lagoon 560-6296
Disney's Hollywood Studios.......................... 560-3720
Disney hotels See Hotels and Resorts
Downtown Disney...................................... 828-3150
ESPN Wide World of Sports.................... 541-5600

MEDICAL CARE
Celebration Health Florida Hospital 764-4000
Emergency Dept.. 303-4034
Fitness Center.. 303-2552
Celebration Dental Emergencies 566-2222
Centra Care In-room care 238-2000
Central Care Walk-in Clinics.................. 200-2273
Formosa Gardens.. 397-7032
Kissimmee.. 390-1888
Lake Buena Vista.. 934-2273
Sand Lake Rd.. 851-6478
Doctors on Call Service (DOCS) 399-3627

EastCoast Medical In-room care................ 648-5252
Reedy Creek Paramedics 560-1990

MEDICAL EQUIPMENT RENTALS
Apria Health Care 291-2229
Care Medical Equipment........................ 856-2273
Turner Drugs 828-8125
Walker Mobility 518-6000

PHARMACIES
CVS W Irlo Bronson Hwy 321 677-0349
Turner Drugs Celebration Blvd 828-8125
Walgreens W Irlo Bronson Hwy 390-1701

PHOTOGRAPHY SERVICES
Disney Photographic Services 827-5099
PhotoPass.. 560-4300

POLICE
Orange County Sheriff 254-7000
Osceola County Sheriff 348-2222
Walt Disney World Security 560-7959
Urgent matters.. 560-1990

RECREATION
Boat rentals.. 939-7529
Camping Groups.. 939-7807
Carriage rides 939-7529
Disney Cruise Line.................................... 566-7000
DisneyQuest Downtown Disney.................... 828-4600
ESPN Wide World of Sports.................... 828-3267
Live operator 939-1500
runDisney 938-3398
Youth group information 939-4263
Fishing Disney excursions............................ 939-2277
Golf Disney tee-time reservations 939-4653
Horseback riding Fort Wilderness 824-2900
Marathons and foot races...................... 938-3398
Miniature golf Fantasia Gardens.................. 560-4753
Winter Summerland...................................... 560-7161
Pony rides Fort Wilderness 824-2788
Reservations Disney recreation 939-7529
Richard Petty Driving Experience.......... 939-0130
Surfing lessons Typhoon Lagoon.................. 939-7873
Tennis Reservations, lessons...................... 621-1991
Wagon rides.. 939-7529
Walt Disney World Speedway 939-0130
Water Sports Sammy Duvall's...................... 939-0754

RESTAURANTS
Big River Grille BoardWalk Resort 560-0253
Bongos Cuban Cafe Downtown Disney 828-0999
Disney restaurants Reservations 939-3463
Dietary requests 824-5967

Index

About the authors

A FORMER WALT DISNEY WORLD concierge supervisor, Julie Neal has spent over 2,500 days at Disney World not counting her time behind the desk. For the production of this year's guide she was at Disney every single day for three months—if there's one thing she's an expert on, it's how to get around. A roller coaster freak and a wildlife enthusiast, she lists Expedition Everest and the Pangani Forest Exploration Trail as her favorite Disney attractions. Her passions outside the world of theme parks include animal rights, reading and old movies.

Julie's husband Mike designed the book and took most of the photographs in it. Unable to go on most rides—even the merry-go-round makes him dizzy—his favorite Disney thing to do is watch the street performers. The couple lives in Orlando with their daughter Micaela, who when she's not scuba diving or going to school at Florida State, helps out in the family business. She vets Julie's writing, takes photos of her own, and does the animal guide. Her favorite Disney attraction: Big Thunder Mountain Railroad.

The Neals share their home with the most important member of their family: Oliver, the world's most cuddly 85-pound rescue dog.

Guidebook magic.

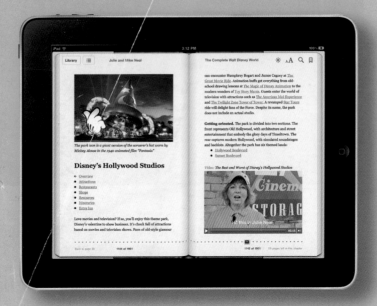

Introducing the definitive *digital* Disney guide book. With content you can search, highlight and add notes to. Hundreds of images that fill your screen. Video. And handy touchscreen navigation with over 3,000 links. For e-readers, tablets and smart phones. It's like magic.

Available at online bookstores worldwide

The Complete Walt Disney World®
eBook edition

Published in September 2014. Features may vary by device.